Fundamentals of
Management Accounting

FUNDAMENTALS OF
MANAGEMENT ACCOUNTING

John A. Tracy
PROFESSOR OF ACCOUNTING
UNIVERSITY OF COLORADO

A Wiley/Hamilton Publication

John Wiley & Sons, Inc.   Santa Barbara   New York   London   Sydney   Toronto

This book was set in Helvetica Light by Cherry Hill Composition, Inc.
It was printed and bound by Halliday Lithograph Corp.
The tables were designed and executed by John Balbalis
with the assistance of the Wiley Illustration Department.
Jerry Wilke was the text designer.
Regina Malone supervised production.

Library of Congress Cataloging in Publication Data:
Tracy, John A
  Fundamentals of management accounting.

  "A Wiley/Hamilton publication."
  Includes index.
  1. Managerial accounting. I. Title.
HF5635.T68   658.1′51   75-26988
ISBN 0-471-88151-1

Printed in the United States of America

10 9 8 7 6 5 4 3 2 1

PREFACE

Most colleges and universities offer two introductory accounting courses. The first deals primarily with the nature, content, preparation, and uses of externally reported financial statements; it is usually called financial accounting. The second concerns internal managerial uses of financial statements and the need of managers for different types of accounting reports and accounting analyses. However, financial accounting is frequently continued into this second course and, consequently, only part of it is devoted to management (or managerial) accounting. Frankly, my preference is for a more even balance between the two and, accordingly, I have written a book for each course: *Fundamentals of Financial Accounting* (Wiley, 1974), and this book, *Fundamentals of Management Accounting*, which is offered for the second introductory accounting course. The range of management accounting subject matter in this volume presents enough material for an entire course. Alternatively, selected topics from this book can be used for the management accounting part of the second introductory accounting course.

This book assumes that the student has completed one introductory financial accounting course. The first chapter sets the stage for the remainder of the book by offering a broad overview of the basic functions of management and the field and concepts of management accounting. The second chapter may appear unnecessary, given the assumption that the student has already completed a first course in financial accounting. It is not. Most students, even the best ones, profit from a brief review of financial accounting. The transition from one course to the next always presents problems of remembering what was learned in the first course. Moreover, the purpose of Chapter Two is not only to review but also to introduce the student to a *manufacturing* company example. Typically, manufacturing costs and accounting procedures are not discussed in much detail in the first accounting course. Hence, part of Chapter Two examines new material for most students, or covers in more detail what they have learned in their first course.

One novel feature of this book is that the company example introduced in Chapter Two is carried through the next six chapters (Chapters Three to Eight). Each successive chapter deals with additional basic management accounting aspects of the same company, such that over these several chapters the student comes to know it very well. This is a holistic sort of approach, one that emphasizes the "building block" or "learning module" sequence. The student can logically add one step to the next as he or she continues through the chapters. Instead of starting with a new example in each chapter, the same facts about the company are carried forward. This allows an economy of discussion because students are already familiar with the background information required. This continuity is especially useful in the three chapters on budgeting (Chapters Six to Eight), since the past experience of the company can be introduced as the basis for building the budget for the following year.

After Chapters One and Two, the book offers flexibility in the sequence of assignments. (Indeed, some instructors may not assign Chapter Two, if their students do not need a review of financial accounting.) The next 12 chapters are organized into packages or modules of three chapters as follows:

A. *Basic Accounting Analysis for Management Control*
   Chapter Three   Basic Measure and Interpretations of Financial Per-
                      formance
   Chapter Four   Basic Analysis of Revenue, Costs, Profit, and Capital
                      Investment Behavior
   Chapter Five   Comparative Analysis of Profit and ROI Performance
B. *Budgeting for Financial Planning and Control*
   Chapter Six   Financial Planning and Profit Budgeting
   Chapter Seven   Budgeting Changes in Financial Position; Budgets and
                      Management Control
   Chapter Eight   Short-term Cash Flow Analysis and Budgeting
C. *Accounting Analysis for Investment Decisions and Special Decision-Making
   Situations*
   Chapter Nine   Capital Investment Analysis: an Introduction
   Chapter Ten   Capital Investment Analysis, Continued
   Chapter Eleven   Relevant Cost Analysis for Special Management Decisions
D. *Cost Accounting Cycle and Standard Cost Systems*
   Chapter Twelve   Product Cost Determination and Accumulation
   Chapter Thirteen   Product Cost Determination and Accumulation (Con-
                      cluded)
   Chapter Fourteen   Standard Cost Systems

These four modules could be assigned in any sequence, although I recommend the order presented in the book. The concluding chapter (Fifteen) offers a brief overview of contemporary developments in management accounting, and stresses that the fundamental concepts and methods of analysis discussed in the book apply with equal importance to nonprofit organizations.

Professor Gary E. White, at the University of Colorado, has prepared a very useful Study Guide for this book. Students should find the Study Guide an excellent supplement to the assigned problems and questions at the end of each chapter. It contains self-checking questions and short problems for each chapter.

I am grateful for the assistance of the staff at Wiley, and particularly thank

P. J. Wilkinson, Bart Grange, and Gary Carlson. Also, several reviewers offered valuable comments and criticisms on early drafts of the book.

Finally I have two more personal notes. This book is written most of all for my father, a businessman for many years. In countless ways he taught me the personal satisfaction and, yes, the personal agonies of being a businessman. My wife Fay was my working partner on this book without whom . . ., well you know the rest.

John A. Tracy
Boulder, Colorado

CONTENTS

Chapter One

Introduction to Management Accounting

INTRODUCTION TO MANAGEMENT ACCOUNTING

The Decision Making Character and Organizational Structure of Management

The Basic Functions of Management

Assume that you are asked to identify the *managers* of a business enterprise, and to distinguish between the managers and the other employees of the business. Your first step might be to investigate who has authority over whom in the organization. It is true that managers hold this power; managers direct the actions of other employees. However, this is only one of the basic functions of management. A well-known author on management theory and practice identifies the basic functions of management as follows:*

Planning   The manager must first decide what he wants done. He must set short- and long-run objectives for the organization and decide on the means that will be used to meet them.

Organizing   In organizing, the manager decides on the positions to be filled and on the duties and responsibilities attaching to each one. But the work done by the members of the organization will necessarily be interrelated; hence some means of coordinating their efforts must be provided.

Staffing   In organizing, the manager establishes positions and decides which duties and responsibilities properly belong to each one. In staffing, he attempts to find the right person for each job.

Direction   Since no one can predict just what problems and opportunities will arise in the day-to-day work, lists of duties must naturally be couched in rather general terms. The manager must, therefore, provide day-to-day direction for his subordinates. He must make sure that they know the results he expects in each situation . . .

Control   In directing, the manager explains to his people what they are to do and helps them do it to the best of their ability. In control, he determines how well the jobs have been done and what progress is being made toward the

* From *Management: Theory And Practice*, pages 4-6, by Ernest Dale. Copyright © 1973 by Ernest Dale. Used with permission of McGraw-Hill Book Company.

goals. He must know what is happening so that he can step in and make changes if the organization is deviating from the path he has set for it.

Innovation   . . . we may number innovation among the true functions of the manager, and the manager may innovate in any one of several ways. . . . It could be argued that the planning function encompasses innovation, since the manager should plan . . . how to change those (future) conditions in order to improve the possibilities open to him. This is logical enough, but it may lead to a lack of emphasis on the need for innovation in all phases of a business, including innovations in the handling of the other management functions.

Representation   Finally, the manager's job includes representing his organization in dealings with outside groups: government officials, unions, civic groups of one kind of another, financial institutions, other companies in the industry, suppliers, customers, and the public generally.

These functions clearly require that the manager be a reasonably good *decision maker,* as well as a person who can implement and carry through his decisions once made. To be a good decision maker a manager must maintain an attitude of objectivity and should distinguish between his or her personal subjective feelings and the facts of the situation. The manager needs a "bag of tools" that can be used to analyze problems, and to determine the best course of action. And, most important, the manager needs to make sure that all available relevant *information* is considered and evaluated in making decisions.

The Need for Management Decision Making Information

It is difficult, if not impossible, to imagine a manager's reaching a decision without mentally processing some information input. The information may be the opinions of others, expressed confidently to the manager. The information may be mainly intuitive, based only on the manager's "gut feelings." The manager relies on many different sources of information inputs into his or her decision-making process. For example, most managers are (or should be) concerned about employee morale. Information sources about employee morale may come mainly from a manager's personal contact with employees, especially by listening to their complaints and grievances.

In short, a manager cannot make a decision in an information vacuum. It seems reasonable to assume that bad information causes or leads to bad decisions. A basic premise of this book is that the better the information input into a manager's decision-making process, the better the decision is likely to be. Of course, good information may not be fully utilized by the manager, or for that matter may not be fully understood. One of the most important functions of a manager is to know what information sources should be used for each decision, and how to use information from each source to reach the "best" or, at least, an acceptable decision.

This book is directed to the *accounting information* needed by managers. Accounting information deals mainly with matters such as costs and revenues, financial position, profit performance measures, and sources and uses of capital. Information cannot be separated from the decision itself. Thus in this book we are also concerned with what managers do with accounting information. As we demonstrate throughout this book, accounting information is especially important in the planning and control functions of management.

The Fundamental Idea of Feedback Information for Management Control and Planning

The concept of *feedback information* refers to the comparison of actual performance and position with the performance and position that was planned for or expected by the manager when decisions were made that led to the activity and operations that are being reported. In simple terms, the use of feedback in information is shown in Exhibit 1.1.

Role of Feedback Information
EXHIBIT 1.1

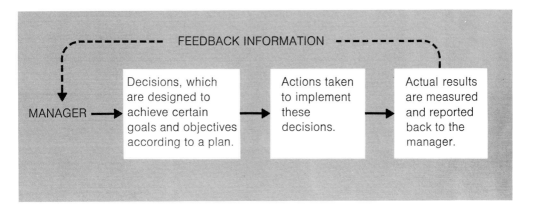

A manager does not make a decision and then simply assume that the results will come out just as expected and predicted. Decisions have to be *executed;* follow-through is just as important as the initial decision. The *actual* results of the decision must be reviewed. In fact, this review of actual against plans is essential for the *next* decision, that is, for planning. If actual performance is falling short, or is deviating from the desired or the necessary performance, then the manager should reconsider the decision and perhaps look for better alternatives to improve performance. In short, feedback information on past decisions provides essential input to present decisions that determine future performance. The essential feature of feedback information is the measurement of current performance against past plans for management control. This comparison for control purposes is also the essential starting point for planning decisions covering the next period, as well as for future periods beyond the next period.

Organizational Structure and Management Decision Making

Almost all business organizations of any size are in some manner subdivided into departments, divisions, or other organizational sub-parts, in order to divide the total effort of the business entity into manageable spheres of activity and responsibility. Generally speaking, the organizational structure of a product-oriented business is based on the following considerations:

1. *Functional specialization.* For example, there may be a manufacturing department responsible for the production of the company's products, a purchasing department responsible for buying the materials and supplies used by the company, a sales department responsible for marketing the products, and so on.

2. *Product lines (groupings).* For example, a company may establish a division that manufactures and sells consumer products which is separate from another division that manufactures and sells industrial products (that is, products bought only by other business firms). Within each of these divisions there may be separate manufacturing and marketing departments.

3. *Territories.* For example, a company may divide its sales personnel into geographical regions, or between foreign and domestic markets.

When we examine an individual manager's span of decision-making authority and responsibility in a business organization, it is useful to distinguish three levels or layers of managers: *top level* managers who have company-wide authorities and responsibilities (usually the president and/or the chairman of the board of directors of the company and a relatively small group of other managers who work directly with the president and/or the chairman); *middle level* managers who are the chief executives of major divisions or departments of the company, and who report to the top level managers; and, *front line* (or *first line*) managers who directly supervise production line workers, sales employees, or office workers, and who report to the middle level managers of their divisions or departments. For example, the organization chart for Admiral Corporation (Exhibit 1.4 page 12) shows that the manager of the Color TV Marketing department reports to the Vice-president of Electronics Marketing, who in turn reports to the Vice-president of Sales and Marketing, who in turn reports to the President of the company. (Admiral merged into Rockwell International Corporation in 1974.)

The approach of succeeding chapters follow a "top down" sequence. The accounting information needs and uses of top level managers for the *business entity as a whole* are the concern of the next several chapters. Later chapters consider the accounting information and analysis needed for *specific decisions* that may be made at the top, middle, or front-line level of management. Also, later chapters consider the type of accounting reports required by different managers in the organization. In designing the accounting reports to a manager it is essential to identify the span of authority and responsibility of that manager. The president of the company receives accounting reports that are considerably different from those received by a production supervisor in one of the manufacturing divisions. The organizational structure of the company is the essential starting point in designing the content and other features of accounting reports to managers in the business entity.

The Information System Nature of Accounting

The Essential Need for a General Accounting System

Many business decisions depend in large part on information about costs, sales revenue, and various profit measures. Creditor and stockholders who invest capital in business enterprises base their decisions on information about the financial condition and net income performance of the business. Taxing authorities depend on information about the business entity's tax base, which may be its total sales revenue, its total payroll, or its taxable income, to determine the amount of tax that should be collected from the business entity. To sum up, the business enterprise depends on and cannot operate without a steady and reliable flow of accounting information.

A business entity must develop a *general accounting system* to collect, process, and report the necessary information to the various persons who need it. Two of the primary user groups of accounting information are *external* to the business entity. These external reporting requirements on the general accounting system are: (1) the preparation and reporting of periodic financial reports to the "outside" (nonmanagerial) investors in the business; and, (2) the preparation of periodic tax returns required to be filed with the appropriate tax authorities. These external communications of accounting information are subject to legal or generally accepted standards, principles, requirements, methods, and customs. In contrast, the *internal* communication of accounting information to managers *within* the business entity (that is, information which does *not* circulate outside the business) is much more flexible and is far less subject to fixed rules and pressures of conformity.

The general accounting information system of a business involves three major steps. Exhibit 1.2 contains a brief description of each step. One type of information input is indispensable; the general accounting system must capture this type of information *as a bare minimum* for reporting to managers, investors, and taxing authorities. This is the information about the *transactions* of the business. Transactions are the economic exchanges between the business entity and the other persons and business entities it deals with. Transactions are the

EXHIBIT 1.2
Basic Steps of the General Accounting System

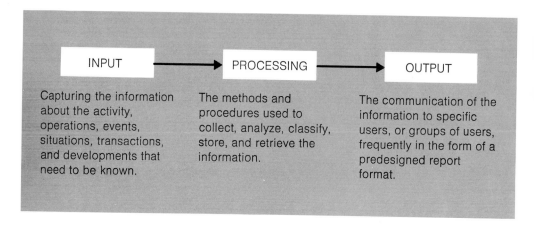

basic financial activity units of a business entity. A business constantly engages in a broad range of economic exchanges to achieve its objectives. (Chapter Two is a survey of the basic cycle of transactions of a business during the year and how these transactions are recorded and reported by the company's accounting system.)

The Three Major Information Reporting Requirements on the General Accounting System

All relevant information about the constant stream of transactions of a business must be captured and processed by the general accounting system to prepare three main outputs, shown in Exhibit 1.3. These are the three major information reporting requirements on the general accounting system of a business entity, which in brief are called *financial accounting, tax accounting,* and *management accounting.*

Management Accounting: The Subject Matter of This Book

Except for a brief review of financial accounting in Chapter Two, this book is directed to management accounting topics. Certain elementary income tax accounting matters are discussed where appropriate throughout the book, since income tax considerations play an important and integral part in many management decisions. However, there is no detailed technical discussion of income taxation laws and procedures.

This book assumes that the student has a basic understanding of financial accounting. Chapter Two is presented as the connecting link between financial

EXHIBIT 1.3
Three Major Information Reporting Requirements on the
General Accounting System

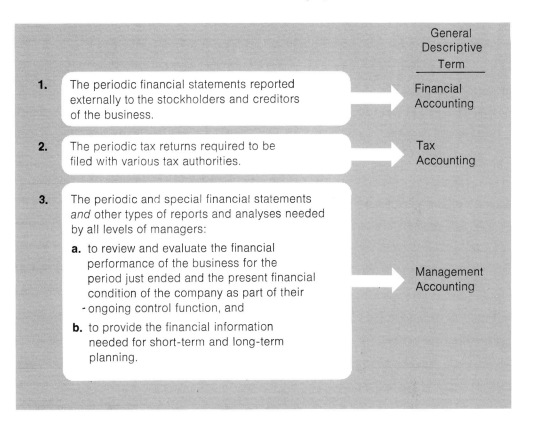

		General Descriptive Term
1.	The periodic financial statements reported externally to the stockholders and creditors of the business.	Financial Accounting
2.	The periodic tax returns required to be filed with various tax authorities.	Tax Accounting
3.	The periodic and special financial statements *and* other types of reports and analyses needed by all levels of managers: **a.** to review and evaluate the financial performance of the business for the period just ended and the present financial condition of the company as part of their ongoing control function, and **b.** to provide the financial information needed for short-term and long-term planning.	Management Accounting

accounting and management accounting. The basic content and structure of the three principal financial statements for the business enterprise as a whole and the basic accounting procedures to prepare these statements are reviewed in Chapter Two. These three statements are: (1) statement of financial condition (balance sheet); (2) statement of net income; and (3) statement of changes in financial position. Together these are the *financial anchor point* of the company. In other words, these three primary financial statements are the most comprehensive and fundamental financial models or financial images of the company which are used by managers in their decision making, especially top level managers. Managers should thoroughly understand financial statements. Later chapters explain the use of financial statements in management control and planning.

Management Accounting Compared with Financial Accounting

The Equal Priority of Management Accounting

Since it is assumed that the student is already familiar with the fundamentals of financial accounting, some differences between management accounting and financial accounting are now discussed. First, management accounting is not an adjunct to or simply an extension of financial and tax accounting. Clearly, management accounting is just as important and necessary as financial and tax accounting. Management accounting should be given equal priority. Indeed, it can be argued that management accounting should be given the first priority, since a viable business entity would not exist without good management decision making, and many management decisions depend on good accounting information.

The majority of companies develop an adequate accounting system to prepare their periodic external financial statements and their various tax returns. Unfortunately, however, some companies do not devote enough time and effort in developing their general accounting system fully and completely to meet the needs of management for accounting information. Thus the company's managers may be making decisions that are based on inadequate, or even misleading accounting information. This book will demonstrate the importance of developing a company's general accounting system fully to meet these needs of management for accounting information, as well as for external financial reporting and tax reporting requirements.

Internal Management Accounting Reports Compared with External Financial Statements

The financial statements reported externally to its stockholders by a company are condensed and summarized, and present the financial condition and financial results of operations for the company as a whole.* Once released to the stockholders the company's financial statements become public and are read with interest by others, for example, labor unions. The external financial statements are general purpose in nature. That is, one and only one set of financial statements are sent to all stockholders (and some creditors) each period, even though the stockholders of a particular company may include a very diverse group of investors.

In contrast, management accounting includes the preparation of several different types of reports to different levels and different decision-making areas of management. Managers differ considerably in their scope of responsibility

---

* It should be noted that in some situations the managers of the company may own *all* the voting stock securities of the company, as well as any other stock outstanding. In this case, the only external financial statements released by the company may be to sources of short- and long-term loans to the company. However, even if the company is relatively small and its stock is closely held among a few stockholders, there may be nonmanagement stockholders to whom financial statements must be reported.

and authority in the organization, as mentioned previously. For instance, the chief executive officer of the company, usually the president or the chairman of the board of directors, needs very comprehensive accounting information for the company as a whole. A general manager of one of the company's divisions needs primarily accounting information about his or her division, and in more detail than is reported to the president of the company. In fact, no two managers in a company have exactly the same scope and area of responsibility— otherwise duplication of management effort would occur.

A first task of the management accountant is to identify the accounting information needs of *each* individual manager in the organization. The accounting information reported to each manager should be relevant to his or her specific functions and scope of responsibility in the organization. This basic concept of management accounting is called *responsibility accounting* and is discussed in more detail below. In short, management accounting must prepare reports for a diverse hierarchy of managers throughout the business organization. On the other hand, (external) financial accounting takes the opposite approach— *one* general purpose set of financial statements is reported to all the stockholders in the company.

External financial statements are presented (in the majority of cases) according to *generally accepted accounting principles,* which with few exceptions are also allowable for determination of the federal taxable income of business corporations. Hence, the accounting methods adopted by most businesses are in conformity with generally accepted principles. More specifically the term "generally accepted accounting principles" means generally accepted *external financial reporting* accounting principles. There are good reasons to adopt the same basic accounting methods for internal management reporting that are used for reporting externally to investors. Or, to be more precise, there are good reasons to start with the same accounting methods and then *perhaps* to modify or expand these accounting methods, if necessary, to meet the needs of managers.

For management purposes a company's general accounting system should report certain current and future information that is not necessary for the preparation of external financial statements and tax returns, which as you know are presented on the historical cost basis. As one example, let us consider the insurance of assets. Managers should understand that the values of assets reported in external financial statements are presented on the historical cost basis. Compared with the *current* replacement cost values of the assets, the historical cost values may be significantly lower. The particular manager making insurance decisions needs to know the current replacement cost values of the assets. He should know better than to assume that the external financial statements report current values. And, the management accountant should know that, when reporting to this manager, current replacement costs estimates are needed.

Managers receive accounting reports monthly, or perhaps even biweekly or weekly. In contrast, stockholders receive very brief quarterly financial reports and depend on the annual financial report for their primary source of information from the company. Managers usually receive their reports sooner also. Stockholders usually have to wait three to six weeks after the close of the period. Managers would not tolerate such a delay and insist on more timely reports, even if certain estimates must be used to prepare the report quickly. Finally, management accounting methods and information are future oriented. External financial statement and tax return accounting methods and information are past (historical) oriented. Management must know the past, but cannot change the past, of course. Management's decision making is concerned with what will or should happen in the future.

The Management Accountant: More Than a "Scorekeeper"

The general role and functions of management accountants in the business organization have evolved over the years. Frankly, a generation or more ago many companies had a rather limited view of what their management accountants should or could do. In many instances management accountants were primarily responsible for the company's cost accounting methods and record-keeping and not much more. Today the majority opinion among business managers seems clearly to be that management accountants should work closely with managers as active consultants and advisers. This modern view goes beyond the traditional role of the management accountant as a collector of facts, or a "scorekeeper", as it has been called.

This current view of the active participative role of management accountants in the management decision-making process is evident in many ways. It is apparent in the budgeting and planning process (which is discussed in Chapters Six and Seven). It is apparent in the setting of standard costs and the interpretation of deviations (called variances) of actual costs from standard costs (which is discussed in Chapter Fourteen). Most important, it is evident in the design of management control reports and the preparation of special purpose analyses (which are discussed in several different chapters).

To sum up, in addition to being management's scorekeeper, the management accountant of today is also expected to provide "attention-directing" and "problem-solving" information and analyses for managers and, in general, to be a close working partner with them. The management accountant does *not* make the decisions, to be sure. This is the manager's job and responsibility. On the other hand, the management accountant should have a very good understanding of how the manager makes decisions. For example, the management accountant needs a good working knowledge of the purchasing, production, marketing, and employment practices of the company to make analyses and to report on the performance in these areas to the appropriate managers.

Different Costs for Different Purposes

A large part of management accounting is directed to the determination, measurement, and analysis of costs. Before you continue to read, stop here and jot down what you think the term cost means. Your answer is probably only "1/n" correct, where n equals the number of *different* meanings of the term cost. For instance, if there were only two meanings of the term cost, then your answer would be "one half correct." Actually there are several different meanings of the general term "cost." *There are different concepts and definitions of cost for different purposes—there is not one all-purpose meaning of the term cost.* One primary function of management accountants is to decide which specific concept and measure of cost is the most appropriate and the most relevant for each management purpose.

To measure periodic net income and profit performance, the cost of manufacturing products must be determined so that the proper *product cost* per unit is allocated to the company's inventory quantities. These product costs are *past costs.* In contrast, for many current management decisions *future costs* must be estimated. For management control reports, *fixed costs* should be separated from *variable costs.* Fixed costs are those costs that remain more or less constant over a wide range of activity during a period of time, whereas variable costs depend on the actual level of activity during the period. Also in management control reports *actual costs* may be compared with *standard* or *budgeted costs,* which are predetermined measures of what the costs should have been for the period.

Some costs are *direct costs* to a particular product being manufactured or to a particular activity or operation being analyzed. Other costs are *indirect costs* which are more removed from any obvious basis of attachment or matching with a particular product, activity, or operation. Some costs are directly affected by a particular decision to be made, whereas other costs would be the same no matter which of several alternative courses of action is selected by the decision maker. Those costs that are different between the alternatives being considered by the decision maker are called *incremental* or *differential costs.* Last, there is a distinction between *full costs* and *partial costs.* Full costs include many fixed and indirect costs and usually span a long period of time. For many purposes, however, partial costs are more relevant. The chapters that follow explain which meaning of cost is required for each management purpose.

Placement of the Management Accounting Function in the Organizational Structure

In most business organizations, responsibility for management, tax, and financial accounting functions is included in the job description of the company's *Controller* (sometimes spelled Comptroller). The place of the Controller in a company's organizational structure differs from company to company. Exhibit 1.4 shows the organizational structure of one large company, Admiral Corporation, with an arrow pointing to this company's placement of the Controller. (In 1974 this company merged into Rockwell International Corporation.) Notice in this chart that the Controller reports to the company's Financial Vice-president.

Except in relatively small organizations, the controller would supervise sev-

EXHIBIT 1.4
Typical Organization Chart

(*Source*. Allen R. Janger, *Corporate Organization Structures: Manufacturing*,
The Conference Board, Inc. 1973, p.16.)

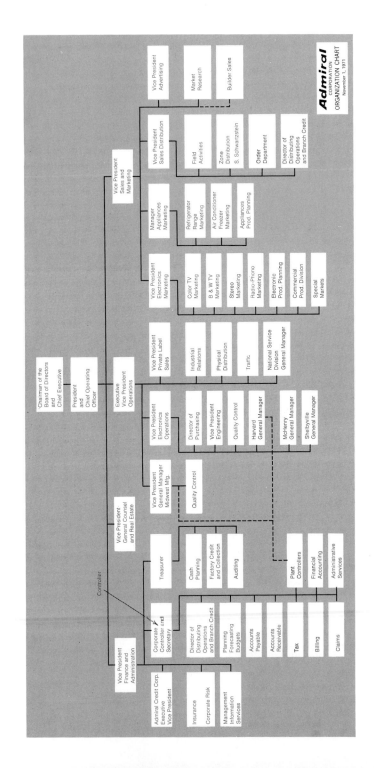

eral accountants, each of whom is responsible for a specialized accounting function. Under the controller there may be a cost accounting department, a budget department, a tax department, and so on. In turn each department may be subdivided. For example, the tax department may be subdivided according to types of taxes, such as income taxes, payroll taxes, and property taxes. Likewise, a cost department may be subdivided according to each major operating division of the company.

The Controller usually is responsible for nearly all of the management, tax, and financial accounting functions in the company. However, the division of certain *financial administration* functions and responsibilities among the Controller, the Secretary, and the Treasurer (corporate positions required by law in most states), and the Vice-president of Finance is *not* a matter of settled opinion or standard practice. For instance, should insurance be the responsibility of another financial officer of the company (most likely the Treasurer or the Vice-president for Finance)? Who should be responsible for the maintenance of bank relations and the negotiation of bank loans? Who should decide whether to lease or to purchase certain assets? Who should be responsible for coordination of the long-run financial planning of the company? The role of the Controller as the chief accounting officer of the business entity does not preclude the Controller from also having other financial administration responsibilities. But, as we just mentioned, it is difficult to generalize. Different companies divide these duties differently between the Controller, Treasurer, and other financial officers.

Finally, it should be observed that the Controller's position is very high in the organizational structure. Usually the Controller is either at the second to top level of management or very close to it. The Controller has reporting responsibilities throughout the whole organization. He generally exercises the predominate role in tax decisions, choices of accounting methods, and in several other accounting related matters. In some instances, the Controller sits on the Board of Directors of the corporation.

Key Management Concepts for Management Accounting

As we have already explained, the primary function of management accounting is the reporting of relevant information to the management decision makers in the organization. To perform this vital function, management accountants need a good working knowledge of management theory and practices. The remainder of this chapter introduces basic concepts of management that have particular relevance and importance to the management accountant.

The Central Importance of Decision Standards

Most management decisions, especially planning and control decisions, require the comparison and evaluation of what has happened or what will happen against *standards*. In general terms, standards are yardsticks, benchmarks, reterence points, or criteria used by managers to judge the "quality of achievement." Students need a standard to judge how well they are doing in school. A student may adopt a minimal standard, such as "as long as I pass all my courses. I'm satisfied." Or the student's standard may be to earn all A's. Judgment of the quality and level of achievement of performance is almost always *relative* to certain standards or criteria against which the performance is compared. To a certain extent, performance is dependent on the standards adopted by the decision maker. If a low standard is used, then low quality performance may be accepted as reasonable, and there may be no incentive for improvement.

Generally speaking, there are three basic types of decision standards:

1. *Past period* or *historical* performance and position of the company—current performance and present position are compared against the prior period, as well as the trend over several periods.
2. *Current period goals* and *objectives* of the company—these standards are measures of achievement for the current period that managers have adopted *before* the period began, based on planning, budgeting, goal setting, and determination of the objectives for the current period.
3. *Competitor's performances* and *economy-wide conditions*—these are external standards that look beyond the company.

In short, managers ask: (1) are we doing better or worse than last period?; (2) are we doing better or worse than we had planned to do this period, or than we should have done this period?; and (3) how are we doing relative to our competitors and relative to the business community and economic conditions in general? All three types of decision standards come into play in many decisions.

To compare this period with prior periods, managers first must understand the financial statements of the company and the basic behavior and relationships of costs, revenue, profit, and capital investment. These are the main topics of Chapters Two to Four. Chapter Five explores interperiod comparative analysis methods, that is, the analysis of this period's performance to last period's performance and position. Next, Chapters Six and Seven examine the general subject of budgeting and the development of performance standards and objectives for the coming period, which are used to evaluate the period's actual performance and position. By this process, sales revenue targets, cost standards, profit goals, and other financial objectives are developed. The third type of decision standards (competitors' performances and general economic conditions) are discussed in several chapters.

Short-run Versus Long-run Decisions

Let us assume that the purchasing agent of a company decides to buy a certain brand and model of pencils to be used by employees. A quantity of these pencils is purchased that should last about two or three weeks. Clearly this example is a *short-run* (or *short-term*) decision. *Short-run* means that the company is committed to this particular course of action (that is, the use of these particular pencils) for a relatively short period of time. When all the pencils are used then the company is free to repurchase the same pencils again, or to change to another brand or type of pencil, or to change to ball-point pens, and so on.

Consider, on the other hand, the purchase of a highly specialized and expensive machine that should last the company 10 years or more. In buying this fixed asset, the company is committing a sizable amount of capital to a particular use (that is, the services provided by the machine) for a relatively long period of time. The company cannot "get out of" this commitment except by disposing of the asset, which in turn may cause a substantial loss. *Long-run* decisions are those that, for most practical purposes, bind the business to a particular course of action for a relatively long period of time. The company may be able to terminate its long-term commitment, but not without some penalty.

Just how long is long-run? There are no firm and clear lines of separation between the long-run and the short-run. The use of one year (12 months) as an arbitrary dividing line is not altogether a bad rule of thumb. On the other hand, any significant commitment of more than three or six months perhaps should be called long-run. In most cases any commitment of less than three to six months probably would be called short-run. Usually the exact length of time is not the critical factor. Much more important are the options open to the company for "getting out of" the commitment without penalty, or the options for changing or modifying the commitment later. For example, the purchase of a building by a company usually is planned as a long-term investment. But the building may be quite marketable, and the company may be able to sell the building without a loss (perhaps even for a gain) anytime it decides to. Or, the company may be able to rent out part of the space in the building on a month-to-month or year-to-year basis.

In general, most long-run decisions involve relatively large amounts of monetary commitment. This monetary commitment usually takes one of two forms: (1) a substantial amount of cost is invested in long-lived assets; or, (2) the company enters into long-term contracts calling for future payments, for example, a labor union contract for three years that sets wage rates over this time period. In the first instance, money is invested *now* in certain resources needed to carry on the operations of the business in the future. In the second instance, no money is invested now; the payment obligations fall due in the future. (Long-term *investment* decisions require the explicit recognition of the cost of capital; this topic is discussed in Chapters Nine and Ten.)

Management by Exception (Selected Emphasis) Versus the "Equal" Management of Everything

The manager's life is a problem-oriented one. Indeed, management is often defined as a problem-solving function. Most decisions made by managers are problems in the sense that there is more than one alternative solution or course of action, and the "best" alternative is not obvious. Managers try to allocate their time among problems more or less in proportion to how serious the problems are. It would be a mistake to allocate an equal amount of time to each and every problem the manager deals with. Some problems are more important than others; these problems demand more attention and time.

The allocation of more management time and effort to the more important problems is called "management by exception." One assumption behind this concept is that a manager already should have solved many of the business's ongoing problems in *prior* periods, such that the activity and performance of the current period should be "fixed" on a proper course of direction. However, some things may (and usually do) go wrong during the current period; certain results may not conform to what was designed to occur. Or, unexpected developments may throw performance off track. In short, management by exception means that a manager should be alert for and focus attention on the *specific* factors that are going wrong in this period out of the whole range of activity and performance under the manager's span of responsibility.

The management emphasis is on the "exceptions" or deviations from what was planned for and programmed in advance by the manager. Those things that are going right (that is, where there are no significant exceptions or deviation) are not ignored by the manager. The manager needs to know about them and depends on accounting reports to include both types of information—what's going right and what's going wrong. The design of accounting reports to managers should implement the management by exception approach, by directing attention to the exceptions. For instance, assume that 20 different cost performance areas of operations are included in the accounting report to a manager, of which 3 are deviating seriously from what was planned. These 3 would be highlighted in that period's report; the other 17 would be reported as "under control."

Guarding Against Information Overload on Managers

A manager has only so much time in which to absorb the information reported to him or her—that is, to digest, interpret, and analyze the information, and then to reach a decision. Only *relevant* information should be reported to the manager; time cannot be wasted on irrelevant information. But which information is relevant and which is irrelevant? How does the accountant sort between the two kinds of information? The first step is to have a good understanding of the decision being made by the manager. The accountant should know the range of possible alternatives and options being considered by the manager. Likewise, the accountant should know the basic objectives and purposes of the organization. The accountant should identify those factors or variables that have the most potential impact on the decision, versus those factors and variables that do not have significant impact no matter which alternative is followed. The accountant should ask which factors and variables would be *different* between each possible alternative course of action open to the manager in the decision situation.

Consider, for instance, a decision facing a manager regarding how to use the factory building space already owned by the company. None of the alternatives being considered involve moving out of the building. In other words, all the decision alternatives are based on the assumption of remaining in the building for some time. In this case, therefore, many of the costs of occupancy and use of the building probably would be the same no matter which alternative were followed. These costs are not relevant to the decision, since they are not different between the various alternatives under consideration by the manager. Such costs would be either suppressed completely and kept out of the accounting information being reported to the manager for this decision, or at least the costs would be deemphasized and given secondary importance in the report. Costs that are different between the alternatives being considered by the manager are the relevant costs and should be given primary emphasis in the report.

If irrelevant information is not filtered out, so that only relevant information reaches the manager, then the manager may be overloaded with too much information. This excess of information may very likely confuse rather than help the decision process. But there is always a problem of sorting relevant from irrelevant information. The possibility of two critical errors plagues the management accountant: (1) irrelevant information may be reported, or (2) some relevant information may not be reported. One or the other error is to be expected sometimes. Which error is more serious? This is a difficult question to answer. There may be a bias to report too much irrelevant information, rather than omit some relevant information. The management accountant should be on constant alert for both types of errors. Hopefully the users of the information (the managers) will tell the accountant if irrelevant information is being reported, or if relevant information is not being reported.

Responsibility Accounting: Following the Organizational Structure

Reporting accounting information to all the different individual managers of a company is based on the *organizational structure* of the company. The term organizational structure refers to the division and relationship of duties, functions, and responsibilities among the managers of the entity. The span of authority and responsibility of each manager first must be clearly identified as the starting point in designing the scope, content, level of detail, and frequency of the accounting reports to each manager. This key concept is called *responsibility accounting.* The president (chief operating executive) of a company needs all-inclusive, summary level accounting reports spanning the company as a whole. (These accounting reports to the president may be supplemented with more specific detailed reports on particular problem areas.)

On the other hand, a general manager of a division or department should receive accounting reports *for this division or department,* in some detail and probably quite frequently. The content, format, and level of detail in these departmental or divisional accounting reports depends on the nature of the functions of this organizational unit, that is, whether it is a manufacturing division, a purchasing department, a sales territory, a personnel department, the data processing department, or the like. A departmental or divisional manager may also receive accounting reports for the company as a whole, to determine how his or her division or department fits in and relates to the business entity as a whole. But these company-wide supplemental accounting reports to a divisional or departmental manager probably would not be in as much detail nor as frequent, since the manager has no direct responsibility and authority beyond his or her division or department. In summary, in preparing the accounting reports to each manager in the business organization, the management accountant should first clearly identify the boundaries of each manager's responsibility, and the specific performance aspects and factors within this responsibility area that each manager is held responsible for planning and controlling.

Controllable Costs

Other than top level managers who have company-wide authority and responsibility, middle level and front-line managers have very definite limits to their authority and responsibility. In reporting cost performance and results, only those specific costs that the manager has authority over and is responsible for should be included in the reports to the manager. These are called *controllable costs*. This is one primary application of the responsibility accounting concept.

For example, consider the purchasing officer for a particular department in one of a company's manufacturing divisions. This individual manager has direct authority and responsibility to purchase the various supplies, materials, and services used by this department. Therefore, these are controllable costs of this particular manager. On the other hand, should the purchasing department be charged with part of the total occupancy cost of the building in which the purchasing office is located, say on the basis of square footage? The purchasing agent does not have any direct authority or responsibility for the several decisions regarding the insurance coverage on the building, maintenance of the building, the proper depreciation method of the building's cost, and so on. Thus these occupancy costs are not controllable *to this particular manager*. Keep in mind, however, that the occupancy costs are controllable costs to some *other* manager, that is, the manager responsible for the insurance, maintenance, heating, and the like, of the building.

As one moves up the organizational ladder, the span of each manager's responsibility becomes wider and wider. Thus, the range of controllable costs reported to higher level managers becomes wider and wider. At the top level of management virtually all costs are controllable, since at this level managers have very wide areas of responsibility. The main meaning of controllable costs involves those costs over which an individual manager has authority. Every particular cost is the responsibility of a particular manager in the organization. One major purpose of the responsibility accounting approach is to identify each cost to the appropriate manager.

Summary

The study of management accounting logically begins with the basic functions of management, which have been identified as planning, organizing, staffing, direction, control, innovation, and representation. A common ingredient of all these functions is decision making. Good decision making depends on good information. Management accounting, in large part, can be summarized as providing accounting information for management decision making. Much of this accounting information is feedback information for the purpose of comparing the actual performance and results of this period with that planned for and intended when the decisions were made that led to the period's actual performance and results. A comparison of this kind is essential for management control of current performance as well as planning for the next period.

Every business entity needs a general accounting system for three main purposes: to prepare external financial statements and reports to investors in the company; to prepare income and other tax returns that must be filed periodically; and, to prepare accounting reports and analyses to all the managers throughout the business organization. These three accounting functions are called in order financial accounting, tax accounting, and management accounting. Clearly management accounting should have equal priority with the other two main requirements on the general accounting system of a company. Financial accounting, tax accounting, and management accounting should not interfer with each other; a company's general accounting system should be designed to meet all three demands.

Financial accounting is subject to generally accepted accounting principles, which in the main agree with allowable income tax accounting methods. Management accounting, on the other hand, is not bound by GAAP and must be more flexible and open-ended to meet the accounting information needs of managers. For instance, current replacement cost values, or future predicted costs and sales prices are essential information for some management decisions. Generally speaking, these values are not reported for financial and tax accounting purposes. The design of accounting reports to individual managers requires that the specific range of responsibility and functions of each manager be considered by the management accountant. The accounting reports to each manager are "custom-made", in other words, whereas the external financial statements constitute one general purpose report that is sent to all stockholders in the corporation.

The modern management accountant is much more than an accounting "scorekeeper." The management accountant of today is expected to play an active consultant role in management decision making. In particular, the management accountant must determine which concept and measurement of cost are most relevant for each management purpose. There are several different meanings of cost, each for a different purpose. In most businesses, the Controller is the chief accounting officer who is responsible for the company's financial, tax, and management accounting functions. The Controller may also be assigned certain other financial administration functions, in addition to the accounting functions. The Controller's position is very high in most companies' organizational structures.

Management planning and control decisions require the adoption of decision standards, against which the planned or actual outcomes of decisions are compared. These are the bench marks or yardsticks used by the decision makers to judge their quality of achievement. Basically there are three types of decision standards—historical (past period) standards, current period planned or budgeted decision standards, and competitive and economy-wide standards. All three are relevant to most decisions. Short-run versus long-run is a useful distinction because it draws attention to how long a company is committed to a particular course of action and to the financial consequences of being committed to that course of action.

Managers usually must allocate their scarce time in proportion to the importance of the problems confronting them. They devote less of their time to those areas that are going according to plans and are under control. This is called management by exception. The main implication of this management technique is that accounting reports to each manager should highlight and direct attention to the "out of control" deviations or exceptions from plans and directions which managers should concentrate on.

The key idea of designing accounting reports to each manager that are consistent with his or her responsibility in the organizational structure of the company is called responsibility accounting. One main implication of responsibility accounting is that controllable costs should be stressed in reports to individual managers. Controllable costs are all those costs that an individual manager has authority over and is thus responsible for. In conclusion, a word of warning: the management accountant should be on guard against reporting too much accounting information, since this causes information overload on managers. The most relevant and significant information may get lost in the deluge of data and, thus, may be overlooked.

Questions

1. 1   For each of the management functions listed by Dale what are some types of information needed for the decisions made by managers in carrying out the function?

1. 2   (a) What is meant by feedback information?
        (b) Give one or two examples of how you use feedback information in your personal life.

1. 3   "Feedback information is necessary both for control purposes and for planning purposes." Do you agree with this statement? Explain.

1. 4   Do all the managers in the business organization need essentially the same accounting information? Briefly explain.

1. 5   Identify the three primary outputs of a company's general accounting system.

1. 6   What are the main differences between internal (management) accounting reports and external accounting reports?

1. 7   What are the three basic steps of a company's general accounting system? Briefly explain each step.

1. 8   "Essentially management accounting is an extension of financial accounting." Do you agree? Explain.

1. 9   What does the term *responsibility accounting* mean? Does the basic idea of this term have any bearing on financial accounting?

1.10   "Most companies keep two or three sets of books." Do you agree? Briefly explain.

1.11   "Management accounting is essentially a detailed bookkeeping function that focuses primarily on costs." Do you agree? Briefly explain.

1.12   (a) What are the main duties of a company's Controller?
(b) What other duties may the Controller be assigned?

1.13   (a) What is meant by the term "decision standards?"
(b) Give one example of how performance may be less than what it could be as a result of poor decision standards.
(c) What are the three basic types of decision standards used in most business decision situations?

1.14   For each decision listed below explain whether this decision is a short-term or a long-term decision, or if it is in the grey area or on the borderline between short-run and long-run.
(a) Purchase of one page of advertising in one issue of *Time* magazine.
(b) Purchase of new IBM electric typewriter.
(c) Hiring a new office worker who must first serve a six-month probationary period being given a regular position.
(d) Purchase of a new forklift truck for use in the company's warehouse.
(e) Signing a year employment contract with the new president of the company which involves an incentive bonus provision that can be renewed annually on the mutual agreement of both parties.

1.15   "If a manager were following the management by exception principle, then he would spend about the same amount of time every period on the same problems." Do you agree? Briefly explain.

1.16   Which error is more serious? Reporting 5% too much irrelevant information in the regular periodic accounting reports to a manager, or failing to report one relevant item out of 20?

1.17   Would an organizational chart be of any use in implementing the responsibility accounting concept? Explain.

1.18 "There is one true meaning of cost." Do you agree? Briefly explain.

1.19 For a particular manager what is the main test to decide if a cost is controllable or not?

Problems

P1. 1 A local camera store is organized into three sales departments: (a) new and used cameras and other photographic and darkroom equipment, (b) film processing services, and film development supplies and chemicals, and (c) new and used hi fi and stereo equipment (which is located in a separate area in the store but is convenient for customers that are in the store just to buy film or to drop off film for processing). The gross profit margin (percent) on sales revenue is considerably different between these three product lines.

There is a different manager for each department, each of whom has almost total authority and responsibility for the profit performance of his department. The three managers report to the president of the company, who owns the majority of the stock issued by the corporation. The president sets the general company-wide objectives and financial policies of the company. The company owns its building.

Required: Based on the information given above (which is no more than a brief overview of the company), answer the following questions.

(1) Should the Controller of this company prepare separate profit performance statements for each department? If so, which types of costs and expenses should be deducted against each department's sales revenue?

(2) Is the building's annual depreciation expense a direct and controllable cost that should be charged against each department's sales revenue?

(3) Employees in department (b) are paid on an hourly wage basis with a guarantee of at least 40 hours per week plus time and a half for overtime. In contrast, employees in the other two departments are paid entirely on the basis of a percentage of the sales they make. Explain the difference in these labor costs and how the costs should be reported to the managers of each department.

(4) The company buys most of its products FOB (free on board) shipping point, which means that the company pays the freight cost of shipping the products to the store. Many shipments contain products for two or even all three departments. Should transportation-in costs of these shipments be allocated to each department?

(5) Should all three departments earn the same total amount of profit (sales revenue less appropriate costs and expenses) each year? If not, briefly explain how the president might compare and evaluate the profit performance of the three departmental managers.

P1. 2 Assume that your accounting class is making a field visit to a nearby company that manufactures and sells restaurant furniture, such as tables, chairs, counters, and the like. The company's Controller has just completed a brief explanation of the company's accounting system, of which he is in charge. He discussed in some detail the various tax returns that are prepared and he distributed to the members of the class recent copies of the quarterly and annual financial reports that were sent to the stockholders of the company. Based on your quick reading of these stockholder reports, the company's financial statements seem very typical in terms of format and detail of the accounting information presented, and the independent auditor's report states that the financial statements have been prepared according to generally accepted accounting principles. However, the Controller said virtually nothing about the company's management accounting system, and he showed the class no management accounting reports.

When a student asked him about what sorts of management accounting reports are prepared for the top and middle levels of managers in the organization, the controller replied that the company is a closely held corporation and all the stock is owned by the top level managers in the company, and thus the financial reports to stockholders could do "double duty." That is, the financial statements to stockholders also are used by the managers for their management purposes.

Required:
(1) Explain whether you agree or disagree with the Controller in this situation. If you disagree, give a few specific examples of the additional types of information needed by managers that are not usually included in financial statements to stockholders.
(2) Assume that the company's president, on reading your answer to part (1), becomes convinced of the urgent need to implement a good management accounting system for the company. In fact, he fires the old Controller and hires a new Controller who is given the primary mission of quickly putting into effect a management accounting system. In basic terms where would the new Controller start in the development of a management accounting system for this company? In other words, what would be some of the first things the new Controller would look at and study as the first steps in designing a management accounting system for the company?

P1. 3 Rental City, Inc., is a typical rental store that rents out a large variety of tools and equipment either by the hour, the day, or the week. All these items are purchased outright by the company. One key success factor is its purchase of those particular items that very few persons or households buy themselves but that are needed on occasion. For instance, Rental City does not rent screwdrivers or hammers, since almost every household buys these tools. But the company does rent moving tools and equipment, such as pads and dollies, since very few households buy these items. Unfortunately the company sometimes buys a special or novelty item that no one wants to rent. In particular, Rental City happened to purchase a waterfall fountain centerpiece for parties that has been rented out only once in two years. Even lowering the rental rate did not help. This item cost $325 two years ago. The company adopted a five-year depreciation life for this asset with an estimated salvage value of $25. The company uses the sum-of-the-years'-digits depreciation method for all of its assets.

Required:

(1) What is the present book value of the asset?
(2) The company has been approached by a hotel who wants to buy the asset. The same centerpiece today sells new for $480. There is no active used (secondhand) market for this item. What is the *relevant cost* that the owner/ manager of the company should use in negotiating a sales price with the hotel?
(3) Assume that the company sells the asset to the hotel for $100. How would this transaction be reported:
   (a) In the external financial statements to stockholders for the year?
   (b) In the internal accounting report to the manager for the year?
   If your answer to (a) is different than (b), explain.

P1. 4   This company is one of several retail shoe stores in a city with a population of 50,000. The owner and general manager is in the process of evaluating and judging the store's profit performance for the year just ended. Certain sources or items of information are listed below.

Required: For each information source or item, identify which one of the basic three types of decision standards for which this information is needed or is most useful.

(1) Prior years' net income statements prepared by the company's accountant for the general manager.
(2) The annual survey just published by the National Retail Shoe Store Association, which reports averages for all the member stores' operating costs, sales revenue, and much other financial data.
(3) A study by the city's Chamber of Commerce, published about 12 months ago, reporting the average income per capita and per family for persons living in the city.
(4) An article in yesterday's *Wall Street Journal* regarding an increase in social security payroll taxes paid by the company that will go into effect next year.
(5) A recent article in *Time* commenting on the increasing number of persons going barefoot during summer, and for that matter even in late spring and in early fall in many cities.

Chapter Two

Brief Review of Financial Accounting

BRIEF REVIEW OF FINANCIAL ACCOUNTING

Financial Statements for a Manufacturing Company

Introduction of Company Example

Financial statements for a typical *manufacturing* company for the two years ending December 31, 1975 and 1976 are presented in the following pages. These are the three principal financial statements for the entity as a whole, and they serve as the example for a brief review of financial accounting. Financial statements are accompanied by additional disclosures, mainly footnotes that explain briefly the major accounting policies of the company and that provide supporting detail to the financial statements. For simplicity, however, no footnotes are presented here, since this additional information is not needed for the review purpose of the chapter.

First, read carefully each of the three statements: (1) Exhibit 2.1, the Statement of Financial Condition (also called the Balance Sheet); (2) Exhibit 2.2, the Net Income Statement (also called the Results of Operations Statement or Profit and Loss Statement); and, (3) Exhibit 2.3, the Statement of Changes in Financial Position (until recently called the Statement of Sources and Uses of Funds). Since some background in financial accounting is assumed, these statements are presented in a form acceptable for reporting externally to investors. Notice, however, that the Net Income Statement includes more detail and description than is customary in external financial reports. This additional information provides a more useful and convenient source of reference for discussion in this chapter.

Brief Overview of the Transactions of a Business Entity

This chapter reviews and analyzes the basic transactions for the year 1976 of the company whose financial statements have just been introduced. To begin, a general overview of the *transactions* of a business entity is shown in Exhibit 2.4. The business entity is pictured as being in the middle of the economic exchange process. The business entity is essentially an intermediary in the production and distribution of goods and services, as well as being an investment intermediary for those who invest capital in the enterprise. In large part, finan-

EXHIBIT 2.1

Statement of Financial Condition at December 31, 1975 and 1976

ASSETS

	1975	1976
Current Assets		
Cash	$ 288,925	$ 346,045
Accounts Receivable	934,500	1,478,125
Raw Materials Inventory	396,400	463,825
Work-in-Process Inventory	123,250	144,826
Finished Goods Inventory	1,417,375	1,560,374
Prepaid Expenses	436,750	491,300
Total	$3,597,200	$4,484,495
Fixed Assets		
Buildings	$1,815,000	$1,815,000
Machinery and Equipment	2,423,200	2,561,700
Vehicles	286,500	319,000
Total, at Original Cost	$4,524,700	$4,695,700
Accumulated Depreciation	872,400	1,253,695
Net of Depreciation	$3,652,300	$3,442,005
Land	675,000	675,000
Total	$4,327,300	$4,117,005
Total Assets	$7,924,500	$8,601,500

SOURCES OF CAPITAL

	1975	1976
Current Liabilities		
Accounts Payable and Accrued Costs	$1,417,000	$1,350,400
Income Tax Payable	56,300	78,492
Short-term Notes Payable	500,000	750,000
Total	$1,973,300	$2,178,892
Long-term Liabilities		
Long-term Notes Payable	$1,500,000	$1,750,000
Owners' Equity		
Invested Capital (40,000 common stock shares outstanding)	$4,000,000	$4,000,000
Retained Earnings	451,200	672,608
Total	$4,451,200	$4,672,608
Total Sources of Capital	$7,924,500	$8,601,500

Note to Student:
Footnotes are an integral part of externally reported financial statements. To simplify this example no footnotes are included with these financial statements.

EXHIBIT 2.2
Statement of Net Income for Years Ending December 31

	1975			1976		
Sales revenue			$10,000,000			$11,825,000
Cost of goods sold:						
Beginning finished inventory cost		$1,133,900			$1,417,375	
Cost of finished goods manufactured during year:						
Beginning work-in-process inventory cost		$ 98,600			$ 123,250	
Cost of raw materials issued to production during the year	$2,250,675			$2,604,375		
Direct labor manufacturing cost for the year	2,926,875			3,336,750		
Manufacturing overhead costs recorded during year	1,293,075			1,464,750		
Total manufacturing costs charged to this year		6,470,625			7,405,875	
Total of work-in-process brought forward plus this year's manufacturing costs		$6,569,225			$7,529,125	
Ending work-in-process inventory cost		123,250			144,826	
Total cost of products finished during year			6,445,975			7,384,299
Total cost of finished goods available for sale			$7,579,875			$8,801,674
Ending finished inventory cost			1,417,375			1,560,374
Cost of (finished) goods sold			6,162,500			7,241,300
Gross profit (before other operating expenses of year)			$ 3,837,500			$ 4,583,700
Operating expenses:						
Marketing expenses		$2,733,000			$3,182,300	
Administration and general expenses		373,500	3,106,500		423,500	3,605,800
Operating profit (before interest and income tax)			$ 731,000			$ 977,900
Interest expense			148,750			180,000
Net income before income tax			$ 582,250			$ 797,900
Income tax expense			272,980			376,492
Net Income			$ 309,270			$ 421,408
Earnings per share			$7.73			$10.54

cial accounting is directed to the recording and processing of the financial effects of the constant stream of transactions engaged in by the business entity, and to the preparation of periodic financial statements from the accounting records of the company.

The business raises capital (usually money) by issuing short-term or long-term debt securities and by the issue of stock securities.* This money (capital) thus becomes available for the business to purchase the various resources and other input factors needed to manufacture and distribute the products and

* Sole proprietorships and partnerships do not issue stock (ownership) securities. The exhibit refers to corporations.

EXHIBIT 2.3
Statement of Changes in Financial Position for Years Ending December 31

	1975	1976
Sources Of Funds		
Net Income for Year (See Net Income Statement)	$ 309,270	$ 421,408
Add Back Depreciation	359,320	381,295
Total Funds from Operations	$ 668,590	$ 802,703
Long-term Borrowing	250,000	500,000
Total	$ 918,590	$1,302,703
Uses Of Funds		
Cash Dividends	$ 100,000	$ 200,000
Payment on Long-term Debt	—0—	250,000
Capital Expenditures	842,500	171,000
Total	$ 942,500	$ 621,000
Net Increase (Decrease) of Funds During Year	($ 23,910)	$ 681,703

Increases (Decreases) in Current Assets and Current Liabilities During the Year Ending December 31:

	1975	1976
Cash	$ (204,294)	$ 57,120
Accounts Receivable	286,425	543,625
Raw Materials Inventory	38,715	67,425
Work-in-Process Inventory	24,650	21,576
Finished Goods Inventory	283,475	142,999
Prepaid Expenses	40,150	54,550
Net Increase of Current Assets	$ 469,121	$ 887,295
Accounts Payable and Accrued Costs	$ 221,831	$ (66,600)
Income Tax Payable	21,200	22,192
Short-term Notes Payable	250,000	250,000
Net Increase of Current Liabilities	$ 493,031	$ 205,592
Increase (Decrease) of Funds During Year	$ (23,910)	$ 681,703

Notes to Student:
1. In this statement funds is defined as the excess of total current assets over total current liabilities, which is the usual definition for external reporting to investors. See, however, the discussion of cash flow in Chapter Eight.

2. In this example depreciation is equal to the increase in the Accumulated Depreciation account during each year, which means that there are no retirements or other disposals of (depreciable) fixed assets during the year. In many cases there are disposals during the year, which decrease the balance of the Accumulated Depreciation account.

EXHIBIT 2.4
A Transactions Overview of the Business Entity

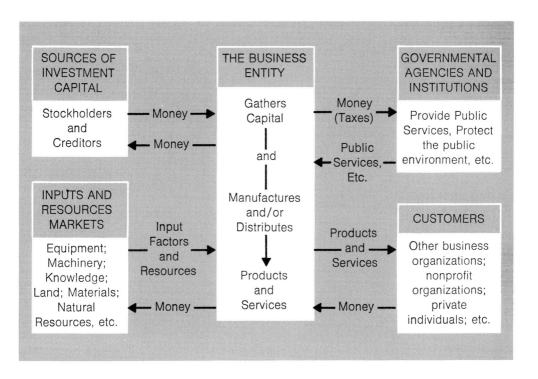

services sold by the business. These products and services are sold to customers. Their sale generates the sales revenue or money inflow to recover the costs of manufacturing and distributing the products and services, and to provide an adequate payment or return on the capital invested in the business. Taxes must be paid to government authorities for the public services provided to the business, as well as to its investors, employees, and customers.

A Special Point: Determining the Cost of Products Manufactured (Finished) During the Period

Notice in particular the format and content of the cost of goods sold section in the Net Income Statement (Exhibit 2.2). This company is a *manufacturer.* Instead of purchasing products in a finished condition ready for resale (which wholesalers and retailers do), this company purchases three basic types of manufacturing factors: (1) raw materials, (2) direct labor, and (3) manufacturing overhead supplies and services. The company combines these three input factors to produce the finished products it sells. These manufacturing costs are accum ulated in the *Work-in-Process Inventory* account during the production process. When the products are completed the total manufacturing cost of the products is transferred from the Work-in-Process Inventory account to the Finished Goods Inventory account by an appropriate accounting entry (which is shown later in this chapter).

It is very important to understand that a company's total manufacturing costs for the year for all the production activity and operations of that year usually is *not* equal to the cost of products finished (completed) during the year. In this example, for instance, a small part of the total manufacturing costs for each year are caused by and, therefore, are charged to the increase of the company's work-in-process inventory. Therefore, the cost of products *finished* (completed) during each year is somewhat less than the total manufacturing costs for each year. To repeat, a small part of each year's total manufacturing activity is due to the increase of the quantity of products still in the process of production at the end of each year.* To summarize these remarks (see Exhibit 2.2 for amounts):

Subtraction of Work-in-Process Inventory Increase from Manufacturing Costs to Determine Cost of Goods Finished During Year

	1975	1976
Total manufacturing costs	$6,470,625	$7,405,875
Less increase of work-in-process inventory (ending inventory cost less beginning inventory cost)	24,650	21,576
Cost of products finished during the year	$6,445,975	$7,384,299

Management's Need to Understand Financial Statements

Managers at all levels, but especially top level managers and the directors of a corporation need to understand thoroughly the three main financial statements for the company as a whole (as one total entity). For one reason, top management has the responsibility of insuring that the externally reported financial statements of their company present fairly the financial condition, performance, and activities of the company. Financial reporting is part of their *fiduciary duties* to the investors in the company. Obviously these managers should understand their own financial communications to investors. And, equally important, top level managers should understand how to interpret the financial condition and performance of their company which is reported in these statements. These interpretations, in fact, are an essential part of their management control and planning functions, and are discussed in following chapters.

---

* In the reverse situation a decrease in the work-in-process inventory during the year is *added* to the manufacturing costs of the period to determine the cost of products finished during the year.

Plan of Chapter

Making Summary Entries for the 1976 Transactions of the Company

In the remainder of this chapter the summary of each basic transaction of the company during 1976 is identified. These summary transactions are recorded in illustrative journal entries, which are then recorded in the accounts for the company.* The set of accounts are shown in Exhibit 2.8, which you should now study. Notice that the beginning balances of the assets, liabilities, and owners' equity accounts are the same amounts reported in the company's December 31, 1975 Statement of Financial Condition (Exhibit 2.1). The revenue and expense accounts start the year with zero balances.

After all of the 1976 summary entries have been recorded in the accounts and the ending balances are determined for each account, we can see that these ending balances agree with the amounts reported in the company's Statement of Financial Condition at December 31, 1976, and its Statement of Net Incomes for the year ending December 31, 1976. Also, from the entries in the accounts we shall be able to determine the amounts reported in the Statement of Changes in Financial Position for the year ending December 31, 1976.

The Three Basic Types of Transactions

Relative to how they are reported in the financial statements, the transactions of a business entity can be divided into three basic groups, which are shown in Exhibit 2.5. Accordingly, the company's 1976 transactions will be presented in the order of these three groups. Each summary transaction is shown as a *journal entry,* which is the original (first) recording of a transaction that shows the specific accounts increased and/or decreased by the transaction. Journal entries in turn are the source of information for recording the increases or decreases to the *accounts.* The collection of accounts (sometimes called the general ledger) are the direct source of information for preparation of the financial statements. A journal entry has the main advantage here of being a convenient and concise way of showing the financial consequences of each transaction. Since it is a complete entry for each transaction, the journal entry shows all the accounts increased or decreased by the transaction. Each summary transaction is keyed with a letter so that you can trace the transaction into the T accounts in Exhibit 2.8. Since a basic understanding of financial accounting on your part is assumed, there is only a very brief discussion of each transmission. However, you may be rusty on the rules of debits and credits. Hence, a plus sign (+) or a minus sign (−) is given for each debit or credit as a reminder.

---

* See the appendix to this chapter for a brief review of recording transactions in T accounts and the rules of debits and credits.

EXHIBIT 2.5
Three Basic Groups of Transactions

1. Revenue and expenses (as well as other income and losses, if any) that determine the net income for the period.

Summaries of these transactions are reported in the Net Income Statement

In addition to net income transactions, other transactions fall into one of two groups:

2. Transactions which change only current asset and/ or current liability accounts, and which therefore do *not* change the amount of *funds*. Funds, by the most common definition for financial statement reporting, is equal to total current assets less total current liabilities. At the start of 1976 the company's amount of funds is determined as follows:

	December 31,1975
Current Assets	$3,597,200
Current Liabilities	1,973,300
Funds	$1,623,900

If the total amount of funds is not changed, then the transaction must be *entirely contained* within the current accounts.

Summaries of these transactions' flows are *not* reported as such; but the supplement to the Statement of Changes in Financial Position includes the net increase or decrease during the period of each current asset and current liability account.

3. All other transactions of the company, most of which are sources or uses of funds and thus increase or decrease funds. (Keep in mind that net income usually is a source of funds also.)

Summaries of these transactions are reported in the Statement of Changes of Financial Position (except for the very few transactions that do not affect funds).

Revenue and Expense Transactions and Manufacturing Costs Also

Sales Revenue

The company's sales revenue generated during 1976 by the delivery of goods (products) totals $11,825,000; assume that all sales were made on credit. Journal entry (A) records the summary of all these sales transactions for the

Debit (+) Accounts Receivable	11,825,000	
Credit (+) Sales Revenue		11,825,000

year. For this and each of the following summary transactions for 1976:

1. Make sure that you understand the journal entry, that is, why the specific accounts are debited or credited (increased or decreased).
2. Trace the journal entry into the company's T accounts in Exhibit 2.8.

To shorten the presentation no explanations are given in the journal entries.

Raw Materials Purchases

Notice the Raw Materials Inventory account in the balance sheet (Exhibit 2.1). Manufacturers purchase raw materials that go into the manufacturing of their finished products. Generally, raw materials (or, at least, part of them) become part of the finished product. For instance, the company in this example may purchase steel sheets from a steel company. Then this company may mold, shape, and cut the steel sheets to form the body for its products.

The Raw Materials Inventory account holds the cost of raw materials that have been purchased until the items are used in the manufacturing process. The purchase cost is carried in this account until the point of release or issue to production, at which time the appropriate amount of cost is transferred out of the account. During 1976 the company purchased raw materials for a total cost of $2,671,800. All purchases are assumed to have been on credit. Summary entry (B) records these purchases during the year. Entry (B) is *not* an expense entry; notice that no expense account is involved. (It is an example of the second type of transaction shown in Exhibit 2.5). However, it is best to

Debit (+) Raw Materials Inventory	2,671,800	
Credit (+) Accounts Payable and Accrued Costs		2,671,800

B

present the raw material purchase entry at this point to follow the manufacturing process in a logical sequence. Purchase of raw materials precedes the use of the raw material in the manufacturing process.

Manufacturing Costs During Year

During 1976 total costs of $7,405,875 were recorded for manufacturing its products (some of which are still in process at the end of the year). This total cost of the company's manufacturing activity and operations during the year consists of several different cost items, which are summarized in Exhibit 2.6. In this exhibit notice in particular the variety of balance sheet (asset and liability) accounts that are decreased or increased in recording these costs. Some costs are raw materials used in production, some are depreciation, some are cash payments to employees, and so on.

These costs of the company's production activity are accumulated in the Work-in-Process Inventory account. The manufacturing costs stay in this account until the products reach the end of the production process. At the point of completion the cost of the finished products is transferred out of the Work-in-Process Inventory account to the Finished Goods Inventory account. Entry Ⓒ shows the recording of the (total) manufacturing costs to the Work-in-Process Inventory account based on the information from Exhibit 2.6.

It should be emphasized that a manufacturing company needs to establish very definite and very detailed cost accounting methods and procedures to determine the cost of its products up to the point of completion, so that the cost of finished products is known. (Manufacturing accounting cost methods and procedures are discussed in Chapters Twelve and Thirteen.) It is assumed that, based on the manufacturing cost accounting records kept during the year, the

Debit (+) Work-in-Process Inventory	7,405,875	
Credit (−) Prepaid Expenses		382,600
Credit (+) Accumulated Depreciation		231,925
Credit (−) Raw Materials Inventory		2,604,375
Credit (+) Accounts Payable and Accrued Costs		318,745
Credit (−) Cash		3,868,230

C

EXHIBIT 2.6
Summary of 1976 Manufacturing Costs

Description of Cost		Balance Sheet Account Credited	Total Cost Shown in Exhibit 2.2
Cost of the raw materials relased into the manufacturing process during 1976.		Raw Materials Inventory	$2,604,375
Cost during 1976 of wages and benefits paid to or on behalf of direct labor employees, that is, those employees working directly on the production line:			
Cash payments during year.	$3,152,570	Cash	
Accrued costs payable at year-end.	184,180	Accounts Payable and Accrued Costs	
Total			$3,336,750
All other costs of manufacturing operations during 1976, which collectively are called *overhead:*			
That part of the beginning balance of Prepaid Expenses charged off to manufacturing operations.	$ 382,600	Prepaid Expenses	
Depreciation of buildings, machinery and equipment, and vehicles allocated to manufacturing operations during 1976.	231,925	Accumulated Depreciation	
Cash payments for supplies, services, etc., during 1976.	715,660	Cash	
Accrued costs payable at year-end.	134,565	Accounts Payable and Accrued Costs	
Total			$1,464,750
Total manufacturing Costs During 1976.			$7,405,875

total cost of all the products completed during 1976 is $7,384,299. Summary entry (D) shows the recording of the cost of products finished (completed) during 1976.

Debit (+) Finished Goods Inventory	7,384,299	
Credit (−) Work-in-Process Inventory		7,384,299 D

Cost of Goods Sold Expense

Most products are manufactured in so-called "batches" or "lots." In other words, a quantity of the product is processed as a group; few products are manufactured one at a time. At the time of making entries during the year to record the completion of each batch, a manufacturing company prepares a detailed *inventory stock record* of some sort. This important inventory record includes the total cost of the batch of products just completed. (The accounting methods and procedures for identifying and measuring the costs of each production batch are discussed in Chapters Twelve and Thirteen.) Dividing the total cost of each production batch by the total quantity produced in this batch gives the cost *per unit.*

Based on these per unit product costs for the several batches completed and entered in the Finished Goods Inventory account during the year, the accountant determines the cost of the units sold during the year according to whichever inventory cost method is adopted (such as First-In, First-Out, or Last-In, First-Out). This company happens to use the LIFO inventory method. According to this method the total cost of all the products sold during 1976 is determined to be $7,241,300. Entry (E) records the summary cost of goods (products) sold during the year.

Debit (+) Cost of Goods Sold Expense	7,241,300	
Credit (−) Finished Goods Inventory		7,241,300 E

Notice that more products were finished during the year ($7,384,299) than were sold ($7,241,300). Hence, the Finished Goods Inventory account increases by $142,999 (which is $7,384,299 less $7,241,300).

Product Costs Versus Expenses: A Short Note at This Point

Manufacturing companies must carefully separate their costs of operations between manufacturing and nonmanufacturing costs. As we have already seen in the entries above, manufacturing costs are accounted for as *product costs*. That is, manufacturing costs are accumulated first in the Work-in-Process Inventory account and then are transferred to the Finished Goods Inventory account. Product costs do not become expenses until the finished products are sold— see entry Ⓔ. Other nonmanufacturing costs of operations are charged to an expense account immediately, at the time the cost is recorded. For example depreciation of manufacturing fixed assets is accounted for as a product cost. Notice in entry Ⓒ that depreciation is one of the costs charged to the Work-in-Process Inventory account. In contrast, depreciation of, for example, the typewriters used in the company's offices is classified as an administration and general expense. This cost is recorded directly to an expense account—see entry Ⓕ below.

In actual practice the line of separation between manufacturing and non-manufacturing costs is not easy to draw for many cost items. For instance, should the annual salary of the Vice-president of Production be classified as a manufacturing cost, or instead as one of the administration and general expenses of the company? What about the costs of handling finished goods as these products leave the production line and are moved into the company's warehouse? Are postproduction handling and storage costs of the inventory part of the total product costs, or should these costs be classified as selling expenses? For income tax purposes some costs that logically could be classified as manufacturing costs are instead charged to expense as soon as recorded. This is done rather than hold the costs in inventory accounts until the products are eventually sold. Thus the current period's taxable income is minimized, but keep in mind that the company's inventory cost value also is understated.

Marketing and Administration and General Expenses

During 1976 the company recorded total nonmanufacturing costs of $3,182,300 that are identified with or are allocated to the marketing operations (selling and delivery of products) during the year. Also, the company recorded administration and general costs which total $423,500. Together these two basic non-manufacturing operating functions of the company cost a total of $3,605,800 during 1976. This total cost consists of several different cost items, which are summarized in Exhibit 2.7. As in the case of Exhibit 2.6, notice that a wide variety of assets are credited (decreased) in recording these costs, and that some of the costs are increases to the liability account. Summary entry Ⓕ records these operating expenses for the year. It should be mentioned that a company does not use conglomerate broad expense accounts such as are charged in entry Ⓕ. In actual practice much more specific expense accounts are established. However, the main purpose of entry Ⓕ is simply to show the basic nature of the expenses.

EXHIBIT 2.7
Summary of 1976 Marketing and Administration and General Costs

Description of Cost	Balance Sheet Account Credited	Amount
Cost of wages and benefits paid to or on behalf of nonmanufacturing employees, salesmen, and officers during 1976:		
Cash payments during year. $1,624,610	Cash	
Accrued costs payable at year-end. 219,330	Accounts Payable and Accrued Costs	
Total		$1,843,940
That part of the beginning balance of Prepaid Expenses charged off to Marketing and Administration and General operations during 1976.	Prepaid Expenses	54,150
Depreciation of buildings, machinery and equipment, and vehicles allocated to Marketing and Administration and General operations during 1976.	Accumulated Depreciation	149,370
All other nonmanufacturing costs recorded during 1976, such as for advertising, office rent, legal fees, data processing supplies, and so on:		
Cash payments during year. $ 705,115	Cash	
Accrued costs payable at year-end. 853,225	Accounts Payable and Accrued Costs	
Total		1,558,340
Total Marketing and Administration and General Costs During 1976		$3,605,800

Debit (+) Marketing Expense	3,182,300	
Debit (+) Administration and General Expense	423,500	
Credit (−) Prepaid Expenses		54,150
Credit (+) Accumulated Depreciation		149,370
Credit (+) Accounts Payable and Accrued Costs		1,072,555
Credit (−) Cash		2,329,725

(F)

Interest and Income Tax Expenses

Interest expense depends on how much money is borrowed, for how long, and at what interest rate per period. Interest is paid usually at the end of short-term borrowing periods and every six months on long-term debt. Therefore, there is some lag in paying interest. In other words, interest expense accures every day money is borrowed even though it is paid only periodically. At the end of the year the accountant usually has to record (through an adjusting entry) some amount of accrued interest expense that has not been paid. The total interest expense for 1976 is $180,000, which is based on the company's debt balance and interest rates in effect during the year. Of this total amount, $17,500 is unpaid at December 31, 1976. The remainder of $162,500 was paid in cash during the year. Entry (G) records the interest expense for 1976.

Debit (+) Interest Expense	180,000	
Credit (−) Cash		162,500
Credit (+) Accounts Payable and Accrued Costs		17,500

(G)

During the year corporations are required to make progress payments toward their estimated federal income tax for the year. (This example omits any state income tax, though many states impose an income tax on business corporations.) The corporation paid total progress payments of $298,000 during 1976. Based on the final determination of its 1976 federal taxable income, the company's total income tax is $376,492. Since $298,000 has been paid during the year, only the balance of $78,492 ($376,492 less $298,000) is payable at December 31, 1976. This amount will have to be paid during the first part of next year (1977). Based on these facts, entry (H) records the company's 1976 income tax expense.

Debit (+) Income Tax Expense	376,492	
Credit (−) Cash	298,000	H
Credit (+) Income Tax Payable	78,492	

Closing the Revenue and Expense Accounts: Recording Net Income to Retained Earnings

One final entry is made now, although this entry is primarily a bookkeeping step rather than an entry for a transaction.* It is called the *closing* enry. The revenue and expense accounts for the year are closed (terminated), and the net difference among the revenue and expense accounts is transferred to the Retained Earnings Account. Entry (I) shows the closing entry at year-end 1976. The credit (+) of $421,408 to the Retained Earnings account is the net income for 1976, that is, sales revenue less all the expenses for the year.

Debit (−) Sales Revenue	11,825,000	
Credit (−) Cost of Goods Sold Expense	7,241,300	
Credit (−) Marketing Expenses	3,182,300	
Credit (−) Administration and General Expenses	423,500	I
Credit (−) Interest Expense	180,000	
Credit (−) Income Tax Expense	376,492	
Credit (+) Retained Earnings	421,408	

Transactions Contained Entirely Within Current Asset and Current Liability Accounts (Other Than the Manufacturing Entries Already Recorded)

During 1976 the company collected total cash of $11,281,375 from its customers, which are payments of their accounts receivables owed to the company. (It is assumed that there are no bad debts in this example.) Summary

---

* Our discussion has omitted adjusting entry procedures at the end of the year. Many manufacturing costs and operating expenses must be brought up to date at year-end with the adjusting entries. However, a description of this booking procedure is not essential to this discussion.

entry (J) records the cash receipts for the year. During 1976 the company paid total cash of $4,147,200 when its accounts payable and other accrued costs became due and payable during the year. Summary entry (K) records these cash disbursements during the year. The income tax payable balance at December 31, 1975 became due during 1976 and was paid. Entry (L) records these payments in 1976.

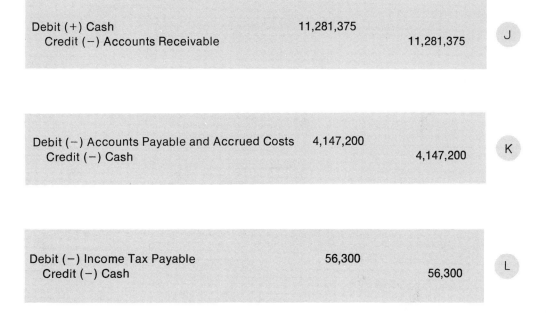

| Debit (+) Cash | 11,281,375 | | J |
| Credit (−) Accounts Receivable | | 11,281,375 | |

| Debit (−) Accounts Payable and Accrued Costs | 4,147,200 | | K |
| Credit (−) Cash | | 4,147,200 | |

| Debit (−) Income Tax Payable | 56,300 | | L |
| Credit (−) Cash | | 56,300 | |

At the start of 1976 the company owed $500,000 on short-term notes payable. These notes became due and were paid during the year. The company borrowed $1,250,000 on new short-term notes during the year all of which were paid before the year-end. Also, in October 1976 the company borrowed $750,000; this note is still outstanding and payable at December 31, 1976. In summary the company received total cash of $2,000,000 ($1,250,000 + $750,000) from short-term borrowing during 1976, and paid $1,750,000 of short-term notes during the year. Perhaps the best way of looking at this borrowing activity is to make two separate entries, one for the cash received and one for the cash paid—see entries (M) and (N). Recall that the interest expense on these short-term notes is recorded above in entry (G).

During 1976 the company paid for certain items that will benefit operations next year. For instance, a one-year fire insurance premium was purchased and paid for in late December 1976. This premium cost is deferred until 1977 by

| Debit (+) Cash | 2,000,000 | | M |
| Credit (+) Short-term Notes Payable | | 2,000,000 | |

| Debit (−) Short-term Notes Payable | 1,750,000 | | N |
| Credit (−) Cash | | 1,750,000 | |

recording the cost to the Prepaid Expenses asset account. Then, in 1977, the cost will be charged off, such as is shown in entries Ⓒ and Ⓕ above. The total of such prepaid costs at the end of 1976 is determined to be $491,300. All of these prepaid costs were paid in cash during 1976. Entry Ⓞ shows the recording of the prepaid costs.

| Debit (+) Prepaid Expenses | 491,300 | | O |
| Credit (−) Cash | | 491,300 | |

In entries Ⓙ to Ⓞ (as well as entries Ⓑ and Ⓓ for that matter), notice that only current asset and/or current liability accounts are changed by the transactions. Recall also that funds is defined (most often) as the *difference* between total current assets less total current liabilities. Hence, the amount of funds is *not* changed by any of these transactions. On the other hand, the amount of *cash* is increased or decreased by every one of these transactions. In other words, do not confuse funds (total current assets less total current liabilities) with cash. External financial statements do *not* report a summary of cash receipts and disbursements during the year.* (For internal management purposes cash flows are reported—see Chapter Eight.) Those transactions increasing or decreasing funds are reported in the external financial statements.

---

* The net increase or decrease during the year of each current asset and current liability account are reported as part of the Statement of Changes in Financial Position for the year. But, a separate schedule of Cash Receipts and Disbursements is not reported.

Sources and Uses of Funds (Which are Reported in the Statement of Changes in Financial Position)

In this example, as in most practical situations, all of the company's sales revenue transactions are increases to a current asset account. Therefore, sales revenue increases the amount of funds. (In some cases, sales revenue may be recorded by an increase to a noncurrent asset account, which means funds are not increased at the point of sale; funds do not increase until the noncurrent asset account is converted into a current asset account.) On the other side, most expenses decrease a current asset account or increase a current liability account, and thereby decrease funds. The primary exception to this general effect of expenses is depreciation. Depreciation is a decrease to long-term fixed asset accounts, thus depreciation does not decrease funds. To measure the increase of funds from net income for the year, the amount of depreciation should not be deducted, or should be added back to the final net income amount. In entires Ⓒ and Ⓕ total depreciation of $381,295 ($231,925 + $149,370) is recorded in 1976. This amount is added back to net income in the 1976 Statement of Changes in Financial Position (see Exhibit 2.3). (All other expenses decrease funds in this example.) Beginning with the funds generated from net income, the remainder of this financial statement reports the other sources and uses of funds during the year, which are the remainder of the company's 1976 transactions.

During 1976 the company borrowed $500,000 on a new *long-term* note payable which has a maturity date sometime after 1977. This long-term financing transaction is recorded in entry Ⓟ. Also, before it became due (which would have been in 1978) the company paid a $250,000 long-term note to avoid the higher interest rate on the note. The company was able to borrow long-term money at a lower interest rate in 1976. Part of long-term borrowing recorded in entry Ⓟ is to substitute new long-term debt with a lower interest rate for part of the old long-term debt. The payment during 1976 of the long-term note is recorded in entry Ⓠ.

Debit (+) Cash	500,000	
Credit (+) Long-term Note Payable		500,000

Ⓟ

Debit (−) Long-term Notes Payable	250,000	
Credit (−) Cash		250,000

Ⓠ

During 1976 the company paid a total of $5 per share of cash dividends to the common stockholders, for a total payment of $200,000. (40,000 shares of common stock are outstanding, and there were no increases or decreases in the number of outstanding shares during 1976.) Summary entry (R) records the cash dividends for the year. (The amount of dividends may be accumulated in a separate Dividends account during the year, which is closed to the Retained Earnings account at year-end.)

Debit (−) Retained Earnings	200,000	
Credit (−) Cash		200,000

(R)

During 1976 the company purchased fixed assets for a total cost of $171,000, which was paid in cash. Machinery and equipment costing $138,500 were purchased, and vehicles costing $32,500 were bought. There were no retirements or disposals of fixed assets during the year. Entry (S) records these *capital expenditures* during 1976.

Debit (+) Machinery and Equipment	138,500	
Debit (+) Vehicles	32,500	
Credit (−) Cash		171,000

(S)

This concludes the 1976 transactions. In many situations there are other examples of transactions which are not illustrated above. However, transactions (A) to (S) are a fairly broad representative basic set of transactions for a typical manufacturing company.

The Accounts for the Company with all 1976 Transactions Entered

The company's 1976 transactions, which have been discussed and analyzed in the preceding pages, are shown entered into the complete set of T accounts for the company in Exhibit 2.8. The ending balances of each account are written below the line drawn across each account. The three principal financial statements of the company are prepared from these accounts of course. Carefully

EXHIBIT 2.8
General Ledger Acconts of Company

Cash

BB	288,925	C	3,868,230
J	11,281,375	F	2,329,725
M	2,000,000	G	162,500
P	500,000	H	298,000
		K	4,147,200
		L	56,300
		N	1,750,000
		O	491,300
		Q	250,000
		R	200,000
		S	171,000
	346,045		

Accounts Receivable

BB	934,500	J	11,281,375
A	11,825,000		
	1,478,125		

Buildings

BB	1,815,000		
	1,815,000		

Machinery and Equipment

BB	2,423,200		
S	138,500		
	2,561,700		

BB = Beginning Balance,
carried forward
from December 31, 1975.

Other letters: see transaction
entry in the chapter that
is keyed with this letter.

Raw Materials Inventory

BB	396,400	C	2,604,375
B	2,671,800		
	463,825		

Work-in-Process Inventory

BB	123,250	D	7,384,299
C	7,405,875		
	144,826		

Finished Goods Inventory

BB	1,417,375	E	7,241,300
D	7,384,299		
	1,560,374		

Prepaid Expenses

BB	436,750	C	382,600
O	491,300	F	54,150
	491,300		

Vehicles

BB	286,500		
S	32,500		
	319,000		

Accumulated Depreciation

		BB	872,400
		C	231,925
		F	149,370
			1,253,695

Land

BB	675,000		
	675,000		

Accounts Payable and Accrued Costs		
K 4,147,200	BB	1,417,000
	B	2,671,800
	C	318,745
	F	1,072,555
	G	17,500
		1,350,400

Income Tax Payable		
L 56,300	BB	56,300
	H	78,492
		78,492

Short-term Notes Payable		
N 1,750,000	BB	500,000
	M	2,000,000
		750,000

Long-term Notes Payable		
Q 250,000	BB	1,500,000
	P	500,000
		1,750,000

Owners' Invested Capital		
	BB	4,000,000
		4,000,000

Retained Earnings		
R 200,000	BB	451,200
	I	421,408
		672,608

Sales Revenue		
I 11,825,000	A	11,825,000
		—0—

Cost of Goods Sold Expense		
E 7,241,300	I	7,241,300
—0—		

Marketing Expense		
F 3,182,300	I	3,182,300
—0—		

Administrative and General Expense		
F 423,500	I	423,500
—0—		

Interest Expense		
G 180,000	I	180,000
—0—		

Income Tax Expense		
H 376,492	I	376,492
—0—		

follow each account's balance into its place in the financial statements. Notice that the revenue and expense accounts have zero balances, since these accounts have been closed to the Retained Earnings account. The total of entries to each account during the year (that is, the balance before the closing entry) is used to prepare the Net Income Statement.

The preparation of the Statement of Changes in Financial Position is *not* prepared from the *ending* balances of the accounts. This statement begins with the net income for the year (from the Net Income Statement), and the amount of any expense that is not a decrease of funds is added back. Depreciation is the only such expense in this example. This gives the amount of funds during the year from net income sources. To determine the other sources and the uses of funds during the year, the accountant examines the long-term (noncurrent) accounts. Most of the transactions entered in these accounts are either increases (sources) of funds, or decreases (uses) of funds. For instance, there is an increase of $500,000 in the Long-term Notes Payable account (see Exhibit 2.8). This transaction records the borrowing of money during 1976, which is a source of funds of course, and therefore this transaction (in summary) is included in the Statement of Changes in Financial Position. Likewise, the accountant would determine the other sources and the uses of funds during 1976.

A Final Note

In this chapter a basic cycle of transactions during the year for a typical manufacturing company is analyzed and recorded in the accounts for the company. This particular company is carried forward as the main example in Chapters Three to Eight. Here we should mention again that managers need more detailed information, particularly regarding the behavior of costs and expenses, than is reported in the financial statements shown in this chapter. Also, managers need to know the sources of sales revenue and the causes of changes in sales revenue and costs from period to period. In other words, for management review, analysis, and decision making, the company's internal accounting reports include various types of explanatory and analytical schedules based on much more detailed information than is given in the summary level information reported in the financial statements in this chapter.

But keep in mind that financial statements for the company as a whole are an essential part (though not all) of the information that managers need for control of and planning for the financial performance and position of the company. Hence, Chapter Three discusses the basic measures and interpretations of financial performance and position that are of most importance to managers. Chapters Four and Five then consider the additional kinds of information and methods of analysis utilized in managerial decision making.

RECORDING TRANSACTIONS IN ACCOUNTS

Transactions are the basic financial activity units of the business that cause the financial condition of the company to change. Transactions are recorded first (originally) in the form of a journal entry, which is a complete concise accounting of the transaction. From the journal entries transactions are then recorded in the particular *accounts* changed by the transactions. Even a relatively small business entity must establish many accounts. The specific design of accounts and the methods of recording and processing transactions through accounts vary from company to company. The essential nature of an account is to provide a basic accounting information record for each asset, liability, and owners' equity, as well as the revenues and expenses of the company. A very helpful way to visualize an account is to use the so-called "T" account form, which is shown in Exhibit 2.9.

One side of the T account is used to show increses to the account and the other side is used to show decreases, which is a very convenient way to separate clearly increases from decreases. The left side of a T account is called the *debit* side and the right side is called the *credit* side. Debits to some accounts are increases and debits to other accounts are decreases; likewise for credits. The basic rules of debits and credits are shown in Exhibit 2.10.

The bracket over the Expenses and Revenues accounts emphasizes that these net income accounts are "stand-ins" as it were for the Retained Earnings

EXHIBIT 2.9
T Account

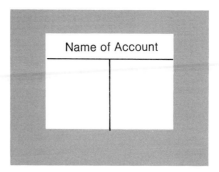

Name of Account

EXHIBIT 2.10

Debit and Credit Rules for Recording Transactions in Accounts

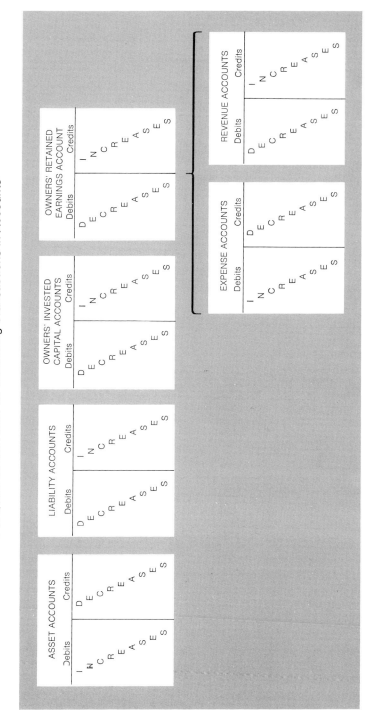

account. Instead of direct debits (decreases) and direct credits (increases) to the Retained Earnings account, expenses and revenues are first recorded to separate accounts, which at the end of the accounting year are closed out to the Retained Earnings account. (See entry I in the chapter for an example of a closing entry.) By following the rules shown in Exhibit 2.10 for the labeling or "tagging" of increases and decreases as either debits or as credits, each and every transaction must be recorded with an equality of (total) debits and (total) credits. This offers an important bookkeeping advantage. It provides a constant check on the balance of each transaction being recorded.

Questions

2. 1   Identify and briefly explain the nature and content of the three principal financial statements reported annually to the stockholders of a corporation.

2. 2   Refer to Exhibit 2.2, the Net Income Statement for the company, a manufacturer. Is the net income statement different for a *retailer*? Be specific regarding any differences.

2. 3   Why does the balance sheet (statement of financial condition) always *balance*? Why couldn't total assets be more or less than a company's total sources of capital?

2. 4   Could a company report a net loss for the year just ended but be in good financial condition nevertheless? Briefly explain.

2. 5   Why isn't Retained Earnings shown as an asset? Evidently many persons think it is an asset.

2. 6   Would you be concerned if total current assets were less than total current liabilities? Why?

2. 7   If the company's total manufacturing costs during the year are more than the cost of goods finished (completed) during the year, explain how this is apparent in the company's financial statements.

2. 8   Although an unusual situation, assume that a manufacturing company began operations in late November and that by the end of December, being in business only a little more than a month, no products have been finished yet.
   (a) Would there be any credits (decreases) in the company's Work-in-Process account?
   (b) Would there be any credits (decreases) in the company's Raw Materials Inventory account?
   (c) What would be unusual about a Net Income Statement prepared for this partial year period?

2. 9   What are the differences between recording transactions in journal entries and recording transactions in accounts?

2.10   Which manufacturer should have the largest balance of work-in-process inventory relative to its finished goods inventory: a company that has a very short production process or a company that has a very long production process?

2.11 Assume that a manufacturing company failed to record the completion of certain products by the end of the accounting year. Those products were on hand in the finished goods warehouse at year-end. What would be the mistakes in:
(a) The year-end balance sheet?
(b) The net income statement for the year?

2.12 Please refer to Exhibit 2.6 in the chapter which summarizes the company's manufacturing costs for the year 1976. Assume that some of the direct labor employees were mistakenly classified as other labor expense during the year, and were not included in the direct labor cost of $3,336,750 shown in the exhibit (though they should have been). What are the consequences of this error?

2.13 Assume that a company deliberately refuses to classify certain manufacturing costs as overhead costs. Instead, the company puts these costs into selling expense or general and administrative expense accounts.
(a) Why might a company do this?
(b) What are the consequences of this error?

2.14 Other than depreciation, give two examples of expenses not decreasing funds. Also, give two examples of revenue not increasing funds.

2.15 Does the recording of the following items increase or decrease funds:
(a) A stock dividend?
(b) Writing off an intangible long-term asset?
(c) Writing off the uninsured loss of inventories destroyed by fire?

2.16 "Financial statements such as those reported to the external investors in the business are irrelevant to the managers of the company." Do you agree? Briefly explain.

2.17 Why are some increases to accounts debits while increases to other accounts are credits?

2.18 Is the debits and credits method of recording transactions in accounts just as useful in computerized accounting systems?

Problems

P2. 1 The purpose of this problem is to reconstruct the basic transactions of the same company example discussed in the chapter for the year 1975 from the information reported in the company's financial statements for 1975, as well as certain other information given below. Assume that the same basic transactions were recorded for 1975 as are shown for 1976 in the chapter—only the amounts are different.

Required:
(1) From the financial statements for the company presented in the chapter

(see Exhibits 2.1 to 2.3) determine the correct amounts for each transaction during 1975 for the company, and make each entry. Label these entries (A) to (S) in the same manner illustrated in the chapter. Then record the transactions to the set of T accounts for the company.

(2) Based on your entries to the T accounts recorded in part (1), determine the *beginning* balances in each asset, liability, and owners' equity account. Having determined these beginning balances, prepare in good form the statement of financial position at December 31, 1974 for the company.

Other information needed to work problem:

(a) $296,530 of the year's manufacturing direct labor and overhead costs are still payable at year-end 1975.

(b) $896,450 of the year's marketing and administration and general expenses are still payable at year-end 1975.

(c) The division of the beginning balance of Prepaid Expenses which were charged off during 1975 is:

Manufactured Costs	= $349,300
Marketing and Administration and General Expenses =	47,300

(d) $211,470 of 1975's depreciation was charged to manufacturing operations.

(e) There is $14,300 of accrued interest payable at year-end 1975.

(f) The total of new borrowings from short-term notes was $1,500,000 during the year.

(g) Of the total capital expenditures shown in Exhibit 2.3 for 1975, $32,400 was for Vehicles and $810,100 was for Machinery and Equipment.

P2. 2   A company's total annual sales revenue is the main measure of activity during the year, which in large part determines the company's expenses, assets, and liabilities. This problem starts with a certain amount of assumed sales revenue for the year, and gives the various *ratios* of expenses, assets, and liabilities to sales revenue. Based on this information, prepare a condensed net income statement for the year and the company's balance sheet at the end of the year.

The total sales revenue for the year is $10,000,000. The company's gross profit is 40% of sales revenue. Marketing and other operating expenses are 30% of sales revenue. Sales revenue is 1.6 times total assets (or 160% of total assets). One half of total assets are supplied from liabilities. Four fifths (or 80%) of the company's total liabilities are interest bearing debts. The average annual interest rate is 8%. The income tax rate on taxable income is a flat 48%. Current assets make up one half of the company's total assets. The company's ending inventories (including raw materials, work-in-process, and finished goods) are equal to one fourth (25%) of the cost of goods sold for the year. The company's ending total accounts receivable is one tenth of sales revenue of the year. The company's ending total prepaid expenses is 2.5% of the total operating expenses (excluding interest and income tax) for the year, including cost of goods sold.

Through the end of the year, 25% of the original cost of the company's fixed assets has been depreciated, except for land, of course. The cost of the land is equal to 5% of the total assets of the company at year-end. Short-term (due in less than one year) interest bearing debts are equal to 40% of all interest bearing debts. The ending income tax payable is equal to 20% of th income tax expense for the year. Finally, the ratio of net income to the total stockholders' equity at year-end is equal to 13.312%.

Required: In as much detail as possible from the above information, and in good form, prepare:

(1) The net income statement for the year.
(2) The statement of financial condition at year-end.

P2. 3   The purpose of this problem is to determine the cash flow effects of the sales and expenses of the company during 1976, which are discussed and analyzed throughout the chapter. The final answer is the (net) cash flow from net income for the year 1976. In most cases the net income for the year, which is accounted for on the accrual basis, is not equal to the (net) cash flow from net income during the year. In fact, in some situations a company may report a net income for the year but there may be a (net) cash outflow during the year from net income, which is important for managers (as well as investors in the company) to understand. As a rough rule of thumb, in growth situations cash flow usually is less than net income, and in declining situations cash flow is more than net income. In stable situations cash flow should be more or less equal to net income. [Projecting the (net) cash flow from net income is very important in management planning and is discussed in more detail in Chapter Eight.]

Required:

(1) Start with the entries made in the Cash T account shown in Exhibit 2.8 in the chapter. Exclude any debits (increases) and any credits (decreases) which are not directly connected to a revenue or expense transaction. For example, entry (M) should be excluded, since this debit (increase) is from borrowings on short-term notes payable. But entry (C) should not be excluded, since these cash payments were for manufacturing costs during the year, and these product costs end up later in the cost of goods sold expense account. After making the appropriate exclusions, determine the net cash increase (or decrease) during the year 1976 from net income.

(2) An alternative approach is to make use of the comparative balance sheet (Exhibit 2.1), and the relevant information in the net income statement (Exhibit 2.2) and the statement of changes in financial position (Exhibit 2.3). In general terms this approach is as follows:

Start with the net income for the year.
Deduct: • Increases in those assets directly connected with making sales and incurring expenses, which are Accounts Receivable, Inventories, and Prepaid Expenses. *Note:* Increases to Fixed Assets are viewed as benefiting future years' net income and thus are *not* deducted from net income of this year.
          • Decreases in those liabilities directly connected with making sales and incurring expenses, which are Accounts Payable and Accrued Costs, and Income Tax Payable.
Add: • Decreases in those assets directly connected with making sales

and incurring expenses. Notice in particular that depreciation is added back to net income even though increases to Fixed Assets are not deducted from net income.

- Increases in those liabilities directly connected with making sales and incurring expenses.

Giving the net cash inflow (or outflow) during the year from net income. *Note:* Cash dividends usually are not deducted to determine the cash flow from net income; cash dividends are a use of, or payment from the cash flow net income.

Final Note: your answer to part (2) of the problem should be the same as your answer to to part (1).

P2. 4   During the year just ended the company recorded the following manufacturing costs: $196,320 direct labor costs, and $157,730 overhead costs, for a total of $354,050 conversion costs. The total cost of raw materials purchased during the year was $235,915. Three different and independent situations are shown below.

Required: For each case below determine the missing amounts.

	Case A	Case B	Case C
Raw Materials Inventory			
Beginning balance	$ 38,400	$ 46,300	$ 38,315
Ending balance	$ 43,900	$ 41,500	$ 38,315
Work-in-Process Inventory			
Beginning balance	$ 29,300	$ 39,400	$ 26,830
Ending balance	$ 42,100	$ 29,800	$ 26,830
Finished Goods Inventory			
Beginning balance	$ 95,800	$ 84,300	$ 76,000
Ending balance	$106,200	$ 80,600	$ 76,000
a. Cost of raw materials issued to production.	$	$	$
Conversion costs (see above).	$354,050	$354,050	$354,050
b. Total manufacturing costs charged to production during the year.	$	$	$
c. Cost of goods manufactured (completed) during the year.	$	$	$
d. Cost of goods sold during the year.	$	$	$

P2. 5   A company, even a relatively small firm, maintains hundreds or separate individual accounts for all its specific assets, liabilities, revenues, and expenses.
To show a realistic complete listing of all accounts for a typical company would
be quite cumbersome and would make this problem too long. Thus the list of
accounts is shortened by grouping similar accounts together. With this in mind,
the following list of accounts of a *retailer* is presented. All year-end adjusting
entries have been recorded and are reflected in the account's balances. (The
accounts are listed in no particular order.)

Accounts Payable	$ 296,400	Depreciation Expense	$ 48,500
Accrued Expenses Payable	14,800	Repair and Maintenance	
Fixed Assets (except Land)	812,300	Expense	68,400
Sales Revenue	3,200,000	General and	
Cost of Goods Sold Expense	2,136,500	Miscellaneous Expenses	19,600
Interest Expense	91,000	Income Tax Payable	12,100
Prepaid Expenses	93,200	Land	196,000
Cash	362,400	Accounts Receivable	331,800
Transportation-in Expense	46,900	Inventory*	498,600
Salaries and Wages Expense	619,300	Accumulated Depreciation	158,700
Common Stock—Par Value	250,000	Transportation-Out	
Paid-In-Capital in		(Delivery) Expense	28,100
Excess of Par	750,000	Income Tax Expense	52,780
Notes Payable†	600,000	Retained Earnings‡	141,580
		Legal and Auditing Expense	18,200

* Beginning inventory at the start of the year was $458,600.
† Of this total, notes having a maturity value of $200,000 are due in one year or less. The remainder
is due more than one year from today.
‡ Cash dividends of $30,000 were paid during the year and have been charged against this account,
but the net income for the year has *not* yet been closed to the account.

Required: In good form prepare:
(1) The net income statement for the year (including the amount of goods
purchased during the year).
(2) The statement of financial condition at the end of the year.
(3) A statement of (changes in) retained earnings for the year; there were no
unusual or extraordinary debits (decreases) or credits (increases) to the
account during the year. (*Note:* This statement is *not* illustrated in the
chapter, but it is reported by many companies even though not required.)

P2. 6   The statements of financial condition at December 31, 1975 and 1976, and the
statements of changes in financial position and the net income statements for
the years ending December 31, 1975 and 1976 are presented below for a *retailer*.
As you should recall, a retailer buys products (goods) in a condition ready for
resale to its customers.

Required: From the information reported in the three financial statements, plus certain other information given below, determine and then record in general journal form a summary entry for each basic transaction of the company during 1976, including the closing entry at year-end 1976. Post these entries to the T accounts of the company; enter the beginning balances in the T accounts from the December 31, 1975 balance sheet of the company. Based on your entries to the T accounts, determine the ending balances at December 31, 1976 and prove these balances with the amounts reported in the 1976 financial statements.

Other information for 1976:

(a) All sales and all inventory purchases are made on credit.

(b) The company records inventory purchases to the Purchases account.

(c) The recording of the operating expenses during the year included cash disbursements of $384,900; the remainder of the expenses were bought on credit except for the charge-off of prepaid expenses and the depreciation for the year.

(d) There were no retirements or disposals of fixed assets during the year.

(e) Total cash receipts from short-term borrowing during the year were $300,000.

(f) Accrued interest payable at December 31, 1976 is $3500.

STATEMENT OF NET INCOME FOR YEARS ENDING DECEMBER 31

	1975		1976	
Sales revenue		$2,500,000		$3,150,000
Cost of goods sold:				
Beginning inventory	$ 180,000		$ 261,250	
Costs of goods purchased during the year	1,706,250		2,060,800	
Total cost of goods available for sale during year	$1,886,250		$2,322,050	
Ending inventory	261,250		306,050	
Total cost of goods sold		1,625,000		2,016,000
Gross profit		$ 875,000		$1,134,000
Operating expenses:				
Marketing expenses	$ 506,200		$ 633,100	
Administration and general expenses	218,300	724,500	238,400	871,500
Operating profit (before interest and income tax expenses)		$ 150,500		$ 262,500
Interest expense		18,000		25,000
Net income before income tax		$ 132,500		$ 237,500
Income tax expense		57,100		107,500
Net income		$ 75,400		$ 130,000
Net income per share		$3.77		$6.50

Note: The LIFO inventory cost valuation method is used.

STATEMENT OF FINANCIAL CONDITION AT DECEMBER 31, 1975 AND 1976

Assets

	1975	1976
Current Assets		
Cash	$ 80,200	$ 96,200
Accounts Receivable	152,175	205,950
Finished Goods Inventory	261,250	306,050
Prepaid Expenses	48,600	53,200
Total	$542,225	$661,400
Fixed Assets		
Buildings	$112,500	$112,500
Machinery and Equipment	49,300	62,700
Vehicles	24,600	35,325
Total, at Original Cost	$186,400	$210,525
Accumulated Depreciation	49,125	72,425
Net of Depreciation	$137,275	$138,100
Land	40,500	40,500
Total	$177,775	$178,600
Total Assets	$720,000	$840,000

Sources of Capital

	1975	1976
Current Liabilities		
Accounts Payable and Accrued Costs	$140,000	$175,000
Income Tax Payable	12,000	23,000
Short-term Notes Payable	100,000	100,000
Total	$252,000	$298,000
Long-term Liabilities		
Long-term Notes Payable	$100,000	$125,000
Owners' Equity		
Invested Capital (20,000 common stock shares outstanding)	$200,000	$200,000
Retained Earnings	168,000	217,000
Total	$368,000	$417,000
Total Sources of Capital	$720,000	$840,000

Note To Student: Footnotes are an integral part of externally reported financial statements. But to simplify this example no footnotes are included with these financial statements.

STATEMENT OF CHANGES IN FINANCIAL POSITION
FOR YEARS ENDING DECEMBER 31

	1975	1976
Sources of Funds		
Net Income for Year (See Net Income Statement)	$ 75,400	$130,000
Add Back Depreciation	19,800	23,300
	$ 95,200	$153,300
Long-term Borrowing	25,000	25,000
Total	$120,200	$178,300
Uses of Funds		
Cash Dividends	$ 50,000	$ 81,000
Capital Expenditures	58,200	24,125
Total	$108,200	$105,125
Net Increase (Decrease) of Funds During Year	$ 12,000	$ 73,175

Increases (Decreases) in Current Assets and Current Liabilities During the Year Ending December 31

	1975	1976
Cash	$ 6,600	$ 16,000
Accounts Receivable	(30,250)	53,775
Finished Goods Inventory	81,250	44,800
Prepaid Expenses	3,100	4,600
Net Increase of Current Assets	$ 60,700	$119,175
Accounts Payable and Accrued Costs	$ 18,400	$ 35,000
Income Tax Payable	5,300	11,000
Short-term Notes Payable	25,000	—0—
Net Increase of Current Liabilities	$ 48,700	$ 46,000
Increase (Decrease) of Funds During Year	$ 12,000	$ 73,175

P2. 7   Certain information is shown below which is taken from a retailer's accounts for the year just ended:

Account	Balance	
	Debit	Credit
Sales revenue		838,500
Sales returns	23,500	
Sales discounts and allowances	18,250	
Inventory (beginning balance)	92,400	
Purchases	532,125	
Purchase returns		27,375

The company sets the selling prices of its products to yield a gross profit exactly equal to 37.5% of the sales price *on all* its products. However, after the point of sale, special discounts or price allowances are given to some customers. Occasionally some products are returned by its customers. Likewise, the company occasionally returns some products purchased to its suppliers. But the company never receives any discounts or allowances from the original purchase price of the products bought.

Required: Based on the above information, determine the cost of the company's inventory that should be on hand at the end of the year, assuming no inventory shrinkage during the year.

P2. 8   This company operates a public warehouse and has applied to a lending institution for a loan to expand its facilities. The company maintains its accounting records and files its federal income tax return mainly on a cash receipts and disbursements basis, except that fixed assets' costs are depreciated over the useful lives of the assets. The lending institution has requested financial statements prepared on the accrual basis. The company's trial balance follows:

TRIAL BALANCE
December 31, 1976

	Debit	Credit
Cash	$ 145,000	
Investments	425,000	
Property, plant and equipment	1,200,000	
Accumulated depreciation		$ 362,000
Common stock		1,000,000
Retained earnings		318,000
Rental income		400,000
Operating expenses	200,000	
Insurance expense	30,000	
Administrative expenses	70,000	
Investment income		15,000
Federal income tax paid	25,000	
	$2,095,000	$2,095,000

Other relevant information follows:

	December 31	
	1975	1976
Accounts receivable	$ 27,000	$ 37,000
Interest income receivable	1,000	2,600
Market value of investments (all investments are corporate bonds)	460,000	475,000
Accounts payable (operating expenses)	8,000	9,700

The amount in the Insurance expense account is a February 1, 1976 payment for insurance premiums: $6000 for a one-year liability insurance policy and $24,000 for a three-year fire insurance policy. The coverage under both policies commenced on January 1, 1976.

All prior year income tax returns (1975 and earlier) have been reviewed by taxing authorities and found to have been properly prepared. Assume that the income tax rate is a flat 48% on taxable income. (*Note:* Not all of 1976's income tax has been paid, and thus not all has been recorded by the end of the year.)

Required: Prepare in good form and on the accrual basis:
(1) The company's statement of financial condition at December 31, 1976.
(2) The company's net income statement for the year ending December 31, 1976.

P2. 9   The following information is taken from the statements indicated for this company. (*Note:* the format and detail of information is rearranged for this problem as compared with normal financial statements.)

BALANCE SHEET
January 1, 1976

Assets

Current assets	$35,000
Buildings and equipment	48,000
Accumulated depreciation—buildings and equipment	(15,000)
Patents	5,000
	$73,000

Sources of Capital

Current liabilities	$ 9,000
Capital stock	27,000
Retained earnings	37,000
	$73,000

STATEMENT OF CHANGES IN FINANCIAL POSITION
FOR 1976

Funds, January 1, 1976		$26,000
Funds provided:		
Operations:		
Net income	$24,000	
Gain on sale—buildings	(4,000)	
Depreciation—buildings and equipment	10,000	
Amortization—patents	1,000	31,000
Issue of capital stock		13,000
Sale of building		7,000
		$77,000
Funds applied:		
Dividends	12,000	
Purchase of land	14,000	
Purchase of buildings and equipment	30,000	56,000
Funds, December 31, 1976		$21,000

Total assets on the Balance Sheet at December 31, 1976 are $105,000. Accumulated depreciation on the building sold was $6000.

Required: Select the correct answer for each of the following questions, and show your supporting computations.

(1) When the building was sold, the Buildings and Equipment account received a credit of
  (a) $17,000.
  (b) $13,000.
  (c) $10,000.
  (d) $9000.
  (e) None of the above or not determinable from the above facts.
(2) The book value of the Buildings and Equipment at December 31, 1976 is
  (a) $65,000.
  (b) $59,000.
  (c) $53,000.
  (d) $40,000.
  (e) None of the above or not determinable from the above facts.
(3) The current liabilities at December 31, 1976 are
  (a) $31,000.
  (b) $21,000.
  (c) $19,000.
  (d) $16,000.
  (e) None of the above or not determinable from the above facts.
(4) The balance in the Retained Earnings account at December 31, 1976 is
  (a) $53,000.
  (b) $49,000.
  (c) $42,000.
  (d) $38,000.
  (e) None of the above or not determinable from the above facts.
(5) Capital stock (plus capital in excess of par or stated value) at December 31, 1976 is
  (a) $40,000.
  (b) $37,000.
  (c) $27,000.
  (d) $14,000.
  (e) None of the above or not determinable from the above facts.

P2.10 This company was established on January 1, 1975 and is a distributor of home air conditioning units. The company purchases the units in large quantities directly from the manufacturer, and then sells the units in smaller quantities to various retail stores that sell the air conditioning units to the final customer. The company's net income statements for 1975 and 1976 were presented to you as shown below.

On closer examination of the company's accounting procedures it is discovered that the company makes sales on two quite different bases:
(1) Some sales are normal sales on credit; legal title and possession passes from the company to the buyer at the point of sale and the buyer (the retail store) must pay the company the amount owed within the credit period offered by the company.
(2) Some air conditioning units are shipped to the retailers on a *consignment basis*; legal title does *not* pass to the retail store at this point. The retailer is

STATEMENTS OF NET INCOME
FOR THE YEARS ENDED DECEMBER 31, 1976 AND 1975

	1976	1975
Sales	$1,287,500	$1,075,000
Cost of Sales	669,500	559,000
Gross profit	618,000	516,000
Selling and administration expense	403,500	330,000
Net income before income taxes	214,500	186,000
Provision for income taxes	96,450	82,780
Net income	$ 118,040	$ 103,220

an agent of the company who sells the units for the company. At the point of the final sale the retailer (the consignee) must pay the company the amount billed for the units sold. Hence, the retailer simply holds the units and does not buy them from the company until the point of final sale to the homeowner.

Both sales methods were in effect in 1975 and 1976. In both years, however, the company treated all shipments as outright sales.

The sales price and cost of the units were the same in 1975 and 1976. Each unit had a cost of $130 and was uniformly invoiced at $250 to customers and to consignees. During 1976 the amount of cash received from consignees in payment for units sold by them was $706,500. Consignees remit for the units as soon as they are sold. Confirmations received from consignees showed that they had a total of 23 unsold units on hand at December 31, 1976. Consignees were unable to confirm the unsold units on hand at December 31, 1975.

The cost of sales for 1976 was determined as follows:

		Units	
Inventory on hand in warehouse, December 31, 1975		1,510	
Purchases		4,454	
Available for sale		5,964	
Inventory on hand in warehouse, December 31,1976		814	
Shipments to: open account customers	3,008		
consignee customers	2,142	5,150 @ $130 = $669,500	

Required:
(1) Compute the correct total cost of the company's inventory at
   (a) December 31, 1976, and
   (b) December 31, 1975.

(2) Determine the correct net income for the company for 1976. Income tax is 48% on the taxable income over $25,000, and only 22% on the first $25,000 of taxable income. Show your computations clearly. Present the revised 1976 net income statement for the company as your answer.

P2.11   This corporation is a retailer. The corporation has approximately 1000 stockholders and its stock, which is traded "over-the-counter," sold throughout 1976 at about $7 a share with little fluctuation.

Below is the corporation's balance sheet at December 31, 1975.

BALANCE SHEET
DECEMBER 31, 1975

Assets		
Current assets		
Cash		$ 4,386,040
Accounts receivable	$3,150,000	
Less allowance for doubtful accounts	94,500	3,055,500
Inventories—at the lower of cost (first-in, first-out) or estimated realizable market		2,800,000
Total current assets		$10,241,540
Fixed assets—at cost	3,300,000	
Less accumulated depreciation	1,300,000	2,000,000
Total assets		$12,241,540

Liabilities and Stockholders' Equity		
Current liabilities		
Notes payable due within one year		$ 1,000,000
Accounts payable and accrued liabilities		2,091,500
Federal income taxes payable		350,000
Total current liabilities		$ 3,441,500
Notes payable due after one year		4,000,000
Stockholders' equity		
Capital stock—authorized 2,000,000 shares of $1 par value; issued and outstanding 1,000,000 shares	$1,000,000	
Additional paid-in-capital	1,500,000	
Retained earnings	2,300,040	
Total stockholders' equity		4,800,040
Total liabilities and stockholders' equity		$12,241,540

Information concerning the corporation and its activities during 1976 follows.

(a) Sales for the year were $15,650,000. The gross profit percentage for the year was 30% of sales. Merchandise purchases and freight-in totaled $10,905,000. It can be assumed that depreciation and other expenses do not enter cost of goods sold.

(b) Administrative, selling, and general expenses other than interest, depreciation, and bad debts expense amounted to $2,403,250.

(c) The December 31, 1976 accounts receivable were $3,350,000, and the corporation maintains an allowance for doubtful accounts equal to 3% of the accounts receivable outstanding. During the year, $50,000 of 1975 receivables were deemed uncollectible and were charged off to the allowance account.

(d) The rate of depreciation on fixed assets is 13% per year and the corporation consistently follows the policy of taking one-half year's depreciation in the year of acquisition. The depreciation expense for 1976 was $474,500.

(e) The total notes of $5,000,000 are payable in 20 equal quarterly installments commencing March 31, 1976 with interest at 9% per annum also payable quarterly.

(f) Accounts payable and accrued liabilities at December 31, 1976 were $2,221,000.

(g) The balance of the 1975 federal income tax paid in 1976 was in exact agreement with the amount accrued on the December 31, 1975 balance sheet.

(h) For purposes of the 1976 estimated tax payments, the controller estimated the company's 1976 taxable income would be $1,200,000. Accordingly, 80% of the tax was paid during the year as progress payments on the company's 1976 income tax. Assume a flat 48% income tax rate to simplify.

(i) During the second month of each quarter of the year 1976, dividends of $0.10 a share were declared and paid. In addition, in July 1976 a 5% stock dividend was declared and paid.

Required: Prepare the following statements in good form, supported by appropriate computations, at or for the year ended December 31, 1976.

(1) Balance Sheet.

(2) Statement of Net Income.

Note: It is suggested that you set up T accounts for the appropriate accounts and enter 1976 transactions in summary in the T accounts. Then, you can prepare the financial statements from the T accounts.

P2.12 *Required:* Identify the financial statement in which each of the following accounts would be reported. Also indicate the specific section in the financial statement in which the account would appear. If you think that the account would not be reported in any usual financial statement, explain.

(a) Cost of goods sold	(f) Merchandise inventory
(b) Purchases	(g) Notes receivable
(c) Buildings	(h) Accounts payable
(d) Accrued salaries payable	(i) Depreciation expense
(e) Office supplies inventory	(j) Long-term notes payable

(k) Rent expense
(l) Cash
(m) Repair and maintenance expense
(n) Freight-in
(o) Common stock—par value
(p) Sales returns and allowances
(q) Machinery and equipment
(r) Accumulated depreciation

(s) Retained earnings
(t) Other income
(u) Short-term notes payable
(v) Accounts receivable
(w) Sales revenue
(x) Allowance for doubtful accounts
(y) Dividends
(z) Treasury stock

P2.13 All of the company's *noncurrent* accounts are shown below; these are all the accounts other than current assets and current liabilities. In addition to the beginning balance at January 1 1976, the summary of the debits and credits to each account during the year ending December 31, 1976 are also given.

Required:
(1) Determine the amount of funds at:
    (a) January 1, 1976.
    (b) December 31, 1976.
(2) Prepare the Statement of Changes in Financial Position for the year ending December 31, 1976, assuming that the entries to the above accounts reflect the most normal or most probable reason for the debits and credits.

Note: This statement is supplemented by a schedule of changes in the current assets and current liabilities, but this supplement cannot be prepared from the information given in this problem.

Buildings		
Beginning		
Balance	156,000	
	37,600	

Accumulated Depreciation—Building		
		Beginning
		Balance 46,800
		6,300

Machinery and Equipment		
Beginning		
Balance	281,400	
	118,300	

Accumulated Depreciation— Machinery and Equipment		
		Beginning
		Balance 139,300
		46,200

Land		
Beginning		
Balance	162,000	

Long-term Notes Payable		
		Beginning
		Balance 250,000
		100,000
	25,000	

Common Stock—Par Value		
		Beginning
		Balance 100,000
		20,000

Paid-in Capital in Excess of Par		
		Beginning
		Balance 250,000
		80,000

Retained Earnings		
		Beginning
		Balance 99,820
		76,200
30,000		

P2.14 An inexperienced bookkeeper prepared the following balance sheet for the company. The company had a relatively large taxable loss for the year just ended and has filed for a refund of income taxes paid in prior years.

Assets		Liabilities and Owners' Equity	
Cash	$ 800	Accumulated depreciation	$ 4,800
Land	14,300	Notes payable (due in	
Inventory	28,400	equal installments of	
Machinery and Equipment	21,400	$500 per month)	30,000
Prepaid expenses	1,850	Allowance for doubtful	
Accounts receivable	36,400	accounts	2,600
Loan to officer (due		Accounts payable	38,200
in three years)	4,500	Owners' equity—invested	
Retained earnings (deficit)	6,300	capital	48,150
Income tax refund		Total credits	$123,750
receivable	9,800		
Total debits	$123,750		

Required: Revise the above balance sheet and present in good form the company's statement of financial condition. Assume that the balances in each account are proper and correct.

P2.15 *Required:* From the information provided prepare in good form the company's Statement of Financial Condition at December 31, 1976.
(a) The Cash balance at December 31, 1976 is $48,000.
(b) Net income for 1976 is $50,000.
(c) The Retained Earnings balance at January 1, 1976 was $75,000.
(d) Cash dividends paid to stockholders during 1976 were $30,000.
(e) The Accounts Receivable balance at January 1, 1976 was $102,800 and the Allowance for Doubtful Accounts had a balance of $2800 at that date; sales made on credit during 1976 total $600,000 and total cash collections from customers during 1974 were $570,000; the company recorded bad debts expense of $5000 during 1976 and wrote off $4800 of uncollectible accounts receivable during the year.
(f) Prepaid expenses at December 31, 1976 total $10,000.
(g) The Accounts Payable balance at December 31, 1976 is $10,000.
(h) The Notes Payable balance at December 31, 1976 totals $50,000, which is due in monthly payments of $2000.
(i) Buildings, machinery, and equipment owned at December 31, 1976 cost the company $80,000 originally, and these assets are one fourth depreciated at December 31, 1976.
(j) The company's Land balance at December 31, 1976 is $20,000.
(k) The stockholders initially invested $100,000 in the company, and have made no additional investment or withdrawal of capital since.
(i) Income Tax Payable at December 31, 1976 is $8000.

Chapter Three

Basic Measures and Interpretations of Financial Performance

BASIC MEASURES AND INTERPRETATIONS OF FINANCIAL PERFORMANCE

Introduction

Purpose of Chapter

Top level managers of a company, as well as many of its other managers, look to the periodic financial statements of the company as a whole for essential information regarding its financial performance and position. A company's financial statements are managers' indispensable primary source of information for measuring and judging how well or how poorly the company is doing financially. It is assumed that management's primary *financial* objective for the (profit motivated) business enterprise is to earn a satisfactory or better amount of net income relative to the stockholders' investment in the company, and relative to the risks involved in earning the net income.* Of course, managers need to determine how successful they are in achieving this basic financial goal of the company. The main purpose of this chapter is to explain the key measures of financial performance used by managers in evaluating how successful or unsuccessful they are in achieving the financial goals of the company.

The Company's Financial Statements

The company example introduced in Chapter Two is continued in this chapter. Although this company's three principal financial statements are shown in Chapter Two (see Exhibits 2.1 to 2.3), we present again here the company's comparative balance sheets and net income statements in abbreviated form for ease of reference. The company's financial condition *in very condensed form* is shown in Exhibit 3.1, and its net income statement in somewhat condensed form is shown in Exhibit 3.2.

---

* A company has other financial objectives, of course, such as remaining solvent. And, a company has many different nonfinancial objectives, such as being a good economic citizen, and so on. There is much debate regarding the real or de facto objectives of managers, and whether their actual objectives are entirely consistent with the goal of earning a satisfactory or better net income on the stockholders' equity in the company. However, space does not permit further discussion of these interesting points.

EXHIBIT 3.1
Statement of Financial Condition

	December 31, 1975		December 31, 1976	
Total assets	$ 7,924,500	100.0%	$ 8,601,500	100.0%
Sources of assets:				
Liabilities	$ 3,473,300	43.8%	$ 3,928,892	45.7%
Stockholders' equity	4,451,200	56.2%	4,672,608	54.3%
Total	$ 7,924,500	100.0%	$ 8,601,500	100.0%

Notice in particular the "step-down" format of the net income statement. Starting with total sales revenue, the cost of goods sold expense is subtracted first to give the gross profit, which is a "first line" measure of profit—that is, profit before any operating expenses for the year are considered and before interest and income tax. Next, the total operating expenses (marketing expenses and administration and general expenses) are subtracted to arrive at a "second line" measure of profit, called *operating profit,* since it is the profit after deducting the cost of goods sold and all operating expenses from sales revenue. This is a critical line in the net income statement. Operating profit is the measure of the ability of a company to sell its products for more than the costs of manufacturing (or purchasing) them and the costs of operating the business entity. Management has to control the ratio of operating profit to sales revenue to provide a sufficient amount to: (1) pay interest (2) pay income tax and (3) leave a residual net income for the stockholders.

Interest expense is subtracted from operating profit, since interest is a deductible expense for determination of taxable income. Roughly speaking, the next line in the net income statement (net income before income tax) is an approxi-

EXHIBIT 3.2
Statement of Net Income For Years Ending

	December 31, 1975		December 31, 1976	
Sales revenue	$10,000,000	100.0%	$11,825,000	100.0%
Cost of goods sold	6,162,500	61.6%	7,241,300	61.2%
Gross profit	$ 3,837,500	38.4%	$ 4,583,700	38.8%
Operating expenses	$ 3,106,500	31.1%	3,605,800	30.5%
Operating profit	$ 731,000	7.3%	$ 977,900	8.3%
Interest expense	148,750	1.5%	180,000	1.5%
Net income before income tax	$ 582,250	5.8%	$ 797,900	6.8%
Income tax expense	272,980	2.7%	376,492	3.2%
Net income	$ 309,270	3.1%	$ 421,408	3.6%

mate measure of a company's taxable income for the year in normal situations. There are several reasons why the two may not agree in some situations, however. In this example, taxable income is equal to the net income before income tax. Only the federal income tax is imposed on the company in this example— there is no state income tax. Thus the total income tax expense each year is equal to the net income before income tax (which is equal to taxable income) times the appropriate federal income tax rate. Currently the first $25,000 of corporate taxable income is taxed at a 22% rate, and the remainder over $25,000 is taxed at a 48% rate.* (If the taxable income is more than $25,000, the total taxable income may be multiplied by 48%, and then $6500 can be subtracted from this amount to give the correct tax for the year.)

Also, certain terminology problems should be mentioned. The term *profit* has no single meaning. It can refer to *gross* profit, *operating* profit, *taxable* profit (that is, operating profit less interest, which is called income before income tax in the net income statement), or *final* profit (that is, profit after *all* expenses, which of course is called *net income*). We shall always make the specific meaning of profit clear in the following discussion. To complicate matters further, the term *income* sometimes is used to mean profit, in which case the proper prefix should be attached such as *net* income. Occasionally the term income is used in a *total* income sense, which should more properly be called *revenue* (and shall be in the following discussion). More often, when it is applied to the typical business entity, income refers to *other sources* of earnings that are in addition to and incidental to the sales revenue of the company. For example, income in this sense may refer to relatively minor amounts of interest income earned by a company, or to its share of the net income of a subsidiary or affiliated company that the company owns stock in.

Return on Investment (ROI)

Two Basic ROI Ratios: Return on Assets and Return on Equity

For 1975 the company in the example earned net income of $309,270 (see Exhibit 3.2). Is this profit performance good, average, or poor? It is impossible to answer this question without also knowing the amount of capital invested to earn this amount of profit. For the majority of business enterprises the most important test or measure of its profit performance is not simply the amount of total profit but is, instead, the *ratio* of profit to capital. In other words, profit must be judged relative to the amount of capital being used to earn the profit. In gen-

---

* Corporations with 10 or fewer stockholders may elect to be treated as a "subchapter S" corporation, which means the corporation itself pays no income tax; instead, the corporation's taxable income must be included in the stockholders' personal income tax returns.

eral terms this relationship is called *Return on Investment,* or *ROI* for short. The term "return" is more or less a substitute for profit. Return means the residual amount left over after deducting expenses from sales revenue for the period.*

To generate sales revenue, almost all product-oriented companies (as well as most service-oriented companies for that matter) need to invest in various assets, such as inventories, fixed assets, and the like. A company must first secure an adequate amount of capital to have enough capital on hand to invest in the necessary assets. The term "investment" in ROI refers to the amount of capital invested to yield the profit earned by the company. The ROI *ratio* is usually expressed as a percent, such as 10.0% or whatever. In general summary:

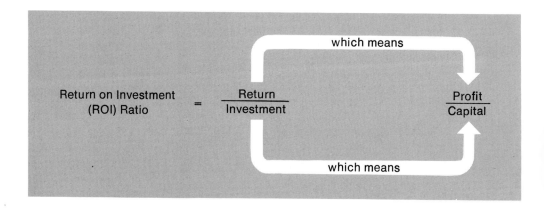

Conceivably *all* of the total capital needed by a corporation for investment in its assets could be supplied from stockholders' equity, that is, through the issue of stock plus retained earnings. In this rather unusual situation, there would be no liabilities— total assets would equal total stockholders' equity. In this rare case there would be only one measure of profit for investors (net income) and only one measure of capital (total assets or total stockholders' equity, since these two would be equal).

But in almost all practical situations some part of a company's total capital (which is invested in its assets) is supplied from liabilities. This is true for the company in the example. For instance, at December 31, 1975, this can be shown as follows (see Exhibit 3.1 for amounts):

---

* Some companies do not sell products or services in the usual sense, and thus they do not have sales revenue. For instance, mutual funds have investment income from their holdings of securities, and banks have interest income from their loans to customers. Hence, return in these situations would be the gross income less the expenses of earning the gross income.

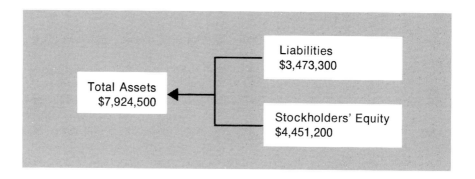

Since there are two basic sources of the total capital invested in a typical company's assets, there are two basic ROI ratios. One is the *return on equity* ratio; it is the ratio of net income to stockholders' equity, or

$$\text{Return on Equity Ratio} = \frac{\text{Net Income}}{\text{Stockholders' Equity}}$$

For this ROI ratio, net income is clearly the proper measure of profit, since capital is defined and is limited to the capital supplied from the stockholders. Net income, of course, is the final residual amount of profit of the company after deducting all expenses, including interest and income tax. Net income "belongs" entirely to the stockholders. (Usually not all of the net income for the year is paid out as a cash dividend.)

The second basic ROI ratio is based on the *total assets* of the company, that is, the total capital supplied from *both* liabilities and stockholders. This ROI measure is called the *return on assets* ratio, and is computed as follows:

$$\text{Return on Assets Ratio} = \frac{\text{"Profit"}}{\text{Total Assets}}$$

What is the proper measure of "profit" for this ROI ratio? Using net income does not make sense, since net income accrues entirely to the benefit of the stockholders, and they supply only part of the total capital. Putting it another way, net income is *after* deducting interest expense. But, clearly, interest is payment for the use of debt capital, and these liabilities provide part of the capital invested in the total assets of the company. Hence, "profit" for the return on assets ratio is set equal to the sum of net income plus interest, or

$$\text{Return on Assets Ratio} = \frac{\text{Net Income} + \text{Interest}}{\text{Total Assets}}$$

The return on assets ratio presents troublesome problems. First, the profit measure in this ROI ratio (net income + interest) does *not* appear on any of the profit lines in most net income statements—see Exhibit 3.2, for instance. This profit mesure must be added from the two different amounts in the net income statement. However, this problem is very minor in comparison with two more serious ones. Adding together net income and interest is like adding apples and oranges from the income tax point of view. Net income is *after* tax, but interest is *before* tax. This is illustrated in the net income statement shown in Exhibit 3.2. Interest is subtracted to arrive at taxable income (net income before income tax). That is, not all of the operating profit is taxed because interest for the year is deducted to give the taxable income.

To earn $309,270 of net income in 1975 the company had to earn $582,250 before tax and after interest. Roughly speaking, a company must earn about $1.92 of pretax profit to keep $1 as net income, since about $.92 (48%) has to be paid as income tax (once the corporation's total taxable income goes over $25,000). On the other hand, to earn interest of $148,750 in 1975 the company had to earn just $148,750 of operating profit, since interest is deductible for income tax purposes. The main implication of the tax difference between net income and interest concerns the total amount of operating profit a company has to earn on its total assets, in order to meet its interest requirements, to pay income tax, and to leave enough net income (after income tax). This topic is considered further in the discussion that follows.

Another serious problem in the computation of the return on assets ratio is that part of a company's liabilities are *noninterest* bearing liabilities. In this example there are two such noninterest bearing liabilities: (1) Accounts Payable and Accrued Costs and, (2) Income Tax Payable. Usually the total Accounts Payable of a company are a significant percentage of its total liabilities, although other noninterest bearing liabilities may not be very material. The total interest amount added to net income to give the measure of profit used in the return on assets ratio computation does *not* include any cost for the use of the capital supplied from noninterest bearing liabilities. This problem is discussed in more detail in later chapters. The essential idea is that interest is payment for the use of debt capital; and since total assets is a measure that includes all capital invested in the business, interest is added to net income to determine the profit earned on the total assets of the company.

The two basic ROI ratios for the company are computed and shown in Exhibit 3.3 for the years 1975 and 1976. The December 31 balances for the asset, liability, and stockholders' equity accounts are used. It can be argued that the average balances during the year should be used for more precise results. Using year-end balances makes the computations much easier to follow, and are not seriously different from the average balances. The amounts in the ROI computations are taken from the financial statements shown in Exhibits 3.1 and 3.2.

Basic Determinants of ROI Ratio

Notice in Exhibit 3.3 that the return on assets ratio increased from 5.8% in 1975 to 7.0% in 1976, which is obviously a favorable change. The improvement

EXHIBIT 3.3

Computation of Return on Investment (ROI) Ratios

			1975	1976
Return on Assets	$=$	$\dfrac{\text{Net Income+Interest}}{\text{Total Assets}} =$	$\dfrac{\$309,270+\$148,750}{\$7,924,500} = 5.8\%$	$\dfrac{\$421,408+\$180,000}{\$8,601,500} = 7.0\%$
Return on Equity	$=$	$\dfrac{\text{Net Income}}{\text{Stockholders' Equity}} =$	$\dfrac{\$309,270}{\$4,451,200} = 6.9\%$	$\dfrac{\$421,408}{\$4,672,608} = 9.0\%$

in this ROI ratio is analyzed and explained in terms of two basic determinants: (1) the *asset turnover ratio*—which is (Sales Revenue/Total Assets) and, (2) the *profit ratio*—which is (Profit/Sales Revenue). These two component ratios are multiplied to determine the ROI ratio as is shown in Exhibit 3.4. Remember that for computation of the return on assets ratio, profit equals (net income + interest).

Each of the two separate determinant ratios are very important and very different measures of management performance. Keep in mind that profit is *not* earned directly. First of all, sales must be made. Management must make good use of the assets of the company to produce sales revenue. This is the starting point to earn profit. The asset turnover ratio is a measure of the ability of management to keep the assets productive, that is, to use the assets to generate sales revenue. Without enough total sales revenue for the period, there is no way a company would be able to earn enough profit for that period.

The second requirement on management, given an adequate turnover of assets, is to keep total expenses for the period less than total sales revenue for the period so that an adequate percentage of the sales revenue remains as profit for the period. When expressed as a percentage of sales revenue the profit residual is the profit ratio.

The importance of separating the return on assets ratio into its two component ratios is brought out in comparing the company's 1976 performance with 1975. It is convenient to use an $100 base unit in discussing ratios, which is employed here. The asset turnover ratio (Exhibit 3.4) reveals that in 1976 the company produced $137 of sales revenue on each $100 of assets. Compared with 1975, this is $11 more sales revenue ($137 less $126) for each $100 of assets. Even if the profit ratio had remained the same, there would have been more profit on each $100 of assets, since for each $100 of assets in 1976 there is $11 more sales revenue yielding profit. Therefore, the return on assets ratio would increase. A company normally tries to increase its asset turnover ratio, as long as its profit ratio is not decreased in the process. If it is already at a satisfactory level, a company attempts at least to maintain its asset turnover ratio.

EXHIBIT 3.4
Two Basic Determinants of ROI Ratio

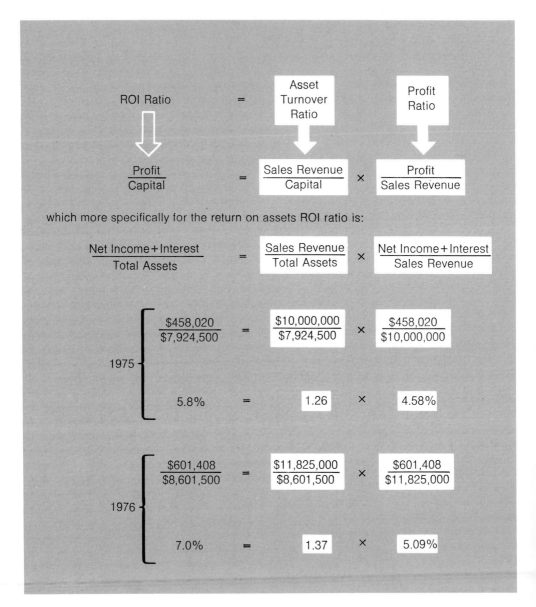

Also, the company's 1976 profit ratio is higher than in 1975. Each $100 of sales revenue resulted in $5.09 of profit in 1976, which is 51 cents more profit than in 1975 ($5.09 less $4.58). Even if the asset turnover ratio had remained the same, each $100 of sales revenue yielded more profit in 1976 which, of course, increases the return on assets ratio. A company normally tries to increase its profit ratio, as long as the asset turnover ratio is not decreased in the process. If its profit ratio is already at a satisfactory level, a company attempts at least to maintain that level.

In summary, the company increased its return on assets ratio rather significantly from 5.8% to 7.0% due to increases in both its asset turnover ratio and its profit ratio in 1976. The same sort of analysis can be applied to the return on equity ratio. Since capital in this ROI ratio is defined as stockholders' equity, the asset turnover ratio might better be called the equity turnover ratio.

What Is an Adequate Rate of Return on Equity? How Can It Be Improved?

Notice that the company earned a 9.0% rate (another term for ratio) of return on its stockholders' equity in 1976. (See Exhibit 3.3.) Is this good enough? It is better than the 6.9% rate earned in 1975. But should it be better? This is a complex question, but it is an essential question that top management of a company must answer. Management should establish a definite rate of return on equity objective for the company. One difficulty concerns determining with what the company's return on equity should be compared. One very relevant comparison group are the companies in the same lines of business. Hence, the managers compare their company's rate of return on stockholders' equity with the company's competitors return on equity performances. Alternatively, a broader group of companies could be used for comparison. It would be appropriate to look at one of the annual surveys of companies that are published yearly by *Business Week, Forbes,* and *Fortune.* These annual reviews highlight the rates of return on stockholders' equity for a very broad cross section of business enterprises. Relative to these broad averages, the company's 9.0% rate of return on equity appears too low. Probably the company should do better.

There are two basic ways of improving its return on equity—(1) increasing its return on assets, by increasing its asset turnover ratio or its profit ratio, or both; and, (2) taking better advantage of *financial leverage.* Financial leverage, in the briefest terms, means borrowing money at interest rates that are lower than the rate of return on assets that can be earned with the capital, such that more return on assets is earned than the interest cost of the debt, which produces additional profit for the stockholders. Financial leverage is discussed in a later section of this chapter. For now, the interest rate and the total liabilities of the company are taken as constants. Thus, here we consider the first alternative.

If the company could have generated more sales revenue from the same amount of total assets, then this higher asset turnover ratio would have increased the company's return on assets *and therefore would also have increased its return on equity rate.* To illustrate this important point, a hypothetical situation is now analyzed. Assume that the company's asset turnover ratio in 1976 had been 1.75 on the same amount of total assets of $8,601,500 (see Exhibit 3.1). This means that the company would have generated $15,052,625 sales revenue for 1976 ($8,601,500 × 1.75 = $15,052,625), which would have been an additional $3,227,625 of sales revenue: ($15,052,625 hypothetical sales revenue less the $11,825,000 actual sales revenue).

Notice in 1976 that the company's operating profit (before interest and income tax) is 8.3% of sales revenue (see Exhibit 3.2). Assume for convenience here that this operating profit percentage would remain the same on the increase of sales revenue (which by the way is *not* a completely valid assumption, as will be explained in Chapter Four). Thus the additional sales revenue would have yielded additional operating profit equal to

$$(\$3,227,625 \text{ additional sales revenue} \times 8.3\%) \; = \; \frac{\$266,917 \text{ additional}}{\text{operating profit}}$$

Since total assets are the same, total liabilities would be the same. Hence, the company's 1976 interest of $180,000 would not have increased. However, the operating profit increase of $266,917 would have increased taxable income by the same amount. Therefore, net income would have increased by only 52% of the operating profit increase (since the federal income tax rate is 48%), which is equal to:

$$\text{increase in net income} = (\$266,917 \times 52\%) = \$138,797$$

Hence, at the higher asset turnover ratio, net income would have been $560,205 ($421,408 reported in Exhibit 3.2 plus the $138,797 increase). The return on equity at the hypothetical higher asset turnover ratio (of 1.75) would have been as follows:

$$\frac{\text{Net Income}}{\text{Stockholders' Equity}} = \frac{\$560,205}{\$4,672,608} = 12.0\%$$

In summary, to have achieved a 12.0% return on equity for 1976 the company's asset turnover ratio would have had to have been 1.75 instead of the actual 1.37 ratio, which gives only a 9.0% return on equity ratio.

Instead of increasing its asset turnover ratio, the other way the company could improve its return on asset ratio and thus its return on equity ratio would be to increase its profit ratio. Say, for example, that the company's goal for

1976 had been to earn a 12.0% return on equity. If the company's total assets ($8,601,500) *and* its asset turnover ratio for 1976 (1.37) are held constant, then total sales revenue would be the same as given, which is $11,825,000 (see Exhibit 3.2). Out of this sales revenue the net income would have had to have been $560,205 to earn a 12.0% return on equity, since ($560,205/$4,672,608 = 12.0%, as shown above). This is $138,797 more net income than the company actually earned in 1976. To earn $138,797 additional *after tax* net income, the net income before tax would have had to increase $266,917 since the company "keeps" only 52% of any increase in operating profit: ($138,797/.52 = $266,917). Or putting it the other way, if operating profit increased $266,917, then income tax would increase by $128,120 (48% of the increase), leaving a net income increase of $138,797.

In summary, the company's 1976 operating profit would have had to have been $1,244,817 ($977,900 actual plus the $266,917 increase). This would have been an operating profit ratio equal to 10.5% of sales revenue ($1,244,817/ $11,825,000 = 10.5%), which is 2.2% higher than the company actually achieved in 1976 (10.5% less 8.3%). This means that the company's operating expenses would have had to have been substantially less. To have reduced operating expenses by 2.2% of sales revenue would have been a formidable task in most situations.

Reporting Expense Ratios in Management Profit Performance Statements

Notice that the percent of each expense to sales revenue is reported in the net income statement shown in Exhibit 3.2. The reporting of expense percents (or ratios) is standard practice in the regular periodic profit performance statements to managers. Profit performance reports to managers are much more detailed than the highly condensed net income statement presented as Exhibit 3.2. In Chapters Four and Five much more information is added to the company's net income statement for management analysis purposes. However, the value and general use of expense ratios can be conveniently introduced with the relatively few expenses shown in Exhibit 3.2.

As we explain in the preceding section, a company must earn a satisfactory (or better) profit ratio to earn a satisfactory (or better) ROI ratio, assuming that its asset turnover ratio is satisfactory. Profit is equal to (Sales Revenue − Total Expenses) of course. So, another way of stating that the profit must be satisfactory, is to say that the total expense ratio must be satisfactory. For instance, if a company wants to earn a 5.0% (or better) profit ratio, then the company cannot allow its expenses to exceed 95.0% of sales revenue. Thus managers watch very carefully the ratio of each expense or expense group to determine if any one of the expense ratios is too high.

Although an oversimplification and certainly not the whole story, a basic profit strategy of management is to keep each expense, or group of closely related expenses, at an acceptable percentage (ratio) of sales revenue. This means that managers need to develop a standard or bench mark ratio for each expense or expense group against which actual expense ratios can be compared. If each and every expense item is kept at (or below) this control limit, then the company's profit ratio objective can be achieved.

Establishing the "proper," or an acceptable control limit ratio for each and every one of the hundreds (if not many more) separate expenses or expense groups is a difficult management problem for most companies. One complication is that some expenses are fixed in total amount for a year and do not vary in response to increases or decreases of sales revenue. For instance, the annual property tax on a company's warehouse (storage) building is usually a fixed cost for the year. The company may keep its warehouse completely full all year because of high sales, or there may be much empty space during the year because of low sales. In either case the property tax expense for the year is the same. Say, for example, that this fixed property tax expense for the year is $10,000. Consider this expense ratio at two different sales revenue levels, one low and one high:

	Low Sales Level	High Sales Level
Property Tax Expense Ratio $=$	$\dfrac{\$10,000}{\$1,000,000} = 1.0\%$	$\dfrac{\$10,000}{\$2,000,000} = 0.5\%$

Notice that this expense ratio would be twice as large at the low sales level than at the high sales level.

Another complication is that some expenses are more or less independent of the actual sales revenue level for the year. For instance, a company's legal expense for the year may depend mainly on how many law suits are brought against it during the year, or on other legal requirements that have little to do with the sales level for the year. Or, another example, a company may suffer a large loss from embezzlement in a given year (when discovered). In most years the company has no such expense (or, at least, does not discover this expense).

Some expenses are discretionary and arbitrary in the sense that their "proper" or "tolerable" level is primarily a subjective decision by managers. In good years managers may decide to travel first class, but in lean years they may decide to travel coach. In good years, entertainment allowances may be generous, but in lean years the company's salesmen and officers may be more restricted in what they can spend. Hence, the expense ratio standard would depend to some extent on management's policy for the year.

Even with these several problems in mind, managers should (and do) analyze the percentage of each expense or expense group to sales revenue. Any significant change year to year, and any significant deviation from the standard on control limit ratio for an expense should be highlighted in the profit performance reports to managers. This basic technique of analysis is illustrated frequently in later chapters. Finally, it should be mentioned that one of the primary purposes of *budgeting* is to establish cost behavior standards and cost performance control limits. Budgeting, among other things, involves the careful analysis of costs to determine what each cost should be if operations are performed at a reasonable level of efficiency relative to the policies, objectives, constraints, and economic environment of the company. Budgeting is discussed in Chapters Six and Seven.

Financial Leverage

Introduction

The previous sections in this chapter explain the two basic ROI ratios of a company, and stress the importance of earning an adequate return on assets in order to earn a satisfactory return on equity. Earning an adequate return on its assets demands that the company keep both its asset turnover ratio and its profit ratio high enough. The preceding discussion is not the whole picture, however, since the capitalization structure of the company is taken as a given. In other words, the total amount of liabilities (as well as the interest rate on debt) and the total amount of stockholders' equity are held constant in the previous discussion. Alternative mixes of total liabilities to total stockholders' equity have not been explored, so that our attention could be focused on fundamentals of ROI ratios and on how an increase (or a decrease) in the asset turnover ratio or the profit ratio would affect the return on equity ratio.

This section, on the other hand, holds the return on asset ratio constant in order to explore the effects of alternative mixes of liabilities and stockholders' equity. In other words, this section is concerned with how the company is financed, which includes how much of the total capital invested in its assets is supplied by liabilities, whether these liabilities bear interest or not, what the interest rates are, and how much of the capital is supplied from stockholders. The main purpose is to explore the advantages and the potential disadvantages of what is called *financial leverage*.

To illustrate financial leverage it is necessary to compare *different* capitalization structures, that is, different mixes or proportions of liabilities and equity (stockholders') capital. To simplify and to make computations easier, a new example is introduced here which is stripped down, but which is comparable to the company analyzed in previous sections. Assume a company has total assets of $1 million. These assets are used by management to generate sales revenue of course. (The company's asset turnover ratio is not relevant here.) Given its sales revenue, the company earns an *operating profit* (before interest and income tax) of $150,000, which is a 15.0% rate of operating profit on total assets: ($150,000/$1,000,000 = 15.0%). Notice that this is a *new* ratio, which is called the *operating profit ratio*. Previously we did not explore this particular rate of return on total assets. However, for the following discussion this operating profit ratio is the best point of departure for analysis. This operating profit ratio is held constant in all the different cases presented below. The mix of liabilities and equity capital is changed in each alternative case.

CASE A: A Rather Extreme Situation—No Liabilities

The first case, called CASE A, is the starting point for the following analysis. This case is shown in Exhibit 3.5. The following explanation for CASE A is quite detailed in order to make clear all the procedures and assumptions. A $1 million amount of capital invested in total assets is assumed to have a convenient base of computation. In other words, each case looks at a $1 million "slice" of the business. The next question concerns where the company raised this amount of capital. How much of the total capital is supplied from liabilities, and how much is supplied from stockholders? In CASE A there are no liabilities; all $1 million of the capital is supplied from stockholders and only one class of common stock is assumed. Of course, having no liabilities is the extreme situation and would be very unusual. This case simply sets the stage for further discussion.

The company earns a 15.0% rate of operating profit on its assets, which is $150,000 (see the first step in Exhibit 3.5). The next step is to consider three "claims" to the operating profit: (1) interest (2) income tax, and (3) the (residual) net income. In CASE A there are no liabilities so there is no interest expense. Taxable income, although not shown in Exhibit 3.5, is equal to the

EXHIBIT 3.5
Case A

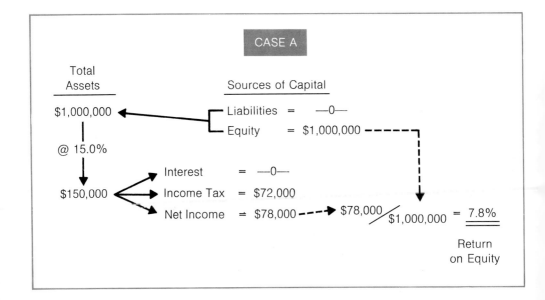

operating profit of $150,000, since there is no interest expense deduction. A *flat* income tax rate of 48% is applied to the taxable income. Actually, the current federal income tax rate on corporations is 22% on the first $25,000 and 48% on the excess over $25,000. However, it is very convenient to hold the income tax to a flat 48%, to avoid the two-step tax computation. Thus the income tax expense in CASE A is $72,000, which is ($150,000 × 48%). Net income, of course, is the residual amount after interest and income tax expense. Thus net income is $78,000 in CASE A. Notice that net income is also equal to 52% of the taxable income—that is, the company "keeps" only 52% (100% less 48%) of its taxable income.

Last, notice in Exhibit 3.5 that net income is extended over and divided by the stockholders' equity to determine the rate of return on the equity for the year, which in CASE A is 7.8%. Can the company's capitalization structure be rearranged to increase the return on equity rate? The basic alternative is to substitute liabilities for some of the stockholders' equity capital invested in the business.

CASE B: Interest Bearing Debt at High Interest Rate

CASE B, shown in Exhibit 3.6, illustrates what would happen if the company financed 40% of its capital needs from interest bearing debt sources and paid

EXHIBIT 3.6
Case B

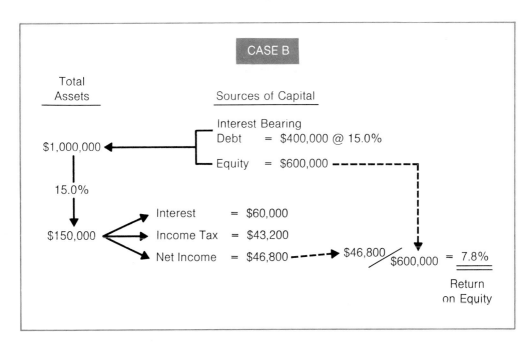

an annual interest rate of 15.0% for this debt. Admittedly, 15.0% is a very high annual interest rate, in fact, a rate that is seldom encountered in most business borrowing unless the company is in drastic circumstances. But the 15.0% rate is used to illustrate a very important point, which can be seen by following through to the disposition of the $150,000 operating profit. (Also, most businesses would have noninterest bearing liabilities; CASE C will consider this point.)

CASE B illustrates that the company can borrow money at an interest rate as high as its rate of operating profit on assets and still *not* decrease its rate of return on stockholders' equity. Observe that the return on equity is still 7.8% in this case. You may be asking: How can the company pay a 15.0% interest rate, which is more than the 7.8% return on equity, and not decrease the 7.8% rate of return on equity?

The main point is that the interest expense of $60,000 ($400,000 × 15.0%) is a *deductible expense* for determination of taxable income. The $60,000 interest expense decreases taxable income by the same amount; thus, income tax is decreased by $28,800 ($60,000 × 48%). The *aftertax* impact of the interest is only a $31,200 decrease to net income ($60,000 less $28,800). In other words, the aftertax impact of interest is only 52% of the interest cost, or $60,000 × 52%, which is $31,200. The company's net income is $31,200 worse off by using debt, but the stockholders in CASE B invest $400,000 less capital in the business. The following comparison can be made:

$$\frac{\text{Net Income}}{\text{Stockholders' Equity}} = \frac{\$\ 78,000}{\$1,000,000} = 7.8\% \qquad \frac{-\$\ 31,200}{-\$400,000} = \frac{\$\ 46,800}{\$600,000} = 7.8\%$$

| | CASE A | CHANGES | CASE B |

CASE C: A More Normal Situation

Normally a company would not have to pay as high an annual interest rate as 15.0% on its debt. And, normally a company would have noninterest bearing liabilities supplying part of its total capital. CASE C assumes that the company pays a 10.0% annual interest rate; also a reasonable amount of *noninterest bearing liabilities* is assumed (see Exhibit 3.7). In this situation there is an increase in net income and an increase in the rate of return on equity in comparison with CASE B.

Notice that interest expense decreases from $60,000 in CASE B to only $30,000 in CASE C. This is due to two reasons: (1) the annual interest rate is

EXHIBIT 3.7
Case C

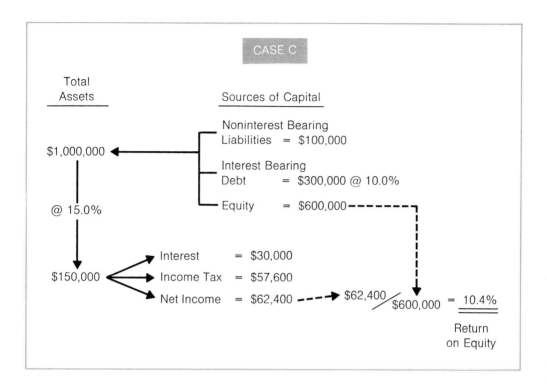

lower (15.0% compared with 10.0%); and, (2) part of the total liabilities are supplied from noninterest bearing liabilities (mainly Accounts Payable). Thus the *average* interest rate *on all liabilities* is only 7.5%: ($30,000 total interest divided by $400,000 total liabilities = 7.5%). Notice that in CASE C the noninterest bearing liabilities constitute one tenth of the total capital ($100,000/ $1,000,000). This is not necessarily a normal or average percentage for all companies, although one tenth is reasonable. The main point is to understand that noninterest bearing liabilities usually make up some part of the total capital sources of a company and, therefore, must be taken into account.

A key question is: Where did the net income increase of $15,600 ($62,400 in CASE C less $46,800 in CASE B) come from? The answer can be explained as follows: The company borrows $400,000 for which it pays an annual interest of $30,000 (given the 10.0% annual interest rate and given that $100,000 is non interest bearing liabilities). The company earns a 15.0% rate of operating profit on this $400,000, which is equal to $60,000 ($400,000 × 15.0%). Thus there is a pretax gain or "spread" on this part of the total capital equal to $30,000 ($60,000 less $30,000). The company also earns a 15.0% rate of operating profit on the other $600,000 of capital (supplied by the stockholders) which is $90,000 ($600,000 × 15.0%).

The company not only earns $90,000 pretax operating profit for the stockholders on their capital invested in the business, but also earns a pretax *leverage gain* of $30,000 on the use of borrowed capital. This gives a total pretax profit after interest for the stockholders of $120,000 ($90,000 + $30,000). This $120,000 is subject to the 48% income tax rate; hence, the income tax equals $57,600. The aftertax net income is thus $62,400 ($120,000 less $57,600). This explanation is summarized in Exhibit 3.8.

CASE D: The Potential Disadvantage of Financial Leverage

Assume the liabilities and interest rate are the same as in CASE C. But assume the company had a very bad year and was able to earn only 5.0% operating profit rate on its assets. In this case, the outcome would be as is shown in Exhibit 3.9. *If* the company had not borrowed on any interest bearing debt, the stockholders would have been *relatively* better off, which can be seen by comparing Exhibit 3.10 with Exhibit 3.9. Financial leverage works against the company in CASE D, since the company's operating rate of profit (5.0%) is less than the average annual interest rate of 7.5%. It would have been better not to have borrowed. The stockholders would have earned at least a 2.9% on their equity, which is better than the 1.7% rate that results if interest bearing debt is used. In short, there would be a leverage *loss* in CASE D, which is summarized in Exhibit 3.11.

In most cases, though by no means in all cases, the business enterprise earns a rate of operating profit on its assets *greater* than the average interest rate on all liabilities. Thus financial leverage works in favor of the company's stockholders. But the risk of not earning a high enough operating profit return on assets is there, and it should be remembered. Finally, financial leverage, especially when it works in favor of the stockholders, is sometimes called "trading on the equity." Briefly, this term means that a company can use its base of stockholders' equity capital to secure borrowed money. The company can "trade" (borrow) on its equity, and hopefully can invest the capital so that financial leverage works to the advantage of the stockholders.

Financial Leverage Analysis of Company's 1976 Profit Performance

The same analysis presented in the last several pages and the same format shown in Exhibit 3.8 are followed in summarizing in Exhibit 3.12 the impact of financial leverage in 1976 for the company example discussed previously in the chapter. The relevant information is taken from the condensed financial statements of the company shown in Exhibits 3.1 and 3.2. Clearly financial leverage works to the advantage of the company. Indeed, financial leverage accounts for about one third of the company's 1976 net income: the $138,671 after tax leverage gain (see Exhibit 3.12) is 32.9% of the total net income of $421,408.

EXHIBIT 3.8
Explanation of Financial Leverage Effects for Case C

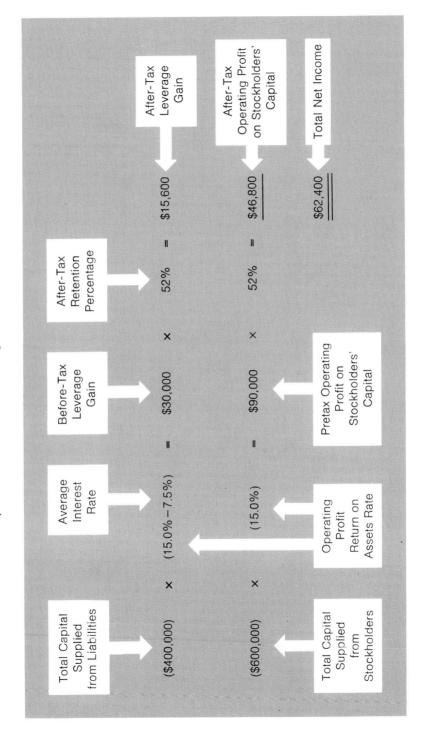

EXHIBIT 3.9
Case D

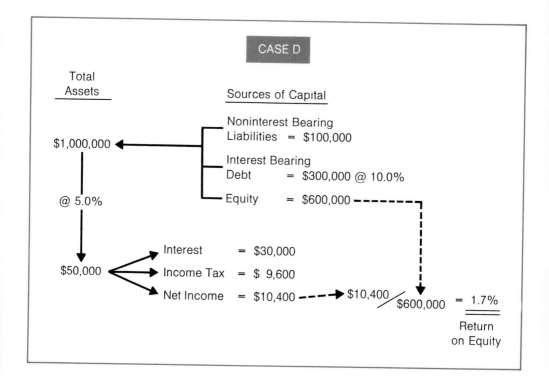

Summary

The primary financial objective of a (profit motivated) business enterprise is to earn a satisfactory net income relative to the stockholders' investment in the company. This requires that the company make good use of its assets to generate sales revenue and to keep its expenses less than sales revenue so that a satisfactory profit results from the sales revenue. The return on investment (ROI) ratio is equal to the company's profit (return) divided by the capital (investment) being used to earn the profit. There are two basic ROI ratios: (1) return on assets, which is (net income + interest) divided by the total assets of the company; and, (2) return on equity, which is net income divided by stockholders' equity. A company must earn a sufficient return on its assets to earn a satisfactory (or better) return on its equity.

To earn a sufficient return on its assets a company must maintain two basic determinants of this ROI ratio at high enough levels: (1) the asset turnover ratio, which is (sales revenue/total assets); and, (2) the profit ratio, which is (profit/

EXHIBIT 3.10
Case D, with No Interest Bearing Debt

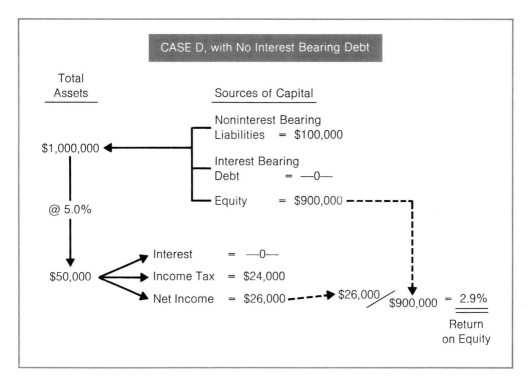

sales revenue). Even relatively slight changes in one or the other of these two components of the ROI ratio can cause dramatic changes in the return on assets ratio. The asset turnover ratio is essentially a sales promotion test; it measures the ability of the company to use its assets to generate sales revenue. On the other hand, the profit ratio is essentially an expense control test; it measures the ability of management to keep expenses within required limits to earn an adequate profit from the sales revenue. Management profit performance reports usually include the ratio (or percent) of each expense (or expense group) to sales revenue. Significant deviations from the standard or control limit ratio for each expense should be highlighted for management's attention and action.

The final impact of a company's return on assets ratio on its return on equity depends also on the financial leverage situation of the company. Financial leverage refers basically to the idea of using liabilities to supply a part of the total capital invested in its assets, hopefully to earn a rate of operating profit (before interest and income tax) on its assets that is greater than the average interest rate paid on all its liabilities. The differential between the rate of operating profit being earned on its assets and the average interest rate on its liabilities when multiplied by the total liabilities is the pretax leverage spread or

EXHIBIT 3.11
Explanation of Financial Leverage Effects for Case D

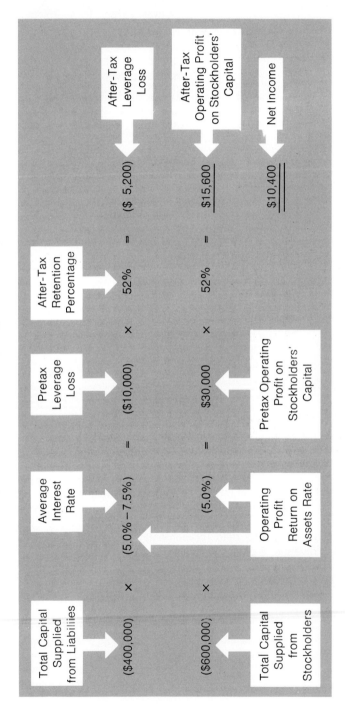

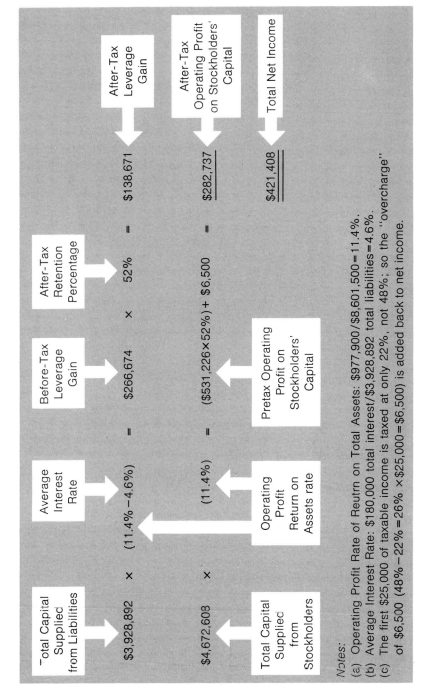

EXHIBIT 3.12
Explanation of Financial Leverage Effects for Company's
1976 Profit Performance

Notes:
(a) Operating Profit Rate of Reutrn on Total Assets: $977,900/$8,601,500=11.4%.
(b) Average Interest Rate: $180,000 total interest/$3,928,892 total liabilities=4.6%.
(c) The first $25,000 of taxable income is taxed at only 22%, not 48%; so the "overcharge"
    of $6,500 (48%−22%=26% ×$25,000=$6,500) is added back to net income.

gain. Even allowing for the taxation of this gain (about 48%), the aftertax lever-age gain can add a significant amount to a company's net income and, thus, can increase the return on its equity.

The average interest rate on a company's liabilities is affected not only by the interest rates negotiated with its sources of debt, but also depends on what percentage of its total liabilities are supplied from noninterest bearing liabilities. There is a basic risk in trading on equity, as financial leverage is sometimes called. A company may not be able to earn a rate of operating profit on its assets equal to or more than the average interest rate on its liabilities. In that case, the company suffers a leverage loss that reduces net income and its return on equity.

Questions

3. 1   What does the term "profit" mean?

3. 2   (a) Explain the main reasons and logic for the step-down format of the net income statement.
(b) What is a "single step" net income statement format?

3. 3   What are the two basic return on investment (ROI) ratios? Explain each factor for both of these ratios.

3. 4   Assume a company had no interest expense for the year. If the company wants to earn $266,500 net income for the year, how much operating profit would the company have to earn?

3. 5   Assume a company has $80,000 interest expense for the year. If the company wants to earn $131,300 net income for the year, how much operating profit would the company have to earn?

3. 6   Briefly explain the two separate determinant ratios of the return on assets ratio. Which of these two component ratios is more important?

3. 7   Which change would be better: an increase in the company's profit ratio from 6.0 to 6.6% or, instead, an increase in the company's asset turnover ratio from 2.0 to 2.2? In answering, you may want to set up numerical examples to prove your point.

3. 8   A company is facing operating cost increase next year that should reduce its profit ratio from 4.0 to 3.0%, even after taking sales prices increases into con-sideration. To keep its return on assets at 12.0%, what will the asset turnover have to be next year? What is the asset turnover ratio this year? Is a change in the asset turnover ratio of this much very practical?

3. 9   Why are the percents of expenses to sales revenue reported in management profit performance statements?

3.10   Managers should adopt a standard or control limit to determine what each expense's percent to sales revenue *should be* for the year. What are some problems in determining these bench mark expense ratios?

3.11   Assume that a retailer's basic sales pricing policy is to mark up the purchase cost of its products by one third of the cost per unit to determine the selling price. In this case, what is the company's bench mark cost of goods expense ratio?

3.12   Refer to question 3.11. Assume that the company's annual profit performance report shows its cost of goods sold expense to be 78.5% of sales revenue.
(a) Is this actual expense ratio more or less than it should be?
(b) What are some possible reasons for the variance between the actual expense ratio and the bench mark ratio?

3.13   What is meant by the term "financial leverage"?

3.14   What is the basic condition or situation in which financial leverage is a disadvantage?

3.15   Assume a company can earn a 12.0% operating profit return on its assets, instead of the 15.0% rate assumed in CASE B and CASE C in the chapter. Would financial leverage be an advantage or disadvantage in each CASE? Briefly explain.

Problems

P3. 1   Assume the following ratios in 1976 for a company:

Return on Assets (ROA) Rate		Asset Turnover Ratio	×	Profit Ratio
15.0%	=	5.0	×	3.0%

Each case described below is a separate and independent situation for next year, 1977:
(1) Assume the asset turnover rate increases to 5.5. The profit ratio remains the same. What is the ROA rate in 1977?
(2) Assume the profit ratio decreases to 2.5%. The asset turnover ratio remains the same. What is the ROA rate in 1977?
(3) Assume the asset turnover ratio increases by 10% (from 5.0 to 5.5) and the profit ratio decreases by 10% (from 3.0 to 2.7%). Would the ROA rate therefore remain the same in 1977? If not, why?
(4) Assume the company is planning to tighten control over the capital invested

in its assets during 1977 such that the asset turnover ratio should increase to 5.5 in 1977. The company is content to earn the same ROA rate in 1977 as in 1976. What is the lowest profit ratio that would permit the company to earn the same ROA rate in 1977 as in 1976?

(5) Assume the company plans to increase sales revenue by 20% in 1977 with no increase in total assets. The profit ratio should be the same. What is the ROA rate in 1977 under these conditions?

(6) The company, being privately owned and rather conservative financially, holds a large excess cash balance equal to about one fifth of its total assets. (That is, the *excess* cash balance is one fifth of its total assets.) If the company distributes this excess cash to its stockholders, and assuming other factors remain the same in 1977, what is the ROA rate in 1977?

(7) Assume that just before year-end 1976 the company raised a large amount of capital by issuing securities. This money was received late in the year and and was immediately invested in assets, but these assets were at work only a short time during the last few days in the year. If the *average* total assets during the year had been used to compute the ratios above, then the total assets measure would have been 10% less. Recompute the ratios for 1976 based on this new information.

P3. 2   Which of the following situations are not very realistic. Briefly describe why you believe each is unrealistic.

	Asset Turnover Ratio	×	Profit Ratio	=	Return On Assets Rate
(a)	4.0	×	3.0%	=	12.0%
(b)	15.0	×	1.0%	=	15.0%
(c)	6.0	×	− 2.0%	=	− 12.0%
(d)	20.0	×	5.0%	=	100.0%
(e)	40.0	×	.5%	=	20.0%
(f)	− 2.0	×	10.0%	=	− 20.0%
(g)	8.0	×	30.0%	=	240.0%

P3. 3   In *very condensed* form the company's financial statements for the year just ended are as follows. (Assume a flat 48% income tax rate.)

Balance Sheet at End of Year			Net Income Statement for Year	
Total Assets	$3,000,000		Sales Revenue	$5,000,000
Acounts Payable and			Operating Expenses	4,580,000
Other Non-Interest			Operating Profit	$ 420,000
Bearing Liabilities	$ 200,000		Interest Expense	20,000
Notes Payable (Short-			Pretax Income	$ 400,000
and Long-Term)	$ 200,000		Income Tax	192,000
Stockholders' Equity	$2,600,000		Net Income	$ 208,000
Total Sources of Capital	$3,000,000			

Required:

(1) For the year just ended determine:
    (a) The return on assets and the two main determinants of this ratio.
    (b) The return on equity.
(2) For the year just ended analyze the effects of financial leverage.
(3) If the company's notes payable had been $1,000,000 and if the stockholders' equity had been $1,800,000 instead of the amounts shown above, then:
    (a) Prepare the net income statement for the year, assuming the same annual interest rate on the notes payable.
    (b) Answer parts (1) and (2) of this problem for this new situation.
(4) If the company's sales revenue had been $6 million for the year and assuming the same operating profit percent to sales revenue as shown above, and assuming the same capitalization structure and same total assets as shown above, then:
    (a) Prepare the net income statement for the year.
    (b) Answer parts (1) and (2) of this problem for this new situation.

P3. 4 The article reproduced on the next page is taken from a recent issue of *Consumer Reports* (Feb. 1974, page 105).

Required: Answer the following questions about the article:

(1) Do you agree with the basic contention of the article that Winn-Dixie should also disclose their return on investment in order to tell the "whole truth"?
(2) Is the article correct basically when it says that "2% is good for a food chain, which depends for its actual earning on high turnover"?

Winn-Dixie's Profit: How Do You Count?

If you live in Florida, Georgia, Alabama or the Carolinas, there's a good chance you do your grocery shopping at a Winn-Dixie supermarket. Although Winn-Dixie confines its operation almost entirely to that area, the food chain appears in a Fortune magazine listing of the nation's 50 largest retailers. That adds up to a high saturation of stores in a relatively few states.

And if you do shop at Winn-Dixie, you're probably familiar with the paper bag they use, shown in the illustration. Not that the message on the bag is easy to understand or interpret. Take "Our Net Profit," given as 2 per cent on the pie graph. Yes, Winn-Dixie's net profit was about that in 1972 (actually, 2.1 per cent, according to Fortune). But 2 per cent is good for a food

Here's what happens to the dollar you spend at Winn-Dixie.

chain, which depends for its actual earnings on high turnover. More meaningful is the annual rate of return on investment, which Fortune quotes at 19.7 per cent in 1972. Quite a difference.

Then there's the anticonsumer message at the bottom. It's a little ambiguous. Does it mean that any costs generated by consumer-protection legislation would be magnani-mously absorbed by Winn-Dixie? Or is it a scare tactic to get across the idea that such legislation will drive the already sky-rocket-ing price of food still higher? Commenting on the latter interpretation, New York Con-gressman Benjamin S. Rosenthal wrote to the chain: "Instead of spending your time and money printing misleading and anti-consumer messages, I respectfully suggest that you attempt to bring about a change in . . . the food situation, so that people can afford food again."

CU also wrote to Winn-Dixie. We asked, among other things, whether the chain would be willing to include on its shopping bag the rate of return on investment. We received no answer from Winn-Dixie. But we did get a comment from an unexpected source: Forbes magazine (October 15, 1973). It quoted James E. Davis, chairman of Winn-Dixie: "It's a bad time for showing profits. Hell, we just got a letter from some guy who is with Consumers Union who insisted we were misleading people. . . . This guy wants us to print on the bag our return on invested capital. . . . How do you satisfy a dumb SOB like that? He's the kind of guy who really wants us to lose money, then print that on our bags."

You can satisfy us dumb SOBs, Mr. Davis, by printing the whole truth.

P3. 5   A company has $5,000,000 total assets. The sources of its assets are: noninterest bearing liabilities, $400,000; interest bearing debts at an average 9.0% annual interest rate, $2,000,000; and, stockholders' equity, $2,600,000. The company is able to earn a 10.0% annual rate of operating profit on its total assets. The income tax rate is a flat 54%, consisting of a 48% federal income tax rate and a 6% state income tax rate. State taxable income is assumed to be equal to federal taxable income (though this is not quite correct in most situations).

Required:

(1) Prepare a diagram for the company as shown in Exhibit 3.7 to analyze the disposition of the year's operating profit of the company.
(2) Analyze the financial leverage effects and prepare a diagram for the com-pany as shown in Exhibit 3.8.
(3) What is the lowest rate of return on assets that the company could earn without financial leverage working to the disadvantage of the stockholders in this situation?

P3. 6   As is noted in the chapter, the basic ROI ratios, turnover ratios, and financial leverage analysis ratios can be based on the *average* balances during the year instead of the ending balances which are used in the chapter.

Required:

(1) For the company example used in this chapter, compute each ratio listed below for 1976 based on the average balance or balances during 1976 appropriate for each ratio; use the *simple average* balance, which means the beginning balance plus the ending balance divided by two.

(a) Return on assets, asset turnover, and profit ratio.

(b) Return on equity, and

(c) Average interest rate.

(2) Based on your answers to part (1), prepare an analysis summary of the financial leverage effects—see Exhibit 3.12 for example.

P3. 7 Refer to the financial statements of the company example introduced in Problem 2.6.

Required: Determine and show computations clearly for:

(1) The company's 1975 and 1976 return on assets, and the determinant ratios of return on assets.

(2) The company's return on equity for 1975 and 1976.

(3) The effects of the company's financial leverage for 1976; see Exhibit 3.12 for example.

(*Note:* Where appropriate use year-end balances in your computations instead of average balances during the year.)

P3. 8 Below is reproduced Caterpillar's 1973 and 1972 net income statements, which are taken without change from the company's published 1973 annual report (page 16). Notice that the two-year net income statement is joined with the statement of changes in retained earnings during the year, which is a not uncommon reporting practice among publicly owned companies. The income tax footnote (note 6) is not reproduced and is not pertinent to this problem.

Required: Rearrange Caterpillar's net income statements for 1973 and 1972 to fit the net income statement format shown in Exhibit 3.2. Exclude Caterpillar's other income items for both years; in other words, terminate each year's statement at net income before the two other income items are included. Thus the "bottom line" net income is $229.1 million for 1973 and $195.4 million for 1972. Also, include the percents for Caterpillar as are shown in Exhibit 3.2.

CONSOLIDATED RESULTS OF OPERATIONS
(Millions of Dollars)

	1973	1972
Sales	$3,182.4	$2,602.2
Costs:		
Inventories brought forward from previous year	706.9	698.9
Materials, supplies, services purchased, etc.	1,701.1	1,271.8
Wages, salaries and contributions for employee benefits	1,076.0	858.9
Depreciation (portion of original cost of buildings,		
machinery and equipment allocated to operations)	106.4	100.8
Interest on borrowed funds	28.7	22.4
Taxes based on income (note 6)	152.5	160.9
	3,771.6	3,113.7
Deduct: Inventories carried forward to following year	818.3	706.9
Costs allocated to year (1)	2,953.3	2,406.8
	229.1	195.4
Equity in profit of affiliated companies	17.0	10.0
Profit of subsidiary credit companies	.7	1.0
Profit for year—consolidated (per share (2): 1973—$4.32;		
1972—$3.62)	246.8	206.4
Profit employed in the business at beginning of year	1,017.2	890.5
	1,264.0	1,096.9
Dividends paid in cash during year (per share:		
1973—$1.50; 1972—$1.40)	85.5	79.7
Profit employed in the business at end of year	$1,178.5	$1,017.2

(1) Includes cost of goods sold: 1973—$2,503.1; 1972—$1,991.2.
(2) Computed on weighted average number of shares outstanding.

P3. 9   The return on equity ratio, instead of being determined in the manner described in the chapter, can be calculated as follows:

$$\text{Return on Equity} = \underbrace{\frac{\text{Net Income}}{\text{Sales Revenue}}}_{(A)} \times \underbrace{\frac{\text{Sales Revenue}}{\text{Total Assets}}}_{(B)} \times \underbrace{\frac{\text{Total Assets}}{\text{Stockholders' Equity}}}_{(C)}$$

Required:

(1) Define and briefly explain each of the three components (A), (B), and (C) in the above formula to compute ROE.

(2) Using the information in the condensed financial statements presented in Exhibits 3.1 and 3.2, compute each component ratio (A), (B), and (C) for 1975 and 1976 for the company. Use year-end balances where appropriate.

(3) Assume for a company the following ratios for 1975 in the above formula:

$$12.0\% = 4.0\% \times 2.0 \times 1.5$$

For each of the following separate and independent situations for next year, 1976, compute the ROE for next year:

(a) Sales revenue increases 50% but total assets remain the same; the other two component ratios remain the same.

(b) Sales revenue increases 50% and total assets increase 50%; most of the increase in total assets is supplied by an increase in liabilities such that the ratio of total liabilities to total stockholders' equity is 1.0 to 1.0 in 1976; ratio (A) remains the same in 1976.

(c) The company's pretax profit ratio (that is, net income after interest but before income tax) to stockholders' equity increases to 10.0% in 1976, and the other two component ratios remain the same; assume a flat 48% income tax rate.

P3.10   The following financial statements were taken from the company's most recent annual report to its stockholders:

STATEMENTS OF NET INCOME AND RETAINED EARNINGS
FOR THE YEARS ENDING DECEMBER 31, 1976 AND 1975
(All Dollar Balances in Thousands)

	1976	1975
Net sales	$48,400	$41,700
Costs and expenses:		
Cost of goods sold	$31,460	$29,190
Selling, general, and administrative	12,090	8,770
Interest	400	440
Income tax	2,136	1,584
Total	$46,086	$39,984
Net income	$ 2,314	$ 1,716
Retained earnings, January 1	8,501	7,345
Total	$10,815	$ 9,061
Dividends:		
Preferred stock, $1.20 per share cash	$ 60	$ 60
Common stock:		
$1 per share cash	525	500
10% stock dividend, at $50 per share market value	2,500	—0—
Total dividends	$ 3,085	$ 560
Retained earnings, December 31	$ 7,730	$ 8,501

BALANCE SHEETS
DECEMBER 31, 1976 AND 1975
(All Dollar Balances in Thousands)

	1976	1975
ASSETS		
Current Assets:		
Cash	$ 2,120	$ 1,881
Accounts receivable, less allowance for doubtful accounts: 1976, $125; 1975, $110)	4,075	3,669
Inventories	7,250	6,803
Prepaid expenses	125	218
Total current assets	$13,570	$12,571
Plant and Equipment, at cost:		
Land and buildings	$13,500	$13,500
Machinery and equipment	9,250	8,520
Total	$22,750	$22,020
Accumulated depreciation	13,470	12,549
Net	$ 9,280	$ 9,471
Total assets	$22,850	$22,042
LIABILITIES AND SHAREHOLDERS' EQUITY		
Current Liabilities:		
Accounts payable	$ 2,950	$ 3,426
Accrued expenses	1,575	1,644
Income taxes payable	470	346
Current portion of long-term debt	500	500
Total current liabilities	$ 5,495	$ 5,916
Long-term liabilities:		
8.0% debentures, $500 due annually until January 1, 1986	$ 5,000	$ 5,500
Shareholders' Equity:		
Preferred stock, $20 par value, 6.0% annual dividend (authorized: 100,000 shares; issued and outstanding 50,000 shares)	$ 1,000	$ 1,000
Common stock, $1 par value (authorized, 900,000 shares; issued and outstanding: 1976, 550,000 shares; 1975, 500,000 shares)	550	500
Capital in excess of par value of common stock	3,075	625
Retained earnings	7,730	8,501
Total shareholders' equity	$12,355	$10,626
Total liabilities and shareholders' equity	$22,850	$22,042

Other information: The cash dividends on both the preferred and common stock were paid in June and December each year. The stock dividend on common stock was distributed in August 1976.

Required:

(1) For 1976 and 1975 compute:
   (a) The return on equity rate based on the ending balance each year.
   (b) The asset turnover and profit ratios to determine the return on assets.
(2) For 1976 analyze the effects of financial leverage on the common stockholders; see Exhibit 3.12 for a basic guideline.
(3) Assume that in 1976 the company had paid a total cash dividend of $6 per share instead of paying the $1 cash dividend and the 10% stock dividend. In this situation, determine the return on equity rate for 1976 and explain why it is different than the rate determined in part (1a).

P3.11 Please refer to Exhibits 3.1 and 3.2 which present the condensed balance sheets and net income statements of the company for 1975 and 1976. The company would like to earn a 15.0% rate of return on equity in 1977.

Required:

(1) If all of the improvement in the ROE rate in 1977 has to come from an increase in the asset turnover ratio, and assuming all other factors remain the same as in 1976 determine what the asset turnover ratio would have to be in 1977. Prove your answer.
(2) If all of the improvement in the ROE rate in 1977 has to come from an increase in the profit ratio, and assuming all other factors remain the same as in 1976, determine what profit ratio would have to be earned in 1977. Prove your answer.
(3) If the maximum feasible asset turnover ratio in 1977 is 2.0, then what would the company's 1977 profit ratio have to be assuming all other factors remain the same as in 1976? Prove your answer.

P3.12 Please refer to the net income statements presented in Problem 3.10, which are used also for this problem.

Required:

(1) Rearrange the format of the company's net income statement for each year to conform with the format shown in Exhibit 3.2.
(2) Compute the expense ratios and enter these ratios in the net income statement prepared for part (1).
(3) Identify which, in your opinion, are the most significant expense ratio changes between 1975 and 1976.

P3.13 A certain company has gone through significant changes in its policy over the years regarding how the company should be financed. Two generations ago the founder, who started the company with a very small personal investment of capital, believed in avoiding all debt. The company was started during the Depression and it is understandable why the "old man" was so conservative. When his son became president after World War II, there was a shift to the use of some debt capital, but for only a relatively small part of the total assets of the company. Just recently the grandson of the founder became president, and he increased the proportion of debt capital to equity capital. In summary, the following information is typical for each generation of the company.

	First Generation	Second Generation	Third Generation
Operating profit (before interest and income tax) on total assets	10%	15%	15%
Percentage of noninterest bearing liabilities to total assets	5%	5%	10%
Percentage of interest bearing liabilities to total assets	0%	20%	50%
Average annual interest rate on interest bearing liabilities	5%	5%	9%
Income tax (federal) rate on taxable income	15%	48%	48%

Required: For each "generation" of the company shown above, analyze the effects of financial leverage on the stockholders. Use a $100,000 "slice" of total assets for each generation to have a convenient base of computation.

P3.14   Please refer to Exhibit 3.7 in the chapter. Certain changes in this example are made below.

Required:

(1) For each separate and independent situation below, determine the return on equity in the manner illustrated in Exhibit 3.7; assume that all factors except as changed below remain the same as shown in the chapter:
   (a) The operating profit rate on total assets is 18.0%.
   (b) The interest rate is 8.0%.
   (c) The combined federal and state income tax rate is 54.0%.

(2) Change each of the following factors by a favorable one percentage point, and determine the return on equity for each of the three new situations:
   (a) The operating profit rate on total assets.
   (b) The interest rate.
   (c) The income tax rate.

Which of these "one percentage point changes" has the most impact on the company's ROE?

P3.15   A company's total assets are $5 million, and its total stockholders' equity is $3 million. For the year just ended the company's total interest expense is $120,000. The income tax rate is a flat 48%. The company's net income is $405,600, which in part is due to a favorable aftertax financial leverage gain of $124,800.

Required: Determine the company's return on assets for the year; show your computations clearly.

Chapter Four

Basic Analysis of Revenue, Costs, Profit, and Capital Investment Behavior

CHAPTER FOUR

BASIC ANALYSIS OF REVENUE, COSTS, PROFIT, AND CAPITAL INVESTMENT BEHAVIOR

Introduction

Consider the company's Net Income Statement presented in Chapter Two (Exhibit 2.2), which is also shown in more condensed form in Chapter Three (Exhibit 3.2). Total sales revenue increased from $10,000,000 in 1975 to $11,825,000 in 1976, which is an increase of $1,825,000, or 18.25%. Should net income also increase *exactly* 18.25%? Intuitively it may seem that an increase of about 18% in total sales revenue should "pull up" net income by about 18%. In other words, it would seem that with a higher sales revenue there should be a corresponding increase in net income. But, on closer examination, do you think that *each and every* expense should increase *exactly* 18.25%, no more and no less? Expenses, in fact, do not move in lock step with increases (or decreases) of sales revenue. Notice that the company's net income increased from $309,270 in 1975 to $421,408 in 1976, which is an increase of $112,138, or about 36%. This is considerably more than the 18% increase in sales revenue.

Chapter Three explains that net income *alone* is not the entire measure of financial success. Net income (or some other measure of profit) must be compared with and divided by the capital investment being used to generate that net income (or other profit measure). As we explain in Chapter Three, a company must earn an adequate return on its assets to earn a satisfactory return on its stockholders' equity. Thus the change in the company's total assets from 1975 to 1976 is also very important to consider. The company's Statement of Financial Condition is reported at the beginning of Chapter Two (Exhibit 2.1), and is also shown in more condensed form in Chapter Three (Exhibit 3.1). Notice that total assets at year-end 1975 were $7,924,500 and are $8,601,500 at the end of 1976, which is an increase of $677,000 or about 8.5%. Total assets increased only 8.5% even though sales revenue increased by more than 18%. The higher asset turnover ratio in 1976 improves the rate of return on assets of the company, assuming, of course, that the company's profit ratio did not decrease and offset the higher ratio of sales revenue to total assets.

The main point of the above comments simply is to raise questions that are discussed in more detail in this chapter:

Given the 18.25% increase in sales revenue why did net income increase by over 36%? How does net income behave generally relative to increases in sales revenue?

Given the 18.25% increase on sales revenue why did total assets increase only 8.5%? In general, how do total assets (total capital investment) behave relative to increases in sales revenue, and what is the impact of this on the return on assets and the return on equity?

Managers need to have a sure grip on the analytical tools needed to answer these questions. The purpose of this chapter is to develop some of these tools for management analysis of profit and capital investment behavior.

Basic Management Dimensions of Profit and Return on Investment (ROI) Performance

Introduction: The Need for Additional Information

The information presented in the Net Income Statement at the start of Chapter Two (see Exhibit 2.2), although satisfactory for external reporting to investors, is *not* adequate for management analysis of the profit performance of the company. An additional dimension of information is needed to begin analysis. In particular, information is needed about: (1) the *quantities* of products manufactured and sold; (2) the *behavior* of the company's manufacturing costs and operating *expenses*; (3) the *sales prices* of the products sold during the period; and, (4) certain information about the *interest* and *income tax* expenses of the period. Before proceeding to the analysis of the company's profit performance that makes use of this additional information, a key assumption is made for the company example.

A Key Assumption for the Example: A One Product Company

The one basic assumption that is made for the company example is that the company manufactures and sells only *one* product, the same product in both 1975 and 1976 of course. Most companies in fact sell two or more products, although some companies come close to selling only one basic product, such as a brewery that sells only one brand of beer. A one product example is a good place to start, and it has the important advantage of avoiding certain problems of analyzing and reporting information for the multiproduct company. In particular, when there are two or more sources of sales revenue, there are two basic problems of accounting for costs which are best avoided in this introductory discussion.

One problem is that most multiproduct companies have several *joint costs*. For example, the annual real estate tax on the company's manufacturing land and buildings is a joint cost that benefits all the products manufactured during the year. In fact, most manufacturing overhead costs are joint costs, which must be allocated in some manner to the various products manufactured during the year. (This allocation is discussed in Chapter Thirteen.) Some raw material and direct labor costs are also joint costs. For example, a direct labor operation may involve the separation of the raw material into two or more parts, each used in a different product. Allocation of joint costs is a rather technical topic that should be avoided at this point in our discussion. By limiting attention to a one product company, all the company's costs relate to one source of sales revenue.

Second, with two or more sources of sales revenue there is the problem of how to summarize sales revenue, cost, and profit information in the periodic reports to managers at different levels in the organization. Imagine, if you would, a company that has 30 or 40 different product lines, a number that is not too unusual. And, within each product line there are distinct product sizes and models. Presenting useful *summaries* of all this sales and cost information while avoiding getting lost in too much detail is a serious reporting problem. This reporting problem is best sidestepped in this introductory discussion. Summarization in reports is not a serious problem with only one product. Total sales revenue, for example, is simply the total quantity sold times the sales price for the product.

Introduction of Basic Management Profit Performance Report for Company

A basic management profit performance report is now represented in Exhibit 4.1. Compared with the net income statement first shown in Chapter Two (Exhibit 2.2), this report includes an additional dimension or "layer" of information that is needed for management control and planning analysis. In particular, for each year the sales volume, selling price, costs per unit, and certain other information is given. Also, fixed costs are separated from variable costs. The reasons for this separation are discussed at some length later in the chapter. Read Exhibit 4.1 carefully and become familiar with the information presented in the report. This information is referred to frequently in the next several sections. You might ask: Where would this information come from? The accounting system of the company is the main source. The company's accountants develop a system to capture, process, store, and retrieve the information so that it is readily available for preparation of profit performance reports to managers.

A word of warning is in order: the particular format, arrangement, and level of detail shown in Exhibit 4.1 is my choice. There is no implication that this is the best or most generally preferred style of management profit reports. The specific design of management reports is, to a large degree, a matter of individual opinion and preference. Furthermore, management profit reports must be adapted to the specific circumstances and particular customs and practices of the company, which may change over time. Exhibit 4.1, therefore, is offered simply as a useful and not unusual format to work with.

Determining Cost of Goods Sold

This company uses the last-in, first-out (LIFO) method to determine cost of goods sold during the year. This means that the most recent (or latest) costs of products manufactured are charged against sales revenue. In this example,

EXHIBIT 4.1
Management Profit Performance Report

Line		1975 500,000 units			1976 550,000 units		
		Percents	Dollar Value per Unit		Percents	Dollar Value per Unit	
(a)	Sales Volume Base						
(b)	Sales revenue	100.0	$20.000	$10,000,000	100.0	$21.500	$11,825,000
	Cost of goods sold:						
	Variable costs—						
(c)	Raw materials	21.4	$ 4.287	$2,143,500	21.5	$ 4.630	$2,546,500
(d)	Direct labor	26.7	5.331	2,665,500	26.4	5.674	3,120,700
(e)	Overhead	4.9	0.982	491,000	4.9	1.046	575,300
(f)	Total variable costs	53.0	$10.600	$5,300,000	52.8	$11.350	$6,242,500
	Fixed costs—						
(g)	Direct labor	1.2	$ 0.244	$ 122,000	1.2	$ 0.258	$ 141,900
(h)	Overhead	7.4	1.481	740,500	7.2	1.558	856,900
(i)	Total fixed costs	8.6	$ 1.725	$ 862,500	8.4	$ 1.816	$ 998,800
(j)	Total cost of goods sold	61.6	$12.325	6,162,500	61.2	$13.166	7,241,300
(k)	Gross profit	38.4	$ 7.675	$ 3,837,500	38.8	$ 8.334	$ 4,583,700
	Operating costs:						
	Variable costs—						
(l)	Marketing	24.3	$ 4.850	$2,425,000	24.0	$ 5.150	$2,832,500
(m)	Administrative and general	0.7	0.150	75,000	0.7	0.160	88,000
(n)	Total variable costs	25.0	$ 5.000	$2,500,000	24.7	$ 5.310	$2,920,500
	Fixed costs—						
(o)	Marketing	3.1	$ 0.616	$ 308,000	3.0	$ 0.636	$ 349,800
(p)	Administrative and general	3.0	0.597	298,500	2.8	0.610	335,500
(q)	Total fixed costs	6.1	$ 1.213	$ 606,500	5.8	$ 1.246	$ 685,300
(r)	Total operating costs	31.1	$ 6.213	3,106,500	30.5	$ 6.556	3,605,800
(s)	Operating profit	7.3	$ 1.462	$ 731,000	8.3	$ 1.778	$ 977,900
(t)	Interest expense	(average debt=$1,750,000×8.5%)		148,750	(average debt=$2,250,000×8.0%)		180,000
(u)	Net income before tax			$ 582,250			$ 797,900
(v)	Income tax	($582,250×48% less $6,500)		272,980	($797,900×48% less $6,500)		376,492
(w)	Net income			$ 309,270			$ 421,408

the company manufactures more units than are sold each year. Hence, by using the LIFO method the cost of goods sold includes only the current year's costs of production. Exhibit 4.2 summarizes the company's production output, products sold, and inventory increases each year. From Exhibit 4.2 we can determine the (total) manufacturing cost per unit produced each year, as follows:

Total Manufacturing Cost per Unit

	1975	1976
$\dfrac{\text{Total Manufacturing Costs}}{\text{Total Production Output}} =$	$\dfrac{\$6,470,625}{525,000} = \$12.325$ per unit	$\dfrac{\$7,405,875}{562,500} = \$13.166$ per unit

In Exhibit 4.1 the cost per unit sold each year [see line (j)] is equal to the manufacturing cost per unit each year shown above. The additional information in Exhibit 4.2 regarding the breakdown between variable costs and fixed costs is useful for later discussion.

Also a report like that shown Exhibit 4.2 is useful for certain managers in determining how well inventories are being controlled relative to the inventory holding policies of the company. For instance, at year-end 1975 the manager would observe that the ending inventories of work-in-process and finished goods are 25% of the year's sales quantity: (125,000 units/500,000 units = 25%). In Exhibit 4.2, work-in-process inventory is combined with finished goods inventory. Except in detailed reports to production managers the breakdown between the two inventories is not too important, since units in process will be finished shortly in most manufacturing situations. The more relevant information is the total inventory situation of the company. The footnotes in Exhibit 4.2 explain the conversion of in-process units into an equivalent number of finished units, which must be done to put the work-in-process inventory on the same basis as finished units to determine production cost per (completed) unit.

The Essential Distinction Between Variable and Fixed Costs

Perhaps the one feature of the management profit performance statement (Exhibit 4.1) that is most noticeable is the separation between *fixed* costs and *variable* costs. For managers to carry out their control and planning analysis, most accounting reports should separate fixed costs from variable costs in each of a company's three basic operating areas:

1. Manufacturing (production);
2. Marketing and distribution (selling); and,
3. Administration and general.

Thus Exhibit 4.1 reports the fixed and variable costs both *in total and* on a *per unit* basis for each of the three operating areas.

EXHIBIT 4.2
Total Production Output, Goods Sold, and Inventory Changes

	1975				1976			
	Quantity (in units)	Variable Costs	Fixed Costs	Total Costs	Quantity (in units)	Variable Costs	Fixed Costs	Total Costs
Total production output	525,000	$5,565,000	$ 905,625	$6,470,625	562,500	$6,384,375	$1,021,500	$7,405,875
Goods sold (LIFO method)	500,000	5,300,000	862,500	6,162,500	550,000	6,242,500	998,800	7,241,300
Increase of Work-in-Process and Finished Good Inventories	25,000	$ 265,000	$ 43,125	$ 308,125	12,500	$ 141,875	$ 22,700	$ 164,575
Beginning Work-in-Process and Finished Goods Inventories	100,000	1,060,000	172,500	1,232,500	125,000	1,325,000	215,625	1,540,625
Ending Work-in-Process and Finished Goods Inventories	125,000	$1,325,000	$ 215,625	$1,540,625	137,500	$1,466,875	$ 238,325	$1,705,200

a. Work-in-Process Inventory units are converted into an equivalent number of finished units in this schedule. For example, at the beginning of 1975 the company has 16,000 units in process which are one-half complete with respect to the costs of manufacturing. These are converted into the equivalent of 8000 finished units. These 8000 equivalent units are added to the 92,000 units of finished products to get the total 100,000 units shown above. Likewise, at the end of 1975 the company has 20,000 units still in process which are one-half complete. These in-process units are converted to 10,000 equivalent units, which are added to the 115,000 finished units to get the total of 125,000 units shown above.

b. The total production output measure for each year also has to take into account the equivalent units in the beginning and ending Work-in-Process Inventory. In 1975, for example, the company completed the beginning Work-in-Process units, which is the equivalent of manufacturing 8000 finished units. The company started and completed 507,000 units during the year, excluding those in the beginning Work-in-Process Inventory. And, the company worked on 20,000 units which are still in process at year-end that are one half complete, which is the equivalent of 10,000 finished units. In total, the manufacturing output for the year is: (8000 units+507,000 units+10,000 units=525,000 units). Keep in mind that the first and third factors in the parentheses are stated in terms of equivalent units.

The *per unit* costs reported in the management profit performance statement need to be understood very carefully. The essential idea is this:

Total Quantity × Variable Cost per Unit   =   Total Variable Cost
Total Fixed Cost/Total Quantity   =   Fixed Cost Per Unit

Notice the direction of causality in these two equations. Total quantity times variable cost per unit *determines* total variable cost—total variable cost *depends on* the total quantity and the variable cost per unit. In contrast, a company starts with a certain total fixed cost for the period which, if divided by total quantity, *determines* the fixed cost per unit. Given a certain total fixed cost, the fixed cost per unit *depends on* the total quantity for the period. The higher the quantity, then the lower the fixed cost per unit. And, the lower the quantity, then the higher the fixed cost per unit. In contrast, the variable cost per unit is constant over a wide range of quantity levels.

Variable costs are those costs that depend on the actual level of activity during the period. As activity increases, these costs increase, and as activity decreases, these costs decrease. For instance the total cost of raw materials used during the period depends on the number of units of raw materials actually withdrawn from the inventory stock of these items and how much each raw material unit cost. Another example is transportation expense, or freight out as it is also called. If more units are sold and delivered, then this expense increases. And if fewer units are delivered, then this expense decreases. Variable costs are the most obvious costs of carrying on operations during the period. Although not as obvious perhaps, fixed costs are just as necessary to carry on operations.

Fixed costs do *not vary* or depend on the level of activity, quantity of output, or volume of operations during a *given time period* (a year in this example). Fixed costs are those costs that for most practical purposes are a constant total amount over a certain range of activity levels during the time period. Many fixed costs are incurred on a *total commitment basis* for a certain period of time. The company enters the time period knowing (or should know) what these fixed costs commitments are for the coming time period.

Costs are fixed for many different reasons, including the following basic reasons:

1. Many employees are hired on a *salary basis* that does not depend on the level or volume of work flow the persons are responsible for. Salaried employees could be laid off in extreme situations, but over a normal range of activity the number of salaried employees tends to remain more or less constant. The company avoids layoffs unless the sales volume has plummeted. Even in this case the company may depend on attrition due to normal causes, such as retirements and employees quiting to take other jobs, rather than actually terminating any employees. In the manufacturing

area most supervisory and higher level production managers are paid on a fixed salary basis.

2. Most machinery, equipment, buildings, tools, and other physical assets used in the production, marketing, and administration operations of the business are depreciated on the basis of a predetermined fixed schedule of depreciation, such as the straight-line or sum-of-the-years'-digits method. The amount of the depreciation charged-off during the period is fixed according to the depreciation method (or formula), and does not depend on the actual level of usage of the fixed assets.

3. Many supportive-type costs, such as janitorial and cleaning, data processing, and insurance, remain relatively constant regardless of fluctuation in operating activity during the year. For instance, the cost of keeping the earnings records on each employee is unaffected by whether the person works 36 hours or 48 hours during a week.

4. The company may rent certain assets for a fixed amount per period.

5. Property taxes are based on the assessed value of the property, which in most instances does not depend on the activity level during the period. The tax is the same amount no matter whether the company has a good year or a bad year.

Before we accept the idea of fixed costs too readily, there are some points and conditions to keep in mind. Some fixed costs are determined by the policies and decisions of the company than by the nature of the cost itself. For instance, the general policy of the company regarding laying off and hiring of employees directly affects the fixed cost of employees paid on a salary basis. The company may decide to keep all employees on the payroll even though this means that not all employees are being fully worked. Management may decide that the best policy is to have an experienced, loyal, and ready work force when the work activity increases in the future. Depreciation is fixed by the accounting policy of using a time-based method, instead of an activity-based method. During slack periods a company could possibly rent out part of its unused building space and in this manner offset some of the fixed costs of its buildings, such as depreciation, property taxes, janitorial work, and the like. But the company may *not* do this, perhaps to have the space readily available in the event production and sales activity picks up.

Some fixed costs are inherent in the general business environment and in this sense are imposed by forces outside the business entity. Real estate taxes are a good example. However, fixed costs for the most part are the result of deliberate decisions by management—decisions that carefully compare costs against benefits. What are the benefits of fixed costs? The main idea is that fixed costs provide *capacity*. Although a complex concept and difficult to measure, essentially capacity is the potential for use measured in terms of either input units or output units for a given time period. For example, if the business owns or rents a building for one year, then so many square feet are available for use during that time period. This square footage is the building's capacity. If a truck is owned or rented, so many miles or ton-miles of delivery potential (capacity) are made available by the ownership or rental of the vehicle. *Production capacity* is the overall aggregate measure (or estimate) of the company's manufacturing output potential for a period (usually a year).

Contribution Margin

Definition of Contribution Margin

One main reason for the separation of fixed and variable costs is that the *contribution margin* can be easily computed from this cost information. Briefly, contribution margin is the difference between sales revenue and the variable cost associated with the sales revenue. Contribution margin usually means sales revenue less *all* variable costs, although it can be determined in steps as follows:

<u>Two-Step Contribution Margin Measurement</u>
<u>Sales revenue</u>
− <u>Variable manufacturing costs</u>
= <u>Gross contribution margin (before other variable costs)</u>
− <u>Variable marketing and administration and general costs</u>
= (Final) contribution margin

Gross contribution margin is the counterpart of gross profit, except that fixed manufacturing costs are not deducted from sales revenue, which is an important difference of course. The term "contribution margin" without any other qualification means the *final* contribution margin, that is, after all variable costs are deducted from sales revenue. This is the meaning of the term in this and subsequent chapters, unless the particular terms "*gross* contribution margin" is used instead.

Usually interest and income tax are *not* deducted as variable costs from sales revenue, since these two expenses do not vary in proportion to sales revenue. Both these expenses vary to be sure: interest depends on the total debt and the average interest rate paid on the debt; and, income tax varies with the taxable income of the corporation. But neither expense varies in a convenient relationship with sales revenue. In contrast, variable operating costs vary in more or less strict proportion with sales revenue. In summary, usually contribution margin is expressed before interest or income tax. More accurately therefore, it could be called *operating* contribution margin since variable operating costs are deducted from sales revenue, but not interest or income tax. The precise meaning is kept in full view in the following discussion, to avoid any confusion.

Analysis of Company's Contribution Magin Each Year

The contribution margin per unit for the company each year is computed and shown in Exhibit 4.3. These are the contribution margins per unit before interest and income tax expenses are considered. Exhibit 4.4 next shows the use of these per unit contribution margins to compute the total contribution margin earned by the company in both years.

EXHIBIT 4.3
Computation of Contribution Margin Per Unit

Exhibit 4-1 Reference	Per Unit	1975		1976	
Line (b)	Sales price		$20.000		$21.500
Line (f)	Variable manufacturing cost	$10.600		$11.350	
Line (l)	Variable marketing cost	4.850		5.150	
Line (m)	Variable administration and general cost	0.150		0.160	
	Total variable cost		15.600		16.660
	Contribution margin		$ 4.400		$ 4.840

Contribution margin is a *profit measure,* although an incomplete one, since fixed costs are not considered. But it is an important measure of profit. A company must earn an adequate contribution margin per unit and must sell enough units to cover its fixed costs *and* provide enough operating profit: (1) to pay its interest expense for the year; (2) to pay its income tax expense for the year; and, (3) to leave a sufficient amount of residual net income for the year. Many managers favor a *contribution margin format* for their periodic profit performance statements. This follows the general approach of first determining total contribution margin, then subtracting fixed costs, and so on. Accordingly, the company's 1975 and 1976 profit performance statements are shown in a contribution margin format (see Exhibit 4.5). Compare the differences in this

EXHIBIT 4.4
Computation of Total Contribution Margin

Year	Total Number of Units Sold During Year	×	Contribution Margin per Unit (Exhibit 4.3)	=	Total Contribution Margin
1975	500,000	×	$4.400	=	$2,200,000
1976	550,000	×	$4.840	=	$2,662,000

EXHIBIT 4.5
Contribution Margin Format for Management Profit Performance Report

Line		1975 — 500,000 units			1976 — 550,000 units		
	Sales Volume Base	Percents	Dollar Value per Unit		Percents	Dollar Value per Unit	
(a)		100.0	$20.000	$10,000,000	100.0	$21.500	$11,825,000
(b)	Sales revenue	100.0	$20.000	$10,000,000	100.0	$21.500	$11,825,000
	Variable costs:						
(c)	Raw materials	21.4	$ 4.287	$2,143,500	21.5	$ 4.630	$2,546,500
(d)	Direct labor	26.7	5.331	2,665,500	26.4	5.674	3,120,700
(e)	Overhead	4.9	0.982	491,000	4.9	1.046	575,300
(f)	Total manufacturing	53.0	$10.600	$5,300,000	52.8	$11.350	$6,242,500
(g)	Marketing	23.4	4.850	2,425,000	24.0	5.150	2,832,500
(h)	Administrative and general	0.7	0.150	75,000	0.7	0.160	88,000
(i)	Total variable costs	77.1	$15.600	7,800,000	77.5	$16.660	9,163,000
(j)	Contribution margin	22.9	$ 4.400	$ 2,200,000	22.5	$ 4.840	$ 2,662,000
	Fixed costs:						
(k)	Direct labor			$ 128,100			$ 145,125
(l)	Overhead			777,525			876,375
(m)	Total manufacturing costs incurred during the year			$ 905,625			$1,021,500
(n)	Less: manufacturing fixed costs charged to increase of inventories during the year— see Exhibit 4.2			43,125			22,700
(o)	Total manufacturing fixed costs charged to the year			$ 862,500			$ 998,800
(p)	Marketing costs			308,000			349,800
(q)	Administrative and general costs			298,500			335,500
(r)	Total fixed costs			1,469,000			1,684,100
(s)	Operating profit			$ 731,000			$ 977,900
(t)	Interest expense			148,750 (average debt=$1,750,000×8.5%)			180,000 (average debt=$2,250,000×8.0%)
(u)	Net income before income tax			$ 582,250			$ 797,900
(v)	Income tax			272,980 ($582,250×48% less $6,500)			376,492 ($797,900×48% less $6,500)
(w)	Net income			$ 309,270			$ 421,408

contribution margin format with the more conventional format shown in Exhibit 4.1.

Fixed costs per unit are *not* shown in the contribution margin format statement (Exhibit 4.5). These per unit costs could be included, but one basic idea of the contribution margin approach is to view fixed costs as a lump sum total amount for the period. Hence, the fixed costs per unit are suppressed in this report. Since the emphasis is on total fixed costs, notice also that *all* manufacturing fixed costs are shown, even though a small part of the company's total fixed manufacturing costs each year are *not* charged off as expense to that year. As is shown in Exhibit 4.2, each year a certain amount of the manufacturing fixed costs for that year is charged to the increase of the company's inventories during the year. In a sense the company "escapes" this part of its total manufacturing fixed costs for the year because the amount is charged to inventory rather than to expense. (There is argument that *all* fixed manufacturing costs should be expensed in the period incurred, and this is discussed in Chapter Thirteen.)

Using Fixed and Variable Cost Information to Analyze Operating Profit Performance: The Break-even Point

Notice in Exhibit 4.3 that the company's total variable cost for each unit sold in 1975 is $15.60 and that the company sells each unit for $20. The company's total fixed costs is $1,469,000 in 1975 (see Exhibit 4.5). Also the company must pay its interest and income tax expense of course. However, interest expense and income tax expense are best kept in the background at this point. Interest expense depends on the amount of debt during the year and the average interest rates. In turn, the amount of debt depends, to some extent, on the levels of sales and production. A lower sales level means a company normally needs less total capital, and the company would borrow less. The income tax expense for the year depends on the amount of interest expense, since interest is a deductible expense for determination of taxable income. Avoiding these factors for the present, we focus in the following analysis on *operating profit,* that is, net income *before* interest and income tax.

How much operating profit would be earned at different sales levels during 1975, assuming that the company's total fixed costs remain constant at $1,469,-000 across a very broad range of sales volumes? Operating profit is computed for a particular sales level as follows:

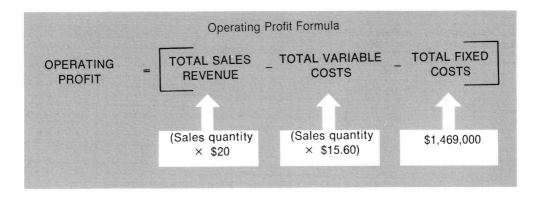

Operating Profit Formula

OPERATING PROFIT = [TOTAL SALES REVENUE − TOTAL VARIABLE COSTS − TOTAL FIXED COSTS]

(Sales quantity × $20)   (Sales quantity × $15.60) $1,469,000

For several different levels of sales this computation yields the results shown in Exhibit 4.6.

If no sales are made, there would be no variable costs, since variable costs depend on the *actual* quantity of units sold. However, the company would incur total fixed costs of $1,469,000, since these costs are the committed costs for the year, and the company cannot or decides not to attempt to decrease these costs.* The result of a zero sales quantity situation, as can be seen in Exhibit 4.6, is an operating *loss* of $1,469,000. This extreme situation is more for the purpose of illustration than a practical possibility. It is very unlikely that the year's sales would turn out to be zero. A going concern that has established a reputation and that has developed many customer contacts and a general product acceptance would not approach zero sales even in a terrible year. The zero sales level is simply a useful point of departure to begin analysis of how operating profit behaves relative to the company's fixed and variable costs.

To illustrate the general behavior of sales revenue, costs, and operating profit (or loss) over a broad range of sales volumes, a *break-even diagram* is shown in Exhibit 4.7. Several important points should be noticed as you study it:

1. The total sales revenue line starts at zero dollars, and then increases $20 for each additional unit sold across the whole range up to 700,000 units. The sales price per unit, in other words, is constant over the entire range of possible sales levels. This probably is an oversimplification. In actual practice, the company may not be able to sell as many as 700,000 units, or even 600,000 units at the $20 sales price; there may not be this much demand at the $20 price. But the purpose of the diagram is to illustrate the sales revenue behavior based on a constant sales price assumption.

2. The total cost line does *not* start at zero dollars—it starts at $1,469,000, and then increases $15.60 for each additional unit sold across the whole

---

* At low sales levels this is a rather severe assumption, and may not be realistic. This point is discussed later in the chapter.

EXHIBIT 4.6
Computations of Operating Profit at Different Sales Levels

Sales volume	Total Sales Revenue	Total Variable Cost	Total Fixed Cost	Operating Profit (Loss)
Zero	Zero	Zero	$1,469,000	($1,469,000)
100,000 units	(100,000 × $20.00) = $ 2,000,000	(100,000 × $15.60) = $ 1,560,000	1,469,000	(1,029,000)
200,000 units	(200,000 × 20.00) = 4,000,000	(200,000 × 15.60) = 3,120,000	1,469,000	(589,000)
300,000 units	(300,000 × 20.00) = 6,000,000	(300,000 × 15.60) = 4,680,000	1,469,000	(149,000)
400,000 units	(400,000 × 20.00) = 8,000,000	(400,000 × 15.60) = 6,240,000	1,469,000	291,000
500,000 units	(500,000 × 20.00) = 10,000,000	(500,000 × 15.60) = 7,800,000	1,469,000	731,000
600,000 units	(600,000 × 20.00) = 12,000,000	(600,000 × 15.60) = 9,360,000	1,469,000	1,171,000
700,000 units	(700,000 × 20.00) = 14,000,000	(700,000 × 15.60) = 10,920,000	1,469,000	1,611,000

EXHIBIT 4.7
1975 Break-even Diagram for Company

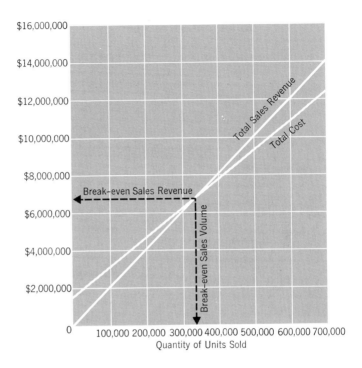

range up to 700,000 units. Even at the zero sales level it is assumed that the company would incur unavoidable fixed costs of $1,469,000. Clearly, this is too pessimistic in practical situations; the company could cut back on some fixed costs at low sales levels. For now, however, this aspect is avoided. In addition to this fixed cost "floor," the company incurs $15.60 variable cost for each unit sold. The variable cost per unit is assumed to remain constant over the entire range of sales volumes. This probably is a simplification also, since at very low levels of production the variable cost per unit may be higher. However, the purpose of the diagram is to introduce cost behavior based on a constant variable cost per unit assumption. Bear in mind that "relevant range" limits should be applied to such a diagram, below which fixed cost may decrease and variables cost per unit may increase, and above which fixed cost may increase somewhat and the variable cost per unit may decrease somewhat. In 1975 the company is within this relevant range.

3. This point of intersection of the total sales revenue line and the total cost line is called the *break-even point*. At this particular level, total sales revenue equals total cost so that the company earns exactly a zero oper-

ating profit (before interest and income tax). Of course, the company wants to do better than this. The break-even point is the crossover point from loss to profit.

The dotted lines in the break-even diagram point to how many units would have to be sold to break-even, and to what the total sales revenue would be at that break-even level. The precise numbers are hard to read directly from a break-even diagram like that in Exhibit 4.7. The exact break-even amounts usually must be computed as shown in Exhibit 4.8.* If the company sells exactly 333,864 units, which is its break-even volume, then the total sales revenue and the total costs would be as follows:

Sales and Costs at Break-even Point

Total Sales Revenue:			
(333,864 units × $20)	=		$6,677,280
Total Costs:			
Fixed Cost	=	$1,469,000	
Variable Cost:			
(333,864 units × $15.60)	=	5,208,280	6,677,280
Operating Profit (before Interest and Income Tax)			$ —0—

EXHIBIT 4.8
Computation of 1975 Break-even Sales Quantity and Revenue

$$\text{Break-even Quantity} = \frac{\text{Total Fixed Costs}}{\text{Contribution Margin per Unit}} = \frac{\$1,469,000}{\$4.40} = \underline{333,864 \text{ units}} \text{ (rounded off to the nearest whole unit)}$$

$$\text{Break-even Sales Revenue} = \left[\text{Break-even Quantity} \times \frac{\text{Sales}}{\text{Price}} \right] = (333,864 \times \$20) = \underline{\$6,677,280}$$

* It can be argued that the company's total fixed manufacturing cost for the year should be used in the break-even computation instead of the manufacturing fixed cost that is charged to expense in the year. In this example the company's work-in-process and finished goods inventories increase during 1975. Thus a part of the company's fixed manufacturing costs are not expensed but are charged to the increase of inventories. Unless there are material differences between the total quantity sold and the total quantity produced during the year, the difference between the total manufacturing fixed cost for the period and the amount of this fixed cost that is expensed to cost of goods sold is not that important. However, it is important to understand that a company does not achieve its break-even point simply by producing units; units must be *sold* to reach the break-even point.

The break-even sales level is a measure of how much sales revenue is needed to cover the company's fixed costs for the year. The company commits itself to fixed costs on the expectation that the coming year's sales volume will be sufficient to justify these fixed costs. But there is always a risk to some degree or another that the company may not reach its sales goals, and thus part of the capacity provided by the fixed costs would go unused. Keep in mind that the break-even point in this example is *not* enough to provide for interest and income tax expenses and to leave a net income residual for the year.

The break-even quantity also can be viewed as a fulcrum point on which operating profit pivots. This general idea is called *operating leverage.* Up to the break-even quantity, all contribution margin goes toward meeting fixed costs. Beyond the break-even quantity, *all* contribution margin provides operating profit. This key idea is illustrated in the *profit/volume graph* for 1975 shown in Exhibit 4.9. At the zero sales level the company's operating loss would be $1,469,000 (making all the assumptions previously discussed.) Each unit sold in 1975 provides $4.40 contribution margin: ($20 sales price less $15.60 variable costs per unit = $4.40 contribution margin per unit). Notice that the profit gap in the profit/volume graph (Exhibit 4.9) begins to expand rapidly beyond the break-even point. Above the break-even quantity, each and every additional unit sold brings in a "pure operating profit" of $4.40 per unit, since the contribution margin from the first 333,864 units has covered all the fixed costs for the year. In 1975 the company sold 166,136 more units than its

EXHIBIT 4.9
1975 Profit/Volume Graph for Company

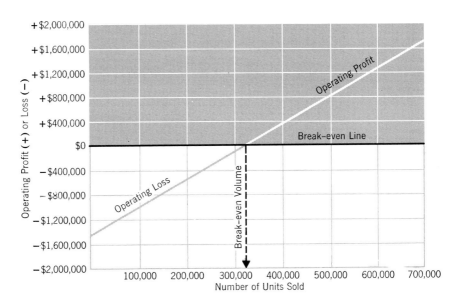

break-even point (500,000 units sold less 333,864 units break-even point= 166,136 units), which yields an operating profit as follows:

$$\begin{array}{c}\text{166,136 units over} \\ \text{break-even point}\end{array} \times \begin{array}{c}\text{\$4.40 contribution} \\ \text{margin per unit}\end{array} = \text{\$731,000 operating profit}$$

The Essential Distinction Between Variable and Fixed Capital

The basic distinction between fixed and variable behavior applies with equal importance to the total capital invested in assets by a company to make sales and carry on operations. The amount of capital invested in some assets depends on the total sales revenue level or the total operating cost level for the period. For instance, as sales revenue increases, the balance in the Accounts Receivable account will also increase, assuming that the company does not change the credit terms given to its customers, assuming that about the same percentage of customers buy on credit, and assuming that its collection experience from customers is about the same at different sales levels. And, as sales volume decreases, then the Accounts Receivable balance should decrease, making the same assumptions.

On the other hand, the amount of capital invested in some assets does *not* decrease with a decrease in sales or production volumes. This company in previous years invested large amounts of capital in its fixed assets. These fixed assets provide the production and operating capacity needed to support the 525,000 units of output in 1975 and the 500,000 units of sales in 1975. But if output or sales had been less, the amount of capital invested in its fixed assets would not have decreased.

In short, the balances of some assets respond to and are sensitive to increases or decreases in sales volume and production volume. But other assets, fixed assets in particular, are not "jacked up and down" with increases and decreases in sales and production volumes. The company is committed to a fixed amount of investment in certain assets whether the expected sales volume is achieved or whether the sales volume happens to be quite poor for the year.

Using Fixed and Variable Capital Investment Information to Analyze ROI Performance

Usually a good part of the total capital secured by a company is invested in its fixed assets. For a short-term period, such as one year, the capital invested in these long-term operating resources is more or less fixed. Refer to the December 31, 1975 balance sheet for the company, which is presented at the start of Chapter Two (Exhibit 2.1). At year-end 1975 the company had more than $4,000,000 invested in its fixed assets. To be more precise, the book value of fixed assets (net of Accumulated Depreciation on the Buildings, Machinery,

Equipment, and Vehicles) was $3,652,300 and the Land account had a balance of $675,000, for a total book value of $4,327,300. Except for Land, these fixed assets result in a certain amount of depreciation being recorded each year, and this depreciation is a fixed cost of that year. As we previously explained, fixed costs are the committed costs for the year that are necessary to provide manufacturing and operating capacity.

Would the $4,327,300 capital invested in its fixed assets at year-end 1975 have been any higher if the company had sold, say, 100 more units in 1975? In other words, could the company have sold 100 more units with the same fixed assets? In all likelihood the answer is yes. Could the company have sold 10,000 more units with the same fixed assets? Again, probably yes. Could the company have sold 25,000 more units? Although this is 5% higher than the actual sales quantity in 1975 (which is 500,000 units), perhaps the company could have sold 525,000 units without having to increase its fixed assets. Much more important to our discussion here are changes in the other direction. Would the company's fixed assets have been any less if the company had sold, say, 10,000 units *less* in 1975? Probably the fixed assets would not have been any less. What if 100,000 fewer units had been sold in 1975? Even such a large drop in sales may not have resulted in any disposals or retirements of the fixed assets.

In general, then, the amount of capital invested in fixed assets is relatively fixed and constant over a wide range of sales levels, especially on the downside. Once a company has acquired certain fixed assets and has them in place and ready for use, the fixed assets cannot be jacked up and down very quickly; major increases or decreases to its fixed assets takes some time. The company acquires the fixed assets it thinks will be needed to provide enough capacity to meet the production and sales demands on this capacity during the coming year. Indeed, most companies prefer to have a certain amount of excess capacity available for any unexpected surges in production and sales. But if production and sales levels turn out to be lower than expected, a company usually cannot quickly decrease the investment in its fixed assets. To analyze this important point without getting into several technical ones, it is assumed that the company's fixed asset investment of $4,327,300 would have been the same from zero sales up to 550,000 units of sales for 1975.

In contrast, investments in most current assets, especially accounts receivable and inventory, are much more responsive to increases or decreases in sales revenue. If the company had sold, say, 10,000 more units in 1975 at the $20 sales price, then total sales revenue would have been $200,000 higher. Thus the ending balance of its Accounts Receivable would have been higher. Likewise, the company probably would have produced more units. Thus, the ending quantity of inventories would have been higher.

Although somewhat oversimplified, assume that the company invests $7.20 of capital in its current assets per unit sold. At the sales volume of 500,000 units in 1975, therefore, this assumption means that the company's investment in its current assets would be $3,600,000. (Actually the company had $3,597,200 of current assets at the end of 1975; the small difference is due to rounding off.) Since the company in this example has no other assets in addition to its current assets and its fixed assets, all assets have been accounted for in these two basic assumptions:

Assumed Capital Behavior for Company

Current assets	=	$7.20 per unit sold
Fixed assets	=	$4,327,300 from 0 to 550,000 units sold

Given these two assumptions, and given the schedule of operating profit developed previously (see Exhibit 4.6), Exhibit 4.10 shows the determination of the company's rate of operating profit on total assets at various sales levels for 1975. Keep in mind that this ratio determines the return on equity.

Notice in Exhibit 4.10 that there is a twofold impact of fixed costs *and* fixed capital on the operating profit return on total assets. Below the break-even point *two* factors work against the company—both the fixed costs and the fixed capital. As we can see, below the break-even point the operating profit return on assets is very poor. But above the break-even point both factors work for the company. The company increases its operating profit *and* the company gets better utilization from its investment in fixed assets. The fixed asset investment of $4,327,300 is spread over more units as the sales volume increases.

Putting this another way, the *average* total capital investment per unit decreases as the sales volume increases. At the 100,000 units sales level the company invests $7.20 of variable capital for each unit sold plus an average of

EXHIBIT 4.10
Computation of Operating Profit Return on Total Assets at Different Sales Levels in 1975

Sales Volume	Fixed Assets (Fixed Capital)	Current Assets (Variable Capital)	Total Assets (Total Capital)	Operating (Loss) or Profit [a]	Operating Profit Rate of Return on Assets[b]
Zero	$4,327,300	Zero	$4,327,300	($1,469,000)	−33.9%
100,000 units	4,327,300	(100,000×$7.20)=$ 720,000	5,047,300	(1,029,000)	−20.4%
200,000 units	4,327,300	(200,000× 7.20)= 1,440,000	5,767,300	(589,000)	−10.2%
300,000 units	4,327,300	(300,000× 7.20)= 2,160,000	6,487,300	(149,000)	− 2.3%
400,000 units	4,327,300	(400,000× 7.20)= 2,880,000	7,207,300	291,000	4.0%
500,000 units	4,327,300	(500,000× 7.20)= 3,600,000	7,927,300	731,000	9.2%
550,000 units	4,327,300	(550,000× 7.20)= 3,960,000	8,287,300	951,000	11.5%

[a] See Exhibit 4.6 for this information.
[b] This ratio equals (Operating Profit/Total Assets).

$43.27 fixed capital, which is ($4,327,300 fixed capital divided by 100,000 units). Hence, the total capital investment per unit sold is $50.47 ($7.20+$43.27). But at the actual 1975 sales volume, for instance, the company's average fixed capital investment is only $8.65 per unit sold, which is ($4,327,300 fixed capital divided by 500,000 units). Hence, the total capital investment per unit sold is $15.85 ($7.20+$8.65). Consider side by side the two sales volumes just mentioned (see Exhibit 4.10 for information):

Comparison of Actual with a Below Break-even Sales Level in 1975

		100,000 units Sales Level	500,000 units Sales Level
Operating Profit Return on Assets	$= \dfrac{\text{Operating Profit per Unit}}{\text{Average Capital Investment per Unit}} =$	$\dfrac{(\$10.29)}{\$50.47} = -20.4\%$	$\dfrac{\$1.46}{\$15.85} = 9.2\%$

Notice that both the numerator *and* the denominator of the ratio of operating profit to assets change favorably at the higher sales volume. The operating profit per unit changes from a loss of $10.29 per unit ($1,029,000 operating loss divided by 100,000 units) to a profit of $1.46 per unit ($731,000 operating profit divided by 500,000 units). And, the average total capital investment per unit decreases from $50.47 per unit to $15.85 per unit, as is explained above. Thus there is a twofold favorable impact on the operating profit return on assets at the higher sales level.

Summary

Operating profit and net income usually do *not* vary in exact proportion to increases or decreases of sales revenue. If sales revenue increases 10.0%, for example, it would be most unusual for operating profit and net income to increase exactly 10.0% in response to the sales revenue increase. Likewise, the return on assets and the return on equity rates usually do not increase exactly 10.0% if sales revenue increases 10.0%. Indeed, operating profit may increase 20.0% or more, given a 10.0% increase of sales revenue. The basic reason for the lack of a simple proportional relationship between increases or decreases of sales revenue and increases or decreases of operating profit is the presence of fixed costs. Fixed costs are those costs over a fairly wide revelant range of sales levels remain constant. Most companies also have made capital investments in fixed assets that over a fairly wide relevant range of sales levels remain constant. Although oversimplified, a basic strategy of management is to make the maximum possible use from the company's fixed costs and fixed capital investments to maximize the company's operating profit and return on assets. In other words, the basic goal is to spread the company's fixed costs and fixed capital investment over the largest number of units that can be sold.

A basic management profit performance report is presented in this chapter which, among several key features, separates between fixed and variable costs. From this information the contribution margin is determined that, in basic terms, is equal to (sales revenue less variable costs). Contribution margin is a profit measure, though an incomplete profit measure, since fixed costs are not considered. Regular periodic profit performance reports to managers may be presented in a contribution margin format, and this is illustrated in the chapter.

One important use of the contribution margin per unit is to compute the break-even sales quantity, or the break-even point as it is called. The company must exceed its break-even point to earn an operating profit. The break-even point in the chapter is defined in terms of operating profit before interest and income tax in order to avoid the problems of dealing with these two expenses, which are considerably different than operating costs. A company does not try just to break even—a company hopes to do much better than this and, indeed, must do better to meet its interest requirements, to pay its income tax, and to leave a sufficient net income residual.

Nevertheless, the break-even point is a useful reference point: it tells managers how many units must be sold to cover the company's fixed costs of the period (usually a year). The break-even quantity is computed as follows:

$$\text{Break-even Point} = \frac{\text{Total Fixed Costs}}{\text{Contribution Margin per Unit}}$$

Below the break-even point, contribution margin earned from sales revenue goes toward covering fixed costs. Above the break-even point, the additional contribution margin is "pure" operating profit. Meeting *and* exceeding the break-even point is always a top priority.

To provide the necessary manufacturing and operating capacity for the coming year (and for several years in the future for that matter) a company invests in many fixed assets, such as land, buildings, and machinery and equipment. A company must acquire enough fixed assets to provide all the capacity that will be needed to meet the anticipated sales and production levels during the coming year. If actual sales fall below the predicted levels, then in most situations a company cannot (or decides not to) decrease its fixed assets. Thus capital invested in its fixed assets is more or less fixed. If sales fall short, there will be excess capacity; the company's fixed assets would not be used to their full potential.

In a sales shortfall situation there is a twofold adverse impact: (1) the company's fixed costs remain constant even though sales revenue and contribution margin decrease; and, (2) the company's fixed assets do not decrease even though operating profit decreases. Thus the operating profit return on assets suffers in two ways. But as sales volume increases, operating profit is benefited by the fixed costs not increasing, and return on assets is benefited by fixed assets not increasing.

Questions

4. 1   Should net income increase or decrease by the exact percentage that sales revenue increases or decreases? Briefly explain why or why not.

4. 2   What basic kinds of information are needed in regular periodic management profit performance reports that are not included in external net income statements?

4. 3   (a) What is a joint cost?
(b) Does a *one product* company have problems accounting for joint costs?

4. 4   Refer to the basic management profit performance report shown in Exhibit 4.1. Compare this report with the company's net income statement shown in Exhibit 2.2.
(a) What basic similarities do you observe?
(b) What basic differences do you observe?
(c) Which is the better statement?

4. 5   Notice that the company in the example discussed in the chapter uses the LIFO inventory method. What are the main advantages and disadvantages of the LIFO method?

4. 6   At year-end 1976 the company in the example discussed in the chapter has 22,000 units of ending work-in-process inventory that are one half through the manufacturing process. Therefore, the number of units started and completed during the year, in addition to the completion of the units in the beginning work-in-process inventory, must have been:
(a) 550,000 units.
(b) 562,500 units.
(c) 541,500 units.
(d) Cannot be determined.
Show your computations to support your answer, or explain why you cannot determine the answer.

4. 7   Last year the company reported an operating loss; this year the company reports an operating profit. Does this necessarily mean that the company crossed over its break-even point this year as a result of selling more units?

4. 8   Analyze the company's 1976 operating profit (see Exhibit 4.1 or 4.5) in terms of going over its break-even point.

4. 9   Refer to Exhibit 4.2. If the company's inventory holding policy is to maintain its combined work-in-process and finished goods ending inventories equal to one fifth of *next* year's predicted sales, then are the company's inventories under control assuming that predicted sales were 575,000 units for 1976 and 700,000 units for 1977?

4.10   How are *variable* costs per unit different than *fixed* costs per unit?

4.11   (a) Is depreciation always a fixed cost? Briefly explain.
       (b) Contrast the labor cost of salesmen who are paid a salary with no incentive bonus versus salesmen who are paid entirely on a sales commission basis.

4.12   What is meant by the "relevant range" for fixed costs?

4.13   "A company should avoid or at least minimize its fixed costs." Is this good advice? Briefly explain.

4.14   (a) Define *contribution margin.*
       (b) "All other things being the same, then the higher the contribution margin per unit the better." Do you agree? Briefly explain.

4.15   Would the company's break-even point in 1975 have been different if the company had manufactured only 500,000 units instead of 525,000 units? Explain with appropriate computations.

4.16   Which assets tend to vary with increases or decreases in sales and production levels? How do these assets differ from fixed asset investments?

4.17   Assume that a company's sales volume decreased 10% this year compared with last year but other factors remained the same. Its return on assets decreased by 25%! Explain the probable major reasons why the company's return on assets decreased more than its sales volume.

Problems

P4. 1   Refer to the company's two-year profit performance statement shown in Exhibit 4.1. As is explained in this chapter, the company uses the LIFO inventory cost valuation method. Also keep in mind that the entire year is treated as one production "batch" for determining the manufacturing cost per unit. (See Exhibit 4.2.)

   Required: Assume that the company uses FIFO instead of LIFO. Also assume that the FIFO cost value of the December 31, 1974 combined work-in-process and finished goods inventories was the same as the LIFO cost value. Determine the cost of goods sold, the ending inventory cost value (combined work-in-process and finished goods), and the gross profit for 1975 and 1976 that would have been reported if the FIFO method had been used. (The raw materials inventory method used by the company is not changed in this problem.)

P4. 2   A company's contribution margin (before interest and income tax) is $5 per unit in the current year. The company's sales department has researched the "demand curve" for the company's product, that is, the quantity that would be bought at different sales prices. Based on this market analysis the sales department is convinced that if the company were to lower its sales price by 10%, then the quantity sold to its customers would increase by 10%. The company is currently operating below its production capacity, and increasing its production by 10% would give a better utilization of its manufacturing plant and facilities, and thus would lower the average fixed manufacturing cost per unit. Should the company lower its sales price for the coming year, assuming that the sales department is correct and that all other relevant factors remain the same next year?

P4. 3   Given below are the cost situations of two different companies that sell essentially the same product. These are the only two companies selling this product. Although the brand names are different, customers view the products as equivalent and equally substitutable for each other. Both companies sell their product for $10 per unit, and this sales price should remain constant throughout the coming year. Assume that each company will not engage in a price war to attract customers away from its competitor. Taken together, the total market demand for the two brands of the product should be about 1 million units, although the actual total demand may turn out to be 200,000 units more or less. The customers in the past have appeared to be rather fickle, and they have capriciously changed from one brand to the other. Formerly the worst that either company has done is to get 40% of the total market.

The cost situation of the two companies, as a result of the time when each company entered the business, are quite different:

	Company F	Company V
Total fixed operating costs for coming year	$2,700,000	none
Total variable operating costs per unit sold for the coming year	$4.00	$9.40

Assume you have the opportunity to invest in one or the other company at the same cost for either investment. In either case you would buy a majority of the stock and thus control the management of the company.

Required: Which investment (between these two alternatives) would appeal more to you? Explain your choice. (As in the chapter, limit your analysis to the operating profit before interest and income tax considerations.)

P4. 4   Because of an unexpected and serious downturn in the economy, during the year just ended the company sold only 100,000 units, which is far below what the company had planned to sell. The company manufactures and sells only one product. In fact, about one third of the company's production capacity stood idle and unused during the year just ended. The company is thinking about a sales price decrease to stimulate sales demand next year. This year's sales price is $20. The company is thinking of decreasing the sales price next year to $18. Due to tighter cost controls next year the company thinks it can lower its total variable cost per unit sold from $12 this year to $11.60 next year. However, next year total fixed costs should remain the same as this year, which in total are $668,000.

(*Note:* The total variable cost per unit includes *all* variable cost elements, that is, manufacturing, marketing, and administration and general. Likewise, the total fixed cost amount includes *all* fixed costs, that is, manufacturing, marketing, and administration and general.)

The total assets of the company next year should remain about the same as this year, which is $1 million. The company does not plan any changes in its capitalization structure, which is 20% noninterest bearing liabilities, 40% interest bearing debt, and 40% stockholders' equity. The average annual interest rate (on its interest bearing debt) is 8.00% this year; this annual rate should be the same next year. The income tax is a flat 48% rate on taxable income each year, which will not change.

Required:

(1) Complete the form given below for the company's net income statement for *this year.* Include quantities and per unit amounts where appropriate in the blank space in the middle.

Sales Revenue	$
Variable Costs	$
Contribution Margin	$
Fixed Costs	$
Operating Profit	$
Interest	$
Taxable Income	$
Income Tax	$
Net Income	$

(2) For *this year* compute the operating profit break-even point, that is, the break-even point before consideration of interest and income tax expenses. Show your computations clearly.

(3) For *next year,* making the assumptions explained at the beginning of the problem, compute the operating profit break-even point. Show your computations clearly.

(4) For *next year,* making the assumptions explained at the beginning of the

problem, determine how many units would have to be sold for the company to earn the same rate of return on (stockholders') equity as the company earned this year. Show all computations clearly.

P4. 5   Refer to the company's two-year profit performance statement shown in Exhibit 4.1 and also to the alternative contribution margin format statement shown in Exhibit 4.5. Unless they are specifically changed in the following parts to this problem assume that all data and information remain the same.

Required:

(1) Compute the company's operating profit break-even point for 1976.

(2) (a) *Assume* that the company had manufactured 600,000 units and had increased its combined work-in-process and finished goods inventories by 50,000 units in 1976 instead of manufacturing 562,500 units and increasing its inventories by 12,500 units (as is shown in Exhibit 4.2). Recompute the operating profit break-even point for 1976 based on these alternative assumptions.

(b) After you have answered part (2a) of the problem, explain whether you think that it might be better to divide the contribution margin per unit into the *total fixed costs* recorded during the year instead of following the procedure explained in the chapter? If this alternative procedure were followed, what does the break-even point mean? Does it mean the number of units that would have to be sold or, instead, the number of units that would have to be produced?

(3) See page 128 for the assumptions regarding the behavior of assets relative to the number of units sold in 1975. Assume that noninterest bearing liabilities constitute 20% of total assets and that interest bearing debts constitute 25% of total assets, at all levels of total assets. The average annual interest rate on its interest bearing debts is assumed to be 8.5%. Given these assumptions, determine the *net income* break-even point for 1975, that is, the sales quantity that would result in net income exactly equal to zero.

P4. 6   Certain information about a company's operations for the last three years is given below; the company manufactures and sells one product.

	1974	1975	1976
Selling price per unit	$10.00	$10.00	?
Manufacturing variable costs per unit	$ 4.50	$ 4.00	$ 5.00
Other variable costs per unit (except interest and income tax expenses)	$ 1.25	?	$ 2.00
Quantity sold	100,000	?	150,000
Quantity produced	105,000	130,000	?
Contribution margin per unit	?	?	?
Total contribution margin	?	$585,000	?
Fixed costs—manufacturing	$105,000	$117,000	$144,000
Fixed costs—other	$155,000	?	$200,000
Operating profit (before interest and income tax)	?	?	?
Operating profit break-even quantity	?	65,000	67,000
Total interest expense	$ 70,000	?	$100,000
Beginning inventory quantity	?	?	?
Ending inventory quantity	20,000	20,000	30,000
Income tax (at a flat 48% rate on taxable income)	?	$102,000	?
Net income	?	?	$163,800

Required: Determine the missing information for each year shown above.

(*Note:* If the missing information cannot be determined from the information given above, explain briefly why not. The company uses the LIFO inventory cost valuation method.)

P4. 7   Assume the following simplified and condensed balance sheet for a manufacturer at the end of the company's year (dollar amounts are in thousands):

ASSETS		SOURCES OF CAPITAL	
Current assets	$10,000	Noninterest bearing liabilities	$ 2,000
Fixed assets (net of accumulated depreciation)	10,000	Interest bearing debt at 8.0%	8,000
Total assets	$20,000	Stockholders' equity	10,000
		Total capital sources	$20,000

The company's contribution margin (before interest and income tax) was $12.08 per unit for the year just ended, and the company sold 500,000 units of its one and only product. Fixed costs for the year (excluding interest and income tax) were $3 million in total.

For the coming year the company plans to raise its selling price 12 cents per unit, to go into effect on the first day of the year, and to sell the same number of units. Variable costs per unit and total fixed operating costs should remain the same. Although more current assets will be needed at the higher sales revenue level, no capital expenditures (fixed asset purchases) will be made, since the production capacity is adequate to produce 500,000 units again during the coming year. The cash flow from net income will be enough to finance the small increase in current assets. The depreciation to be recorded on fixed assets next year, in fact, should equal the increase in current assets. Thus total assets will increase only by the portion of net income retained. (The company will not increase or decrease any of its liabilities next year, and no stock will be issued or retired during the year.) The company's policy is to distribute a cash dividend equal to 50% of its net income for the year. The interest rate (8%) and the income tax rate (48%) should remain the same next year.

Required: Given the above information and assumptions, for the coming year:
(1) Determine the operating profit (before interest and income tax) break-even quantity.
(2) Determine the net income.
(3) Determine the return on equity (use year-end balance).

P4. 8   Mr. Calderone started a pizza restaurant in 1972. For this purpose he rented a building for $400 per month. Two ladies were hired to work full-time at the restaurant, and six college boys were hired to work 30 hours per week delivering pizza. An outside accountant was hired for tax and bookkeeping purposes. For this service, Mr. Calderone pays $300 per month. The necessary resturant equipment and delivery cars were purchased with cash. Mr. Calderone has noticed that expenses for utilities and supplies have been rather constant.

Mr. Calderone increased his business between 1972 and 1975. Profits have more than doubled since 1972. Mr. Calderone does not understand why his profits have increased faster than his volume.

A projected Income Statement for 1976 has been prepared by the accountant and is shown below:

PROJECTED INCOME STATEMENT
FOR THE YEAR ENDED DECEMBER 31, 1976

Sales		$95,000
Cost of Food Sold	$28,500	
Wages and Fringe Benefits of Restaurant Help	8,150	
Wages and Fringe Benefits of Delivery Boys	17,300	
Rent	4,800	
Accounting services	3,600	
Depreciation of Delivery Equipment	5,000	
Depreciation of Restaurant Equipment	3,000	
Utilities	2,325	
Supplies (Soap, Flour Wax, etc.)	1,200	73,875
Net Income before Taxes		$21,125

(*Note:* It is assumed in the above statement that the average pizza will sell for $2.50 in 1976.)

Required:

(1) Determine the break-even point in number of pizzas that must be sold in 1976.

(2) Mr. Calderone would like a before-tax net income of $30,000. What volume must be reached in number of pizzas to obtain this profit in 1976?

(3) Briefly explain to Mr. Calderone why his profits have increased at a faster rate than his sales.

P4. 9 This company has one production department that manufactures only two products, which are two sizes of metal discs—"large" and "small." The manufacturing process begins with the cutting of doughnut-shaped rings from rectangular strips of sheet metal; these rings are then pressed into discs. The sheets of metal, each 4 feet long and weighing 32 ounces, are purchased at $1.36 per running foot. The department has been operating at a loss for the past year as shown below:

Sales for the year	$172,000
Expenses	177,200
Net loss of the department	$ 5,200

The following information is available.

(a) Ten thousand 4-foot pieces of metal yielded 40,000 large discs, each weighing 4 ounces and selling for $2.90, and 40,000 small discs, each weighing 2.4 ounces and selling for $1.40.

(b) The company has had no spoilage in the cutting step of the process. The skeletons remaining after the rings have been cut are sold for scrap at $0.80 per pound.

(c) The variable manufacturing conversion cost of each large disc is 80% of the disc's direct material cost and the variable manufacturing conversion cost of each small disc is 75% of the disc's direct material cost. Variable conversion costs are the sum of direct labor and variable overhead costs.

(d) Fixed manufacturing costs for the year were $86,000.

(e) No other costs or expenses are considered in this problem; in other words, the loss shown above is before other expenses such as the selling and general administrative expenses of the company.

Required:

(1) For each of the products manufactured, determine:
(a) Unit material cost after deducting the value of salvage.
(b) Unit variable conversion cost.
(c) Unit contribution margin.
(d) Total contribution margin of all units sold for the year.

(2) Assuming that you computed the material cost for large discs at $0.85 each and for small discs at $0.51 each, compute the number of units the company must sell to break even based on a normal production capacity of 50,000 units of each product during the year.

P4.10   Please refer to the financial statements of the retail company example introduced in Problem 2.6. The following additional information is now presented
for these financial statements. Assume that the company sells only one product.

	1975	1976
Sales price per unit	$125	$140
Total quantity sold	20,000 units	22,500 units
Total quantity purchased	21,000 units	23,000 units
Beginning inventory quantity	3,000 units	4,000 units
Ending inventory quantity	4,000 units	4,500 units
Marketing variable expenses	$262,800	$331,200
Marketing fixed expenses	$243,400	$301,900
Administration and general variable expenses	$ 36,100	$ 45,900
Administration and general fixed expenses	$182,200	$192,500

Required: Prepare a two-year management profit performance report for the
company based on the above information plus the information included in the
financial statements presented in Problem 2.6. Follow the guidelines and format
shown in Exhibit 4.1, keeping in mind that some modifications are necessary
because this company is a retailer, not a manufacturer.

P4.11   This problem builds on the financial statements introduced in Problem 2.6 and
the additional information about the company presented in Problem 4.10. Please
refer to these two sources of information in order to complete the following
requirements.

Required:
(1) For both 1975 and 1976 determine the company's operating profit (before
interest and income tax) break-even point. Show your computations clearly.
(2) Compute the company's contribution margin per unit for each year, as well
as the total contribution margin each year.
(3) Assuming that the variable costs per unit and the total fixed costs remain
the same over the entire range shown below, compute the company's operating profit (before interest and income tax) for 1976 at the following sales
levels:
(a) 5,000 units.
(b) 10,000 units.
(c) 15,000 units.
(d) 25,000 units.

(*Note:* You do not have to prepare a formal net income statement for each case; compute the
operating profit in the quickest manner possible but show your computations.)

P4.12   For the year just ended this company sold 80,000 units of the only product
manufactured by the company for an average sales price of $75 per unit. For
the coming year the company does not plan to change the sales price. Since

the product is basically a nonessential "luxury" item, the total sales demand depends on consumers' disposable income over and above the amount needed by consumers to buy more essential products and services. However, the company is reasonably sure that next year's sales demand should be no less than 60,000 units and no more than 100,000 units. This shall be called the *relevant range* in the following parts of this problem.

For the coming year the following assumptions should be made for the company:

(a) Total current assets—$15.00 per unit sold over the relevant range.
(b) Total fixed assets—$1,200,000 over the relevant range.
(c) Variable costs per unit—$50.00 over the relevant range.
(d) Total fixed costs—$1,750,000 over the relevant range.
(e) Items (c) and (d) do *not* include any interest or income tax expenses.

Required: Starting with a sales volume of 60,000 units and at each 10,000 units increment point (70,000 units, 80,000 units, etc.) prepare a schedule like that shown in Exhibit 4.10 to determine the rate of operating profit on total assets over the relevant range.

P4.13   Refer to the example and assumptions introduced in Problem 4.12; this problem contains certain additional information regarding the company's capitalization structure (that is, the company's mix of capital sources). Make the following additional assumptions over the relevant range:

(f) Total interest bearing liabilities = 25% of total current assets.
(g) Total interest bearing liabilities = $600,000 + 35% of total current assets.
(h) Total stockholders' equity = $600,000 + 40% of total current assets.
(i) The average interest rate = 8.0% per year.
(j) The income tax rate is a flat 48% of taxable income.

Required: Starting with a sales volume of 60,000 units and at each 10,000 units increment point (70,000 units, 80,000 units, etc.) over the relevant range compute the return on equity. Show your computations clearly.

P4.14   A new motion picture company was established to produce and distribute a "blockbuster" film for which the company has great hopes. One year later the company had invested $10,000,000 in the film, and the film is now ready for distribution to movie theaters. The company receives one half of the ticket sales receipts for the showing of the film. The average ticket price after the initial "premier" showing period will be $2.50. During the premier showing period, which should be the first three months, the average ticket price should be $4. Once the film is "in the can" (completed and ready for distribution), the company's out-of-pocket costs are for all practical purposes fixed each month that the film is showing, because in any one month the same number of movie theaters show the film— though, of course, prints of the film move from one city to another over the run of the movie. The company's fixed costs of operations as long as the film is showing should be $250,000 per month. As soon as the audience potential for the film is exhausted, the company will sell all rights to the film to a network television company and at that point the company will be dissolved. In fact, a television network has already offered $2 million for the film which can be accepted by the company anytime during the next two years.

Required:

(1) Assume that the monthly audience for this film will be 2 million paid attendances. Determine how many months the film will have to run for the company to break even, before interest and income tax expenses are considered.

(2) Identify the main differences between this break-even analysis situation and the example discussed and analyzed in the chapter.

Chapter Five

Comparative Analyses of Profit and ROI Performance

COMPARATIVE ANALYSIS
OF PROFIT AND ROI PERFORMANCE

Managing Change

One basic function characterizes the role of managers as much as any other. To the extent possible, a manager must plan for and control *changes* in the many factors that affect and ultimately determine the success of the organization, or that segment of the organization the individual manager is responsible for. For a profit-motivated business entity, managers focus on those factors most important and most directly relevant to the profit and ROI performance of the entity. Few, if any, of these factors remain constant and unchanging very long. Admittedly the term "factor" is very broad and general. It includes, for example, wage rates, work rules, productivity, labor laws, the availability and costs of raw materials, production machinery and technology, consumer preferences, marketing methods, selling prices, income tax laws, managerial training and executive development, and so on. Needless to say, the list is very long and comprehensive.

Either directly or indirectly these "success factors" are reflected in accounting measurements reported to managers. For instance, an increase in the cost per unit of the raw materials used by the company shows up directly in the management profit performance reports. Productivity, on the other hand, shows up more indirectly in profit performance reports. Productivity generally refers to the ratio of inputs to output. Labor productivity, for instance, refers to the ratio of the number of direct labor hours required to produce one unit of product.

Assume that last year it took 20 hours to produce a unit of product and this year it takes 19 hours. In this case there is a 5.0% labor productivity gain (one hour less compared with 20 hours). But the labor cost per unit of output may *not* decrease in this hypothetical example because the wage rate per hour may increase by 5.0% or more. The labor cost per unit produced depends both on labor productivity and wage rates. Likewise for raw materials. By reducing the quantity of raw materials used for each unit of output, there is a gain in raw material productivity. But this may be offset by raw material purchase cost increases. In any event, the final effects of these changes show up in the management profit performance reports, especially in the cost per unit amounts. Other changes, such as hiring and promoting top quality managers, show up much more indirectly, and are reflected in the ability of the company to earn an

ROI and profit that are consistently above the performance of other companies in the same industry.

The preceding chapter stresses the importance of managers' understanding the basic relationships of revenue, costs, and capital investment, especially the distinction between fixed costs and variable costs and between fixed capital investment and variable capital investment. The basic premise of this chapter is that managers also need to compare the current period's financial performance with the immediate past period to pinpoint changes in factors between the two periods: to see why and how much financial performance improved or worsened, and what may happen next period. This interperiod comparative analysis does *not* supply *all* the information the manager needs to know. But it does provide a very useful starting point for planning for and controlling what will happen next period.

The management profit performance report shown as Exhibit 4.1 in Chapter Four (and shown also in an alternative format in Exhibit 4.5) is continued as the example throughout this chapter. This statement is a realistic, although somewhat simplified portrayal of a relatively small business. The example also is realistic for an autonomous division of a middle size company, or even for, say, one separate product line of a division of a large company. The orientation of this chapter is to managers who have broad authority and responsibility for the operating profit and ROI performance for this company, or for this segment of a larger company. True, the responsibility of many managers in a company's organizational structure does not extend to the final "bottom line" profit performance. For example, a production manager's span of authority and responsibility is limited to manufacturing costs, production scheduling, and so on. Even for these managers, however, the comparative analysis techniques discussed throughout the chapter are very useful within his or her area of authority and responsibility.

Reasons for Comparative Analyses

For management control purposes the financial performance of the current period (just ended) is compared with the preceding period, in order to identify *which specific* factors changed and how much difference each major change caused. Furthermore, to plan ahead and to predict how the factors may change next period, this interperiod comparative analysis is indispensable—it provides the base of experience from which to project the future. Comparative analysis does not provide all the answers, of course. Assume, for instance, that one factor increased 6% this year compared with last year. A manager should *not* simply assume that this factor will increase exactly 6% again next year. However, knowing the pattern of how each major factor changed this year compared with last year does provide a point of departure for prediction, although not the final answer.

The aims of interperiod comparative analysis are to pinpoint each major factor that changed *and* to determine the impact of this change on profit and ROI.

The manager then has to decide if the change was acceptable or not. Should the factor have changed? Was the change predicted accurately a year ago? Could the manager have prevented it from changing? Should the change have been more or less than it actually was? Will the change repeat itself again next year? Were the company's competitors hurt worse or less by these changes? These questions return to a basic point discussed in Chapter One concerning "decision standards," which are the criteria used by managers to judge the quality of achievement for the company, or for the segment of the organization they are responsible for.

As we mention in Chapter One (pages 13 to 14), there are three basic types of decision standards: (1) past period historical performance, (2) current period goals and objectives, and (3) competitors' performances and general economic conditions. In other words, managers compare their company's performance against its own performance of the prior period (or periods), against the goals and objectives for this period that were established at the start of the period, and against its competition and general economic conditions. Usually all three comparisons are relevant in judging a company's performance each year.

This chapter explains certain basic analytical tools for comparing accounting measurements for this period with last period. The main purpose is to provide an explanation of why operating profit (and net income) changed, and why the company's ROI rates changed this year compared with last year. This sort of analysis directs the attention of managers to the key factors that determine the financial performance of the company. The same analytical techniques are used in comparing the actual performance of this period with the goals and objectives for this period. Chapters Six and Seven discuss the development of *budgets,* which are a formal means of expressing the financial goals and objectives of a company for the coming period. The basic analytical techniques discussed in this present chapter are not repeated in the following two chapters.

Percent Increase/Decrease Types of Reports: A Starting Point

One place to start in the interperiod* comparative analysis of profit performance is a report that shows the percent increase or decrease of the company's sales revenue and each expense this year compared with last year. See Exhibit 5.1 for an example of this report. In actual practice, this type of report usually includes much more detail regarding the company's different sources of sales revenue and its many different expenses. In this example, however, the company manufactures and sells only one product. The general nature of this type of comparative profit performance report can be illustrated just as well with only a relatively few expenses. The information in Exhibit 5.1 is taken from the information originally presented in Exhibit 4.1, which would be appropriate to review briefly here.

* A period can be almost any length of time, such as a month, a week, or a quarter (three months). In this example the year is the basic time period.

EXHIBIT 5.1
Comparative Profit Performance Statement

Line[a]		1975	1976	Percent Change
(b)	Sales revenue	$10,000,000	$11,825,000	+18.25
(j)	Cost of goods sold expense	6,162,500	7,241,300	+17.51
(k)	Gross profit	$ 3,837,500	$ 4,583,700	+19.44
(l) (o)	Marketing expenses	$ 2,733,000	$ 3,182,300	+16.44
(m) (p)	Administrative and general expenses	373,500	423,500	+13.39
(r)	Total operating expenses	$ 3,106,500	$ 3,605,800	+16.07
(s)	Operating profit	$ 731,000	$ 977,900	+33.78
(t)	Interest expense	148,750	180,000	+21.01
(u)	Net income before income tax	$ 582,250	$ 797,900	+37.03
(v)	Income tax	272,980	376,492	+37.92
(w)	Net income	$ 309,270	$ 421,408	+36.26

[a] Lines refer to information given in Exhibit 4.1.

Perhaps the most interesting disclosure in Exhibit 5.1 is that sales revenue increases 18.25% but that the company's operating profit increases nearly twice as much, that is, by 33.78%, even though the cost of goods sold and marketing expense percent increases are about the same as the sales revenue increase. This sort of "revelation" is both the strength and the weakness of these types of reports. The reports do call attention to important changes, such as the ones just mentioned. But the reports do *not* provide much information or explanation of *why* the change occurred. These types of comparative reports usually do not do much more than set the stage for more detailed analysis, which must dig deeper into the reasons for the changes. Why did sales revenue increase by 18.25% Were more units sold or did the sales price increase, or both? Why did operating expenses increase by less than the percent increase in sales revenue? Although the type of report shown in Exhibit 5.1 raises these important questions, not enough information is available in the report to answer them.

Sales Revenue Changes: Sales Price Changes and Volume Changes

In the most simple situation either the quantity sold changes or the sales price per unit changes, but not both. In 1975 the company in the example sold 500,000 units at $20 per unit. If the quantity sold increases 10% and the sales price remains the same, then total sales revenue would increase 10%. All the increase would be attributable to the *volume change* factor:

Change in Sales Volume with Constant Price

	Volume		Sales Price		Sales Revenue
Last Year	500,000 units	×	$20	=	$10,000,000
This Year	550,000 units	×	20	=	11,000,000
Percent Change	+10.0%		None		+10.0%

In this hypothetical case, all the sales revenue increase is due to the 10.0% increase in volume, which can be computed as follows:

Analysis of Sales Volume Change

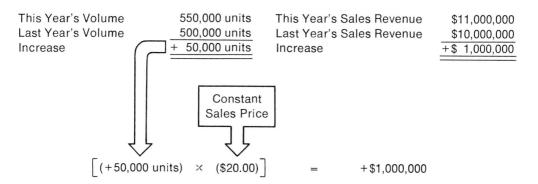

This Year's Volume	550,000 units	This Year's Sales Revenue	$11,000,000
Last Year's Volume	500,000 units	Last Year's Sales Revenue	$10,000,000
Increase	+ 50,000 units	Increase	+$ 1,000,000

Constant Sales Price

$$\left[(+50{,}000 \text{ units}) \times (\$20.00)\right] \quad = \quad +\$1{,}000{,}000$$

In this situation the marketing managers would be given "management credit" for selling 10% more items at the same price, which generates $1 million more sales revenue.

Assume, on the other hand, that the total quantity (volume) sold remains the same but that the sales price per unit increases from $20 last year to $21.50 this year, which is an increase of 7.5%:

Change in Sales Price with Constant Volume

	Volume		Sales Price		Sales Revenue
Last Year	500,000 units	×	$20.00	=	$10,000,000
This Year	500,000 units	×	21.50	=	10,750,000
Percent Change	None		+7.5%		+7.5%

In this hypothetical situation all the sales revenue increase is attributable to the sales price change, which is computed immediately below. In this situation the marketing managers would be given "management credit" for selling the same volume as last year for a selling price 7.5% higher than last year, which generates $750,000 more sales revenue.

Analysis of Sales Price Change

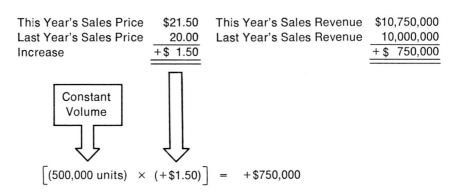

This Year's Sales Price	$21.50	This Year's Sales Revenue	$10,750,000
Last Year's Sales Price	20.00	Last Year's Sales Revenue	10,000,000
Increase	+$ 1.50		+$ 750,000

$$\left[(500{,}000 \text{ units}) \times (+\$1.50)\right] = +\$750{,}000$$

The comparative management profit performance statement shown as Exhibit 4.1 shows that *both* changes occurred in 1976 as compared with 1975—volume increases 10% *and* the selling price increases 7.5%:

Changes in Both Sales Price and Sales Volume

	Volume		Sales Price		Sales Revenue
1975	500,000 units	×	$20.00	=	$10,000,000
1976	550,000 units	×	21.50	=	11,825,000
Percent Change	+10.0%		+7.5%		+18.25%

Notice that sales revenue increases 18.25% or by $1,825,000, which is $75,000 more than the sum of the two separate changes determined above (the $1 million volume increase and the $750,000 sales price increase). This $75,000 additional sales revenue is caused by the *joint change* of both factors increasing at the same time.

In the prior analysis the volume increase of 50,000 units is multiplied by the constant price of $20 per unit, *as if the sales price did not change*. And, the sales price increase of $1.50 per unit is multiplied by the constant volume of 500,000 units, *as if the volume did not change*. But since both factors change together, the increase of 50,000 units are sold for $1.50 more than last year's sales price:

Analysis of Joint Change Effect

Volume Increase		Sales Price Increase		Joint Change Effect
(+50,000 units)	×	(+$1.50)	=	+$75,000

The diagram shown as Exhibit 5.2 presents the sales price and volume increases graphically. The inner area represents 1975 sales revenue, that is, $20.00×500,000 units. The outer area represents 1976 sales revenue, that is, $21.50×550,000 units. Clearly the joint change effect has to be counted, but counted *only once*. For most management analysis purposes it is *not* useful to separate the total sales revenue increase into *three* components. The best course of action usually is to report only *two* effects—the volume change effect and the sales price change effect. Thus the joint change effect is included with the volume or the sales price change (but not both).

In this book the joint change effect is included with the sales price change. This means that the increase in the sales price is multiplied by the *current*

EXHIBIT 5.2
Comparison of 1975 and 1976 Sales Revenue

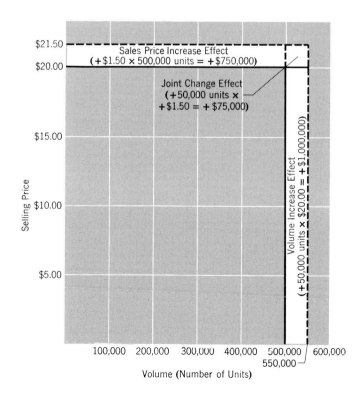

period's volume, not last period's volume. Refer again to Exhibit 5.2. There, this means that the sales price change effect is *all* of the horizontal bar in the diagram—the small corner is added to the sales price change effect. This procedure seems more in accord with management's thinking: the higher sales price has no effect until the units are sold, and the current period's sales volume is the main point of reference in management's analysis. Accordingly the increase in sales revenue is analyzed as follows:

Analysis of Change in Sales Revenue

Sales Price Change Effect				
Increase in Sales Price		This Year's Volume		
+$1.50	×	550,000 units	=	+$ 825,000
Volume Change Effect				
Last Year's Sales Price		Increase in Volume		
$20	×	+50,000 units	=	+$1,000,000
Total Increase in Sales Revenue			=	+$1,825,000

Variable Cost Changes: Cost per Unit Changes and Volume Changes

The company sold 50,000 more units in 1976 than in 1975. The question logically arises: How much increase in total cost is caused by the increase of 50,000 units sold? To answer this question it is necessary to distinguish between fixed costs and variable costs. As is explained in Chapter Four, fixed costs during a year do *not* increase in response to an increase in volume, unless the increase is sufficiently large to move outside the relevant range for the fixed costs. *Year to year,* however, inflation may cause fixed costs to increase, or the company may increase its capacity, which increases fixed costs. Fixed cost changes from 1975 to 1976 are analyzed in the next section. This section is concerned with the changes in the *variable* costs between the two years. Variable costs, it should be recalled, are those costs that change in more or less direct proportion to changes in the volume of activity. Thus a 10% increase in the quantity of goods sold leads to the expectation that, *other things being the same,* the total variable costs in 1976 should have increased 10%.

But other things usually do not remain the same; the variable cost *per unit* may change. Indeed, the $1.50 per unit sales price increase suggests that variable costs per unit probably did increase in 1976. The 7.5% increase in the selling price may have been based in part—perhaps in large part—on increases in the variable costs per unit. Increases in the variable costs per unit may have "pushed up" the sales price. The $825,000 favorable sales price change effect in sales revenue (see the analysis above) may be offset substantially by increases in the variable costs per unit. Managers cannot ignore this relationship.

There are three different types of variable costs: (1) manufacturing (2) marketing, and (3) administration and general. Each should be analyzed separately; each is a separate management area of responsibility in most middle size and large business organizations. All three types of costs may increase for the same basic reason, such as an increase in wage rates that applies to employees in all three areas of the business. But each area is usually a separate organizational unit, under control of different managers, and each area usually faces some problems that are local to that area. For instance, increases in raw material prices apply to the manufacturing area, but not to the other two areas. On the other hand, increases of paper costs and other office supply items would affect the administration and general area mainly. Likewise, an increase in salesmen's commission rates would affect the marketing area but not the other two areas.

Exhibit 5.3 shows the analysis of the changes of the total variable cost for each of the three basic operating areas for 1976 compared with 1975. For each area the volume change effect and the cost per unit change effect is computed. Please read the footnotes to the schedule. Also, keep in mind that the company is using the LIFO inventory method. If the FIFO method had been used the manufacturing cost per unit sold in 1976 would have been accounted for differently.

Contribution Margin Changes: Dollar per Unit Changes and Volume Changes

The analysis given in the two preceding sections is used to determine the impact of these changes on the company's *contribution margin*. Recall that contribution margin is equal to sales revenue less variable costs. Combining the preceding analysis leads to the following summary (the dollar per unit change refers to the sales price per unit change or the cost per unit change, as the case may be):

Summary of Sales Revenue and Variable Costs Changes

	Volume Change Effects	Dollar per Unit Change Effects	Total
Sales Revenue	+$1,000,000	+$ 825,000	+$1,825,000
Variable Costs	+ 780,000	+ 583,000	+ 1,363,000
Contribution Margin	+$ 220,000	+$ 242,000	+$ 462,000

If we refer back to the contribution margin format of the management profit performance report (Exhibit 4.5), we can see that the company's contribution margin did Increase $462,000: ($2,662,000 in 1976 less $2,200,000 in 1975= +$462,000).

EXHIBIT 5.3
Comparative Analysis of Changes in Variable Costs

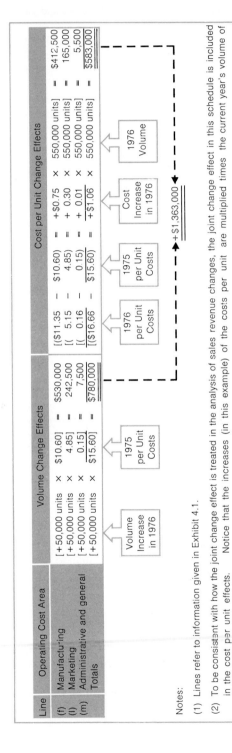

Line	Operating Cost Area	Volume Change Effects						Cost per Unit Change Effects								
(f)	Manufacturing	[+50,000 units	×	$10.60]	=	$530,000		[($11.35	−	$10.60)	=	$0.75	×	550,000 units]	=	$412,500
(l)	Marketing	[+50,000 units	×	4.85]	=	242,500		[(5.15	−	4.85)	=	+ 0.30	×	550,000 units]	=	165,000
(m)	Administrative and general	[+50,000 units	×	0.15]	=	7,500		[(0.16	−	0.15)	=	+ 0.01	×	550,000 units]	=	5,500
	Totals	[+50,000 units	×	$15.60]	=	$780,000		[($16.66	−	$15.60)	=	+$1.06	×	550,000 units]	=	$583,000

1975 per Unit Costs — Volume Increase in 1976

1976 per Unit Costs — 1975 per Unit Costs — Cost Increase in 1976 — 1976 Volume

+$1,363,000

Notes:

(1) Lines refer to information given in Exhibit 4.1.

(2) To be consistent with how the joint change effect is treated in the analysis of sales revenue changes, the joint change effect in this schedule is included in the cost per unit effects. Notice that the increases (in this example) of the costs per unit are multiplied times the current year's volume of 550,000 units

In 1975 the contribution margin per unit was $4.40: ($20.00 selling price less $15.60 total variable cost per unit). In 1976 the contribution margin per unit is $4.84: ($21.50 selling price less variable cost per unit of $16.66). Therefore, in 1976 the company managed to increase its contribution margin per unit by $.44 ($4.84−$4.40) and also managed to sell 50,000 more units at this higher contribution margin per unit. The contribution margin increase can be analyzed on a per unit basis as follows:

Analysis of Contribution Margin Increase

Volume Change Effects	= (+50,000 units) ×	$4.40	= $220,000
Dollar per Unit Change Effects	= 550,000 units ×	(+$0.44)	= + 242,000
Total Change in Contribution Margin			+$462,000

At the risk of some oversimplification, what the above analysis says is that *if* the dollar per unit values (sales price and variable cost) had *not* changed, then the company's contribution margin would have been $4.40 and the company would have generated $220,000 more contribution margin in 1976. But, in fact, the selling price increased $.44 more than the increase in total variable costs per unit. Therefore, $.44 more contribution margin per unit was earned on 550,000 units, for a favorable effect of $242,000. This amount can be crudely called an "inflation gain." The selling price was inflated by $1.50 per unit; this was partly offset by the inflation of the total variable costs per unit of $1.06. This cost increase leaves the company with a net "inflation gain" of $.44 per unit. However, fixed costs are higher in 1976, which also must be taken into account.

Fixed Cost Changes

First, it should be repeated that most fixed costs are the costs of providing capacity. Clearly manufacturing fixed costs provide production capacity. Also it can be properly said that marketing fixed costs provide sales capacity, and that administrative fixed costs provide what might be called "management capacity." In most situations, production capacity is the most binding constraint. There is nothing to sell and nothing to manage if the company cannot produce it in the first place. Conceivably a company could have too small a sales capacity relative to its production capacity or its management capacity. For instance, for lack of salesmen the company may fail to make sales of products that it could manufacture. Possibly management capacity could be too small, such that the company simply refuses to sell products that it could produce and sell because there are not enough managers to go around. But in the majority of cases, production capacity is the primary constraint.

Thus far in the example no specific information or measures have been given regarding the company's production capacity in 1975 or 1976. Of course, the example assumes that manufacturing capacity in each year is adequate to produce the output of that year, which is 525,000 units in 1975 and 562,500 units in 1976 (see Exhibit 4.2). The measurement of manufacturing capacity and the proper accounting for the use of this production capacity involve certain rather involved accounting procedures, which are discussed in Chapter Thirteen. For the present it simply is assumed that production capacity each year is equal to the number of units manufactured that year, which means there is no excess or idle capacity either year. Thus in 1975 production capacity equals 525,000 units, and in 1976 it is 562,500 units. This means that each year the company is operating at exactly 100% of its production capacity, so there are no accounting problems regarding unused capacity. (Chapter Thirteen considers the problems of accounting for unused capacity.)

The interperiod comparative analysis of change in total manufacturing fixed cost should start with the separation between those cost changes caused by increases (or decreases) of the company's production capacity and those cost changes due to higher or lower purchase costs of those factors making up the total manufacturing fixed cost for the period. To explain: given the assumption regarding production capacity just made, the company increased its production capacity from 525,000 units in 1975 to 562,500 units in 1976. *If* there had been no purchase price inflation of the various cost factors making up the fixed manufacturing costs of the company, then the company would expect its manufacturing fixed costs to increase as follows in 1976:

1976 Expected Fixed Manufacturing Cost Based on Production Capacity Increase (Assuming No Cost Inflation)

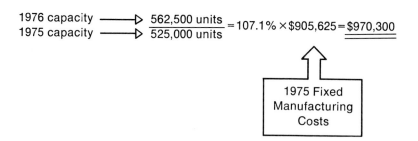

$$\frac{\text{1976 capacity} \longrightarrow 562,500 \text{ units}}{\text{1975 capacity} \longrightarrow 525,000 \text{ units}} = 107.1\% \times \$905,625 = \$970,300$$

1975 Fixed Manufacturing Costs

Notice, however, that the *actual* 1976 manufacturing fixed costs are $1,021,500 (see Exhibit 4.2). Hence, the cost inflation part of the increase can be determined roughly as follows:

Comparison of 1976 Expected Manufacturing Fixed Costs
(Based on Production Capacity Increase) with Actual Costs

Actual 1976 manufacturing fixed costs	=	$1,021,500
"Expected" 1976 manufacturing fixed costs based on increase in capacity (see computation immediately above)	=	970,300
Increase due to inflation of costs of the factors making up manufacturing fixed costs	=	$ 51,200

Based on this sorting out of the cost factor inflation effect, $51,200 in 1976, the next step would be to identify the most significant items that account for the $51,200 increase. Keep in mind that the company does not gain any increase of its production capacity due to cost factor inflation increase. Instead, the same factors simply cost more in 1976 than in 1975. For example, the annual fire insurance cost on the company's manufacturing plant and facilities may have increased, say $3800. (This assumes that this particular cost factor is included in the fixed manufacturing overhead accounts, which it should be since it is a necessary cost of the production process.) This one item is a sizable part of the total increase of $51,200, and thus it probably would be reported to the manager responsible for controlling this particular cost factor, as well to the top level managers of the company who make an overall review of the company's production operations. On the other hand, not every single small cost increase should be identified and reported separately to managers. Some "lumping" together of the smaller and more insignificant cost factor increases is necessary, to focus management's attention on the major cost factor increases.

The fixed marketing and the fixed administration and general costs both increase in 1976, as is shown by comparing 1976 with 1975 on these cost lines in Exhibit 4.1. For these fixed costs it is much more difficult to separate that part of the fixed cost increase due to expansion of capacity from that part due to cost factor inflation. It is not usual for a company to make a formal or explicit measure of its sales capacity or its "management capacity." Thus usually there is no practical way to estimate how much of the increase in these fixed costs is attributable to a capacity increase and how much is attributable to cost factor inflation increases. Nevertheless, in the analysis of each major cost factor making up these fixed costs, part of the increase may be due to adding more salesmen or more managers (paid on a fixed salary basis). This reason for a fixed cost increase is considerably different than increasing the salaries of the marketing and management personnel. As in the case of manufacturing fixed costs, usually only the more significant cost increases are reported to managers. The smaller changes are lumped together to put emphasis on the more significant cost factor increases which usually are more deserving of managers' attention.

Comparison of Break-even Point Each Year

Given the contribution margin in 1976 which is $4.84 per unit (see Exhibit 4.5), and given the total fixed cost deducted from sales revenues in 1976, which is $1,684,100 (see fixed costs reported in Exhibit 4.5), the 1976 operating profit break-even point can be computed and compared with 1975, as follows (see Exhibit 4.8 for 1975's break-even computation):

Comparison of 1975 and 1976 Break-even Points

	1975	1976
$\dfrac{\text{Total Fixed Costs}}{\text{Contribution Margin per Unit}} =$	$\dfrac{\$1,469,000}{\$4.40} = 333,864 \text{ units}$	$\dfrac{\$1,684,100}{\$4.84} = 347,955 \text{ units}$

Even though the contribution margin per unit increases, the increases in total fixed costs causes the company's operating profit break-even point to increase by almost 4% (347,955 units/333,864 units=104.2%).

Comparison of ROI Performance

Changes in Operating Profit Rate of Return on Total Assets

To this point in the chapter the analysis has explained the increase in the operating profit (before interest and income tax) from 1975 to 1976, which is briefly summarized as follows:

Summary of Major Changes in Operating Profit

Contribution Margin Increase—see Schedule on page 153				$462,000
Increase of Fixed Costs—see Exhibit 4.5:				
Operating Cost Area	1975	1976	Change	
Manufacturing	$862,500	$998,800	+$136,300	
Marketing	$308,000	$349,800	+$ 41,800	
Administrative and General	$298,500	$335,500	+$ 37,000	
Total Increase				215,100
Increase of Operating Profit				$246,900

The total operating profit for the year is "split up" among three major claims: (1) interest on (some) liabilities (2) income tax on the taxable income resulting from the operating profit less interest (which is deductible for determination of

EXHIBIT 5.4
Comparative Analysis of the Company's Distribution of
Operating Profit Each Year

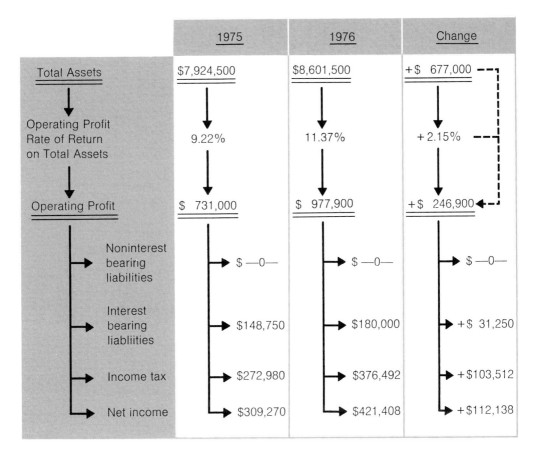

	1975	1976	Change
Total Assets	$7,924,500	$8,601,500	+$ 677,000
Operating Profit Rate of Return on Total Assets	9.22%	11.37%	+2.15%
Operating Profit	$ 731,000	$ 977,900	+$ 246,900
Noninterest bearing liabilities	$ —0—	$ —0—	$ —0—
Interest bearing liabliities	$148,750	$180,000	+$ 31,250
Income tax	$272,980	$376,492	+$103,512
Net income	$309,270	$421,408	+$112,138

taxable income); and (3) the residual net income for the stockholders. There are two quite different types of liabilities—noninterest bearing and interest bearing. To indicate this, therefore, Exhibit 5.4 includes a zero distribution to noninterest bearing liability sources of capital, which after all do provide part of the capital invested in the total assets, although the company makes no explicit payment for the use of this "free" capital.

Why did the operating profit rate of return on total assets increase by 2.15 percentage points, as is shown in Exhibit 5.4? As explained in Chapter Three (pages 78 to 81), it is useful to compute the asset turnover ratio and the profit ratio to analyze changes in return on assets. Exhibit 5.5 shows these computations for each year. To explain the impact of the changes in the asset turnover ratio and the profit rate, consider the following schedule which computes what

EXHIBIT 5.5
Comparative Determinant Analysis of Return on Assets

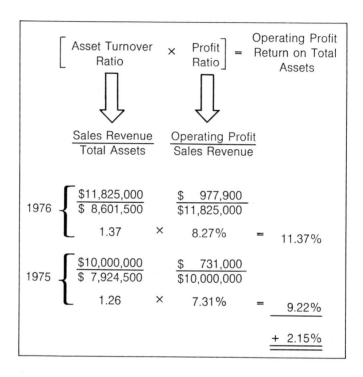

the operating profit would have been in 1976 if the asset turnover and the profit ratio had been the same as in 1975:

Determination of What 1976 Operating Profit Would Have Been at 1975 Ratios

	Total Assets	Asset Turnover Ratio	Sales Revenue	Profit Ratio	Operating Profit
At 1976 ratios:	$8,601,500 ×	1.37 =	$11,825,000 ×	8.27% =	$977,900
At 1975 ratios:	8,601,500 ×	1.26 =	10,854,300 ×	7.31% =	793,450
Increase in operating profit due to improvement of both ratios					+$184,450

As is shown by this comparison, the improvements in the asset turnover ratio and the profit ratio result in an operating profit increase of $184,450 from what it would have been. This additional operating profit increases the return on assets by 2.15% ($184,450/$8,601,500=2.15%).

Changes in Return on Equity

Of particular importance to top management, as well as the stockholders, is the rate of return on equity, that is, net income divided by stockholders' equity. This key measure of financial performance is computed as follows (see Exhibit 2.1 in Chapter Two for stockholders' equity amounts, and Exhibit 4.1 or 4.5 for net income amounts):

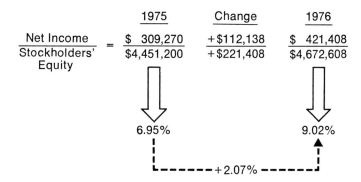

	1975	Change	1976
$\dfrac{\text{Net Income}}{\text{Stockholders' Equity}} =$	$ 309,270 / $4,451,200	+$112,138 / +$221,408	$ 421,408 / $4,672,608
	6.95%		9.02%

+2.07%

The most obvious reason for this increase of 2.07 percentage points in the return on equity is that net income increases by more than $112,000, whereas the stockholders' equity increases by only about $221,000. Since there were no issues or retirements of stock during 1976, the stockholders' equity increases by the amount of net income less the cash dividends paid during the year: ($421,408−$200,000=$221,408). Why did net income increase? (The company's operating profit increase of $246,900 has been already analyzed—see the summary schedule on page 156)?

From Exhibit 5.4 we can see that the company paid about $31,000 more interest expense in 1976 than in 1975, since the interest bearing debt increased in 1976 (though the average interest rate on its debt decreased). This increase of interest is deductible for determination for taxable income. In summary (see Exhibit 5.4 for amounts):

Net Income Increase Resulting from Operating Profit Increase

Operating Profit Increase (see page 156)	$246,900
Increase of Interest Expense (which also decreases Taxable Income by the same amount)	31,250
Remainder of Increase of Operating Profit (which is also an increase of Taxable Income)	$215,650
Income Tax at 48%	103,512
Net Income Increase	$112,138

Comparative Analysis of Financial Leverage

Financial leverage is working better for the stockholders in 1976 than the year before. Even though the average rate of interest on its *interest bearing* debts decreased in 1976 (see Exhibit 4.1 or 4.5), a larger percentage of its total assets is supplied from interest bearing debts in 1976 and, as a result, the average rate of interest on *all* liabilities increased in 1976, which is indicated as follows (using year-end balances—see Exhibit 2.1 or 3.1 for liability balances):

Determination of Average Interest Rates on All Liabilities

	1975	1976
$\dfrac{\text{Total Interest}}{\text{All Liabilities}} =$	$\dfrac{\$148,750}{\$3,473,300} = 4.28\%$	$\dfrac{\$180,000}{\$3,928,000} = 4.58\%$

Comparing the average interest rate on all liabilities with the operating profit rate of return on total assets for each year shows that the financial leverage "spread" increases:

Determination of Financial Leverage "Spread" in Rates
(in Percent)

	1975	1976
Operating Profit Rate of Return on Total Assets (see Exhibit 5.4)	9.22	11.37
Average Interest Rate on All Liabilities	4.28	4.58
Financial Leverage Spread Between Rates	4.94	6.79

The larger leverage spread in 1976 increases the aftertax financial leverage gain in 1976—for the computations see Exhibit 5.6.

The computation of the beforetax and aftertax leverage gain for each year in Exhibit 5.6 follows the discussion of financial leverage presented in Chapter Three (see pages 85 to 91). However, perhaps a few words of explanation are needed. The stockholders' equity is multiplied by the operating profit rate of return on assets each year to determine the before-tax income earned on their capital. This before-tax income is next multiplied by the aftertax retention percent, which is 52%, and then $6500 is added back. (The first $25,000 of taxable income is taxed at only $5500; 48% of $25,000 is $12,000, which is $6500 more than the $5500 tax on the first step of taxable income.)

Exhibit 5.6 shows that the aftertax leverage gain increases from $89,256 in 1975 to $138,670 in 1976, which is an increase of $49,414. In short, the significant increase in the operating profit rate of return on total assets (from

EXHIBIT 5.6
Comparison of Financial Leverage Gain in 1976 and 1975

		Before Income Tax						After Income Tax		
1976	Computation of Leverage Gain on Liabilities	=$3,928,892	×	6.79%	=	$266,674	× 52%		=	$138,670
	Computation of Operating Profit on Stockholders' Equity	=$4,672,608	×	11.37%	=	$531,226	× 52%	+ $6,500	=	282,738
	Total Net Income =									$421,408
1975	Computation of Leverage Gain on Liabilities	=$3,473,300	×	4.94%	=	$171,646	× 52%		=	$ 89,256
	Computation of Operating Profit on Stockholders' Equity	=$4,451,200	×	9.22%	=	$410,603	× 52%	+ $6,500	=	220,014
	Total Net Income =									$309,270

9.22% to 11.37%), even allowing for the increase in the average interest rate on all liabilities, gives the company a much larger spread to work with and thus the leverage gain improves accordingly.

Summary

One basic function of managers is to plan for and to control changes in the many factors that determine the success and quality of achievement of the organization. In profit-motivated business entities, managers are mainly concerned with those factors that directly or indirectly determine the profit and the return on investment (ROI) performance of the company. A key function of management accounting is to prepare reports that focus on the most important factors of financial success, and that highlight the most s gnificant changes from period to period in these factors. Managers make interperiod comparative analyses of profit and ROI results to judge the performance of the present period against the last period and, equally important, to lay the foundation for planning for changes that will take place in the next period. Planning begins with the most recent changes that have occurred; this is the base of experience for projecting what changes will take place in the future. In short, interperiod comparative analysis is essential for management control and also is the essential first step of management planning.

Interperiod comparative management profit reports that disclose the percent increases or decreases across the lines in these statements are useful to point out significant changes of revenue and expenses, and whether these percent changes are generally consistent or deviant with one another. However, the more important management questions concern why sales revenue and expenses increase or decrease, not just how much or by what percentage these key accounting measures change from one period to the next. Thus, an increase (or decrease) of sales revenue is analyzed in terms of two basic causes for the change: (1) the volume change effect, which is the increase (or decrease) of the quantity of units sold times last period's sales price; and, (2) the sales price change effect, which is the increase (or decrease) of the sales price per unit times this period's quantity of product sold. The distinction between these two causes of an increase (or decrease) of sales revenue is very significant to management. Selling more units is a different management problem and achievement than raising the sales price.

The interperiod comparative analysis of total variable cost changes follows the same method that is used for analyzing sales revenue increases or decreases. The volume change effect is separated from the variable cost per unit change effect. The volume change effect is the increase (or decrease) of total quantity sold times last period's variable cost per unit. The cost per unit increase (or decrease) is multiplied times this period's total quantity sold to determine the total effect of the change in variable cost per unit.

Given the two-way analysis of the increase or decrease of sales revenue and the corresponding increase or decrease of total variable costs, the same approach is applied to the increase or decrease of total contribution margin. In the company example analyzed in the chapter, both the contribution margin per unit increased (due to a larger increase in the sales price than the total variable cost per unit), and the total quantity (volume) sold increased. Hence, both changes increased the company's total contribution margin. But the company's fixed costs also increased as would be expected because of the inflation reflected in the company's sales price and variable costs per unit. In most instances, a company can measure or reasonably estimate its manufacturing (production) capacity for the year. This is important to the interperiod comparative analysis of manufacturing fixed costs changes.

Part of an increase of a company's manufacturing fixed costs may be due to the expansion of its production capacity. This is entirely different, and should be separated from the increases due to the inflation of the cost factors making up the company's manufacturing fixed overhead costs. The same logic applies to the interperiod comparative analysis of fixed marketing and fixed administrative and general costs, although the measurement of capacity in these two areas is much more difficult and not as common. Nevertheless, increases of these fixed costs due to adding more sales or office personnel, for example, is different from the same number of employes being given salary raises.

Once increases or decreases of sales revenue, variable costs, and fixed costs of this period compared with last period are analyzed in the manner just discussed, the managers in essence have explained the increase (or decrease) of the company's operating profit before interest and income tax. Of prime importance is the operating profit rate of return on total assets. The increase (or decrease) of this key ROI measure is best explained by comparing the company's asset turnover ratio and its profit ratio for each year. The change in the operating profit rate of return on total assets, and the change in the average interest rate on all liabilities explain why the return on (stockholders') equity increased or decreased. To round out the analysis, a comparison of financial leverage effects for each year is useful. For instance, a favorable increase in the operating profit rate of return on total assets may be offset in large part by an unfavorable financial leverage change.

ANALYSIS OF SALES MIX CHANGES

The company example used in this and previous chapters is a one product company. This key assumption avoids certain analysis problems facing the multiproduct company, in particular changes in the company's *sales mix*. Sales mix refers to the relative proportions of the different products making up total sales revenue. This appendix considers briefly the analysis of sales mix and changes in sales mix.

Assume that the company in the example manufactures and sells *three* products, instead of just one. These three products are called X, Y, and Z. Exhibit 5.7 reports the sales quantity, prices, and revenue, as well as the variable costs and contribution margin for each product each year. Notice that the *total* units sold, the *total* sales revenue, the *total* variable costs, and the *total* contribution margin from all three products combined is the same in both years as for the one product company in the chapter. (See Exhibit 4.5 to check this point.)

First, it should be understood that each of the footnoted items in Exhibit 5.7 is a *weighted average*. A weighted average can be determined in one of two ways. To explain, consider the $20 weighted average sales price in 1975:

Determination of Weighted Average Sales Price

(1) $\dfrac{\text{Total Sales Revenue}}{\text{Total Quantity Sold}} = \dfrac{\$10,000,000}{500,000 \text{ units}} = \dfrac{\$20.00}{}$ weighted average sales price

(2) Determine the proportion of each item's quantity to the total quantity, multiply this fraction times each item's sales price, and then add these adjusted sales prices together:

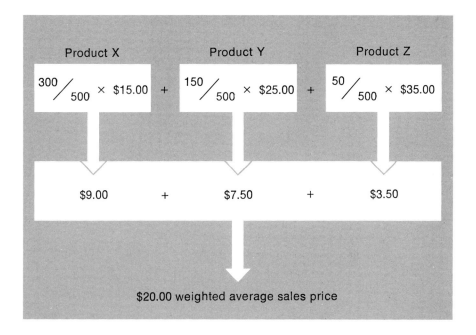

The second method has the advantage of focusing attention on the proportion of each product's quantity sold to the total quantity sold. For instance, observe that product X accounts for (300/500) or 60% of the items sold.

A comparative schedule of sales revenue, variable costs, and contribution margin reporting each product separately such as is shown in Exhibit 5.7 clearly is very informative to managers. Not every point can be mentioned here, but some of the more important ones are as follows. Product X shows the most significant improvement in 1976. It accounts for about 65% ($1,725,000/$2,662,-000=64.8%) of the company's total contribution margin in 1976, up from about 55% in 1975. Clearly product X is the mainstay of the company. The quantity sold increased 15% in 1976 (from 300,000 units to 345,000 units), and the contribution margin increased from $4 to $5 per unit in 1976, which is a 25% gain in this critical "first-step" measure of profit (before fixed costs, interest, and income tax expenses).

Product Y shows some improvement in 1976, though not nearly as much as product X. The company sold 10,000 more units in 1976. However, the company was not able to improve the contribution margin per unit; the increase in the sales price was entirely offset by the increase of the variable cost per unit. The volume increase accounts for all the contribution margin increase from product Y. Thus the total contribution from this product improved by $65,000: (10,000 more units × $6.50 contribution per unit).

Product Z looks to be in very poor shape. The company lowered the sales

EXHIBIT 5.7
Example of Sales Mix Report

SALES REVENUE

	1975			1976		
Product	Quantity Sold	Sales Price	Sales Revenue	Quantity Sold	Sales Price	Sales Revenue
X	300,000	$15.00	$ 4,500,000	345,000	$18.00	$ 6,210,000
Y	150,000	25.00	3,750,000	160,000	26.00	4,160,000
Z	50,000	35.00	1,750,000	45,000	32.33	1,455,000
Totals	500,000	$20.00[a]	$10,000,000	550,000	$21.50[a]	$11,825,000

TOTAL (MANUFACTURING, MARKETING, AND ADMINISTRATIVE AND GENERAL) VARIABLE COSTS

	1975			1976		
Product	Quantity Sold	Variable Cost per Unit	Total Variable Cost	Sold Quantity	Variable Cost per Unit	Total Variable Cost
X	300,000	$11.00	$ 3,300,000	345,000	$13.00	$ 4,485,000
Y	150,000	18.50	2,775,000	160,000	19.50	3,120,000
Z	50,000	34.50	1,725,000	45,000	34.62	1,558,000
Totals	500,000	$15.60[a]	$ 7,800,000	550,000	$16.66[a]	$ 9,163,000

CONTRIBUTION MARGIN

	1975			1976		
Product	Quantity Sold	Contribution Margin per Unit	Total Contribution Margin	Quantity Sold	Contribution Margin per Unit	Total Contribution Margin
X	300,000	$ 4.00	$ 1,200,000	345,000	$ 5.00	$ 1,725,000
Y	150,000	6.50	975,000	160,000	6.50	1,040,000
Z	50,000	0.50	25,000	45,000	(2.29)	(103,000)
Totals	500,000	$ 4.40[a]	$ 2,200,000	550,000	$ 4.84[a]	$ 2,662,000

[a] This dollar per unit amount is a weighted average.

price in 1976, but still sold 10% fewer units in 1976 (5000 units decrease from the 50,000 units sold in 1975). Furthermore, the contribution margin slipped from a small although positive $.50 per unit in 1975 to a *negative* $2.29 per unit in 1976. As Exhibit 5.7 indicates, there is a *contribution loss* of $103,000 from product Z in 1976. Unless this can be reversed, the company should consider dropping product Z, or at least should consider ways of decreasing variable costs per unit or of increasing the sales price so that an adequate contribution margin per unit is achieved.

Clearly the breakout* by each product of quantities sold, dollar values per unit (sales price, variable cost, and contribution margin), and total amounts is necessary for management analysis. Looking only at totals for all products combined would not reveal the vast differences between the three products. However, these sorts of reports can become quite detailed in practical situations, involving many hundreds (or more) different products sold by a company. In a sense, a good thing can be carried too far. Some grouping by product lines or by product models may be necessary in the reports to middle and upper management levels.

The sales mix of products determines the weighted average contribution margin earned from all products sold and, therefore, the company's break-even point depends on its sales mix. As is shown in the chapter (see page 156), the 1976 break-even point for the company is 347,955 total units at the contribution margin of $4.84 per unit. Given the 1976 sales mix reported in Exhibit 5.7, the weighted average contribution margin (for all three products) is also $4.84 per unit. Consequently, assuming the same total fixed costs ($1,684,100), the three product company has the same break-even point as the one product company example discussed in the chapter.

On the other hand, assume that the 1976 mix had not changed but had been the same as the 1975 mix. This would have resulted in a different weighted average contribution margin per unit, which is computed as follows (see Exhibit 5.7 for information):

Computation of 1976 Break-even Point Based on 1975 Sales Mix (Instead of Actual 1976 Sales Mix)

Product	1975 Sales Mix		1976 Contribution Margin per Unit		
X	300/500	×	$5.00	=	$3.000
Y	150/500	×	6.50	=	1.950
Z	50/500	×	(2.29)	=	($0.229)
Weighted average contribution margin per unit				=	$4.721

$$\text{Break-even Point} = \frac{\text{Total Fixed Costs}}{\text{Contribution Margin per Unit}} = \frac{\$1,684,100}{\$4.721} = 356,725 \text{ units}$$

* The term "breakdown" (instead of breakout) is often used with the same meaning.

As this computation shows, the break-even point would have been higher if the company had not shifted to a more favorable sales mix in 1976. The 1975 (less favorable) sales mix would have resulted in less operating profit in 1976, since the weighted average contribution margin per unit would have been only $4.721 (based on the 1975 sales mix), compared with $4,840 given the actual 1976 sales mix. The difference of $0.119 in contribution per unit ($4.840 − $4.721) when multiplied times the 1976 sales volume of 550,000 units is more than $65,000 difference in operating profit for the year.

Questions

5. 1   Assume that the company's production line employees are bargaining for a 5.0% across the board wage rate increase since the company increased its labor productivity 5.0% this year:
(a) Is this a "fair" demand?
(b) If the wage increase is granted, what are the consequences on the labor cost per unit of product manufactured?

5. 2   What are the main management reasons for the interperiod comparative analysis of financial performance?

5. 3   What three basic types of decision standards are used by managers in evaluating current period performance?

5. 4   What are the main advantages and disadvantages (or limitations) of profit performance comparison reports that show percent increases and decreases such as Exhibit 5.1?

5. 5   Which is better: a 5% increase in sales price or, instead, a 5% increase in volume sold? In answering, remember the fixed versus variable cost distinction explained in Chapter Four. You might set up a simple numerical example to support your answer.

5. 6   (a) What are the arguments for including the joint change effect with the sales price change effect?
(b) What are the arguments for including the joint change effect with the sales volume change effect?
(c) Under what conditions is the joint change effect *negative*?

5. 7   Without doing any detailed computations, determine whether the manufacturing cost per unit sold in 1976 would be more or less if the company used FIFO instead of LIFO (see Exhibit 4.1)? Briefly explain why.

5. 8   (a) If sales price increases 8.0% and total variable costs per unit increase 5.0%, then does the contribution margin per unit increase by 3.0%? Explain your answer with a simple numerical example.
(b) If sales price increases 8.0% and total variable costs per unit increases by

10.0%, then does the contribution margin per unit decrease by 2.0%? Explain your answer with a simple numerical example.

5. 9 "Inflation always works to the advantage of companies because their contribution margins per unit increase." Do you agree? Explain briefly.

5.10 Identify two different fixed costs that are subject to cost inflation year to year, and one fixed cost that is not or, at least, most of which is not.

5.11 "If the company's total fixed costs increase 7.5% and the company's contribution margin per unit increases 7.5%, then the company's break-even point will not change." Do you agree? Explain briefly; a simple numerical example to support your answer would be helpful.

5.12 If the company's contribution margin per unit had not changed in 1976, then given the company's fixed costs reported in Exhibit 4.5 what would the company's operating profit break-even point have been in 1976? Show computations clearly.

5.13 Does an increase in operating profit this year compared to last year necessarily mean:
(a) An increase in net income?
(b) An increase in the return on equity?

5.14 If a company increases its operating profit rate of return on assets, does this necessarily mean a larger financial leverage spread?

5.15 "As a general though oversimplified rule of thumb, a company should attempt to shift its sales mix so that the product with the highest contribution margins per unit make up a higher proportion of the total sales quantity." Do you agree? Briefly explain.

Problems

P5. 1 Last year the company sold 100,000 units at $50 per unit. Last year its variable operating costs per unit sold were $30 and its total fixed operating costs for the year was $1,500,000. The company's total assets were $3,000,000, one half of which were fixed assets. The company's capitalization structure was: 15% noninterest bearing liabilities, 40% interest bearing debt at an average 9% annual interest rate, and 45% stockholders' equity. This year the company sold 110,000 units at $48 per unit. Also for this year operating costs per unit sold are $28.50 per unit and its total fixed operating costs are $1,567,500. Fixed assets did not increase at the higher sales and production volumes this year because there was more than 10% unused capacity last year. Current assets, on the other hand, increased in proportion to the increase in sales revenue. The mix of capital sources (and the average annual interest rate) did not change. Assume a flat 48% income tax rate.

Required:

(1) In brief and condensed form prepare:
   (a) The two-year comparative profit performance statement for the company, and
   (b) The two-year comparative statement of financial condition for the company at the end of last year and this year.

(2) Analyze the change in the company's sales revenue this year compared with last year.

(3) Analyze the change in the company's contribution margin this year compared with last year.

(4) Analyze the change in the company's operating profit break-even point this year compared with last year.

(5) Analyze the change in the company's return on assets this year compared with last year.

(6) Analyze the change in the company's financial leverage effects this year compared with last year.

P5. 2   The purpose of this problem is to prepare next year's (1977) profit performance statement for the main example discussed in the chapter. In particular, see the company's 1975-1976 profit performance statement shown in Exhibit 4.1. Interperiod comparative analyses between 1977 and 1976 are also required. For purposes of this problem, assume the following for 1977 (all other assumptions for the company are the same as are discussed in the chapter):

(a) The company will sell 600,000 units at $23.50 per unit.
(b) Variable manufacturing costs per unit will be:

Raw materials	$4.782
Direct labor	$6.015
Overhead	$1.132

(c) The combined ending inventory of work-in-process and finished goods will be 150,000 units, that is, one fourth of the sales for 1977.
(d) Total fixed manufacturing costs will be:

Direct labor	$175,175
Overhead	$1,048,600

(e) Marketing expenses will be:

Variable	$5.365 per unit
Fixed	$440,400

(f) Administration and general expenses will be:

Variable	$0.712 per unit
Fixed	$373,800

(g) Average debt during the year will be $2,700,000 and the average interest rate will be 9.0%.

Required:

(1) Prepare the 1977 profit performance statement for the company:
   (a) in the format shown in Exhibit 4.1, and
   (b) in the alternative contribution margin format shown in Exhibit 4.5.
(2) Analyze the change in sales revenue and the change in contribution margin between 1977 and 1976.

P5. 3 A company manufactures and sells three basic products, which we will call A, B, and C in this problem. A new president of this company has just been appointed. The schedule given below has just arrived on the desk of the new president, which is a comparison of this year's sales to last year's:

Sales Revenue by Product Lines

	Last Year			This Year		
Product	Total Units Sold	Average Sales Price	Total Sales Revenue	Total Units Sold	Average Sales Price	Total Sales Revenue
A	100,000 ×	$10.00 =	$1,000,000	120,000 ×	$11.00 =	$1,320,000
B	100,000 ×	10.00 =	1,000,000	90,000 ×	9.10 =	819,000
C	100,000 ×	10.00 =	1,000,000	110,000 ×	9.50 =	1,045,000
Total	300,000 ×	$10.00 =	$3,000,000	320,000 ×	$ 9.95 =	$3,184,000

The president does not have the time to make computations for the interperiod comparisons of sales. Instead, he asks you, the chief accountant of the company, to prepare a useful analysis of the interperiod sales of the three products, that he can review.

Required:

(1) For each of the three products, separately determine the sales price change effect and the volume change effect to explain the increase or decrease of total sales revenue for each product.
(2) This part of the problem concerns the analysis of the total revenue of the entire company, that is, the bottom line in the above schedu!e.
   (a) Notice the average sales price this year is $9.95. How is this $9.95 average sales price determined? What does It mean? Why does the average sales price decrease 5 cents?

(b) For the company's total sales revenue performance, determine the sales price change effect and the volume change effect to explain the increase this year compared with last year.

(c) Which level of interperiod comparative analysis—each product separately or all products in total—in your opinion is more useful to the president? Would your answer to this question be the same if the company manufactured and sold 30 products instead of 3? What about 300 products? Or, 3000 products?

P5. 4 This problem continues from Problem 5.3. The company's manufacturing variable costs are identified and measured for each of the three separate products manufactured and sold by the company. On the other hand, the variable marketing and the variable administrative and general expenses are not accounted for by each product separately, since most of these costs are joint costs that depend on the total quantity (of all three products) sold. Fixed costs for each year are not the concern of this particular problem. From the accounting records of the company the following schedule has been prepared:

Variable Manufacturing Costs by Product Lines

	Last Year			This Year		
Product	Total Units Sold	Average Variable Mfg. Cost per Unit	Total Variable Mfg. Cost	Total Units Sold	Average Variable Mfg. Cost per Unit	Total Variable Mfg. Cost
A	100,000 × $6.00 =		$ 600,000	120,000 × $6.60 =		$ 792,000
B	100,000 × 7.00 =		700,000	90,000 × 6.72 =		604,800
C	100,000 × 8.00 =		800,000	110,000 × 7.52 =		827,200
Total	300,000 × $7.00 =		$2,100,000	320,000 × $6.95 =		$2,224,000

Required:

(1) For each of the three products separately determine the volume change effect and the cost per unit change effect to explain the increase or decrease of the variable manufacturing cost this year compared with last year.

(2) For the total variable manufacturing costs of all three products determine the volume change effect and the cost per unit change effect to explain the increase in the company's total variable manufacturing cost this year compared with last year.

(3) Using your answers to part (2) of this problem and part (2b) of Problem 5.3, determine the volume change effect and the dollar per unit change effect to explain the total change in the gross contribution margin of this division.

(*Note:* Gross computation margin is the contribution margin before determining the variable costs of marketing and administration.)

P5. 5 Please refer to the retailer company example whose financial statements are introduced in Problem 2.6, and also refer to the additional information presented in Problem 4.10 for this company.

Required:

(1) In the format shown in Exhibit 5.1, prepare a two-year comparative profit performance statement for the company for the years ending December 31, 1975 and 1976.

(2) For each of the following, present a comparative analysis to show the reasons for the increase (or decrease) from 1975 to 1976:
  (a) Sales revenue.
  (b) Cost of goods sold expense.
  (c) Variable marketing expenses.
  (d) Variable administration and general expenses.
  (e) Contribution margin.
  (f) Operating profit break-even point.
  (g) Return on assets.

(3) For each year (1975 and 1976) analyze the effects of financial leverage on the return on equity. (See Exhibit 5.6, for example.)

P5. 6 Two years ago, in 1974, this company's raw material and direct labor manufacturing costs were as follows:
For one unit of finished product—

(a) 100.00 pounds of raw materials were required.
(b) The average cost per pound of raw material was $10.
(c) 100.0 hours of direct labor were required.
(d) The average cost per direct labor hour was $5.

In 1975 and again in 1976 the production department was able to make changes to decrease the weight of raw materials used to manufacture one unit of finished product by 5.0% of the preceding year's raw material's weight. Also, in 1975 and again in 1976 the company made changes to improve labor productivity; the number of direct labor hours needed to manufacture one unit of finished product decreased by 4.0% of the hours needed in the preceding year. The sum of a company's raw material and direct labor costs is called the *prime cost.*

Required:

(1) If the raw material purchase cost and the direct labor hour wage rate had not changed since 1974, determine the company's prime cost in 1976 of manufacturing this particular product.

(2) Determine the maximum raw material purchase cost and the maximum direct labor wage rate for 1976 which would be permitted by the productivity gains so that the company's prime cost is the same as it was in 1974.

(3) Assume that the raw material purchase cost is $11.50 per pound in 1976 and that the direct labor wage rate per hour is $5.75. Assume that other manufacturing costs per unit have remained the same since 1975.

(a) Determine the "cost of inflation" per unit of finished product in this situation.

(b) Who pays for this cost of inflation?

P5. 7   Treat each situation below as an independent and separate case.

(a) Last period the company sold 100,000 units at $5 per unit. This period's total sales revenue is $577,500. From your interperiod comparative analysis you determine that the volume change effect is an increase of $50,000. *Required:* Determine this period's sales price per unit.

(b) This period the company sold 48,000 units at $4.50 per unit. From your interperiod comparative analysis you determine that the sales price change effect is an increase of $9600. *Required:* Determine last period's sales price per unit. From the information given can you also determine last period's sales volume?

(c) Last period the company sold 30,000 units at $10 per unit. This period's total sales revenue is $275,000. From your interperiod comparative analysis you determine that the volume change effect is a decrease of $50,000. *Required:* Determine this year's sales price per unit.

(d) This year the company reduced its sales price per unit by 10.0% compared with last year, and sold 10.0% more units than last year. *Required:* Would the company's total sales revenue this year be the same as last year? If not, would the negative price change effect be larger than the positive volume change effect (and thus cause total sales revenue to be less), or would the reverse be true?

P5. 8   Last year the company (a retailer) sold 300,000 units at $25 per unit. The company's total expenses, excluding interest and income tax, were $6,400,000, which includes total fixed costs of $1,600,000. Interest expense last year was $100,000 and the income tax expense was a flat 48% of taxable income. This year the company sold 324,000 units at $27.50 per unit. Total expenses, excluding interest and income tax, were $7,632,000, which includes total fixed costs of $1,800,000. Interest expense this year was $118,800, and the income tax expense increased by an amount equal to 48% of the increase in taxable income.

Required:

(1) In brief form present a two-year comparative net income statement for the company; see Exhibit 5.1 for example.

(2) Analyze the changes in sales revenue, variable costs per unit, and contribution margin between this year and last year.

(3) Last year the company operated at exactly 100% of its inventory storage capacity. The company rents all the inventory storage space needed from a public warehouse. Therefore, at the start of this year to provide for the anticipated increase in sales volume, the company increased capacity by renting 10.0% additional inventory storage space, which caused the rental expense to increase by 10.0%. This year the rental expense was $880,000;

the cost per square foot rented this year was the same as last year. Last year the company's total labor cost was $700,000. All employees are paid a fixed salary per month. All employees were given a 15.0% wage increase starting on the first day of this year. However, no new employees were hired and none left the company this year. The remainder of the fixed costs include a variety of different cost items, most of which cost more this year than last year. Based on this information, analyze in as much detail as possible the change in the company's fixed costs this year compared to last year.

(4) Compare the operating profit break-even point this year with that of last year.

P5. 9   This year the company's average selling price on all its products sold was $52 and the average variable cost per unit sold was $47. Certain changes may happen next year which are described below. Treat each situation as a separate and independent case.

(a) Next year the company expects no change in the mix (relative proportions) of products sold, but all sales prices will be increased by 5.0%. All variable costs per unit should also increase exactly by 5.0%. The total volume sold will be the same.
Required: Will the company's total contribution margin earned next year increase or decrease? If so, by what percentage? If not, why does the contribution margin remain the same?

(b) Next year the company expects no change in the mix of the products sold, and the company expects to offset the higher purchase costs of raw materials, labor, and other inputs by increases in productivity such that the variable cost per unit sold should remain the same. The company expects to lower the selling prices on all its products by 5.0% and as a result to sell 20.0% more quanity of each and every item.
Required: Will the company's total contribution margin earned next year increase or decrease? If so, by what percentage? If not, why does the contribution margin remain the same?

(c) Next year the company expects to change its sales mix such that the average sales price will increase by 4.0%. The average variable cost for this sales mix should decrease by 3.0%. The total sales volume will remain the same.
Required: Will the company's total contribution margin earned next year increase or decrease? If so, by what percentage? If not, why does the contribution margin remain the same?

(d) Please refer to case (b) again. Instead of a 20% increase in sales volume, determine by what percentage the sales volume would have to increase for the company to earn the same total contribution margin next year as this year.

P5.10   Certain information about the company is given below for the accounting year ended September 30, 1975 and 1976:

	1975	1976
(a) Sales revenue	$3,025,390	$2,791,740
(b) Operating profit	145,219	139,587
(c) Interest expense	26,207	31,121
(d) Income tax expense	50,626	45,564
(e) Net income	68,386	62,902
(f) Average total assets	963,500	915,325
(g) Average total noninterest bearing liabilities	42,394	54,920
(h) Average total interest bearing liabilities	327,590	366,130
(i) Average total stockholders' equity	593,516	494,275
(j) Cash dividends paid	38,449	30,759

Early in fiscal year 1976 the company's president retired, and the company purchased the stock owned by the president and immediately retired and canceled the stock. This was required under the employment contract with the president. No new stock shares were issued either year.

Required: For each of the following prepare a comparative analysis between 1976 and 1975 (show your computations clearly):

(1) Return on assets, including the two determinants of this ratio.
(2) Return on equity, including effects of financial leverage.

P5.11   The company has asked your assistance in determining the best sales and production mix of their products for 1977. The company manufactures a line of dolls and a doll dress sewing kit. The company's sales department provides the following data:

Doll's Name	Estimated Demand for 1977 (Units)	Net Price
Laurie	50,000	$5.20
Debbie	42,000	2.40
Sarah	35,000	8.50
Kathy	40,000	4.00
Sewing kit	325,000	3.00

To promote sales of the sewing kit there is a 15% reduction in the net price for a kit purchased at the same time that a doll is purchased. From accounting records you develop the following data:

(a) The production costs per unit:

Item	Raw Material	Direct Labor
Laurie	$1.40	$0.80
Debbie	0.70	0.50
Sarah	2.69	1.40
Kathy	1.00	1.00
Sewing kit	0.60	0.40

(b) The labor rate of $4 per hour is expected to continue without change in 1977. The plant has capacity of 65,000 labor hours per year on a single-shift basis. Present equipment can produce all of the products.

(c) The total fixed costs for 1977 will be $100,000. Other variable costs (in addition to raw material and direct labor costs) will be 50% of direct labor cost.

(d) The company has a small inventory of its products that can be ignored.

Required:

(1) Compute the contribution margin of a unit of each product.

(2) Compute the contribution to profit of a unit of each product per direct labor hour expended on the product.

(3) Prepare a schedule computing the total direct labor hours required to produce the estimated sales units for 1977. Indicate the item and number of units that you would recommend be increased (or decreased) in production to attain the company's effective productive capacity.

P5.12 Assume the following for a one product retailer company for this year and last:

	Last Year	This Year
Sales revenue	$300,000	$315,000
Cost of Goods sold	200,000	216,000
Gross profit	$100,000	$ 99,000

Treat each situation below as a separate and independent situation.

(a) It is known that the sales volume this year is 10.0% less than last year.

Required:

(1) Determine the percent increase in the sales price this year compared with last year.

(2) Can you determine *the amount* of the volume change effect and the sales quantity for each year? If so, compute each.

(b) It is known that the sales volume this year is 4.0% less than last year.

Required:

(1) Determine the percent increase in the purchase cost per unit this year compared with last year.

(2) Can you determine *the amount* of the volume change effect and the cost per unit change effect, even though you do not know the sales quantity for each year? If so, compute each.

(c) It is known that the sales volume this year is 8.0% more than last year.

Required:

(1) Determine the percent increase or decrease in the selling price and the purchase cost per unit this year compared with last year.

(2) Analyze the decrease in the gross profit this year compared with last year.

P5.13   The management of this company has engaged you to assist in the development of information to be used for managerial decisions. The company has the capacity to process 20,000 tons of cotton seed per year. The yield of a ton of cottonseed is as follows:

Product	Average Yield per Ton of Cottonseed (in pounds)	Average Selling Price per Unit
Oil	300	$ 0.15 per pound
Meal	600	50.00 per ton
Hulls	800	20.00 per ton
Lint	100	3.00 per hundred weight
Waste	200	

A special marketing study revealed that the company can expect to sell its entire output for the coming year at the average selling prices shown above. You have determined the company's cost to be as follows:

Processing costs

    Variable: $9 per ton of cotton seed put into process
    Fixed: $108,000 per year

Marketing costs

    All variable: $20 per ton sold.

Administrative and general costs

    All fixed: $90,000 per year.

Required:

(1) If the average cost per ton of cottonseed will be $30.80 during the coming year, determine the company's operating profit break-even point.

(2) Shortly after you presented your break-even computation information based on the $30.80 per ton cost of cotton seed, a widespread flood occurred that destroyed a large part of the cotton crops, and as a result the cost per ton will increase. In view of these changed conditions, management would like to know the average maximum amount that the company can afford to pay for a ton of cottonseed. Management has defined this average maximum amount as the amount that would result in the company's having losses no greater when operating than when closed down under the existing cost and revenue structure. Management states you are to assume that the fixed costs shown in your break-even point report will continue unchanged even when the operations are shut down. Determine this maximum cost per ton.

(3) The company has no interest bearing liabilities. The stockholders consider the minimum satisfactory return on their investment in the business to be 25% before corporate income taxes. The stockholders' equity in the company is $968,000. Compute the maximum average amount that the company can pay for a ton of cottonseed to realize the minimum satisfactory return on the stockholders' investment in the business, if the company operates at full (100%) of capacity:

(a) Assuming that the company wants to recover fixed costs through its sales revenue; and, alternatively,

(b) Assuming that the company takes the attitude explained in part (2), that is, that the fixed costs, at least for the coming year, are unavoidable and already lost anyway.

(4) Is the approach (or attitude) adopted in parts (2) and (3b) above good management policy in the short-run? In the long-run?

P5.14   This company mines a commonly used mineral. The following information is available from the company's accounting records:

	1976	1975	Increase (Decrease)
Sales revenue	$891,000	$840,000	$ 51,000
Cost of goods sold	688,500	945,000	(256,500)
Gross profit	$202,500	($105,000)	$307,500

The following information is also available:

(a) The sales price of the mineral was increased from $8 per ton to $11 per ton on January 1, 1976.

(b) New mining machinery was placed into operation on January 1, 1976 which reduced the cost of mining from $9 to $8.50 per ton.

(c) The company's quantity of inventory at the end of 1976, 1975, and 1974 has remained the same; inventory is valued on the LIFO basis.

Required: Prepare an analysis to explain the change in the gross profit, as well as sales revenue and cost of goods sold, from 1975 to 1976. Your analysis should include the effects of changes in the selling price, cost per unit sold, and volume sold.

P5.15 The following information is available from the local gas utility company's accounting records:

	Last Year	This Year	Increase (Decrease)
Average number of customers	27,000	26,000	(1,000)
MCF scales	486,000	520,000	34,000
Revenue	$1,215,000	$1,274,000	$59,000

Required: To explain the increase in operating revenues, prepare an analysis accounting for the effect of changes in:

(1) Average number of customers.
(2) Average gas consumption per customer.
(3) Average rate per MCF sold (MCF = thousand cubic feet).

Chapter Six

Financial Planning and Profit Budgeting

FINANCIAL PLANNING AND PROFIT BUDGETING

Introduction—The Constant Pressure To Maintain or To Improve Profit Performance*

A Brief Review of the Company's Most Recent Profit Performance

The company in the example discussed in Chapters Two to Five earned a 9.0% rate of return on its stockholders' equity in 1976. This key return on investment (ROI) measure is the critical test of profit performance. It depends directly on the company's operating profit (before interest and income tax) rate of return on total assets, which is 11.4% in 1976. The company's average interest rate on its total liabilities (including some noninterest bearing liabilities) in 1976 is 4.6% which, given the 11.4% operating profit rate of return on total assets, yields a financial leverage gain in 1976. These basic financial measures of the company's performance in 1976 are tied together and summarized in Exhibit 6.1. (As previously, the company's year-end asset, liability, and stockholders' equity balances are used.)

The Need To Improve Return on Equity: How To Do It?

For most industrial (that is, product manufacturer) companies, a 9.0% return on equity is not acceptable, at least not in the long run. The board of directors of this company, following a comparison with the company's competitors and with prevailing general economic conditions, concludes that this company should be earning at least a 12.0% annual return on equity. Accordingly the directors have made it clear to the president and to other top level managers of the company that reaching a 12.0% return of equity is the number one financial priority for 1977. How can the company improve its return on equity?

There are two focal points in answering this sort of question: (1) the operating profit rate of return on total assets, called return on assets for short; and, (2) the financial leverage situation of the company. Improving the financial leverage gain usually means increasing the proportion of liabilities to total assets (that is, using a higher *debt to equity ratio*), or lowering the average interest rate on all

---

* This opening section builds heavily on previous discussion, especially Chapter Three which discusses ROI measures and the analysis of financial leverage effects.

EXHIBIT 6.1
Summary of Key Financial Ratios and Measures and How They
Determine Rate of Return on Equity

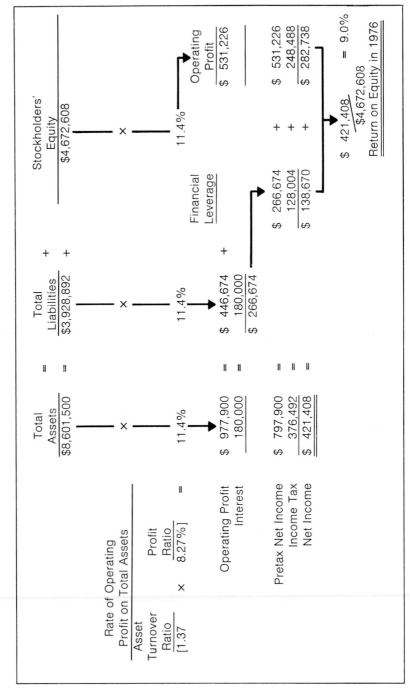

liabilities. The latter course means borrowing money at a lower interest rate or increasing the proportion of noninterest bearing liabilities to total liabilities.

Essentially the financial leverage question is a financial policy decision for top level management to make, which goes beyond the subject matter of this book. However, notice that the liabilities already make up about 46% of total assets (see Exhibit 3.1), and this may mean that the company cannot increase its ratio of liabilities to total assets to any significant extent. It is assumed, therefore, that the mix of liabilities and stockholders' equity capital will remain about the same in 1977.

In this situation, top management would concentrate on how to improve the company's rate of return on assets in 1977. Although the amount of total assets may increase in 1977, this scaling-up, in itself, will *not* help the *ratio* of operating profit to total assets. As just explained, the mix of liabilities and stockholders' equity will be about the same in 1977. In other words, an increase of total assets will mean an increase of liabilities and an increase in stockholders' equity such that liabilities still supply about 46% of the company's total capital and stockholders still supply about 54%. Hence, it is the *rate* of operating profit on total assets that has to be improved.

For convenience of analysis at this point, the implications of what is necessary to achieve a 12.0% return on equity is demonstrated for the total assets at year-end 1976, which is $8,601,500 (see Exhibit 3.1). Assume, to be conservative, that the average interest rate on all liabilities in 1977 will increase to, say, 6.0%. What rate of operating profit on total assets would the company have to earn in 1977 in order to yield a 12.0% return on equity? This "required" operating profit can be computed backward, or from the bottom up, starting with the 12.0% return on equity (see Exhibit 3.1 for stockholders' equity and liability amounts):

Computation of "Required" Rate of Operating Profit on Total Assets To Earn 12.0% Return on Equity

Stockholders' Equity = $4,672,608×12.0%	=	$ 560,713	Net Income
[(48% × pretax net income) − $6,500]	=	505,081	Income Tax
[($560,713 − $6,500)/52%]	=	$1,065,794	Pretax Net Income
Total Liabilities = $3,928,892×6.0%	=	235,734	Interest
		$1,301,528	Operating Profit

"Required" Rate of Operating Profit on Total Assets = $1,301,528 / $8,601,500 = 15.1%

As you can see, the company would have to increase its actual operating profit rate of return on total assets to 15.1% in 1977 to earn a 12.0% return on equity. (In 1976 the company earned only 11.4% operating profit return on its assets, as is shown in Exhibit 6.1.) To increase its return on assets, the company must increase its asset turnover ratio or increase its profit ratio, or both. For instance, if all the improvement in the return on assets has to come from an increase in the asset turnover ratio, then the 1977 "required" asset turnover ratio would be determined as follows (see Exhibit 6.1 for profit ratio):

Determination of "Required" Asset Turnover Ratio

Return on Assets		Asset Turnover Ratio		Profit Ratio
15.1%	=	?	×	8.27%
Answer: 15.1%/8.27%	=	1.83		

On the other hand, if all the improvement in the return on assets has to come from an increase in the profit ratio, then the 1977 "required" profit ratio would be determined as follows (see Exhibit 6.1 for asset turnover ratio):

Determination of "Required" Profit Ratio

Return on Assets		Asset Turnover Ratio		Profit Ratio
15.1%	=	1.37	×	?
Answer: 15.1%/1.37	=			11.01%

Increasing the asset turnover ratio means generating more total sales revenue with the same amount of total assets, or increasing sales revenue proportionally more than the percent increase in total assets. But from exactly where will the additional sales revenue come? Increasing the profit ratio means that some operating expenses will have to be reduced as a percentage of sales revenue. But *which specific* expense ratios can be reduced? Top level managers cannot simply "give orders" to increase sales and to reduce expense ratios. There must be management *planning* to determine where and how to increase sales revenue and to reduce expense ratios. Managers do not sit back and hope for a better year. Definite plans must be formulated that, in specific terms, deal with how to reach the company's financial goals.

Also, the balances in the company's various asset accounts must be maintained at proper levels, neither too high nor too low, compared with total sales revenue and total expenses during the year. And liabilities must be paid on time. An adequate cash balance for day to day—every day, in fact—is necessary. Securing additional capital (if needed) from long-term creditors and stockholders has to be prepared for in advance, and usually cannot be decided on at the last minute.

Central Importance of Planning

Planning is a very broad and comprehensive concept. In simplest terms, planning consists of at least a minimal amount of thinking ahead, in sufficient detail, such that adequate preparations are taken in time to carry out intended objectives. It is impossible not to do any planning at all. Indeed, did you read this sentence without some "planning"? Could you make a trip without some idea of your destination, and without at least a rough "plan" of how you will get there? It is hard to imagine a business not doing *some* planning.

Well managed business enterprises are characterized by an adequate amount of good planning. One of top management's most basic functions is planning. Top level managers, and even middle level managers to a lesser degree, should set aside some of the time they use for the day-to-day pressing problems of the business for this process. At the top level of management it is difficult to distinguish clearly and cleanly between policy making, setting objectives and goals, adopting strategy, and planning. Different authors use these terms with different meanings; there is much overlap in management literature among these concepts. But no doubt exists that top management should spend a good deal of their time doing these essential functions.

Policies, strategies, objectives, and goals span many different dimensions and aspects of the modern business enterprise including, for instance, relations with legislative and regulatory branches of government, environmental issues and concerns, racial relations and civil rights, labor relations and working conditions, and so on. Clearly such a list can be very long for today's business enterprise. Management accounting is concerned primarily with *financial* dimensions of the business enterprise, although we must quickly add that many of the other dimensions of the business have financial consequences that managers have to consider. The main thrust of the following discussion concerns financial planning and the exercise of financial control by management relative to these plans.

Financial planning begins with the setting of the company's financial goals and objectives, and the adoption of the broad guidelines of financial strategy and policy to reach these goals and objectives. Financial goals and objectives have been more or less taken for granted in previous chapters. In other words, it is assumed that a business wants to earn (at least) a sufficient rate of return on its stockholders' equity. Most businesses, it seems apparent, would like to do better than earning just a sufficient or adequate rate of return on equity. In any case, what is a *sufficient* rate of return on equity? How much risk is the business firm willing to take to earn a higher rate of return? And, given the answers to these questions, what is the best or optimal manner to finance the capital needs of the business? These are essential questions in the field of *business finance.*

This book does not explore the complex questions and issues that customarily are assigned to the field of business finance. Where necessary, however, a reference is made to these issues. It is assumed that management has established financial objectives, goals, policies, and strategies for the business entity. Whether they are the best ones is not debated. It is fair to say that management accounting is directed more to the *implementation* of the company's financial objectives, goals, policies, and strategies, instead of the establishment of them. But it should also be said that management accounting provides the essential financial information regarding the company's actual performance and progress toward these financial bench marks. Management accountants must thoroughly understand the business entity's financial objectives, goals, policies, and strategies.

Informal Versus Formal Planning: Nature of Budgeting as Formal Financial Planning

In many business enterprises, especially smaller firms, financial planning is not formalized or done in any systematic fashion. That is, the specific person or persons who do the financial planning are not clearly designated, and what they do is not "written down," documented, or made explicit. Indeed, some businesses seem to succeed in spite of their lack of financial planning. What financial planning is done may be done mainly on what is called an "urgency basis" —the manager waits until the financial problem is so clear that anyone could see it, and then decides to "solve" the problem in the most expedient manner, with little if any thought about the implications of this decision to the other financial goals and objectives of the business, and without too much thought about the long-run financial goals of the business.

However, the quick "solution" to urgent financial problems may cause other financial problems, or may not prevent the same problem from reappearing in the future. For example, a manager may decide to borrow on short-term notes at a very high interest rate to get over what is thought to be a temporary cash bind. Equally important, the manager should also determine why the company is short of cash in the first place, and should decide what is the best *ongoing* solution for the future cash needs of the company.

In short, *formal and systematic* financial planning usually is very important to the success of the business entity. "Formal" and "systematic" means that certain managers in the organization regularly allocate part of their time and effort to this task, and that the financial planning is carried out reasonably well, which includes communication *to and from* most other top and middle level managers in the organization. In larger business enterprises, financial planning requires several staff specialists to assist top level managers in this task, and they may be organized in a separate department. In smaller firms, on the other hand, one manager may do all the financial planning, perhaps with some outside consulting advice and help, for example, from a CPA.

Budgeting is the most common term used to describe formal systematic financial planning. Financial plans, when expressed in some detail and in a time frame (such as for next year), are called *budgets.* Plans are made to be broken in one sense; it has been quipped that "we need a plan so that we know what we're deviating from." In a more serious sense, budgets (financial plans) should be realistic: a good budget is an *achievable* financial plan. Unless the assumptions and forecasts of the plan turn out to be wrong, then the plan remains in force and, therefore, budgets are the bench mark and point of reference against which actual performance is compared. In this way budgets are used for financial *control* purposes as well as for financial planning. Control should *not* be thought of in the restrictive sense of prevention or limiting action. Rather, control should be thought of in the more positive sense of staying on course; that is, the course outlined in the budget. In summary, budgets are an *expression* of financial plans that are also used to judge the *execution* of those plans.

Three Basic Areas of Financial Planning and Budgeting

Financial planning can be divided into three basic areas of management responsibility: (1) *profit* planning, (2) *capital sources and investment* planning, and, (3) *cash flow* planning. Each of these areas of management planning can be subdivided into *short-term* planning (usually meaning one year) and *long-term* planning (usually meaning more than one year).

Profit planning deals primarily with future sales revenue, future operating costs, and future interest and income tax expenses, as well as with the future rate of return on assets and rate of return on equity. Obviously, for profit-motivated enterprises, profit planning is a primary function of management. Profit planning begins with forecasts of future sales prices and forecasts of the quantities that can be sold at those prices. It also involves forecasting future operating costs that are based on predictions and estimates of raw material purchase prices, labor wage rates, and productivity. All this detailed profit planning, which may be done by several different managers, is eventually brought together and summarized in a profit budget document or report. This budget document usually is expressed in essentially the same format as the regular periodic profit performance reports to managers, such as is shown in Exhibit 4.1. It is proper to call this type of profit budget document a *budgeted net income statement,* or by a similar title such as *profit budget.*

In many instances, the profit planning for next year requires more than one cycle of effort by the various managers involved in this budgeting process. For instance, when all the details and separate parts of next year's profit budget are finally put together and summarized, the budgeted net income statement may reveal that operating profit for next year would not be enough for the company to earn a sufficient rate of return on its assets. Hence, the managers would "go back to the drawing boards" to try to find ways of improving the profit plan. During this second cycle the managers may have to reconsider many factors, such as sales prices, productivity ratios, and so on. Hopefully, a satisfactory *and* achievable profit plan will emerge. The final budgeted net income statement should be a practical and reasonable set of goals for the coming year.

Profit planning also requires a good deal of related planning of a more *non-financial* nature. There must be logistics and facilities planning to ensure an adequate inflow of raw materials and supplies, and so that there will be adequate manufacturing and other operating capacity availble to carry out production and sales during the coming year. Likewise, the profit plan leads to a good deal of personnel planning to have an adequate and well-trained work force available when needed to carry on the production and sales work reflected in the profit plan. In most cases, sales revenue is the *key index* of most other levels of activity throughout the company. For example, assume a 10% increase in sales volume is budgeted for next year. This step-up in total sales volume is "translated" into how many additional employees will be needed (if any) to handle the larger sales and production level, and so on, throughout all areas of the business organization.

Profit planning is the starting point for other financial planning, that is, capital sources and investment planning and cash flow planning. Capital sources and investment planning is directed to the economic resources needed to carry out the budgeted production and sales activity reflected in the profit budget. Given the profit plan, managers must also analyze and plan for the various assets that will be needed, and for how much capital will have to be invested in those assets to support the sales revenue and the production and other operations being budgeted for next year.

Starting with the profit budget for next year, managers must ask questions like the following: Based on the budgeted sales revenue will accounts receivable increase? Will finished goods inventories increase? Based on the budgeted production output for next year, will raw materials and work-in-process inventories increase? How much of the increases in these current assets can be provided by increases in current liabilities, in particular, accounts payable and short-term notes payable? Will new fixed assets have to be acquired to increase production, storage, and delivery capacity for next year's budgeted production and sales levels?

Capital sources and investment planning quite naturally subdivides into: (1) *short-term* planning, which is concerned mainly with current assets and current liabilities; and, (2) *long-term* planning, which is concerned mainly with long-lived assets and the long-term sources of capital to the company. Planning for an increase of accounts receivable due to a budgeted increase of sales revenue for next year, for example, is quite different than purchasing a fixed asset that has a 4-, 10-, or 20-year useful life.

Cash flow planning usually is treated as a *separate* planning function in the business organization, not just as one aspect of capital sources and investment planning. Almost every transaction of the company sooner or later results in a cash receipt or a cash payment. Thus, cash flow planning is very involved and comprehensive. Running out of cash is not only embarrassing, it could be disasterous. Clearly a company needs to maintain an adequate cash balance day to day so that all cash payment obligations can be met on time. The *precise timing and the exact amounts* of cash receipts and payments is very important. Cash flow planning and budgeting focuses on relatively short time intervals, usually no more than a month.

The remainder of this chapter explores profit planning. The next chapter (Chapter Seven) deals with short-term capital sources and investment planning. Chapter Eight discusses cash flow analysis and budgeting. Chapters Nine and Ten consider long-term capital investment planning and analysis. A one-year profit plan for the company example discussed in Chapters Two to Five is developed for next year (1977). Many companies plan profit only one year in advance; that is, they plan profit *in detail* only one year in advance. Profit planning can be done for 2 years, 5 years, or even 10 years.

For the purpose of explaining fundamentals of profit budgeting in this chapter, a one-year profit plan is by far the most convenient to discuss. Longer-term profit planning is much more complex, and in many regards much less precise (though no less important than short-term planning). One-year profit plans usually are quite detailed and thus provide more *control points* against which actual sales revenue and actual operating costs can be compared. The longer the profit plan, as a general rule, the more aggregate and the more summarized is the nature of the profit plan. For instance, a company's 10-year profit "plan" may be no more than a very general statement to "double sales revenue and net income." A company does not leap from one decade to the next. Instead, a company must deal with one year at a time but without ignoring longer-term trends, of course.

Communication and Motivation Aspects for Budgeting: A Brief Note

One approach of developing a profit budget for the coming year is to involve only top level managers, perhaps with the assistance of their staff, that is, without any involvement of middle or lower level managers. In this situation the profit budget tends to be "dictated from the top down" to the lower level managers, who have had very little to say in the development of the budget but who will have the brunt of the responsibility in achieving the profit budget's goals and objectives. It seems foolhardy to ignore the input and experience of middle level and front-line managers in formulating forecasts and estimates for the many different factors that must be considered in the profit planning process. Thus, in many companies these managers are actively involved in the formulation of the profit budget. The profit budgeting process involves the cooperative effort of many different managers at different levels, which should help both management communication within the organization and the motivation of managers.

Communication among managers in the organization should be improved because the profit budget is expressed in fairly specific details instead of in broad general comments. In the budgeting process a good deal of dialogue occurs between different managers. Misunderstandings and disagreements between managers with responsibilities for different parts of the total profit plan come into sharper focus *before* a final decision has to be made and *before* action is taken. Time is available to reach common understanding and mutual agreement, rather than trying to resolve problems under pressure where an urgent decision is necessary. Managers of one department or division should be better able to understand how their decisions and policies interact with and are mutually dependent on other departments and divisions. The sales manager should appreciate production scheduling problems better, and the production manager should better appreciate the competitive pressures on selling the company's products.

Although there is serious debate on the point, there are potential motivational advantages of a profit budgeting process that involves participation of lower and middle levels of managers in "building up" the total profit budget. This cooperative participatory approach, it is argued, should produce more commitment to the achievement of the profit goals and objectives expressed in the budget. Managers, by contributing their part to the total budget, are in essence making a "promise" that they will actually achieve these goals and objectives. Hence, they will try harder to do so than if the goals and objectives were imposed from the top down. This approach to profit budgeting facilitates what is called "management by objectives," which generally refers to the participatory involvement of lower levels of managers with higher levels in the setting of objectives, policies, and strategy.

Sales Forecasting

Profit budgeting starts with the forecast sales revenue for next year. Sales forecasting requires prediction of how many units of each product will be sold at the specific sales prices the company intends to establish for the products. A company must forecast the sales revenue for each product it sells, although different models or sizes of the same basic product may be grouped together. In this example the company sells only one product, which greatly simplifies the amount of detail that must be discussed and analyzed. Usually a company makes *two levels* of sales forecasts: (1) the total market demand for all products of the same basic type, including those products that are direct competitors or close substitutes to the company's products; and, (2) the share or fraction of this total market demand that the company hopes and expects to capture. The company's share of the total market depends on many factors, all subject to change over time, such as price differences, product image and qualitative differences that customers are aware of, differences in the product's warranty and guarantees, and many other differences between the company's product and all the competitive products sold by other companies.

Many serious practical problems complicate the forecasting of total market demand, competition effects, and the company's market share. Forecasting problems are caused by changes in product differentiation, advertising, and customer loyalties to certain brands, as well as shifts in consumer preferences and servicing the product after point of sale. For this example it is assumed that the company's sales managers have done the required analysis of these several factors, and that they have determined the estimated quantity that could be sold at a certain sales price. In summary, the company's vice-president of sales decides that the company's product should be priced at $23 per unit in 1977. At this sales price the best estimate is that 650,000 units will be sold in 1977. The vice-president of sales readily admits that this 650,000 units volume forecast is the center of a possible sales *range,* which extends from 625,000 to 675,000 units. In other words, at the $23 sales price the company may sell 25,000 fewer or 25,000 more than 650,000 units. Basically the forecast sales volume of 650,000 is the most probable estimate for next year.

These "final sales numbers" are only the tip of the iceberg with regard to what must be done in sales forecasting and in communicating the sales goals to all sales managers and salesmen in the organization. The 650,000 units sales volume forecast has to be identified with either specific customers or with specific territories. Specific sales managers and specific salesmen are usually allocated their shares or *quotas* of the total 650,000 units. The total sales forecast is based on the assumption of effective advertising and effective fieldwork by the company's salesmen. The sales price should take into account the type and amount of services the company will provide before and after the sale of the product, as well as the guarantees on the product. In setting the sales price, the costs of manufacturing and distributing the product, as well as the other expenses of the company must also be considered.

Cost Estimation and Forecasting

Fixed Budgeting Versus Variable Budgeting Approaches

A major factor in deciding on the selling price of $23 per unit for next year are the company's budgeted costs for next year, of course. This is not to suggest that a company simply adds a certain percentage markup to cost to determine sales price. Competition, product demand, and many other factors have to be taken into account. In any case, once selling price is established and the forecast sales quantity at the sale price is estimated, attention focuses on the costs of production and operations that will be needed to support the budgeted sales activity. One general cost budgeting approach is to budget costs for the forecast 650,000 units sales level, *and only for that particular sales volume.* This one-level budgeting approach is called *fixed budgeting.* The cost budget is constructed for a fixed sales volume of 650,000 units, without any explicit recognition that the actual sales volume may turn out to be higher or lower than this quantity.

The alternative cost budgeting approach is called *variable budgeting.* The cost budget for next year by this method takes into account that the sales volume may be as much as 25,000 units higher or lower than the forecast of 650,000 units in 1977. The variable budgeting approach determines the *behav-*

ior of costs over the predicted range of sales volumes in 1977, which in this example is from 625,000 to 675,000 units (see discussion above). Few companies can predict their next year's sales volume within one tenth of 1%, or even 1%. Indeed, a company may not be able to forecast its sales volume for next year within plus or minus 10%.

There is nothing wrong with using the sales department's best estimate of sales volume next year as the "center point" for the cost budget, and with building the budgeted net income statement for next year based on this most likely sales forecast of 650,000 units. Indeed, a profit budget for 1977 is presented below that is based on the 650,000 units sales volume level. However, if the actual sales volume in 1977 turns out to be, say, 630,000 units, then the total costs budgeted for a 650,000 units sales level would not be appropriate for the comparison of actual costs (at 630,000 units sales volume) with the original cost budget (at 650,000 units sales volume). The company would need to know what costs should have been at the actual 630,000 units sales level to be able to make meaningful comparisons. The variable budgeting approach anticipates this need. The company budgets its costs over the predicted sales *range* during the original cost budgeting process. At the end of the year, when the actual sales volume is known, the budgeted costs for this particular sales level have been already determined, and they can be immediately referred to for comparison of actual costs with budgeted costs for the year.

Budgeting Production Output: Inventory Changes

Product oriented companies must adopt inventory holding policies. In this example, it is assumed that the policy of the company is to maintain a combined *ending* inventory of finished goods and work-in-process equal to one fourth of the year's sales volume. Remember that products that are only part way through the manufacturing process at the end of the year are converted into an equivalent number of finished units. (See Exhibit 4.2 for review.) Any reasonable mix of work-in-process and finished goods units that gives a total quantity equal to one fourth of the sales volume for the year is acceptable. In this example, therefore, the combined ending quantity of work-in-process and finished goods inventories should be: (650,000 units $\times \frac{1}{4}$ = 162,500 units). The 1977 beginning inventory of work-in-process and finished goods (brought forward from the end of 1976) is equal to 137,500 units—see Exhibit 4.2. Hence, these inventories must increase by a total of 25,000 units in 1977 (162,500 units less 137,500 units). To sum up, the company's production output for 1977 should be budgeted at 675,000 units, which includes 650,000 units to be sold plus the 25,000 units increase of work-in-process and finished goods inventories during the year.

Budgeting Manufacturing Costs

The budgeting of *manufacturing* costs for the production output level of 675,000 units divides into two parts: variable costs and fixed costs. Variable manufacturing costs include many different specific costs, which fall into one of three basic types: raw materials, direct labor, and variable overhead (indirect manufacturing costs). The determination, allocation, and accumulation of these product costs is quite involved, and is discussed in detail in Chapters Twelve to Fourteen. It is assumed that the company's production managers have made all the detailed analysis to determine the company's variable manufacturing costs during 1977.

Without going into all the details of analysis regarding the budgeting of variable manufacturing costs, we mention two primary factors that bear most directly on a company's production costs. The first is the most obvious—the *purchase prices* of raw materials, direct labor, and the many other production inputs and services that are used in the manufacturing process. The second factor is not so obvious—*productivity ratios*. Most companies constantly strive to increase productivity from raw materials, labor, and other inputs and services. Roughly speaking, productivity is the ratio of output to input. For example, one hour of labor produces so many units of output (on average). An increase in productivity means that more units of output result from one hour of labor. Forecasting productivity ratios for the coming year may not be any easier than forecasting purchase prices, although the company's past manufacturing experience may be a better base of experience for predicting productivity next year than the historical purchase prices of materials and labor.

Manufacturing *fixed* costs can be divided into two quite different types: (1) *depreciation* of manufacturing fixed assets (and any amortization of deferred costs that is charged to manufacturing operations), which generally is based on predetermined systematic methods of allocation of these assets costs to each year of useful life of the assets; and (2) *out-of-pocket* costs which, roughly speaking, are paid in cash during the year (for example, fixed salary labor costs). To be more precise, some of these costs may be prepaid a few months in advance (such as insurance premiums), and some may be incurred on a short-term credit basis. Nevertheless, in general, the term out-of-pocket cost is appropriate.

Usually production managers have responsibility for budgeting all manufacturing costs, both variable costs and fixed costs. Budgeting manufacturing depreciation for next year starts with the fixed assets already in use. Then the production manager considers whether any additions or retirements of manufacturing fixed assets are budgeted for next year that would increase (or decrease) the manufacturing depreciation for next year. In this example, notice that the company plans a 20% increase in production output during 1977 compared with 1976: 675,000 units of output are budgeted for 1977 (see above) compared with 562,500 units produced in 1976 (see Exhibit 4.2). This is an increase of 112,500 units, or 20% higher than 1976. The immediate question is: Will the company have to acquire additional fixed assets to expand its production capacity?

We assumed previously (see pages 153 and 154) that the company operated at its practical production capacity level in 1976. Thus the company will need additional production capacity to provide for the budgeted 20% output increase in 1977. Included are a major expansion to the building, which should cost $726,000, new machinery and equipment, which cost $600,000, and additional vehicles, which should cost $66,000. The cost of these items adds to total budgeted capital expenditures of $1,392,000 during 1977.* No additional land is needed. Including the budgeted costs of the new fixed assets, and based on the depreciation methods used by the company, the total manufacturing depreciation to be charged off during 1977 is computed. Probably the accounting department would provide these depreciation amounts to the production manager. (It is assumed no fixed assets will be retired during the year.)

Budgeting the out-of-pocket fixed manufacturing costs for next year requires that each major cost item be carefully estimated based on any changes and new conditions predicted for the following year. Several of these fixed costs may increase as a result of the increase in the budgeted production output for 1977. For example, more production supervisors (paid on a fixed salary basis) may have to be hired at the higher level of production. Real estate taxes will increase, since new buildings will be constructed. Real estate taxes may also increase because of increases in tax levy rates for the coming year. The annual fire insurance premium on the manufacturing buildings, machinery, and equipment will increase because more of these assets will be insured next year. Also, insurance rates may be going up in general. The fixed salaries of production supervisors, maintenance workers, and other manufacturing overhead labor may be higher next year as a result of higher wage levels. Payroll taxes may be higher. And so on.

Fixed manufacturing costs would be analyzed and determined for the budgeted production output level of 675,000 units. But the production managers and accountants who are developing the production budget also should keep in mind that if the actual production level in 1977 turns out to be only, say, 650,000 units, then the company's fixed manufacturing costs could be somewhat less. The lower output level, if this happens, would be known to the production managers before the end of the year, and they would take appropriate action to step down some of the fixed costs, wherever possible. For instance, one or more fixed salary production supervisors may be laid off before the end of the year. Or, the purchase of some of the new fixed assets may be delayed and held over for purchase in 1978, which would avoid depreciation on these assets in 1977. However, total fixed manufacturing costs probably would not decrease very much if the production output level falls short of 675,000 units, since the company is "locked in" to many fixed costs which cannot be decreased quickly. The difference in total fixed manufacturing costs at a lower production level would be only slightly less than the amount budgeted for 1977 at the 675,000 units production output level. But even a small difference is important when one compares budgeted costs with actual costs, which is demonstrated in Chapter Seven.

---

* See Chapters Seven and Nine for a discussion of the management plannnig and analysis leading to these decisions.

Budgeting,Marketing and Administration and General Costs

Budgeting next year's marketing and administration and general costs generally follows the same basic procedures that are discussed above for budgeting manufacturing costs. One important difference is that these other operating costs are based primarily on the budgeted *sales* volume for next year, whereas manufacturing costs are based on the budgeted *production* output for next year. In both the marketing and the administration and general areas there are fixed costs and variable costs. Employees paid on a fixed salary basis account for a large part of the annual fixed costs in each area, although there are many other employees in these two areas who are paid on an hourly basis and these employees would be a variable cost. Salesmen may be paid on an incentive commission basis, which makes these marketing expenses a variable cost.

Some costs have both a fixed *and* a variable component. For instance, the total telephone cost for the year may include a fixed base amount, since a certain number of telephone calls are made each year. whether the company has high or low sales, and since a fixed number of telephones are installed on the company's premises. Beyond this basic number of local and long-distance calls, the number of additional calls may vary in more or less direct proportion to the number of sales orders received and delivered during the year. Delivery costs frequently include both a fixed base cost amount for the year plus a variable cost component. For instance, the company in this example owns a certain number of delivery trucks. The depreciation recorded on its delivery trucks in 1977 will be the same whether 600,000 units are sold and delivered next year, or whether 700,000 units are sold and delivered. But other delivery expenses, such as gas and oil and the number of new truck tires that must be replaced, will vary in more or less direct proportion to the number of units sold and delivered. The annual audit fee charged to the company by its independent CPA's may be fixed in large part. But, the audit bill may increase somewhat as the company's sales revenue increases, since there is a larger volume of transactions and larger asset and liability balances to audit at a higher sales level. In short, many costs are *semifixed* and *semivariable*, that is, part fixed and part variable. Some costs are all fixed, such as the depreciation on the company's office equipment for next year. Some costs are all variable, such as commissions paid salesmen which are a certain percentage of sales revenue. But many of a company's nonmanufacturing operating costs include both a fixed cost component and a variable cost component. These "mixed" costs must be budgeted in two steps.

First, the fixed cost "floor" of the total cost is determined. Then, the variable cost component is determined and usually is expressed as a certain amount per unit of product sold or as a certain percentage of sales revenue. Each such "semifixed/semivariable" cost is a different problem. For one example, consider again the company's annual telephone cost. On analysis of past experience the management accountant or budget analyst may find that each year there are a certain number of required local calls and that this number of local calls is the same whether the company's sales volume is at the low end of its predicted range or at the high end next year. On the other hand, the number of long-distance calls may vary in proportion to the number of sales orders processed.

Given these assumptions, therefore, next year's budgeted telephone expense might be computed somewhat as follows:

Computation on Next Year's Budgeted Telephone Expense		
Fixed Cost	Estimated cost of local calls, based on telephone charges for local calls for next year (which probably depends mainly on the number of telephones installed on the company's premises)	$xx,xxx
Variable Cost	Expected number of long distance calls (based on budgeted sales volume expressed in number of sales orders) times the average cost per long-distance call (based on long-distance toll charges predicted for next year)	xx,xxx
Total Cost		$xx,xxx

As this one example indicates, budgeting each and every marketing and administration and general cost item in this much detail would be time-consuming. Companies may use more approximate "quick and dirty" techniques. For instance, many separate but related cost items may be grouped together. Only the more material cost items are scrutinized as closely as indicated in the telephone expense example.

Finally, some of the fixed costs of marketing and some of the administration and general fixed costs could be stepped down if the company's actual sales volume next year turns out to be lower than the budgeted sales volume. For instance, the company in this example plans to spend a sizeable amount on advertising to promote the budgeted sales volume of 650,000 units at the budgeted $23 sales price. Most of this advertising outlay budgeted for next year is a fixed cost once the decision is made to run an advertisement on television or in a newspaper. If actual sales in 1977 fall short of 650,000 units, then some of the planned advertising may be eliminated or scaled down to reduce this cost. Some employees paid on a fixed salary basis could be laid off. As some employees quit, the company may not replace them in order to reduce its fixed salary expense for the year.

Summing up: Presentation of Next Year's Budgeted Net Income Statement of Company

Exhibit 6.2 presents the company's budgeted net income statement for 1977, which is basd on all the preceding discussion and assumptions in this chapter. As we have already indicated, the "final numbers" shown in the profit plan

EXHIBIT 6.2
1977 Budgeted Net Income Statement with Comparison to 1976

Line		1977 650,000 units			1976 550,000 units		
		Percents	Dollar Value per Unit		Percents	Dollar Value per Units	
(a)	Sales Volume Base						
(b)	Sales revenue	100.0	$23.000	$14,950,000	100.0	$21.500	$11,825,000
	Cost of goods sold:						
	Variable costs—						
(c)	Raw materials	20.5	$ 4.721	$3,068,650	21.5	$ 4.630	$2,546,500
(d)	Direct labor	24.9	5.716	3,715,400	26.4	5.674	3,120,700
(e)	Overhead	4.8	1.103	716,950	4.9	1.046	575,300
(f)	Total variable costs	50.2	$11.540	$7,501,000	52.8	$11.350	$6,242,500
	Fixed costs—						
(g)	Direct labor	1.5	$ 0.312	$ 202,800	1.2	$ 0.258	$ 141,900
(h)	Overhead	8.0	1.863	1,210,950	7.2	1.558	856,900
(i)	Total fixed costs	9.5	$ 2.175	$1,413,750	8.4	$ 1.816	$ 998,800
(j)	Total cost of goods sold	59.7	$13.715	8,914,750	61.2	$13.166	7,241,300
(k)	Gross profit	40.3	$ 9.285	$ 6,035,250	38.8	$ 8.334	$ 4,583,700
	Operating costs:						
	Variable costs—						
(l)	Marketing	23.9	$ 5.500	$3,575,000	24.0	$ 5.150	$2,832,500
(m)	Administrative and general	0.7	0.170	110,500	0.7	0.160	88,000
(n)	Total variable costs	24.6	$ 5.670	$3,685,500	24.7	$ 5.310	$2,920,500
	Fixed costs—						
(o)	Marketing	2.5	$ 0.580	$ 377,000	3.0	$ 0.636	$ 349,800
(p)	Administrative and general	2.8	0.635	412,750	2.8	0.610	335,500
(q)	Total fixed costs	5.3	$ 1.215	$ 789,750	5.8	$ 1.246	$ 685,300
(r)	Total operating costs	29.9	$ 6.885	4,475,250	30.5	$ 6.556	3,605,800
(s)	Operating profit	10.4	$ 2.400	$ 1,560,000	8.3	$ 1.778	$ 977,900
(t)	Interest expense	(average debt=$3,000,000×9.0%)		270,000	(average debt=$2,250,000×8.0%)		180,000
(u)	Net income before tax			$ 1,290,000			$ 797,900
(v)	Income tax	($1,290,000×48% less $6,500)		612,700	$797,900×48% less $6,500)		376,492
(w)	Net income			$ 677,300			$ 421,408

(Exhibit 6.2) are built up from a great deal of detailed analysis. For instance, the budgeted raw material cost per unit—see line (c) in Exhibit 6.2—is the sum of a very detailed schedule that lists all the different material items used in the manufacturing process, the predicted purchase prices of each item, and the raw material usage predictions about each item such as the expected percentage of raw material wastage and spoilage that is normal for most production processes. In short, a voluminous amount of detail is contained in the supporting schedules that dovetail into each line shown in the budgeted net income statement (Exhibit 6.2).

A few final comments about the company's 1977 profit budget are in order here. The budgeted operating profit ratio for 1977 is 10.4%—see line (s) in Exhibit 6.2. Earlier in the chapter (page 185) it is shown that the company needs to earn a 15.1% return on assets to achieve its return on equity goal of 12.0% in 1977. Given the budgeted 10.4% profit ratio for 1977, the company's asset turnover ratio in 1977 will have to be as follows:

Return on Assets	=	Asset Turnover Ratio	×	Profit Ratio
15.1%	=	?	×	10.4%
Answer: 15.1%/10.4%	=	1.45		

In 1976 the company's asset turnover ratio is 1.37 (see Exhibit 6.1). Whether the company can achieve the 1.45 asset turnover ratio depends on how much its total assets will increase all the higher sales revenue in 1977.

The company's total assets should not increase above $10,309,685 in order to keep the company's asset turnover ratio at or above 1.45: ($14,950,000 budgeted sales revenue divided by 1.45 asset turnover ratio=$10,309,685). Compared with the $8,601,500 total assets at year-end 1976, total assets, therefore, should not increase more than $1,708,385 during 1977: ($10,309,685 less $8,601,-500=+$1,708,385). As mentioned above, capital expenditures (purchases of new fixed assets) of $1,392,000 are planned for 1977 (see page 196). And, the company plans to increase its work-in-process and finished goods inventories during 1977 (see pages 193 and 194). Hence, these two asset increases approach the limit before there is any consideration of increases in accounts receivable and other assets.

In the next chapter we discuss budgeting for asset increases, which is based on the budgeted net income statement for 1977. We also examine planning for the amounts and sources of capital needed to increase the company's asset investments. Nothing discussed in this chapter explains the increase in the average debt to $3 million—see line (t) in Exhibit 6.2. However, it is useful to present a *complete* budgeted net income statement for next year, including the interest expense and the income tax expense, so that the final net income can be shown.

In conclusion, the company's budgeted net income statement for 1977 (Exhibit 6.2) is the main connecting link between this and the next chapter. From this key budget document the managers can plan for and budget the specific asset increases that will be needed next year to support the higher level of sales revenue and manufacturing and other operating costs. Based on these budgeted asset increases, the managers can then analyze how much additional capital will be needed, which in turn leads to the analysis of how much of this total capital will be provided from net income, how much from increases in accounts payable, how much may have to be borrowed on interest bearing debts, and whether any additional capital will have to be provided from stockholders.

Finally, and most important, the 1977 budgeted net income statement is the main source of information for the comparison of the company's *actual* profit performance in 1977 against what the company budgeted for and should have achieved in 1977. By making this comparison of actual against budget, managers can determine where and why actual profit performance deviated from the profit plan for the year, which is the essential starting point for management control.

Questions

6. 1   If a company's return on equity is too low, what are the basic changes management would try to make to improve the rate of return on equity?

6. 2   If a company is able to improve its asset turnover ratio by 5.0% (for example, from 2.00 to 2.10) and also improves its profit ratio by 10.0% (for example, from 10.0% to 11.0%), then how much improvement would result in the operating profit rate of return on assets? You might want to set up a simple numerical example to show support for your answer.

6. 3   The general manager of a small business believes he is too busy for planning, which he says is not much more than "feet on the desk, wishful thinking" anyway. Do you agree? How would you respond to this manager?

6. 4   "The Controller is the chief management officer of the company who establishes the company's financial goals, objectives, policies, and strategies." Do you agree? Briefly explain.

6. 5   "The best long-term plan is to solve each short-run problem as the problem arises; long-term plans are too general to anticipate all the day-to-day short-run problems that come up." Do you agree? Briefly explain.

6. 6   What are the three basic areas of financial planning, and which is most important?

6. 7   "The basic plan of any business organization is *survival.*" Comment on this statement. What are some of its implications, assuming this statement is correct?

6. 8   What is the difference between *budgeting* and *budget?*

6. 9 (a) Why is total sales revenue a good general index of other activity levels throughout the business organization?

(b) What is the importance of the key index nature of sales revenue for budgeting?

6.10 Why is cash flow planning (and budgeting) treated as a *separate* management planning function?

6.11 How does budgeting improve communication among managers?

6.12 (a) Should budgeting have a positive role in the motivation of managers and other employees?

(b) Might budgeting be a *dis*-motivation factor? How?

6.13 Where does profit budgeting for next year begin? Briefly explain.

6.14 In general terms what are some of the basic factors that a company's sales department considers in developing the sales forecast for the coming year?

6.15 What is the main difference between the fixed budgeting approach and the variable budgeting approach for budgeting costs?

6.16 Assume that the company in the example discussed throughout the chapter decides to change its inventory policy in 1977. Instead of holding a combined ending inventory of work-in-process and finished goods equal to one fourth of the year's sales, the company decides that its ending inventory should be one fifth of sales:

(a) Based on this different policy, how many units would be manufactured in 1977? Show your supporting computations.

(b) Given the revised budgeted production output you determined in part (a), what are some of the major changes in budgeted manufacturing costs for 1977? Only discuss these changes; do *not* make any computations.

6.17 Contrast the budgeting of manufacturing depreciation for next year with the budgeting of manufacturing fixed out-of-pocket costs for next year.

6.18 What is one key difference between budgeting manufacturing costs for next year versus budgeting marketing and administration and general costs for next year?

6.19 What is a semifixed cost?

6.20 Other than the examples used in the chapter, can you think of two or three non-manufacutring fixed costs that could be stepped down during the year if actual sales fall short of budgeted sales?

Problems

P6. 1 A company's financial condition at the close of its most recent year in extremely condensed form and in terms of percents only is as follows:

		Noninterest Bearing Liabilities	5%
		Interest bearing Debts (at 9.5% average	
		annual interest rate)	30%
		Stockholders' Equity	65%
Total Assets	100%	Total Capital Sources	100%

For the year just ended the asset turnover ratio was 2.57 and the company's operating profit ratio was 5.00% of sales revenue. Assume a flat 48% income tax rate on the company's taxable income. The company is not satisfied with its return on equity performance. Indeed, the company would like to earn a 12.0% return on equity next year.

Required:

(1) Compute the company's rate of return on equity for the year just ended. Show your work clearly.
(2) If all the improvement must come from an improvement in the operating profit ratio, determine what the operating profit ratio will have to be next year to achieve a 12.0% return on equity.
(3) If all the improvement must come from an improvement in the asset turnover ratio, determine what the asset turnover ratio would have to be next year to achieve a 12.0% return on equity.
(4) If all the improvement must come from an improvement in financial leverage effects, and assuming that the percent of noninterest bearing liabilities to total assets will not change and that the average annual interest rate on all debt will not change, determine how much of the stockholders' equity would have to be replaced with interest bearing debt to achieve a 12.0% return on equity next year.

P6. 2 In brief and condensed form the company's financial statements for the year just ended are as follows (in thousands of dollars):

Total assets	$2,400	Sales revenue	$9,080
Noninterest bearing		Cost of goods sold	5,902
liabilities	$ 200	Gross profit	$3,178
Interest bearing		Operating expenses	2,724
liabilities	640	Operating profit	$ 454
Stockholders' equity	1,560	Interest expense	64
Total capital sources	$2,400	Taxable income	$ 390
		Income tax	195
		Net income	$ 195

In planning for next year the company has decided that its return on equity should be at least 15.0%.

Required: Assume that the company can change only one of the following basic factors next year and that all other key factors remain the same. Thus all of the improvement in the company's return on equity performance must come from the one factor that is changed next year. Determine what each of the following would have to be next year to achieve the company's return on equity goal:

(1) Asset turnover ratio.

(2) Operating profit ratio (as percent of sales revenue).

(3) Average interest rate on all liabilities.

(4) Replacement of stockholders' equity with interest bearing liabilities.

(5) Replacement of stockholders' equity with noninterest bearing liabilities.

P6. 3 For the year just ended the company's financial performance is summarized by the following key ratios and dollar balances:

(a) Asset turnover ratio = 2.50.

(b) Operating profit (before interest and income tax) ratio of sales revenue = 4.00%.

(c) Total assets = $400,000.

(d) Total liabilities = $150,000 (including $25,000 noninterest bearing liabilities).

(e) Total stockholders' equity = $250,000.

(f) Total interest expense = $10,000.

(g) Income tax expense = 50% of taxable income (including federal and state taxes).

Required:

(1) Determine the return on assets and return on equity of the company for the year just ended.

(2) Assume that the company's Board of Directors establishes a 9.0% return on equity goal for next year.

　　(a) If all of the improvement must come from the asset turnover ratio and all other factors remain the same next year, determine what the asset turnover ratio would have to be next year to reach the ROE goal.

　　(b) If the maximum feasible asset turnover ratio next year is 3.00 and the remainder of the improvement in the ROE ratio must come from increasing the profit ratio, and assuming other factors remain the same next year, determine what the profit ratio would have to be next year to reach the ROE goal.

(3) Assume that the company's Board of Directors establishes a 12.0% return on equity goal for next year. And, assume that the company expects to increase its profit ratio to 6.00% and increase its asset turnover ratio to 2.75.

　　(a) Would these changes be sufficient to reach the ROE goal?

　　(b) If not, assume that the average interest rate on liabilities will remain the same but that the company can replace some stockholders' equity capital with interest bearing liabilities. Determine how much increase in interest bearing liabilities (in substitution for stockholders' equity) would be needed to reach the company's ROE goal.

P6. 4 For several years this company has followed a very conservative financial policy of using no interest bearing debt. In fact, noninterest bearing liabilities have also been minimized and on average have been only about 5.0% of total assets. For the year just ended the company earned a return on assets of 23.75% on total assets of $14,300,000. The company's asset turnover ratio has been very close to

2.50 for several years. To expand production and sales capacity, the company plans to purchase an existing plant (buildings and machinery) from a competitor who is quitting business. The purchase cost of these additional fixed assets is $4,290,000. Actually, this purchase will give the company more additional capacity than is immediately needed over the next two to three years, but in the long run the purchase of the plant is far cheaper than building a new building and buying new machinery and equipment. However, the president is concerned that the additional fixed assets will cause the company's asset turnover ratio next year to decrease to 2.20.

Also, the stockholders' have expressed some reluctance to put up another $4 million unless the company can maintain or improve its return on equity performance. But the president believes there is no way to improve the profit ratio. Therefore, he has decided to borrow $4,290,000. The annual interest rate on this debt will be 8.5%. The income tax rate is a flat 48% of taxable income.

Assume that next year's sales revenue is $44,987,800 and that total assets (ending balance) are $20,449,000 (which includes the purchase of the additional fixed assets described above). There were no borrowings on interest bearing debt other than for the purchase of the additional fixed assets described above, and no payments were made on this liability during the year.

Required: In the manner shown in Exhibit 6.1 present an analysis of the company's return on equity for:
(1) The year just ended.
(2) Next year, based on the above assumptions and information.

P6. 5 Refer to Exhibit 6.1 for the analysis of reutrn on equity in 1976 for the example discussed in the chapter. This problem begins with the data and information shown for the company in Exhibit 6.1. Assume that the Board of Directors of the company establishes a 15.0% return on equity goal for 1977.

Required:
(1) If all of the improvement must come from an improvement in the profit ratio, determine what the company's 1977 profit ratio would have to be to reach the ROE goal, assuming all other factors remain the same in 1977.
(2) Assume that the asset turnover ratio can be increased to 2.0 in 1977, but that no improvement can be made in the profit ratio.
  (a) If the percent of liabilities to total assets is not changed, determine what the average interest rate on liabilities would have to be to provide enough leverage gain to reach the ROE goal in 1977. To standardize computations use the 1976 operating profit ratio of 8.27% as a precise percent (even though this is a rounded off percent).
  (b) If the average interest rate on liabilities is not changed, and assuming interest bearing liabilities could be substituted for stockholders' equity capital, determine what percentage of the company's total assets would have to be supplied by liabilities to reach the company's ROE goal in 1977.

P6. 6 The company in this problem manufactures and sells three basic products. The sales performance of each product for the last five years is given below:

Year	Product A			Product B			Product C		
	Sales Quantity	Sales Price	Sales Revenue	Sales Quantity	Sales Price	Sales Revenue	Sales Quantity	Sales Price	Sales Revenue
1972	1,210,000	$1.50000	$1,815,000	500,000	$10.0000	$5,000,000	100,000	$ 5.0000	$ 500,000
1973	1,331,000	1.65000	2,196,150	501,000	10.5000	5,260,500	90,000	5.5000	495,000
1974	1,464,100	1.81500	2,657,342	499,500	11.0250	5,506,988	81,000	6.0500	490,050
1975	1,610,510	1.99650	3,215,383	500,000	11.5763	5,788,150	72,900	6.6550	485,150
1976	1,771,561	2.19615	3,890,614	500,200	12.1551	6,079,981	65,610	7.3205	480,298

The general sales manager of the company is preparing a sales forecast for next year, 1977, for each product line. The first step is to find out if there is any detectable pattern of consistency over the last five years that might be a good clue for forecasting next year's sales. Of course, this does not mean that the sales manager simply assumes that history will repeat itself exactly. But the historical pattern, if there is one evident in the data, is a good starting point for forecasting next year's sales.

Required: For each product line analyze the last five years of sales data and, based on your findings, predict next year's sales if the same pattern holds for 1977 that is demonstrated for the past five years.

P6. 7   As we discussed in the chapter, a sales forecast for the coming year cannot be expected to provide a pinpoint estimate of exactly how many units of a product will be sold, down to the last digit. Instead, a sales forecast usually provides a range or interval within which actual sales next year should probably fall. This forecast range for the company example is stated to be 625,000 to 675,000 units for 1977. You can see in Exhibit 6.2 that the midpoint of this forecast range, that is, 650,000 units, is used to prepare the budgeted net income statement for 1977.

The president of the company would like to know what net income in 1977 would be if the "worst" happens and the company sells only 625,000 units (at the $23 budgeted sales price). Also, he would like to know what 1977 net income would be if the "best" happens and the company sells 675,000 units (at the $23 budgeted sales price).

Required: Determine net income for 1977 for the "worst" case and for the "best" case. You do *not* have to prepare a formal, completely detailed budgeted profit statement for each case, such as is shown in Exhibit 6.2. But you should show enough of your supporting computations to make clear your expense amounts.

(*Note:* Assume that all fixed costs and interest expense in 1977 are the same across the entire sales forecast range. This is probably not completely realistic, but it does simplify the problem considerably. Also, assume that the production output for 1977 is based on the original sales budget volume of 650,000 units, and that this quantity is produced during the year even though the sales volume falls short in the "worst" case and the sales volume is higher in the "best" case.)

P6. 8   This company sells three basic products, called X, Y, and Z. The sales prices, sales quantities, and variable costs for the year ended December 31, 1976 were as follows:

Product	Total Units Sold	Average Sales Price	Variable Manufacturing Costs Labor	Raw Materials	Total Sales Revenue	Total Variable Costs
X	68,000	$18.250	$6.500	$4.000	$1,241,000	$ 714,000
Y	31,000	23.500	6.500	5.000	728,500	356,500
Z	26,000	32.500	6.500	6.500	845,000	338,000
Totals	125,000				$2,814,500	$1,408,500

All other operating costs are fixed costs, which in 1976 were as follows:

Manufacturing	$ 525,000
Marketing	271,000
Administration and general	328,800
Total	$1,124,800

Next year the labor cost per hour will increase 10.0% starting January 1, 1977 under the terms of the union contract with the company. However, labor productivity on average should increase 4.0%, which means for example that if a particular operation took 10.0 hours in 1976 only 9.6 hours should be required in 1977. Raw materials' purchase prices in 1977 will probably increase by 20.0% on all items. The company does not see any way to improve the raw materials' productivity ratios next year. The sales manager has prepared the following sales forecast for 1977:

Product	Sales Quantity	Sales Price
X	75,000 units	$18.50
Y	32,000 units	25.00
Z	30,000 units	35.00

Fixed costs should increase by 15.0% on average in 1977.

Required: Prepare the 1977 budgeted operating profit performance statement for the company, with comparison to 1976 actual operating profit performance, in as much detail as is possible from the information given above. Do *not* include interest and income tax expenses in your statement. Also, ignore inventory changes during each year.

P6. 9   Refer to the company example introduced in Problem 2.6 and the additional information for this company presented in Problem 4.10. In particular, it is assumed that you have prepared the two-year management profit performance report for the company for 1975 and 1976.

The following forecasts and estimates have been made by various managers in the organization for 1977:

(a) Sales price per unit $156.50
(b) Sales volume   24,000 units to 28,000 units
(c) Inventory quantity policy: ending inventory equals one fifth of year's sales volume

(d) Marketing variable expenses per unit $ 16.00
(e) Purchase price per unit $ 98.75
(f) Administration and general variable expenses per unit $ 2.31
(g) Fixed costs should increase by 10.0%.
(h) Total interest bearing debt should average $275,000 and the average annual interest rate should be 10.0%.
(i) Income tax rate should not change.

Required: Prepare the company's budgeted 1977 net income statement based on the above information for three different sales levels:

(1) The "worst" case (24,000 units),
(2) The "most probable" case (26,000 units), and
(3) The "best" case (28,000 units).

Assume that fixed costs and the interest expense are constant over the entire sales range. However, assume that the company strictly observes its ending inventory policy [see item (c) above] in all three cases. It is suggested that you include three columns in your statement, one for each case.

P6.10 The company has adopted the following flexible budgeting assumptions for the coming quarter (three months) for one of its production plants that manufactures only one product:

Raw material	15 pounds	×	$6.25 per pound	=	$ 93.75
Direct labor	4 hours	×	7.50 per hour	=	30.00
Variable overhead	4 hours	×	3.15 per hour	=	12.60
Total variable manufacturing cost per unit					$136.35

Fixed overhead:
24,000 to 32,000 hours	=	$316,875
32,001 to 36,000 hours	=	356,400
36,001 to 40,000 hours	=	389,550

This production plant ships the finished products to a warehouse and has no further responsibility for the goods after the manufacturing process is completed. The plant's maximum production output capacity for three months, under normal working conditions, is 40,000 direct labor hours.

For each coming quarter the general manager must prepare a production budget for the plant which is forwarded to the general office of the company and is included in the overall budget for the entire company. The plant budget is prepared on the flexible budgeting basis, as the data shown above illustrate.

Required: Prepare the production costs budget for the coming quarter for the plant for three different production output levels:

(1) 7500 units of product,
(2) 8800 units of product, and

(3) 9800 units of product.

Include in your budget the manufacturing cost per unit at each output level.

(*Note:* Problem 7.8 will compare the plant's actual costs for the quarter against the production budget for the quarter.)

P6.11   The administrator of Community Hospital has presented you with a number of service projections for the year ending June 30, 1977. Estimated room requirements for inpatients by type of service are:

Type of Patient	Total Patients Expected	Average Number of Days in Hospital		Percentage of Regular Patients Selecting Types of Service		
		Regular	Medicare	Private	Semiprivate	Ward
Medical	2100	7	17	10	60	30
Surgical	2400	10	15	15	75	10

Of the patients served by the hospital 10% are expected to be Medicare patients, all of whom are expected to select semiprivate rooms. Both the number and proportion of Medicare patients have increased over the past five years. Daily rentals per patient are: $40 for a private room, $35 for a semiprivate room, and $25 for a ward.

Operating room charges are based on man-minutes (number of minutes the operating room is in use multiplied by number of personnel assisting in the operation). The per man-minute charges are $.13 for inpatients and $.22 for outpatients. Studies for the current year (1976) show that operations on inpatients are divided as follows:

Type of Operations	Number of Operations	Average Number of Minutes per Operation	Average Number of Personnel Required
A	800	30	4
B	700	45	5
C	300	90	6
D	200	120	8
	2,000		

The same proportion of inpatient operations is expected for next fiscal year (1977), and 180 outpatients are expected to use the operating room. Outpatient operations average 20 minutes and require the assistance of three persons.

Required: Prepare statements showing the computation of:
(1) The number of patient days (number of patients multiplied by average stay in hospital) expected by type of patients and service.
(2) The total number of man-minutes expected for operating room services for inpatients and outpatients. For inpatients show the breakdown of total operating room man-minutes by type of operation.
(3) Expected gross revenue from routine services.
(4) Expected gross revenue from operating room services.

P6.12 This company mines and processes rock and gravel. It started in business on January 1, 1976 when it purchased the assets of another company. The adjusted trial balance of the company at the end of the first year of business is as follows:

ADJUSTED TRIAL BALANCE
December 31, 1976

Cash	$ 21,000	
Accounts receivable	24,000	
Mining properties	60,000	
Accumulated depletion		$ 3,000
Equipment	150,000	
Accumulated depreciation		10,000
Accounts payable		30,000
Federal income taxes payable		4,000
Notes payable to officers		40,000
Capital stock		100,000
Premium on capital stock		46,000
Sales revenue		300,000
Production costs (including depreciation and depletion)	179,000	
Administrative expense (including interest)	77,000	
Federal income tax expense	22,000	
	$533,000	$533,000

Assume the following information for 1977:
(a) The total yards of material sold is expected to increase 10% and the average sales price per cubic yard will be increased from $1.50 to $1.60.
(b) The estimated recoverable reserves of rock and gravel were 4 million cubic yards when the properties were purchased.
(c) Production costs in 1976 include direct labor of $110,000 of which $10,000 was attributed to inefficiencies in the early stages of operation. The union contract calls for 5% increases in hourly rates effective January 1, 1977. Production costs, other than depreciation, depletion, and direct labor, will increase 4% in 1977.

(d) Administrative expense, other than interest, will increase $8000 in 1977.

(e) The company has contracted for additional movable equipment costing $60,000 to be in production on July 1, 1977. This equipment will result in a direct labor hour savings of 8% as compared with the last half of 1976. The new equipment will have a life of 20 years. All depreciation is computed on the straight-line method. The old equipment will continue in use.

(f) The new equipment will be financed by a 20% down payment and a 9.0% three-year installment loan. Interest and equal principal payments are due semiannually on June 30 and December 31, beginning December 31, 1977. The notes payable to officers are demand notes on which 6% interest is provided for and was paid on December 31, 1976. (A full year's interest was paid.)

(g) Accounts receivable will increase in proportion to sales. No bad debts are anticipated. Accounts payable will remain substantially the same amount.

(h) For income tax purposes the company must deduct depletion based on the cost of its mining properties, or must deduct 5% of sales revenue instead of depletion based on cost, whichever is larger. If the second alternative is followed, then the depletion deduction is limited to 50% of taxable income before depletion is deducted.

(i) It is customary in the rock and gravel business not to place any value on stockpiles of processed material that are awaiting sale.

(j) Assume a flat income tax rate of 50% and to retire the notes payable to officers before any cash dividends are paid.

(k) The company has decided to maintain a minimum cash balance of $20,000.

Required: Prepare the 1977 budgeted net income statement for the company, with a comparison to the 1976 actual net income statement.

(*Note:* Problem 7.9 will also make use of the above information as well as your budgeted net income statement for 1977.)

P6.13 Niwot College has asked your assistance in developing its budget for the coming 1977-78 academic year. The college operates on the semester basis; there are two semesters per academic year, of course. The college does *not* offer any summer session courses. You are supplied with the following data for the current (1976-77) year:

(a)

	Lower Division (Freshman-Sophomore)	Upper Division (Junior-Senior)
Average number of students per class	25	20
Average salary of faculty member	$15,000	$18,000
Average number of credit hours carried each year per student	33	30
Enrollment including scholarship students	2,500	1,700
Average faculty teaching load in credit hours per year (8 classes of 3 credit hours)	24	24

For 1977-78, lower division enrollment is expected to increase by 10%, while the upper division's enrollment is expected to remain stable. Faculty salaries will be increased by a standard 5%, and additional merit increases to be awarded to individual faculty members will be $136,125 for the lower division and $153,000 for the upper division.

(b) The current budget is $346,500 for operation and maintenance of plant and equipment; this includes $148,500 for salaries and wages. Experience of the past three months suggests that the current budget is realistic, but that expected increases for 1977-78 are 5% in salaries and wages and $14,850 in other expenditures for operation and maintenance of plant and equipment.

(c) The budget for the remaining expenditures for 1977-78 is as follows:

Administrative and general	$396,000
Library	264,000
Health and recreation	123,750
Athletics	198,000
Insurance and retirement	437,250
Interest	79,200
Capital outlay	495,000

(d) The college expects to award 25 tuition-free scholarships to lower division students and 15 to upper division students. Tuition is $36 per credit hour and no other fees are charged.

(e) Budgeted revenues for 1977-78 are as follows:

Endowment income	$188,100
Net income from auxiliary services	387,750
Athletics	297,000

The college's remaining source of revenue is an annual support campaign held during the spring.

Required:

(1) Prepare a schedule computing for 1977-78 by division (a) the expected enrollment, (b) the total credit hours to be carried, and (c) the number of faculty members needed.

(2) Prepare a schedule computing the budget for faculty salaries by division for 1977-78.

(3) Prepare a schedule computing the tuition revenue budget by division for 1977-78.

(4) Prepare a schedule computing the amount that must be raised during the annual support campaign to cover the 1977-78 expenditures budget.

P6.14 This company operates a ski shop, restaurant, and ski lodge during the 120-day ski season from November 15 to March 15. The proprietor (general manager) is considering changing his operations and keeping the ski lodge open all year. Results of the operations for the year ended March 15, 1976 were as follows:

	Ski Shop		Restaurant		Ski Lodge	
	Amount	Percent	Amount	Percent	Amount	Percent
Revenue	$ 27,000	100%	$ 40,000	100%	$108,000	100%
Costs:						
Cost of goods sold	14,850	55	24,000	60	—	—
Supplies	1,350	5	4,000	10	7,560	7
Utilities	270	1	1,200	3	2,160	2
Salaries	1,620	6	12,000	30	32,400	30
Insurance	810	3	800	2	9,720	9
Property taxes on building	540	2	1,600	4	6,480	6
Depreciation	1,080	4	2,000	5	28,080	26
Total costs	$ 20,520	76	$ 45,600	114	$ 86,400	80
Net income or (loss)	$ 6,480	24%	$ (5,600)	(14%)	$ 21,600	20%

Other pertinent information follows:
(a) The lodge has 100 rooms and the rate from November 15 to March 15 is $10 per day for one or two persons. The average occupancy rate from November 15 to March 15 is 90%.
(b) Ski shop and restaurant sales vary in direct proportion to room occupancy.
(c) For the ski shop and restaurant, cost of goods sold, supplies, and utilities vary in direct proportion to sales. For the lodge, supplies and utilities vary in direct proportion to room occupancy.
(d) The ski shop, restaurant, and lodge are located in the same building. Depreciation on the building is charged to the lodge. The ski shop and restaurant are charged with depreciation only on equipment. The full cost of the restaurant equipment became entirely depreciated on March 15, 1976 but the equipment has a remaining useful life of three years. The equipment can be sold for $1200 but will be worthless in three years. All depreciation is computed by the straight-line method.
(e) Insurance premiums are for annual coverage for public liability and fire insurance on the building and equipment. All building insurance is charged to the lodge.
(f) Salaries are the minimum necessary to keep each facility open and are for the ski season only with the exception of the lodge security guard who is paid $5400 per year.

Two alternatives are being considered for the future operation by the general manager (proprietor):

(a) The proprietor believes that during the ski season the restaurant should be closed because "it does not have enough revenue to cover its out-of-pocket costs." It is estimated that lodge occupancy would drop to 80% of capacity if the restaurant were closed during the ski season. The space utilized by the restaurant would be used as a lounge for lodge guests.

(b) The proprietor is considering keeping the lodge open from March 15 to November 15. The ski shop would be converted into a gift shop if the lodge should be operated during this period with conversion costs of $1000 in March and $1000 in November each year. It is estimated that revenues from the gift shop would be the same per room occupied as revenues from the ski shop, that variable costs would be in the same ratio to revenues, and that all other costs would be the same for the gift shop as for the ski shop. The occupancy rate of the lodge at a room rate of $7 per day is estimated at 50% during the period from March 15 to November 15 whether or not the restaurant is operated.

Required: (Ignore income taxes and use 30 days per month for computational purposes.)

(1) Prepare a projected income statement for the ski shop and lodge from November 15, 1976 to March 15, 1977, assuming the restaurant is closed during this period and all facilities are closed during the remainder of the year.

(2) Assume that all facilities will continue to be operated during the four-month period of November 15 to March 15 of each year.
  (a) Assume that the lodge is operated during the eight months from March 15 to November 15. Prepare an analysis that indicates the projected marginal income or loss of operating the gift shop and lodge during this eight-month period.
  (b) Compute the minimum room rate which should be charged to allow the lodge to breakeven during the eight months from March 15 to November 15 assuming the gift shop and restaurant are not operated during this period.

P6.15 A few weeks ago a few investors pooled their capital and organized a corporation to begin the manufacturing and selling of a new technical and high-priced product for which the corporation has just secured a patent, which should limit direct competition against this product for some time. At the present time, December 31, 1976, all the various machinery and equipment has been purchased and installed, and the company is ready to begin manufacturing the product. In fact, several orders have been already received even though the company's salesmen do not yet have an actual sample of the product to show customers. The company is quite optimlstic about thc sales of the product.

The balance sheet of the company at December 31, 1976 is as follows:

Cash	$515,000	Long-term Notes Payable	
Prepaid Expenses	10,000	(at 8% annual interest	
Buildings	100,000	rate)	$250,000
Machinery and Equipment	250,000	Stockholders' Equity:	
Accumulated Depreciation	—0—	Invested Capital	700,000
Land	75,000	Retained Earnings	—0—
Total Assets	$950,000	Total Sources of Capital	$950,000

The company's president studied budgeting in his college days and is convinced of the value of good budgeting for financial planning and control purposes. Since the company has not yet employed an experienced accountant, the president has engaged a CPA to come in and prepare a budget for the next year, which will be the first year of manufacturing and selling the new product. Based on interviews with the managers in charge of production, selling, and finance, the CPA has compiled the following list of basic assumptions, forecasts, and information.

(*Note:* All references are to the calendar year 1977 and apply to the total year unless stated otherwise. For instance, the forecasted selling price means that this sales price will be in effect during the entire year.)

(1) The company's sales manager estimates that 2100 units will be sold at the selling price of $2600 per unit. Thirty days credit will be offered to all customers, with no cash discounts for early payment. It is expected that all customers will take full advantage of the credit period, and then will pay their debts owed to the company. For simplicity, it is assumed here that the sales will be level during the year, although in fact the sales in the first month or two may be less than in the later months. Hence, assume a constant amount of sales each month during the year.

(2) The company's production manager estimates that the variable manufacturing costs per unit *produced* will be as follows:

Raw materials (including all items)	$ 400
Direct labor (including all manufacturing operations)	550
Variable overhead (including all costs)	100
Total variable manufacturing cost per unit	$1050

These are all *out-of-pocket costs.* Out-of-pocket costs are those costs paid for in cash either immediately at the time of recording the cost or are those items purchased on short-term trade credit (accounts payable). Assume that one tenth of this *total* cost for the year will be payable at year-end. This ending balance in the Accounts Payable takes into account the buildup of raw materials inventory during the year, see (3) below, and the buildup of finished goods inventory, see (4) below.

(3) The company's production manager would like to carry a large supply of raw materials to prevent any stock-outs that would interrupt production. But the financial manager points out that capital must be invested in the raw materials inventory and the cost of capital is too high to permit any excess investment in raw materials. Thus the production manager has agreed to limit the raw material average balance to no more than one tenth of the annual usage. That is, the raw materials inventory balance should be about one tenth of the total cost of raw materials released into production during the year.

(*Note:* The ending balance of Accounts Payable described in (2) takes into account this raw materials inventory policy.)

(4) The company's sales manager would like to carry a large quantity of finished goods so that no sales are lost because the company's product is not in stock and cannot be delivered immediately to customers. However, the financial manager points out the cost of capital, as he did to the production manager. Hence, the sales manager agrees that the finished goods inventory quantity should not exceed two months of annual sales, that is, one sixth of the annual sales volume.

(*Note:* The ending balance of Accounts Payable described in (2) takes into account this finished goods inventory policy. To simplify, assume that products started in process during the year are completed by the end of the year. Thus there is no ending balance of work-in-process inventory.)

(5) The company's production manager estimates that the fixed manufacturing costs for 1977 will be: depreciation of fixed assets = $15,000; out-of-pocket costs = $658,750, of which one tenth will be payable at year-end. The company's maximum practical production capacity for 1977, given its present manufacturing facilities and plant, is 2750 units.

(6) The company's nonmanufacturing *fixed* costs of operations are estimated as follows for 1977: marketing = $550,000; administration and general = $215,000. Total depreciation of $5000 is included in these costs. The remainder are out-of-pocket costs. The largest part of the fixed marketing expense for 1977 is a promotion campaign to advertise the new product. One tenth of these nonmanufacturing out-of-pocket costs will be payable at year-end.

(7) The company's nonmanufacturing *variable* operating costs per unit sold are estimated as follows for 1977: marketing = $650 per unit; administration and general = $150 per unit. One tenth of these out-of-pocket costs will be payable at year-end.

(8) Looking ahead to the end of 1977, the company's financial manager estimates that the prepaid expense balance at that time will be about 2% of the total operating costs during 1977, that is, the total of both fixed and variable costs of manufacturing, marketing, and administration and general. Treat these prepayments as an additional cash payment over and above the expenses and costs described in (2), (3), (4), (5), (6), and (7).

(9) The financial manager predicts that the company should be able to borrow

on short-term notes payable an amount equal to 40% of its total current assets *excluding* cash. Assume that the average annual rate of interest on the short-term notes payable will be 8% in 1977, and that the notes are borrowed during the entire year.

(10) No purchases of new fixed assets are planned during 1977, although if the company is successful in 1977, it probably will consider expansion of its production capacity in 1978. Of course, no retirements of any fixed assets are anticipated during 1977, which is the first year of business.

(11) The stockholders are content to receive no cash dividends during 1977, since the company will need all its available capital to build up its inventories and accounts receivable balances.

(12) The corporation is subject to federal income tax, of course, which is 22% on the first $25,000 of taxable income and 48% on the excess over $25,000. By the end of the year, 80% of the income tax for the year must be paid to the International Revenue Service. The remaining 20% balance is paid the following year in two installments, in March and June.

(13) The company's beginning cash balance at the start of 1977 is $515,000, which will not be sufficient to meet all the demands for cash during the year, given all the above information, assumptions, and forecasts. The company's financial vice-president thinks that the ending cash balance should be about 4.0% of the sales revenue for the year. For the additional money needed assume that the company will borrow $150,000 on the basis of *long-term* notes payable at an annual interest rate of 8%. Assume that this long-term borrowing will take place at mid year, that is, at July 1, 1977, so that the additional debt would be outstanding for only six months during 1977. (If part (b) of this problem is not assigned, then assume that total interest expense for 1977 is $44,089.

Required: Based on the foregoing information, assumptions, and forecasts for 1977, prepare in sufficient detail:

(a) The budgeted profit performance statement for 1977, and

(b) The budgeted balance sheet at December 31, 1977.

Chapter Seven

Budgeting Changes in Financial Position; Budgets and Management Control

BUDGETING CHANGES IN FINANCIAL POSITION; BUDGETS AND MANAGEMENT CONTROL

Budgeting Current Asset and Current Liability Changes Next Year

Budgeting Changes in Current Assets

The company's inventory policy is to maintain a combined ending quantity of work-in-process and finished goods equal to one fourth of the year's sales volume. As is explained above in Chapter Six (see page 194), this means that the company will have to manufacture 675,000 units in 1977, which is 25,000 more units than the budgeted sales of 650,000 units. The procedures of budgeting manufacturing fixed and variable costs are discussed in Chapter Six. These budgeting procedures result in the manufacturing costs budget for 1977, which is shown in Exhibit 7.1. Keep in mind that total fixed manufacturing costs *must be reduced* to a per unit cost: total fixed manufacturing costs of $1,468,125 are divided by the 675,000 units budgeted output to determine the $2.175 per unit shown in Exhibit 7.1. Variable costs, because of their very nature, are budgeted on a per unit basis. Notice that the per unit production costs in Exhibit 7.1 are the same as shown in the company's budgeted net income statement for 1977 (see Exhibit 6.2). In summary, the 25,000 units inventory increase will cost $342,875; ($13.715 per unit × 25,000 units = $342,875).

EXHIBIT 7.1
Manufacturing Costs Budget for 1977 (at 675,000 units Output)

Fixed Costs:		
Direct labor	$ 210,600	
Overhead	1,257,525	
Total fixed costs	$1,468,125	or $ 2.175 per unit
Variable Costs:		
Raw materials —for 675,000 units	$3,186,675	at $ 4.721 per unit
Direct labor —for 675,000 units	3,858,300	at 5.716 per unit
Overhead —for 675,000 units	744,525	at 1.103 per unit
Total variable costs	$7,789,500	at $11.540 per unit
Total Manufacturing Costs	$9,257,625	$13.715 per unit

The company's raw materials inventory policy is to maintain a total stock of raw materials at year-end equal to one sixth of the total usage during the year. Thus the company's ending raw materials inventory cost balance should be about $531,000: ($3,186,675 budgeted raw materials cost from Exhibit 7.1 divided by six equals $531,000). Some manufacturing companies use many different raw material items, and may have different holding policies for their different items. The one-sixth rule for this company is the composite average for all the different raw material items used in the manufacture of its product. Given this inventory policy the company will increase its raw material inventory from $463,825 at year-end 1976 to $531,000 at year-end 1977, for an increase of $67,175. (*Note*: In the next several pages there are many references to balances in the asset, liability, and owners' equity accounts at the end of 1976—refer to Exhibit 2.2 in Chapter Two for this information.)

Based on the company's credit sales terms and its normal cash collection experience, the ending balance of accounts receivable should be no more than 10% of total sales revenue for the year. This guideline is based on many factors, such as the ratio of cash sales to credit sales, what percentage of customers pay their bills on or before the last day of the credit period given by the company, and how many customers take longer to pay than the credit period allowed by the company. At the end of 1975 the ending balance of accounts receivable was just under this 10% guideline: ($934,500 ending balance ÷ $10,000,000 sales revenue = 9.345%). During 1976, however, many customers abused the credit period terms offered by the company and paid their bills one or two months late. As a result, the company had 12.5% of its sales revenue uncollected at year-end 1976: ($1,478,125 ending balance ÷ $11,825,000 = 12.5%). The credit manager has taken action to prevent this from happening in 1977. The ending balance of accounts receivable should be no more than 10.0% of sales revenue, or no more than $1,495,000: (10.0% × $14,950,000 budgeted sales revenue). Thus the company's accounts receivable should increase only $16,875 during the year: ($1,495,000 budgeted ending balance − $1,478,125 actual beginning balance).

Before we examine the company's cash balance during 1977, the company's other current asset is considered—prepaid expenses. This account consists of many different short-term prepaid cost items, such as insurance premiums paid in advance, certain real estate taxes which are paid in advance, office supplies, maintenance and cleaning supplies, and the like. One simple method is to measure the balance in this account as a percentage of total expenses for the year excluding interest and income tax (since these two expenses are not prepaid and are not operating expenses). Although it can be done more precisely, this "quick and dirty" approach probably is reasonably accurate in most instances. In 1976 the ending balance of prepaid expenses ($491,300) is about 4.5% of total expenses. In 1977, total expenses (excluding interest and income tax) are budgeted at $13,390,000 (see Exhibit 6.2 for information). Thus the ending balance of prepaid expenses should be $602,300: ($13,390,000 × 4.5% = $602,300). In summary, this current asset should increase $111,000 during 1977: ($602,300 budgeted ending balance − $491,300 actual beginning balance).

Deciding on a proper cash balance policy is a controversial problem. Clearly a company should avoid two extreme situations: (1) not having enough cash on hand to cover all cash payment obligations as they come due; and, (2) having too much cash on hand, which means that a good part of the company's capital is not invested in profit-producing assets. Some companies carry very large cash balances, and some carry very small balances. In this example it is assumed that the company's policy is to maintain an ending cash balance equal to 3.0% of sales revenue for the year. Thus the ending balance should be $448,500: ($14,950,000 budgeted sales revenue × 3.0%). The cash balance should therefore increase $102,455 during 1977: ($448,500 budgeted ending balance less $346,045 actual beginning balance).

The company's cash policy does *not* mean that its cash balance should be exactly 3.0% of sales revenue each and every day during the year, or even at the end of every month during the year. Like many companies this company's sales revenue is subject to seasonal fluctuation during the year. Sales in some months are much larger than other months, which results in wide fluctuations of cash collections from customers month to month. Cash flow budgeting of next year's cash receipts and payments month by month may be necessary to anticipate when the company will have to make short-term borrowings during the year and, in general, to plan for adequate cash balances throughout the year. Cash flow analysis and budgeting procedures are discussed in Chapter Eight.

The budgeted changes in the company's current assets are summarized in Exhibit 7.2. An immediate concern of management is how to provide the $640,000 (rounded off) additional capital that will be needed to increase the current asset balances.

Budgeting Changes in Current Liabilities

In this example the company has three basic short-term (current) liabilities: (1) accounts payable and accrued costs, (2) income tax payable, and (3) short-term notes payable. Given the $640,000 budgeted increase of current assets during 1977 (see Exhibit 7.2), the managers first would determine how much of this increase can be provided by an increase in accounts payable (and accrued costs). The company purchases most raw materials, many supplies, and some services on credit. Since the company's total production and operating costs will increase next year, the company's total purchases on credit in 1977 will increase. Thus the balance of accounts payable and accrued costs should also increase (unless the credit periods offered to the company were shortened, or unless the company increases its cash purchases compared to its credit purchases next year).

The company's purchasing department estimates that the company's 1977 ending balance of accounts payable and accrued costs should be about one eighth of total expenses for next year, exclusive of interest and income tax. In actual practice, a company may make more detailed analyses of each major item bought on credit, instead of using a rough ratio to total expenses. Also, to be more precise, some manufacturing costs and other operating expenses are

EXHIBIT 7.2
Budgeted Changes in Current Assets During 1977

Current Asset	Budgetary Assumption	Actual 1976 Year-end Balance	Budgeted 1977 Year-end Balance	Budgeted Increase During 1977
Cash	3.0% of sales revenue	$ 346,045	$ 448,500	$102,455
Accounts Receivable	10.0% of sales revenue	1,478,125	1,495,000	16,875
Raw Materials Inventory	One sixth of raw material usage	463,825	531,000	67,175
Work-in-Process and Finished Goods Inventories	Combined quantity equal to one fourth of year's sales volume	1,705,200	2,048,075	342,875
Prepaid Expenses	4.5% of total expenses (excluding interest and income tax)	491,300	602,300	111,000
Totals		$4,484,495	$5,124,875	$640,380

not purchased on credit. Depreciation is the most obvious example. But most raw materials, many supplies, and some services are bought on credit. Basing the ending liability balance on the total expenses budgeted for next year usually is a reasonably accurate method.

The 1976 ending balance of accounts payable and accrued costs is about one eight of the company's 1976 total expenses (exclusive of interest and income tax): ($1,350,400 year-end balance ÷ $10,847,100 = 12.4%, or about one eight). Unless this ratio changes in 1977 the balance of accounts payable and accrued costs at year-end 1977 should be $1,673,750: ($13,390,000 budgeted expenses for 1977 ÷ 8 = $1,673,750). Hence, this current liability account should increase $323,350 during the year: ($1,673,750 budgeted ending balance − $1,350,400 actual beginning balance).

Corporations must estimate their federal income tax liability for the coming year, and based on this estimate make total progress payments during the year equal to 80% of the estimated income tax for the year. The remaining 20% is due after the close of the year. In Exhibit 6.2—see line (v)—the budgeted income tax expense is $612,700 for 1977. About 80% of this would be paid during 1977; therefore, about 20% or $112,500 would be payable at the end of the year. Hence, this current liability would increase $44,008: ($122,500 budgeted ending balance less $78,492 actual beginning balance). (Many companies have much more complicated income tax problems than the company in this example, and budgeting for the income tax payments and year-end liability may not be as simple as just explained here.) Notice that the budgeted taxable income in Exhibit 6.2—see line (u)—assumes an average total notes payable balance of $3 million during 1977. Short-term notes payable are discussed next.

Borrowing on short-term notes payable is limited because banks (and other sources of short-term loans) insist that the company keep its *current ratio* high enough to ensure short-term solvency. Recall that the current ratio is total current assets divided by total current liabilities. It is tempting to fall back on simple rules of thumb; for example, that the current ratio should not be lower than 2.0 to 1.0, which is thought to be a good standard for most companies. However, this "standard" ratio may be too *low* for some companies and may be excessively conservative for other companies. It is true that at year-end 1976 the company's current ratio is 2.06 to 1.00: ($4,484,495 current assets ÷ $2,178,892 current liabilities = 2.06). However, at year-end 1975 the current ratio was only 1.82 to 1.00 and the company did not experience any payment problems during 1976.

The "proper" current ratio for a company depends on many factors, including the company's policy regarding how much margin of safety it wants in being able to pay all its current liabilities on time. An extended discussion of this topic would probe deeply into the field of business finance. It is simply assumed, therefore, that the company "can live with" a current ratio as low as 1.80 to 1.00, although the general policy is to keep the ratio somewhat above this minimum. Relative to this policy, the company's financial vice-president decides that increasing the company's short-term notes payable balance by $100,000 during 1977 would be reasonable. Therefore, the budgeted ending balance of this liability account is $850,000: ($750,000 actual beginning balance + $100,000 budgeted increase during 1977).

The budgeted changes in the company's current liabilities during 1977 are summarized in Exhibit 7.3. Notice that the budgeted current ratio at year-end 1977 is 1.94 to 1.00: ($5,125,075 current assets, from Exhibit 7.2, ÷ $2,646,250 current liabilities).

Cash Flow from Budgeted Net Income Next Year: A Brief Note

The company is budgeting sales revenue at $14,950,000 next year, which is an increase of $3,125,000 or more than 26% above 1976. This sales growth will require total current asset increases of $640,000 during 1977, as discussed above (see Exhibit 7.2). Current liabilities are budgeted to increase $467,000 (rounded off) during 1977 (see Exhibit 7.3). Hence, the company will need the additional $173,000 ($640,000 − $467,000) from other capital sources during next year. Also, the company plans capital expenditures of $1,392,000 in 1977 (see page 196). These two demands for capital total $1,565,000. Where will this more than one and one-half million dollars of capital come from?

EXHIBIT 7.3
Budgeted Changes in Current Liabilities During 1977

Current Liability	Budgeting Assumptions	Actual 1976 Year-end Balance	Budgeted 1977 Year-end Balance	Budgeted Increase During 1977
Accounts Payable and Accrued Costs	One eighth of total expenses (excluding interest and income tax)	$1,350,400	$1,673,750	$323,350
Income Tax Payable	20% of income tax expense for year	78,492	122,500	44,008
Notes Payable	Discretionary within limit of minimum current ratio	750,000	850,000	100,000
Totals		$2,178,892	$2,646,250	$467,358

Before managers consider long-term borrowing or additional stock issues for capital, they first need to determine how much cash flow will be generated *internally* from net income next year. They must decide how much of this cash flow from net income will be retained in the business and not paid out as cash dividends during the year. Earning net income yields a positive cash flow to the company, although it should be quickly added that in most cases the *amount* of net cash inflow is *not* equal to the amount of net income. Net income is budgeted at $677,000 (rounded off) for 1977 (refer to Exhibit 6.2). But cash flow from net income for the year will be different than this amount. One major reason is depreciation, which as you know is not a cash outlay in the period the depreciation is recorded.

The simplest approach of adjusting or converting net income to its cash flow effect is to add the amount of depreciation for the period to the amount of net income, as follows:

"Simple" Approximation of Cash Flow from Net Income in 1977

Budgeted net income (see Exhibit 6.2)	$ 677,000
Budgeted depreciation (from company's fixed asset schedules)	438,000
Budgeted cash flow (before consideration of other adjustments needed to convert net income to its more correct cash flow effect)	$1,115,000

Adding back depreciation to net income is only a first step toward determining the more precise cash flow from net income. Other factors also must be considered. In Chapter Eight there is a more complete discussion of cash flow analysis and cash flow budgeting procedures. Here it is sufficient to work with the "rough" estimate of cash flow from net income just computed, which is $1,115,000 for 1977.

Based on this budgeted cash flow from net income the president plans to recommend to the company's Board of Directors a cash dividend of $7.50 per share of common stock during 1977, which is a total dividend payment of $300,000 based on 40,000 shares of common stock outstanding at the start of 1977. This would be an increase from the $5 cash dividend per share paid in 1976 (see Exhibit 2.3). (If the company falls short of its profit plan in 1977, then the Board of Directors probably would reduce the cash dividend per share.) If a $300,000 cash dividend is assumed for 1977, the *cash retention* from net income in 1977 would be $815,000: ($1,115,000 budgeted cash flow − $300,000 budgeted cash dividend).

The Long-Term Debt Decision

As our discussion above indicates, this company's budgeted cash retention from net income should be $815,000 during 1977. But this is $750,000 short of the $1,565,000 capital needed to increase current assets more than the increase in current liabilities, and to pay for the capital expenditures planned for 1977. (See page 225.) The company has two basic alternative sources for this $750,000 additional capital: (1) new long-term debt borrowings; or, (2) an additional stock issue. Deciding between these alternatives, or perhaps a mix of both, is a business finance issue that goes beyond management accounting. The management accountant would be asked to furnish analyses of the consequences of debt versus equity financing, including the financial leverage effects and the impact on future earnings per share. The final decision rests with the company's Board of Directors, and usually depends heavily on the recommendation of the company's president and vice-president of finance.

It is assumed that the company decides to increase its long-term debt early in 1977 by $750,000 to provide the additional capital needed for purchase of the new fixed assets, and to increase its current assets (over the amount provided by the increase in current liabilities). Even though interest rates in 1977 are projected to increase, the company's financial vice-president favors the long-term debt alternative, to avoid the issue of new shares of common stock. (There should be no retirements of common stock during 1977.) The company will borrow the $750,000 in February or March. Also, the $100,000 increase of short-term notes payable (see Exhibit 7.3) will occur early in the year. Based on this budgeted timetable for borrowing, the interest bearing debt should average $3 million during 1977. The weighted average interest rate, including the interest rate on the old long-term debt and on the new short-term and new long-term borrowings, is estimated to be 9.0% during 1977. Thus the total interest expense for 1977 is budgeted to be $270,000—see line (t) in Exhibit 6.2.

Investment in Fixed Assets: Another Brief Note

The decision to purchase and construct new fixed assets costing a total of $1,392,000 is more or less taken for granted in the preceding discussion. The brief explanation is that more production capacity will be needed in 1977 to provide for the increase in production output caused by the budgeted increase of sales volume for 1977. In actual practice, these long-term investment decisions involve a great deal of *engineering* and *economic* analysis. The engineering analysis concerns many technical aspects, such as the exact specifications of the types, models, and sizes of the new equipment and facilities that the company will need to expand its production capacity. The building construction being planned by the company has to be analyzed from many architecture and engineering points of view, such as how much weight per square foot the floor space will have to carry, the electric power distribution system in the building, the sewage and waste handling capacity of the building's plumbing system, and whether fire safety codes are being met.

The economic analysis involved in making long-term investment decisions deals primarily with the question of whether the assets can "pay their way." Generally, this means whether the cost invested in the assets can be recovered through future sales revenues (or from other income generated by the asset), and whether the company can earn a satisfactory (or better) rate of operating profit return on these investments. Chapters Nine and Ten discuss the economic analysis of long-term investments decisions in some detail. For now, we assume that the managers and their staff personnel have done all the engineering and economic analysis that justifies the investment of $1,392,000 in the new fixed assets.

Statement of Budgeted Changes in Financial Position During Next Year

Based on the company's budgeted net income statement for 1977 (refer to Exhibit 6.2) and the preceding discussion in this chapter concerning the budgeted changes in assets and liabilities during 1977, the company's changes in financial position during 1977 and the budgeted balance sheet at the end of 1977 is prepared (see Exhibit 7.4). The actual balances at year-end 1976 are taken from the company's balance sheet at December 31, 1976 (see Exhibit 2.1). The budgeted increases and ending balances have been explained in the previous sections in this chapter (see Exhibits 7.2 and 7.3 in particular). The amounts shown in Exhibit 7.4 are rounded off to the nearest thousand dollars.

EXHIBIT 7.4
Budgeted Changes in Financial Position During 1977

Balance Sheet Account	Actual Balance at Year-end 1976	Budgeted Change During 1977	Budgeted Balance at Year-end 1977
Cash	$ 346	+$ 102	$ 448
Accounts Receivable	1,478	+ 17	1,495
Raw Materials Inventory	464	+ 67	531
Work-in-Process Inventory } Finished Goods Inventory }	1,705	+ 343	2,048
Prepaid Expenses	492	+ 111	603
Total Current Assets	$4,485	+$ 640	$ 5,125
Buildings	$1,815	+$ 726	$ 2,541
Machinery and Equipment	2,562	+ 600	3,162
Vehicles	319	+ 66	385
Total	$4,696	+$1,392	$ 6,088
Accumulated Depreciation	1,254	+ 438	1,692
Net	$3,442	+$ 954	$ 4,396
Land	675	—0—	675
Total Assets	$8,602	+$1,594	$10,196
Accounts Payable	$1,351	+$ 323	$ 1,674
Income Tax Payable	78	+ 44	122
Short-term Notes Payable	750	+ 100	850
Total Current Liabilities	$2,179	+$ 467	$ 2,646
Long-term Notes Payable	$1,750	+$ 750	$ 2,500
Stockholders' Equity:			
Invested Capital	4,000	—0—	4,000
Retained Earnings	673	+ 377[a]	1,050
Total	$4,673	+$ 377	$ 5,050
Total Sources of Capital	$8,602	+$1,594	$10,196

Notes:
[a] Net income of $677 thousand less cash dividends of $300 thousand.

(Also, notice that the work-in-process and finished goods inventories are grouped together as one balance.)

Budgeted Return on Assets and Return on Equity

Given the company's budgeted net income plan for 1977 (Exhibit 6.2) and the budgeted changes during 1977 in its assets, liabilities, and stockholders' equity

(Exhibit 7.4), the company's budgeted return on assets and return on equity can be determined (as previously, year-end balances are used):

Computation of Budgeted Return on Assets for 1977

$$\text{Return on Assets} = \frac{\text{Operating Profit}}{\text{Total Assets}} = \boxed{\text{Asset Turnover Ratio} \times \text{Profit Ratio}}$$

$$\frac{\$1,560,000}{\$10,196,000} = \boxed{\frac{\$14,950,000}{\$10,196,000} \times \frac{\$1,560,000}{\$14,950,000}}$$

$$15.3\% = 1.47 \times 10.4\%$$

Computation of Budgeted Return on Equity for 1977

$$\text{Return on Equity} = \frac{\text{Net Income}}{\text{Stockholders' Equity}} = \frac{\$677,300}{\$5,050,000} = 13.4\%$$

At the beginning of Chapter Six it is explained that the company's primary financial goal for 1977 is to earn a 12.0% return on equity, which would require the company to earn a return on assets of 15.1% (see pages 183 to 185). Thus the company will meet these goals if the profit plan and the asset investments plan for 1977 can be actually achieved. But many things can go wrong. The managers responsible for achieving the budgeted goals and objectives have to monitor actual profit performance and investments against the budget for 1977.

Implementing the Profit Plan

The two key budget documents developed in the previous discussion—the budgeted net income statement for 1977 (Exhibit 6.2) and the budgeted changes in financial position during 1977 (Exhibit 7.4)—are called the *master budget.* These budget statements are prepared *in summary for the whole company for the entire year.* Once the master budget has been formally adopted by the company's top level managers, each management responsibility center in the organization (divisions, departments, etc.) develops a detailed budget that serves as its plan of action over the coming year. These departmental and divisional budgets tie into and are coordinated with the master budget, of course.

For instance, the master budget sets a sales volume goal of 650,000 units for next year, which will require a production output of 675,000 units during 1977. Given this budgeted output for next year, the chief production manager develops a detailed manufacturing budget for each month over the coming year. First, the production output quantity for each month is scheduled. Based on this month by month production output schedule the budgeted manufacturing costs of each raw material item, each labor operation, and each overhead cost factor are determined. If the company uses a standard cost system (discussed in Chapter Fourteen), these budgeted manufacturing costs would be the standard costs that are established for each production cost factor. The detailed monthly production budget serves as an "action plan" for the coming months. Based on this production budget the purchasing agent would determine the quantity of raw materials needed over the coming months; the personnel department would determine if any additional employees need to be hired over the coming months, and so on.

Shortly after the end of each month the production manager receives a report of the actual production output and the actual manufacturing costs, which includes a side-by-side comparison with the budgeted output and the budgeted costs. Differences between budget and actual are called *variances*. Reporting variances is a key management accounting function. Variances are a prime example of *feedback information* for management control. In other words, they point out deviations from plans. In this manner, the actual to budget monthly report serves as an "early warning system." The detection of deviations from plans *soon enough* so that managers can take action before the problems get out of hand is essential for management control.

The particular details of the budgets and the actual to budget monthly reports which are reported to each manager in the business organization vary from one area to another. A sales manager's budget and monthly actual to budget reports focus on sales volume, sales prices, and the direct selling expenses under his authority and responsibility. In contrast, the production manager, as described above, needs budgets and monthly reports that emphasize production output and manufacturing costs. Top level managers, in particular the president or chief executive officer, work with the master budget and receive actual to budget reports for the business as a whole. Top level managers typically receive monthly reports of actual to budget, although in some situations quarterly (three months) reports may be adequate.

Managers usually also make a final *year-end review* of actual against budget of the entire year's performance. This year-end review is a critical first step in planning and constructing the budget for the following year. In the developing of the 1977 budget, recall how frequently reference is made in the previous discussion to the company's 1976 performance. For convenience the discussion that follows focuses on the year-end review of actual to budget for the entire year. The basic procedures of actual to budget comparisons apply to any time period, whether a month or the entire year. Keep in mind that the managers do not wait until the end of the year to compare actual to budget. In fact, by the end of the year managers should have a good idea of exactly where and by how much actual performance falls short or exceeds the budgeted goals and performance for that year.

Managers need to be aware as soon as possible of any significant deviations from the profit plan. They need to take corrective action as soon as the problem arises, not several months later. For instance, the company's sales manager receives a monthly report that compares actual sales performance for each territory, and perhaps for each salesman as well, against the budgeted sales quotas. Any significant variances would be highlighted. Also, the monthly actual to budget report would include the specific expenses under the sales manager's authority and responsibility. Expenses running over the budgeted amount for the month, and/or year-to-date would receive attention.

Comparison of Budget to Actual: A First Step of Management Control

Management Control: An Accomplishment Oriented Concept

More than anything else, management *control* means the achievement of the entity's goals and objectives. In other words, control is an *accomplishment-oriented* concept. This point is mentioned at the outset since, unfortunately, the term "control" has restrictive or preventive meanings in the minds of many. Management control consists, in part, of preventing nongoal-directed performance. But the most important aspect of management control is the promotion and motivation of goal-directed performance. There are many aspects and theories of management control. This section is concerned with the uses of budgets for financial control.

An Overview Analysis of the Year's Actual Profit Performance Compared to that Budgeted

The *actual* 1977 report for the company is shown in Exhibit 7.5, which also includes the original profit budget for 1977 for comparison. (See Exhibit 6.2 for the original profit budget.) As Exhibit 7.5 shows, the company's actual 1977 net income falls short of that budgeted for the year. The reasons are many. One basic way of explaining the shortfall of net income is to compare actual *operating profit* for the year with that budgeted (see Exhibit 7.6). The company sold 10,000 more units than budgeted which at the budgeted profit per unit of $2.400 produced $24,000 favorable volume variance. But each of the 660,000 units that were sold generated $.215 less profit than they should have, which is an unfavorable variance of $141,900 ($.215 × 660,000 units = $141,900).

In summary:

Analysis of Operating Profit Variances in 1977

Volume Variance	(+10,000 units × $2.400 per unit) =	+$ 24,000 (favorable)
Operating Profit per Unit Variance	(−$.215 per unit × 660,000 units) =	− 141,900 (unfavorable)
Net Effect	(as shown in Exhibit 7.6)	−$117,900 (unfavorable)

EXHIBIT 7.5
Management Profit Performance Report

Line	Sales Volume Base	1977 Actual 660,000 units Percents	Dollar Value per Unit		1977 Budgeted 650,000 units Percents	Dollar Value per Unit	
(a)	Sales Volume Base						
(b)	Sales revenue	100.0	$22.900	$15,114,000	100.0%	$23.000	$14,950,000
	Cost of goods sold: Variable costs—						
(c)	Raw materials	21.2	$ 4.864	$3,210,240	20.5	$ 4.721	$3,068,650
(d)	Direct labor	24.9	5.700	3,762,000	24.9	5.716	3,715,400
(e)	Overhead	4.9	1.114	765,875	4.8	1.103	716,950
(f)	Total variable costs	51.0	$11.678	$7,707,480	50.2	$11.540	$7,501,000
	Fixed costs—						
(g)	Direct labor	1.4	$ 0.314	$ 207,240	1.5	$ 0.312	$ 202,800
(h)	Overhead	8.0	1.838	1,213,080	8.0	1.863	1,210,950
(i)	Total fixed costs	9.4	$ 2.152	$1,420,320	9.5	$ 2.175	$1,413,750
(j)	Total cost of goods sold	60.4	$13.830	9,127,800	59.7	$13.715	8,914,750
(k)	Gross profit	39.6	$ 9.070	$ 5,986,200	40.3	$ 9.285	$ 6,035,250
	Operating costs: Variable costs—						
(l)	Marketing expenses	23.9	$ 5.486	$3,620,760	23.9	$ 5.500	$3,575,000
(m)	Administrative and general	0.8	0.174	114,840	0.7	0.170	110,500
(n)	Total variable costs	24.7	$ 5.660	$3,735,600	24.6	$ 5.670	$3,685,500
	Fixed costs—						
(o)	Marketing	2.6	$ 0.583	$ 384,780	2.5	$ 0.580	$ 377,000
(p)	Administrative and general	2.8	0.642	423,720	2.8	0.635	412,750
(q)	Total fixed costs	5.4	$ 1.225	$ 808,500	5.3	$ 1.215	$ 789,750
(r)	Total operating costs	30.1	$ 6.885	4,544,100	29.9	$ 6.885	4,475,250
(s)	Operating profit	9.5	$ 2.185	$ 1,442,100	10.4	$ 2.400	$ 1,560,000
(t)	Interest expense	(average debt = $3,000,000 × 9.1%)		273,000	(average debt = $3,000,000 × 9.0%)		270,000
(u)	Net income before tax			$ 1,169,100			$ 1,290,000
(v)	Income tax	($1,169,100 × 48% less $6,500)		554,668	($1,290,000 × 48% less $6,500)		612,700
(w)	Net income			$ 614,432			$ 677,300

EXHIBIT 7.6
Comparison of Actual and Budgeted Operating Profit

	Operating Profit per Unit		Sales Volume	Total Operating Profit
Budgeted:	$2.400	×	650,000 units =	$1,560,000
Actual:	2.185	×	660,000 units =	1,442,100
Variances:	$0.215		10,000 units	$ 117,900
	Unfavorable		Favorable	Unfavorable

Why did the actual operating profit per unit fall below the amount budgeted for the year? Exhibit 7.7 shows the major variances of sales price and expenses. Each of these per unit variances would be broken down into their major parts for more detailed analysis. For example, the cost of goods sold per unit unfavorable variance would be analyzed in terms of each of the manufacturing costs. We can see in Exhibit 7.5 that there is a *favorable* direct labor variable cost per unit variance ($5.716 budgeted compared with $5.700 actual), but that there is an *unfavorable* raw materials cost per unit variance: ($4.721 budgeted compared with $4.864 actual = $.143 unfavorable variance). A more detailed comparison of actual to budget of all raw material items may reveal that several items were under budget but that two or three raw material items were over budget.

Analysis of Manufacturing Cost and Operating Expense Variances

Variances between budget and actual can be divided into an *efficiency* factor and *purchase price* factor for *variable* manufacturing costs and operating ex-

EXHIBIT 7.7
Sales Price and Expense Variances

	1977		
	Budgeted	Actual	Variance
Sales Price	$23.000	$22.900	$0.100 unfavorable
Cost of Goods Sold per Unit	13.715	13.830	0.115 unfavorable
Gross Profit per Unit	$ 9.285	$ 9.070	$0.215 unfavorable
Marketing Plus Administrative and General Expenses	6.885	6.885	No variance
Operating Profit per Unit	$ 2.400	$ 2.185	$0.215 unfavorable

penses. For example, consider the following summary of manufacturing direct labor cost of a production department for one month:

Summary of Budgeted and Actual Direct Labor Costs for Month

Actual direct labor	10,500 hours	$59,325
Budgeted direct labor	10,000 hours	54,000
Variances	500 hours	$ 5,325
	unfavorable	unfavorable

The budgeted direct labor hours for this month are determined by multiplying the actual output for the month times the budgeted (or standard) number of direct labor hours allowed for each unit of output. The budgeted total direct labor cost shown above is determined by multiplying the budgeted number of hours times the budgeted (or standard) cost per direct labor hour. In other words, from the above schedule it can be determined that the budgeted cost per direct labor hour is $5.40: ($54,000 ÷ 10,000 hours = $5.40 per hour).

The production department worked 500 more hours than was "allowed" and each hour cost $5.65 per hour: ($59,325 ÷ 10,500 hours = $5.65). Hence, each hour cost $.25 more than budgeted: ($5.65 − $5.40 = $.25 unfavorable variance per hour). In summary,

Analysis of Direct Labor Variance for Month

Efficiency Factor	(500 hours × $5.40 per hour)	=	$2700 unfavorable
Purchase Price Factor	($.25 per hour × 10,500 hours)	=	2625 unfavorable
Total Variance			$5325 unfavorable

Although the specific details vary for each manufacturing cost or operating expense, generally speaking, it is useful to separate these variances into their efficiency and purchase price components, as just shown for direct labor cost. On the other hand, *fixed* costs and expenses require a different sort of analysis.

Consider the annual real estate tax paid by the company, which is a fixed cost for the year. This cost total depends on the assessed value of the buildings and land owned by the company and the mill levy (tax rate) per $1000 of assessed value. The variance between budget and actual for the year for this particular fixed cost may be due to a change in the mill levy rate that was not predicted in the initial budgeting process. Or, the variance may be due to a larger (or smaller) assessed value on the real estate, either because the company acquired new real estate that was not planned at the start of the year or disposed of some real estate that was scheduled in the budget. Or, perhaps, the property assessment procedures of the county government were changed during the year. In contrast, variance between budgeted depreciation for the year and the actual depreciation recorded would be analyzed differently. Depreciation variance may be due, for example, to higher actual purchase costs of new fixed assets bought during the year than were budgeted. Or, perhaps, some of the new fixed assets were not installed until later in the year than were budgeted, so a smaller fraction of first-year depreciation was recorded on these assets. Each fixed cost or expense is a separate case; it is difficult to generalize.

The analysis of variance between budget and actual just discussed for fixed costs and expenses refers to the *total* cost or expense for the year. As mentioned previously, fixed costs and expenses are fixed only over a *relevant range* of production output and sales volumes. In this example, the actual sales volume in 1977 is 10,000 units higher than the budgeted sales volume for the year (see Exhibit 7.5) which is only about a 1.5% increase over the budgeted sales volume.* It is unlikely that any of the fixed manufacturing costs or the fixed operating expenses had to be stepped up to handle the slightly higher production and sales volumes during the year. In other words, the actual sales and production volumes are within the relevant range over which these costs and expenses remain fixed. Thus the amounts originally budgeted for 1977 are the proper base amounts against which to compare actual fixed costs and expenses. On the other hand, if sales and production volumes had been, say, 10% higher than the budgeted volumes for the year, it is likely that many of the fixed costs and expenses would have been stepped up to provide for the higher level of activity. In this situation the originally budgeted amounts should be adjusted and put on the basis of the actual volume that falls outside the relevant range for the fixed costs and expenses in the original budget.

Finally, care should be taken to distinguish between *total* fixed cost variances and fixed cost *per unit* variances. For example, assume that the company's advertising expense was budgeted at $171,600 for the year and that this is a fixed expense for 1977. Assume also that the company's actual total advertising expense for the year is exactly the same amount. Thus no variance exists between the budgeted and the actual total fixed advertising expense. But on a per unit basis there is a variance:

Comparison of Fixed Cost per Unit Variance

		Budget		Actual
Fixed Advertising Expense per Unit	=	$\dfrac{\$171,600}{650,000 \text{ units}} = \$.264$		$\dfrac{\$171,600}{660,000 \text{ units}} = \$.260$

* Production output in 1977 is 687,500 units, which is only 1.9% more than the 675,000 units originally budgeted (refer to Exhibit 7.1).

As this comparison shows, there is a small variance per unit: ($.264 budgeted − $.260 actual = $.004 favorable variance per unit). The same total fixed expense is spread over a slightly larger number of units. This is due to the very nature of fixed costs and expenses. (For *manufacturing* fixed costs there may be an inventory cost valuation problem with unfavorable fixed cost per unit variances. This is discussed in Chapters Twelve and Thirteen.)

Comparison of Budgeted and Actual Changes in Financial Position During the Year

To achieve the return on assets and return on equity objectives for the year, managers must control the company's investments in assets during the year, as well as achieving the year's budgeted operating profit and net income goals. For example, a company may reach its operating profit goal for the year but may increase its assets more than budgeted, and thus the actual return on assets would be less than the budgeted return on assets for the year. The discussion above is concerned with the analysis of variances between the budgeted and actual profit during 1977. In brief, the company fell somewhat short of its profit goals for the year (see Exhibit 7.5). But this is not the whole story. How does the company's actual rate of return on assets and its actual rate of return on equity compare with the budgeted rates for 1977?

Exhibit 7.8 presents the comparison of the company's budgeted and actual changes in financial position during 1977. Some of the variances between the budgeted and the actual changes are not too significant. For instance, the actual purchase costs of all the fixed assets during 1977 are $11,000 more than planned: ($1,403,000 actual − $1,392,000 budgeted). The increase in Accounts Payable is $42,000 more than budgeted ($365,000 − $323,000) as a result of the higher level of operating costs in 1977 (see Exhibit 7.5). The increase in the Income Tax Payable account is $11,000 less because the actual taxable income in 1977 is lower than budgeted—again, refer to Exhibit 7.5. Since net income was budgeted at $677,000 but actually is only $614,000 for 1977, the Retained Earnings account would have increased $63,000 less than budgeted, but the company paid only $250,000 cash dividends during the year which is $50,000 less than the amount budgeted. Hence, the Retained Earnings account increased only $13,000 less than budgeted.

One significant variance shown in Exhibit 7.8 is the $72,000 difference between the budgeted increase in Accounts Receivable of $17,000 compared with the actual increase in Accounts Receivable of $89,000. Sales revenue is $164,000 more than budgeted: ($15,114,000 actual − $14,950,000 budgeted— see Exhibit 7.5). Using the 10% rule developed previously (see page 222), this sales revenue variance means that the ending balance of Accounts Receivable should have increased about $16,000 more than was originally budgeted. But as mentioned above, the actual increase is $72,000. Thus the credit manager has not been completely successful in keeping customers' receivables col-

EXHIBIT 7.8
Comparison of Actual and Budgeted Financial Position Changes
During 1977 (in thousands)

Balance Sheet Account	Actual Balance at Year-end 1976	Budgeted Change During 1977	Budgeted Balance at Year-end 1977	Actual Change During 1977	Actual Balance at Year-end 1977
Cash	$ 346	+$ 102	$ 448	−$ 25	$ 321
Accounts Receivable	1,478	+ 17	1,495	+ 89	1,567
Raw Materials Inventory	464	+ 67	531	+ 77	541
Work-in-Process Inventory } Finished Goods Inventory	1,705	+ 343	2,048	+ 380	2,085
Prepaid Expenses	492	+ 111	603	+ 127	619
Total Current Assets	$4,485	+$ 640	$ 5,125	+$ 648	$ 5,133
Buildings	$1,815	+$ 726	$ 2,541	+$ 732	$ 2,547
Machinery and Equipment	2,562	+ 600	3,162	+ 598	3,160
Vehicles	319	+ 66	385	+ 73	392
Total	$4,696	+$1,392	$ 6,088	+$1,403	$ 6,099
Accumulated Depreciation	1,254	+ 438	1,692	+ 439	1,693
Net	$3,442	+$ 954	$ 4,396	+$ 964	$ 4,406
Land	675	—0—	675	—0—	675
Total Assets	$8,602	+$1,594	$10,196	+$1,612	$10,214
Accounts Payable	$1,351	+$ 323	$ 1,674	+$ 365	$ 1,716
Income Tax Payable	78	+ 44	122	+ 33	111
Short-term Notes Payable	750	+ 100	850	+ 100	850
Total Current Liabilities	$2,179	+$ 467	$ 2,646	+$ 498	$ 2,677
Long-term Notes Payable	$1,750	+$ 750	$ 2,500	+$ 750	$ 2,500
Stockholders' Equity:					
Invested Capital	4,000	—0—	4,000	—0—	$ 4,000
Retained Earnnigs	673	+ 377[a]	1,050	+$ 364[b]	1,037
Total	$4,673	+$ 377	$ 5,050	+$ 364	$ 5,037
Total Sources of Capital	$8,602	+$1,594	$10,196	+$1,612	$10,214

Notes:
[a] Net income of $677 thousand less cash dividends of $300 thousand.
[b] Net income of $614 thousand less cash dividends of $250 thousand.

lected on time. Another significant variance between budget and actual is the cash balance. The company's ending cash balance should be $453,000, using the 3.0% rule developed earlier (see page 223): ($15,114,000 actual sales revenue × 3.0% = $453,000). But the actual cash balance is only $321,000, which is $132,000 less than budgeted. Clearly management should give the cash balance situation close attention.

Comparison of Budgeted and Actual Return on Assets and Return on Equity

The actual return on assets is compared with budget as follows (see Exhibits 7.5 and 7.8 for sources of information):

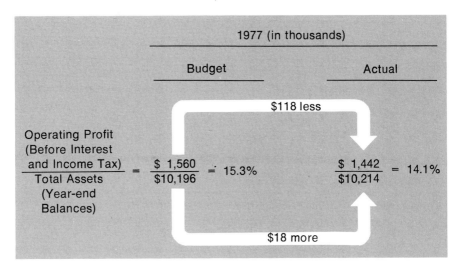

As this comparison indicates, both factors worked against achieving the return on assets goal in 1977: operating profit is $118,000 less than budgeted and total assets are $18,000 more than budgeted. Even so, the actual return on assets is still 14.1% for 1977.

The 1977 rate of return on (stockholders') equity for the company is compared as follows (see Exhibits 7.5 and 7.8 for sources of information):

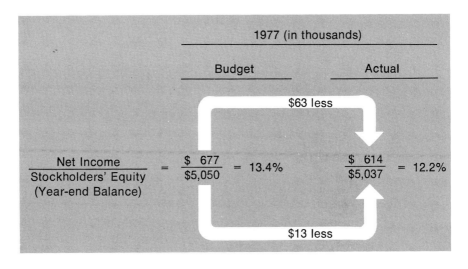

Although less than budgeted, the company did slightly better than its minimum 12.0% return on equity goal for 1977.

Problems of Budgeting

Our discussion here and in Chapter Six stresses the uses and advantages of budgeting. However, budgeting is far from an "all good and no bad" management tool. There are several basic problems of budgeting, or that may be caused by budgeting. These problems are considered briefly in the remainder of this chapter.

Sorting Between Significant and Insignificant Variances

Variances between budget and actual are designed to be feedback information for management control. Variances serve as "red flags" to alert management to deviations from plans, and to pinpoint problems that have developed. However, a basic difficulty is how to sort between significant and insignificant variances. Generally, "significant" means that the variance is deserving of management's attention and investigation, so that proper action may be taken to correct and to prevent repitition of an unfavorable variance; or advantage may be taken of the improvements shown by favorable variances.

Actual performance is never *exactly* equal to the budget down to the last dollar and down to the last unit of sales or production output. In comparing actual to budget there will be *some* variance (favorable or unfavorable) in almost every item in every budget report. A good deal of estimation, prediction, and forecasting is inherent in the budgeting process. A budget, no matter how carefully formulated, is nothing more than a reasonably close approximation of what is expected to happen and what can be achieved. In other words, it is possible for the budget to be "wrong" and the actual performance to be "right." A variance may be the result of a poor budget estimate or prediction, which means that the company's budgeting methods should be improved. The actual performance may be the best the company could have done.

Assuming that the budgeted amounts and quantities are "good," there is still the basic problem of deciding which of the variances are most deserving of a manager's attention and action. It may be tempting to use a rule of thumb, such that any variance 2% more or less than budget is treated as significant, and any variance within ± 2% of budget is treated as insignificant. It is true that *very* small variances, in general, probably are not worthy of management's attention, unless they are consistently favorable or unfavorable over several periods, in which case there may be a pattern that is worth looking into. But where can a line be drawn? A company has to rely on its own past experience to a great extent. Managers occasionally will spend time (and money) investigating what turn out to be insignificant variances. Hopefully, this "wasted motion" provides guidelines for the future. The most important management purpose is to use the investigation of variances as the basis for constructive and positive change in the future.

Budgets and Behavior

If they are not well managed, one or more steps in the budgeting process may lead to *dysfunctional behavior* by managers and employees in the business organization. "Dysfunctional" means contrary to or not supportive of the objectives, goals, and policies of the business organization. At the very outset, one problem to overcome is the "cost control" image of budgets. Many managers and employees tend to view budgeting as no more than an elaborate facade to implement tight, if not unreasonable constraints and demands on the decisions and performance of individuals in the organization. They view budgets as a straitjacket that prevents individual initiative. In their minds, budgets are evidence that the company does not trust individuals. Managers should be aware that budgets suffer from this image, and that they will have to work to overcome this poor attitude in seeking the support and cooperation of the individuals in the organization who are involved in and affected by the budgeting process.

A more positive theme of budgeting is summed up in the phrase "profit planning." Of course, earning profit requires the control of costs, that is, keeping costs within certain limits relative to sales revenue. The profit-planning nature and purpose of budgeting is certainly valid. Nevertheless, top level managers have to do a good job of communicating this function and purpose to middle and lower level managers, as well as to other employees who are far removed from any direct participation in the profit performance of the company. Convincing these employees that better profit performance means more job security and higher wage and salary levels is not easy.

The communication among managers regarding *unfavorable* variances is a difficult human relations problem. Unfavorable variances cause managers to "run for cover" to avoid having the blame laid at their doorstep. However, managers must work together to explore the reasons for the variances, and to decide what should be done to improve performance next period. In different periods the variances may be due to different reasons. Managers may take quite different action in one period compared with another.

The budgeting process cannot be separated from the basic management philosophy and style of management of the company. One distinction is between what is called the top down, authoritarian, giving orders style of management, on the one hand, versus the open, participative, management by objectives style, on the other hand. The budgeting process usually reveals which basic philosophy and style of management the company follows. If the company favors the authoritarian management approach, then the budgeting procedures will show this very clearly. The middle and lower level managers (as well as other employees) probably will view the budget as being "forced" on them. Given this top down, highly centralized management style, the budget may receive poor acceptance from those who have to execute it. In situations of this kind the formal budget may have low credibility, such that the effectiveness of the budgetary process is seriously hampered. If, on the other hand, the company has adopted a more participative nonauthoritarian style of management, then the budget may receive better acceptance and may be a valuable means of communication throughout the organization. In any case, it is too much to expect the budget to work against the grain of the company's management philosophy and practices.

With respect to the individual manager or employee who is involved in the budgeting process, there is a good deal of debate regarding several aspects of budgeting. Although general agreement exists that one basic purpose of budgeting is to motivate and to maintain high standards of performance of employees and managers, there is disagreement on how best to accomplish these basic goals. How "tight" or how "loose" should budgeted performance standards and quotas be set? Does a tight and demanding budget encourage peak performance? Or, does this discourage peak performance if the individual views the budget target as unrealistic and unfair? How should the investigation of variances be conducted? How should the budget-to-actual "track record" of a manager or supervisor be used (if at all) to evaluate the person for promotion and salary increases? These questions point up some of the management problems of budgeting.

Summary

Good management is characterized by good planning. Budgeting is the main method of formal financial planning. Once developed and adopted, budgets are the bench mark against which actual performance can be compared. Through this comparison, deviations (called variances) from plans can be determined. This is the essential feedback information that managers need, to carry out their control functions. The budgetary process begins with forecasting sales revenue for the next period. The budgeted sales revenue is the key index of overall activity throughout the organization during that period. Budgeting the manufacturing costs and operating expenses for next period depends directly on the sales budget. Budgeting increases or decreases in assets and liabilities during the coming period depends on the budgeted net income statement (profit plan) for next period. Budgeting is not a cure-all, and it may involve many management problems. But, on balance, budgeting is very valuable for management planning and control.

Questions

7. 1   How do the company's inventory-holding policies affect the budgeting of inventory changes during the coming year?

7. 2   In budgeting the increase or decrease in the company's Accounts Receivable balance during the coming year, what are the most important factors the accountant would have to analyze?

7. 3   "In budgeting current liabilities changes during the coming year a company should plan its short-term notes payable borrowings to keep the company's current ratio no lower than 2.0 to 1.0." Do you agree? Explain briefly.

7. 4   "As sales revenue increases, the company's average Accounts Payable balance should also increase, though not necessarily by the same percent." Do you agree? Briefly explain.

7. 5   "If sales revenue is budgeted to increase by 10.0% next year, then the ending balance in the company's Income Tax Payable should also increase by 10.0%." Do you agree? Briefly explain.

7. 6   "Cash flow from net income is determined by adding back depreciation to the amount of net income."" Do you agree? Briefly explain.

7. 7   In deciding whether to make long-term investments in new fixed assets, what basic kinds of analyses are required?

7. 8   What does the term *master budget* refer to?

7. 9   Is the master budget the document that the various individual managers in the organization use to plan and control operations in their specific areas of responsibility? Briefly explain.

7.10   If actual to budget comparisons are made each month during the year, what is the purpose of the *year-end* review of actual to budget profit performance?

7.11   Assume that actual total operating profit for the year is exactly equal to the amount budgeted. Does this mean that there are no variances between budgeted sales revenue, manufacturing costs, and operating expenses compared with actual sales revenue, manufacturing costs, and operating expenses?

7.12   Contrast the analysis of variances (between budget and actual) for *variable* manufacturing costs and operating expenses and *fixed* manufacturing costs and operating expenses.

7.13   "If actual production and sales volumes for the year are outside the relevant range for the company's fixed costs and expenses, then the analysis of variances should not use the originally budgeted amounts for the fixed costs and expenses." Do you agree? If so, with what would the actual fixed costs and expenses be compared?

7.14   Assume that a company's actual total fixed costs and expenses for the year exactly equal the amounts budgeted for the year for each item. Therefore, there would be no variances between budgeted and actual fixed costs (and expenses) per unit. Do you agree? Briefly explain.

7.15   "If the company achieves its operating profit and net income budget goals for the year, then the company also will achieve its budgeted return on assets and return on equity goals." Do you agree? Briefly explain.

7.16   What are some of the more important management problems of budgeting?

7.17 "If the sales forecast is subject to error, then there is no purpose of budgeting."
Do you agree? Briefly explain.

Problems

P7. 1 Refer to the company's actual 1977 profit performance shown in Exhibit 7.5.
Assume that all these data and information are the same except as they are
changed in this problem. Instead of the $22.90 actual sales price given in
Exhibit 7.5, assume that the actual sales prices during 1977 had been as follows:

Period	Units Sold	Sales Price in Effect During the Period
January through April	220,000	$22.25
May through August	220,000	23.25
September through December	220,000	24.25

Required:

(1) How much would the 1977 net income of the company have been given the
above sales prices during the year, assuming that the operating costs and
interest expense were the same as are shown in Exhibit 7.5? To answer,
prepare the (revised) 1977 profit performance statement for the company. To
save time, you may abbreviate and condense this statement as appropriate.

(2) Based on the sales prices given above, compare the budgeted sales revenue
for 1977 with the actual sales revenue. In particular, compute the volume
variance and the price variance. In reporting these variances to the sales
manager(s) should the sales price changes during the year be included in
the explanation of the variances?

(3) Based on the sales prices given above, compare actual and budgeted
operating profit for 1977, and compute the operating profit variances for the
year.

P7. 2 Refer to the company's actual 1977 profit performance shown in Exhibit 7.5.
Assume that all these data and information are the same except as they are
changed in this problem. Instead of the quantity sold during the year this is
given in Exhibit 7.5, assume that the actual quantity sold at the sales price of
$22.90 per unit is 640,000 units. The company adjusted its production output
accordingly and manufactured 662,500 units during 1977. Instead of the costs
reflected in Exhibit 7.5, assume that the company's operating costs are as
follows during 1977:

	Total Fixed Costs	Total Variable Costs
Manufacturing costs (based on actual production level)	$1,423,050	$7,740,650
Marketing costs (based on actual sales level)	372,480	3,527,680
Administration and general costs, (based on actual sales level)	403,200	115,200

Required:

(1) How much would the 1977 net income of the company have been given the above sales quantity and the above operating costs during 1977? To answer, prepare the (revised) 1977 profit performance statement for the company. To save time you may abbreviate and condense this statement as appropriate.

(2) Based on the sales and production levels and the costs given above, compare the budgeted operating costs with the actual operating costs for 1977. In particular, compute the appropriate variances for the fixed and variable costs. Analyze the variances between actual and budgeted costs in the manner you think is most appropriate.

(3) Based on the sales quantity and the costs given above compare actual and budgeted operating profit for 1977, and compute the operating profit variances for the year.

P7. 3 Refer to the budgeted manufacturing costs for 1977 statement for the company that is shown as Exhibit 7.1 In particular, notice the raw material cost. To simplify, assume that only one raw material item is used in the manufacture of the company's product. The budgeted raw material cost for 1977 was determined as follows:

Total budgeted production output	675,000 units
Raw material weight per unit of finished product	× 4.8 pounds
Total raw material weight required	3,240,000 pounds
Normal wastage allowance	135,000 pounds
Total raw material weight allowed	3,375,000 pounds
Budgeted cost per hundredweight (cwt)	× $94.42 cwt
Budgeted raw material usage cost for 1977	$3,186,675

Exhibit 7.5 shows the actual performance of the company in 1977. Assume that the *actual* raw material cost per hundredweight issued to production in 1977 is

$100, and that raw material wastage was normal. During 1977 687,500 units were manufactured, which is 27,500 more units than sold (see Exhibit 7.5), according to the company's inventory holding policy of maintaining its ending inventory equal to one fourth of the units sold during the year.

Required: Analyze the variance between the actual and the budgeted total cost of raw materials used during 1977.

P7. 4   This company happens to lease all of its fixed assets from outside leasing companies. Not a single fixed asset is owned; all are leased. Otherwise the business is a typical manufacturing company that produces and sells a variety of products on credit. The company carries normal stocks of raw materials, work-in-process, and finished goods inventories.

Required:

(1) Discuss the main differences in this company's budgeting procedures compared with the more typical company example discussed in Chapters Six and Seven.

(2) Would the "simple" method of determining cash flow from budgeted net income next year work in this situation? Explain.

P7. 5   Two businessmen are having their usual coffee break. One is the owner and general manager of a local men's clothing store, which has grown rapidly in recent years and is planning a major expansion and remodeling of its premises. The other is the owner and general manager of a 1000-seat movie theater next door to the men's clothing store, which has been in the same location for several years. As is customary, a certain fraction of the gross ticket sales receipts is paid to the distributor of each feature film shown. Both businesses have done reasonably well. The clothing store manager this particular morning is explaining that his company's budgeting procedures and actual to budget reports are very useful for planning and control. The movie theater manager replies that budgeting is not needed in his business and would be a waste of effort and money. "You either show movies that people want to see, or you don't," is his basic management philosophy.

Required: Do you agree with the movie theater manager? Would budgeting be "wasted effort" for his business? Explain.

P7. 6   Refer to the retailer company's financial statements introduced in Problem 2.6 and the additional information presented in Problem 4.10. Also, refer to the budget information and the "most probable" budgeted net income statement of the company for the year 1977 that you prepared in Problem 6.9. This problem builds directly on that preceding information. The president of the company has requested you, the chief accountant of the company, to prepare a budgeted statement of financial condition at year-end 1977 and a budgeted statement of changes in financial position during 1977. These budget documents are to be presented to the company's Board of Directors for their formal approval. From your analysis of the company's past policies and practices, and from conversations with the president and other top managers of the company, you believe that the following assumptions and forecasts are reasonably accurate and reliable for 1977:

(a) The company's ending inventory holding policy will continue to be the same as described in Problem 6.9—see information item (c) in that problem.

(b) The company will give slightly more liberal credit terms to its customers in 1977, which means that about one month's sales will be uncollected at year-end 1977. (Sales are spread evenly over each month during the year; ignore bad debts in this problem.) There are no cash sales.

(c) Purchases and other supplies and services bought on credit should be made under the same credit terms, which means that the year-end balance of accounts payable and accrued costs should be close to 6.0% of the total cost of purchases and operating expenses, excluding depreciation.

(d) Prepaid expenses at year-end 1977 should be about 6.5% of total operating expenses, excluding depreciation (and excluding cost of purchases during the year).

(e) About 20.0% of 1977 income tax expense should still be payable at year-end 1977; the other 80.0% will have to be paid during the year.

(f) Based on the planned retirements of certain fixed assets, which will be fully depreciated by the date of disposal in 1977, the company will make the following capital expenditures in 1977 to provide the storage and delivery capacity needed to support the forecast sales range for 1977:

Buildings	$35,000
Machinery and equipment	28,300
Vehicles	14,700
Total cost	$78,000

The cost of the fixed assets retired during the year will be:

Buildings	$ —0—
Machinery and equipment	17,500
Vehicles	13,200
Total cost	$30,700

Based on the above planned purchases and retirements, the 1977 depreciation should be $28,400.

(g) The company would prefer to maintain a year-end cash balance at least equal to 3.0% of total sales revenue for the year.

(h) No payment on the long-term debt falls due during 1977, and the company does not plan on making any early payment on this debt obligation. Indeed, the company expects to borrow an additional $50,000 from long-term debt sources during the year, and also to increase the year-end balance of short-term notes payable by $50,000. The average balance of interest bearing debt during 1977, based on these borrowing plans, should be $275,000 on which an average annual interest rate of 10.0% will be paid.

(i) The company intends to pay the same cash dividend per share in 1977 that was paid in 1976, and it does not intend to issue any new shares of stock or to retire any outstanding shares.

Required: Prepare in good form and sufficient detail a statement of the budgeted changes in financial position and balance sheet at year-end 1977. (See Exhibit 7.4 for example.)

P7. 7   This problem is continued from Problems 7.6 and 6.9, and depends on your answers and computations for them.

Required:

(1) Based on the 1977 budgeted net income at the 26,000 units sales volume and based on the budgeted balance sheet at year-end 1977, determine for 1977 the company's budgeted:
   (a) Return on assets, including the asset turnover ratio and operating profit (before interest and income tax) ratio.
   (b) Return on equity.

(2) If the actual sales volume turns out to be only 24,000 units in 1977, but assuming the other net income budget assumptions and forecasts are correct, and assuming that the company follows the budgeting assumptions made in Problem 7.6 (including capital expenditures of $78,000), determine for 1977 the company's budgeted:
   (a) Return on assets, including the asset turnover ratio and operating profit (before interest and income tax) ratio.
   (b) Return on equity.

P7. 8   Refer to Problem 6.10, in which you prepared the production budget for the coming quarter of one of the company's production departments. The actual cost and output for this quarter was as follows:

(a) Total output	9,500 units
(b) Total direct labor hours	38,475 hours
(c) Total direct labor costs	$284,715
(d) Total variable overhead costs	$123,120
(e) Total raw materials used	138,700 pounds
(f) Total cost of raw materials used	$865,488
(g) Total fixed overhead costs	$394,300

Required:

(1) Prepare a detailed comparative analysis between the budgeted and actual costs of this production department for the quarter.

(2) Based on your answer to part (1), indicate which particular variance, or variances between budget and actual is (or are) probably the most important, that is, the most significant to the manager in charge of this production department.

P7. 9   Refer to the example introduced in Problem 6.12. Its information is used in this problem.

Required:

(1) Prepare the 1977 statement of budgeted balance sheet changes and year-end balances (see Exhibit 7.4 for example).

(2) Assume that the company actually sells 15% more cubic yards than in 1976 and that the actual average sales price is $1.65 per cubic yard. However, the company's actual operating costs, as explained in items (b) to (e) in particular, are exactly as they were budgeted. Also the company's actual interest expense turned out to be as budgeted. Of course, the company's actual income tax expense depends on the company's actual taxable income for the year. Based on this information, prepare the company's 1977 net income statement.

P7.10   This company manufactures and sells three quite different products, although all three products are manufactured at the same location with the same machinery and equipment. The company has organized three separate sales divisions, each in charge of a sales manager. All production, on the other hand, is in charge of one production manager. The company very carefully accounts for all variable manufacturing costs and has developed an excellent cost accounting system to assign the variable costs to one of the three products manufactured by the company. On the other hand, virtually all of the fixed manufacturing overhead costs are joint costs that cannot be objectively matched or attached with one of the three products. Thus the company prepares a contribution margin report that matches all variable costs with each of the three product's sales revenue. But no fixed cost is allocated between the three products sales revenue.

The company for many years has followed a formal budgeting system, and the year-end review of budget against actual is an important step. The sales managers know that the budget to actual performance of their division is very well remembered when the president decides on their salaries for the following year, as well as their eventual consideration for a promotion in the company. For the year just ended, the summary report comparing budget to actual has just arrived on the president's desk. You should find this report fairly straightforward, although one aspect needs explaining. Notice the two indexes reported in the statement. The quantity index is computed as follows, for example, where the budgeted quantity is 100 and the actual quantity sold is 105:

$$\text{Quantity Index} = \frac{\text{Actual Quantity}}{\text{Budgeted Quantity}} = \frac{105}{100} = 1.05$$

The dollar per unit refers to either the sales price or the variable cost per unit. This index is computed as follows, for example, where the budgeted sales price is $100 and the actual sales price is $98:

$$\text{Dollar per Unit Index} = \frac{\text{Actual Sales Price}}{\text{Budgeted Sales Price}} = \frac{\$\,98.00}{\$100.00} = .98$$

Budget Versus Actual Annual Report

	Budgeted	Actual	Dollar per Unit Index	Quantity Index
Sales revenue				
Product A	$5,300,000	$5,620,650	1.01	1.05
Product B	2,600,000	2,930,200	.98	1.15
Product C	1,400,000	1,303,400	.95	.98
Total	$9,300,000	$9,854,250	?	?
Variable manufacturing costs				
Product A	$3,180,000	$3,405,780	1.02	1.05
Product B	1,430,000	1,578,720	.96	1.15
Product C	630,000	648,270	1.05	.98
Total	$5,240,000	$5,632,770	?	?
Variable selling costs				
Product A	$ 424,000	$ 467,460	1.05	1.05
Product B	234,000	322,920	1.20	1.15
Product C	175,000	137,200	.80	.98
Total	$ 833,000	$ 927,580	?	?
Contribution margin				
Product A	$1,696,000	$1,747,410	?	1.05
Product B	936,000	1,028,560	?	1.15
Product C	595,000	517,930	?	.98
Total	$3,227,000	$3,293,900	?	?

Required:

(1) Complete the budget to actual report by determining the index ratios to enter where each question mark appears.

(2) In the manner suggested in Exhibit 7.6, analyze the variance between budgeted and actual contribution margin for each of the three products as well as the total of all three products.

(*Note:* Exhbiit 7.6 focuses on operating profit whereas this problem focuses on contribution margin—before any fixed costs are considered.)

(3) Which sales manager seems to have done the best, assuming that the budgeted amounts are realistic and achievable? Explain briefly.

P7.11 Assume that you happen to meet a friend of your father who owns and is president of a company, and who likes to talk a great deal about his business. He rambles quite a bit and does not want to divulge how profitable his business is. But later you become very curious regarding just how profitable the business may be. You recall from your conversation that the president made the following forecasts for the coming year:

(a) Total sales revenue	$20,000,000
(b) Variable operating costs	65% of sales revenue
(c) Total assets:	
—current assets	40% of sales revenue
—fixed assets	$4,000,000
(d) Total fixed operating costs	$5,020,000
(e) Noninterest bearing liabilities	10% of total assets
(f) Interest bearing liabilities	40% of total assets
(g) Average annual interest rate	10.0%
(h) Federal income tax rate	48% of taxable income

Required:

(1) In condensed and brief form prepare the budgeted net income statement and the balance sheet for the company based on the above information, and also determine the budgeted return on equity.

(2) A year later you meet the president again and he mentions that he exceeded his expected sales revenue by 5% but that variable cost increases cut his contribution margin to one third of sales revenue. Assuming the other forecasts were true, determine the company's actual return on equity for the year.

P7.12   A small group of investors have just purchased 100% of the common stock of a privately owned corporation. Until now, the stock had been owned by members of a family for three generations. There are no family members that are willing to continue the business, especially since the profit performance of the company the last several years has been going from bad to worse. The financial statements for the year ending December 31, 1976 were made available to the new investors. They are shown below.

STATEMENT OF FINANCIAL CONDITION
AT DECEMBER 31, 1976

Cash	$ —0—	Accounts payable	$ 187,500
Accounts receivable	400,000	Accrued costs and	
Inventories	625,000	expenses	$ 170,000
Prepaid expenses	85,000	Total current	
Total current assets	$1,110,000	liabilities	$ 357,500
Fixed assets, at cost	$1,000,000	Stockholders' equity:	
Less accumulated		Common stock	$ 250,000
depreciation	600,000	Retained earnings	902,500
Net	$ 400,000	Total	$1,152,500
Total assets	$1,510,000	Total sources of	
		capital	$1,510,000

STATEMENT OF NET INCOME
FOR YEAR ENDING DECEMBER 31, 1976

Sales revenue		$5,000,000
Cost of goods sold:		
Raw materials used	$1,500,000	
Direct labor	1,000,000	
Variable overhead	500,000	
Fixed overhead	750,000	
Total		3,750,000
Gross profit		$1,250,000
Other operating expenses		
Variable expenses	$ 750,000	
Fixed expenses	500,000	1,250,000
Net income		—0—

Depreciation recorded in 1976 included $80,000 charged to manufacturing costs and $20,000 charged to other operating expenses. The reason for the zero cash balance is that the company paid a cash dividend to the old stockholders to reduce the cash balance to zero. This was part of the agreement between the old and new stockholders. The new owners believe that the current replacement values of the other assets are very close to their book values, and accordingly they paid the old stockholders $1,152,500 for the stock. To raise the necessary cash to operate the business, the new owners have arranged two loans from a bank. One is a 12-month loan (due December 31, 1977), and the second is a five-year loan. The short-term loan's principal amount is $300,000 and the long-term loan's principal is also $300,000. The long-term loan's annual interest rate is 9.0%, and the short-term loan bears a 12.0% annual interest rate. Both loans will be executed immediately—as soon as the new owners start business the first working day in January 1977. The short-term loan probably can be renewed one year from now, *if* the company can make a substantial profit improvement from last year.

The new president of the company, based on detailed analyses prepared by the new Controller, has reached the following conclusions and has made the following forecasts for 1977:
(a) Except for the cash balance, the year-end 1976 balances of the current assets and the current liabilities are in the proper ratios to the sales and expenses for 1976, and no changes in these ratios are expected during 1977. It should be noted that all raw materials are purchased on credit and no other credit entries are made to the Accounts Payable account.
(b) Depreciation in 1977 should be the same as in 1976, since no additions or retirements of fixed assets are planned in 1977.
(c) The new sales manager expects to increase the average sales price by 5% and to increase total volume by 10.0%.

(d) The new purchasing manager believes that the average raw material purchase price can be held the same in 1977, and that no change will occur in the raw material productivity in 1977.

(e) The new production manager has planned several changes that he thinks will increase labor productivity by 10.0%. But the average labor wage rate should increase by 12.5%. Variable overhead costs depend on direct labor hours; on average the purchase costs of the various variable overhead items should increase by 5.0%.

(f) Fixed manufacturing overhead, exclusive of depreciation, should increase by 6.0% in 1977.

(g) The president believes that the average purchase cost of the various items making up the variable nonmanufacturing operating expenses can be held constant in 1977, but that the fixed expenses will probably cost 5.0% more in 1977, exclusive of depreciation.

(h) The federal income tax will be 22% on the first $25,000 of taxable income and 48% on the remainder. Eighty percent of the estimated total income tax for the year must be paid during the year.

Required:

(1) Prepare the budgeted net income statement for the company for 1977.

(2) Prepare the company's budgeted balance sheet at December 31, 1977, assuming that a new short-term bank loan is made to the company at year-end 1977.

(3) Based on your answers to (1) and (2), determine the budgeted return on assets and return on equity for 1977.

P7.13   The company's management profit performance statement for the year ending December 31, 1976 is shown below. Following this financial statement are certain budgeting forecasts and assumptions for the next year. This company is a *retailer* that purchases products in condition for resale to its customers. In other words this company is not a manufacturer; it does not in any way process the products it sells. To simplify, it is assumed that this company sells only one product.

MANAGEMENT NET INCOME STATEMENT FOR THE YEAR ENDING
DECEMBER 31, 1976

Sales revenue (500,000 units @ $10)			$5,000,000
Cost of Goods Sold:			
Beginning Inventory (50,000 units @ $5.75)		$ 287,500	
Purchases, in chronological "price groups"			
(a price group is the total quantity of			
purchases bought at the same purchase			
price per unit)			
(100,000 units @ $5.79)	$579,000		
(125,000 units @ $5.90)	737,500		
(150,000 units @ $6.04)	906,000		
(137,500 units @ $6.20)	852,500		
Total (512,500 units)		3,075,000	
Cost of Goods Available for Sale (562,500 units)		$3,362,500	
Ending Inventory (62,500 units @ $6.20)		387,500	2,975,000
Gross profit before operating expenses			$2,025,000
Product ordering, receiving, storage, and handling costs:			
Fixed costs	$162,400		
Variable costs (512,500 units @ $.52)	266,500	$ 428,900	
Selling, promotion, and transportation-out costs:			
Fixed costs	$ 87,800		
Variable costs (500,000 units @ $1.15)	575,000	662,800	
Administrative and general costs:			
Fixed costs	$289,300		
Variable costs (500,000 units @ $.16)	80,000	369,300	1,461,000
Operating profit (net income before interest and income tax)			$ 564,000
Interest Expense ($800,000 average debt × 8.0%)			64,000
Net income before income tax			$ 500,000
Income tax (at flat 48% rate)			240,000
Net income			$ 260,000

Budget forecasts and assumptions for next year (1977):

(a) The sales demand for the company's product, that is, the number of units that would be bought by customers at different sales prices, is estimated by the sales manager to be as follows for 1977:

Sales Price per Unit	Total Demand for Company's Product
$ 9.50	575,000 units
10.00	535,000 units
10.50	500,000 units
11.00	470,000 units
11.50	445,000 units

(b) The purchasing agent expects the purchase price for the product to increase immediately to $6.40 per unit and then to stabilize at this cost per unit throughout the year. There are no plans to change the company's inventory turnover policy, which is to maintain its ending inventory quantity equal to a certain percentage of the sales quantity for the year.

(c) All operating costs will be affected by cost inflation next year; to simplify, it is assumed that the cost inflation will be 5% next year on all costs; in other words, $1 of an operating cost this year will cost $1.05 next year as a result of the higher cost levels next year. Productivity ratios in all three operating areas will remain the same next year; hence, none of the inflation will be offset by productivity gains.

(d) Although the actual sales volume in 1977 turns out to be lower than in 1976 (see below), the decrease is *not* enough to allow the company to step down or eliminate any fixed cost elements in 1977. For instance, no fixed salary employee is laid off.

(e) The total amount of interest bearing debt and the annual interest rate should remain just about the same next year; also, there is no reason to expect any change in the income tax rate.

Required:

(1) The company set its sales price at $10.50 for the year and actually sells 485,000 units. Compare the budgeted sales revenue for the year 1977 with the actual sales revenue. Compute the variances between budget and actual.

(2) The company has just prepared its *actual* management profit performance statement for the year ending December 31, 1977, in the same format as shown above. This statement begins with the actual sales revenue of $5,092,500 (485,000 units @ $10.50). Following the same format, prepare the *budgeted* management profit performance statement against which the 1977 actual profit statement should be compared, based on the actual sales volume for 1977. The comparison between budgeted and actual sales revenue has already been completed in part (1). This part of the problem is directed to determining the budgeted costs against which the company's actual costs should be compared.

Chapter Eight

Short-Term Cash Flow Analysis and Budgeting

SHORT-TERM CASH FLOW ANALYSIS AND BUDGETING

Importance of Cash Flow Planning and Control

Cash flow is the lifeblood of a business. Cash constantly circulates in and out of the business, and the business must maintain an adequate cash balance every day through the year. Over the course of a year the basic sources (inflows) and uses (outflows) of cash can be summarized as is shown in Exhibit 8.1. This exhibit adopts the usual one-year (12 months) time period as the dividing line between short-term and long-term. Notice that for each basic source there is a "natural" opposite use. For instance, earning net income results in a net cash inflow for the year (in most cases). On the other side, cash dividends are paid to stockholders (in most cases). This chapter is concerned with the analysis and budgeting of *short-term* cash inflows and outflows for management planning and control purposes.

Short-term cash flow analysis and budgeting (or some kind of less formal planning) is necessary for two basic management purposes:

1. To provide adequate cash balances throughout the year to support and maintain the profit-making activity of the company, and to avoid any interruptions or curtailments of this activity that would limit the *profit performance* of the company.

2. To provide adequate cash balances when needed throughout the year to pay all liabilities as they come due, which means to maintain the *continuous solvency* of the company and thereby protect the ability of the company to make purchases on credit and to borrow money when and as needed.

The consequences of poor cash flow planning on the profit performance of a company can be very serious. By neglecting short-term cash flow planning, a company could find itself in an inadequate cash position. The result might be that it could not pay all its employees in full on time, or that production output would have to be curtailed or temporarily suspended. A work stoppage or an inventory stock-out would result in lost sales, and thus there would be lost profit opportunities. In short, inadequate cash flow would result in inadequate profit performance. Short-term cash flow analysis and planning are essential to main-

EXHIBIT 8.1
Basic Sources and Uses of Cash During Year

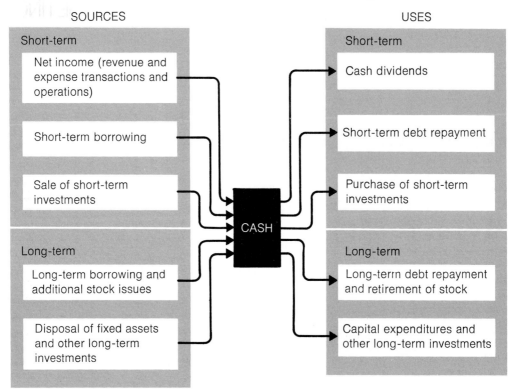

tain sufficient cash balances during the year to carry on the profit-making trans-actions and operations of the company.

Equally important, a business must have adequate cash balances when needed to pay liabilities as these payment obligations come due. Otherwise the company is at the "mercy" of its creditors, who have certain legally enforceable options that go into effect if the terms and provisions of liability contracts and arrangements are violated by the company. One or more such unpaid creditors may have the legal right to force the company into involuntary bankruptcy. How-ever, in most situations some agreement among the creditors and the company is reached to extend the term (time period) for payment of the liabilities. Cred-itors may not want to force bankruptcy on the company. The company may be able to pay more of its liabilities as a going concern than if it were forced out of business. In these situations the creditors usually demand more of a voice in management, and they impose tight financial constraints. This generally makes life much more difficult for the company, and causes the stockholders some loss of their normal rights. The stock's market value usually suffers and may, in fact, become almost worthless.

Although the main thrust of this chapter is short-term cash flow analysis and planning, it should be emphasized that long-term planning of the demands for and sources of capital over the next two to five years (or longer) should be coordinated with the company's short-term cash flow planning.* Determining cash flow over the coming year and the budgeted cash position of the company at the end of the coming year is the essential starting point for planning the longer range sources and demands for cash. Managers need to know the cash flow over the immediate future (next year), and what the company's cash balance is likely to be one year from now in order to plan from that time forward.

Cash Flow Analysis of Budgeted Net Income

In Chapter Seven the budgeted depreciation for the coming year (1977) is added back to the budgeted net income for the year to obtain a quick and approximate measure of the budgeted cash flow from net income sources for the year (see page 226). However, this "depreciation add-back" method is not a complete nor necessarily accurate measure of cash flow from net income. In fact, this approach may be seriously misleading in some situations. Depreciation is the most obvious difference between the cash basis and the accrual basis of net income accounting. But on closer examination, it is clear that the total sales revenue reported in the annual net income statement is not equal to the total cash receipts from customers during the year (unless the company makes only cash sales). And, the total cash payments during the year for most expenses are not equal to the accrual basis amounts reported in the net income statement. For short-term cash flow planning purposes a *more complete and more accurate* estimate of the cash flow from budgeted net income for the coming year is preferable in most situations. The same company example discussed and analyzed in Chapters Six and Seven is continued in this chapter.

Sales revenue is budgeted to be $14,950,000 during 1977—see line (b) in Exhibit 6.2. Most of the company's sales are on credit. Thus most sales revenue is *not* collected in cash at the point of recording the sales revenue. The cash is not collected until 10, 20, 30, or more days after the sale is recorded. Indeed, the *ending* balance of Accounts Receivable is simply the amount of uncollected sales revenue recorded during the year. On the other hand, the *beginning* balance of Accounts Receivable carried forward from the previous year would (for all practical purposes) be collected during this year, although none of these cash collections are recorded as sales revenue this year. (These sales were recorded last year, of course.) In short, a dollar in the ending balance of Accounts Receivable is a dollar recorded as sales revenue but not collected in cash during the year. In reverse, a dollar in the beginning balance of Accounts Receivable is a dollar of cash collected during the year but not recorded as sales revenue during the year.

---

* Chapters Nine and Ten discuss the basic nature of long-term investment decisions and the accounting information and analysis needed for these decisions.

Therefore, if the ending balance is more than the beginning balance, this increase of Accounts Receivable should be subtracted from total sales revenue for the year to determine the total cash collected from customers during the year. Accordingly, the total cash that will be collected from its customers during 1977 by the company in the example, based on the information presented in its budgeted financial statements (see Exhibits 6.2 and 7.4), is determined as follows (in thousands, rounded off):

Cash Flow Analysis of Sales Revenue for 1977
(in Thousands)

	(Budgeted) Sales Revenue	$14,950
+	(Actual) Accounts Receivable balance at start of year	1,478
	Total That Could Be Collected	$16,428
−	(Budgeted) Accounts Receivable balance at end of year	1,495
=	(Budgeted) Cash collected from customers during year	$14,933

Some manufacturing costs and operating expenses are recorded on a "pay as you go" basis; the amount of the cost or expense is a decrease to cash at the time of recording the item. But *most* costs and expenses are either: (1) prepaid in cash *before* the amount is recorded as an expense in the net income statement; or (2) the cost or expense is paid in cash *after* being recorded. Prepayments are recorded as increases to asset accounts. For example, raw materials when purchased are charged to an inventory account. Prepayments of insurance costs are charged to the Prepaid Expenses asset account. And, "prepayments" of depreciation are charged to fixed assets accounts. In contrast, delayed (deferred) payments are recorded as increases to liability accounts. For example, the advertising expense recorded for the month may be paid for after the end of the month. When the advertising expense is recorded (in the month that the ads appeared) the Accounts Payable account is increased. *Later* the Accounts Payable amount is paid in cash.

In short, a dollar in the *beginning* balance of an inventory or prepaid expense account was prepaid before the start of the year. When this dollar is charged off to expense during the year, the company does *not* pay out this dollar in cash again. In reverse, a dollar in the *ending* balance of an inventory or prepaid expense account is paid out during the year, although this dollar has not yet appeared as an expense in the net income statement. Therefore, if the ending balance is more than the beginning balance, the increase of the inventory or prepaid expense account should be added to the total expenses for the year to determine the total cash outlays during the year that are related to the expenses.

A dollar in the *beginning* balance of Accounts Payable is a dollar that must be paid during the year, although this dollar is not included in the total expenses for the year. (The expense was recorded last year.) In contrast, a dollar in the *ending* balance of Accounts Payable is included in the total expenses for the year but is not paid out during the year. Therefore, if the ending balance is more than the beginning balance, this increase of Accounts Payable is sub-tracted from the total expenses for the year to determine the cash outlay for expenses during the year.

Instead of a detailed specific cost-by-cost and expense-by-expense analysis according to the discussion above, a summary analysis of all expenses for 1977 is now presented (amounts in thousands, rounded off); see Exhibit 8.2. (The amounts in Exhibit 8.2 are taken from Exhibits 6.2 and 7.4.) As we explain above the amount of depreciation charged off during the year is not a cash outlay during that year. Thus the amount of depreciation is deducted from the total operating expenses for the year. (Based on the depreciation schedules for 1977, including the new fixed assets to be purchased during 1977, the com-pany's depreciation to be recorded in 1977 should be $437,500, or $438,000 rounded off.) Sooner or later a company has to replace the fixed assets being depreciated, to continue business. However, the replacement of fixed assets is not tied to the method of depreciating them. If a company records, say, $100,000 of depreciation this year, this does not mean that it will purchase

EXHIBIT 8.2
Cash Flow Analysis of Budgeted Operating Expenses for 1977
(in thousands)

Budgeted cost of goods sold expense	$8,915	
Budgeted marketing expenses	3,952	
Budgeted administration and general expenses	523	
Total budgeted operating expenses		$13,390
Less:		
Beginning balance of raw materials inventory	$ 464	
Beginning balance of work-in-process and finished goods inventories	1,705	
Beginning balance of prepaid expenses	492	
Ending balance of accounts payable	1,674	
Total		4,335
Net difference		$ 9,055
Plus:		
Ending balance of raw materials inventory	$ 531	
Ending balance of work-in-process and finished goods inventories	2,048	
Ending balance of prepaid expenses	603	
Beginning balance of accounts payable	1,351	
Total		4,533
Total		$13,588
Less: Budgeted depreciation for year		438
Cash outlay for expenses during year		$13,150

$100,000 of new fixed assets this year. In short, purchases of new fixed assets are treated as capital expenditures (long-term investments) separate from the cash flow from net income.

Exhibit 8.3 brings together the above analysis into one general statement, and also includes the other two expenses for 1977—interest expense and income tax expense. The format of this exhibit is somewhat different: the budgeted net increase or decrease during 1977 in each balance sheet account that is directly involved in recording sales revenue or expenses is added or subtracted to the net income account. (These budgeted increases and decreases are taken from Exhibit 7.4.) In closing, notice that the cash flow determined by the depreciation add-back method in Chapter Seven, which is $1,115,000 (see

EXHIBIT 8.3
Cash Flow Analysis of 1977 Budgeted Net Income
(in thousands)

	Budgeted Net Income Statement (See Exhibit 6.2)	Brief Explanation (See Exhibit 7.4 for Amounts)		Cash Flow
Sales Revenue	$14,950	Less $17 increase of Accounts Receivable		$14,933
Cost of Goods Sold	8,915	Plus increase of Raw Materials Inventory	$ 67	
Marketing Expenses	3,952	Plus increase of Work-in-Process and Finished		
Administrative and General Expenses	523	Goods Inventories	343	
Total Operating Expenses	$13,390	Plus increase of Prepaid Expenses	111	
		Total increases	$521	
		Less increase of Accounts Payable	$323	
		Less depreciation	438	
		Total decreases	$761	
		Net decrease	$240	13,150
Operating Profit	$ 1,560			$ 1,783
Interest Expense	270	(Assume paid entirely in cash during year)		270
Net Income Before Income Tax	$ 1,290			$ 1,513
Income Tax	613	Less $44 increase of Income Tax Payable		569
Net Income	$ 677	Net cash inflow from Net Income		$ 944

page 226), is considerably different than the complete and accurate cash flow of $944,000 shown in Exhibit 8.3. Finally, keep in mind that this discussion and analysis are for only one example; there is no suggestion that cash flow usually is more than net income for the year. In many instances it is less than net income, and in some cases there may be a net cash *outflow* from net income during the year.

Short-term Solvency Analysis

The Current Ratio: A Point of Departure for More Detailed Analysis

Solvency means basically the ability of the company to pay its liabilities as these payments become due. One of the most popular "quick and dirty" approaches to test the *short-term* solvency prospects of a company is to compute its *current ratio,* also called the *working capital ratio.* This ratio is determined by dividing total current assets by total current liabilities at the balance sheet date. For the company in the example the current ratios are computed as follows (in thousands, rounded off; see Exhibit 7.4 for amounts):

		December 31	
		1977 (Budgeted)	1976 (Actual)
Total Current Assets / Total Current Liabilities	=	$\dfrac{\$5,125}{\$2,646} = 1.94$	$\dfrac{\$4,485}{\$2,179} = 2.06$

In other words, at year-end 1976 current assets were 2.06 times current liabilities, and at year-end 1977 there should be $1.94 of current assets for each $1 of current liabilities. (Keep in mind that the dollar amounts are the book *values* of the current assets and the current liabilities). A popular rule of thumb is that the current ratio should be at least 2 to 1. But is this "standard" of 2 to 1 necessarily a good ratio for *this* company? Should it be higher? Is a lower ratio really adequate? For that matter, why should current assets be more than current liabilities?

The Short-term Operating Cycle and the Short-term Credit Cycle

Perhaps the best way to answer these questions about the current ratio is to consider how long it takes the company to complete its *operating cycle,* and then to compare this period to the average *short-term credit period.* The basic flows of each cycle are shown in Exhibit 8.4. First, the company spends money to manufacture its products. Cash is "converted" into finished goods during the manufacturing process. The manufacturing time from start to finish for this com-

EXHIBIT 8.4
Short-term Operating and Credit Cycles

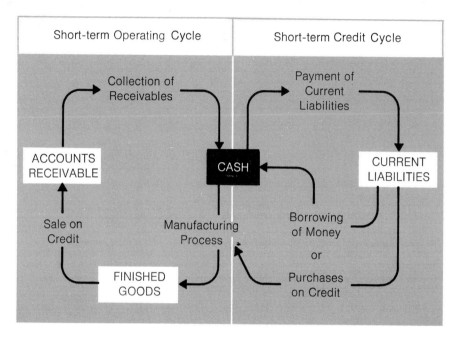

pany is 25 days on average.* In other words, it takes the company 25 days on average to get from cash to finished goods. Hence, the first leg on the short-term operating cycle shown in Exhibit 8.4 takes 25 days.

The finished goods inventory is held in stock until the point of sale and delivery to customers. As is discussed in Chapter Six (see page 194), finished goods inventory is held 91 days on average before sale. In other words, the company's finished goods inventory is equal to about one fourth of its annual sales volume, which is one fourth of a year, or 91 days. Thus it takes another 91 days to

---

* This 25-day period is a weighted average of two quite different types of manufacturing costs: (1) raw materials, and (2) all other manufacturing costs. In this example raw materials constitute about one third of the total manufacturing costs (see Exhibit 6.2 for review). Raw materials are bought in advance of when needed and are carried in stock until released to the manufacturing process. In this example, the company holds raw material in inventory 60 days on average before it is used in the manufacturing process. (See discussion on page 222 for review.) The actual manufacturing process, that is, the working on the raw materials and making these materials into a finished product, is assumed to be a fairly short process—about one week from start to finish. Hence, one third of the manufacturing cost (the raw materials cost) takes 60 days from point of purchase to point of use, but the other two thirds is spent in about one week. Weighing the two factors together gives a combined average of about 25 days for *all* manufacturing costs: [(⅓ × 60 days) + (⅔ × 7 days) = 25 days].

complete the second leg of the short-term operating cycle. In this example, it is assumed that most goods are sold on credit, and that the average customer credit period is 37 days: the ending balance of Accounts Receivable is budgeted to be one tenth of the year's sales, and $1/10 \times 365$ days = 37 days. In summary, it takes 153 days to complete one turn of the short-term operating cycle $(25 + 91 + 37 = 153)$. In other words, it takes the company 153 days to get from cash back to cash.

In this case the company has capital invested in its inventories and accounts receivable for 153 days on average before the assets are converted back to cash. This company, like the majority of companies, uses two major *short-term* sources of capital: (1) accounts payable (purchases of raw materials, supplies, and services on credit); and, (2) short-term notes payable. In this example there is one other current liability—Income Tax Payable—but, since it is relatively immaterial, this other short-term liability is ignored. As Exhibit 7.4 shows, the company has about twice as much Accounts Payable compared with Notes Payable. That is, its short-term capital sources are about two thirds Accounts Payable and one third Notes Payable. The average Accounts Payable period is about 42 days and the average Notes Payable period is 150 days. Thus the combined weighted average short-term credit cycle is 78 days: $(^2\!/_3 \times 42$ days) + $^1\!/_3 \times 150$ days) = 78 days.

Therefore, it takes the company 153 days to get from cash to cash on the current asset side (as explained above). But the company has to pay its current liabilities every 78 days. How can this be done? The basic answer is that current assets must be sufficiently more than current liabilities. In fact, the following ratio can be computed to determine the "proper" ratio of current assets to current liabilities for this company.

Minimum Required Current Ratio

$$\frac{\text{Short-term Operating Cycle}}{\text{Short-term Borrowing Cycle}} = \frac{153 \text{ days}}{78 \text{ days}} = \underline{1.96}$$

Every 78 days the current liabilities have to be paid. Roughly speaking, only about one half of the current assets would be converted into cash in this time, since it takes almost twice as long for the current assets to complete one operating cycle (from cash back to cash). Thus the current assets should be about twice the current liabilities, so that within one short-term borrowing period there would be enough current assets converted into cash to pay the current liabilities. It is computed above (see page 225) that the 1977 budgeted year-end current ratio for the company is 1.94, which is almost exactly equal to the "required" current ratio of 1.96.

The analysis of short-term solvency is not as simple as it might appear to be from this brief discussion. Managers should consider several other factors as well, especially how large the company's average cash buffer (safety reserve) should be. The main point, however, is that managers must establish policies about the credit periods to grant to the company's customers, the credit periods to bargain for from its suppliers, the borrowing periods on short-term notes payable, and the average inventory quantities to carry in stock. And, management has to determine carefully the time required (or that should be required) to manufacture its products. All these time periods must be known to determine the short-term operating cycle and the short-term liability periods of the company. From these two basic periods the company's minimum required current ratio can be determined, as is shown above.

Short-term Operating Turnover Ratios

Certain managers in the organization need regular periodic accounting reports regarding how well or not the company is staying within its established inventory holding and accounts receivable collection periods. If either of these periods become too long, this may cause short-run solvency problems and may indicate a slow response on the part of managers to take appropriate action. For instance, the manager in charge of customer credit may decide, in consultation with other sales' managers, that the company should extend 30 days credit to the company's customers. Accounts receivable should be collected within this time limit, except for the small percentage of customers who are late payers.* For control purposes the manager needs to know the *actual* collection experience from its customers relative to the credit policy of the company. When capital becomes tight, for instance, many customers become slow payers, and the company must know if and to what extent this is happening. Likewise, if the company's policy is to hold its finished goods inventory level equal to 91 days of sales, then those managers who have inventory control responsibility need regular periodic reports regarding *actual* inventory stock levels relative to current and expected sales demands for the products.

Certain *turnover ratios* are computed and reported to managers for their comparison of the actual accounts receivable collection period and the actual inventory holding period with how long these periods should be. Recall from the discussion above that these two periods are as follows in this example:

Average accounts receivable collection period = 37 days
Average finished goods inventory holding period = 91 days

These periods are based on the normal conditions and practices in this particular industry. Keep in mind, however, that these periods vary from industry to industry, or from year to year in the same industry sometimes.

The *accounts receivable turnover* ratio is a quick and reasonably accurate measure of the actual average accounts receivable collection period. It is com-

* The late payers explain why the average customer credit period adopted above is 37 days instead of 30 days.

puted as follows for 1976 for the company in this example (amounts in thousands, rounded off; see Exhibits 6.2 and 7.4 for information):

Accounts Receivable Turnover Ratio

$$\frac{\text{Sales Revenue}}{\text{Ending Accounts Receivable}} = \frac{\$11,825}{\$1,478} = 8.0$$

From this ratio we observe that sales revenue for 1976 is 8.0 times the ending balance of accounts receivable; accounts receivable were "turned over" or collected 8.0 times in 1976. Expressed another way, there were 8.0 accounts receivable collection cycles completed during the year. Based on the average credit period of 37 days, however, there should have been 10.0 turnovers or collection cycles during the year: (365 days ÷ 37 days = 10.0). Hence, the actual accounts receivable turnover ratio of 8.0 is too low compared with the expected or normal ratio of 10.0 times. As was previously explained in Chapter Seven (see page 222) in the latter part of 1976 some customers abused their credit terms, and the ending accounts receivable balance is abnormally high.

An *average* accounts receivable balance during the year could be used to compute the accounts receivable turnover ratio, which may give a more useful result in some cases. Also, other more technical aspects may have to be considered that are beyond the purpose of this discussion. The main point is that a ratio of 8.0 is seriously different from the normal turnover ratio of 10.0 which would be obtained if customers were paying their accounts receivable on time.

The company's *inventory turnover ratio* is a quick although not necessarily accurate measure of its average inventory holding period. Usually the company's finished goods inventories are the main concern of managers, though raw materials inventory may also be a problem. For 1976 the company's *finished goods* inventory turnover ratio is computed as follows (amounts in thousands, rounded off; see Exhibit 6.2 and 2.1 for information):

Finished Goods Turnover Ratio

$$\frac{\text{Cost of Goods Sold}}{\text{Ending Finished Goods Inventory}} = \frac{\$7,241}{\$1,569} = 4.6$$

Total cost of goods sold in 1976 is 4.6 times the ending finished goods inventory cost balance, which means that the finished goods inventory was "turned over" or sold 4.6 times during the year. Putting it another way, there were 4.6 finished goods inventory holding cycles completed during the year. Based on the average holding period of 91 days,* there should have been only 4.0 turnovers or

* Technically, this period is a little too long since the company's policy is to maintain its *combined* work-in-process and finished goods inventory quantity to equal one fourth of the year's sales. But finished goods make up the large majority of the combined inventory.

holding cycles completed during the year (365 days ÷ 91 days = 4.0). Thus *it appears* that the company is holding finished goods less time on average than the normal holding period established by the company; that is, finished goods are being turned over more rapidly than planned.

However, keep in mind that the company uses the LIFO inventory method. Therefore, to some extent, there is a "mismatch" in the two factors used in the inventory turnover ratio computation. Cost of goods sold reflects the *current year's* manufacturing costs, but the ending finished goods inventory balance reflects (for the most part) *prior years'* manufacturing costs which in this example are lower. In situations of this kind, it may be more useful to determine the inventory turnover ratio based on a revised FIFO cost value estimate of the ending inventory.

Turnover ratios can be determined also for the raw materials inventory holding period, the manufacturing period, the accounts payable borrowing period, and even the short-term notes payable borrowing period. In most instances the accounts receivable turnover ratio and the finished goods inventory turnover ratio are the two most important ratios for managers' attention.

Short-term Cash Flow Budgeting Analysis and Procedures

Introduction

One of the most important practical demands on a business is to maintain an adequate cash* balance day to day so that all liabilities and other cash payment obligations (such as payroll) can be paid on time and without delay. All businesses need to do some type of planning, or forecasting, or prediction of cash receipts and payments over the short run. It would be foolhardy to simply assume, without any analysis, that cash receipts will be larger and sooner than cash payment obligations such that the company will always have a positive cash balance for every day over the next several months or year. Cash flow planning and control are so important that formal cash flow budgeting analysis and procedures are needed, or at least are very useful in most cases.

However, attempting to forecast cash receipts and payments on a day-by-day basis is not practical for many reasons. First, a company cannot predict the exact days when its sales over the coming period will be made. Even if sales day by day could be predicted accurately, a company cannot predict the exact day when the cash will be received from customers for sales made on credit. Customers may pay a few days early or a few days late. Although the day on which some cash payments will be made can be predicted accurately, such as the dates employees are to be paid, the timing of many other cash payments is more flexible. Managers have the discretion to authorize some payments

---

* Usually the term "cash" means primarily the amount of money on deposit in the company's demand deposit checking accounts with commercial banks, although cash also includes coin and currency on hand.

before the deadline when the obligations have to be paid, or they may delay some payments until after the time when they should be made.

The majority of companies maintain a large enough cash balance to serve as a *buffer* or *safety reserve* to cover any unusual delays in receiving cash or any unusual early payments. For example, the chief financial officer may decide to maintain a cash balance equal to one week's average cash receipts (or one week's average cash payments). Or, a company's policy may be more conservative, and the safety cash balance may be maintained at an amount equal to two weeks' average cash receipts, or even a month's average cash receipts. Recall in Chapter Seven that it is assumed the company in the example decides that its 1977 ending cash balance should be equal to 3.0% of its sales revenue for 1977. It is not suggested, however, that this ratio is necessarily typical. Many companies prefer higher ratios and some get by on lower ratios.

By and large companies use the month as the basic time period to analyze and to budget short-term cash flows. Generally speaking, a month is the shortest time interval for which sales revenue can be forecast with reasonable accuracy. Also, the month is a very convenient period for budgeting the cash outgo for expenses and production costs. One of the primary purposes of preparing a monthly cash flow budget is to determine if, when, how much, and for how long money may have to be borrowed during the coming year. Without a cash flow budget or some other sort of short-term cash flow forecast, it is conceivable that the manager would not know of the need to borrow until it is too late, or almost too late. Last-minute desperation attempts to borrow do not make a favorable impression on bankers, to say the least, and might be the main reason for refusing a loan to the business. Also the company needs to know the timing of cash flows during the year from net income, in order to know when and how much cash dividends can be paid during the year.

The company example introduced and developed in previous chapters is continued at this point to explain the preparation of a monthly cash flow budget for the coming year. In particular, the 1977 budgeted profit performance statement (see Exhibit 6.2) and the 1977 budgeted financial position changes statement (see Exhibit 7.4) are the two main points of departure for the following discussion. Also, the other points developed in Chapters Six and Seven are assumed to be the same.

Budgeting Monthly Cash Receipts from Sales Revenue

Preparing a month-by-month cash flow budget for the coming year begins with the monthly sales forecast, that is, the estimate of sales quantities and total sales revenue month by month for the coming 12 months. It is assumed that this company makes both cash sales and sales on credit. The company's sales manager furnishes the following monthly sales forecast for 1977 (see Exhibit 8.5). Notice that the total budgeted sales quantity (650,000 units) and total budgeted sales revenue ($1,853,800 + $13,096,200 = $14,950,000) agrees with the sales volume and sales revenue in Exhibit 6.2. The company's sales are seasonal and reach a peak in the months of September to November. Finally, Exhibit 8.5 assumes a constant sales price of $23 during all of 1977.

EXHIBIT 8.5
Monthly Sales Forecast

Month	Total Quantity	Sales Revenue	
		Cash Sales	Credit Sales
January	35,000	$ 115,000	$ 690,000
February	35,000	115,000	690,000
March	35,000	115,000	690,000
April	35,000	115,000	690,000
May	35,000	115,000	690,000
June	40,000	138,000	782,000
July	50,000	161,000	989,000
August	60,000	184,000	1,196,000
September	90,000	230,000	1,840,000
October	100,000	276,000	2,024,000
November	85,000	161,000	1,794,000
December	50,000	128,800	1,021,200
Totals	650,000	$1,853,800	$13,096,200

The company's customer credit manager, based on past experience and the predicted sales credit terms to be offered customers during 1977, estimates that cash collections from credit sales during 1977 will be as shown in Exhibit 8.6. Two points should be mentioned regarding this exhibit. Notice that 100% of credit sales are expected to be collected; thus, the assumption is that there will be no bad debts during 1977. Most companies suffer some bad debts from their credit sales, usually considerably less than 1.0% of total credit sales. But to simplify, bad debts are ignored in this example. Second, the collection experience predicted in Exhibit 8.6 is for the credit sales to be made during 1977, *not* to the beginning balance of Accounts Receivable at the start of 1977. As is mentioned in Chapter Seven (see page 222) the company's normal sales credit terms had been abused by customers during the late part of 1976, which resulted in a higher than normal balance of Accounts Receivable at year-end

EXHIBIT 8.6
Predicted Cash Collection from Credit Sales

	Percent
Credit sales collected in month of sale	25
Credit sales collected in month following sale	40
Credit sales collected in second month following sale	30
Credit sales collected in third month following sale	5
Total collected	100

1976. The credit manager predicts that this balance of Accounts Receivable should be collected as follows during 1977:

Predicted Collection of Beginning Accounts Receivable Balance

Month of Collection	Amount
January 1977	$1,200,000
February 1977	200,000
March 1977	78,125
Total	$1,478,125

Based on the above forecasts the monthly cash receipts from sales for 1977 are budgeted as shown in Exhibit 8.7. Notice that the 12 months' total cash receipts ($14,933.1 thousand) agrees exactly with the cash flow from sales revenue for the year already analyzed and shown in Exhibit 8.3. The main purpose of preparing the monthly budget of cash receipts from sales (Exhibit 8.7)

EXHIBIT 8.7
1977 Monthly Budget of Cash Receipts from Sales (in thousands)

Month	Beginning Accounts Receivable Balance	Cash Sales During Month	Credit Sales During Month (25%)	Credit Sales Last Month (40%)	Credit Sales Two Months Ago (30%)	Credit Sales Three Months Ago (5%)	Total Cash Collected
January	$1,200.0	$115.0	$172.5	a	a	a	$ 1,487.5
February	200.0	115.0	172.5	$276.0	a	a	763.5
March	78.1	115.0	172.5	276.0	$207.0	a	848.6
April		115.0	172.5	276.0	207.0	34.5	805.0
May		115.0	172.5	276.0	207.0	34.5	805.0
June		138.0	195.5	276.0	207.0	34.5	851.0
July		161.0	247.3	312.8	207.0	34.5	962.6
August		184.0	299.0	395.6	234.6	34.5	1,147.7
September		230.0	460.0	478.4	296.7	39.1	1,504.2
October		276.0	506.0	736.0	358.8	49.4	1,926.2
November		161.0	448.5	809.6	552.0	59.8	2,030.9
December		128.8	255.3	717.6	607.2	92.0	1,800.9
Total							$14,933.1

a These amounts are included in the collection of the beginning balance of Accounts Receivable shown in the first column.

is to determine the *timetable* of cash receipts during the year, rather than simply assuming that one twelfth of the year's total cash receipts will be received each month. As Exhibit 8.7 shows, the monthly cash inflows are very uneven during the year, which has extremely important consequences regarding whether the company will have to borrow during the year and how to plan the company's production output during the year.

Budgeting Monthly Cash Payments for Production Costs and Expenses During the Year

The next step in the cash flow budgeting process is to analyze the cash payments month by month that will be required by the company's production operations and operating expenses during the year, as well as the interest and income tax payments for the same interval. Starting with the manufacturing operations first, the basic question is how the company plans to schedule production output during the coming year. The company may decide to stabilize monthly production output for the year, that is, to manufacture about an equal quantity of products each month during the year. Spreading production output evenly over the year has several important advantages. The company could employ a relatively constant number of employees during the year, instead of hiring additional workers during some months who may have to be laid off after the busy season. And, the company could avoid paying employees for overtime hours, or at least could minimize overtime hours worked. Overtime hours worked by hourly paid employees cost the company 150% of their normal wage rates under current labor laws and most union contracts. Also, if production output is equalized each month throughout the year, then the capacity requirements of the company's manufacturing machinery and equipment would be less than if output in some months is double or triple other months. Therefore, the company's investment in these fixed assets is minimized by a stabilized production output policy.

Alternatively, the company could decide to set production output each month more or less equal to the predicted sales volume for the month following. This production scheduling approach avoids the accumulation of inventory during the slow sales months that occurs if production output is equalized each month during the year. If production output is stabilized in 1977 the company in this example would produce about 56,250 units each month: (675,000 units/12 = 56,250 units). But notice that in the first seven months (January to July) the units sold each month would be less than output (see Exhibit 8.5 for sales quantities). Going into August the company would have produced 128,750 more units than it sold during the first seven months. In August to November the company plans to sell 335,000 units, which is 110,000 more units than would be manufactured during these four months. Thus most of the inventory accumulation during the first seven months is depleted during the four heavy sales months.

From the cash flow standpoint the main impact of a stable production output each month is that cash outlays for production costs would have to be made in the early months, *before* the cash is received from sales later in the year. Instead of a detailed analysis of each production cost and expense, it is assumed to simplify discussion that:

1. The company decides to stabilize production output each month during the year, which means the cash payments for these manufacturing costs should be relatively equal each month; and,

2. Cash payments for all other operating expenses (in addition to the costs of production) are relatively constant from month to month. For most *fixed* expenses this is a reasonably accurate assumption.

For most *variable* operating expenses, however, this may be a somewhat inaccurate assumption. By and large cash payments for variable expenses do not occur until or somewhat after the units are sold. Exhibit 8.5 shows that the peak sales months are later in the year. Hence, the cash payments in the early months are being overstated. Also, interest expense payments may not be made in equal monthly installments. And, the current year's income tax expense requires *four* payments at different dates during the year, and is not paid monthly. More precisely, therefore, a company should separately analyze each production cost and each major operating expense, as well as the predicted interest and income tax payments during the coming year. To keep the discussion within reasonable limits, it is simply assumed that all these expenses result in *about* equal monthly cash outlays during the coming year.

Based on the two key assumptions just mentioned, the total cash payments for production costs and expenses would be about equal each month. In Exhibit 8.3 we observe that the cash flow effects of the company's budgeted expenses for the year 1977 are (in thousands, rounded off):

Expenses for the Year 1977

Total operating expenses	$13,150
Interest	270
Income tax	569
Total	$13,989

Therefore, cash outlays for expenses each month would be one twelfth, or $1165.8 thousand.

Exhibit 8.8 compares the monthly cash receipts from sales (determined in Exhibit 8.7) with the monthly cash payments for expenses, and shows the impact on the company's cash balance each month. Cash dividends are budgeted at 7.50 per share, or 300,000 in total for the year, based on 40,000 shares of stock outstanding. This point has been discussed in Chapter Seven (see page 237). The company's president decides to recommend to the Board of Directors

EXHIBIT 8.8
1977 Monthly Operating Cash Flow Budget Including Cash Dividends
(in thousands)

Month		Net Income Cash Flow				Ending Cash Balance Before Borrowing (Negative)
		From Sales[2]	For Expenses[3]	Net Inflow (Outflow)	Dividends[4]	
December	1976	—	—	—	—	$ 346.0[1]
January	1977	$1487.5	$1165.8	$321.7		667.7
February	1977	763.5	1165.8	(402.3)		265.4
March	1977	848.6	1165.8	(317.2)	$ 50.0	(101.8)
April	1977	805.0	1165.8	(360.8)		(462.6)
May	1977	805.0	1165.8	(360.8)		(823.4)
June	1977	851.0	1165.8	(314.8)	50.0	(1188.2)
July	1977	962.6	1165.8	(203.2)		(1391.4)
August	1977	1147.7	1165.8	(18.1)		(1409.5)
September	1977	1504.2	1165.8	338.4	50.0	(1121.1)
October	1977	1926.2	1165.8	760.4		(360.7)
November	1977	2030.9	1165.8	865.1		504.4
December	1977	1800.9	1165.8	635.1	150.0	989.5

(1) See, for example, Exhibit 2.1 for the December 31, 1976 cash balance.
(2) Exhibit 8.7 develops the monthly cash receipts from sales.
(3) See discussion on pages 272 to 273; a key assumption is that the company equalizes production output each month through the year.
(4) See discussion on this page for cash dividend plan of company for 1977.

that the company pay $1.25 per share at the end of March, June, and September, and a year-end (December) dividend of $3.75. This cash dividend payout schedule decision depends heavily on a monthly net income cash flow budget for the year such as is shown in Exhibit 8.8. Also the monthly operating cash flow budget for 1977 (Exhibit 8.8) reveals another very important point. The company will not have any cash flow from internal sources during the first eight months of 1977. If the company's new fixed assets are to be constructed or purchased during the first part of the year, which is probably true, then the company will have to arrange long-term borrowing during the early part of the year to pay for these capital expenditures.

Last, a monthly cash flow budget schedule, such as shown in Exhibit 8.8, is essential for planning short-term borrowing during the coming year. Exhibit 8.8 clearly reveals the need for short-term loans during the middle months of the year, and indicates about how large these borrowings will have to be. This cash flow budget also indicates when cash flow will be adequate to repay the loans, during the later months.

Summary

An adequate cash balance day to day is needed to sustain the profit-making operations of a company, as well as to pay liabilities as they come due. Inadequate cash balances usually lead to inadequate profit performance and may cause insolvency. Thus the analysis and planning of short-term cash flows is essential to the financial health and success of a business. Net income and short-term borrowing are the two main sources of cash inflow over the short-term, usually defined to be one year. However, the amount of cash flow from net income usually is not equal to the amount of net income earned and recorded for the period.

Analysis of the cash flow timings from sales revenue and for expenses is necessary to determine the net cash inflow (or possibly outflow!) from net income operations during the year. The amount of cash realized over the year may be substantially lower or higher than the net income earned. Managers need to know how much cash flow will be realized from net income to decide the company's cash dividend policy for the coming year, and to plan short-term borrowing during the year. Also, long-term planning of the company's capital sources starts with the cash flow budget for the coming year. Next year is the first year of the long-term, of course.

Short-term solvency analysis is concerned with the ability of the company to pay its current liabilities as they come due. The company's debt-paying ability depends on its cash position. Its cash position depends very much on how long it takes the company to complete one operating cycle from cash through inventory and then through accounts receivable back to cash. The longer the company's inventory holding period and the longer its customer credit terms, the longer is its operating cycle period. The company's short-term credit cycle depends on its mix and periods of short-term debt and accounts payable. The longer the short-term borrowing period and the longer the credit terms offered by accounts payable sources, then the longer is the short-term credit cycle. Normally a company's operating cycle is considerably longer than its short-term credit cycle. Hence, the company needs more total current assets than total current liabilities, in order to convert enough current assets into cash soon enough so that current liabilities can be paid as they come due.

A 2 to 1 ratio of current assets to current liabilities is considered a good standard or rule of thumb. However, an individual company should divide its operating cycle period by its short-term credit cycle period to determine its proper current ratio, given the company's particular circumstances and policies. The company's proper current ratio may be considerably higher or lower than the "standard" 2 to 1 guideline. For management control it is useful to compute the accounts receivable turnover ratio and the inventory turnover ratio. Managers can compare these ratios of actual performance against the company's customer credit terms and inventory holding period. These comparisons bring to the managers' attention any serious deviation that may require immediate attention.

In most instances, cash receipts from sales revenue each month during the year and cash payments for expenses each month during the year are not simply one twelfth of the total year's cash flows. Cash receipts each month depend on the pattern of monthly sales revenue during the year, and cash payments each month depend on the company's production output schedule during the year as well as its mix of fixed and variable manufacturing costs and fixed and variable operating expenses. The preparation of a monthly operating cash flow budget for the coming year is very useful. This short-term cash flow budget provides essential information for planning the precise timing and amounts of short-term borrowing and repayments during the year; for deciding cash dividend amounts to be paid during the year; and for determining when and how much internal cash flow will be available to help pay for the capital expenditures planned during the coming year.

Questions

8. 1 What are the basic sources and uses of cash during a year?

8. 2 What are the two basic management reasons for short-term cash flow analysis and budgeting?

8. 3 Why is the quick and simple "depreciation add-back" approach not necessarily an adequate method for the cash flow analysis of net income?

8. 4 Describe a feasible (theoretically possible) although not necessarily practical situation in which the cash flow from net income *would equal* net income earned for the year.

8. 5 In this situation the company's accounts receivable, inventories, and prepaid expenses increase during the year. Therefore, the cash flow from net income must be less than net income. Do you agree? Briefly explain.

8. 6 Would it be possible to have a net cash *outflow* from net income during the year? If so, explain how. If not, explain why not.

8. 7 If a company's short-term operating cycle is 155 days and its short-term credit cycle is 62 days, then what should its minimum current ratio be? Briefly explain.

8. 8 Indicate whether each of the following changes, assuming all other relevant factors remain the same, would increase or decrease the company's minimum required current ratio:

(a) Holding a smaller quantity of raw materials in inventory.

(b) Offering longer credit terms to its customers.

(c) Shortening the production process by purchasing more automated and faster equipment to speed up the production process.

(d) Increasing the amount of notes payable relative to accounts payable (notes payable are longer-term than accounts payable).

(e) Increasing the average quantity of finished goods held in inventory.

8. 9 (a) If a company's basic credit terms are 2/10, n/30 (2% cash discount if paid 10 days or less following the date of sale, otherwise the full amount is due no later than 30 days after the date of sale), and if one third of its customers take advantage of the discount, then what should its accounts receivable turnover ratio be? Show your computations.

(b) Why might the company's normal average collection period be somewhat longer than your answer to (a)?

8.10 Refer to Exhibit 8.7, which gives the predicted cash collection from sales revenue during 1977. Is this schedule of predicted cash collections from sales consistent with the 37 days average cash collection period used in the chapter? Show why or why not. Remember that the 37 days average period is based on *total* sales, including cash sales.

8.11 Given the use of LIFO, would you prefer to measure the finished goods inventory turnover ratio in terms of number of units instead of the number of dollars? Why or why not? Briefly explain.

8.12 (a) In general terms, how would the 1977 monthly operating cash flow budget of the company (see Exhibit 8.8) be changed if the company scheduled production output each month to equal the next month's predicted sales volume, instead of stabilizing production output during the year as is assumed in Exhibit 8.8?

(b) What decisions probably would be different if the change described in (a) were made?

8.13 "Cash flow analysis and budgeting is not necessary in our situation, since our company maintains a very large cash balance," remarked the president of the company. Do you agree? Briefly explain.

8.14 (a) Why doesn't a company lengthen its short-term credit cycle so that it can get by on a low current ratio, such as 1.2 to 1.0, or even 1.0 to 1.0?

(b) Why doesn't a company shorten its operating cycle so that it can get by on a low current ratio, such as 1.2 to 1.0, or even 1.0 to 1.0?

Problems

P8. 1 This manufacturing company has two types of credit customers. Most are extended normal trade credit terms of 30 days, with a 2.0% cash discount for prompt payment (within 10 days). Some are such poor credit risks that the company demands advances before their order is even started in the production process. These advance deposits are credited (increased) to the "Customers' Advances" liability account. When the order is delivered, the remaining balance (total sales price less advance payment) is billed COD (cash on delivery). The company makes no cash sales as such. All customers fall in one or the other types just discussed. Certain information from the company's financial statements of the last four years is shown below:

Account	1973	1974	1975	1976
Net sales revenue	$5,864,000	$7,130,000	$8,643,000	$10,453,000
Accounts Receivable*	880,000	763,000	804,000	916,000
Customers' Advances*	153,000	184,000	105,000	127,000

* Year-end balances.

Required: Determine the cash flow from sales revenue during the years 1974, 1975, and 1976.

P8. 2   This company is a land developer who has bought several square miles of undeveloped land and has subdivided the land in 5- to 10-acre-size lots. This company has graded the lots and has put in a sewer system, and curb and gutter. Each lot is sold for a relatively small down payment, usually 5 to 10% of the total purchase price. The buyer signs a 10-year note for the remaining balance of the purchase price. The company records the entire purchase price as sales revenue at the time of sale. Certain information from the company's financial statements of the last 4 years is shown below:

Account	1973	1974	1975	1976
Land sales revenue	$1,500,000	$3,000,000	$5,000,000	$ 8,000,000
Notes receivable from land sales (ending balance)	2,400,000	4,850,000	9,040,000	15,250,000

Required:

(1) Determine the cash flow from sales revenue for the years 1974, 1975, and 1976.
(2) Would the company's total cash flow from net income be positive or negative each year? Why? If negative, how can this company keep Its "head above water," that is, remain solvent?

P8. 3   This company makes all sales for cash; there are no credit sales. Certain information has been taken and summarized from the company's financial statements of the last five years, which is as follows:

	1972	1973	1974	1975	1976
Sales revenue		$2,800,000	$4,300,000	$3,450,000	$6,250,000
All expenses, except depreciation		2,635,000	4,079,000	3,441,100	5,861,100
Depreciation expense		89,000	94,500	92,100	103,500
Net income (loss)		$ 76,000	$ 126,500	($ 83,200)	$ 285,400
Inventories plus prepaid expenses*	$ 537,500	$ 618,300	$ 764,800	$ 518,400	$ 983,400
Accounts payable and accrued costs plus income tax payable*	$ 132,500	$ 146,500	$ 159,300	$ 147,300	$ 161,800

* Ending Balances.

Required:

(1) Determine the cash flow from net income for the years 1973, 1974, 1975, and 1976. Show your analysis.
(2) In which year is the cash flow the largest? Why? Do you find anything unusual in this year?

P8. 4 All three of the following companies have a 2 to 1 current ratio based on information from their most recent financial statements, which is as follows:

	Company A	Company B	Company C
Cash	$ 300,000	$ 200,000	$ 150,000
Marketable securities	—	—	200,000
Accounts receivable	675,000	540,000	450,000
Inventories	1,350,000	540,000	450,000
Prepaid expenses	88,000	72,000	46,000
Total current assets	$2,413,000	$1,352,000	$1,296,000
Accounts payable and accrued costs	$ 702,000	$ 390,000	$ 248,000
Income tax payable	36,500	26,000	28,000
Short-term notes payable	468,000	260,000	372,000
Total current liabilities	$1,206,500	$ 676,000	$ 648,000
Sales revenue	$5,400,000	$5,400,000	$5,400,000
Cost of goods sold expense	$4,050,000	$2,700,000	$2,700,000

For all three companies assume that the average borrowing period of its accounts payable and accrued cost liabilities is 30 days, and that its average short-term notes payable borrowing period is 90 days.

Required:

(1) On the basis of the composition of current assets compared with the composition of current liabilities, rank the companies in terms of the most solvent, the second-most solvent, and the least solvent.

(2) Based on an analysis of their minimum required current ratios, rank the three companies in terms of solvency. Show your computations clearly. To simplify your analysis, it is suggested that you exclude income tax payable from the analysis of the short-term credit cycle.

P8. 5   Certain information about several different companies is given below.

Required: For each company determine the minimum required current ratio that the company should maintain to protect its short-term solvency.

Company	(1) Average Manufacturing Period	(2) Average Finished Goods Holding Period	(3) Average Customer Credit Period	(4) Average Accounts Payable and Accrued Costs Borrowing Period	(5) Average Short-term Notes Payable Borrowing Period	(6) Percent Mix of (4) and (5)
A	10 days	50 days	30 days	30 days	60 days	50%—50%
B	10 days	80 days	30 days	30 days	120 days	50%—50%
C	33 days	120 days	45 days	30 days	120 days	60%—40%
D	33 days	90 days	45 days	30 days	120 days	40%—60%
E	50 days	145 days	45 days	30 days	180 days	40%—60%

P8. 6   The short excerpt reproduced below appeared in a recent issue of *Business Week* magazine (December 21, 1974, page 99). First, study the example.

Required: Do you agree with the analysis shown in this example?

FIFO vs. LIFO

Here's how one company's books would look under FIFO and LIFO accounting, assuming it started the year with an inventory of 1000 widgets valued at $4 each. During the year, the company sold 600 widgets at $9 each and replaced them in inventory with 600 widgets for which it paid $6 each.

INCOME STATEMENT	FIFO		LIFO	
Sales	$5400		$5400	
Cost of goods sold		$2400		$3600
Selling costs		1000		1000
		$\overline{3400}$		$\overline{4600}$
Pretax income	2000		800	
Taxes @ 48%	960		384	
Net income	$\overline{\$1040}$		$ \overline{416}$	
Ending inventory		$5200		$4000
Net cash flow	−$160		+$ 416	

In particular, show how the "net cash flow" effects on the bottom line were determined and state whether you agree with the example's main points.

P8. 7   Please refer to the retailer's budgeted financial statements that you prepared for Problems 7.6 and 6.9. These statements are used for this problem.

Required: Prepare a cash flow analysis of the company's budgeted net income for 1977. (See Exhibit 8.3 for example.)

P8. 8   The 1974 and 1973 net income statements and the 1974 and 1973 statements of changes in financial position for Cook Electric Company are reproduced on the next two pages. These two financial statements are taken from *Cook Electric— Annual Report—1974* (pages 12 and 13).

Required: In the manner illustrated in Exhibit 8.3, prepare an analysis of the cash flow from net income for Cook Electric for
(1) 1974, and
(2) 1973.

P8. 9   This company, a retailer, makes 67.0% of its annual total sales in December of each year during the three weeks before Christmas. Sales during the remainder of the year are spread evenly over each month. All sales are for cash. From January to November the company purchases and accumulates inventory in preparation for the Christmas rush. The success of the company depends on the ability of the company's managers to predict in advance which items will sell well as Christmas gifts, and to purchase these items at the best possible cost. In many cases this means buying the items several months before December. The non-December sales are certain basic items that have a fairly stable, ongoing sales demand; the company gets its share of these sales simply because it is one of several stores in the area that sell these items. During the last week in December, after Christmas, the company pays all the notes payable borrowed on during the year to finance the accumulation of the Christmas inventory. Indeed, all of these notes have a December 31 maturity date.

The company has a "line of credit" arrangement with its bank, which commits the bank to lend money to the company during the year when and as requested by the company, up to a certain total credit limit. At the start of each year the

COOK ELECTRIC COMPANY AND SUBSIDIARIES
STATEMENT OF CONSOLIDATED INCOME

	Year Ended June 30	
	1974	1973
Net sales	$29,557,725	$22,855,069
Interest income	193,577	147,747
	29,751,302	23,002,816
Costs and expenses:		
Cost of products sold	18,753,967	14,193,913
Selling and administrative	5,357,914	4,261,146
Provision for depreciation	485,244	426,677
Interest	217,168	240,292
	24,814,293	19,122,028
Income Before Income Taxes	4,937,009	3,880,788
Federal and state income taxes:		
Currently payable	2,357,000	1,840,000
Deferred	88,000	45,000
	2,445,000	1,885,000
Net Income	$ 2,492,009	$ 1,995,788
Net income per common and common equivalent share	$ 1.30	$ 1.05

company must submit an inventory accumulation budget to the bank which is the basic document for deciding the total credit limit for the coming year. For the year ended December 31, 1976 the company's net income statement down to the operating profit line is:

Net sales		$8,325,000
Costs of goods sold		5,178,150
Gross profit		$3,146,850
Selling expenses	$1,634,850	
Administrative and general expenses	725,600	2,360,450
Operating profit before interest and income tax		$ 786,400

Other pertinent information for 1976 and 1977 is as follows.

(a) The company's non-Christmas inventory is fairly constant during the year and is financed largely from normal accounts payable, that is, by buying these items on credit. These inventory needs are *not* part of the line of credit agreement with the bank. The average gross profit on the non-

COOK ELECTRIC COMPANY AND SUBSIDIARIES
STATEMENT OF CONSOLIDATED CHANGES IN FINANCIAL POSITION

	Year Ended June 30	
	1974	1973
Additions to working capital:		
From operations:		
Net income for the year	$ 2,492,009	$ 1,995,788
Income-statement items not requiring use of working capital:		
Provision for depreciation	485,244	426,677
Provision for deferred income taxes	88,000	45,000
Other	68,350	—
Total from Operations	3,133,603	2,467,465
Reclassification of deferred items	61,200	—
Proceeds from exercise of stock options	18,300	165,625
Total Additions	3,213,103	2,633,090
Deductions from working capital:		
Additions to property, plant and equipment, less disposals (1974—$8,106; 1973—$91,741)	1,004,365	346,353
Reduction of long-term debt	210,525	421,050
Treasury shares purchased	—	18,435
Cash dividends on Common shares	764,491	600,913
Total Deductions	1,979,381	1,386,751
Increase for the Year	1,233,722	1,246,339
Working capital at beginning of year	8,410,104	7,163,765
Working Capital at End of Year	$ 9,643,826	$ 8,410,104
Changes in components of working capital:		
Increases (decreases) in current assets:		
Cash	$ 422,401	$ 98,710
Short-term investments	(2,613,331)	510,688
Receivables	1,494,425	878,476
Inventories	3,527,971	250,298
Prepaid expenses	27,839	38,666
	2,859,305	1,776,838
Increases in current liabilities:		
Accounts payable	869,686	171,600
Accrued expenses	542,426	115,919
Dividend payable	38,453	10,510
Federal and state income taxes	175,018	232,470
	1,625,583	530,499
Increase in Working Capital	$ 1,233,722	$ 1,246,339

Christmas items was one third of the sales price in 1976 and is expected to be the same in 1977.

(b) All of the Christmas inventory accumulation during the year is financed by borrowing on notes payable under terms of the line of credit with the bank. The average gross profit on Christmas items was 40.0% of the sales price in 1976, and is expected to be the same in 1977.

(c) The company's best estimate is that total sales revenue in 1977 should be about 15.0% higher than in 1976. In both years the mix of Christmas and non-Christmas sales (described above) will be the same.

Required:

(1) Determine the maximum line of credit the company should negotiate for to provide ample borrowing ability to accumulate Christmas inventory during the year. Include supporting computations and present your report in a form that should be understandable to the banker.

(2) Assume that the company borrows the money on the first day of the month following the purchase of Christmas inventory. For example, to pay for the Christmas inventory purchased in March, the company would borrow an amount equal to the purchases on April 1. All notes will have the same maturity date—December 31, 1977. The annual effective annual interest rate charged by the bank is 12.0%. Based on past experience, the company's Christmas inventory purchases should be distributed as follows during 1977 (in percent):

January	0	July	10
February	5	August	10
March	5	September	20
April	5	October	20
May	5	November	10
June	10	December	0

Prepare a monthly schedule showing the "takedown" (borrowing) on the company's line of credit, and determine the budgeted total interest expense for 1977.

P8.10 This company manufactures molded plastic containers. In October 1976 the company determined that it needed cash to continue operations. The company began negotiating for a one-month bank loan of $100,000 that would be discounted at 12% per year, on November 1. On considering the loan, the bank requested a projected income statement and a cash budget for the month of November.

The following information is available:

(a) Sales were budgeted at 120,000 units per month in October 1976, December 1976, and January 1977, and at 90,000 units in November 1976.

The selling price is $2 per unit. Sales are billed on the fifteenth and last day of each month on terms 2/10 net 30. (That is, a 2% discount from the gross price billed is offered to the customer if cash payment is made within 10 days after the billing date.) Past experience indicates sales are even throughout the month, and 50% of the customers pay the billed amount within the discount period. The remainder pay at the end of 30 days, except for bad debts, which average ½% of gross sales.

(b) The inventory of finished goods on October 1 was 24,000 units. The finished goods inventory at the end of each month is to be maintained at 20% of sales anticipated for the following month. There is no work-in-process.

(c) The inventory of raw materials on October 1 was 22,800 pounds. At the end of each month the raw materials inventory is to be maintained at not less than 40% of production required for the following month. Materials are purchased as needed in minimum quantities of 25,000 pounds per shipment. Raw material purchases of each month are paid in the next succeeding month on terms of net 30 days (no cash discount).

(d) All salaries and wages are paid on the fifteenth and last day of each month for the period ending on the date of payment.

(e) All manufacturing overhead and selling and administrative expenses are paid on the tenth of the month following the month in which they are incurred. Selling expenses are 10% of gross sales. Administrative expenses, which include depreciation of $500 per month on office furniture and fixtures, total $33,000 per month.

(f) The standard cost of a molded plastic container, based on normal production of 100,000 units per month, is as follows:

Materials—½ pound	$ .50
Labor	.40
Variable overhead	.20
Fixed overhead	.10
Total cost per unit	$1.20

Fixed overhead includes depreciation on factory equipment of $4000 per month. Any remainder of fixed overhead cost that is not charged to the production output of the month is charged off as an expense against sales revenue that month.

(g) The cash balance on November 1 is expected to be $10,000.

Required: Prepare the following for the company, assuming that the bank loan is granted:

(1) Schedules computing inventory budgets by months for:
   (a) Finished goods production in units for October, November, and December.
   (b) Raw material purchases in pounds for October and November.

(2) A projected net income statement for the month of November, down to the net income before income tax expense.

(3) A cash forecast for the month of November showing the opening balance, receipts (itemized by dates of collection), disbursements, and balance at end of month.

P8.11   In brief and condensed form a retailer's budgeted net income statement for next year with comparison with the actual net income for this year (the year just ended) is shown as follows:

	Next Year (Budgeted)	This Year (Actual)
Sales revenue	$5,625,000	$4,500,000
Cost of goods sold	3,825,000	3,170,000
Gross profit	$1,800,000	$1,330,000
Variable operating expenses	703,125	562,500
Contribution margin	$1,096,875	$ 767,500
Fixed operating costs*	337,500	227,500
Operating profit	$ 759,375	$ 540,000
Interest expense	54,000	48,000
Income before income tax	$ 705,375	$ 492,000
Income tax	332,080	229,660
Net income	$ 373,295	$ 262,340
* Includes depreciation of	$ 39,400	$ 28,600

At the end of this year (the year just ended) the company's current asset and current liabilities are as follows:

Current Assets		Current Liabilities	
Cash	$ 150,000	Accounts payable and	
Accounts receivable	270,000	accrued expenses	$ 397,940
Inventory	634,000	Income tax payable	45,932
Prepaid expenses	76,140	Notes payable	158,500
Total	$1,130,140	Total	$ 602,372

The company considers that its current assets and current liabilities at the end of this year are in a normal and stable relationship with sales revenue and expenses, and it plans no changes in these relationships for next year. The relationships are determined as follows:

—Accounts receivable depends on sales revenue.
—Inventory depends on cost of goods sold.

—Prepaid expenses depends on operating costs, excluding cost of goods sold and depreciation.

—Cash depends on sales revenue.

—Accounts payable and accrued expenses depends on all expenses, excluding income tax and depreciation.

—Income tax payable depends on the income tax expense.

—Notes payable (short-term) depends on inventory; in particular, the company's bank is willing to loan the company an amount equal to one fourth of its inventory.

Required:

(1) Determine the budgeted balances for current assets and current liabilities at the end of next year.

(2) In the manner suggested in Exhibit 8.3, analyze and determine the budgeted cash flow from net income for next year.

P8.12 For the next accounting year beginning July 1, 1977 the local campus bookstore, based on its sales experience over the past several years, estimates that its total sales revenue for the year will be distributed over the 12 months as follows:

	Percentage of Year's Sales Revenue		Percentage of Year's Sales Revenue
July	2	January	30
August	3	February	3
September	30	March	3
October	3	April	2
November	4	May	2
December	8	June	10

The heavy sales in September and January are due to the start of the fall and spring semesters.

The total projected student enrollment from the office of the Dean of Admissions is 20,000 full-time students during the fall and spring semesters, plus 8000 students for the summer session, which is held from June to August. The bookstore has a monopoly on the textbook market in this town—there is no other convenient store to purchase books and other school supplies. Last year each student purchased $170 on average of books and supplies during the academic year (September to May), and each summer student purchased $75 of books and supplies on average during the three-month summer period. This average purchase per student should remain the same during the coming year, except that textbook and other prices have increased 7.5%. The company collects cash from sales revenue as follows:

	Percentage of Month's Sales Revenue
Cash collected in month of sale	90
Cash collected in next month following sale	8
Cash collected in second month following sale	2

Required:

(1) Prepare a forecast of monthly sales revenue for the coming year based on the above information and assumptions.
(2) Assuming the company begins the year with an Accounts Receivable balance equal to the amount implied in the above information and assumptions, prepare a forecast of the monthly cash receipts from sales revenue for the coming year. Also, determine what the Accounts Receivable balance will be at the end of next year (at June 30, 1978).

P8.13 In very brief and condensed form the most recent financial statements of this small retail business, an unincorporated sole proprietorship, are as follows:

ASSETS		EQUITIES	
Cash	$ 24,000	Accounts payable	$ 28,560
Accounts receivable	37,500	Accrued expenses	5,280
Inventories	51,000	Current liabilities	$ 33,840
Prepaid expenses	6,600		
Current assets	$119,100		
Fixed assets, net of accumulated depreciation on straight-line basis	23,500	Owner's equity	108,760
Total	$142,600	Total	$142,600

NET INCOME STATEMENT

Sales revenue	$300,000
Cost of goods sold	204,000
Gross profit	$ 96,000
Operating expenses	66,000
Net profit	$ 30,000

The owner is 60 years old and plans to quit business and retire five years from now. Sales demand for this type of product has been slipping and probably will continue to decline during this period. Thus, the owner has not found anyone interested in buying the business, and he plans to liquidate it over the next five years. The fixed assets have a five-year remaining useful life and probably will have no salvage value. The owner predicts that sales revenue will decrease about $50,000 each year, starting next year. Each current asset and current liability will be decreased in proportion to the sales revenue decline. To simplify, assume no changes in the sales prices or the purchase prices of the products handled by the business over the next five years. Also, assume that the owner can decrease his total operating expenses proportional to the decrease in sales revenue each year.

Required: The owner would like to know how much total cash he can plan to take out of the business each year over the next five years, based on the above assumptions. Determine this annual cash take-out amount. Show your computations.

P8.14   The Unitog Company (headquartered in Kansas City, Missouri) is unusual in that it offers to sell *or to rent* its products, which are industrial uniforms (such as those worn by postal service employees). The following information was taken from Unitog's 1974 annual report for the accounting year ending January 27, 1974:

	(in Thousands)
(a) Net sales revenue	$22,658
(b) Net rental revenue	5,937
(c) Average accounts receivable balance (which it is assumed applies entirely to *sales* revenue)	2,196
(d) Cost of sales	12,339
(e) Cost of rentals	3,546
(f) Average inventories balance (of goods held for sale)	6,053
(g) Average rental garments inventories balance	1,095

Required:

(1) Compute the company's short-term operating cycle based on the above information. For this problem use only two steps—the average inventory holding period (which includes the manufacturing process) and the average customer credit period. Show your computations.

(2) *If* the company's average short-term credit cycle were 50 days (based on *all* current liabilities), then determine the appropriate minimum current ratio for the company.

P. S. For your information Unitog's current ratio at the end of the last four years was: 1974, 3.54; 1973, 4.44; 1972, 4.90; 1971, 4.25.

Chapter Nine

Capital Investment Analysis: An Introduction

CAPITAL INVESTMENT ANALYSIS: AN INTRODUCTION

Managing Asset Investments: Current Assets Compared with Long-Term Assets

Almost all business entities must invest capital in various assets to carry on their operations and transactions. A company's total assets on the one side are matched with an equal total amount of capital sources on the other side. Except for noninterest bearing liabilities a company's sources of capital have a "cost." Interest is paid on debt, and a company needs to earn at least a minimum rate of return on its stockholders' equity. Thus the most essential financial objective of a company is to earn a sufficient amount of *operating profit* (before interest and income tax) on its total assets each year, to meet its interest requirements and to earn an adequate aftertax rate of return on its stockholders' equity. (Chapter Three discusses the meaning and measurement of return on assets and return on equity, which you may want to review briefly at this point.)

Clearly managers should carefully analyze and control the investments in all the company's various assets. Managers should avoid investing too much capital in any asset, that is, more capital than is needed to support the company's level of sales activity and operations. Excessive investment in assets means that higher than normal operating profit will have to be earned. If not, then the company's return on assets performance will be penalized, since its operating profit will be divided by an excessive amount of total assets.

The general field of asset investment management quite naturally divides into two basic areas—current assets and long-term assets. Current assets include cash, accounts receivable, inventories, and prepaid expenses. By their very nature, there is a constant flow of transactions through the current assets accounts. Current assets are high turnover accounts. Managers can make continuous adjustments in the level of investments in these assets. For instance, a manager may decide to increase finished goods inventories and, therefore to step up the company's production output within the week. Managers constantly monitor the investment levels in these assets. Given a month or two, a company can substantially increase or decrease the investments in its inventories and accounts receivable, especially if there have been substantial increases or decreases in the company's sales revenue.

Investments in fixed assets are quite different than current asset investments. Fixed assets are long-term investments that commit the company for many years. A company cannot easily reduce or reverse its investments in fixed assets once these long-term economic resources are purchased or constructed. Also, many fixed asset investments cannot be increased "just a little," as is possible for current assets. A manager may decide to increase finished goods inventories by 1%. On the other hand, a company usually cannot add such a small increment to its existing production plant and manufacturing facilities. Fixed asset investments, for the most part, are "lumpy," which means that these capital expenditures are made in relatively large amounts each time. Large increments of fixed assets must be purchased or constructed at one time, which is especially true for buildings and major items of machinery and equipment.

In short, investments in assets by a business require that an equal amount of capital be invested in the business. Except for noninterest bearing liabilities these sources of capital have a cost of using the capital each year, which the company has to meet by earning a sufficient rate of operating profit on its assets each year. All asset investments are important. But fixed asset investments are especially important. Relatively large amounts of capital have to be invested for relatively long periods of time. The *cost of capital* to the company is an especially important factor to consider in the analysis of fixed asset and other long-term investment decisions.

Determining the Company's Cost of Capital

Exhibit 9.1 presents the condensed financial position of a typical company at the end of its most recent year. This company's capitalization structure is used as the main example in this and the next chapter. Notice that in Exhibit 9.1 the company's noninterest bearing liabilities (all short-term) are separated from its interest bearing debts. This is convenient for the analysis that follows. But keep in mind that this format is not the usual one for the external reporting of financial statements. In most balance sheets, *all* current liabilities, both interest bearing and noninterest bearing, are grouped together in one section.

This company has $10 million capital invested in its assets. Thus the company needs to earn an adequate amount of profit before tax and interest that is sufficient to pay the interest on its debts and to leave an adequate amount of after-tax net income for its stockholders. Broadly speaking, this "required profit" is earned from two sources or in two ways: (1) through the normal ongoing sales of its products and services the company should be able to earn an *operating profit*; and, (2) the company may have other sources of income in addition to the sales of its products and services, which generally are called *nonoperating profit* or *other income*. Up to this point in the book, our discussion has been concerned with operating profit, since this is the main ongoing source of profit for most companies. However, a company may make investments that are secondary or incidental to the main business of the company. For instance, a company may make temporary investments in short-term marketable securities to keep its excess cash invested until the money is needed for future investments in operating assets, such as inventories or fixed assets.

EXHIBIT 9.1
Financial Position of Company

Cash	$ 1,250,000	Accounts Payable	$ 900,000
Accounts Receivable	1,000,000	Income Tax Payable	100,000
Inventories	2,500,000	Total Noninterest	
Prepaid Expenses	250,000	Bearing Liabilities	$ 1,000,000
Total Current Assets	$ 5,000,000		
		Interest Bearing Debt:	
		Short-term	
		(10.0% average	
		annual rate)	$ 1,500,000
Fixed Assets (Net of		Long-term	
Accumulated		(8.0% average	
Depreciation)	5,000,000	annual rate)	2,500,000
			$ 4,000,000
		Stockholders' Equity	
		(only one class of	
		Common Stock)	$ 5,000,000
		TOTAL CAPITAL	
TOTAL ASSETS	$10,000,000	SOURCES	$10,000,000

Assume that the company in this example derives all its "required profit" from normal operating sources (through sales of its products and services) and has no other source of income. Also assume that the $10 million total assets is a relatively stable base of capital during the coming year which is adequate, although not excessive, for the company's level of sales activity and operations next year. (Chapters Six and Seven discuss the detailed planning and budgeting of changes in assets and sources of capital for the coming year.) Given these assumptions: How much operating profit should the company earn during the coming year?

The interest cost for next year can be computed since the interest rates are known (refer to Exhibit 9.1). On the other hand, there is no fixed contractual rate of net income promised to the stockholders on their equity investment of $5 million. The problem of deciding what is an adequate or sufficient rate of net income on stockholders' equity goes far into the field of business finance, beyond the boundaries of management accounting (although the two fields overlap to a great extent). Certainly management accountants should understand how managers determine the company's rate of return on equity goal. A thorough and complete discussion of this problem is beyond the purpose of this book.* Therefore, a *reasonable* annual rate of return on equity is assumed to

---

* See, for example, James C. Van Horne, *Financial Management And Policy*, Prentice-Hall, Englewood Cliffs, N.J., 1974, pages 101-128.

continue this example. A return on equity goal of 13% per year is adopted. Based on recent surveys of actual rates of return on equity, this is about average, although this company probably would like to do better if possible.

Assuming a 13% return on equity goal for next year, the computation of the amount of operating profit (before interest and income tax) "required" to be earned next year by the company is shown in Exhibit 9.2. In it, the operating profit is determined from the "bottom up." The first step is shown on the bottom line. The stockholders' equity of $5,000,000 (see Exhibit 9.1) is multiplied by the 13.0% return on equity rate to determine the required net income for the year, which is $650,000. Next, this net income of $650,000 is divided by the 52% *aftertax retention percent,* based on the assumption of a flat 48% corporate income tax rate. (To simplify, the lower tax rate on the first $25,000 of taxable income is ignored.) This gives the following: ($650,000 aftertax net income divided by 52% = $1,250,000). This $1,250,000 amount is the *before-tax net income,* or the taxable income. As Exhibit 9.2 indicates, 48% of this taxable income is equal to $600,000. The annual interest of $350,000 (see Exhibit 9.2) is then added to the $1,250,000 to arrive at the $1,600,000 operating profit. The total sales revenue and total expenses are not of any direct concern here and are not shown in Exhibit 9.2.

In summary, therefore, the company needs to earn a 16.0% annual return on assets (ROA):

$$\frac{\text{Required Operating Profit}}{\text{Total Assets}} = \frac{\$1,600,000}{\$10,000,000} = 16.0\% \text{ RETURN ON ASSETS}$$

This 16.0% annual ROA depends on the company's capitalization structure, that is, the mix of liabilities and stockholders' equity capital invested in the

EXHIBIT 9.2
Computation of Company's Required Operating Profit for Next Year

Sales Revenue	$ xx,xxx,xxx
Operating Expenses	xx,xxx,xxx
Operating Profit (Before Interest and Income Tax)	$ 1,600,000
Interest:	
Short-term debt: $1,500,000×10.0%=$150,000	
Long-term debt: $2,500,000× 8.0%=$200,000	350,000
Net Income Before Income Tax (Assumed Equal to Taxable Income for Year)	$ 1,250,000
Income Tax (at Flat 48% Rate)	600,000
Net Income (Equal to $5,000,000 Stockholders' Equity×13.0% Annual Rate)	$ 650,000

EXHIBIT 9.3
Computation of Required (Pretax) Rate of Return on Assets (ROA)

Source of Capital	Percentage of Total Capital Sources (See Exhibit 9.1)		Before Tax Average Annual Cost		Weighted Cost
Noninterest bearing liabilities	10%	×	0.00%	=	0.0%
Interest bearing debt	40%	×	8.75%[1]	=	3.5%
Total liabilities	50%	×	7.00%[2]	=	3.5%
Stockholders' equity	50%	×	25.00%[3]	=	12.5%
Total capital sources	100%				16.0%

Notes:
(1) $350,000 total interest divided by $4,000,000 debt=8.75%.
(2) $350,000 total interest divided by $5,000,000 *total* liabilities=7.0%.
(3) 13.0% after tax rate divided by 52% after tax retention percent=25.0%.

business as well as the annual cost of each capital source. Given the particular capitalization structure shown in Exhibit 9.1, the 16.0% return on assets determined above (see Exhibit 9.2) can be double checked by an alternative method of computation which uses the percent of total capital supplied from each source and the annual cost of each source—see Exhibit 9.3.

The term *cost of capital* (COC) refers to the basic idea that a company must earn a sufficient amount of operating profit each year (plus other income, if any) relative to the total capital (assets) used to generate this operating profit. This is so that interest may be paid, and so that the aftertax net income objective of the company may be achieved. The term *return on assets* (ROA) generally is used in the actual performance sense. Cost of capital, on the other hand, generally is used in the normative or "ought to" sense; it refers to the return on asset *goals* and the return on equity *objectives* for the coming year.

It should be stressed that the 16.0% cost of capital for the company in this example is the *before interest and before income tax* rate. To illustrate this point, consider a $1000 "slice" of the company's total assets. Assume that the company can, in fact, earn a 16.0% rate of operating profit before interest and income tax. The *disposition* of this operating profit is shown in Exhibit 9.4. This "disposition breakout" method of analysis is useful in later discussion in this and the next chapter. Also, this approach is extremely useful in analyzing financial leverage (see Chapter Three, pages 85 to 93).

Evaluating Investment Opportunities

Introduction: Basic Types of Investments by a Business Entity

A basic assumption of most business management theories is that managers put a very high priority on achieving the company's return on equity objective and

EXHIBIT 9.4
Disposition (or Breakout) of "Required" Operating Profit
on $1000 Slice of Total Assets

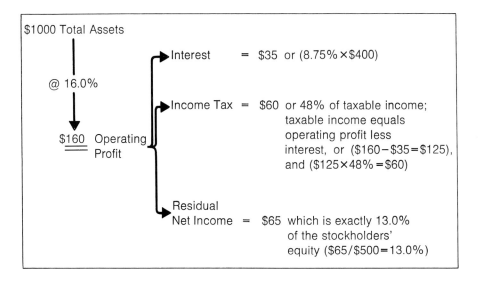

$1000 Total Assets

@ 16.0%

$160 Operating Profit

Interest = $35 or (8.75% × $400)

Income Tax = $60 or 48% of taxable income; taxable income equals operating profit less interest, or ($160 − $35 = $125), and ($125 × 48% = $60)

Residual Net Income = $65 which is exactly 13.0% of the stockholders' equity ($65/$500 = 13.0%)

are not satisfied if this goal is not reached. This means that the business must generate enough sales revenue and must control its operating expenses such that the ratio of its annual operating profit (before interest and income tax) to its total assets equals or exceeds its pretax cost of capital rate. Here this means that the company must earn an operating profit rate of 16.0% on its total assets, as explained above. If the company's actual performance falls short of this goal, then managers make use of the several analytical tools discussed in previous chapters to decide what must be changed to improve the return on assets (ROA) performance of the company. Plans for changes may be put into a formal budgeting framework, as is discussed in Chapters Six and Seven.

The main concern of the rest of this chapter is the evaluation of the *marginal* investment opportunities that are available to an established company. Marginal means *additional* or *incremental* to the existing ongoing operations and investments of the company. Generally speaking, these new investment opportunities can be classified as follows for most businesses:

1. *Replacements of fixed assets* which have reached the end of their useful lives to the company; new fixed assets of a similar nature (of a like kind) are purchased to continue the operations of the company.

2. *Expansion of production and distribution capacity.* New fixed assets are purchased not to replace old assets that have worn out but, instead, to increase the manufacturing and/or delivery capacity of the company because of:

(a) Planned increases in the sales volume of the company's existing product lines, or

(b) The company plans to enter new product lines in addition to its existing product lines.

(At higher sales levels the company may have to increase its investments in current assets, as well as fixed assets.)

3. *Cost savings investments.* Frequently these investments involve purchases of new fixed assets that are more efficient than the company's present manufacturing machinery and equipment and, thus, would result in labor or raw material cost savings in the future.

4. *Nonoperating investments.* These investments are not an integral part of the normal manufacturing and sales operations of the company, but are not inconsistent with its primary business and offer certain advantages that make sense. For example, a company may purchase a building much larger than it needs for its immediate office or warehouse purposes, and a large part of the building may be rented out for several years until the company needs the space. There are many such examples that vary from company to company.

Each type of investment involves special problems of analysis. Before getting into these more technical problems, there are certain fundamental concepts and techniques of analysis that apply to the evaluation of all investment opportunities. These basic ideas and methods are explained in the remaining pages of this chapter. Then in Chapter Ten we explore some of the more specialized problems that are associated with particular kinds of investments.

The Two Basic "Demands" on the Future Returns from an Investment

Although obvious, nevertheless it is necessary to mention at the start of this discussion that it is assumed no rational investment decision maker commits capital to an investment unless the *future returns* of capital from the investment are predicted to be adequate, relative to the purpose and risks of the investment. For almost all business investment decisions there are two primary "demands" or conditions that the future returns from the investment must satisfy to be adequate:

1. First, the total amount of capital invested must be recovered in the future returns. The initial amount of capital invested can be called the *entry cost* of the investment. Thus the total of the future returns must at least be equal to the entry cost of the investment. But this alone is not enough to make an investment attractive.

2. Second, during the life of the investment the company, over and above the recovery of the entry cost of the investment, needs to earn a sufficient rate of profit on the amount of capital committed to the investment.

Assume the company in the example can make a certain investment today that has an entry cost of $100,000. The specific nature of the investment is not our concern here. One year from today it is predicted that the total return from the investment will be $116,000. There are no other returns before or after this date. The $116,000 is *net* of any expenses or costs that are required to generate this return. Of course, a company can hardly ever be absolutely (100%) certain that exactly $116,000 will be received precisely one year from now. (The problems of uncertainty in making predictions of future returns and how to incorporate the probabilities of being too high or too low into the analysis are rather complex, and are best avoided at this point.)

Before we proceed, it is extremely important to understand that investment analysis deals with *cash flows*. In other words, the $100,000 entry cost given above means that $100,000 *of cash* would have to be paid out today to enter the investment. And, the $116,000 future return means that $116,000 *of cash* would be received one year from today. It is very critical to keep this cash basis in mind. Also, it is essential to define precisely which cash outlays have or have not been deducted to arrive at the predicted future cash returns. In this example, interest and income tax cash payments have *not* yet been deducted. In other words, the $116,000 future cash return to be received one year from today is *before* interest and income tax payments are considered. But all other cash outlays that are made to generate the future return from the investment have been deducted. With these important points in mind, the key question is whether this is an attractive investment to the company.

As was shown previously in Exhibit 9.3, the company should earn an 16.0% annual rate of profit (before interest and income tax) on its investments. Assuming that this cost of capital (COC) rate is appropriate to this investment, then the minimum future return the company should receive from this one-year, one-return investment can be determined as follows:

Determination of Minimum Future Return Needed to Meet Company's COC Requirements

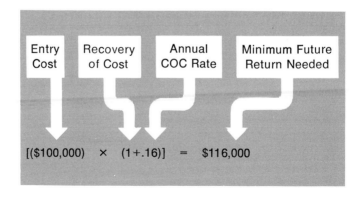

Entry Cost	Recovery of Cost	Annual COC Rate	Minimum Future Return Needed

$$[(\$100,000) \times (1+.16)] = \$116,000$$

The minimum future return is compared with the predicted future return, which is also $116,000. Hence, this investment's future return is adequate, but no more than adequate, to meet the company's minimum objective of recovering the amount of capital invested and earning, at least, a 16.0% profit on the amount of capital invested each year.

The Two Basic Methods of Analyzing Future Returns from an Investment: Finding the Investment's Internal Rate of Return (IRR); and, Finding the Investment's Present Value

If the future returns from an investment can be predicted, and assuming that the entry cost of the investment is known, of course, there are two basic methods of evaluating the future returns relative to the entry cost. One method is to determine the *internal rate of return* (IRR), which is implicit in the future returns. This IRR is compared with the company's "required" cost of capital rate to determine if the investment's IRR is higher or lower than the company's COC. For the same example explained in the preceding section, the IRR method of analysis is shown as follows:

Determining the Internal Rate of Reutrn (IRR) from the Future Return

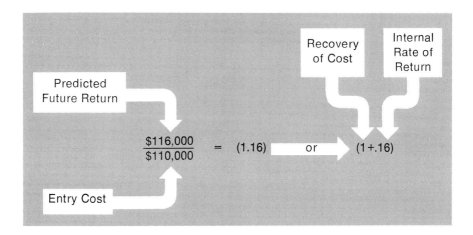

The term Internal Rate of Return might better be called the "internal rate of *profit*", since it refers to the ratio of the profit residual of the future return over and above the recovery of the entry cost of the investment. However, the term Internal Rate of Return is very well established and, therefore, is used in the following discussion. In this example the IRR of the investment is exactly equal to the company's cost of capital (COC) rate, both being 16.0%.

In this simple example there is only one future return from the investment, and finding the IRR is not difficult. However, *long-term* investments usually involve two or more future returns. In such investment situations, finding the IRR is not easy if done by hand computations. (Computers can be programmed to find the IRR, which overcomes most of these computation problems.) As the later discussion in this and the next chapters show, some trial and error usually is necessary to find the precise rate of internal reutrn from a long-term investment.

A more convenient method is to divide each future return by a *fixed* and *known* discount factor to find the *present value* of the investment, which may be more or less than its entry cost. This method is first explained for the one-year, one future return investment example explained above. For this investment example the discount factor is equal to (1 + COC), where COC is the company's cost of capital rate, which is 16.0%. The present value method of analyzing this investment example is shown as follows:

Determining the Present Value of the Investment

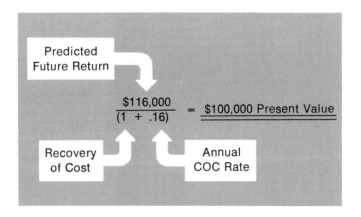

$$\frac{\$116,000}{(1 + .16)} = \$100,000 \text{ Present Value}$$

The essential idea of dividing the future return by the discount factor (1 + COC) is that the future return must be large enough both to recover the investment's entry cost *and* to earn a 16.0% profit. The investment's present value is compared with its entry cost, which is also $100,000. Both the IRR and present value (PV) methods are next applied to two different one-year, one return investment situations, in which the IRR does *not* equal the company's COC, and in which the entry cost does *not* equal the present value of the investment.

Assume that the future return one year from today (before interest and income tax) is predicted to be $121,800 from a certain investment. The entry cost is still the same—$100,000—and all other assumptions made above are the same. This investment is analyzed as follows:

Analysis of Investment Having One Future Return of $121,800 One Year from Today

IRR
Method
$$\left[\frac{\$121,800}{\$100,000}\right] = (1+.218), \text{ or } 21.8\%$$ rate of profit, which is more than the company's 16.0% COC.

PV
Method
$$\left[\frac{\$121,800}{(1+.16)}\right] = \$105,000, \text{ or } \$5,000$$ more than the $100,000 entry cost, which is called the *excess present value.*

By either method of analysis this investment opportunity looks attractive. Notice that the present value of the investment is $5000 more than the enrty cost, which is called the *excess present value* of the investment.

Assume on the other hand, that the investment's future return is predicted to be only $110,200 one year from today. Both methods reveal the inadequacy of this investment:

Analysis of Investment Having One Future Return of $110,200 One Year from Today

IRR
Method
$$\left[\frac{\$110,200}{\$100,00}\right] = (1+.102), \text{ or } 10.2\%$$ rate of profit, which is less than the company's 16.0% COC.

PV
Method
$$\left[\frac{\$110,200}{(1+.16)}\right] = \$95,000, \text{ or } \$5,000$$ less than the $100,000 entry cost.

Thus it is unlikely the company would enter this investment.

Two or More Years of Waiting for a Future Return: The Compounding Concept

If the company must wait more than one year* for a future return from an investment, then there is one additional element in the analysis which it is extremely important to understand. As previously, the best way to explain this new aspect is with a specific example. Assume that the same company could invest $100,000 today and *two years* from today would receive one future return of $134,560 (before interest and income tax) from the investment. As shown above (see Exhibit 9.3), this company needs to earn 16.0% profit (before interest and income tax) *annually* on its investment. Thus at the end of the first year the company "should" receive $16,000 profit on its investment: ($100,000 × 16.0% = $16,000). But in this case nothing is received.

Clearly the initial capital investment of $100,000 has to carry forward to the second year—the company needs to earn 16.0% again during the second year on this amount, since none of the $100,000 capital has been recovered. The

* One year is adopted as the most intuitive investment earning period in this discussion. Actually, any time interval can be used, such as a quarter (three months), one month, or one day.

key question concerns the $16,000 of profit "needed" to be received at the end of the first year which, in fact, is *not* received then. The key answer is that this "required" profit is added to the initial capital investment and the combined total ($100,000 entry cost + $16,000 unreceived profit = $116,000) is treated as the capital investment base for determining the required profit needed to be earned during the second year. This adding-in of unreceived profit is called *compounding*—the unreceived profit is added into or compounded into the initial capital investment, which increases the capital base on which profit has to be earned during the next year.

To sum up, the following computations can be made to determine what the future return would have to be at the end of the second year, to justify this investment relative to the company's cost of capital:

Determination of Minimum Future Return Needed Two Years from Today

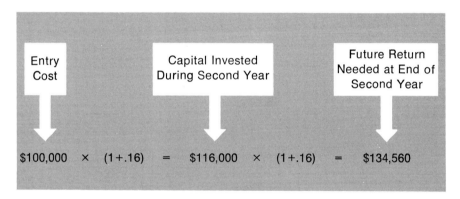

Instead of computing the intermediate value of $116,000, which is the capital invested during the second year (including the unreceived profit of $16,000 that is compounded with the initial entry cost), it is more direct to make this sort of computation as follows:

Direct Computation of Minimum Future Return Needed Two Years from Today

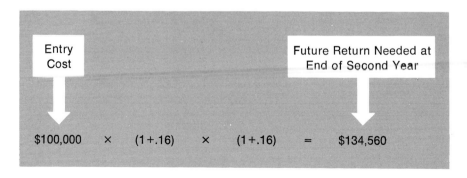

This sort of repetitive computation is more usually written as follows:

More Usual Manner of Showing Computation

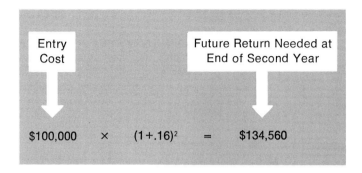

Entry Cost

Future Return Needed at End of Second Year

$100,000   × $(1+.16)^2$ = $134,560

Observe that the predicted future return from this two-year investment is exactly equal to what it should be. That is, the internal rate of return (IRR) from this investment would be 16.0%, which is exactly equal to the company's cost of capital rate. Obviously, this example is "rigged" to come out exactly equal to a 16.0% IRR.

What if the future return two years from today is predicted to be, say, $139,240. What is the IRR in this case? To answer we would have to solve for r in the following equation:

This equation must be solved in order to find investment's IRR (r in the equation)

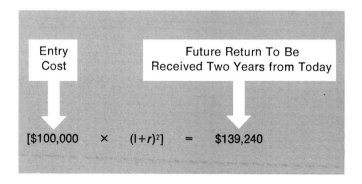

Entry Cost

Future Return To Be Received Two Years from Today

[$100,000   × $(1+r)^2$]   = $139,240

By now it is evident that r would be higher than 16.0%, since the future return ($139,240) is higher than what it would have to be at the 16.0% rate ($134,560). But it is *not* convenient to solve for r, is it?

To test whether or not the future return is enough to earn a profit rate equal to the company's cost of capital, the present value (PV) approach is much more convenient. The PV method uses the company's COC rate instead of solving for r in the above equation. To find the present value of the $139,240 future return received two years from today, the following computation is made:

Determining the Present Value of the Future Return Received Two Years from Today

$$\left[\frac{\$139,240}{(1+.16)^2}\right] = \$103,478, \text{ which is } \$3,478 \text{ more than the } \$100,000 \text{ entry cost}$$

Of course, we need to know the value of $(1+.16)^2$ to make the above present value computation.

Nature and Uses of Compound Interest and Present Value Tables

There are two basic options to determine a value such as $(1+.16)^2$: (1) a calculator can be used if one is available; or, (2) the value can be determined from the tables that have been prepared for various combinations of rate of profit and the number of years. These are called *compound interest tables,* and are presented at the end of this chapter. The original demand for these tables was in long-term *interest* income earning investment situations. This is why the term "interest" is used. More properly, they should be called compound income or compound profit tables. Either way, we should find that $(1+.16)^2$ equals 1.3456.

Last, in determining present values, it is usually more convenient to do the necessary calculations as follows (using the same example again):

$$\$139,240 \times \left[\frac{1}{(1+.16)^2}\right] = \text{Present Value}$$

In other words, multiplying the future return by the factor in the brackets is easier than dividing it by $(1+.16)^2$ if one is doing the work with pencil and paper. The "1" in the numerator of the fraction in the brackets can be thought of as *one dollar* of future return. Hence, the value of the fraction in the brackets is the present value of one dollar of future return to be received two years from today.

Present value tables are prepared to show the values for various combinations of rate of profit and the number of years. A present value table is also presented at the end of this chapter. In this table we can find that

$$\left[\frac{1}{(1+.16)^2}\right] = 0.743163$$

This means that if you invest $.743163 today and receive $1 return two years from today, you would earn 16.0% each year on your investment, keeping in mind that the unreceived income for the first year is compounded with the original investment to determine the capital investment for the second year. The total return in this investment example is $139,240; hence, the investment's present value can be quickly determined as follows:

$139,240 × (.743163) = $103,478, which is the same Present Value amount determined above

The basic procedures just explained for a two-year investment period apply to any number of years. For instance, assume the company could invest $100,000 today and receive $174,901 (before interest and income tax) four years from today. The IRR method would begin with the following equation and then solve for r.

$$\$100,000 \times (1 + r)^4 = \$174,901$$

The compound interest table at the end of the chapter is very helpful to find r. Notice that $(1 + r)^4$ is equal to 1.74901, that is, ($174,901 ÷ $100,000 = 1.74901). In the compound interest table we can find that $(1 + .16)^4$ equals 1.81064. Therefore, r is less than 16.0%. By shifting over to the next column on the left, we can see that $(1 + .15)^4$ equals 1.74901. Therefore, r equals 15.0% in this investment example. Hence, the internal rate of return from this investment is less than the company's cost of capital rate (16.0%).

This less than satisfactory rate of profit is also shown by the present value method. From the present value table at the end of the chapter we can see that $\left[\dfrac{1}{(1 + .16)^4}\right]$ equals .552291. The present value of the four-year investment is

$174,901 × (.552291) = $96,596 Present Value

Of course, the entry cost ($100,000) is more than this present value, so the company would not find this an attractive investment.

Recovery of Capital During Life of Investment

Suppose that the company could invest $100,000 today, and one year from now would receive a return of $66,000 and two years from today would receive a second return of $58,000. As previously, these future returns are before interest and income tax. Is this an attractive investment opportunity? One approach is to compute the present value of each future return, and then add these separate present values to get the total present value of the investment. As explained above, the company's cost of capital is used as the discount rate in the present value computations:

Computation of Total Present Value of Investment

	Future Return	Discount Factor		Present Value
Present value of future return to be received one year from today:	$66,000 ×	$\left[\dfrac{1}{(1+.16)^1}\right]$	=	$ 56,897
Present value of future return to be received two years from today:	$58,000 ×	$\left[\dfrac{1}{(1+.16)^2}\right]$	=	$ 43,103
Total present value of both future returns:				$100,000

Based on this present value analysis the investment is just attractive enough, since the total present value equals the entry cost of the investment.

It is also important to understand the recovery of capital at the end of the first year, and what impact this has on the amount of profit that must be earned during the second year. Since the present value equals the entry cost, we know that the investment's IRR equals 16.0%. Thus the following analysis can be made of the investment—see Exhibit 9.5. In this exhibit notice in particular that the $66,000 return at the end of the first year is divided between: (1) profit equal to 16.0% of the capital investment balance at the start of the year; and (2) the residual amount ($66,000 − $16,000) which is the amount of capital that is recovered at that time. Thus the capital investment balance at the start of the second year is reduced to $50,000: ($100,000 original capital less the $50,000 recovered at the end of the first year). The $50,000 capital recovered from *this* particular investment is available for *other* investments by the company. Finally,

EXHIBIT 9.5
Analysis of Two Year Investment

Year	Investment Balance at Start of Year	Return Received at End of Year	Cost of Capital (at 16%)	Amount of Capital Recovered
First	$100,000	$66,000	$16,000	$ 50,000
Second	$ 50,000	$58,000	$ 8,000	50,000
				$100,000

also notice that the total capital recovered by the end of the second year equals $100,000, which is equal to the entry cost of the investment.

Instead of the unequal future returns given in the example discussed above, assume that the company could invest $100,000 today and would receive a return of $62,296 one year from today and a second return of $62,296 two years from today. Since the future returns are equal, a "shortcut" in the computation procedures for the total present value of the investment can be made as follows:

Computation of Present Value for Two Equal Future Returns

Total present value of both future returns $= \$62,296 \times \left[\dfrac{1}{(1+.16)^1} + \dfrac{1}{(1+.16)^2} \right]$

From the present value table at the end of the chapter we can find that the present values of the two terms in the brackets are .862069 and .743163. These two are added together to give 1.605232, so the present value computations becomes:

$$\$62,296 \times (1.605232) = \$100,000 \text{ Present Value}$$

The 1.605232 is the present value of an *annuity* of $1 received at the end of each of two years. Generally, an annuity refers to equal amounts received at equal intervals. Present value tables for annuities are also available, and are also presented at the end of this chapter, although the investments discussed below and in Chapter Ten do not involve equal future returns. However, some problems at the end of these two chapters involve equal future returns, and the annuity tables are useful for these problems.

Comparison of Alternative Patterns of Future Returns Whose Present Values are in Excess of the Entry Cost of the Investment

The preceding discussion makes one very important assumption. If the present value of the future returns (discounted at the company's cost of capital rate) is not equal to or more than the entry cost of the investment, then the company should not proceed with the investment. However, this is rather simplistic. For instance, assume that the future returns were such that the investment would yield an annual operating profit (before interest and income tax) rate of only 15.3%, which is below the company's 16.0% "required" cost of capital rate. Should the company so quickly reject this investment? This depends on whether better investments are actually available. It may be that the 15.3% investment is the best opportunity the company knows about. If so, perhaps it should go ahead with the 15.3% investment. Indeed, if capital would otherwise go uninvested, then the company may be under some pressure to make the investment. Alternatively the company may retire some of its outstanding liabilities or common stock. These decisions are primarily ones of financial policy. Their consideration is beyond the scope of this book. The following discussion is concerned with those situations in which the future returns of the investment opportunities known to the company promise *more* than its minimum cost of capital rate.

Three Alternative Patterns of Future Returns: Determining Their Excess Present Values and Internal Rates of Return

Assume the company could invest $850,000 today in any one of three different investments. The company has only enough cash presently to make one of these investments. Each investment promises a different pattern of future returns, which are shown in Exhibit 9.6. Which pattern of future returns is "best," or should be preferred by the company? One possible way of comparing the three alternatives is simply to add the future returns and find the total returns to be received from each investment. This would give the following: Investment (1) = $1,290,000; Investment (2) = $1,210,000; and, Investment (3) = $1,313,384. In comparing these three sums it may appear that Alternative no. 3 is the best, Alternative no. 1 is the second best, and Alternative no. 2 is the worst. If we accept this sort of comparative analysis, we have missed the essential point of the previous discussion regarding the cost of capital. This kind of analysis is not acceptable and may be seriously misleading because it ignores *when* the future returns are to be received. It treats all future dollars as the same, whether received at the end of year one or at the end of year four.

One proper method of analysis is to determine the *yield,* or *internal rate of return* (IRR) from each alternative timetable of future returns. This means finding what rate of annual operating profit would be earned from each investment alternative. The highest of these rates normally is the most attractive investment

EXHIBIT 9.6
Three Alternative Future Return Schedules

Future Return Received at End of		Investment Alternative No. 1	Investment Alternative No. 2	Investment Alternative No. 3
Year One	=	$370,000	$490,000	$328,346
Year Two	=	330,000	346,000	328,346
Year Three	=	290,000	218,000	328,346
Year Four	=	300,000	156,000	328,346

opportunity. In studying the three patterns of future returns it is not obvious which one would produce the highest IRR. A useful starting point is to determine the *present value* of each investment's future returns, based on the company's cost of capital rate, which is the lowest internal rate of return the company should earn. In this manner the investment alternative with the highest *excess present value* can be identified.

Each future return in Exhibit 9.6 is multiplied by $\left[\dfrac{1}{(1+.16)^n}\right]$ where n equals the number of years from the point of investment to the point of receipt. The values for the expression in the brackets are given in the present value table at the end of the chapter. The present values for each future return of each investment are added to give the total present value of each investment alternative. Without showing all the detailed computations (which you should know how to determine by now), the total present values of each investment alternative and their excess present values are:

Present Values of Each Investment

		Total Present Value	Excess Present Value (over $850,000)
Investment Alternative No. 1	=	$915,687	$65,687
Investment Alternative No. 2	=	$905,369	$55,368
Investment Alternative No. 3	=	$918,771	$68,771

Thus it would appear that Investment Alternative no. 3 is the best, since it has the highest present value and the highest excess present value.

However, it happens that all three alternatives have the same IRR, which is 20.0%. This is shown in Exhibit 9.7 in two different ways:

1. The 20.0% rate is applied to the capital investment balance each year to determine the profit each year; the excess of the future return that year over the profit is the amount of capital recovery that year, which is subtracted to get the next year's capital balance.

2. The IRR rate is used to discount the future returns to obtain the present value of the future returns at this (20.0%) rate (instead of the company's cost of capital rate).

The two approaches give the same result, of course. We may ask how the correct and precise 20.0% IRR is found. Essentially a trial and error method is used. Since all three of the investments have an excess present value, then the IRR must be higher than 16.0% (which is the company's COC). Thus a guess at the rate is made, and the results are computed by using this rate. If this rate is too high, then it is lowered and the computations are made again. Eventually the precisely correct rate is found.

EXHIBIT 9.7
Proof of 20% Annual IRR for the Three Different Patterns of Future Returns

	Year	Determining Capital Recovery Approach				Present Value (Discounting) Approach
		Unrecovered Capital Balance at Start of Year	Future Return Collected at End of Year	Profit at 20% of Capital Balance	Capital Recovery	Present Value of Future Returns
INVESTMENT ALTERNATIVE NO. 1	One	$850,000	$370,000	$170,000	$200,000	$\frac{\$370,000}{(1+.20)^1} = \$308,333$
	Two	650,000	330,000	130,000	200,000	$\frac{\$330,000}{(1+.20)^2} = \$229,167$
	Three	450,000	290,000	90,000	200,000	$\frac{\$290,000}{(1+.20)^3} = \$167,824$
	Four	250,000	300,000	50,000	250,000	$\frac{\$300,000}{(1+.20)^4} = \$144,676$
	Totals				$850,000	$850,000
INVESTMENT ALTERNATIVE NO. 2	One	$850,000	$490,000	$170,000	$320,000	$\frac{\$490,000}{(1+.20)^1} = \$408,333$
	Two	530,000	346,000	106,000	240,000	$\frac{\$346,000}{(1+.20)^2} = \$240,278$
	Three	290,000	218,000	58,000	160,000	$\frac{\$218,000}{(1+.20)^3} = \$126,157$
	Four	130,000	156,000	26,000	130,000	$\frac{\$156,000}{(1+.20)^4} = \$75,232$
	Totals				$850,000	$850,000
INVESTMENT ALTERNATIVE NO. 3	One	$850,000	$328,346	$170,000	$158,346	$\frac{\$328,346}{(1+.20)^1} = \$273,621$
	Two	691,654	328,346	138,331	190,015	$\frac{\$328,346}{(1+.20)^2} = \$228,018$
	Three	501,639	328,346	100,328	228,018	$\frac{\$328,346}{(1+.20)^3} = \$190,015$
	Four	273,621	328,346	54,725	273,621	$\frac{\$328,346}{(1+.20)^4} = \$158,346$
	Totals				$850,000	$850,000

Investment Alternative no. 3 has the highest excess present value in the previous computation (using the company's cost of capital rate as the discount rate) because it has the slowest pattern of capital recovery. In other words, Alternative no. 3 has the largest capital investment balance each year (as we can see in Exhibit 9.7), and thus more profit is earned each year. This will show up as additional excess present value compared with the other two alternatives. It is best to solve for each investment alternative's IRR in addition to comparing their excess present values. (In some instances one investment alternative may have the highest IRR but the lowest excess present value.)

Capital Recovery Pattern of Each Investment Alternative: The Preference for Early Capital Payback

As shown in Exhibit 9.7, the annual rate of profit (the internal rate of return) is the same for all three investments, even though the timetable of future returns is different in each case. It may appear, therefore, that management would be indifferent between the three investment alternatives. Clearly if one alternative happened to yield a higher IRR, for example, 22%, while the other two yielded only 20%, then the decision would favor the highest IRR. But is IRR the only test? Is there a secondary factor to consider choosing among three equal IRR investment alternatives?

Notice in Exhibit 9.7 that Alternative no. 2 recovers more capital in year one, or in the first two years, or in the first three years, than the other two investment alternatives. In the first two years, for instance, we can see that Alternative no. 2 recovers $560,000 ($320,000 plus $240,000), whereas Alternative no. 1 recovers only $400,000 and Alternative no. 3 recovers only $348,361 ($158,346 plus $190,015). The more rapid recovery of capital usually is considered to be an advantage. The cash flow returning to the company sooner gives the company more *liquidity flexibility.* In other words, from investment Alternative no. 2 the company has more money available during the first two years, which can be invested in other investment projects, or which can be used for payment of liabilities or to meet other demands for cash.

The "quickness" or rapidity of capital recovery from an investment is measured by its *payback period.* To measure the payback period, future returns are accumulated until their total equals the entry cost. Alternative no. 1 has total returns of $700,000 over the first two years ($370,000 + $330,000), so another $150,000 is needed to reach the $850,000 entry cost (the total capital invested). Observe in Exhibit 9.7 that during year three there is $290,000 total return, almost twice the $150,000 remainder needed to reach the $850,000 mark. Thus investment Alternative no. 1 takes about two years and six months to payback the entry cost. Likewise the payback periods for the other two investment alternatives can be determined: Alternative no. 2 equals two years and one month; and, Alternative no. 3 equals two years and seven months. In some situations the investment alternative that has the shortest payback period may not have the highest IRR. Managers may have to make a trade-off decision between which is more important: the quick recovery of capital, or the highest IRR.

The quick recovery of capital may not always be an advantage, since one or two years from today the company may actually *not* need the money. The company at that time may not have an investment opportunity that would yield as much as a 20% annual rate of profit. The argument can be reversed, as it were, to favor Investment Alternatives nos. 1 and 3, since these projects leave more money invested (more capital is unrecovered) at the 20% earnings rate for a longer period of time than Alternative no. 2. (This is why they have the largest excess present values—see page 309.) To understand this point, add up the total profit over the four-year period for each investment, which is as follows: Alternative no. 1 = $440,000; Alternative no. 2 = $360,000; and, Alternative no. 3 = $463,384. In short, much depends on the future cash flow needs and the future investment opportunities of the company.

A Final Word

The next chapter discusses specific types of investments that businesses make and how the future returns from the investments are determined. In this chapter the future returns are simply taken for granted, without any discussion of what the returns consist of or how they are determined. In other words, here our discussion is limited to the basic relationships between the future returns and the entry cost of an investment, and to the analysis and evaluation of investments relative to the company's cost of capital requirements. This basic understanding of investments is essential to the more detailed and technical discussion in the next chapter. In the next chapter we also consider other more technical points, for example, the favorable impact of income tax provisions in certain investment situations.

The term *capital budgeting* refers to the comparative analysis of two or more alternative investment projects when capital is limited in supply and the company must allocate or ration the capital it has available. The alternative investments are ranked relative to their internal rates of return and excess present values and then compared on these bases, as has been shown in the above discussion. However, this discussion barely touches on many other problems of capital budgeting.* An adequate treatment of capital budgeting goes far into the field of business finance, which is beyond the scope of this book. In any case, capital budgeting analysis begins with a sound understanding of the fundamentals of investment analysis which are examined in this chapter.

---

* The term "capital budgeting" sometimes is used in a very broad sense, including *all* aspects of investment analysis and decision making, not just the *comparative* analysis of two or more investment opportunities. In this broader sense of the term, virtually all of this chapter deals with "capital budgeting."

Summary

Based on its mix of capital sources and the cost of each source, a company determines its cost of capital rate. In this chapter the term *cost of capital* refers to the company's required rate of operating profit (before interest and income tax) on its total assets, which has to be earned to achieve its return on stockholders' equity goal. Given a budgeted or estimated amount of total assets for the coming year, a company multiplies its total assets by its cost of capital rate to determine the total operating profit that should be earned during the year.

The cost of capital rate is essential to bring into the analysis of new or marginal capital investment opportunities being considered by a company, especially long-term investments. The two basic demands on the future returns from an investment are to recover the entry cost (the initial amount of capital invested) and to earn an adequate amount of profit each year, at least equal to its cost of capital. Given the predicted future returns from an investment, there are two basic methods of evaluating the investment. The investment's internal rate of return (IRR) can be determined, which is the annual rate of profit that would be earned each year on the amount of unrecovered capital invested each year. If the investment's IRR yield is more than the company's COC rate, then the investment is attractive. For long-term investments, finding the precise IRR requires some trial and error, and is not convenient if it is done by hand. Alternatively, the company's cost of capital rate is used to discount the future returns in order to find the investment's present value. If the investment's present value is more than its entry cost, then the investment is attractive.

Normally the key test in choosing between two or more investment alternatives is which one has the highest IRR, or the highest excess present value. If the internal rates of return among the investment alternatives are fairly close, then the company also should look to which investment has the most rapid recovery of capital, that is, the quickest capital payback period. In any case, for cash flow planning it is very important to know the capital recovery patterns of investments. Present value computations are made considerably easier with the use of present value tables, such as the ones at the end of this chapter.

Compound Interest Table for Values of $[(1+r)^n]$

(r)

Number of Years (n)	6.0%	8.0%	10.0%	12.0%	14.0%	16.0%	18.0%	20.0%	22.0%
1	1.06000	1.08000	1.10000	1.12000	1.14000	1.16000	1.18000	1.20000	1.22000
2	1.12360	1.16640	1.21000	1.25440	1.29960	1.34560	1.39240	1.44000	1.48840
3	1.19102	1.25971	1.33100	1.40493	1.48154	1.56090	1.64303	1.72800	1.81585
4	1.26247	1.36049	1.46410	1.57352	1.68896	1.81064	1.93878	2.07360	2.21533
5	1.33823	1.46933	1.61051	1.76234	1.92541	2.10034	2.28776	2.48832	2.70271
6	1.41852	1.58687	1.77156	1.97382	2.19497	2.43640	2.69955	2.98598	3.29730
7	1.50363	1.71382	1.94872	2.21068	2.50227	2.82622	3.18547	3.58318	4.02271
8	1.59385	1.85093	2.14359	2.47596	2.85259	3.27841	3.75886	4.29982	4.90771
9	1.68948	1.99900	2.35795	2.77308	3.25195	3.80296	4.43545	5.15978	5.98740
10	1.79085	2.15892	2.59374	3.10585	3.70722	4.41143	5.23383	6.19174	7.30463
15	2.39656	3.17217	4.17725	5.47356	7.13794	9.26552	11.97375	15.40702	19.74228
20	3.20713	4.66096	6.72750	9.64629	13.74349	19.46075	27.39303	38.33759	53.35762

Compound Interest Annuity Table for Values of $[(1+r)^1 + (1+r)^2 + \ldots + (1+r)^n]$

(r)

Number of Years (n)	6.0%	8.0%	10.0%	12.0%	14.0%	16.0%	18.0%	20.0%	22.0%
1	1.06000	1.08000	1.10000	1.12000	1.14000	1.16000	1.18000	1.20000	1.22000
2	2.18360	2.24640	2.31000	2.37440	2.43960	2.50560	2.57240	2.64000	2.70840
3	3.37462	3.50611	3.64100	3.77933	3.92114	4.06650	4.21543	4.36800	4.52425
4	4.63709	4.86660	5.10510	5.35285	5.61010	5.87714	6.15421	6.44160	6.73958
5	5.97532	6.33593	6.71561	7.11519	7.53551	7.97748	8.44197	8.92992	9.44229
6	7.39384	7.92280	8.48717	9.08901	9.73048	10.41388	11.14152	11.91590	12.73959
7	8.89747	9.63662	10.43589	11.29969	12.23275	13.24010	14.32699	15.49908	16.76230
8	10.49132	11.48755	12.57948	13.77565	15.08534	16.51851	18.08585	19.79890	21.67001
9	12.18080	13.48655	14.93743	16.54873	18.33729	20.32147	22.52130	24.95868	27.65741
10	13.97165	15.64547	17.53117	19.65458	22.04451	24.73290	27.75513	31.15042	34.96204

Present Value Table for $\left[\dfrac{1}{(1+r)^n}\right]$

(r)

Number of Years (n)	6.0%	8.0%	10.0%	12.0%	14.0%	16.0%	18.0%	20.0%	22.0%
1	.943396	.925926	.909091	.892857	.877193	.862069	.847458	.833333	.819672
2	.889996	.857339	.826446	.797194	.769467	.743163	.718184	.694444	.671862
3	.839619	.793832	.751315	.711780	.674971	.640658	.608631	.578704	.550707
4	.792094	.735030	.683013	.635518	.592080	.552291	.515789	.482253	.451399
5	.747258	.680583	.620921	.567427	.519369	.476113	.437109	.401878	.369999
6	.704960	.630169	.564474	.506631	.455586	.410442	.370431	.334898	.303278
7	.665057	.583490	.513158	.452349	.399637	.353829	.313925	.279082	.248588
8	.627412	.540269	.466507	.403883	.350559	.305025	.266038	.232568	.203761
9	.591898	.500249	.424097	.360610	.307508	.262953	.225456	.193807	.167017
10	.558394	.463193	.385543	.321973	.269744	.226683	.191064	.161505	.136899
15	.417265	.315241	.239392	.182696	.140096	.107927	.083516	.064905	.050652
20	.311804	.214548	.148643	.103666	.072761	.051385	.036505	.026084	.018741

Present Value Annuity Table for $\left[\dfrac{1}{(1+r)^1} + \dfrac{1}{(1+r)^2} + \cdots + \dfrac{1}{(1+r)^n}\right]$

(r)

Number of Years (n)	6.0%	8.0%	10.0%	12.0%	14.0%	16.0%	18.0%	20.0%	22.0%
1	.943396	.925926	.909091	.892857	.877183	.862069	.847458	.833333	.819672
2	1.833392	1.783265	1.735537	1.690051	1.646660	1.605232	1.565642	1.527777	1.491534
3	2.673011	2.577097	2.486852	2.401831	2.321631	2.245890	2.174273	2.106481	2.042241
4	3.465105	3.312127	3.169865	3.037349	2.913711	2.798181	2.690062	2.588734	2.493640
5	4.212363	3.992710	3.790786	3.604776	3.433080	3.274294	3.127171	2.990612	2.863639
6	4.917323	4.622879	4.355260	4.111407	3.888666	3.684736	3.497602	3.325510	3.166917
7	5.582380	5.206369	4.868418	4.563756	4.288303	4.038565	3.811527	3.604592	3.415505
8	6.209792	5.746638	5.334925	4.967639	4.638862	4.343590	4.077565	3.837160	3.619266
9	6.801693	6.246887	5.759022	5.328249	4.946370	4.606543	4.303021	4.030967	3.786283
10	7.360084	6.710080	6.144565	5.650222	5.216114	4.833226	4.494085	4.192472	3.923182

Questions

9. 1 Assume that a company's operating profit rate of return on assets is 12.0%, but that this company's total assets are 10.0% higher than need be to support the company's level of sales revenue and operations. If the company had managed its asset investments better, what operating profit rate of return on assets could have been earned?

9. 2 If a company had no liabilities at all (either interest bearing or noninterest bearing) and its return on equity goal is 15.6%, what rate of operating profit (before tax) would the company have to earn on its assets to achieve its return on equity objective?

9. 3 Please refer to Exhibit 9.4 in the chapter:
(a) If the company were able to earn a 17.0% return on its assets (instead of the 16.0% shown in the exhibit), what rate of return on equity would result?
(b) If the company wanted to earn a 18.2% rate of return on equity, what would the operating profit rate of return on assets have to be?

9. 4 A company's preinterest, pretax cost of capital rate is 20.0%. A certain investment would cost $65,000 to enter today, and one year from today a one-time future return of $78,000 in cash net of all expenses except interest and income tax would be received. Evaluate this investment opportunity according to:
(a) The method of determining what the minimum future return from the investment would have to be,
(b) The IRR method, and
(c) The present value method.

9. 5 "If the investment's IRR is higher than the company's COC, then the present value of the investment must be more than its entry cost." Do you agree? Briefly explain why or why not.

9. 6 A company's annual COC rate is 15.0%. A certain investment opportunity is open to the company that would cost $100,000 today and that would return $130,000 two years from today. Since the company would earn 30.0% over the two years on this investment, which is two times the 15.0% annual COC rate, the company would be justified to make the investment. Do you agree? If so, explain why. If not, determine how much the future return two years from today would have to be to justify the investment.

9. 7 The IRR from an investment is 14.0% and the company's COC is 15.0%. However, the manager who proposed this investment argues that the company's COC is somewhat arbitrary and, anyway, the 14.0% is "close enough" to justify going ahead with the investment. Do you agree? Briefly discuss.

9. 8 Should a company accept an investment that yields a 14.0% IRR if it has a second investment that yields 18.0%, assuming that its COC is 16.0%? Briefly explain.

9. 9 (a) How long would it take you to double your money if you make an invest-

ment that yields an annual income (net of income tax and all other expenses) of 8.0% on your investment, assuming income is reinvested each year over the life of the investment?

(b) How long would it take to double your money if you make an investment that yields an annual income (net of income tax and all other expenses) of 8.0% on your investment, assuming income is withdrawn each year from the investment?

9.10   "If the present value equals the entry cost of the investment, then the IRR must equal the company's COC." Do you agree? Briefly explain.

9.11   What is an annuity? Can you use a compound interest table to find the present value of an annuity? If so, explain how. If not, how would you determine the present value of an annuity?

9.12   A company's COC is 15.0%. An investment opportunity is available that has an entry cost today of $100,000, and which promises a future return of $15,000 one year from today and a second and final return of $115,000 two years from today. Is this an attractive enough investment for the company to consider seriously? Explain your answer.

9.13   If the future returns from an investment are discounted at the company's COC rate and the present value of the investment is less than its entry cost, what does this mean?

9.14   "If two alternative investments have the same IRR and assuming that this IRR is is higher than the company's COC, then the company should be indifferent between the two and may as well flip a coin to decide which investment to make." Do you agree? Explain briefly.

9.15   (a) Why would a business prefer rapid capital payback from its investments?
       (b) If an investment promises an IRR higher than the company's COC, wouldn't the company prefer slow capital recovery instead of rapid capital payback?

9.16   "If one investment has a shorter payback period than another, then it must be the better investment opportunity." Do you agree? Explain briefly.

Problems

P9. 1   Refer to Exhibit 9.1, which shows the financial position of the company, in particular its capitalization structure. Instead of a 13.0% annual return on equity goal, assume that the directors decide that the company should earn at least 15.6% return on equity next year. All other assumptions discussed for the example in the chapter remain the same.

Required:
(1) In the manner shown in Exhibit 9.2, determine the amount of operating profit the company would have to earn next year.

(2) In this case what is the company's cost of capital?

(3) If the company's asset turnover ratio next year is expected to be 2.0, then what (operating) profit ratio will the company have to earn next year? Show your computations.

P9. 2   Refer again to Exhibit 9.1, which shows the financial position of the company, in particular its capitalization structure. Instead of the long-term debt of $2,500,000 shown, assume that the company is more conservative and uses *no long-term debt*, although all the short-term liabilities are the same as shown. The stock-holders' equity is $2,500,000 higher in this case, which is the result of using no long-term debt. All other assumptions discussed for the example in the chapter remain the same.

Required:

(1) In the manner shown in Exhibit 9.2, determine the amount of operating profit the company would have to earn next year.

(2) In this case what is the company's cost of capital?

(3) If the company's (operating) profit ratio next year is expected to be 8.0%, then what must the company's total sales revenue be next year? Show your computations.

P9. 3   Refer to Exhibit 9.1, which shows the financial position of the company, and to Exhibit 9.2, which shows the determination of the company's required oper-ating profit next year relative to its cost of capital. Based on this analysis the company has set its selling prices for next year to earn the required amount of operating profit. Shortly after the year begins, however, it becomes apparent that the interest rate on its short-term debt should average only $7\frac{1}{3}\%$ during the year. All other assumptions discussed in the chapter for the example remain the same.

Required:

(1) If the company leaves the selling prices next year as originally determined and earns the amount of operating profit originally planned, then what return on equity would be earned next year? Show your computations.

(2) Assume instead that the company wants to adjust its selling prices and to pass along the interest expense savings to its customers. Assume an average sales price of $100 and assume the company's profit ratio is 10.0%. What would be the adjusted average sales price? Show your computations.

P9. 4   Please refer to Exhibit 9.1, which shows the financial position of the company, in particular its capitalization structure. Also, refer to Exhibit 9.2, which shows the determination of the company's required operating profit next year relative to its cost of capital. In addition to the federal tax rate of 48% on taxable income, assume that the company is subject to a state income tax of 5% on its taxable income. For federal tax purposes the state income tax is deductible, and for state tax purposes the federal income tax is deductible. All other assump-tions discussed in the chapter for the example remain the same.

Required: Determine how much additional operating profit the company would have to earn in this situation in order to earn its return on equity goal.

(*Note:* A trial and error approach probably would be the best way to approach this problem.)

P9. 5   A company's noninterest bearing (short-term) liabilities average about 12.5% of its total assets. Its interest bearing debts average about one half of its total assets at an average interest rate of 8.5% per year. Assume a flat income tax rate of 50%. The company establishes its annual cost of capital (operating profit return on total assets) rate at 15.5%.

Required:

(1) Determine the company's return on equity goal. Show your computations.
(2) For a $1000 amount of total assets, show the disposition of the operating profit earned on this capital base, assuming the company exactly earns its cost of capital rate. (See Exhibit 9.4 in the chapter for example.)
(3) If the company can achieve an asset turnover ratio of 3.0 and an (operating) profit ratio of 6.0%, then what rate of return on equity would be earned? Show your computations.

P9. 6   *Short Compound Interest Computations*

(1) Assume that you invest $10,000 today in a savings account, with the instructions that you want all income automatically reinvested. Three years later you withdraw $11,910.16 from your savings account.

   Required: Determine your annual rate of income from this investment.

(2) What if at the end of three years you withdrew $12,597.12 from your savings account?

   Required: Determine your annual rate of income from this investment.

(3) A friend asks to borrow some money against an inheritance of $5000 which he will receive on his twenty-first birthday—four years from today. Assume that you could earn 8.0% income on your investments each year.

   Required: Determine how much you would be willing to loan to your friend.

(4) Assume you invest $100,000 today in a savings account that advertises a 6.0% income rate. One year later you return to withdraw your balance and you are given the sum of $106,167.72. You point out that there must be a mistake, since you only expected to receive $106,000. What is the explanation for the difference?

(5) Assume that you put $10,000 in a risky investment, receive no income, and two years later cash out for $8836.

   Required: Determine your annual rate of *loss* on this investment.

   (*Warning:* You cannot use the compound interest tables at the end of the chapter to solve this part of the problem.)

P9. 7   A company's annual cost of capital rate is 18.0%. Several possible investments are described below. Each alternative is a separate and independent situation from the others.

Required: For each investment shown below determine its internal rate of return and its present value.

Investment Alternative	Entry Cost Today	Future Return(s)
1	$50,000	$ 59,000 one year later
2	$50,000	$ 56,000 one year later
3	$50,000	$ 61,000 one year later
4	$50,000	$ 34,000 one year later plus $29,500 two years later
5	$50,000	$ 31,936 one year later plus $31,936 two years later
6	$50,000	$ 33,523 one year later plus $33,523 two years later
7	$50,000	$103,680 four years later
8	$50,000	$ 34,810 two years later plus $48,469 four years later

P9. 8   A company's annual cost of capital rate is 14.0%. Several possible investments are described below. Each alternative is a separate and independent situation from the others.

Required: For each investment shown below determine its internal rate of return *and* its present value.

Investment Alternative	Entry Cost Today	Future Return(s)			
		One Year Later	Two Years Later	Three Years Later	Four Years Later
1	$100,000	$ 14,000	$114,000		
2	100,000		129,960		
3	100,000			$156,090	
4	100,000	5,000	5,000	135,956	
5	100,000	35,738	35,738	35,738	$ 35,738
6	100,000	− 20,000[a]	152,760		
7	100,000		− 40,000[a]	220,800	
8	100,000	54,000	38,400	24,200	11,400

[a] These are called "negative returns." At this point the company has to make an additional capital investment of the amount shown.

P9. 9   The company can make one and only one of the following investments. Each investment requires an entry cost of $600,000 today. The predicted future returns from each investment alternative are as follows:

Future Return at End of Year	Investment Alternative		
	A	B	C
One	$284,000	$183,246	$158,000
Two	156,000	183,246	149,000
Three	142,000	183,246	140,000
Four	128,000	183,246	131,000
Five	114,000	183,246	472,000

The company's annual cost of capital is 16.0%.

Required: Analyze the pattern of future returns from each investment alternative, and recommend the best alternative to management. Show your computations and make your assumptions clear.

P9.10   A company can purchase the new computer system it has just decided to install in place of its old computer equipment. The purchase cost is $1,865,000 for the entire system. Alternatively, the company could enter into a long-term lease for the identical computer hardware. A third party leasing company quotes the company an annual rent of $300,946 for 10 years. Each rent payment is due on the *first* day of the year. At the end of the tenth year the company has no equity in the computer hardware; the leasing company still owns the computer system at that time, and the company would have to negotiate a new lease then for any further use of the hardware. The company estimates that the new computer system would have a useful life of 10 years with a salvage value equal to 15% of its original cost. The company's cost of capital is set at 18.0% per year.

Required: Should the company buy or lease the computer?

(*Hint:* determine the internal rate of return to the leasing company and compare this IRR to the company's cost of capital, or determine the present value of the future rental payments and compare this to the purchase cost of the computer system. Also, keep in mind that the rental payments are made on the first day of each year and do not forget about the salvage vaue of the computer at the end of its tenth year.)

P9.11   A company has just hired 10 additional salesmen, and each is provided a new car at company expense. The company receives a quote of $4800 for each car from its local Ford dealer. The company replaces its salesmen cars every four years. Based on past experience, the "blue-book" (actual) disposable value of this model four-year old Ford is about 25% of its original cost. The company could lease the same car for $652 per half-year. Each rent is due at the end of each six-month period. At the end of the four years the company would reutrn the cars to the leasing company and would have no equity in the cars. The company's annual cost of capital is 16.0%.

Required: Should the company buy or lease the new cars?

(*Hint*: Determine the internal rate of return to the leasing company and compare this IRR with the company's cost of capital, or determine the present value of the future rental payments and compare this with the purchase cost of the cars. Also, keep in mind the salvage value of the cars at the end of four years.)

P9.12   In this investment situation the company can control the timing of the future returns, but in all cases the investment will yield the same internal rate of return, which is 18.0% per year. Three alternative patterns of future returns have been presented to the manager, all of which, he is told, will yield an 18.0% annual return on the investment:

Future Return Received at End of Year	Investment Alternative		
	A	B	C
One	$200,739	$232,200	$313,200
Two	200,739	207,900	220,320
Three	200,739	183,600	137,160
Four	200,739	159,300	63,720

Required:

(1) Determine the entry cost of the investment and prove that it is the same for all three alternatives.
(2) Determine the amount of capital recovery and profit earned each year on the investment for each of the three alternatives. (For example see Exhibit 9.7 in the chapter.)
(3) If the company's cost of capital is expected to increase in the near future, which investment alternative should be preferred?
(4) If the company's cost of capital is expected to decrease in the near future, which investment alternative should be preferred?

P9.13   For the year just ended the company's financial statements, in very brief and condensed form, are as follows (in thousands):

STATEMENT OF FINANCIAL CONDITION AT YEAR-END

ASSETS		LIABILITIES AND STOCKHOLDERS' EQUITY	
Cash	$ 450	Accounts Payable	$ 700
Marketable Securities	2,000	Income Taxes Payable	100
Accounts Receivable	1,500	Notes Payable (10.0%)	800
Inventories	1,800	Total current liabilities	$1,600
Total current assets	$5,750	Long-term Notes	
Fixed assets (net of		Payable (8.0%)	1,750
accumulated depreciation)	2,250	Stockholders' Equity	4,650
Total Assets	$8,000	Total capital sources	$8,000

NET INCOME STATEMENT FOR YEAR

Sales revenue	$18,000
Cost of goods sold and other operating expenses	16,950
Operating profit	$ 1,050
Income from marketable securities investments	120
Total operating profit and other income	$ 1,170
Interest expense	220
Net income before income taxes	$ 950
Federal and state income taxes	475
Net Income	$ 475

The company is reconsidering its investment in marketable securities. These securities were purchased 18 months ago with the intention at that time of holding the securities only a few months, until the company's new warehouse construction was started at which time the securities would be sold to pay for the new warehouse. However, sales demand has fallen off, and the company has just decided to postpone construction of a new warehouse, which at current sales levels is not needed.

Required:
(1) Assume that at the start of the year the company had sold the marketable securities for what they had cost, and with the sale proceeds had reduced long-term debt by $750,000 and had distributed the other $1,250,000 to its stockholders. Restate the company's ending balance sheet and net income statement for the year assuming the company had taken this action.
(2) Compare the company's return on equity in the two situations, that is, first as shown above, and second based on the action described in part (1).
(3) Based on your answer to part (1), determine the company's annual cost of capital rate if the company wants to earn 15.0% return on equity.

(4) Based on your answers to parts (1) and (3) determine how much total sales revenue there would had to have been to achieve the company's return on equity goal of 15.0%.

P9.14   In this particular industry there are four companies manufacturing and selling essentially the same product, and these four companies are very competitive. All four companies have the same total assets—$50,000,000. Also, all four companies were in the same operating cost situation (excluding interest and income tax), which for the year just ended was:

Fixed operating cost for the year = $23,850,000
Variable operating costs = $70 per unit sold.

However, each of the four companies have a different capitalization structure, which are summarized as follows:

Sources of Capital	Company A	Company B	Company C	Company D
Noninterest bearing liabilities	$ 2,500,000	$ 5,000,000	$ 5,000,000	$ 7,500,000
Interest bearing debt at 9.0% average annual interest rate	$ none	$15,000,000	$15,000,000	$25,000,000
Preferred stock at 8.00% annual dividend rate (if earned)	$ none	$ none	$15,000,000	$ none
Common stockholders' equity (common stock plus retained earnings)	$47,500,000	$30,000,000	$15,000,000	$17,500,000
Total Capital Sources	$50,000,000	$50,000,000	$50,000,000	$50,000,000

(1) Assume all four companies set their selling price at $100 per unit and each company sold 1 million units during the year just ended.

   Required: Compute the return on the (common stockholders') equity for each company. Assume a flat 50% income tax rate.

(2) Assume that, initially at the start of last year, each company thought it could sell 1 million units as long as its selling prices were not too much out of line with the other three companies. Each company wanted to earn a 15.0% rate of return on its (common stockholders') equity for the year.

   Required: Based on the assumption of 1 million units sales volume, determine the selling price that each company would have had to establish to earn a 15.0% return on its equity.

(3) Assume that all four companies have the same return on equity goal of 15.0% annually.

Required: (a) Compare the companies' cost of capital rates, and explain the differences. (b) Based on a uniform industry sales price of $100 per unit, determine each company's "cost of capital break-even point." This is the sales volume that would enable the company to earn exactly its cost of capital.

P9.15 A company has been renting office space in a prestige address building. The company's current lease is expiring, and the landlord has indicated that the quarterly rent will be increased by $800, although the landlord is offering a four-year-lease contract and the rent cannot be raised during the term of the new lease. The company could move to another nearby office building which offers the same amount of space on a four-year lease at the same quarterly rent the company is now paying. The costs of moving to the new location would be $9100. The company's annual cost of capital is 16.0%. Under both leases, rent is paid on the first day of each quarter (three months).

Required:
(1) From the financial point of view which alternative is better? Show your computations.

> (*Note:* Unless you go to other compound interest tables than those at the end of the chapter or use a calculator, you will have to be a little less precise and assume that rent payments are made on the first day of each half-year (six months).)

(2) What other factors probably would influence the decision? Briefly discuss.

P9.16 Reducing the company's financial condition to a $1000 "slice" shows the following:

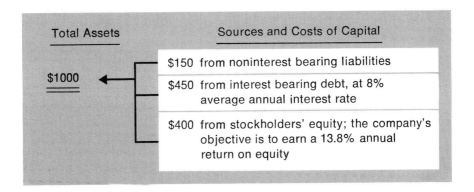

Assume a flat combined state and federal income tax rate of 54% on the company's taxable income. In the following parts of the problem, return on assets means the ratio of annual operating profit before interest and income tax expenses on total assets.

Required:

(1) If the company earns a 15.6% return on its assets, show the disposition of the operating profit on each $1000 of total assets. (See Exhibit 9.4 in the chapter for example.)

(2) If the company earns a 12.8% return on its assets show the disposition of the operating profit on each $1000 of total assets.

(3) If the company earns a 20.0% return on its assets show the disposition of the operating profit on each $1000 of total assets.

(4) If the company's asset turnover ratio is 3.0 times, determine the necessary operating profit ratio so that the company can achieve its return on equity objective.

(5) If the average annual interest rate is 10.0% instead of 8.0%, but everything else remains the same, determine the necessary return on assets rate so that the company can achieve its return on equity goal.

Chapter Ten

Capital Investment Analysis, Continued

CAPITAL INVESTMENT ANALYSIS, CONTINUED

Cost Savings Investments

From the Previous Chapter to this Chapter

The company example introduced and analyzed in Chapter Nine is continued in this chapter. Given the capitalization structure of the company which is shown in its current balance sheet (refer to Exhibit 9.1), we determined in the preceding chapter that the company's annual cost of capital rate is 16.0% (see Exhibits 9.2 and 9.3). In other words, the company should earn operating profit (before interest and income tax) equal to, at least, 16.0% of the assets being used to earn the operating profit. (The company does not have other sources of income, it is assumed.)

In Chapter Nine the nature and source of the future returns from an investment are not discussed. In this Chapter, on the other hand, two main investment examples are analyzed to demonstrate what future returns consist of and how these future cash flows are determined. The first main example is a *cost savings* investment. Most established companies over the years have invested in a relatively large complex or group of different types of fixed assets that provides the production and distribution facilities and capacity which is needed by the company to make sales and to carry on its operations. As a general rule, each year some of a company's fixed assets are replaced as they reach the end of their useful lives to the company. In many of these fixed asset replacement situations the future sales revenues of the company would be the same no matter which *particular* new fixed assets are acquired by the company, as long as the fixed assets acquired do, in fact, provide the required services and capacity needed by the company.

Essentially the decision situation facing managers in these fixed asset replacement circumstances is which specific asset to acquire, and whether to purchase or to rent (lease) it. For example, the future sales revenue of a company would be the same whether the company uses manual or electric typewriters, and whether the company owns or rents the typewriters. The purchase versus rent (lease) choice is essentially a financial management question which involves alternative capitalization structures. The choice between which of two or more available new assets should be purchased is the concern of the discussion that follows.

Given that there are two or more alternative assets that could be purchased to provide the needed services and capacity, the problem is to choose the best alternative. Frequently one asset may cost more to purchase now but will cost less to operate in the future, compared with another asset (assuming that both the alternatives provide sufficient capacity to meet the needs of the company). In short, one alternative requires more capital investment today in exchange for future *cost savings* (compared with the other alternative). The key question is: Is the larger investment today worth the future cost savings?

Example Introduced

It is assumed that the company needs to replace a certain production machine. The old machine has reached the end of its useful life; it has become too undependable and too costly to repair and maintain. The need for a new machine, or to be more precise the need for specific manufacturing services provided by a new machine is taken for granted. In other words, the company is reasonably sure that the sales demand for the product manufactured with the machine will continue for sometime into the future. This is always a key assumption, of course.

The production manager's first thought is the newest model of the old machine being replaced, which has just been introduced on the market. The main advantages of this new model are that it could be "slipped into place" with only minimal interruption of the manufacturing activities of the company, it would require very little installation cost, and it would involve very few "breaking-in" costs (for example, training employees how to operate the machine), since the new model is very similar to the old one. However, another machine has come to the attention of the production manager that would provide the needed services and capacity equally well. To distinguish the two machines being considered, the following descriptive names are used in the following discussion:

"Replaceo" = Essentially the newest model of the old machine being replaced.
"Automato" = Substantially different type of machine, which is more automatic than "Replaceo."

Automato requires considerably less direct labor hours to operate than Replaceo. The production manager has estimated how much direct labor costs would be saved each year if Automato were purchased instead of Replaceo, based on the forecast production output levels over the next several years. Of course, these output levels are subject to change and may turn out to be too high or too low. But the output levels are reasonably reliable forecasts. Based on these forecasts the production manager determines the differential direct labor cost savings obtained by purchasing Automato (shown in Exhibit 10.1).

EXHIBIT 10.1
Differential Direct Labor Cost Savings Due to Purchase of Automato

Year One	$ 66,000
Year Two	94,400
Year Three	108,000
Year Four	118,400
Year Five	135,600

The estimated useful life of either machine is five years. The production manager estimates that five years from today Automato would have a $50,000 higher salvage value than Replaceo. On the other hand, Automato's purchase cost is $350,000 more than Replaceo's purchase cost. Automato's installation and breaking-in costs would be higher, since the Automato is a considerably different type of machine than the old machine. These breaking-in costs are deducted from the estimated direct labor cost savings shown for year one in Exhibit 10.1. Thus, notice that the cost savings in year one are considerably less than in year two. The cost savings increase over the years because production output levels are forecast to increase over the next five years. The essential financial question facing the production manager is: Are the future cost savings from the Automato machine (see Exhibit 10.1) worth the additional $350,000 capital investment today?

Determining the Present Value of the Differential Cost Savings for Comparison with Differential Capital Investment

To simplify the following analysis, it is assumed that the future cost savings take place entirely at the end of each year, although this is rather conservative, since the savings would take place during each month over the year. The additional purchase cost of Automato is being viewed as a capital investment of $350,000, which will generate direct labor cash outlay savings shown in Exhibit 10.1. These are the future returns from the $350,000 investment. Also, the investment has a $50,000 higher disposable value at the end of the five-year investment period.

In the discussion to this point the purchase cost of each machine has *not* been presented, nor have the total labor costs for each year for each machine been given. This is intentional, to emphasize that the relevant costs for this type of decision are the *differential* costs between the two alternatives. These are the costs (in the future) that would be different depending on which machine is purchased. Many other production costs would be the same in the future no matter which machine were purchased, such as the production manager's salary, or the annual janitorial cost of the plant, and the like.* Costs that would be the same are *not* relevant to this investment decision. Differential costs are the relevant costs, which means that the differential costs are the only costs that are controlled or are affected by which alternative is decided on. The differential future returns (cost savings in this case) are compared with the differential amount of capital that would have to be invested to achieve the future returns. In this case the company would have to invest $350,000 additional capital to purchase Automato. This is the differential amount of capital investment that is analyzed relative to the differential future returns from the investment.

As it is developed in Chapter Nine (refer to Exhibit 9.3 in particular), the company's annual cost of capital rate on total assets is 16.0%. Therefore, the company should earn, at least, this minimal rate of annual operating profit on the $350,000 differential capital investment made if Automato is purchased. The 16.0% cost of capital rate is used to discount the future returns to their total present value. This total present value of the investment is then compared with the $350,000 entry cost. The present value computations of the future returns from the investment in Automato are shown in Exhibit 10.2. (See the end of Chapter Nine for present value table.)

---

* A careful and detailed scrutiny should be made of each operating cost to identify all those costs that may be different depending on which machine is purchased. In this example it is assumed that only direct labor costs are affected by the choice of machine, although in an actual situation there may be other costs affected by the choice.

EXHIBIT 10.2
Computation of Present Value of Future Cost Savings

Year	Future Returns (Cost Savings)		Present Value Factor		Present Value
One:	$ 66,000	×	$\frac{1}{(1+.16)^1}$	=	$ 56,897
Two:	94,400	×	$\frac{1}{(1+.16)^2}$	=	70,155
Three:	108,000	×	$\frac{1}{(1+.16)^3}$	=	69,191
Four:	118,400	×	$\frac{1}{(1+.16)^4}$	=	65,391
Five:	135,600	×	$\frac{1}{(1+.16)^5}$	=	64,561
Disposable Value:	50,000	×	$\frac{1}{(1+.16)^5}$	=	23,805
Total Present Value of Cost Savings and Disposable Value					$350,000

Notice that the total present value of the future returns (cost savings) is exactly equal to the additional capital investment in Automato. Thus the purchase of Automato is justified from the cost of capital point of view. If the total present value had turned out to be less than $350,000, then the investment would not be attractive. The company may have other investment opportunities for the $350,000 of capital that promise more than a 16.0% rate of annual operating profit. But the differential (additional) investment of $350,000 of capital in Automato would at least "pay its own way," since a 16.0% annual rate of operating profit would be earned. In fact, if the income tax factor is analyzed more closely, this is a very attractive investment.

A Closer Look at the Income Tax Factor in Investment Analysis

The federal income tax law allows the cost of fixed assets that have limited useful lives to be charged against sales revenue (or other income sources to the business) according to one of the acceptable methods of depreciation, to determine the annual taxable income of the company. Depreciation, therefore, can be thought of as a *tax shield,* just like any deductible expense. This means that deductible expenses "shield" an equal amount of sales revenue (or other income) from taxation, since there is no taxable income unless sales revenue (plus other income, if any) for the year *exceeds* the total deductible expenses for the year. Tax is paid only on the *excess* of sales revenue (plus other income) over and above the total deductible expenses for the year. Depreciation is singled out as a special tax shield (deductible expense), since the federal income tax laws are very permissive and quite favorable to taxpayers, by allowing *accelerated* depreciation methods to be used to determine the annual taxable income of a company. These accelerated depreciation deduction methods that are allowed for tax purposes generally have very favorable cash flow results, which can be a decisive factor in many investment decisions.

The fixed asset replacement investment decision discussed in the preceding section is a good example of the importance and consequences of accelerated depreciation for income tax purposes. As is explained, the company could invest an additional $350,000 in the machine called Automato. The total present value of the future returns (cost savings) from the investment, when discounted at the company's cost of capital rate, is exactly equal to $350,000 (see Exhibit 10.2). Thus it would appear that this is a "break-even" sort of investment opportunity. However, the previous discussion makes a critical but implicit assumption about the timing of depreciation deductions with respect to the additional purchase cost of Automato. Recall that Automato costs $350,000 more to purchase but has a $50,000 higher salvage value at the end of its five-year estimated useful life. Thus the company would have $300,000 additional depreciation to deduct over the five years of the investment: ($350,000 additional cost less $50,000 additional salvage value equals $300,000 additional cost to depreciate).

In the previous discussion and analysis, both in this chapter and in Chapter

Nine, there is an implicit assumption that the taxable income each year equals the following: return that year less interest that year less *capital recovery that year*. Although it was never explicitly stated, it is assumed in the preceding discussion that the depreciation deducted for tax purposes each year equals the amount of capital recovery that year. This assumption is very helpful in simplifying the income tax aspects of the investment analysis of future returns. This rather important point is very difficult to grasp in the computations of the present value of the future returns, as shown in Exhibit 10.2 for example. It is necessary to analyze the *disposition* of the future returns each year over the life of the investment to see this point. Exhibit 10.3 shows the disposition, or breakdown of each future return (cost savings in this example) between the annual 16.0% operating profit and the capital recovery each year. Exhibit 10.3 also shows the breakdown of the operating profit each year between interest, income tax, and the net income residual. This disposition breakdown analysis follows the approach first shown in Exhibit 9.4, which you may want to review at this point.

The notes in Exhibit 10.3 explain how each year's amounts are determined. These notes are not repeated here, except to expand on the determination of the income tax amount each year. In Exhibit 10.3 it is assumed that the depreciation deducted each year for income tax purposes is equal to the amount of capital recovered that year. In other words, taxable income is assumed to be equal to the operating profit less interest for the year, which is then multiplied by 48% to determine the income tax for that year. Clearly this is a poor assumption in this example if we study the capital recovery pattern over the five years. The company would not depreciate the fixed asset in this manner.

The company probably would use either the straight-line or an accelerated depreciation method. In particular, assume that the company uses the sum-of-the-years-digits (SOYD) depreciation method. Hence, Automato's $300,000 additional depreciable cost ($350,000 additional cost less $50,000 additional salvage value) would be deducted as follows:

Computation of Annual SOYD Depreciation Amounts

Year	Total Depreciable Cost		Fraction		Annual Depreciation
One	$300,000	×	5/15	=	$100,000
Two	300,000	×	4/15	=	80,000
Three	300,000	×	3/15	=	60,000
Four	300,000	×	2/15	=	40,000
Five	300,000	×	1/15	=	20,000
Total					$300,000

This pattern of depreciation deductions to determine each year's taxable income is quite different than the pattern of capital recovery shown in Exhibit 10.3. Thus the company's actual cash payments for income tax each year would be

EXHIBIT 10.3
Analysis of Annual Returns and Operating Profit from Investment in Automato

	(1) Investment Balance at Start of Year	(2) Return (Cost Saving)	Disposition of Return		Disposition of Operating Profit			
Year			Operating Profit at 16% (3)	Capital Recovery (4)	Interest (5)	Income Tax (6)	Residual Net Income (7)	Total (3)
One	$350,000	$ 66,000	$ 56,000	$ 10,000	$12,250	$21,000	$22,750	$56,000
Two	340,000	94,400	54,400	40,000	11,900	20,400	22,100	54,400
Three	300,000	108,000	48,000	60,000	10,500	18,000	19,500	48,000
Four	240,000	118,400	38,400	80,000	8,400	14,400	15,600	38,400
Five	160,000	135,600	25,600	110,000	5,600	9,600	10,400	25,600
Total before salvage value				$300,000				
Salvage Value				50,000				
Total				$350,000				

Notes:

(1) Starting with the initial cost of $350,000 in Year One, the capital recovered each year is subtracted to get next year's capital investment balance.

(2) See Exhibit 10.1 for the future returns (cost savings).

(3) This is the company's cost of capital rate (16%) multiplied times the investment balance that year.

(4) This is the return that year less the operating profit that year determined by step (3).

(5) Given the capitalization structure of this company (see Exhibits 9.1 and 9.3), one half of its capital is supplied by liabilities at an annual average interest cost of 7%. Hence interest each year equals one half of the investment balance times 7%.

(6) This is the operating profit part of the return each year—see step (3)—less interest and less the capital recovery each year, which gives taxable income that is then multiplied times the income tax rate of 48%.

(7) This is the operating profit less interest and income tax.

quite different than are shown in Exhibit 10.3. The difference in income tax payments each year between the *assumed* depreciation from Exhibit 10.3 and the *actual* depreciation deductions each year are computed in Exhibit 10.4.

Although the same total amount of depreciation ($300,000) is deducted over the five-year span of the investment and the same total income tax is paid, the SOYD depreciation method minimizes the income tax payments in the first two years. The company would avoid tax payment of $43,200 at the end of year one and $19,200 at the end of year two, although in years four and five these temporary tax "savings" must be paid back, as can be seen in Exhibit 10.4. Certainly the company should be able to make good use of the capital provided by the tax deferrals in the first two years. It would have the use of $43,200 of capital for four years, from the end of year one to the end of year five. And, it would have the use of $19,200 of capital for two years, from the end of year two until the end of year four. Not only can the purchase of Automato be justified on the basis of the original analysis shown in Exhibit 10.3, but the tax payment deferrals caused by the use of an accelerated depreciation method make this more than simply a break-even investment opportunity.

There is more than one way to analyze the value of the income tax payment deferrals from using an accelerated depreciation method, that is, from deducting depreciation sooner for income tax purposes than capital is recovered from future returns. One approach is to compute the present value of the amounts shown in the "Change in Income Tax" column in Exhibit 10.4. (At the 16.0% rate of discount we can determine that the present value would be $20,338; you should definitely check this by your own computations.) Another approach is to solve for the internal rate of return (IRR) from the investment based on the actual schedule of income tax payments that would be made if the SOYD depreciation method were used. This second approach becomes rather complex, although we observe that the IRR from this investment would be higher than 16.0%, since capital would be recovered quicker, which gives a lower capital

EXHIBIT 10.4
Income Tax Effects of SOYD Depreciation Method

Year	Assumed Depreciation (See Exhibit 10.3)	Actual (SOYD) Depreciation	Change in Taxable Income	Change in Income Tax (at 48%)
One	$ 10,000	$100,000	−$90,000	−$43,200
Two	40,000	80,000	− 40,000	− 19,200
Three	60,000	60,000	—0—	—0—
Four	80,000	40,000	+ 40,000	+ 19,200
Five	110,000	20,000	+ 90,000	+ 43,200
Total	$300,000	$300,000	$ —0—	$ —0—

investment during each year such that the same future returns yield a higher IRR. In summary, usually it is useful to prepare an analysis of the capital recovery pattern over the life of a fixed asset investment, such as is shown in Exhibit 10.3, and to compare this capital recovery pattern with the depreciation amounts that will be deducted for income tax purposes each year. If material differences exist between the two, then the favorable income tax effects should be considered in the evaluation of the investment.

New Product Line Investment Opportunity

Example Introduced

Assume that the same company in the example developed in Chapter Nine is considering seriously a proposal made by its sales department that the company should enter a new product line. A four-year projected sales revenue and cost statement has been prepared by the sales department to support this proposal—see Exhibit 10.5. According to this projected profit and loss statement, the new product line would show an operating loss in the first two years. In these first two years the company would have to establish and build up awareness and acceptance of the new products. But in years three and four notice that the company would earn a respectable operating profit from this new product line, according to this forecast.

To enter the new product line the company would have to purchase new production machinery and equipment at a cost of $850,000. These new fixed assets have an estimated useful life of four years for income tax purposes, and could be sold for an estimated salvage value of $50,000 at the end of the four years. The major financial question, of course, is whether the new product line investment can be justified relative to the company's cost of capital. To answer this question requires a rather detailed analysis of this investment opportunity, starting with the cost forecasts included in Exhibit 10.5.

A Closer Look at Future Costs: The Incremental Approach

First, are *all* the future costs presented in Exhibit 10.5 *relevant* to this analysis? In particular, which costs would be spent if the project were entered into, and which would not? Only the future *differential or incremental* costs caused by entering the new product line are relevant to this investment analysis. These are the additional costs of manufacturing and marketing the new products, which would not be incurred if the company does not proceed with the new product line. For each cost in the sales department's statement (Exhibit 10.5) the question is: Is this cost actually a future *out-of-pocket* cost that is directly the result of manufacturing and selling the new products?

The direct variable manufacturing costs (raw material and direct labor) are incremental costs—there would seem to be little doubt about this. There may be one possible qualification to this conclusion, however. Some of the employees of the company already on the payroll may be used to work in the manu-

EXHIBIT 10.5
Sales Revenue, Cost, and Profit Projections for New Product Line

	Year One	Year Two	Year Three	Year Four
Sales Revenue	$ 600,000	$1,350,000	$3,000,000	$4,500,000
Cost of Goods Sold:				
Beginning Inventories	$ —0—	$ 69,000	$ 160,000	$ 391,600
Manufacturing Costs:				
Direct Variable Costs:	$ 300,000	$ 687,500	$1,507,000	$2,192,000
Overhead Costs:				
Out-of-pocket costs	$ 171,000	$ 264,000	$ 564,000	$ 819,000
Depreciation on new machinery and equipment	200,000	200,000	200,000	200,000
Allocated building space costs	49,000	61,000	118,000	160,000
Total Overhead Costs	$ 420,000	$ 525,000	$ 882,000	$1,179,000
Total Manufacturing Costs	$ 750,000	$1,212,500	$2,389,000	$3,371,000
Beginning Inventory Plus Total Manufacturing Costs	$ 750,000	$1,281,500	$2,549,000	$3,762,600
Ending Inventories	69,000	160,000	391,600	646,800
Cost of Goods Sold	681,000	1,121,500	2,157,400	3,115,800
Gross Profit (Loss)	($ 81,000)	$ 288,500	$ 842,600	$1,384,200
Marketing, General, and Administrative Expenses:				
Out-of-pocket costs	$ 250,000	$ 190,000	$ 545,000	$ 617,185
Allocated building space costs	50,000	86,000	164,000	234,000
Total	300,000	276,000	709,000	851,185
Operating Profit (Loss) Before Interest and Income Tax Expenses	($ 381,000)	($ 47,500)	$ 133,600	$ 533,015

facturing of the new products. If these employees were not used for the new product manufacturing, they may have to be paid anyway if the company's policy is to avoid firing or laying off workers. To avoid this complication, it is assumed that to manufacture the new products the company will hire new employees. Clearly the raw materials needed to manufacture the new products would not be purchased if the company does not enter the new product line, so these costs are entirely incremental.

The overhead costs and the other operating costs shown in Exhibit 10.5 are incremental, with one major exception. Some of the space needed for the new machinery and equipment and for the inventory storage of the new products would be provided by building space now owned by the company but standing vacant. This space is not now being used by the company and probably will not be used for the next four years. (This may not be true in different situations, of course.) Since the new fixed assets and the inventory of new products will occupy some of the company's existing space, the company's cost accounting department has told the sales department that the new product line will have to absorb its share of the company's total space costs, which includes depreciation and real estate taxes on the building, general building cleaning and maintenance expenses, and the like. The cost accounting department has worked out the allocation of these space costs that would be charged to the new product line for each of the four years—notice in Exhibit 10.5 that these *allocated* costs are shown separately in the overhead costs section and in the marketing, general, and administration expenses section.

Although the allocation of some of the company's total building space costs to the new product line may be correct and proper for other management accounting reasons in the future, these allocated costs should *not* be deducted against sales revenue for analysis of the new product line investment, because these costs are *not* incremental costs in the future. These space costs would be incurred whether or not the company enters the new product line. The costs are *not additional* costs caused by entering the new product line. The effect of such allocation would be that the existing products being sold by the company would be "relieved" of the amount of space cost allocated to the new product line each year. The "old" product lines would thereby look more profitable, since some of the company's space cost is shifted to the new product line. The correct approach is to analyze the new product line investment on a strict incremental cost basis.

Cash Flow Investment Analysis and Depreciation

The next point in the analysis of the new product line investment proposal concerns depreciation of the new fixed assets. As we can see in Exhibit 10.5, the straight-line depreciation method is used, based on the purchase of $850,000 less the salvage value of $50,000 of the new fixed assets. This total depreciation of $800,000 is *incremental* depreciation. That is, this $800,000 cost would not be incurred if the company does not enter the new product line and does not purchase the new fixed assets. But to determine the future returns from the new product line investment, depreciation should *not* be deducted against the future sales revenue.

Investment analysis is concerned primarily with the timing and amounts of the *cash inflows* and the *cash outflows* of an investment. In capital investment analysis one must shift mental gears as it were, away from the accrual basis of measuring and reporting sales revenue and expenses to a strict cash flow basis. Depreciation is the prime example of the difference between the two. The cash outlay at the time of the purchase of a fixed asset is a prepayment of the total depreciation to be charged off over the useful life of the fixed asset. For both external reporting to investors and normal periodic internal reporting to management, depreciation is charged off to each period of use, to measure the operating profit for each period (as well as for product costing and inventory cost valuation purposes). This is quite proper and necessary.

But in the analysis of long-term investments, depreciation is *not* a cash outflow *in the future years,* and it should *not* be deducted against the future returns from the investment. The total depreciation is imbedded in the purchase cost of the fixed assets, which is a cost outlay *today* not in the future years. Cash flows must be considered when paid or when received in investment analysis. In short, depreciation is already counted in the entry cost of the investment; this capital investment outlay paid *today* has to be recovered in the *future* returns from the investment, that is, the future net *cash* inflows over the life of the investment.

To sum up the preceding discussion regarding the costs included in the four-year new product line profit forecast statement (Exhibit 10.5), the allocated costs and the depreciation are subtracted from the total costs each year to determine the future incremental cost outlays from entering the new product line—See Exhibit 10.6. These are the relevant cost totals to deduct against the forecast sales revenue each year, in order to determine the net future returns from the new product line investment each year.

EXHIBIT 10.6
Determination of Incremental Cost Outlay Each Year

	Year One	Year Two	Year Three	Year Four
Costs: from Exhibit 10.5				
Cost of goods sold	$ 681,000	$1,121,500	$2,157,400	$3,115,800
Other operating costs	300,000	276,000	709,000	851,185
Total costs	$ 981,000	$1,397,500	$2,866,400	$3,966,985
Allocated overhead costs	$ 49,000	$ 61,000	$ 118,000	$ 160,000
Allocated other				
operating costs	50,000	86,000	164,000	234,000
Depreciation	200,000	200,000	200,000	200,000
Total costs excluded	$ 299,000	$ 347,000	$ 482,000	$ 594,000
Total incremental cost				
outlay each year	$ 682,000	$1,050,500	$2,384,400	$3,372,985

Cash Flow Timing Problems and "Rounding Off" Approximations

It would be convenient if all the incremental cost outlays (see Exhibit 10.6) and if the sales revenue amounts for each year shown in the four-year forecast (Exhibit 10.5) were equal to their cash flows each year. However, this probably is not true. It is preferable to convert the sales revenue and the incremental cost outlays into their cash flow effects each year. (The cash flow analysis of revenue and costs is discussed in Chapter Eight.) To keep the analysis within reasonable limits, the annual sales revenue amounts shown in Exhibit 10.5 and the annual incremental cost outlays determined in Exhibit 10.6 are accepted as close approximations of their cash flow effects each year. Also, all cash flows are assumed to take place entirely at year-end for purposes of the following analysis, even though the cash flows would be distributed throughout the year. In some situations these approximations may be too "crude" compared with the actual cash flow timing. But, on the other hand, the four-year profit forecast (Exhibit 10.5) is based on many estimates in the first place.

Determining Additional Future Capital Investment Outlays

In the cost savings investment example discussed previously in this chapter, the only capital required to be invested was the purchase cost of the new fixed asset. No future capital had to be invested over the life of the investment. In contrast, the new product line investment requires two major capital investments during the life of the investment, in addition to the initial investment of $850,000 in the fixed assets. The company's Accounts Receivable and Inventories would be increased each year as a result of entering the new product line.

The company will extend credit to its customers who buy the new products. And, the company must carry a stock of finished goods inventory of the new products. The capital that would have to be invested in Accounts Receivable and Inventories is *incremental* to the new product line investment. Therefore, these future capital investment outlays must be considered in the analysis. It is assumed that the ending balance in Accounts Receivable will equal one eighth of the sales revenue each year. The ending balance is used as the measure of the amount of capital invested in Accounts Receivable in the following analysis, although this somewhat overstates the capital investment each year, since the average balance during the year would be less. The ending Inventory balances required by the new product line are shown in Exhibit 10.5. The ending balance in the Inventories is used to measure the capital invested in this asset, although the average balance could be used. The ending balances are easier to follow through the analysis. The company's Raw Materials Inventory and Prepaid Expenses probably would increase also as a result of entering the new product line. But, to simplify, these two other incremental investments are ignored in the analysis below.

EXHIBIT 10.7
Cash Flow and Investment Schedule for the New Product Line Project

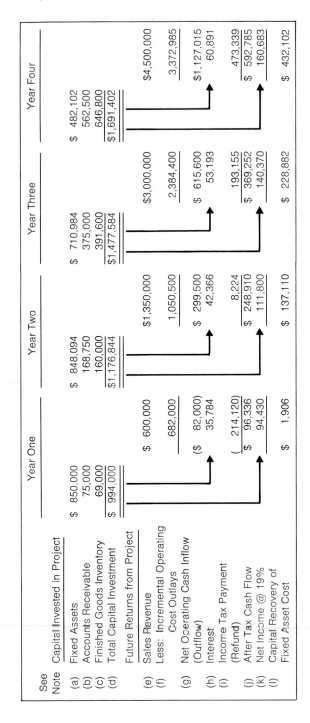

See Note	Capital Invested in Project	Year One	Year Two	Year Three	Year Four
(a)	Fixed Assets	$ 850,000	$ 848,094	$ 710,984	$ 482,102
(b)	Accounts Receivable	75,000	168,750	375,000	562,500
(c)	Finished Goods Inventory	69,000	160,000	391,600	646,800
(d)	Total Capital Investment	$ 994,000	$1,176,844	$1,477,584	$1,691,402
	Future Returns from Project				
(e)	Sales Revenue	$ 600,000	$1,350,000	$3,000,000	$4,500,000
(f)	Less: Incremental Operating Cost Outlays	682,000	1,050,500	2,384,400	3,372,985
(g)	Net Operating Cash Inflow (Outflow)	($ 82,000)	$ 299,500	$ 615,600	$1,127,015
(h)	Interest	35,784	42,366	53,193	60,891
(i)	Income Tax Payment (Refund)	(214,120)	8,224	193,155	473,339
(j)	After Tax Cash Flow	$ 96,336	$ 248,910	$ 369,252	$ 592,785
(k)	Net Income @ 19%	94,430	111,800	140,370	160,683
(l)	Capital Recovery of Fixed Asset Cost	$ 1,906	$ 137,110	$ 228,882	$ 432,102

Notes of Explanation:

(a) Initial investment in Fixed Assets is equal to purchase cost of $850,000; this investment balance is reduced by the capital recovery of fixed asset investment each year, as indicated on line (l).

(b) Ending balance in this account, which is assumed to be one eighth of the total sales revenue for the year.

(c) Ending balance in this account; see Exhibit 10.5.

(d) The sum of the first three items—Fixed Assets, Accounts Receivable, and Finished Goods Inventory—which is the direct, incremental capital associated with this investment project. In practice a company may assign additional capital to this project based on estimates of additional (incremental) cash balances that may be required by the higher sales volume, as well as any other additional capital investment that may be required.

(e) These annual amounts are taken directly from Exhibit 10.5; it is assumed that all sales revenue is received in cash during the year, which is not quite correct, of course. In practice it may be necessary to convert the sales revenue into its cash effects.

(f) These are the operating cost outlays (excluding allocated cost and depreciation) from Exhibit 10.6; these cost amounts should also be adjusted to determine the actual cash outflows each year, but these adjustments are not made in this analysis to simplify.

(g) This is item (e) less item (f).

(h) Interest each year is equal to one half of the capital balance in the project times the average interest rate of 7% on *all* liabilities; see Exhibit 9.3 for review.

(i) Income tax each year is equal to the taxable income times a flat 48% rate. Taxable income is equal to the net operating cash inflow less interest and less SOYD depreciation for the year. Note in Year One there is a taxable loss. Thus it is assumed that the company has other sources of taxable income against which this taxable loss is offset, which means this project generates a tax savings.

(j) This is item (g) less items (h) and (i).

(k) This annual rate on the stockholders' equity must be determined from the other information given. In other words, there is some rate which if applied to the stockholders' share of the total capital investment (one half of the capital) will give a capital recovery pattern that adds up to $800,000, which added to the salvage value of $50,000 equals $850,000.

(l) This is the residual cash flow "left over" after all the above deductions. The total of these amounts for the four years must equal the total fixed asset cost to be recovered, that is, $800,000, which is the total cost of the fixed assets less the salvage value of $50,000 at the end of the fourth year.

Determining the Projected Rate of Return on Stockholders' Equity from the Investment

Based on the above discussion and assumptions, Exhibit 10.7 is now presented to show the analysis of the cash flows and investments in the new product line project. Read carefully the several footnotes in the exhibit, which explain how the cash flow and capital investment amounts each year are determined. In most respects this analysis follows the method explained previously for the cost savings investment (refer to Exhibit 10.3 in particular). However, there are some important differences. Instead of solving for the internal rate of return on this investment, the analysis shown in Exhibit 10.7 solves for the rate of return on (stockholders') equity.

The reason for this different approach is that the interest rate on liabilities is a *fixed* rate. If an investment promises to yield an internal rate of return higher than the company's cost of capital rate—which is true in this case—then the return on equity will be higher than the minimum ROE goal used to determine the COC rate. For a simple example that clearly reveals this effect on the ROE, consider again Exhibit 9.4, which shows the disposition (or breakout) of the operating profit earned on a $1000 "slice" of total assets. In this exhibit the company earns an operating profit rate of return on total assets exactly equal to its cost of capital rate. Therefore, the ROE is exactly equal to the 13.0% minimum goal established by the company. On the other hand, what would be the ROE if the company were able to earn, say, a 20.0% rate of operating profit on total assets, that is, $200 operating profit before interest and income tax on $1000 of total assets? The interest "share" of this operating profit remains fixed at $35. Taxable income would be $165: ($200 operating profit less $35 interest). At the 48% tax rate the income tax "bite" is $79.20. Thus the residual net income (after income tax) is $85.80 which, divided by the stockholders' equity of $500, gives a ROE of over 17%, considerably more than the 13% ROE goal used to establish the company's COC rate. In investment situations such as this new product line opportunity, managers want to know the ROE from the new investment. Thus Exhibit 10.7 is set up to solve for this ROE rate.

The 19.0% rate of return on equity shown in Exhibit 10.7 is found by the trial and error method. The key idea is this: There is some ROE rate that, when applied to stockholders' part (½) of the total capital investment balance each year, will give the "correct" net income for each year. If the interest, income tax, and "correct" net income is subtracted from the net operating cash flows each year, then the total capital recovery of the fixed asset cost over the four years will equal exactly $800,000. The fixed assets' salvage value at the end of the four years is $50,000 in this example. Thus $800,000 of capital recovery is needed from this investment in addition to the salvage value of $50,000, to recover the purchase cost of $850,000. The bottom line in Exhibit 10.7 is the fixed asset capital recovery each year. If the annual rate of net income on stockholders' equity (ROE) is set at 19.0%, then the sum of these capital recovery amounts each year are as follows:

Capital Recovery of Fixed Assets' Cost If ROE Is Set Equal to 19.0%

Year One	$ 1,906
Year Two	137,110
Year Three	228,882
Year Four	432,102
Total	$800,000

If a rate of return on equity lower than 19.0% is tried, then more than $800,000 total capital is recovered. Conversely, if a ROE rate higher than 19.0% is tried, then less than $800,000 of capital is recovered. Hence, the ROE rate has to be exactly 19.0% to recover exactly $800,000 of capital. Finding the *exact* ROE rate by hand calculations is very tedious since repetitive trial and error procedures are applied. (If this sort of analysis is programmed on a computer the ROE rate can be found very quickly.) A good place to begin is the lowest acceptable ROE rate, which in this example is 13.0% per year. (See Exhibit 9.3 for review.) If this rate were "plugged into" the analysis for a first pass at the solution, we would see that much more capital than $800,000 is recovered, which means that the investment yields much more than a 13.0% ROE rate. (Problems at the end of the chapter minimize the computational aspects of this type of investment analysis.)

A question might arise regarding the recovery of the capital invested in Accounts Receivable and Inventories. It is assumed that both of these assets are fully recovered in the normal course of operations. For instance, at the end of the fourth year in this example, Accounts Receivable has a balance of $562,500 and Finished Goods Inventories are $646,800. It is assumed, of course, that the Accounts Receivable will be collected and that the inventories will be sold. In this way the capital invested in these assets is recovered.

In conclusion, the new product investment opportunity promises an annual 19.0% rate of return on the stockholders' equity, which is considerably more than the company's minimum ROE goal of 13.0% per year. But keep in mind the several assumptions made in the above analysis. If we change one or more of the assumptions, then the annual ROE rate would be different. Indeed, the manager may want to change some of the assumptions to determine just how much difference these changes would cause. If programmed on a computer this sort of *sensitivity analysis* is quite feasible, and gives the manager a range of answers for different sets of assumptions. In any case, the 19.0% "answer" developed above should be accepted as no more than a *contingent* ROE rate which depends on whether the sales revenue, costs, and capital investment forecasts turn out to be correct in the future.

Summary

The basic concepts and procedures of investment analysis developed in the preceding chapter are applied in this chapter to two basic practical types of investments that are made by most business entities. Most companies have a choice between two or more alternatives when replacing fixed assets, or when expanding the fixed assets of the company. In many of these situations one fixed asset may have a higher purchase cost today than the others, but this fixed asset will allow lower operating costs in the future years of using the asset. These are called cost savings investments—an additional amount of capital can be invested in the higher cost fixed asset in exchange for lower operating costs in the future. The first step is to measure the differential future operating costs between the fixed asset alternatives. Different costs are those costs that would be different depending on which fixed asset is purchased.

Given the predicted cost savings each year in the future, these future returns are evaluated relative to the differential (additional) purchase cost of the fixed asset with the lower operating costs. The present value of the future returns is determined, using the company's cost of capital as the discount rate. If the present value of the future returns (cost savings) is more than the differential purchase cost, then the investment is attractive. If the amounts of capital recovery each year from the investment are substantially different from the annual depreciation amounts that are deducted for income tax purposes, then the favorable effects of using an accelerated depreciation for tax purposes also should be considered in evaluating the investment.

The second investment example discussed is whether to enter a new product line, which would require the purchase of new fixed assets. (The new product line investment is very similar to capital investments made to expand the production and sale of existing product lines.) Analysis of the new product line investment is more complex than the cost savings investment example. In both cases the future cash returns for each year must be determined. However, in the new product line investment case both costs and sales revenue have to be forecast, and there are many more costs to analyze than in the cost savings case. The relevant costs are those costs requiring future out-of-pocket cash outlays. Depreciation of the new fixed assets should not be deducted against future sales revenues since the total depreciation is imbedded in the purchase cost of the fixed assets.

The net cash future returns each year are analyzed to determine the rate of return on equity (ROE) that would be earned from the investment. Determination of the ROE rate must take into account that future capital investment outlays are made in addition to the initial purchase cost of the fixed assets. The incremental increases of Accounts Receivable and Inventories due to entering the new product line have to be determined for each future year, to determine the total amount of capital invested each year. A trial and error method is used to solve for the ROE rate that would be earned on the investment balances each year. If this ROE rate is below the company's established minimum return on equity objective, then the investment is not attractive.

Questions

10. 1 If the composite average life of all a company's fixed assets is 10 years, does this mean that one tenth of its fixed assets are replaced each year? Briefly explain.

10. 2 What are *differential* costs? How are these costs determined? How are these costs analyzed in fixed asset replacement decisions?

10. 3 Consider the present value computations of the cost savings example shown in Exhibit 10.2. Why might the manager prefer to use a profit rate *higher* than the company's COC rate in determining the present value of the cost savings?

10. 4 (a) "Since the future returns from a cost savings investment opportunity are merely estimates of the future which may turn out to be completely wrong, there is no point to the sophisticated analysis of these investments such as the present value method." Do you agree? Briefly explain.
   (b) In general terms, how would you propose to deal with prediction (forecast) errors in the analysis of cost savings investment opportunities?

10. 5 As a "belt tightening" measure a company is considering putting radial tires on all its salesmen's cars, since that type of tire wears enough longer to justify the higher initial purchase cost.
   (a) Is this an example of a cost savings investment? Why or why not?
   (b) If so, explain how you would go about analyzing this investment by the company.

10. 6 Please refer to the cost savings schedule shown in Exhibit 10.1 for the purchase of the Automato machine:
   (a) Assume that the total cost savings over the five years is the same, but that the cost savings occur later than is shown in the exhibit. In this case would the company earn more or less than its COC on this investment? Explain briefly.
   (b) Assume that the total cost savings over the five years is the same, but that the cost savings occur sooner than is shown in the exhibit. In this case would the company earn more or less than its COC on this investment? Explain briefly.
   (c) What would be the effects of disposing of the machine at the end of the fifth year for more or less than the $50,000 differential salvage value predicted in Exhibit 10.3?

10. 7 Assume that electric typewriters allow each typist to turn out on average 25% more work than manual typewriters, but that the electric typewriters cost three times as much. Both typewriters last an average of 10 years. The typists are paid the same in either case.
   (a) Is it "rational" to purchase electric typewriters instead of manual typewriters? (*Hint:* Set up a simple numerical example to analyze this situation.)
   (b) What other factors may be important in making this decision?

10. 8 "All deductible expenses are tax shields; therefore, why single out depreciation as a special case?" How would you answer this question?

10. 9 Please refer to Investment Alternatives Nos. 1 and 2 shown in Exhibit 9.7, in particular to the capital recovery pattern of each investment. Assume that the company will use the SOYD depreciation method for $800,000 of the entry cost of the investment. The other $50,000 is the salvage value recovered at the end of year four (and is included in the future return for that year). Given these facts, which alternative is more attractive? Why?

10.10 Are the future sales revenues predicted for a new product line investment (such as are shown in Exhibit 10.5) always *entirely* incremental? What if sales of the new product would cause some loss of sales of old products? How would this negative sales impact be handled in the analysis of the new product line investment?

10.11 Assume that a restaurant has been approached by a neon sign company that offers to put an attractive and eye-catching sign on the building. The sign company argues that this sign would attract customers who otherwise would not notice the restaurant, and the general manager of the restaurant tends to agree. However, the neon sign would cost $5000 installed. If you were the general manager of the restaurant how would you go about deciding whether or not to put up the neon sign? (Ignore the alternative of putting up a cheaper sign.)

10.12 Why isn't depreciation on the fixed assets that are purchased to enter a new product line a proper cost to deduct against each future year's sales revenue of the new product line? It would seem that this depreciation is an incremental cost that would not be incurred if the new product line investment is not made.

10.13 What are the major differences between the cost savings investment example and the new product line investment example which are discussed in the chapter?

10.14 "If the IRR on an investment is higher than the company's COC rate, then the ROE from the investment is higher than the company's minimum return on equity goal." Do you agree? Briefly explain.

10.15 Does the basic model and analysis developed in the chapter for a new product line example (see Exhibit 10.7 in particular) apply to the analysis of capital investments made to expand the production and sale of existing product lines? Briefly explain why or why not.

Problems

P10. 1 A company's production manager is deciding between two new machines, either of which is adequate to the company's manufacturing needs. He provides the following information:

Cost Factor	Machine X	Machine Y
a. Purchase cost	$198,300	$164,300
b. Useful life estimate	5 years	5 years
c. Salvage value	—0—	—0—
d. Depreciation per year (straight-line)	$ 39,660	$ 32,860
e. Required labor hours of operation each year	4,000 hours	6,000 hours
f. Annual repair and maintenance expense	$ 8,322	$ 5,000
g. Annual power usage cost	$ 1,500	$ 1,500

Each hour of labor should cost an average of $6 next year (on either machine), and is predicted to increase $.50 per hour each year thereafter. The company's annual cost of capital is 18.0%.

Required:

(1) Identify the relevant costs to this decision, and briefly explain why each is relevant.
(2) Present your analysis regarding which machine should be purchased to the production manager. (Ignore the depreciation method used for income tax purposes.)

P10. 2 Refer to the decision situation explained in Problem 10.1. Assume that the company uses the SOYD (sum-of-the-years'-digits) depreciation method for all its fixed assets for income tax purposes.

Required:

(1) Prepare a schedule that compares the annual capital recovery on the incremental capital investment in Machine X with the annual SOYD depreciation of this incremental capital investment. (See Exhibits 10.3 to 10.4 for guidelines.)
(2) Based on your answer to part (1) would you reconsider your recommendation to the production manager? Explain.

P10. 3 A company has just opened a new production plant which centralizes all its manufacturing in one location. The new plant is highly automated compared with its old plants. The company has disposed of all its old plant buildings, machinery, and equipment, with one exception. Another company has offered to lease the company's Sioux City plant as is, including all the machinery and equipment in the old plant. All the fixed assets in this plant as well as the building have been fully depreciated for income tax purposes. The potential lessee offers to pay $5000 rent every six months (half-year) on the last day of each rent period, and to sign a five-year noncancelable lease. Since the company has not yet found another interested buyer for the Sioux City plant, it is interested in this opportunity to lease it. The company's annual cost of capital is 16.0%. Five years from today the value of the plant building should be about $25,000, but the machinery and equipment would be worthless.

Required:

(1) Relative to this lease opportunity the company would like to know the minimum price it should accept from a buyer in the event such a willing buyer were found. Determine this value. Show your computations.

(2) Two years later the lessee offers to buy the building and its contents for $36,000. Determine whether the company should sell at this price. Show your computations and assumptions

P10. 4 A local radio station could probably receive permission from the Federal Communications Commission to increase its broadcasting output wattage, to reach a broader audience area. Based on this larger audience the company could increase its advertising rates for commercials played on the station. The company's broadcast tower antenna would have to be raised, and certain other equipment would have to be purchased. In all, the capital expenditures would be $75,000 to make the conversion. Based on a study by its advertising sales manager, the additional revenue due to charging higher rates based on the larger audience base would be:

Year	Incremental Advertising Revenue
One	$15,000
Two	20,000
Three	25,000
Four	25,000
Five	25,000

Beyond 5 years it is difficult to predict. The broadcast tower antenna and other equipment has very little secondhand value. The company uses a 10-year-life estimate for these fixed assets. Its annual cost of capital is 20.0%.

Required: Present your analysis of whether the company should increase its broadcast power. Show your computations and explain your assumptions clearly.

P10. 5 The balance sheet (condensed and simplified) of a company at December 31, 1976, the close of its most recent accounting year, is as follows:

Cash	$ 5,500,000	Accounts Payable	$ 4,500,000
Accounts Receivable	3,000,000	Income Tax Payable	400,000
Inventories	6,000,000	Total noninterest	
Prepaid Expenses	500,000	bearing liabilities	$ 5,000,000
Total Current		Interest Bearing Debts:	
Assets	$15,000,000	Short-term @ 9.0%	$ 2,000,000
Fixed Assets, Net of		Long-term @ 10.25%	8,000,000
Accumulated		Total	$10,000,000
Depreciation	10,000,000	Stockholders' Equity:	
Total Assets	$25,000,000	500,000 outstanding	
		shares of common	
		stock	$10,000,000
		Total Capital Sources	$25,000,000

This company has just completed a major disinvestment (liquidation) out of an unprofitable product line. All of the fixed assets that were being used to manufacture these products, as well as the entire inventory of these products, were sold to another company for cash. Thus the company has a rather large cash balance at the present time—see its balance sheet above. The company's controller estimates that of its total $5,500,000 cash balance only $1,500,000 is needed to support its ongoing regular sales and operations during next year. The question is what to do with the excess cash balance of $4,000,000. Each of the following parts of this problem explore different alternatives. Treat each part as separate and independent of the others. In all cases, however, the company's goal is to earn, at least, an annual return on equity of 15.6%. (Assume a flat 48% income tax rate in all cases.)

(1) Assume that at the start of 1977 the company decides to invest the $4 million in safe, one-year government securities which should yield a 8.0% interest income before tax. Thus this part of the company's total assets will generate $320,000 of interest income during the year. The remainder of the assets, therefore, will have to generate operating profit.

Required: Assuming no significant changes in the capitalization structure of the company, and assuming total assets remain at $25 million, determine how much total operating profit (in addition to the interest income) the company would have to earn from its sales during 1977 to reach its return on equity goal.

(2) Assume that at the start of 1977 the company decides to pay a special one-time cash dividend of $8 per share to its common stockholders.

Required: Assuming no significant changes in the company's capitalization structure other than the payment of the cash dividend, of course, determine how much total operating profit the company would have to earn from its ongoing sales during 1977 to meet its return on equity goal.

(3) Assume that at the start of 1977 the company decides to retire $4 million of

its long-term debt. The company's long-term debt consists of callable bonds. Therefore, the company calls one half of the outstanding bonds and immediately cancels long-term debt of $4 million.

Required: Assuming no significant changes in the company's capitalization structure other than the retirement of $4 million long-term debt, of course, determine how much total operating profit the company would have to earn from its ongoing sales during 1977 to reach its return on equity goal.

P10. 6 Refer to the company example introduced at the start of Problem 10.5. The same situation is assumed for purposes of this problem. Knowing of this company's surplus cash position, a major customer approaches it and asks if the company would be interested in purchasing fixed assets (heavy machinery and equipment) and immediately leasing these assets to the customer. Evidently this customer has had some trouble securing enough capital on their own to finance the purchase of these fixed assets. From what the sales manager and the other top level officers of the company know about this particular company, this customer is a well managed company that because of its rapid growth has not generated enough internal cash flow from its net income. Evidently this customer's stockholders do not have any more capital to invest in their business, and the company has not been able to borrow enough money to meet all of its capital needs. This customer purchases a relatively large quantity of the company's products each year. Since the quantity may very well increase in the future, the company is seriously looking into purchasing the fixed assets and leasing them to the customer.

The customer would pay all costs of using the fixed assets; the company would incur no costs of owning the fixed assets except for the minor incidental cost of collecting rent from the customer, and the like. The total purchase cost of the fixed assets would be $4 million. The composite useful life of these fixed assets is five years. At the end of five years the estimated salvage value of the fixed assets is $300,000, and the customer would agree to purchase the fixed assets at that time for that amount. (The estimated useful life for federal income tax purposes is also five years.) To simplify, the following analysis assumes that annual rents would be received by the company at the end of each of the five years. (In actual practice, monthly or quarterly rents are more likely.) Assume a flat 48% federal income tax rate.

Required:

(1) Given the above information and assumptions about this fixed asset lease-out opportunity, determine the minimum schedule of rents that should be received at the end of each year by the company to recover the capital invested in these fixed assets on the straight-line basis, and to earn an operating profit each year on this investment equal to the company's cost of capital requirements. Assume straight-line depreciation is used by the company for income tax purposes. Your answer should be the minimum rental schedule that should be quoted to the customer. Of course, the company may want to earn a higher rate of operating profit on this investment for

several reasons, but this additional aspect of the problem is not explored here. (See Exhibit 10.3 for guidelines.)

(2) Assume that before the company had the chance to quote the rental schedule you determined in part (1), the customer offers to pay $1,237,178 rent at the end of each of the five years; at the end of five years the customer would own the assets, and no additional payment would be made. Is this a better rental receipts schedule for the company? In particular, is the annual rate of return on its investment in these assets better than the rate you determined in part (1)?

P10. 7 Assume that this company's annual cost of capital is 20.0%. The company has an investment opportunity very similar to the asset lease-out example discussed in the preceding problem (Problem 10.6). The company could purchase the assets to be leased out for a total cost of $590,000. Three different companies are "bidding" for the assets, and each offers to pay a different schedule of rental payments:

| Year | Rental Payments Offered by | | |
	Company A	Company B	Company C
One	$226,000	$298,000	$190,565
Two	204,400	226,000	190,565
Three	182,800	161,200	190,565
Four	161,200	103,600	190,565
Five	139,600	53,200	190,565
Purchase payment at end of Year Five	50,000	50,000	50,000

Assume, to simplify the analysis, that each year's rent is received entirely at the end of the year; that the company's annual depreciation for income tax purposes is equal to the amount of capital recovered that year; and that each year's income tax is paid entirely at the last day of the year. There are no other incremental costs of making this asset lease-out investment during the five years of the investment. The assets to be leased-out have a five-year useful life with an estimated salvage value of $50,000 at the end of the fifth year.

Required: Analyze each rental receipts schedule and determine which one is the best investment for the company. Explain any assumptions you make or any other points that may be relevant to your analysis.

P10. 8 Refer to the company's present financial condition as reported in its balance sheet at the beginning of Problem 10.5. The same conditions and assumptions described at the beginning of that problem apply to this problem. This problem considers another alternative for investment of the company's excess cash balance.

The company has an opportunity to purchase a smaller company that manufactures and sells a product line the company has never entered, even though this new product line would be complementary to the company's existing products. The smaller company wants to sell on the following terms: all its fixed assets and all its inventories would be sold for cash, it would keep all its cash and accounts receivable. All rights, trademarks, customers' lists, and the like would be transferred to the buyer. Under no circumstances would the smaller company reenter the manufacturing or selling of these products for a period of 10 years. In fact, on the sale of its fixed assets and inventories, and on the collection of its accounts receivable, the company plans to pay off all its liabilities and liquidate the corporation.

The sales manager has analyzed the past performance of the other company and has prepared a five-year forecast of future sales revenue from this new product line, which is as follows:

Year	Forecast Sales Revenue
One	$ 8,000,000
Two	10,000,000
Three	12,000,000
Four	14,000,000
Five	15,000,000

Relative to this assumed sales volume over the next five years, the production manager, financial vice-president, and controller of the company have analyzed the requirements of selling the new product line if the other company's fixed assets and inventories are purchased. No additions to the fixed assets would be required over the next five years, since intially the fixed assets would not be utilized up to capacity and would approach 100% of capacity only in the fifth year. They agree that the following assumptions are reasonable:

(a) Out-of-pocket operating costs (including all production, marketing, and general and administration costs) would be as follows:

Year	Total Fixed Costs for Year	Total Variable Costs as Percentage of Sales Revenue
One	$2,900,000	60
Two	3,200,000	60
Three	3,500,000	60
Four	3,600,000	60
Five	3,600,000	60

The above costs do not include depreciation on the fixed assets to be acquired.

(b) The composite group remaining life of the fixed assets to be purchased is estimated to be five years, with no salvage value in all likelihood. The company will use straight-line depreciation for income tax purposes.

(c) To simplify, assume that the total inventory (finished goods, work-in-process, and raw materials) required for the new product line would be 25% of the total sales revenue each year.

(d) The company's average accounts receivable balance will increase by an amount equal to one tenth of sales revenue each year from the new product line.

The other company is asking $2 million for its inventories, an amount which is very close to the current replacement cost of the items. On the other hand, the company has *not* set an asking price for the fixed assets; it will accept the highest (cash) price offered for them.

Required: Based on the above information and assumptions, determine the highest price the company should offer for the fixed assets, and still meet its cost of capital requirements on the investment that is necessary to enter this new product line. (See Exhibit 10.7 for guidelines).

P10. 9 An unincorporated fast copy center just off the campus of a large college has been in business several years. The owner rents a xerox machine from the manufacturer for $1500 per month. The rental contract can be terminated by either party with one month's notice, although the manufacturer rarely if ever has canceled a rental contract unless the rent is not paid. To simplify in the following analysis, assume that all the year's rent ($18,000) is paid on the last day of the year. The owner has very little capital invested in the business since the building space is also rented. He does have to stockpile paper, but he is able to buy this paper on short-term trade credit. For all practical purposes, therefore, virtually no capital is invested in the business. Recently the owner has considered buying a xerox machine instead of continuing to rent one. An identical new machine would cost $41,250. If the machine is owned instead of rented, the owner would have to pay a monthly service contract of $300 to the manufacturer. The service contract cost is already included in the monthly rental amount (see above) if the machine is rented. The owner could borrow $20,000 from a local bank at a 10.0% annual interest rate, but would have to put up the remainder of $21,250. Presently the owner has more than $25,000 in a personal savings account that earns 6.0% annually (before income tax).

If purchased, the new machine would have at least a five-year useful life, perhaps longer. Whether the machine is owned or rented should make no difference in the future annual sales revenue and operating costs except for the $300 monthly service contract cost explained above. (Assume, to simplify, that all the year's service contract cost is paid on the last day of the year.) The owner is in the 40% marginal income tax bracket.

Required: Ignoring the risks of a serious sales downturn or going out of business in the next five years, determine whether you, *as owner*, would purchase the new xerox machine. Show your computations.

P10.10 A competitor of this company just declared bankruptcy. The bankruptcy trustee, as required by law, is liquidating all the assets of the corporation to raise money to pay the creditors as much as possible. One of the assets being offered for sale is a partially completed machine being constructed for a customer. This company, in fact, had lost out on the bidding for the machine contract because the other company had submitted a very low bid. However, now the other company is bankrupt. The customer for this machine is willing to have this company take over the completion of the construction of the machine, and is willing to negotiate a new contract price.

It would take this company 18 months to complete the construction of the machine, a time period acceptable to the customer. This company had already prepared a very detailed cost analysis for this machine contract as part of the original contract bidding. The following cost schedule and timetable would apply to the completion of the machine over the next 18 months beginning today. July 1, 1977.

Costs	Three Months Ending					
	9-30-77	12-31-77	3-31-78	6-30-78	9-30-78	12-31-78
Direct labor	$15,000	$15,000	$20,000	$25,000	$30,000	$40,000
Fixed overhead	4,500	4,500	6,000	7,500	9,000	12,000
Variable overhead	8,000	8,500	10,000	12,000	15,000	18,000

Notice that no materials' costs are included in this cost schedule. The bankrupt company already purchased all the materials, parts, and subassemblies required for this machine, and they are being sold by the bankruptcy trustee. This company would not have to purchase any additional materials to complete the machine.

The company has more than enough production capacity to take on this additional construction contract over the next 18 months. In fact, the company is operating more than 20% below capacity, and the forecast over the next two years does not look optimistic. According to the company's accounting policy, fixed overhead costs are applied (allocated) to each job based on a certain percentage of the direct labor cost assigned to the job. The company's annual cost of capital is 20.0%. The bankruptcy trustee is asking $100,000 for the partially completed machine, including all the materials, of course. Assume a flat 48% income tax rate. The customer will pay cash on delivery of the machine on December 31, 1978.

Required: Detremine the minimum price this company should quote to the customer for the machine construction contract. Show all your work clearly.

P10.11 A retailer is opening a new store and has ordered several new display cases, which have been especially designed and manufactured for the store. The manufacturer offers to sell all the display cases for $35,185, which includes the cost of installing the cases. Alternatively, the manufacturer offers to lease (rent) the display cases to the retailer for 10 years for $6000 per year, each year's rent being due and payable on the *first* day of the year. At the end of 10 years the display cases would be sold to the retailer for $1. If the display cases are rented, the retailer must pay $5000 for installation of the cases in addition to the annual rents. Assume a flat 48% income tax rate for both the retailer and the manufacturer. The display cases can be depreciated over 10 years with no salvage value for income tax purposes, even though such equipment may be used more than 10 years by some retailers:

Required: Analyze the purchase versus lease alternatives and make a recommendation to the retailer. Show your computations clearly.

P10.12 Refer to Exhibit 9.6 (Chapter Nine) which shows the future return schedules of the three alternative investment opportunities, and to Exhibit 9.7 which shows, among other things, the annual capital recovery from each investment. Assume that in all three cases the investment would be in a fixed asset that has a cost of $850,000, an estimated useful life of four years, and an estimated salvage value of $50,000 at the end of the fourth year. Assume that for income tax purposes the company uses the SOYD (sum-of-the-years'-digits) method. The company's cost of capital is 16.0%, although all three investments promise a 20.0% internal rate of return yield, as is shown in Exhibit 9.7. The income tax rate is a flat 48%; to simplify, assume each year's income tax is paid in one amount on the last day of the year.

Required:
(1) For each of the three investment alternatives analyze the income tax consequences of using the SOYD depreciation method for tax purposes.
(2) Based on your answer to part (1), which investment alternative is the most attractive? Explain why.

P10.13 As part of its workmen's compensation insurance coverage this company's production plant is inspected once a year by a safety and productivity expert sent in by the insurance company. The plant is given a safety risk rating based on this inspection report. The company's annual workmen's compensation insurance premium depends on its safety risk rating. This annual safety inspection has just been completed. Although the company is not violating any safety laws, the inspection report strongly urges a complete overhaul and upgrading of the lighting throughout the plant. There would be two main advantages of a better lighting system: (a) a better safety risk rating, which means a lower annual insurance premium, and (b) an increase in productivity (output per man hour). Based on the current annual premium, the company would save about $10,000 next year with the better safety risk rating. This cost differential should increase about $1000 each successive year in the future, given the general inflationary trend of the economy. The cost savings due to higher productivity depends on what the total output demand will be each year in the future. The company's production manager has computed the annual production cost savings for two different output levels—the lowest predicted output and the highest predicted output for each year. These forecast production cost savings are as follows:

Year	Production Cost Savings at	
	Lowest Output Level	Highest Output Level
One	$25,000	$30,000
Two	30,000	37,000
Three	35,000	44,000
Four	40,000	51,000
Five	45,000	58,000

The improvement of the plant's lighting system would cost $164,550. The company's annual cost of capital is 16.0%.

Required: Based on just a five-year "payoff" from this investment (that is, ignoring future returns beyond five years from now), analyze whether or not the company should improve its plant's lighting system. Show all your computations clearly. What recommendation would you make to management in this situation.

P10.14 For several years this manufacturing company has been renting warehouse space to store its finished goods inventory. The company signs one-year rental contracts with the owner of the building. Each year the contract is renegotiated; usually the annual rent has increased. The owner of the building pays all costs of ownership, of course, such as real estate taxes, fire insurance on the building, utilities, repairs and maintenance, security guard, and so on. The company has been quite satisfied with its landlord and has had no complaints about the space being rented. However, the company is now considering buying another warehouse building that has just been put up for sale.

The warehouse building for sale is virtually the same size and just as convenient and efficient for storage of its finished goods inventory as the space being rented. Although quite old, the building is structurally sound. But, the building is located in an area recently designated for urban renewal. The building could be used for only four years, at which time it would be demolished. The urban renewal agency will rent the land for four years, but the building on the land must be purchased. Hence, if the company does buy the building (and rent the land), four years from today the company must vacate the building.

To compare the two alternatives—continuing to rent space in the same building as before, or buying the other warehouse—the managers of the company have prepared the following information and estimates.

(a) The projected annual rentals that will be paid if the company continues to rent the same building are estimated as follows (to simplify, assume that each year's rent is paid entirely at the end of the year):

Year One	$46,000
Year Two	47,500
Year Three	49,000
Year Four	51,000

(b) The expenses of using the building purchased from the urban renewal agency over the next four years are estimated as follows.

Expense	Year One	Year Two	Year Three	Year Four
Land rental	$ 5,000	$ 5,000	$ 5,000	$ 5,000
Fire insurance	2,000	2,000	1,500	1,500
Utilities	500	590	609	620
Repairs and maintenance	3,500	3,900	3,000	4,300
Security guard	2,500	2,800	3,000	3,300
Depreciation	25,000	25,000	25,000	25,000

(*Note:* The security guard expense is an allocated share of the total cost of each year of the company's security guard force. The company's security force could patrol the new warehouse building (if purchased) without any additional personnel; the existing force would be reassigned to include regular tours of the new warehouse. For income tax purposes the cost of the building may be fully depreciated over its four-year remaining useful life by the straight-line method. Except for depreciation, assume that the expenses shown above are paid entirely at the end of each year.)

(c) The company's annual cost of capital is 20.0%.
(d) The urban renewal agency is asking $100,000 for the building, which must be paid in cash on purchase.

Required: Based on the above information and assumptions, determine whether the company should purchase the building from the urban renewal agency or should continue to rent the same building. Show your analysis clearly.

P10.15 Thorne Transit, Inc., has decided to inaugurate express bus service between its headquarters city and a nearby suburb (one-way fare $.50) and is considering the purchase of either 32- or 52-passenger buses, on which pertinent estimates are as follows.

	32-Passenger Bus	52-Passenger Bus
Number of each to be purchased	6	4
Useful life	8 years	8 years
Purchase price of each bus (paid on delivery)	$ 80,000	$110,000
Mileage per gallon	10	7½
Salvage value per bus	$ 6,000	$ 7,000
Drivers' hourly wage	$ 3.50	$ 4.20
Price per gallon of gasoline	$ .30	$ .30
Other annual cash expenses	$ 4,000	$ 3,000

During the four daily rush hours all buses would be in service and are expected to operate at full capacity (state law prohibits standees) in both directions of the route, each bus covering the route 12 times (six round trips) during that period. During the remainder of the 16-hour day, 500 passengers would be carried and Thorne would operate only four buses on the route. Part-time drivers would be employed to drive the extra hours during the rush hours. A bus traveling the route all day would go 480 miles, and one traveling only during rush hours would go 120 miles a day during the 260 working-day year. The company's annual cost of capital is 12.0%.

Required: Determine which size bus the company should purchase. Limit your analysis to the two alternatives: the purchase of six 32-passenger buses or four 52-passenger buses. To simplify, assume all cash flows each year occur entirely on the last day of the year.

Chapter Eleven

Relevant Cost Analysis for Special Management Decisions

RELEVANT COST ANALYSIS FOR SPECIAL MANAGEMENT DECISIONS

The Additional Functions of Management Accounting

As we have described in previous chapters, managers rely on the regular flow of periodic accounting reports for a large part of their decision-making information. They depend on these routine accounting reports to direct their attention to problems that have developed and to deviations from plans. Maximizing the usefulness of these basic accounting reports is a primary responsibility of management accounting. Maximizing their own understanding of these basic accounting reports is a primary responsibility of managers. Previous chapters explain that managers need to understand how costs are measured (which is not always obvious!), how to analyze changes in sales revenue and expenses from period to period, how costs behave relative to increases or decreases in volume, the effects of financial leverage, and the cost of capital in analyzing investment decisions. These topics might be called the "accounting fundamentals" for management planning and control.

In short, the regular periodic accounting reports are an indispensible foundation of information for management decision making and problem solving. Yet, this is not the whole of management accounting. Managers encounter problems and initiate the consideration of opportunities that call for cost and other accounting information which is not found in the routine accounting reports. These *special decision situations* deal with an aspect of management that we have barely explored.

An established business organization has an enormous amount of momentum which tends to preserve the status quo, to continue having things done the same way as in the past. In other words, a company's history in large measure determines its future. This is not all bad, of course. The cumulative experience of the business entity should result in reasonably effective sales efforts and reasonably efficient manufacturing and other operating costs. A company that has been in business many years has the advantage of learning from its past mistakes. But a company's managers cannot afford to be complacent. Managers continuously reexamine the established ways of doing things in all areas of the business with an eye toward maintaining and, if possible, improving the profit and return on investment performance of the company. In short, managers frequently ask: What if we did this differently . . . ? These special questions call for special types of accounting analysis.

Examples of such special questions include: (1) whether to make major rearrangements in the layout of the company's manufacturing plant and facilities to decrease production costs; (2) whether to begin to manufacture certain raw material items instead of purchasing them from another company; (3) whether to relocate the company's manufacturing plants and inventory warehouses; (4) whether to increase or decrease the average purchase and inventory quantities of raw materials and supplies; and, (5) whether to accept a sales order at reduced prices from a customer whom the company does not normally deal with. The list of these questions is very long and varies from company to company. Not every question is raised every period, of course. But these special questions are considered seriously from time to time and, when they are, the accountant is expected to supply the cost and other accounting information needed in the decision analysis. The company's historical based accounting system does not provide all the necessary cost data and other accounting information for such decisions. Much of the accounting information must be developed especially for these decision situations.

Developing Relevant Costs for Special Decisions

General Meaning of Relevant Costs (and Other Relevant Accounting Information)

The guiding principle in supplying cost and other accounting information for special management decisions is to identify and measure the *relevant costs* for the decision and, if appropriate, the *relevant revenue* (or other income). First, the manager must identify and define the decision situation or problem. Next the manager must identify and define each feasible alternative course of action that should be considered in the decision situation. In many instances there are just two basic alternatives which are in the nature of "Yes" or "No" alternatives, or "Go" and "No Go" alternatives. In other situations the main point of the decision analysis is to find the best answer over a broad range of possibilities such as deciding on the optimal order size for purchasing raw materials, which can vary from a very small order quantity to a very large order quantity.

Generally, each decision problem or opportunity is considered separately, although a manager should be alert for the consequences of his or her decision throughout the organization. In a large organization there are hundreds or thousands of individual decision makers. Keeping all their decisions mutually consistent and coordinated is a major problem. All managers, especially top level managers, should be concerned with "decision coordination" throughout the organization to avoid *suboptimization*. Suboptimization refers to taking actions in one part of the organization which may have the best results in that *localized* area, but which cause off-setting negative effects in other areas of the organization. "Solving" one problem which is considered in isolation may cause even more serious problems elsewhere in the organization. For example, to minimize the purchase cost of a raw material item the purchasing manager may buy the cheapest grade available. But this low grade may fail so often in the production process that the company would have much lower direct labor costs if a better grade raw material item were bought that does not fail so frequently.

Once the problem or opportunity has been identified and clearly defined the manager, working together with the management accountant, should identify *all* the specific cost-causing and revenue-causing factors that are *different* for each alternative course of action. Usually costs are more difficult to measure or to estimate than revenue. Also, one alternative may require significantly more or less capital investment than the other alternatives, and if so, then the differential amounts of capital investment between the alternatives are relevant to the decision analysis. (See the cost savings investment example discussed in Chapter Ten, pages 329 to 333.)

Relevant costs are those costs that would be *different* between each alternative course of action. Assuming all relevant costs have been identified, the next step is to measure or to estimate *how much different* each cost would be between the alternatives, so that the manager can compare the total cost differential among the alternatives being considered. Likewise, the relevant revenues (or other income) between the alternatives are identified and measured. Based on this comparative analysis of the relevant costs and relevant revenues between the alternatives, the manager should have adequate accounting information for the decision.

Historical Sunk Costs: An Example of Their Irrelevance to Current Decisions

The relevant costs for management decision making are the *future incremental costs* to be affected by the *current* decision, in contrast with the *historical sunk* costs of the company, which are the results of *past* decisions. For example, assume a company owns a particular piece of production machinery which has been used for five years. This fixed asset has an eight-year useful life estimate for depreciation purposes, therefore, three years of depreciation remains to be recorded. The company has just stopped manufacturing the product for which this particular machine was used. The company's production vice-president now is considering how best to use the machine elsewhere in the company's production plant, or whether to sell the asset. Two different production departments in the company are asking for the machine; both could use it in their manufacturing operations over the next three years. Obviously there are many relevant factors to consider in this decision situation. The discussion here is limited to the consideration of the *relevant cost* of the machine in the comparative analysis of the alternatives being considered by the manager.

If one or the other department does not receive the old machine, then another machine would have to be purchased. The department that receives the old machine will avoid this purchase cost. If the old machine is sold, then both departments would have to purchase another machine. Assume that Department A would be able to purchase an equivalent used machine for $35,000 to meet its needs over the next three years. Department B estimates that the cost of a used machine to meet its particular needs over the next three years would cost $50,000. Both used machines would have exactly a three-year useful life, it is assumed. Hence, Department A would avoid a $35,000 purchase cost if it receives the old machine, and Department B would avoid a $50,000 purchase cost. The company could sell the old machine for $42,000.

The purchase costs of the used machines that may be purchased clearly are relevant to this decision. However, the book value of the old machine owned by the company is *not* relevant to this decision and, in fact, has not even been mentioned. Rather, the *disposable value* of the old machine is the relevant value to be considered. It is assumed that an equipment dealer offers $42,000 for the old machine as is. (For income tax analysis purposes the book value of the old machine probably is the tax basis of the asset for determining the gain on sale of the asset, or for determining the depreciation deductions in the future years if the asset is kept.) The book value of the old asset is not relevant *today* when the manager is deciding how best to use the machine in the future or whether to sell the machine. Given the above information, the best course of action is to transfer the old machine to Department B, which would have to pay $50,000 for a similar machine, rather than selling it for $42,000 or giving it to Department A. The company can avoid a cost outlay of $50,000 even though it is giving up revenue of $42,000 by not selling the old machine. (Income taxes may have to be paid on the sale if the book value is less than $42,000.)

As may be apparent, in this example the old machine owned by the company has a remaining useful life of three years, and both the other machines that could be purchased by the production departments are used machines with three-year remaining useful lives. This is to simplify the comparison among the alternatives. Actually, of course, the production departments could purchase new machines that have longer useful lives, and that may have lower future operating costs during the next three years compared with the old machine owned by the company. In this situation the decision becomes a cost savings *investment* problem. The purchase costs of the new, longer-lived machines would be more than the $42,000 disposable value of the old machine. The main question is: For either or both new machines, would the differential amount of capital investment (Purchase Price of New Machine less Disposable Value of Old Machine) be justified based on the future cost savings, given the company's cost of capital? This type of analysis is discussed and analyzed in Chapter Ten (see pages 329 to 333).

Historical book values of most fixed assets are *not* good indicators of their *current* replacement or disposable values. Yet the current replacement and disposable values of fixed assets are the relevant values to consider in decisions regarding the future use of the assets. (Again, note that book values usually determine the income tax consequences of the continued use or disposal of assets.) The irrelevance of book values of assets for current decisions about the future use of assets is not a condemnation of the generally accepted historical cost accounting principle which is used for external financial reporting and for the regular periodic accounting reports to managers in the organization. There is an often argued theory that accounting reports should be based on current value accounting methods, but the argument has found little acceptance. In any case, managers should know that historical book values are poor indicators of current replacement or disposable values.

Plan of Chapter

To explain the development and analysis of relevant costs we next examine in detail two main examples of special decision situations. Studying these two examples will provide a good appreciation of the basic principles of relevant cost analysis, in particular, the emphasis on the future incremental costs (and revenues, if appropriate) that are triggered by the decision. Following the discussion of these two main examples, we briefly consider several other special decisions situations.

Isolated Sales Market

Example Introduced

At this point, recall the company example used in Chapters Two to Seven. In particular, review Exhibit 7.5 (page 233), which reports the profit performance of the company for the twelve months ending December 31, 1977. In the discussion that follows it is assumed that all the transactions reported in Exhibit 7.5 remain the same. Some *additional* revenue and costs for the last two months will now be considered. Assume that late in October 1977 a large national retailer approaches the company's sales manager and asks if the company would be interested in manufacturing its product for the retailer. The retailer's own private brand will be placed on the product, and in no way would the retailer identify who manufactures the product. Several large retail chains, such as J. C. Penney, Sears, and Ward contract with other companies to manufacture products sold under their national brand names. For example, these retailers purchase tires from various tire manufacturers, but the tires are marketed under the brand names of the national retailers, and the customers do not know (without some investigation on their part) who manufactures the tires. In any case, assume that the sales manager is interested in this proposition.

Of course, there are several marketing questions that the sales executive should consider. The national retailer would be competing against the company with the company's own product. On the other hand, this sort of competition may not cause any loss of sales if, in fact, the company cannot reach the same customers through its own marketing efforts and channels of distribution. In other words, products sold by the national retailer may be to customers who would not buy the products from the company anyway. *If* this is true, then selling to the national retailer is an *isolated market,* which means that selling to the national retailer does not have any adverse effects in the company's normal established markets.

The retailer offers to purchase 20,000 units of the company's product. The company would avoid some of its normal selling and delivery costs in filling this special order. The retailer knows this and is asking for a lower price than the company's normal price to its regular customers. In 1977 the company sells its product for $22.90 per unit, as is shown in Exhibit 7.5. The retailer offers only $17.50 per unit, which is $5.40 less per unit than the normal sales price of $22.90. Since the operating profit per unit shown in Exhibit 7.5 is only $2.185 per unit, it might seem that the company could not give up $5.40 per unit "off the top" and still make a profit on the deal. But relevant cost analysis of this special (isolated market) sales order opportunity reveals that it could make a profit.

First, it is assumed that the company could, in fact, manufacture an additional 20,000 units during November and December, given its existing production plant, machinery, and equipment, although this additional production output would push total output during the two months to the company's maximum practical capacity. If the company would have to give up production of 20,000 units that could be sold at the normal sales price of $22.90 to make room for 20,000 units that could be sold at $17.50, then this trade-off would force a different sort of analysis (which is one of the problems at the end of the chapter). In short, the company does *not* have to reduce its sales to normal customers if this special sales order is accepted.

Measuring Incremental Costs and Incremental Revenue To Determine Incremental Contribution Margin from Special Sales Order

The relevant costs for the analysis of the special (isolated market) sales order opportunity are the incremental future costs of producing and delivering the 20,000 units to the retailer. The relevant revenue is the incremental or additional sales revenue directly generated from the special order. The total incremental costs are subtracted from the total incremental revenue to determine the incremental contribution margin from the special order. As is explained above, the company does not have to expand its manufacturing fixed assets to produce the additional 20,000 units. It is assumed that the units will be delivered as soon as produced, so there would be no increase of inventory caused by the sales order. Also the retailer is willing to make immediate payment for products delivered; consequently, there would be no increase of Accounts Receivable caused by the additional sales order. Thus, in total, there would be no incremental investment of capital caused by accepting the special order.

Producing 20,000 additional units would increase the company's *variable* manufacturing costs by $11.678 per unit, for a total of $233,560 (20,000 units × $11.678)—see line (f) in Exhibit 7.5 for this manufacturing cost per unit. (More precisely, the variable manufacturing cost per unit for November and December should be used; it is assumed that the average variable manufacturing cost per unit reported in Exhibit 7.5 is a current measure for the last two months of the year.) The company would avoid variable manufacturing cost outlays of $233,560 by not producing this special order. Hence, quite clearly, the company needs to recover at least $11.678 per unit sold to the retailer. The more difficult question is whether other costs would be higher as a result of producing and delivering the 20,000 units for the special order.

Would *fixed* manufacturing costs be higher? To simplify, it is assumed that the company's total fixed manufacturing costs for 1977 would be the same whether this special order is produced or not. If there were incremental fixed manufacturing costs directly caused by producing the additional 20,000 units, then these additional costs would be relevant to the decision analysis. This leads in turn to consideration of the company's marketing expenses. The company's normal costs of promotion and distribution of the product to its regular customers do not apply to this special sales order. However, some incremental marketing expenses are directly caused by this special order, such as the cost of delivering the products to the retailer. The *fixed* marketing costs for the year probably would remain the same, whether this special order is accepted or not. It is unlikely that the company would have to increase any fixed marketing cost to fill this special order. On the other hand, there are bound to be some *variable* marketing expenses that would increase as a result of it. The manager analyzing this special order should identify which specific variable expenses would increase because of this special order.

A very helpful distinction in this regard is between *order getting* costs and *order filling* costs. The term "order getting" costs refers to the various costs of advertising and promoting the product, the salaries and commissions of salesmen, and many other costs of making customers aware of the company's product and convincing the customers to purchase the product. "Order filling" costs refer to the costs of processing sales orders once they are received from the customers, the costs of delivering the products, as well as other costs that are caused by processing the order and backing up the product after the sale. In this special sales order situation it is likely that incremental order getting variable costs would be minimal. But incremental order filling costs should be examined closely. Based on this analysis the manager's estimate is that the incremental marketing costs of filling this special order would be $3.75 per unit, or a total of $75,000 (consisting largely of delivery costs).

The same incremental cost analysis procedures are applied to the administration and general expenses of the company. That is, which of these costs would increase as a result of accepting the special order? Notice in Exhibit 7.5 that most of these expenses are fixed costs for the year. The manager's best estimate is that none of the administrative or general *fixed* costs would increase, but that the *variable* administration costs would increase by about $2500. It should be emphasized that the manager should not "pad" (intentionally inflate) the estimates of incremental costs that are associated with the special order. There is no point in intentional overestimation of the incremental costs, since no one outside the company should see the cost estimates.

The incremental costs of the special sales order opportunity are summarized in Exhibit 11.1. By knowing the incremental costs, the incremental contribution margin that would be earned from the special sales order can now be determined:

EXHIBIT 11.1
Summary of Incremental Costs of Special Sales Order

Manufacturing costs: ($11.678 variable cost per unit ×20,000 units) $233,560
Marketing costs ($3.75 variable cost per unit×20,000 units)   75,000
Administration costs   2,500
Total Incremental Costs $311,060
Incremental Cost per Unit:

$$\frac{\$311,060}{20,000 \text{ units}} = \$15.553 \text{ per unit}$$

Incremental Contribution from Special Order

Incremental sales revenue ($17.50×20,000 units)	=	$350,000
Incremental costs (see Exhibit 11.1)	=	311,060
Incremental contribution margin		$ 38,940

Hence, the special sales order would increase the company's operating profit (before income tax) by $38,940. The decision to accept the order looks attractive.

One final point deserves brief mention. If the company and the retailer are satisfied with the initial order of 20,000 units, this may lead to much larger orders in the future, which means that the company would have to expand its production capacity. This changes the character of the decision to that of a long-term investment analysis situation, a topic that is examined in Chapters Nine and Ten. The preceding discussion is limited to a *one-time* isolated market sales order opportunity which can be met with the company's existing production capacity which, otherwise, would stand idle, and which involves no long-term commitments. However, the basic analytical procedure of measuring incremental costs and incremental revenues is fundamental to both types of decisions.

Relevant Cost Analysis for Economic Order Quantity Decisions

Example Introduced

Assume that a manufacturer plans to produce a certain output of finished goods during the coming year which will require 554,400 units of a particular raw material. No wastage or spoilage of this particular raw material occurs during the manufacturing process. Hence, the company will need exactly 554,400 units of the item during the coming year. A sufficient quantity of these raw materials need to be on hand when and as needed in the manufacturing process. The consequences of a raw materials *stock out* could be serious. The monthly usage forecast over the coming year is prepared by the production manager, and this information is communicated to the purchasing manager. To simplify, it is assumed that a fairly stable need exists for this raw material item each week throughout the year. (In actual practice, production output may vary week to week, but this fluctuation would add an additional layer of complexity in the following analysis that is best avoided.)

Determining the Relevant Costs

The purchase prices in effect during the coming year for this raw material item are shown in Exhibit 11.2. Quantity discounts are offered for larger orders, as is indicated in the exhibit. Thus it might appear that the best course of action is to purchase more than 200,000 units each time in order to buy at the lowest purchase price. However, large orders result in large inventory balances, and the costs that depend on the inventory size are also relevant to analysis.

The cost of capital invested in the raw material inventory is a very relevant cost to consider in the analysis. The higher the average inventory balance, then the higher the cost of capital invested in the inventory. Determination of a company's cost of capital is explained in Chapter Nine (see pages 291 to 295). It is assumed that this company's annual cost of capital is 15.0%. This is the "required" rate of operating profit before interest and income tax that should be earned on assets. For example, on each additional (or incremental) $100 of capital invested in raw material inventory, the company should earn an additional $15 of operating profit, so that the interest, income tax, and net income demands on this $100 increment of invested capital can be satisfied.

This company, like almost all companies, has several different raw material inventory *holding costs*. These costs include items such as fire insurance on

EXHIBIT 11.2
Raw Material Purchase Price Schedule

Order Quantity	Price per Unit
Less than 1,000 units	$8.65
1,000– 4,999 units	8.40
5,000– 9,999 units	8.25
10,000– 24,999 units	7.75
25,000– 49,999 units	7.40
50,000– 99,999 units	7.15
100,000–199,999 units	7.00
Over 200,000 units	6.95

the inventory, storage space costs, inventory handling labor costs, and the like. The *relevant* holding costs are those that vary depending on the average size of the inventory. Many holding costs are more or less fixed for the year, such as the labor cost of employees who work on the receiving dock and in the warehouse. These employees are usually paid a fixed salary, or are paid for a fixed number of hours each week, and those would be the same regardless of the average raw material inventory quantity on hand. Likewise, over the short run most of the company's building space costs, such as depreciation and real estate taxes, would be fixed and would not vary with the average size of the raw material inventory. But several variable holding costs would increase as the average inventory increases, such as the cost of fire insurance on the inventory and personal property tax on inventory (in those states and localities that levy this tax). In short, it is assumed that the *variable* raw material holding costs equal 5.0% per year of the average cost balance of the raw material inventory.

The costs of ordering the raw materials during the year, that is, of preparing and placing each purchase order, usually include both fixed and variable costs. The purchasing manager's salary for the year, for example, is a fixed cost. Many other labor costs of the employees who process purchase orders are fixed also. On the other hand, some ordering costs may depend on the number of orders placed during the year, although these are minor in most instances, such as the cost of mailing the purchase order. In this example it is assumed that the company's ordering costs are fixed for the year, and are the same regardless of the number of orders placed and the average raw material inventory balance. Thus these ordering costs are irrelevant to this decision analysis because the costs are the same for any (reasonable) number of orders placed during the year.*

Finding the Economic Order Quantity (EOQ)

Given the above information and assumptions, the main question facing the purchasing manager is: How many purchase orders should be placed during the coming year for these raw materials? Or, putting the question in a different manner: What is the *economic order quantity*, or how many units should be ordered with each purchase?

The analysis required to answer these questions is shown in Exhibit 11.3. The first line in the exhibit starts with one purchase order for the entire 554,400 units, which would last for the entire year. On each successive line the number of purchase orders placed during the year is increased by one. (It is assumed that purchase orders are placed with enough lead time so that there is never a raw materials stock out.) The *average* inventory cost balance is used to deter-

---

* In determining the optimal number of job orders to be processed during a year, there may be a significant "set up" cost necessary for each separate job order. This would be a significant cost factor in the analysis. Problems at the end of the chapter explore this type of decision situation.

mine the annual holding costs and is equal to one half the purchase order quantity.* The total holding and total purchase costs are determined, which are added together to get the total raw material cost for the year. The objective is to find the purchase order quantity that minimizes the total raw material cost for the year. This quantity is called the economic order quantity, or EOQ for short. Study Exhibit 11.3 in some detail at this point. The footnotes that explain the computations and assumptions of the analysis are very important.

This purchase order quantity decision is one example of *trade-off* analysis. There is one basic trade-off in this decision situation. The larger the purchase order quantity, then the lower the purchase price per unit—see Exhibit 11.2. But the smaller the purchase order quantity, then the smaller the average inventory balance and, thus, the smaller the inventory holding costs. Starting with the top line in Exhibit 11.3 it is evident that one purchase of all 554,400 units enable the company to buy at the lowest purchase price ($6.95 per unit). But this would result in a very large average inventory balance during the year, which causes the annual holding costs to be more than $385,000. The next line in the schedule is a rather obvious trade-off to make.

By buying twice a year the company purchases 277,200 units each time, the lowest purchase price of $6.95 per unit is still received, and the average inventory balance is reduced by one half. Thus the inventory holding costs are also reduced by one half, which results in a cost savings of more than $192,000 for the year. Clearly the company should go to the "trouble" of ordering twice during the year to save more than $192,000. Furthermore, there appears to be no undesirable *side effects* of making two purchases instead of one. Side effects (also called "externalities") are those aspects of the problem that are not dealt with *explicitly* and *openly* in the analysis. Indeed, it probably would be impossible for the company to order only once a year, since the company would have to have enough inventory storage space to hold all 554,400 units for a while.

Having gone one step in the trade-off, one's natural inclination is to continue this same line of logic until the trade-off does not yield any cost savings. Should the company place three purchase orders during the year instead of two? The answer seems to be a clear yes. The sum of the total purchase cost plus the total annual holding cost if three orders are placed is $4,010,160, which is less than the $4,045,734 if only two orders are placed—see column (j) in Exhibit 11.3. Even with three purchase orders per year, each purchase shipment is more than 184,000 units, and the company may not be able to store this many units at one time.

Notice what happens if three (equal size) purchases are made during the year: 184,800 units are ordered each time, so the purchase price increases to $7 per unit. This causes the total purchase cost to increase by 5 cents per unit, or a total of $27,720: ($0.05 × 554.400 units = $27,720). However, the annual holding costs decrease by $63,294: ($192,654 − $129,360 = $63,294). The trade-

* If the raw material inventory quantity never is allowed to reach zero, then the average quantity would be higher than one half the purchase order quantity.

EXHIBIT 11.3
Analysis of Inventory Holding and Purchase Costs

(a) Number of Orders	(b) Order Quantity	(c) Purchase Price Per Unit	(d) Average Inventory Quantity	(e) Annual Holding Cost Per Unit	(f) Total Annual Holding Cost	(g) Change in Total Annual Holding Costs	(h) Total Purchase Cost	(i) Change in Total Purchase Cost	(j) Total Cost (f)+(h)
1	554,400	$6.95	277,200	$1.39	$385,308		$3,853,080		$4,238,388
2	277,200	6.95	138,600	1.39	192,654	−$192,654	3,853,080	—0—	4,045,734
3	184,800	7.00	92,400	1.40	129,360	− 63,294	3,880,800	+$ 27,720	4,010,160
4	138,600	7.00	69,300	1.40	97,020	− 32,340	3,880,800	—0—	3,977,820
5	110,880	7.00	55,440	1.40	77,616	− 19,404	3,880,800	—0—	3,958,416
6	92,400	7.15	46,200	1.43	66,066	− 11,550	3,963,960	+$ 83,160	4,030,026
7	79,200	7.15	39,600	1.43	56,628	− 9,438	3,963,960	—0—	4,020,588
8	69,300	7.15	34,650	1.43	49,550	− 7,078	3,963,960	—0—	4,013,510
9	61,600	7.15	30,800	1.43	44,044	− 5,506	3,963,960	—0—	4,008,004
10	55,440	7.15	27,720	1.43	39,640	− 4,404	3,963,960	—0—	4,003,600
11	50,400	7.15	25,200	1.43	36,036	− 3,604	3,963,960	—0—	3,999,996
12	45,200	7.40	23,100	1.48	34,188	− 1,848	4,102,560	+$138,600	4,136,748

Notes:

(a) It is assumed equal size orders are placed at equal intervals during the year.

(b) Order quantity is the total annual need, 554,400 units, divided by the number of orders.

(c) See Exhibit 11.2 for the purchase price schedule in effect.

(d) A constant rate of usage is assumed; thus, the average quantity is one-half the order size.

(e) The purchase price is multiplied by 20% to determine the annual holding cost per unit. The 20% is equal to the 15% cost of capital plus the variable holding cost of 5% per year.

(f) This amount is the average inventory quantity times the annual holding cost per unit.

(g) Equals the holding cost on this line less the holding cost at one fewer orders (on the preceding line).

(h) Equals the purchase price per unit times the total annual need of 554,400 units.

(i) Equals the total purchase cost on this line less the total purchase cost on the preceding line.

(j) Equals the total purchase cost plus the total annual holding cost. This is the total cost to be minimized, by placing the optimal number of orders during the year. This total cost is lowest if 5 orders are placed, so the economic order quantity (EOQ) is 110,880 units.

off, although not nearly so favorable, still results in a cost savings of more than $35,000. Other factors probably would strongly favor a smaller average inventory balance, since the company's available storage space for this one raw material item is limited. Three purchases a year still results in a rather large average inventory balance of raw materials, which should be more than adequate as a safety stock for unexpected demands from the production floor, or for unexpected delays in the supplier's delivery of raw materials. But keep in mind that these two aspects begin to become more important as the average inventory quantity of raw materials decreases.

Based on the trade-off analysis procedures just explained, follow down to the lowest total cost line in Exhibit 11.3, which is 5 purchase orders for the year. The $7 purchase price is still in effect with this purchase order quantity, and the average inventory balance is lower. Thus, there are holding cost savings that favor making 5 purchases. Making 6 purchases means that less than 100,000 units are ordered with each purchase, and the purchase price would increase 15 cents per unit for a total purchase cost increase of $83,160: ($.15 × 554,400 units = $83,160). The lower inventory holding costs caused by making 6 purchases cannot overcome this purchase cost increase. Even if the company were to place 11 purchase orders a year (see the second to the last line in the schedule) the inventory holding cost savings cannot overcome the purchase price jump. Beyond 11 purchases a year the purchase order quantity drops below 50,000 units; hence, the purchase price would increase by another 25 cents per unit for a total purchase cost increase of $138,600, which makes further analysis unnecessary.

Another Consideration

An interesting question raised by the analysis in Exhibit 11.3 is whether the manager would, in fact, place 5 purchase orders during the year, which clearly is the lowest total cost line in Exhibit 11.3, or whether the manager might place 11 purchase orders during the year. By ordering 11 times a year it is true that the total cost shown in Exhibit 11.3 is $41,580 higher: ($3,999,996 for 11 orders less $3,958,416 for 5 orders = $41,580). But if 11 purchases are made, then only 50,400 units of raw materials are ordered each time, and the inventory storage space needed for this raw material item would be less than one half as much if 110,880 units are ordered each time (by making 5 purchase orders during the year). If 11 purchase orders are made during the year, this purchase order quantity gives the company about five weeks of raw materials supply with each purchase shipment, which may be adequate to meet any unexpected demands from the production floor or to cover unexpected slowdowns in delivery from the supplier. The final decision may therefore depend on how much raw material inventory storage space is available relative to the other demands for the storage space. In any case, Exhibit 11.3 shows the manager the incremental (relevant) cost of going from 5 purchase orders per year to 11 purchase orders per year.

The EOQ Formula

Assume that the purchase price per unit in the above example is the same for all size purchase quantities, and that no quantity discounts are given. Then the company should minimize its inventory holding costs by ordering the smallest size purchase quantity that is feasible. In other words, the company should place as many orders as practical during the year. The more the orders, then the smaller the order size and the smaller the average inventory, which means the inventory holding costs would be minimized. As a practical matter it may not be possible to place an order more often than every week, or every two weeks. If, on the other hand, there were a significant incremental, variable cost of placing each purchase order, then this relevant cost would have to be considered. The trade-off would be between decreasing the inventory holding costs by increasing the number of purchase orders, on the one hand, and decreasing the ordering costs by limiting the number of orders placed, on the other hand.

In the preceding discussion it is assumed that all purchase ordering costs are fixed for the year, regardless of the number of purchase orders placed, and therefore were irrelevant to the analysis. Assume, in contrast, that each purchase order requires a variable cost outlay of $3880, and that the purchase price per unit is $7. regardless of the quantity ordered. The other facts are assumed to be the same: 554,400 units are needed; and, the annual holding cost is 20%. Thus, one unit held one year costs $1.40 ($7.00 × 20.0% = $1.40). In this situation the economic order quantity (EOQ) can be found by the following formula:

$$\text{EOQ} = \sqrt{\frac{2 \times (\text{Total Quantity Needed}) \times (\text{Cost of Each Order})}{(\text{Holding Cost per Unit for Year})}}$$

For this particular situation, this EOQ formula is

$$\text{EOQ} = \sqrt{\frac{2 \times 554,400 \times \$3880}{\$1.40}}$$

Doing these computations (on a calculator) gives an answer of 55,434 units per order, or about 10 (equal size) orders per year. Normally the answer has to be rounded off to the nearest "whole number" of orders to place each year.

Brief Discussions of Other Special Decisions Requiring Relevant Cost Analysis

From the main examples discussed above, it should be evident that any special decision is usually more complex than it appears, and that these decisions have many other ramifications throughout the organization that should be considered by the decision maker. In this section we briefly examine other examples of relevant cost analysis for special decisions. Keep in mind that not every assumption and caution is given for each decision situation.

Make or Buy Decisions

Assume that a company has some idle manufacturing capacity. One possible way to make use of this excess production capacity is to begin to manufacture (make) some of the raw material or other supply items that the company has been purchasing. The company's *incremental* costs of manufacturing the items may be less than the purchase cost of the items, which is entirely incremental of course. The company's fixed manufacturing costs probably would not be increased by starting to manufacture the items, if the idle capacity would otherwise go unused. The company may have to invest in some new machinery and equipment, which it does not now own, to begin manufacturing the items. But even taking this incremental capital investment into account, the cost savings from making the items instead of buying them may be worth it. As a general rule, this make-instead-of-buy option is most feasible for relatively simple types of raw materials and supplies which do not require mass production to get the average cost per unit down to a reasonable level.

Dropping an Unprofitable Product Line

Assume that the company's regular periodic management accounting reports include a breakdown of sales revenue and operating costs for each of the company's several different product lines. For several years one product line has shown an operating loss each year, despite efforts to increase sales volume of these products. The company's sales manager predicts that the sales volume of the product line should remain about the same in the near future. Sales prices cannot be raised because of competition in this product line. Should the company drop the unprofitable product line? Maybe not!

Dropping a product line means dropping the sales revenue and dropping the *variable* costs of manufacturing and selling these products. Thus the contribution margin (sales revenue less all variable costs) from the product line would be dropped. If the product line's variable costs are more than its sales revenue, then clearly the company should drop the product line (unless sales of other products would suffer). In many cases, however, the product line is earning a positive contribution margin. The product line shows a loss only when fixed costs are subtracted from the contribution margin. Hence, the decision depends on what would happen to the fixed costs being charged against the product line if the product line were dropped. Many of these fixed costs may not be avoidable in the short run even if the product line is dropped. If the product line is discontinued the production capacity used to manufacture these products would be available for other uses.

But what if there are no other immediate demands for this freed-up production capacity? Say, for example, that the unprofitable product line earns $150,000 contribution margin each year, but that $275,000 of fixed costs are charged against the product line, which results in a $125,000 operating loss. If the company actually could decrease its fixed cost cash outlays by more than $150,000 over the next year, then dropping the product would be best. Or, if the company could make use of the freed-up production capacity (by dropping the product line) to earn more than $150,000 contribution margin from an alternative use of the capacity (assuming future fixed cost cash outlays remain the same amount), then the company should drop the product line and shift the production capacity to the other use. In many practical situations a company has to gradually shift away or phase out from a product line rather than abruptly dropping it.

Optimizing Sales Mix Relative to Contribution Margin

Given limited manufacturing capacity, a company may have to make trade-off decisions regarding the sales mix that would make best use of its limited production output. Over the long run the company would expand its manufacturing capacity to meet sales demand, as long as the investment can be justified relative to the company's cost of capital (see Chapter Ten in particular). But in the short run a company may not be able to produce enough output to meet the total demand for all the products it could sell. Assuming the company's total annual fixed costs are more or less the same no matter which sales mix is sold, then the company should attempt to maximize its total contribution margin. To achieve the greatest total contribution margin, one might think that the company should give priority to the products with the highest contribution margins per unit. But this is not always true.

Assume that a company manufactures three products called for convenience X, Y, and Z. The relevant information concerning the company's short-run situation is shown in Exhibit 11.4. The manufacture of all three products requires the use of highly skilled labor. The company has 52,000 man-hours available for the coming year but cannot expand this capacity over the short run, since

EXHIBIT 11.4
Market Demand and Contribution Margin Information

	Product X	Product Y	Product Z
Total market demand	5000 units	5000 units	5000 units
Sales price per unit	$162.70	$157.30	$149.90
Variable costs per unit:			
Raw materials ($2.60/lb)	$ 78.00	$ 52.00	$ 26.00
Direct labor ($8.25/hr.)	33.00	49.50	66.00
Overhead	13.20	19.80	26.40
Selling and delivery	22.50	15.00	7.50
Total	$146.70	$136.30	$125.90
Contribution margin per unit	$ 16.00	$ 21.00	$ 24.00

a shortage exists of these skilled craftsmen, and new employees require more than a year of training for this specialized work.

At first glance it might appear that the best sales strategy is to make 5000 units of Product Z, since it has the highest contribution margin per unit, and then to sell as many units of Product Y that can be manufactured with the remaining production capacity which is not used in the production of 5000 units of Product Z. If this sales mix is decided on, the company's total contribution margin would be as follows:

Computation of Total Contribution Margin

5,000 units of Product Z	×	$24 per unit	=	$120,000
2,000 units of Product Y	×	21 per unit	=	42,000
Total contribution margin				$162,000

The production of 5000 units of Product Z would require 40,000 direct labor hours, since each unit requires 8 hours: ($66 direct labor cost ÷ $8.25 cost per hour = 8 hours). Hence, only 12,000 hours are available from capacity after producing the 5000 units of Product Z. Product Y requires 6 hours per unit: ($49.50 direct labor cost ÷ by $8.25 cost per hour = 6 hours). Hence, only 2000 units of Product Y could be manufactured: (12,000 remaining hours ÷ by 6 hours per unit).

However, the approach just explained misses a key point. The company should maximize the contribution margin *per direct labor hour* available, not the contribution margin per unit sold. Direct labor hours are the limiting factor, or the most binding constraint in this situation. The contribution margins per direct labor hour that are required to manufacture each product are computed in Exhibit 11.5. This exhibit reveals that the company should first maximize the sale of Product X, since it has the highest contribution margin per direct labor

EXHIBIT 11.5
Contribution Margin Per Direct Labor Hour of Each Product

	Product X	Product Y	Product Z
Contribution margin per Unit (see Exhibit 11.4)	$16.00	$21.00	$24.00
Direct labor hours per unit (direct labor cost divided by $8.25 cost per hour)	4 hours	6 hours	8 hours
Contribution margin per direct labor hour	$ 4.00	$ 3.50	$ 3.00

hour, then should shift remaining hours to Product Y, and finally to Product Z. This approach would yield total contribution margin as follows:

Contribution of Total Contribution Margin

5,000 units of Product X	×	$16 per unit	=	$ 80,000
5,000 units of Product Y	×	21 per unit	=	105,000
250 units of Product Z	×	24 per unit	=	6,000
Total contribution margin				$191,000

The production of 5000 units of X requires only 20,000 direct labor hours, leaving 32,000 remaining hours. The production of 5000 units of Y uses 30,000 of these hours, which still leaves 2000 hours available for the production of 250 units of Z. As we can see, the total contribution margin is $29,000 higher than the sales mix discussed above: ($191,000 − $162,000 = $29,000).

A Final Note

Cost, revenue, and capital investment factors, important as they are to any decision, are not the whole of the decision analysis. In almost all decision situations the manager must consider factors that are not reducible to an accounting measure. The manager has to consider "benefits" and "costs" that are not susceptible to any form of measurement. For example, a manager may be trying to decide between continuing to pay the company's employees overtime, or adding several additional new employees to the company's work force. Since the overtime rate of pay is 150% of the hourly base rate, the labor cost of the new employees would be considerably less than paying overtime to the present employees for the same number of hours. But would the relevant cost analysis *alone* decide the matter? The nonmeasurable aspects and consequences of the decision alternatives must be considered by the manager.

The manager may believe that the morale of the present employees may be seriously damaged by taking away overtime work and giving these hours to new employees. There may be a union contract coming up for renegotiation in the near future. Perhaps the company is planning to modernize some of its machinery and equipment within the next few years; this may reduce the number of labor hours needed in the coming years. Or, the company may be thinking of changing the location of its manufacturing operations, although this is not yet definite. One decision is usually intertwined with other decisions. As mentioned previously, managers must be careful not to suboptimize, that is, to make a decision that looks good in isolation but that causes problems with worse consequences elsewhere or at some later date.

Summary

The regular periodic accounting reports to managers in the business organization provide an indispensable foundation of information for decision making, especially for managers' planning and control functions. However, these basic routine accounting reports do not provide all the information needed for the wide variety of unusual problems and special opportunities that managers encounter or investigate from time to time. Managers call on accountants to develop the relevant cost and other pertinent accounting information needed in the analysis of these special decisions. Relevant costs are the future incremental cash outlays that depend on which specific course of action will be taken in the future. Usually each alternative being considered in the decision has different relevant costs. The main purpose of the analysis is to determine the comparative cost differential between the alternatives. Future incremental revenue differences between the decision alternatives also must be brought into the analysis. Identifying all relevant costs and measuring these costs usually is the more difficult side of the analysis, although forecasting future revenues is always a problem.

Future incremental costs are not found in the historical cost based accounting system of the company. These relevant costs have to be developed especially for each decision. Also, historical cost book values of assets are not the relevant values for those decisions regarding the future use or disposal of the assets. The manager needs to know the current replacement value or the current disposable value of the asset, which frequently is much different than its book value.

A company may accept a special sales order below its normal selling price if the total incremental costs of manufacturing and delivering the products is less than the incremental sales revenue from the sales order. In most cases there are two critical conditions that must be met to make this a favorable decision. First, the company must have production capacity available that would otherwise go unused; second, the customer must be in an isolated market which does not affect the normal sales price or demand from its other customers. The economic order quantity decision is a prime example of trade-off analysis. The lowest purchase price achieved by ordering large quantities results in the highest inventory holding costs. The manager has to compare the incremental cost savings of holding a lower average inventory against the higher purchase costs caused by ordering smaller quantities.

The application of relevant cost analysis to other special decision situations reveals that the "common sense" solution is not necessarily the best course of action. Incremental cost analysis in situations where the company has idle manufacturing capacity may show that it is cheaper to make some raw material items than to purchase them. By dropping what appears to be an unprofitable product line, a company may sacrifice contribution margin without a corresponding decrease in its future incremental fixed cost outlays. A company should not necessarily maximize the sales of those products with the highest contribution margins given a limited production capacity. Last, it is important to remember that any decision is surrounded by several "nonmeasurable" factors which are not dealt with in the quantitative accounting analysis. These intangible subjective factors do not lessen the importance of the quantitative accounting analysis, however.

Questions

11. 1 "The preparation of the regular periodic accounting reports to managers in the organization is the main task of management accounting." Do you agree? Briefly explain.

11. 2 What does *suboptimization* mean? What are the dangers of suboptimization? How do managers avoid this?

11. 3 What are relevant costs? Is the company's historical based accounting system an adequate source of information for developing relevant costs?

11. 4 How do the so-called "special" problems and opportunities discussed in the chapter arise? What produces these special decision situations?

11. 5 What are some of the generally accepted "principles" of relevant cost analysis for special decisions?

11. 6 Are historical costs generally irrelevant with respect to current decisions? Why or why not?

11. 7 A company has a stock of discountinued inventory items that it no longer manufactures or sells. The FIFO cost value of these products is $50,000. A discount department store offers $25,000 for the entire stock of these items. Should the company accept the offer? What is the relevant cost of the products for this special decision?

11. 8 A company has an opportunity to make a special sale of a large quantity of its product in an isolated market. To determine the minimum sales price that it will accept for this special order the company subtracts all its fixed costs per unit from its normal selling price. Do you agree with this method? Explain.

11. 9 The production manager of the company in the special sales order opportunity example discussed in the chapter has followed all the logic of the incremental cost analysis for this situation, and he observes that an incremental contribution margin would *seem* to be earned from the special sales order. But he objects to the exclusion of fixed manufacturing costs from the analysis. He argues that the 20,000 units produced for the special order should be charged with their fair share of the fixed overhead costs, which as is indicated in Exhibit 7.5 are more than $2 per unit. He points out that this would show that the special order really would cause a loss, since the contribution margin per unit is less than $2 from the special order. Do you agree? Carefully explain your position.

11.10 "For management decision-making analysis relevant means incremental." Do you agree? Explain.

11.11 What are the main similarities *and* the main differences in the analysis of the special (isolated market) sales order opportunity discussed in this chapter and the new product line investment opportunity discussed in Chapter Ten?

11.12 What is the basic trade-off in the economic purchase order quantity main example discussed in the chapter?

11.13 Instead of the purchase price schedule shown in Exhibit 11.2 for the purchase order quantity decision example discussed in the chapter, assume that no quantity discounts are offered—the same price applies to any quantity purchased. In this case, what is the EOQ (economic order quantity)? Explain fully.

11.14 "A company should get out of an unprofitable product line as soon as possible." Do you agree? Explain.

11.15 Assume that one of a company's product lines shows an operating loss for the year just ended. The preceding chapters in this book discuss several points and factors that managers would analyze for the purpose of improving a situation of this kind. What are some of these basic points and factors that managers would analyze *before* they would seriously consider dropping the unprofitable product line?

11.16 "A company should give priority to the products with the highest contribution margins per unit in deciding on the optimal sales mix from its limited production capacity (in those cases where not all products which could be sold can be manufactured)." Do you agree? Explain.

11.17 What is the most important test or the best way to measure a salesman's performance?

11.18 If a company does not have enough production capacity, might relevant cost analysis for the make or buy decision reveal that the company should stop making some particular items and start buying them?

Problems

P11. 1 A company was moving all its office equipment and machines into a new office building. Unfortunately three electric typewriters were lost in the confusion of the move, and this loss is *not* covered by the company's insurance policies. (There is a possibility of theft, which the company will investigate, but recovery of the typewriters seems unlikely.) The cost accounting department and the purchasing officer of the company supply the following information about the three lost typewriters.

Typewriter No.	Purchase Cost	Depreciation Method	Realistic Useful Life Estimate	Estimated Salvage Value	Present Age	Replacement Cost	
						New	Used
1	$435	Straight–line	8 years	$35	7 years	$600	$100
2	475	Straight–line	8 years	35	5 years	600	285
3	525	Straight–line	8 years	45	2 years	600	415

The company needs to replace the three typewriters very soon.

Required:

(1) What is the amount of loss for the three typewriters that would be recorded on the books (that is, in the accounting journal entry to record this loss)?

(2) What is the amount of loss of the three typewriters from the management decision-making point of view?

(3) Assuming all the information in the above schedule is accurate, should the company replace the lost typewriters with new machines or the equivalent used machines?

P11. 2 Three years ago the company began a cost reduction program and started to "tighten its cost belt." The company's operating profit from its main sales revenue sources had slipped, and because of competitive sales price pressures the company could discover no way to increase its sales prices. Every operating cost was critically reexamined to determine if the cost could be lowered without any adverse effects on sales revenue. Thus the company switched from buying full-size intermediate-priced cars for its traveling salesmen to compact-size cars, which not only cost less to purchase but also give better gas mileage and lower repair and maintenance bills.

At the present time about two thirds of the fleet of salesmen's cars have been converted to compacts. As the other one third of the older intermediate-priced cars reach the end of their useful life, the company expects to replace them with new compacts. The company has adopted a strict four-year replacement cycle for its salesmen's cars. At the end of the forty-eighth month of use every car is "automatically" replaced with a new car. The salesman is given the opportunity to purchase the car at its book value at that time. In almost all cases the salesman does buy the car at that price. The company uses the SOYD depreciation method for income tax, external reporting, and internal management reporting purposes.

Despite the company's fairly successful cost-reduction efforts, our territory has consistently shown operating losses. The general sales manager and executive committee of the company have just decided to abandon it. Among other things this means laying off five salesmen who travel this territory. Thus, five cars are no longer needed by these five salesmen. As it happens all five of these cars are compacts. The salesmen being laid off are *not* entitled to buy these cars, since the cars have not reached the end of their useful lives. Within the next month the company needs to replace five cars in other sales territories. Information about the five cars from the territory to be abandoned is as follows:

Car No.	Age	Original Purchase Cost	Original Estimated Salvage Value	Type	Used Car Dealer Prices	
					Wholesale (Buying) Price	Retail (Selling) Price
1	36 months	$3200	$480	Compact	$1700	$2000
2	36 months	3200	480	Compact	1700	2000
3	24 months	3500	525	Compact	2400	2800
4	24 months	3500	525	Compact	2400	2800
5	12 months	3800	570	Compact	3100	3600

Each territory is a decentralized and autonomous division of the company. The general manager of the division is judged on the operating profit performance of that division. It happens that two different territories both need five replacement cars for their salesmen during next month. Normally they would purchase new compacts, and accordingly both general managers have priced new compacts. The purchase cost would be $4000. (It is assumed that the old cars will be bought by the salesmen involved.) However, the company's headquarters has asked these two general managers whether they would want to "buy" the five compacts from the territory being abandoned, instead of buying new compacts. The "purchase" cost of these five used compacts would be charged to the territory "buying" them. Keep in mind that taxable income (or loss) results only if the company sells the used compacts to an external party. An internal "sale" is not recognizable for income tax purposes.

Required:

(1) For the company as a whole, what is the best course of action to adopt regarding the five used compacts from the territory being abandoned? Show all your computations.
(2) Assume you were the general manager of either of the two territories needing five new compact cars.
  (a) *If* headquarters would "sell" you the five used compacts at their present book values, would you buy these cars, or would you instead purchase five new compacts?
  (b) *If* headquarters opened the "purchase" of the five used compacts to bidding, what is the maximum total "purchase" price you would bid for them?

P11. 3 A job order manufacturing company produces a certain product for stock (inventory). The coming year's total sales demand for this product is budgeted at 24,000 units. Based on past experience, the same quantity is sold and delivered every month during the year. The budgeted costs of manufacturing this product, *excluding* the initial set-up cost of preparing for each job order, are as follows for the coming year:

Cost Factor	Per Unit
Raw materials	$ 5.20
Direct labor	8.00
Variable overhead burden rate	2.00
Fixed overhead burden rate	2.80
Total cost	$18.00

In addition to these costs, each job order requires certain set-up costs, which consist of resetting the machines and equipment to handle the special demands of running the job order. This is the only product manufactured by the company that requires these special preparation costs to get ready for each job. The set-up cost to prepare for each job order is $3000. The company's annual cost of capital (rate of operating profit on total assets) is set at 15.0%. Storage and other holding costs are $.90 per unit of inventory per year.

Required: Based on the above information determine the economic job order quantity and the number of job orders to be processed during the year (assuming that an equal quantity is manufactured in each job order). Show your computations clearly.

P11. 4 This company manufactures a wide assortment of relatively low-priced products, all of which are quite heavy and all of which are sold FOB destination point. Thus the company's delivery expense is a major cost of operations, and it is very concerned about minimizing its total annual delivery expense. The company uses various trucking firms to pick up and deliver its products. Basically there are three types of shipments:

(1) *Express:* these are small size shipments; they have the highest cost per pound of delivery.
(2) *Less than carload:* these are larger size shipments, but still do not fill an entire truck trailer on one pickup; the cost per pound is less than the express rate.
(3) *Carload:* these are the largest size shipments; an entire trailer is filled on one pickup, and the cost per pound is the lowest possible rate.

In the past the company has delivered many sales orders in less than carload sizes and even express sizes many times because it did not have enough production capacity to accumulate inventories that were large enough always to consolidate several sales orders in one carload size shipment. Many items were frequently out of stock and, therefore, the pickup had to go off at less than carload size or even express size. Recently the company completed a major expansion of its manufacturing plant and warehouse space; hence, larger inventories can be carried. Based on a detailed cost analysis the company's shipping department estimates that $850,000 delivery costs could be saved if *all* shipments were consolidated in carload sizes, but that this would require a $3,450,000 increase in the company's average inventory during the year. An alternative is to eliminate all express shipments but to allow some shipments to go out at less than carload size. This alternative would save $350,000 delivery costs per year and would cause the average inventory to increase only $1,200,000. If no change is made, the company's total delivery cost for the year will be $2,415,800 and its average inventory balance will be $7,500,000. The company's annual cost of capital is 20.0%, and the holding cost of inventory is estimated at 8 cents per dollar per year.

Required: Which alternative is best for the company? Show your computations clearly.

P11. 5 A wholesaler buys and sells a particular product by the gross (one gross equals 12 dozen). A gross is the smallest purchase and sales unit. The manufacturer of this product controls the retail selling price of the product at $800 per gross. The wholesaler buys the product at a trade discount of 40% off retail list price. The manufacturer sells the items to the wholesaler FOB (free on board) shipping point. Freight cost is $20 per gross to the wholesaler's location. The wholesaler expects to sell 36 gross during the coming year, and demand should be level through the year. The cost of placing each purchase order is $70 and the cost of receiving each order is $20. Space storage cost is $12 per year for each gross stored. Insurance and property taxes on inventory are about 5.0% of the delivered purchase cost of average inventory. The company's cost of capital is set at 15.0% per year.

Required: Determine the economic order quantity and the number of orders to place during the year, assuming uniform size order quantities, except that the last order placed during year (if necessary) can be one gross higher to make up a total of 36 gross for the year.

P11. 6 Assume that a retailer has budgeted next year's sales volume at 665,280 units. To simplify, it is assumed that the company sells only one product. Just about the same quantity is sold each month. The company's basic capitalization structure for a $10,000 "slice" of total assets is shown as follows (the cost of equity rate is the aftertax net income on stockholders' equity goal established by the company):

	Source of Capital	Amount	Annual Rate
Total Assets = $10,000 ← Noninterest bearing liabilities	=	$2000 @	0.0%
Interest bearing debt	=	$2000 @	10.0%
Stockholders' equity	=	$6000 @	14.3%

Assume a flat 48% income tax rate.

The inventory ordering, receiving, handling, and storage costs for next year have been budgeted as follows (this does *not* include cost of capital):

Fixed Costs	$300,000
Variable Costs	
(a) Those costs dependent on *dollar cost value* of average inventory	$1.50 per year per $100 average cost value
(b) Those costs dependent on average *quantity* of inventory, independent of cost value	$3.00 per year per unit of inventory
(c) Those costs dependent on number of separate orders placed and received, independent of quantity of order and purchase price per unit	(see below)

The absolute maximum storage capacity limit at any one time of the company's warehouse (including some items stacked in the aisles) is 150,000 units. The average time between ordering a shipment and the receipt of the shipment is one month. The supplier will not ship more than one order each month.

Required: Determine the optimum purchase order quantity (and thus the best number of purchase orders) for next year in each of the following separate and independent cases, given the above information, constraints, and assumptions:

(1) The supplier does not give quantity discounts; the purchase price per unit next year will be $20. The variable cost per order will be $1000.

(2) The supplier does not give quantity discounts; the purchase price per unit next year will be $10. The variable cost per order will be $25,000 (a rather high amount to be sure).

(3) The supplier offers quantity discounts, as follows:

Size of Order	Purchase Price per Unit
Less than 65,000 units	$52.00
65,001 to 80,000 units	50.00
80,001 to 90,000 units	49.50
90,001 to 100,000 units	49.15
100,001 to 125,000 units	49.00
Over 125,000 units	48.90

The variable cost per order will be $1000.

P11. 7 *The "Bottleneck" Machine.** A company has just received two orders from different customers (for different products). Both customers urgently need delivery of their orders within one week; otherwise the order will be withdrawn. Unfortunately the company cannot process both orders within one week, given its limited production facilities. One order will have to be refused. The sales manager's opinion is that it would make little difference on future sales to either customer if one order of theirs were refused, since both customers appreciate the limited capacity problems of the company. Hence, the sales manager asks the production manager to accept the order that will yield the most profit. Relevant data concerning the two orders are shown below:

	Product A	Product B
Order Quantity	3000 units	5000 units
Sales price per unit	$1.00	$1.00
Costs per unit:		
Variable costs	$ .55	$ .70
Fixed costs	.10	.10
Total costs	.65	.80
Operating profit per unit	$ .35	$ .20

The company's production capacity is limited by a "bottleneck" machine through which all job orders must pass. Until the company can purchase another one of these machines the company's weekly output cannot exceed the capacity of this particular bottleneck machine. No other production work has to be scheduled for the coming week, so either of the customers' orders described above could be manufactured. Product A can be produced at the rate of 600 per day on the bottleneck machine, whereas Product B can be produced at the rate of 1000 per day. The company works five days a week.

Required:

(1) Which sales order should the production manager accept? Show all your computations clearly.
(2) Assume that instead of the fixed sales prices assumed above, the sales manager could negotiate either sales price up a little. Based on your answer to part (1), how much would the other product's sales price have to be to make both sales orders equally profitable? Show your work.

P11. 8 Refer to the information presented in Exhibit 11.4. Instead of the limited number

---

* Adapted from an example in *Management Services Newsletter*, March 1973 issue, published by Main Lafrentz & Co., Certified Public Accountants; with permission.

of direct labor hours available during the period, assume that the company can hire as many skilled employees as it needs. However, the raw material item used to make all three products (which is the only raw material item used) is in short supply. The company will be able to purchase a maximum of 150,000 pounds during the period. The company's beginning inventory of this raw material is 40,000 pounds.

Required: Determine the optimal sales mix for the period. Show your computations clearly.

P11. 9 The top level managers of the company are reviewing the profitability of the company's four products and the potential effects of several proposals for varying the product mix. Information from the latest annual management profit performance statement is as follows:

Latest Year's Product Line Profit Performance

	Totals	Product P	Product Q	Product R	Product S
Sales	$62,600	$10,000	$18,000	$12,600	$22,000
Cost of goods sold[a]	44,274	4,750	7,056	13,968	18,500
Gross profit	$18,326	$ 5,250	$10,944	($ 1,368)	$ 3,500
Operating expenses[b]	12,012	1,990	2,976	2,826	4,220
Income (loss) before interest and income taxes	$ 6,314	$ 3,260	$ 7,968	($ 4,194)	($ 720)
Units sold		1,000	1,200	1,800	2,000
Sales price per unit		$ 10.00	$ 15.00	$ 7.00	$ 11.00
[a] Variable cost of goods sold per unit		$ 2.50	$ 3.00	$ 6.50	$ 6.00
[b] Variable operating expenses per unit		$ 1.17	$ 1.25	$ 1.00	$ 1.20

Four different possible actions are listed below. Treat each alternative as independent and separate from the others. Assume that over the short run the company cannot decrease its total fixed costs. In all four cases ignore income tax effects.

Required:

(1) If Product R is discontinued, what would be the short-run effect on income?
(2) If Product R is discontinued and a consequent loss of customers caused a decrease of 200 units of sales of Product Q, what would be the short-run effect on income?
(3) If the sales price of Product R is increased to $8 with a decrease in the number of units sold to 1500, what would be the short-run effect on income?

(4) The capacity now being used to manufacture Product R can be used instead to produce a new product, Product T. The total variable costs and expenses per unit for Product T would be $8.05, and it is estimated that 1600 units could be sold at $9.50 per unit. What would be the short-run effect on income if Product R is discontinued and Product T is introduced?

P11.10 A company has just constructed a new manufacturing building next door to its old plant building, and has moved most of its machinery and equipment into this new building. Not all of the old machinery and equipment was moved, however. Some of the older, out-of-date machines and equipment were left in the old building. The company could sell these unmoved machines and equipment for about $15,000 but would have to spend about $3000 to move them out of the old building. The old building is immediately adjacent to the company's new plant building, and there is no convenient access to the old building from any street. Hence, the immediate market value of the old building is zero; it is very doubtful that a buyer could be found. The company plans to use some of the old building for temporary overflow inventory storage space, and as a convenient place to store some supplies that could be kept outside but would be safer inside.

The production manager has just pointed out that the machinery and equipment left behind in the old plant building could be used to make a certain raw material item which the company has been purchasing from outside suppliers. He estimates that for next year's budgeted total need for this raw material item of 50,000 units, the production costs would be as follows:

Cost Factor	Total Amount
Materials and supplies	$ 86,000
Direct labor	70,000
Fringe benefit costs of direct labor	23,000
Building depreciation*	7,500
Machinery and Equipment depreciation*	5,000
Real estate taxes on old building	2,500
Electrical power	8,500
Total costs	$202,500

* These amounts are from the depreciation schedules for these fixed assets based on their original costs. The machinery and equipment has a remaining life of four years. The old building has an estimated remaining life of 10 years.

The company paid $3.50 per unit for this raw material item last year. This purchase price is expected to increase about 10.0% during the coming year.

Required:

(1) Present your analysis regarding whether the company should start to make

the raw material item or should continue to purchase the item from outside suppliers.

(2) Briefly discuss the assumptions you make in your analysis and any other important factors that should be considered in making the decision to make or to buy.

P11.11 Management asked for your assistance in arriving at a decision whether to continue manufacturing a part or to buy it from an outside supplier. The part, which is named Faktron, is a component used in some of the finished products of the company. From your investigation you develop these data:

(a) The annual requirement for Faktrons is 5000 units. The lowest quotation from a supplier is $8 per unit.

(b) Faktrons have been manufactured in the company's Precision Machinery Department. If Faktrons are purchased from an outside supplier, certain machinery will be sold that would realize its book value of about $4500.

(c) Following are the *total* costs of the Precision Machinery Department for the most recent year, during which 5000 Faktrons and many other parts were made:

Account	Amount
Materials	$67,500
Direct labor	50,000
Indirect labor	20,000
Light and heat	5,500
Power	3,000
Depreciation	10,000
Property taxes	8,000
Payroll taxes and other benefits	9,800
Other (out-of-pocket) costs	5,000

(d) The following Precision Machinery Department costs apply to the manufacture of Faktrons: material, $17,500; direct labor, $28,000; indirect labor (fixed salaried production supervisors), $6000; power, $300; other, $500. The sale of the equipment used for Faktrons would reduce the following costs by the amounts indicated: depreciation, $2000; property taxes and insurance, $300.

(e) The following additional costs would be incurred if Faktrons were purchased from an outside supplier: Freight, $0.50 per unit; indirect labor for receiving, materials handling, inspection, and the like, $5000 annually.

Required:

(1) Present your analysis of whether the company should continue to make the part (Faktron) or to purchase it from an outside supplier.

(2) Discuss the considerations, in addition to the cost factors, that you would bring to the attention of management in assisting them to arrive at a decision

whether to make or buy Faktrons. Include in your discussion the considerations that might be applied to the evaluation of the outside supplier.

P11.12 For many years this company has manufactured a very high priced quality hi-fi tape recorder, which it advertises heavily and sells directly to hi-fi retail stores. Last year the company manufactured and sold 30,000 units, but its production capacity was 50,000 units. Its manufacturing costs, operating expenses, and sales revenue for last year were as follows:

Sales revenue		$9,450,000
Manufacturing costs:		
Purchased materials and supplies	$2,340,000	
Variable labor and other costs	2,850,000	
Fixed labor and overhead costs	2,400,000	
Total		7,590,000
Gross profit		$1,860,000
Operating expenses:		
Variable expenses	$1,260,000	
Fixed expenses	1,100,000	
Total		$2,360,000
Operating profit (loss)		($ 500,000)

The entire hi-fi industry, including the tape-recorder segment, is plagued with overcapacity, which should discourage any new companies from entering the industry. Recently, several national retail chains have started to upgrade the line of hi-fi equipment carried in their stores. One national retailer has approached this company and has asked if it would bring out a more economical version tape recorder that would be sold under the private label of the retailer. The retailer offers to buy 10,000 units of this "economy model" over the next year at $185 per unit. The production manager estimates that compared with its standard model, the company could reduce the material and supplies cost by $18 per unit, and could save $23 per unit on the variable manufacturing labor and other costs. There would be no other operating costs associated with the sale to the national retailer. The company's production manager does not like the idea of bringing out a "cheap" model, but in any case he argues that the company should not lower its price to the retailer by more than the $41 cost savings on the economy model, especially in view of the current operating loss of the company. The company expects to sell 35,000 units of its standard model next year. To simplify, ignore any cost increases next year and assume the company's sales price remains the same also.

Required:

(1) What is the company's break-even point next year, before consideration of the special sale to the retailer? Show your computations.

(2) Show your analysis of whether the company should accept the special order from the retailer. Determine the company's operating profit with and without the special sale to the retailer.

(3) Assuming that the special order by the retailer is accepted, determine the amount of profit earned per unit from the standard model and the economy model.

(4) What is the company's break-even point next year, assuming the special order to the retailer is accepted? Show your computations.

P11.13 This company purchases three basic raw material items for its production needs. Demand for each raw material item is level through the year. Information for the coming year for each raw material item is as follows:

	Item A	Item B	Item C
Purchase price per unit	$60.00	$20.00	$5.00
Total quantity needed	72 units	1440 units	18,000 units
Variable cost of placing each purchase order	$15.00	$100.00	$312.50

The company's cost of capital is 20.0% per year. Variable inventory holding costs, excluding cost of capital, equal 5.0% of the average inventory cost balance.

Required: Determine the economic order quantity (EOQ) for each raw material item. Also, determine how many (equal size) orders would be placed during the year for each item.

P11.14 A retail store has experienced heavy shoplifting losses for several years, most of which probably is done by customers, although employees may be responsible for some of the loss. The trend seems to be getting worse. The retail value of the store's inventory shortages for the last five years and each year's total sales revenue were as follows:

	1972	1973	1974	1975	1976
Sales revenue	$4,000,000	$5,000,000	$7,500,000	$10,000,000	$13,000,000
Retail value of inventory shortage	$ 60,000	$ 100,000	$ 168,750	$ 250,000	$ 357,500

The company's average gross profit is one third of sales revenue.

The general manager has considered different alternatives of reducing the store's shoplifting loss. In particular, an electronic tag system is available that

involves attaching a small unnoticeable "bug" on each product which is neu-
tralized by the salesclerk when writing up the sale. If a customer attempts to
walk out without paying, the bug will activate a warning sound as the customer
exits through the door. This system would require an initial installation cost of
$20,000 for all the equipment, and each bug would cost 15 cents. The com-
pany's employees would have to attach the bug to each product. The average
sales price per unit sold in 1976 was $6.50. Whether the present number of
employees would have time to "bug" all the products is questionable. The
company may have to hire one or two more persons, who would be paid at least
$6500 per year.

Required: Analyze whether or not the company should implement the electronic
bug system.

(Note: This problem is somewhat open-ended, and you will have to make some assumptions
in your analysis. Indicate your assumptions clearly.)

P11.15 This company is engaged in manufacturing and wholesaling two principal products. You have been asked to advise management on sales policy for the coming
year. Two different plans are being considered by management. These proposals
are as follows.

Plan 1—Premium Stamp Books

It is proposed that each package of Product A will contain 8 premium stamps,
and each package of Product B will contain 4 premium stamps. Premium stamp
books will be distributed to consumers, and when a book is filled (100 stamps),
it will be redeemed by the award of a cash prize in an amount indicated under an
unbroken seal that is attached to the book at the time of distribution. Every
10,000 books distributed will provide for prizes in accordance with this schedule:

Number of Books	Prize for each	Total Prizes
1	$150.00	$ 150
5	50.00	250
14	20.00	280
50	10.00	500
160	5.00	800
1,020	1.00	1,020
8,750	.40	3,500
10,000		$6,500

This schedule is fixed and is not subject to alteration or modification. The cost
of this plan will be as follows.

Books, including distribution cost	$ 15 per 1000 books
Stamps	$ 1 per 1000 stamps
Prizes	$650 per 1000 books

The premium stamp book plan will take the place of all past advertising, and previously established selling prices will be maintained.

Plan 2—Reduced Selling Prices

It is proposed that the selling price of Product A be reduced by 8⅓% and that of Product B by 5%, and to increase the advertising expenditures over those of the prior year. This plan is an alternative to Plan 1, and only one will be adopted.

Management has provided you with the following information about the previous year's operations, and about anticipated changes.

	Product A	Product B
Prior year's operations:		
Quantity sold	200,000 units	600,000 units
Production cost per unit	$.40	$.30
Selling price per unit	$.60	$.40
Selling expenses were 18% of sales, of which one third was for advertising. Administrative expenses were 5% of sales.		
Expected changes:		
Increase in unit sales volume:		
Plan 1	50%	50%
Plan 2	40%	25%
Decrease in unit production cost:		
Plan 1	5%	10%
Plan 2	7½%	6⅔%
Advertising		
Plan 1	None	None
Plan 2	8% of sales	7% of sales
Other selling expenses:		
Plan 1	15% of sales	12% of sales
Plan 2	12% of sales	12% of sales
Premium book expenses:		
Plan 1	As indicated above	
Plan 2	None	None
Administrative expenses:		
Plan 1	4% of sales	4% of sales
Plan 2	Same dollar value as prior year	

Required: Prepare an analysis for submission to management comparing operations of the previous year with those under both proposed plans.

Chapter Twelve

Product Cost Determination and Accumulation

PRODUCT COST DETERMINATION AND ACCUMULATION

Why Inventory?

From one point of view, holding a stock of inventory is "all bad." Capital is invested in inventory, and the company must earn an adequate amount of operating profit on its investments to meet its cost of capital requirements. There are risks that some of the inventory items may never be used or sold. Some, moreover, may be held too long before they are sold. Because of product obsolescence or competitive pressures, some of the inventory items may have to be sold too cheaply to yield an adequate gross profit. Inventory is usually insured against fire and theft, at a cost to the company. On the other hand, some damage and deterioration to inventory is not insurable, and the company must absorb losses of this kind. Determining the optimal inventory policy, and controlling the quantities, locations, and delivery methods and routes are difficult management problems, which require a fair amount of management cost.

Thus it might seem that the ideal solution is to carry no inventory. But this is not practical for several reasons. Most retailers must have products on hand for inspection by customers, and they may have to make immediate delivery. Classical economic theory describes the functions of the retailer as providing *place utility,* and *time utility,* that is, having the right products at the right place at the right times. This and the next two chapters, on the other hand, are concerned with *manufacturers.* The manufacturing process "creates" or "puts together" a product that was not a product before—the product is given *form utility.* Manufacturers carry three basic types of inventory to operate their production process: (1) raw materials, (2) work-in-process, and (3) finished goods. Each is briefly discussed in turn.

Conceivably, a manufacturer could purchase raw materials on a "hand-to-mouth" basis: the raw material items would arrive shortly before they were needed in the manufacturing process such that the company would not have to hold a quantity of raw materials for a period before using them. But in the majority of situations this is not practical. Most manufacturers must accumulate and have on hand a stock of various raw materials. In this way manufacturers provide an adequate and reliable supply of these items, so that the raw materials are available when they are needed without causing any delay or interruption of the manufacturing process. In this sense the raw materials inventory is a *buffer* or *safety reserve,* to insure that the items are available in adequate quantities when needed.

Also, a company may order relatively large quantities of raw materials that provide for one, two, or three months of usage requirements to obtain a lower purchase price per unit which is offered if large quantities are ordered (see Chapter Eleven, pages 370 to 376). The cost savings due to these so-called *quantity discounts* may be more than the costs of carrying an excess inventory, that is, more than just the minimum level of raw materials needed for an adequate safety stock. (This inventory level and order quantity problem is discussed further in Chapter Eleven.) Furthermore, frequently there are delays in delivery of raw materials to the company, or unexpected shortages may develop. A company is not always able to control the time interval between the ordering of raw materials and the actual arrival of the items at its plant. Last, a company sometimes cannot predict exactly when specific raw materials will be needed for future production but, nevertheless, to be sure that the items are available if and when needed, the company will carry a stock of them. In short, almost all manufacturers carry a raw materials inventory equal to several weeks production demand for these items.

In the majority of cases the manufacturing process takes several days, weeks, or perhaps even several months from start to finish. During this period the manufacturing costs of carrying on production operations are accumulated in the *Work-in-Process Inventory* account, which is explained in the following discussion. The manufacturer has no choice but to carry a work-in-process inventory until the manufacturing process is completed and the products are finished. With the exception of those manufacturers who have very short production periods such as a day or less, the company must carry some work-in-process inventory. The longer the production process, the larger the average Work-in-Process Inventory balance.

Generally speaking, manufacturers are not able to sell their product immediately, that is, as soon as the products come off the end of the production line. Some manufacturers produce to order—specific products are manufactured on the basis of a specific order from a customer. In these cases a customer enters into a contract to buy a certain quantity of the company's product. In fact, the customer may even make partial or full payment before the products are delivered. In this situation the sale is assured before the production process begins. This is a common arrangement when a customer *custom orders* products that must be specially designed to his specific demands. The customer may be the only one who purchases this *particular* product from the company. For example, most sales of a printer are custom orders for items such as sales pamphlets, stationery letterhead, and the like.

Most manufacturers, on the other hand, manufacture products *for stock,* which means that the products are manufactured and placed in finished goods inventory and, then, are held in stock for some time awaiting sale. For instance, General Motors manufactures Chevrolets for stock. The products are produced before they are sold, and the company sells from its stock of finished goods inventory. In many industries the average quantity of the finished goods inventory is equal to more than one month of sales, although it is difficult to generalize. The normal finished goods inventory level of a company depends on many factors. Most companies want to avoid a finished goods inventory *stock out* that causes lost sales. Thus most manufacturers carry a finished goods *buffer stock* to meet unexpected surges in sales demand for their products. There is a seasonal fluctuation of sales demand for many products. During slack demand periods many manufacturers produce more units than are sold, so as to create a buildup of finished goods stock to have ready for the peak seasonal demand period.*

In summary, manufacturers hold three basic kinds of inventory: (1) raw materials, (2) work-in-process, and (3) finished goods. These three assets constitute a relatively significant percentage of the total assets of many manufacturers. The following discussion describes how the manufacturing *costs* of these inventories are determined and accumulated in the inventory accounts.

Basic Types of Manufacturing Costs

Although the proportions of each vary from industry to industry, all manufacturers have three basic types of manufacturing costs: (1) raw materials, (2) direct labor, and (3) overhead.

Raw Materials

Raw materials is a fairly broad term referring to all the materials bought by the manufacturer, most of which become part of the finished product. The term "raw" means that *this* company has not yet worked the materials. For example, consider a paper box and container manufacturing company, which purchases paperboard and cardboard from a papermill. To this company the paperboard and cardboard are raw materials that are cut, folded, glued, and stapled to make paper boxes and containers. But to the papermill the paperboard and cardboard are finished products.

Raw materials is a very general and all-inclusive term that covers many different types of items. Examples of raw materials include the following:

1. Natural resources and agricultural products, such as trees, cotton, corn, iron ore.
2. Partly processed materials, such as steel sheets, newsprint, paperboard.
3. Major component and subcomponent parts, such as tires for automobiles, electric motors for appliances.
4. Major subassemblies, such as the truck chassis for a motor home.
5. Various "hardware" items, such as nuts and bolts, screws, and braces.

---

* The implications of this finished goods inventory accumulation during slow sales months on cash flow is discussed in Chapter Eight (see pages 272 to 274).

It is impractical to list all types of raw materials because this would have to be done industry by industry. It should be stressed that, from the accounting point of view, raw materials inventory can be viewed as a special type of prepaid manufacturing cost, which is held in the Raw Materials Inventory account until the items are released to and used in the production process.

Direct Labor

"Direct labor" refers generally to those employees who directly operate the manufacturing machinery and equipment, or who directly handle the raw materials, work-in-process, and finished goods. The key test is whether the work done by a particular person can be clearly identified with the production of a particular product or a specific group of products. For instance, an employee may operate a drill press and the products that pass through this step of the production process can be specifically identified. Thus the drill press operator is accounted for as direct labor. Generally speaking, the majority of production line workers are accounted for as direct labor, although there may be some difficulty in allocating each worker's total time each workday or workweek among the different products manufactured during that period.

Many factory employees, however, do *not* work on the production line. For example, consider the employees who work in the company's warehouse storage area. These employees receive and place in storage raw materials and move the products to the finished goods warehouse after the production process is completed. Are these workers classified as direct labor? Probably not. Theoretically, their time for a week (or some other period) could be allocated to each and every specific raw material item or each and every finished product item handled. But in most situations this is either not practical or such detailed recordkeeping would be too costly. Each employee would spend too much time keeping a record of what items are being handled, and how many minutes (or fraction of a minute) is spent handling the item. *Off production line* employees generally are accounted for as *indirect labor,* that is, labor that cannot be or is not identified with particular products being manufactured. The cost of indirect labor is allocated among the products making up the company's production output during the period by some reasonable method of distribution of these costs. For instance, for every three hours of direct labor worked, the company may need on average one hour of indirect labor. Thus a simple crude method would be to allocate the average cost of one indirect labor hour for every three hours of direct labor spent working on particular products. In contrast, direct labor is attached or matched with individual products or specific groups of products that are being worked on.

Overhead

Overhead costs include all *manufacturing* costs other than raw materials and direct labor. Raw materials and direct labor, as just explained, are the *direct* manufacturing costs that can be associated and identified with particular products as they are being manufactured. But many manufacturing costs cannot be directly associated with particular products. *Overhead* is the catchall term for a company's *indirect* manufacturing costs. A surprisingly large percentage of total production costs include items like the following.

1. Depreciation of the buildings, machinery, equipment, tools, and vehicles used in the manufacturing process, as well as many out-of-pocket costs of ownership and use of these fixed assets, such as property taxes, repair and maintenance, and utilities (electricity, water, gas).

2. Indirect labor, including the off production line employees, supervisory employees, and production managers.

3. General employee related costs, such as the costs of a company's personnel department, safety programs, in-house cafeteria, rest rooms, medical services, uniforms, sick pay, and training programs.

We emphasize that overhead costs must be *manufacturing* costs, that is, costs caused by the production operations of the company, or costs required to provide the production capacity for the period. Nonmanufacturing operating costs are *not* included in this term. A strict line of separation must be drawn between (manufacturing) overhead costs, which are allocated to and included in *product costs,* and nonmanufacturing operating costs, which with few exceptions are treated as *period costs* and expensed in the period recorded. Product costs enter the inventory accounts of the company, whereas period costs go directly into expense accounts (except a few costs that are charged to deferred cost accounts). Costs of advertising products, salesmens' salaries or commissions for selling the products, costs of delivery of the products from the company's warehouse to the customers, costs of filling sales orders, and costs of the middle and top level sales managers are all accounted for as marketing expenses and are not treated as manufacturing costs.

As may be apparent, there are some particular costs that fall in a grey area between where manufacturing ends and selling begins. One such grey area is the costs of packaging finished products. As you are aware, many products are put in a package or some sort of container. Is the cost of the package a manufacturing cost, or more of a selling cost? If the products cannot be sold loose, or must be protected in a package/container, then one could reasonably view the packaging costs as part of the manufacturing cost. What about the printing on the package or container? Some of this printing is for identification only, and thus could be viewed as a manufacturing cost. But some printing is more for sales promotion purposes. Accountants have to draw a line of separation between manufacturing costs and selling costs, even though the separation may be somewhat arbitrary. In any case, the rules of separation should be followed consistently from period to period.

There are also some practical accounting problems of separation of administration and general expenses from manufacturing costs. For instance, should the annual salary of the vice-president of production be included in the manufacturing overhead classification? Or is this an administration and general expense? There are many practical pressures on a company in deciding what is classified as a manufacturing cost. To minimize federal taxable income, managers may prevail on the company's accountants to classify certain costs as current period expenses instead of manufacturing (product) costs. This causes inventory costs to be lower than a reasonable measure of the full or complete cost of manufacturing the products. The evidence suggests that many companies have gone too far in this direction. Recently (1973) the Internal Revenue Service has adopted stricter guidelines which require the inclusion of all overhead costs reasonably related to the manufacturing process.

Summary

Raw materials and direct labor costs together are called the *prime cost* of manufacturing a product. However, this term should not suggest that overhead costs are unnecessary or are secondary in importance. Overhead costs in many instances are just as large, or even larger than either the raw materials or direct labor costs. Manufacturing overhead costs are allocated among all the products making up the total production output for the period. Most prime costs are variable costs, whereas a good part (though not all) of manufacturing overhead costs are fixed costs. The problem of *fixed* overhead costs is very troublesome, and is discussed further at the close of Chapter Thirteen.

The Production Lot: Job Order Compared with Continuous Processing Manufacturing Systems

Seldom is one unit of a product manufactured at a time. This may be true for a very expensive custom-ordered product, such as a luxury yacht which is manufactured to a customer's exact specification under a specific contract. If we investigated how most products are manufactured, we would find that a certain quantity of the product is manufactured each time. In other words, most products are manufactured in groups. The group of products may be the total output over a period of time from a *continuous processing* manufacturing system. Every period the same products are manufactured on a more or less nonstop basis. Or, the group of products may be manufactured as a separate *batch* or *job order.*

Generally, continuous processing manufacturing plants and production lines are special purpose in nature and are relatively efficient for the mass production of the specific products that the facilities are designed to process. On the other hand, job orders are processed in manufacturing plants whose production facilities are more general purpose in nature. They are flexible enough to permit the processing of several different products during one period and to shift between different products from one period to the next. Both types of manufacturing processes are usually organized into *production departments,* each of which performs specialized functions and operations. In the case of job order systems each production department may work on several job orders for different products during one period. Also some jobs may not be worked on by some departments. In the case of continuous processing systems, on the other hand, the production departments are sequentially connected, and the products flow from one department to the next in order. In short, job order system production departments are somewhat independent of one another, whereas continuous processing system production departments are an integrated sequence of manufacturing operations.

A job order (batch) is a group of products that moves through the manufacturing sequence as a separate production unit, and that is physically distinct from other production batches (jobs) of the same product which are manufactured at different times. A job is "ordered" to replenish the stock of finished inventory of the product, or in response to a customer's order for a certain quantity of the product. Job orders (production batches) have a definite start and a definite finish point in the flow of manufacturing operations. The job may be interrupted, and may stand unworked for a time until the employees get back to the job. But just as frequently the job goes "straight through" the production process without a stop. A job order may take only a few days, or it may take months.

In contrast to the "start and finish" nature of job orders, many products are manufactured continuously. The production line never stops turning out these products, although this may not mean that the company operates 24 hours every day of the year. An example of a continuous manufacturing process is the refining of crude oil into gasoline and other petrochemical products. Crude oil is constantly fed into the manufacturing system as raw material, and gasoline and other products keep coming out the other end of the production process on a nonstop basis. In most continuous processing manufacturing systems there are no physically separate groupings, or batches of the products. Instead a more-or-less constant stream of the products comes off the production line. The total output *for a given period of time* is arbitrarily grouped into a "time batch." The manufacturing costs of this time period are matched with the number of units of products processed during this time period.

In summary, most products are manufactured in groups. The group is either a job order, which is a separate batch of products manufactured as a distinct unit; or the group is the output over a certain time period from a continuous processing manufacturing system. The term *production lot* is used in the following discussion to refer to both types of groups—mainly to emphasize that manufacturing costs must be accumulated and matched (or allocated) to each production lot of products, whether produced as a job order or by continuous processing.*

---

* In the company example discussed in Chapters Two to Eight the entire year's output is treated as one production lot, which is an assumption of convenience only. In actual practice, each production lot's costs are determined separately throughout the year.

Basic Cycle of Manufacturing Costs Through the Accounts

The basic cycle of accounting entries for manufacturing costs during a period are shown in Exhibit 12.1. Notice in particular the entries in the following four accounts.

1. *Raw Materials Inventory.* This account holds the purchase cost of raw materials until the items are released into the manufacturing process. In one sense this account is a prepaid manufacturing cost account.

2. *Work-in-Process Inventory.* This account is a cost accumulation holding account, which is used to collect together the various manufacturing costs during the production process. The manufacturing costs stay in this account until the products reach the end of the manufacturing process, that is, until the products are finished. At the point of completion, the total cost of the finished products is removed from this account and is transferred to the Finished Goods Inventory account.

3. *Manufacturing Overhead Costs.* This is a temporary holding and clearing account for the accumulation of actual manufacturing overhead costs during the period. By their very nature these costs are *indirect* costs of manufacturing. Therefore, these costs cannot be directly identified with particular production lots (batches) as the costs are being recorded. Instead, overhead costs are "piled up" in this account first. The total overhead costs for the period is allocated from this account to the production lots worked on during the period.

4. *Finished Goods Inventory.* This account holds the cost of finished (completed) products until the point of sale, at which time the cost of the goods (products) sold is removed from this account and is transferred to the Cost of Goods Sold Expense account. Instead of removing the cost of the item sold *as soon as* sold (which is called the *perpetual* inventory method), a company may wait and make a *summary entry* for all the items sold during the period at the end of the period (which is called the *periodic* inventory method).

The illustrative diagram shown in Exhibit 12.1 is somewhat simplified. Only the basic nature of the key accounts used in recording manufacturing costs are shown. For instance, some manufacturers first charge all their direct labor costs to a *Direct Labor Cost Clearing* account. The costs are then taken out of this account and are charged to specific production lots at a later date. Also Exhibit 12.1 implies that *all* of the total manufacturing overhead costs for the period are allocated to the Work-in-Process Inventory account. As is explained in the next chapter, part of the total overhead cost accumulated in this holding account during the period may *not* be allocated to particular production lots. Unallocated overhead cost is charged off as expense to the period. In any case, all the total overhead cost must be disposed of and removed from the account.

In conclusion, keep in mind that the final total product cost that "ends up"

EXHIBIT 12.1
Basic Cycle of Manufacturing Costs Through the Accounts

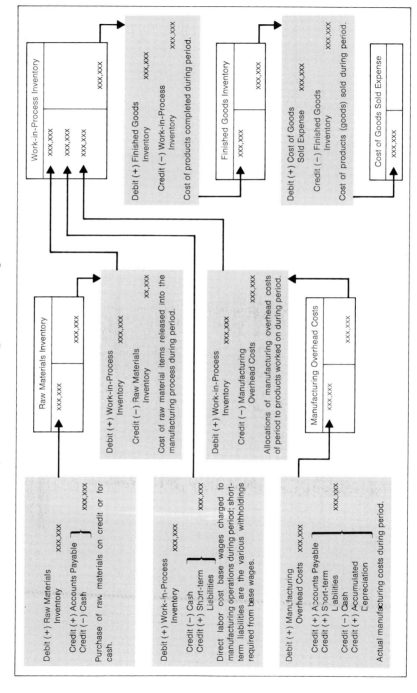

in the Finished Goods Inventory account and from there in the Cost of Goods Sold expense account is a *composite cost* that consists of prime costs, which are directly assigned to each production lot, plus indirect overhead costs, which must be allocated among production lots. Quite clearly the "correctness" of a production lot's total cost depends on: (1) the reliability of the company's cost accounting system in matching the correct and full prime costs with each production lot; and, (2) the reasonableness and fairness of the company's methods of allocating indirect overhead costs among production lots.

Assumption of Reasonably Efficient Manufacturing System to Determine per Unit Product Costs

As we discuss in the preceding section, one of the main purposes of the company's manufacturing cost accounting procedures is to identify the *production lots* being worked on during the period, and to match or to allocate the manufacturing costs to these *product cost accumulation units*. These units are either separate job orders or the total output of the product over the period in the case of a continuous processing manufacturing system. When the products are finished, the total cost of the production lot is divided by the total quantity of products in the lot to determine the *per unit cost* of manufacturing the (finished) product:

$$\frac{\text{Total Cost of Production Lot}}{\text{Total Number of Units in Production Lot}} = \text{Cost per Unit of (Finished) Product}$$

These *per unit product costs* are extremely important information to managers, of course. In other chapters we demonstrate the importance of these per unit product costs. Per unit product costs are compared with budgeted costs (see Chapter Seven), with standard costs (see Chapter Fourteen), and with past period costs (see Chapter Five). Sales price decisions may depend, in part at least, on per unit product costs—what these costs have been, what they are presently, and predictions regarding the future product costs. It is difficult to exaggerate the central importance of per unit product costs for many management decisions. The composition of these product costs—that is, how much is raw material cost, how much is direct labor cost, and how much is overhead—is also important. See, for instance, the management profit performance statements shown as Exhibits 4.1, 4.5, and 6.2.

Unless evidence exists in the contrary, manufacturing cost accounting methods and procedures are based on one critical assumption—that the company's manufacturing process is reasonably efficient, and that there are no unusual and unnecessary wasteful manufacturing operations. In other words, it is assumed that the total manufacturing cost of each production lot *excludes* excessive, wasteful, or unproductive costs. Otherwise the total cost of the production lot would be too high, and consequently the per unit product cost would be too high. This in turn could result in poor management decisions and could cause seriously misleading accounting results.

For instance, assume that the company's cost accountant, without any consideration of the efficiency of the manufacturing operations during the period, accumulates all manufacturing costs for a particular production lot. The accountant then divides this total cost by the total quantity of the lot, which gives a per unit product cost of $15.93. Included in this per unit cost is $6.84 of raw materials cost per unit. Because of several inexperienced workers who are new on their jobs, a substantial amount of the raw materials issued to this production lot were spoiled and had to be thrown away. In fact, about twice as much raw materials were used than are required by normal operations. The cost accountant failed to notice the excessive abnormal raw material usage cost that was charged to this production lot. Thus the total raw material cost in this production lot includes a substantial amount of wasted, or unnecessary raw materials cost. The normal raw material usage cost would be one half of the $6.84 raw materials cost per unit, or only $3.42. The excessive raw material costs should be excluded from the production lot. The per unit product cost should be only $12.51: ($15.93 less the $3.42 wasted raw material cost per unit).

A major manufacturing cost accounting problem is how and where to draw the line between *reasonably* efficient productivity of the manufacturing system and inefficient, wasteful manufacturing performance. In most situations it is unavoidable that a small percentage of the raw materials released to each production lot is "wasted" as a result of cutting, fitting, shrinkage, loss of weight, trimming, and so on, during the manufacturing operations. However, if the raw material wastage exceeds a *normal* percentage of the total raw material input, then the excessive wastage should *not* be charged to the production lot. The excess raw materials wastage cost should be expensed immediately. Unless stated otherwise, the discussion that follows assumes an acceptable level of manufacturing efficiency for raw materials, direct labor, and manufacturing overhead costs during the period (As is explained in Chapter Thirteen, overhead costs are usually the major problem in this regard.)

Recording Raw Materials Purchase and Usage

Recording Purchases

Usually raw materials are bought on credit by manufacturers; cash purchases are not too common. Often the credit terms offered by the supplier include a cash discount for prompt payment. Thus there is the question whether the *gross* (credit) price or the *net* (cash) price should be recorded as the cost of the raw materials. For example, assume that a manufacturer buys a shipment of certain raw materials for a total gross price of $10,000, subject to a 1% discount if paid within 10 days. Therefore, only $9900 would be paid if the shipment is paid within 10 days after receipt of the materials. (Usually the receiving date is the date from which the discount period begins to run, although the date on the purchase invoice may be the first day of the discount period; the purchase invoice date may be a few days before or after the actual receipt of the raw materials by the buyer.)

In this example which cost, $10,000 or $9900, should be recorded as the cost of the raw materials? Prevailing opinion favors the net price as the proper cost. The gross price includes a "penalty" of $100 for late payment, which is more in the nature of a finance cost that should not be charged to the Raw Materials Inventory account. Keep in mind that any cost charged to the Raw Materials Inventory account eventually "ends up" in the Finished Goods Inventory account and becomes part of the total cost of the finished product. Accordingly, the entry for the raw material purchase example is recorded as follows:

Debit (+) Raw Materials Inventory	9900	
Credit (+) Accounts Payable	9900	PURCHASE OF RAW MATERIALS ON CREDIT (NET PURCHASE PRICE RECORDED)
Purchase of raw materials on credit; gross purchase price is $10,000, subject to a 1% discount for prompt payment within 10 days following receipt of shipment; net purchase price recorded.		

Raw materials purchase entries are supported by three main types of source documents: (1) the purchase order, (2) the raw materials receiving report, and (3) the purchase invoice from the vendor (supplier). Accordingly, the company's cost accountant should establish that: (1) the raw materials have been properly ordered by the purchasing agents of the company, who have the authority to place such orders; (2) that the exact quantities and exact items ordered have been received in satisfactory condition; and, (3) that the purchase invoice agrees with the terms of the purchase order and with the quantities of each item actually received. Any differences between these three source documents should be reconciled and explained. For instance, the purchase prices according to the purchase invoice may be higher than the prices shown on the purchase order. This would have to be explained and approved by the purchasing officer before the purchase invoice cost was recorded.

Additional Raw Materials Costs

In most situations the manufacturer incurs several other costs that are related to incoming shipments of raw materials. One obvious cost is the transportation-in cost, if paid by the manufacturer (who is the buyer). Raw materials may be bought FOB (Free On Board) *destination point,* in which case the transportation cost is paid by the seller (supplier) and the delivery cost is included in the purchase price of the raw materials. Alternatively, raw materials may be bought FOB *shipping point,* which means that the manufacturer (buyer) pays the transportation costs to bring the raw materials to the company's location. The transportation cost of the shipment is easy enough to identify with the shipment. But one shipment may consist of several *different* raw materials items that are grouped together into one shipment to minimize transportation costs.

In this case, the allocation of the total freight cost of the shipment among the several different raw material items making up the shipment may take some time and may have to be somewhat arbitrary. For instance, the total freight bill may be based on the total weight of the shipment. This suggests that the weight of each lot of raw material items included in the shipment should be determined, so that if one kind of raw materials accounts for, say, 10% of the total shipment weight, then these raw material items should be allocated 10% of the total transportation cost. Obviously, this may not be very practical in many situations. Even if it were practical, it would take time, and the manufacturer may decide that the allocation effort is not worth it.

In short, transportation-in costs of raw materials shipments are *not* charged to the Raw Materials Inventory account in many (perhaps most) situations. These inbound freight costs are therefore charged immediately to an expense account. This accounting treatment understates the full cost of the raw materials, and thus understates the full cost of the finished product. One conceivable alternative is to charge transportation-in costs to the Manufacturing Overhead Cost account. The total of all overhead costs is allocated to the various production lots worked on during the period. In this manner the transportation costs would find their way into the cost of finished products.

Several other costs are related to raw material acquisition, in addition to transportation-in costs. The manufacturer may pay an insurance premium cost to cover raw materials shipments while in transit. Also there are more indirect costs, such as the salary of the purchasing officers who place the purchase orders. Generally speaking, few (if any) of these additional costs are charged directly to the Raw Materials Inventory account. The recorded cost of raw materials is generally the (net) purchase price. Some of the additional raw materials' costs may be charged to the Manufacturing Overhead Costs account. But probably most of the additional costs related to raw material purchases simply are expensed immediately when paid or accrued.

Releasing Raw Materials to Production—FIFO, LIFO, or Average Cost?

When raw materials are released to the manufacturing process, an accounting entry is made to remove the cost of raw materials from the Raw Materials Inventory account and to charge this cost to the Work-in-Process Inventory account. Determining which and how many units of each raw materials item are released to production is not an accounting problem. A raw materials requisition form is prepared, which contains all these details as well as identifying specifically to which job orders the raw materials are being charged. In the case of continuous processing production systems the cost of raw materials is charged to the particular production department requisitioning the materials. In some situations only the first production department requisitions raw materials, but usually two or more departments are issued raw materials. In any event, the total raw material cost of the finished products includes the raw materials costs charged to all production departments to which raw materials are issued during the production process.

It should be emphasized that the Work-in-Process Inventory account is a *summary* account that records *all* of the company's manufacturing costs during the period. The charges to this summary account are supported by *detailed* cost records for each separate job order (or for each production department, as the case may be). The relationship between the Work-in-Process Inventory account and the detailed cost record for a job order manufacturing system is illustrated

EXHIBIT 12.2
Recording Cost of Raw Materials Issued to Production

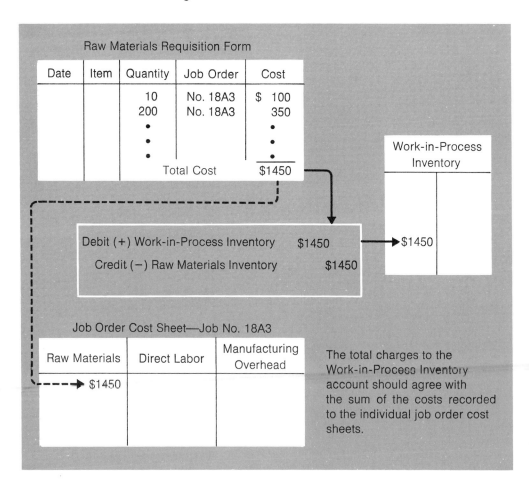

Raw Materials Requisition Form				
Date	Item	Quantity	Job Order	Cost
		10	No. 18A3	$ 100
		200	No. 18A3	350
		•		•
		•		•
		•		•
		Total Cost		$1450

Debit (+) Work-in-Process Inventory $1450
   Credit (−) Raw Materials Inventory $1450

Work-in-Process Inventory

$1450

Job Order Cost Sheet—Job No. 18A3		
Raw Materials	Direct Labor	Manufacturing Overhead
$1450		

The total charges to the Work-in-Process Inventory account should agree with the sum of the costs recorded to the individual job order cost sheets.

in Exhibit 12.2, which shows how raw material cost is charged to a job order. The *job order cost sheet* accumulates all the details of the manufacturing costs identified with or allocated to each specific job order. In short, no cost is charged to the Work-in-Process Inventory account without the same cost being entered on a job order cost sheet (or in a departmental cost summary report in the case of continuous processing manufacturing systems).

A major accounting question regarding the recording of the cost of raw materials released into production is usually studied in the introductory accounting course. There are three generally accepted inventory "charge-out" methods— FIFO (first-in, first-out), LIFO (last-in, first-out), and Average Cost. For an example see Exhibit 12.3, which shows the inventory cost record for a particular raw material item. Based on the information in this inventory record, we can determine that the company purchased 3600 units during the year for a total cost of $37,324.50. It is assumed that no units were on hand at the start of the year, to simplify the example. (The beginning inventory, if there had been any, would be valued at a per unit cost according to the inventory accounting method already adopted by the company.) The purpose of this example is to compare the three different inventory accounting methods, and it is convenient not to have a beginning inventory carry forward.

EXHIBIT 12.3
Raw Material Item Example

	Purchases					Requisitions			
Date	Order No.	Quantity	Cost per Unit	Total Cost	Date	Requisition No.	Quantity	Cost per Unit	Total Cost
1-18	A36	500	$ 9.43	$ 4,715.00					
3-28	A146	250	9.52	2,380.00	4-27	563	550		
6-16	A381	1,000	10.18	10,180.00	7-8	941	1,050		
9-14	A516	650	10.63	6,909.50	10-14	1801	575		
11-8	A817	1,200	10.95	13,140.00	11-19	2043	1,150		

Generally speaking, raw materials cost should be charged out as soon as the items are released to the manufacturing process, although a company's cost accounting system may be designed to permit the periodic recording of raw materials usage cost over an entire month instead of for each requisition. It is assumed that the manufacturer makes a cost removal entry each time raw materials are requisitioned, which is called the perpetual inventory method.

We may consider the FIFO inventory method first, since it appears from the inventory record (Exhibit 12.3) that the company buys raw materials in anticipation of their immediate future need for this item. Although the purchase quantities are not exactly paired off with the requisition quantities, clearly there is a "purchase—then—requisition" sequence. According to the FIFO method, the cost of raw materials released to production in the first (April 27) requisition would be determined as follows:

Determination of Raw Materials Cost Charged to April 27 Requisition by FIFO Method

500 units from the January 18 purchase lot	
@ $9.43 per unit for a total of	$4715.00
50 units from the March 28 purchase lot	
@ $9.52 per unit for a total of	476.00
550 units from the two purchase lots for a total cos. of	$5191.00

Immediately after the April 27 requisition, the FIFO method would leave in the Raw Materials Inventory account the remainder of the March 28 purchase lot, which is $1904 (200 units × $9.52). This remaining cost balance from the March 28 purchase lot then becomes next in line for removal, which in this example would be assigned to the July 8 requisition. And so on during the year.

According to the Average Cost Method the raw materials cost to charge to the April 27 requisition is determined differently. At the point of requisition, that is, at April 27, the company has a stock of 750 units of this particular raw material item, and the total cost of these 750 units is $7095. Dividing the two gives an average cost of $9.46 per unit ($7095/750 units = $9.46 per unit). This average cost per unit is charged to the April 27 requisition, which gives a total cost removal of $5203 (550 units × $9.46 = $5203). Notice that this cost is $12 more than the FIFO method shown above ($5203 Average Cost − $5191 FIFO = $12).

According to the LIFO inventory method the cost of the raw materials to charge to the April 27 requisition is determined as follows:

Determination of Raw Materials Cost Charged to April 27 Requisition by LIFO Method

250 units from the March 28 purchase lot	
@ $9.52 per unit for a total of	$2380.00
300 units from the January 18 purchase lot	
@ 9.43 per unit for a total of	2829.00
550 units from the two purchase lots for a total cost of	$5209.00

The remainder of the first (January 18) purchase lot is $1886 (200 units @ $9.43 per unit = $1,886); this amount would be left in the Raw Materials Inventory account. This remainder becomes the oldest and thus the last purchase lot to be "reached back to " according to the LIFO method. For the next requisition of 1050 units on July 8 the company would first charge out the cost of the 1000 units purchased on June 16, and then would reach back for only 50 units from the January 18 purchase lot. It is apparent that the LIFO method results in a cost removal for the April 27 requisition that is $18 more than FIFO ($5209 LIFO − $5191 FIFO = $18).

Which inventory method is best? Accountants do not agree on the answer to this question. If a company were to buy raw materials on a true hand-to-mouth basis, that is, if all of the quantity of one purchase is released to production before any more of the same raw material item is purchased, then all three inventory accounting methods (when applied on the perpetual basis) would give the same result. There would be *only one* raw material per unit cost at each date of requisition. More typically, a company will make another purchase of the same item before its stock of this raw material item is completely depleted. Indeed, a company may build up a large stock of it in anticipation of future needs. If the raw material purchase prices are significantly different from one purchase to the next, then the choice between the raw material inventory accounting methods may cause a significant difference over a year in how much total raw materials cost is charged out to the job orders (or to the production departments).

Remember that the cost of the finished products manufactured during the year is directly affected by the choice of which raw materials inventory accounting method is adopted. Managers should be very aware of this. If, for example, the manager thinks that the latest (most recent) raw material purchase costs should be included in the finished product cost, then LIFO is the clear choice. On the other hand, the FIFO method usually corresponds more closely to the actual physical in- and outflow of the raw materials. If raw material purchase prices bounce up and down, then the Average Cost method has the advantage of smoothing out the fluctuations. There are many other arguments for and against each of the three inventory methods. Sometimes it is argued that the choice of which inventory method to adopt only concerns the historical cost valuation of inventory for the preparation of the company's external financial statements and its income tax returns. It is pointed out that for most management decisions either current or future raw material costs are more relevant, which certainly is true. But, in fact, a company's *internal* management profit performance reports also are prepared on the historical cost basis. Hence, the choice of raw material inventory method to adopt affects *both* the internal and the external measurement and reporting of inventory cost values and profit performance.

Once the raw materials inventory method has been decided on, the following basic entry is made to record the release of raw materials to production, in this example for the April 27 requisition, assuming the FIFO method:

Debit (+) Work-in-Process Inventory	5191.00		RELEASE OF
Credit (−) Raw Materials Inventory		5191.00	RAW MATERIALS
Cost of raw materials released to production			TO PRODUCTION

Two other points regarding the recording of raw materials usage cost deserve brief mention. As discussed above, if more than a reasonably normal amount of raw materials are charged to a job order, then the cost of *excessive* amounts of raw materials used to complete the products should be removed from the Work-in-Process Inventory account. The excessive raw material wastage cost should be expensed, instead of being included in the cost of the finished product. Occasionally some of the raw materials requisitioned to a job order may later be returned to the warehouse because these items were not needed to complete the job order. In this situation the reverse of the entry shown above should be made for *that part* of the original requisition being returned. The cost of the raw materials being returned would be debited (+) to the Raw Materials Inventory account and the Work-in-Process Inventory would be credited (−) the same amount.

Recording Direct Labor Cost

Gross Wage Cost

As explained previously, direct labor refers basically to production line workers, that is, those employees who work directly on the products at various steps in the flow of the manufacturing operations. A manufacturer keeps very detailed data on the hours worked by each employee during each period and the specific job orders or production departments to which the hours should be charged. Individual time cards are kept to record the specific starting times and stopping times each working day for each employee. Many other types of labor forms and records are prepared to determine exactly how many direct labor hours of each employee or group of employees (such as a work station) should be charged to each job order. In continuous processing manufacturing systems, direct labor costs are determined for each production department through which the products flow.

The company's accounting department calculates the *gross wages* earned during each payroll period by each production line employee (as well as all other employees). For hourly paid employees the correct wage rate per hour is multiplied by the number of hours worked. Some hours may be paid at a higher rate, such as overtime hours worked or second shift hours. In addition to the weekly time cards, an employer needs to maintain quite detailed year-to-date earnings' records for each employee. The proper amount of OASDI (Old Age, Survivors, and Disability Insurance) federal tax to withhold from each employee's gross pay for the current period depends on the employee's cumulative wages earned thus far during the year. If an employee is already over the maximum earnings limit for the year, then no further OASDI tax should be withheld. On the other hand, if the employee's cumulative earnings are less than this cutoff limit, then the current period's gross wage amount is subject to this tax, which must be withheld from the employee's gross pay. To determine the proper amount of federal income tax to withhold from each employee's gross wages, the manufacturer (employer) needs to know how many personal exemptions are claimed by the employee. Usually this information is kept on the year-to-date earnings' record for each employee, rather than on the employee's time card for each pay period. There are several other required withholdings from most employees' gross wages that also depend on the information maintained in the year-to-date employees' records.

In most situations the calculation of the gross pay for each employee is fairly straightforward, assuming, of course, that the direct labor source documents contain all the needed data and that these data are accurate. And, the assignment (distribution) of the gross-pay amounts to particular job orders or to specific production departments is not a major problem. The following entry shows the basic nature of recording direct labor cost for a period:

Debit (+) Work-in-Process Inventory   xxx,xxx.xx

    Credit (−) Cash   xxx,xxx.xx GROSS

    Credit (+) OASDI Tax Payable   xx,xxx.xx WAGES
OF DIRECT

    Credit (+) Withheld Income Tax Payable   xx,xxx.xx LABOR FOR

Recording direct labor cost during period. (There   PERIOD
may be several other accounts credited.)

It should be mentioned again that an entry to the Work-in-Process Inventory (summary) account also requires corresponding "entries" in the individual job order cost sheets for the jobs worked on during the payroll period. Or, in the case of continuous processing systems, each departmental cost summary for the period is charged with its part of the total direct labor cost. The amount of gross wage cost being charged to each job order is entered in the direct labor column of each job order cost sheet (see Exhibit 12.2 for a general illustration of a job order cost sheet). The total debit (increase) to Work-in-Process Inventory account equals the sum of all the "entries" to the specific job order cost sheets, or to specific production departments as the case may be.

One accounting problem is concerned with the likelihood that some direct laborers may have some unassigned time during the payroll period. There may be a certain number of hours paid for that were nonproductive ("dead time"), which cannot be charged to any specific production lots. A certain amount of unassigned time is not unusual, or at least is not unusual for some employees out of a company's total direct labor work force. For instance, there may be production line breakdowns and some employees are paid to "stand around" and wait until the production line is started up again. Or, as a result of poor production scheduling, some of the direct labor employees may not be kept fully busy on production line work during the period. It can be argued that the cost of a *normal* amount of such nonproductive time should be charged to the Manufacturing Overhead Costs account, which in turn is allocated to the Work-in-Process Inventory account (see Chapter Thirteen). However, if there is an excessive number of nonproductive direct labor hours during the period, the cost of these abnormal direct labor hours should be charged to expense in the period the hours are paid.

Additional Direct Labor Costs

A major manufacturing cost accounting problem is the measurement of the several additional supplementary costs of direct labor employees, and the allocation of these costs to specific job orders or to particular production departments. These supplementary labor costs are sometimes called "fringe benefits," but the term *fringe* is a poor choice of words. Most of these supplementary labor costs have become rather permanent and would be difficult, if not impossible, to eliminate. For example, consider federal and state payroll taxes, in particular social security (OASDI) and unemployment taxes. The employer must match the amount of OASDI tax withheld from employees. In 1975, for example, the first $14,100 of wages was subject to a tax of 5.85% on the employee *and* an equal tax of 5.85% on the employer. Hence, for each employee earning $14,100 or more over the year, the company pays an employment tax of $824.85. Also most employers are subject to the joint federal-state unemployment tax, which is a maximum of 4.2% on the first $4200 of wages of each employee that is paid *entirely* by the employer. None of this tax is deducted from the employees' gross wages.

There are many other fringe benefit labor costs paid in whole or in part by employers. Most manufacturers are required to carry workmen's compensation insurance, which provides insurance payments to employees injured or disabled from work-related causes. Many manufacturing companies, either voluntarily or as a provision of a labor union contract, have established retirement and pension plans for eligible employees. Normally a company's contribution in these plans is a significant percentage of the employees' gross wages each period. A company may pay for all or part of a group accident and health insurance policy covering its employees and their dependents (beyond workmen's compensation insurance coverage). The company may provide free parking space for its employees, which may have to be guarded. Some in-house medical services may be provided at no cost to the employees. Many other fringe benefits could be listed. In summary, it is not unusual for these supplementary (fringe) labor costs to add up to 20 or 30% of the gross wages earned by the employees.

The major question facing the cost accountant, once the costs of various fringe benefits are determined, is how to allocate them to production lots being worked on. For example, assume that last week 5.2 hours worked by Jerome Scott, a production line employee, is assigned to Job Order No. 34C-823. Thus 5.2 hours of Jerry's gross wage for the period would be charged to this particular job order. If Jerry earns a base wage rate of $4.50 per hour, then $23.40 of his gross wage for the period should be charged to this job order ($4.50 × 5.2 hours = $23.40). What about the supplementary fringe benefit costs of these 5.2 hours worked by Jerry? It is tempting to assume that all these fringe benefits' costs could be reduced to a simple average cost per hour, for instance, an additional $0.97 per hour for Jerry. But, in fact, many supplementary labor costs are *indirect* costs, such as the costs of providing parking for employees or those of providing medical services. Therefore, many of the supplementary labor costs are charged to the Manufacturing Overhead Cost account. The total overhead costs for the period are allocated to the separate job orders (or production departments). We consider the allocation of manufacturing overhead costs in the next chapter where we also discuss the recording of the completion of products and other manufacturing accounting topics.

Questions

12. 1 What are the disadvantages of holding inventory?

12. 2 Why do manufacturers carry an inventory of raw materials?

12. 3 Which company's normal Work-in-Process Inventory balance would be larger: Caterpillar Tractor Company who manufactures bulldozers and heavy earth moving equipment, or General Mills who manufactures breakfast cereal and packaged food products? Why?

12. 4 (a) What is the typical ratio of finished goods inventory quantity divided by a company's sales volume?
     (b) What is the reverse (or reciprocal) of this ratio called?

12. 5 Which is more serious: a finished goods inventory stock out, or an excessive inventory of finished goods?

12. 6 (a) Consider the last pair of shoes you purchased. What are the main raw material items the shoe manufacturer purchased to make the shoes?
     (b) Is the box the shoes came in a manufacturing cost or a selling expense? What difference would this accounting decision make?

12. 7 Assume that a brewery "manufactures" only one brand of beer, although this beer is sold in barrels to taverns and in bottles and cans in different sizes through distributors for purchases by individuals.
     (a) In this case, is the distinction between direct and indirect labor important as far as determining the cost of brewing the beer up to the point of putting the beer into barrels, bottles, or cans?
     (b) Would the distinction between direct and indirect labor be important in determining the costs of bottling, canning, or "barreling" the beer?

12. 8 Given the increasing trend toward automation, is there a shift away from prime costs to overhead costs? Briefly explain.

12. 9 "All overhead costs are fixed costs." Do you agree? If not, identify two or three examples of *variable* overhead costs.

12.10 What are the differences between products manufactured in job orders and in continuous processing systems?

12.11 Sometimes the term *conversion cost* is used to refer to certain manufacturing costs. This term is *not* defined in the chapter, but what do you think the term means?

12.12 Which are the four key accounts used to record manufacturing costs, and what is the basic nature of each account?

12.13 What is one key assumption made in determining *per unit* product (manufacturing) costs? What are the effects if this assumption is not true?

12.14 Why is the net purchase price of raw materials the preferred cost to record instead of the gross price?

12.15 What is the basic nature and purpose of the *job order cost sheet*?

12.16 Name one advantage and one disadvantage of each of the three generally acceptable raw material inventory methods.

12.17 Assume that all job orders in the company's production plant pass through the company's Inspection Department, which is the last step in the manufacturing process. In general terms, how would the direct labor cost of this production department be assigned to different job orders worked on during a week?

12.18 (a) What are some of the major "fringe benefits" costs of direct labor employees?
      (b) Can these supplementary direct labor costs be easily allocated to specific job orders or to particular production departments?

Problems

P12. 1 Imagine, if you would, a manufacturing process that requires no manufacturing overhead costs—none at all. Admittedly this is not very realistic. But since the accounting procedures for manufacturing overhead costs are not discussed until the next chapter, assume for this problem that the only manufacturing costs are raw materials and direct labor. In other words, the prime costs are the total manufacturing costs in this problem.

During the calendar year just ended the company completed four job orders for a particular product as follows:

Job Order No.	Number of Units Manufactured	Date Job Order Completed
13A	100 units	March 31
13B	150 units	June 30
13C	100 units	September 30
13D	150 units	December 31

To simplify, it is assumed that only one raw material item is required in the manufacture of this product, and that only one direct labor operation is required. (In most situations, of course, several different raw materials are needed, and many direct labor operations are required.) The raw material item is used only to manufacture this particular product. The raw material inventory stock record for the year is shown below; notice that no cost amounts have been removed from the account (this is part of the problem). The abbreviations in the stock records are as follows: JO = job order; Req. = requisition; Sup. Req. = supplemental requisition.

Raw Materials Inventory Item		
1- 1 Beginning Balance	450 lb @ $0.50 = $225.00	
7- 7 Purchase	600 lb @ 0.50 = 300.00	2- 6 Req. to JO 13A 1000 lb
2-18 Purchase	200 lb @ 0.55 = 110.00	3-20 Sup. Req. to JO 13A 50 lb
4-25 Purchase	1,600 lb @ 0.45 = 720.00	5- 9 Req. to JO 13B 1500 lb
6- 9 Purchase	500 lb @ 0.55 = 275.00	6-19 Sup. Req. to JO 13B 160 lb
7-13 Purchase	700 lb @ 0.60 = 420.00	8-12 Req. to JO 13C 1000 lb
10- 2 Purchase	1,400 lb @ 0.70 = 980.00	11-20 Req. to JO 13D 1500 lb
11-21 Purchase	400 lb @ 0.75 = 300.00	12-27 Sup. Req. to JO 13D 100 lb

When recording the weekly payroll, the company does not yet know how the direct labor cost will be distributed among all the job orders worked on during the period. Thus the company first accumulates direct labor costs into an account called "Direct Labor Cost Clearing Account." Based on the direct labor cost distribution summary prepared for each period the appropriate amount of direct labor cost is removed from the clearing account and charged to work-in-process for each job order.

From the company's direct labor cost distribution summaries, the direct labor charges assigned to the four job orders in this problem are as follows:

Job Order No.	Total Direct Labor Cost
13A	220 hours @ $6.25 per hour = $1375.00
13B	280 hours @ 6.50 per hour = 1820.00
13C	195 hours @ 6.60 per hour = 1287.00
13D	315 hours @ 6.75 per hour = 2126.25

From the accounting records maintained for each finished good, the beginning inventory and the quantity sold of the particular product in this problem are as follows for the year:

Beginning inventory: 100 units @ $16.50   = $1,650.00
Sales by Quarters:
    Three months ending March 31   =   90 units
    Three months ending June 30   =   80 units
    Three months ending September 30   =   170 units
    Three months ending December 31   =   100 units

Required: In general journal form prepare a summary entry for each quarter (three months) during the year to record the following:

(1) The issuance of raw materials to the job orders (the purchases of raw materials during the year do not have to be recorded),
(2) The direct labor cost assigned to the job orders,
(3) The completion of the job orders, and
(4) The sales of the finished products that is, the cost of goods sold).

(*Note:* The company has adopted the FIFO method for all its inventory accounting.)

P12. 2 This problem is continued from Problem 12.1. You need to refer to your answers from Problem 12.1 to do this problem.

Required:

(1) Would LIFO be equally acceptable in this situation as far as you can tell from the information given in the problem?
(2) If the company had used LIFO for charging out raw materials cost and for recording the cost of goods sold, determine in the quickest manner possible (without making a complete series of entries) how much different the LIFO results would have been compared with the FIFO results. Since the LIFO cost values of the beginning inventories are not given, assume that these are the same as the cost values given in Problem 12.1.
(3) The company has 160 units of finished goods (of this particular product) on hand in inventory at December 31. Looking ahead over the next three months, the production manager predicts that the raw material needed to manufacture this product will increase to $1 per pound, and that the direct labor cost will increase to $7.25 per hour. The president of the company, based on these forecasts, is concerned that the historical cost value of the ending inventory at December 31 determined by the FIFO method is a poor indicator of the replacement cost of the 160 units. In fact, he asks (orders?) the company's accountant to give some sort of recognition to the replacement cost. In talking with the president, the accountant clearly realizes that the president favors "replacement cost accounting," which means that the replacement cost (as best as can be estimated) is taken into account before any profit for the year is recognized.

Required: If you were the company's accountant, what action would you take in this situation?

P12. 3 Refer to the raw materials example shown in Exhibit 12.3. The purpose of this problem is to determine the total raw material cost that would be charged out to production during the year (either to specific job orders or to particular production departments). Notice that the raw materials cost charged out to the first requisition already has been determined in the discussion in the chapter (see pages 413 and 414). Therefore, you should determine the cost to be charged out to the remaining three requisitions during the year.

Required: Determine the raw materials cost that should be charged to the second, third, and fourth requisitions shown in the example:
(1) According to the FIFO method,
(2) According to the moving average cost method, and
(3) According to the LIFO method.

P12. 4 (1) A company puts its product in a very expensive package, which actually costs more than the total cost of raw materials, direct labor, and manufacturing overhead costs of the product. The company accounts for all packaging costs as a marketing (selling) cost, not as a product cost. Packaging costs are expensed as soon as recorded, and they are not included in the inventory cost value of the product. For this product, certain information for the year just ended is as follows:

Finished Goods	Number of Units	Raw Materials, Direct Labor, and Overhead Costs	Packaging Costs
Beginning inventory	10,000	$ 4,500	
Units manufactured during year	52,000	23,400	$33,800
Ending inventory	12,000	5,400	

Required:
(1) Determine how much different the company's operating profit for the year just ended would be if the packaging costs were treated as a product cost instead of by the company's present accounting method.
(2) For each product's package listed below, indicate whether the cost of the package should be accounted for as a product (manufacturing) cost or as a marketing (selling) cost:
(a) The tube for toothpaste.
(b) The "dust jacket" for a new book.
(c) A rather large cardboard "blister pack" holding a small box of razor blades.

(d) An egg carton for a dozen eggs.

(e) The styrofoam mold encasement that holds hi-fi equipment in place securely in the shipping box.

P12. 5 This company manufactures one basic product continuously in its one plant by by operating one shift (eight working hours) five days (Monday to Friday) each week during the year. Because the company is relatively small and has only one manufacturing plant, the production process is *not* divided into separate departments. The company accumulates raw material purchase costs in the raw materials inventory accounts during the year, but it does not record the cost of raw materials used until the end of the year. The company uses two raw materials in manufacturing its product. The two raw materials inventory accounts during the year ending December 31, 1976 contain the following purchase entries:

Raw Material—Item A				Raw Material—Item B			
Explanation		Debits	Credits	Explanation		Debits	Credits
Beginning Balance	1,000 units	$ 3,000		Beginning Balance	4,200 units	$10,080	
2/16/76	2,500 units	8,125		1/18/76	7,500 units	17,250	
5/28/76	3,450 units	11,730		3/ 8/76	8,100 units	17,415	
9/ 8/76	3,200 units	11,520		5/27/76	7,800 units	16,068	
11/29/76	3,400 units	13,090		7/31/76	8,400 units	16,380	
				10/ 3/76	9,000 units	17,100	
				12/ 8/76	8,600 units	15,910	

At December 31, 1976 the company makes a physical count of each raw material item actually on hand, which gives the following data:

Raw Material—Item A	1400 units
Raw Material—Item B	5000 units

As you can see from the two inventory accounts, no entries have been made during the year to record the cost of raw materials used in the manufacturing process during the year. Based on its ending inventory count of raw materials, the company records the total cost of raw materials used during the entire year.

For the entire year the company completed and transferred to the finished goods warehouse 12,000 units of product. The beginning work-in-process inventory consisted of 1500 units of product which were 100% complete regarding raw material cost, since both raw materials are issued to production as the first step in the manufacturing process and no further raw materials are added during the manufacturing process. The ending work-in-process inventory consists of 1650 units of product which are also 100% complete regarding raw material cost.

Required: For 1976, determine the total cost to remove from each raw material inventory account for the raw materials used in 1976, and determine the average raw material cost per unit of finished product according to:

(1) The FIFO method of charging out raw material cost.
(2) The LIFO method of charging out raw material cost.
(3) The average cost method of charging out raw material cost.

P12. 6 The total direct labor cost by each quarter for the year ending December 31, 1976 of this company is as follow:

First quarter	$2,500,000
Second quarter	$2,550,000
Third quarter	$2,601,000
Fourth quarter	$2,653,020

From a detailed analysis of the direct labor costs and production activity during 1976, you determine the following:

(a) Exactly the same number of labor hours were worked each quarter during the year.
(b) A cost of living escalator clause in the company's union contract required the company to increase every employee's hourly wage rate by 2.0% each quarter; these increases went into effect on the first day of each quarter.
(c) The total number of completed units produced each quarter (there is no work-in-process) is as follows:

First quarter	1,000,000 units
Second quarter	1,010,000 units
Third quarter	1,020,100 units
Fourth quarter	1,030,301 units

Required:

(1) Determine whether increases in the company's direct labor productivity from quarter to quarter is enough to offset the labor wage rate increases. Prove your conclusion by computing the direct labor cost per unit of finished product each quarter.

(2) Assume that the company's finished goods (products) ending inventory increased from 1,000,000 units at December 31, 1975 to 1,030,301 units at December 31, 1976. (Remember that there is no work-in-process inventory.) The finished goods inventory at December 31, 1975 included $2,500,000 of direct labor cost. Determine the amount of direct labor cost that would be charged to the cost of products completed during the year according to:

(a) The LIFO method.

(b) The FIFO method.

Also, determine the amount of direct labor cost that would be included in the company's ending finished goods inventory at December 31, 1976 by each method.

P12. 7 This company has been in the business of manufacturing a variety of products for just two years, that is, during 1975 and 1976. Last year (1975), during the first year of business, the company decided to adopt the FIFO inventory method. Accordingly, the ending inventories of finished goods and work-in-process are determined from the cost of the most recent production lots of each product manufactured. The company's 1976 management net income report through the gross profit line is shown in summary as follows:

NET INCOME REPORT
FOR THE YEAR ENDING DECEMBER 31, 1976

Sales revenue			$1,850,000
Cost of goods sold:			
Beginning work-in-process inventories		$ 64,799	
Manufacturing costs during year:			
Raw materials	$478,170		
Direct labor	614,790		
Overhead	273,240	1,366,200	
Total		$1,430,999	
Ending work-in-process inventories		68,310	
Cost of goods completed		$1,362,689	
Beginning finished goods inventories		194,397	
Total cost of goods available for sale		$1,557,086	
Ending finished goods inventories		204,930	
Cost of goods sold			$1,352,156
Gross profit			$ 497,844

The ending quantity and mix of finished goods and work-in-process inventories at December 31, 1975 and December 31, 1976 are virtually the same. The higher cost value of the 1976 ending inventories is attributable entirely to higher manufacturing costs in 1976 than the year before. Top management of the company has just decided to switch to the LIFO inventory method, and has asked you to determine what the LIFO inventory values would be for the December 31, 1976 inventories. Rather than going back and examining in detail all the job order cost sheets for the different products, management first wants you to make a quick estimate of how much different the LIFO cost values would be. If the difference is significant enough, then management will probably authorize the more detailed cost analysis to put each product on a precise LIFO cost basis. To estimate the total LIFO cost value for the ending inventories at December 31, 1976, management supplies this information regarding manufacturing costs during the late part of 1976 compared with the early part of 1975:

(a) Raw material purchase costs on average are 12.5% higher in 1976. But raw material productivity on average improved by 4.0%. For instance, if a product required 100 pounds of raw materials in early 1975, it requires only 96 pounds in late 1976.

(b) Direct labor costs on average increased by 25.0% in 1976, but because of a rather significant "learning curve" effect, direct labor efficiency improved by 8.0% in 1976. For instance, if a product required 100 hours in early 1975, it requires only 92 hours in late 1976.

(c) Manufacturing overhead costs in 1976 on average are 10.0% higher than in 1975.

Required: Based on the above information, determine the LIFO cost value estimate of the company's beginning and ending inventories of work-in-process and finished goods in 1976.

(*Note:* Assume that the composition of manufacturing costs in the inventories are in the same proportion as the company's 1976 manufacturing costs shown in the net income report presented above.)

P12. 8 Presented below are *summaries* of the debit entries and credit entries to certain accounts of a manufacturer during the year just ended, with the beginning balances indicated in each account if appropriate. These debit and credit summary amounts for the year are normal routine entries; there are no unusual or abnormal entries during the year. (Year-end closing entries have *not* been made yet.)

Raw Materials Inventory		Work-in-Process Inventory	
Beginning		Beginning	
Balance 35,000		Balance 48,300	
280,000		265,000	
	265,000	315,000	
		186,700	761,800

Direct Labor Costs Clearing Account		Manufacturing Overhead Costs	
315,000	315,000	186,700	186,700

Finished Goods Inventory		Cost of Goods Sold	
Beginning			
Balance 86,400		762,900	
761,800			
	762,900		

Required: Prepare the cost of goods section of the company's net income statement for the year. See Exhibit 2.2 for the recommended format of this section.

P12. 9 The cost sheet for a job order begun and completed during the year just ended shows the following:

Explanation	Raw Materials	Direct Labor	Overhead
Requisition of Jan. 10, 1976	$ 89,570		
Payroll ending Jan. 31, 1976		$ 45,050	$ 13,515
Supplemental requisition of February 18, 1976	24,380		
Payroll ending February 28, 1976		46,110	13,833
Supplemental requisition of March 23, 1976	19,610		
Payroll ending March 31, 1976		29,680	8,904
Payroll ending April 30, 1976		8,480	2,544
Totals	$133,560	$129,320	$ 38,796

Total units manufactured: 10,600
Number of units rejected: 600

Units transferred to
finished goods warehouse: 10,000

The raw material requisitions are for those raw materials items required and used to process this job order, of course. The direct labor costs are based on the hours of those employees working on this job order each month the job was in process; all direct labor costs are accumulated during each month, and at the end of the month they are distributed to the job orders. To simplify, it is assumed that overhead costs are allocated to job orders based on a certain percentage of the direct labor costs assigned to the job order. At the end of the year, 2500 of the units produced by this job order are in the company's ending finished goods inventory, and 7500 units have been sold.

Required:

(1) Assuming that the raw material usage and the direct labor hours required to process the job order are within normal limits, and assuming that the rejection ratio is also within a normal range, determine the correct cost value of the ending inventory of the products manufactured by this job order and the cost of the units sold.

(2) Assume that appropriate entries were made during the year based on your costs determined in part (1). At the end of the year, there is a review of all manufacturing costs. This review reveals that during the first four months of the year several new employees were being trained on the job, and that as a result raw material wastage was 10.0% over normal and that labor efficiency was 5.0% below normal. Since this job order was processed during this period, the company's Controller approves an adjustment in the cost of the products manufactured by the job order. Based on the above information, make the adjusting entry needed at year-end, and determine the adjusted cost per unit of the products manufactured by this job order. Show your computations clearly.

(3) Instead of the inefficiencies assumed in part (2), assume that by year-end, as compared with the early part of the year, the company had made several improvements in its manufacturing operations which have reduced the amount of raw materials needed by 10.0% and have increased labor efficiency by 5.0%. Would you make the same year-end adjusting entry in these circumstances that you made in part (2)?

P12.10 This company has organized its manufacturing process into two production departments. The company manufactures pencils on a continuous basis. The first production department starts with the raw materials (wood, graphite, etc.) and ends with the unpainted pencils. The second department receives these unmarked pencils and paints and imprints slogans, company names, and the like on the pencils to fulfill specific sales orders for special markings, or to replenish the company's stock of standard marked pencils. Although the markings or color of the pencils are different, the cost of painting and imprinting are virtually the same for all pencils and, therefore, all pencils produced, whether for special customer orders or for inventory, are allocated the same costs. The departmental cost summary sheet for the first department for July 1976 is shown below. (In actual practice these cost reports are much more detailed regarding each cost element.)

FIRST DEPARTMENT
DEPARTMENTAL COST SUMMARY—JULY 1976

	Raw Materials	Direct Labor	Overhead
Beginning work-in-process inventory: 100,000 pencils; raw materials, 50% complete; labor and overhead, 25% complete	$ 1,100	$ 850	$ 340
Manufacturing costs for month	56,100	87,550	35,020
Total costs to account for	$57,200	$88,400	$35,360
2,500,000 pencils transferred out	55,000	85,000	34,000
Ending work-in-process inventory: 200,000 pencils; raw materials, 50% complete; labor and overhead, 50% complete	$ 2,200	$ 3,400	$ 1,360

The second department had no work-in-process at the beginning or the end of July. This department's costs for July were: raw materials $8500, direct labor $30,000, and overhead $7500. During each month the company accumulates all direct labor costs and all manufacturing overhead costs in separate clearing accounts. Then at the end of each month the totals in these accounts are allocated between the two production departments.

Required:

(1) Make appropriate summary entries in general journal form for July to record the manufacturing costs charged to each department, the transfer of products from the first to the second department, and the transfer of products from the second department to the finished goods inventory.

(2) Determine the per unit cost of the products manufactured during July. Is the cost of the ending work-in-process inventory higher or lower than the per unit cost of the products completed during July? Show supporting computations.

P12.11 The following series of events concern one particular item of raw material that was used for the first time this year. That is, before this year this particular raw material item had not been used in the company's production process.

Date	Event
2–18–76	Received 5,000 pounds, as ordered, for total gross purchase invoice cost of $20,000, subject to 2.0% discount if paid within 10 days from today. Gross price payable in 60 days.
2–20–76	Returned 400 pounds of materials received on 2–18–76 for credit, because these materials were below minimum quality specifications as ordered; these were sent FOB shipping point.
2–24–76	Paid freight bill of $460 for shipment received 2–18–76.
2–27–76	Paid amount owed for 2–18–76 purchase.
3–26–76	Received 8,000 pounds, as ordered, for gross purchase invoice cost of $34,000, subject to 2.0% discount if paid within 10 days from today; gross price due in 60 days.
3–29–76	Paid freight bill of $736 for shipment received 3–26–76.
4– 4–76	Issued 10,000 pounds to job order No. 46AZ1.
5–18–76	Return of 400 pounds from job order No. 46AZ1, which was not needed to complete the job order.
5–28–76	Paid amount owed for 3–29–76 purchase.

Required: In general journal form record an entry for each event listed above. If you must choose between alternative accounting methods clearly indicate your choice in the explanation of your entries. Assume the company uses the FIFO inventory method.

P12.12 In this problem one troublesome aspect of accounting for raw materials found in many manufacturing situations is briefly considered. This problem is not discussed in the chapter, so you will have to "think out" your own solution. Assume that this company purchases a natural resource as its only raw material input. Most of the natural resource is used in the manufacturing process, but some of the raw material is not used and is sold off as a *by-product.* Immediately on receipt of the raw material, the company strips off the by-product (like shaft from wheat). The by-product is accumulated until a large bin is full and then is sold to a by-products company who removes the bin and replaces it with an empty bin, and so on. Assume for the year just ended that the company recorded the following:

Cost of raw materials purchased	$3,846,000
Sales of by products during year	173,070

To simplify assume that the company had no bgeinning or ending inventory of by-product, and that the beginning inventory of raw material equals the ending inventory.

Required: How would you account for the cost of raw materials used in the manufacturing process during the year? Identify and explain at least two alternative methods that you believe might be generally acceptable.

P12.13 Listed below is the sequence of purchases of three raw material items, beginning with the first purchase of each item at the time when the raw material began to be used in the company's manufacturing process and continuing to the present. The total annual quantity of each item released to production is given below also.

			Raw Material		
Date	Quantity	Cost per Unit	Item A	Item B	Item C
1975:					
1–18	400	$8.25	$ 3,300		
2–6	350	$6.18		$ 2,163	
3–14	1,200	$3.28			$ 3,936
3–28	650	$8.40	$ 5,460		
4–19	450	$6.08		$ 2,736	
5–27	1,500	$3.25			$ 4,875
7–3	500	$8.60	$ 4,300		
7–28	600	$5.90		$ 3,540	
8–4	1,400	$3.30			$ 4,620
10–18	700	$8.80	$ 6,160		
10–29	500	$5.80		$ 2,900	
11–5	1,200	$3.25			$ 3,900
12–14	600	$9.00	$ 5,400		
12–21	800	$5.65		$ 4,520	
1976:					
1–16	1,400	$3.25			$ 4,550
2–17	800	$9.10	$ 7,280		
2–19	900	$5.60		$ 5,040	
4–16	1,600	$3.30			$ 5,280
6–2	1,100	$9.20	$10,120		
6–18	1,200	$5.50		$ 6,600	
8–3	1,500	$3.26			$ 4,890
9–18	1,200	$9.35	$11,220		
10–4	1,300	$5.40		$ 7,020	
11–15	1,400	$3.25			$ 4,550
12–7	1,100	$9.40	$10,340		
12–14	1,600	$5.35		$ 8,560	

Total Quantity Issued to Production:	Item A	Item B	Item C
1975	2,100	1,800	4,500
1976	4,050	4,800	5,500

Required:

(1) Determine the cost of raw materials issued to production and the cost of the raw materials ending inventory for 1975 and 1976 for each of the three raw material items shown above according to:
   (a) The FIFO method.
   (b) The LIFO method.
(2) Would the LIFO method be appropriate for raw material item B? Explain.

P12.14 This problem considers the serious accounting question regarding how to match cost of goods sold with sales revenue during periods of inflation. To simplify, assume that this company manufactures and sells just one product. The company maintains an inventory equal to the next three months sales forecast. The company makes very accurate sales forecasts; each quarter the company produces exactly the quantity to be sold the following quarter. All inventory is finished by the end of each quarter; there is no work-in-process inventory still in production at the end of each quarter. 1976 is the first year the company sold any of its product. During the last quarter (three months) of 1975 the company manufactured a quantity of product that then was sold during the first quarter of 1976. The company's policy is to set the selling price to equal 150% of its production cost per unit. For 1976, the following information is available:

Beginning inventory: 10,000 units at $100.00 cost per unit
Manufacturing output during year:
    First quarter   11,000 units at $105.00 cost per unit
    Second quarter   12,000 units at $110.00 cost per unit
    Third quarter   13,000 units at $115.00 cost per unit
    Fourth quarter   14,000 units at $120.00 cost per unit
Sales during year:
    First quarter   10,000 units
    Second quarter   11,000 units
    Third quarter   12,000 units
    Fourth quarter   13,000 units

Notice that the selling price in effect each quarter is *not* shown above. This information is given below.

Required:

(1) Without knowing precisely which selling prices were in effect during each quarter, are you nevertheless willing to make a decision on which inventory method (FIFO, LIFO, or Average Cost) should be used?
(2) Assume the selling prices in effect each quarter were as follows: first quarter, $150.00; second quarter, $157.50; third quarter, $165.00; and fourth quarter, $172.50. Which inventory method is "best" in this situation?
(3) Assume the selling prices in effect each quarter were as follows: first quarter,

$157.50; second quarter, $165.00; third quarter, $172.50; and, fourth quarter, $180.00. Which inventory method is "best" in this situation?

(4) Assume that the selling prices each quarter were as given in part (2). Determine the gross profit that would be reported for 1976 according to:
   (a) The FIFO method.
   (b) The LIFO method.

(5) Assume that the selling prices each quarter were as given in part (3). Determine the gross profit that would be reported for 1976 according to:
   (a) The FIFO method.
   (b) The LIFO method.

P12.15 The company's total gross wages earned by all employees during the year is $16,795,250. From an analysis of the distribution of annual wages it is known that the total gross earnings of the 350 employees who each earned more than $14,100 during the year is $6,489,000.

Required:

(1) Determine the company's total OASDI (social security) tax expense for the year.

(2) Explain the difference in allocating this fringe benefit labor cost to job orders (or production departments) between those employees who earn $14,100 or less during the year versus those who earn more than $14,100.

(3) From the above information could you determine the number of employees who earn less than $14,100 during the year? Explain how, or why not.

Chapter Thirteen

Product Cost Determination and Accumulation (Concluded)

PRODUCT COST DETERMINATION AND ACCUMULATION (CONCLUDED)

In the preceding chapter we examine the measurement and accumulation of the *prime* (or *direct*) costs of manufacturing products, which are raw materials and direct labor costs. In this chapter we complete this discussion by considering the third basic type of manufacturing costs—overhead costs. Overhead costs present the most difficult problems of manufacturing cost accounting. A company's total manufacturing overhead costs for a year may equal or exceed its total raw materials cost or its total direct labor cost during the year. The proper accounting for manufacturing overhead costs is just as important as the proper accounting for raw materials and direct labor costs.

Manufacturing Overhead Costs

As we discussed previously, the term "overhead" refers to a wide range of different types of *indirect* manufacturing costs. Some overhead costs do not present any serious problems of accounting measurement. For instance, property taxes on the company's manufacturing plant (land and buildings) and its manufacturing equipment is a fairly obvious amount for the year. Likewise, the fire insurance premium cost on the company's manufacturing buildings, machinery, and equipment is a fairly definite amount for each year, although the total cost of each insurance policy must be allocated (usually on a straight-line basis) over the months covered by each fire insurance policy. In short, there are many manufacturing overhead costs that are "easy" to measure. The total cost and the period (or periods) to which the cost applies are relatively clear, and present no accounting problems.

On the other hand, many other manufacturing overhead costs are rather difficult to measure and to relate to specific periods. For example, consider depreciation of the company's manufacturing buildings, machinery, and equipment. From your previous study of financial accounting you know that depreciation accounting depends on three basic estimates: (1) the estimated useful lives of each fixed asset, or composite group of fixed assets; (2) the estimated salvage or disposable values of the fixed assets at the end of their useful lives; and, to a lesser extent, (3) the estimated pattern of usage of the fixed assets over their useful lives. Also, there may be a problem in determining the initial purchase (or construction) cost of the fixed assets. Several costs connected with the acquision of fixed assets should perhaps be capitalized in theory, but may not be in fact.

Since a familiarity with depreciation accounting problems is assumed, we make no attempt here to present a full discussion. The evidence seems clear that most companies adopt rather conservative estimates of their fixed assets' useful lives and salvage values, and that they use a predetermined schedule of depreciation instead of activity based methods. Most often, either the straight-line method or an accelerated depreciation method is adopted. Hence, the annual depreciation cost is a *fixed* overhead cost. Or, to be more precise, it is accounted for as a fixed cost because a predetermined schedule of depreciation allocation is followed by the company, which does not depend on the actual volume of use of the fixed assets during each period.

Another relatively significant class of overhead costs are *indirect labor* costs, which generally consist of two types of labor: (1) supervisory employees whose time cannot be matched with particular cost accumulation units (production lots); and, (2) other employees in the manufacturing process whose time cannot be directly identified with or easily associated with particular job orders or production departments, such as general janitorial employees, employees who repair and service the production machinery and equipment throughout the whole plant, workers who handle materials and products but who do not work on the production line, and the like. Some indirect laborers are paid a fixed salary. Even many of those who are paid on an hourly rate wage basis tend to work at least 40 hours every week so their base pay for 40 hours is fixed also. Thus a large part of indirect labor is a fixed cost. Also it should be repeated that the supplementary (fringe benefits) cost of *direct* labor may be treated as manufacturing overhead—see the discussion at the close of Chapter Twelve (pages 418 and 419). Supplementary labor costs of indirect labor are accounted for as manufacturing overhead cost, of course.

Many different manufacturing supplies and services are purchased from other business firms or individuals, which are accounted for as manufacturing overhead costs because these input factors cannot be identified with particular production lots. For example, most companies purchase lubricants for their production machinery and equipment. It would be very difficult and time-consuming (if not impossible) to identify the lubricants' costs with specific pieces of machinery and equipment. For another example, the company may have its entire plant fumigated once a year by a pest control firm that charges a flat total amount. No practical way exists to match this cost with particular job orders or production departments in most situations.

In summary, during the course of a year a manufacturer records many different manufacturing overhead costs. Some are fixed by the very nature of the cost, such as property taxes or fixed salaries. Some are fixed because of the method of accounting for the cost; depreciation is the main example. Some are variable costs, such as the total power (electricity and gas) cost during the period, which depends on the total volume of work processed during the year. As is explained in Chapter Twelve, the Manufacturing Overhead Costs account is a holding account that is used to accumulate the *actual* manufacturing costs recorded during the period.* This account is a temporary collecting device to hold the actual overhead costs until the costs are allocated to the products being manufactured. It may be appropriate to review Exhibit 12.1 at this point to see the flow of costs in *and* out of this account. The recording of overhead costs is shown in the following illustrative summary entry:

Debit (+) Manufacturing
         Overhead Costs   xxx,xxx.xx

    Credit (+) Cash   xxx,xxx.xx ILLUSTRATIVE
ENTRY TO SHOW
    Credit (−) Accounts Payable   xxx,xxx.xx RECORDING OF
ACTUAL
    Credit (+) Accumulated   MANUFACTURING
         Depreciation   xxx,xxx.xx COSTS DURING
    Credit (−) Prepaid Expenses   xxx,xxx.xx PERIOD

General nature of entries made during the year to record various manufacturing overhead costs.

Allocation of Manufacturing Overhead Costs to Production Lots

Indirectness Requires Allocation

Raw material and direct labor manufacturing costs are directly matched with particular job orders or particular production departments, as the case may be. In contrast, manufacturing overhead costs must be *allocated* to these cost accumulation units. "Allocated" means apportioned or distributed among the various job orders or production departments. In this way each cost accumulation unit is charged with its "share" of the company's total manufacturing overhead cost for the year. There is no direct or obvious basis of attachment of overhead costs to the products being manufactured. Thus the company must develop methods or formulas of allocation that are logical and reasonable. In actual situations this is a monumental task. It is impossible to do full justice to the problems of overhead cost allocation in the relatively brief description that space allows.

One basic approach is to identify a *common denominator or general index* of manufacturing activity among all the job orders or production departments. The common denominator should be in some sense a common *cause* of manufacturing overhead costs, or at least it should be highly correlated with manu-

---

* In actual practice a company may use two or more Manufacturing Overhead Costs accounts, one for each plant location, or one for each overhead cost class. Hence, the total overhead costs for the year would be the sum of the balances in the separate overhead cost accounts maintained by the company.

facturing overhead costs. That is, the higher the manufacturing activity (as indicated by the common denominator), then the higher the total overhead costs. The lower the manufacturing activity, then the lower the overhead costs. Many overhead costs are fixed costs, which means that these costs do not depend on the actual level of manufacturing activity over the short run. In other words, the common denominator's correlation with overhead costs is a long-run basic relationship that tends to hold true.

In many instances direct labor hours is a reasonable and practical (though not perfect) *overall* common denominator. This is the basic general index of manufacturing activity used in the rest of the chapter. However, it should be emphasized that in some situations: (1) direct labor hours may not be the best overall common denominator or index of manufacturing activity; and, (2) two (or more) different common denominators may be used, one for some of the overhead costs and another for other overhead costs. For example, the weight or quantity of raw materials of each job order or production department may be a better overall index for some manufacturers, or for some overhead costs. Some overhead costs may be allocated on the basis of direct labor hours, and other overhead costs may be allocated on the basis of raw material weight processed.

Basic Concept of Burden Rate

Suppose a manufacturer expects that its total manufacturing (production) output for the coming year will require 50,000 direct labor hours. This estimate is based on the analysis of the total projected production output for the coming year. If the company uses formal budgeting procedures, this information is an essential part of the forecasts and estimates for next year (refer to Chapter Six). If not, the projections may be less certain, but some estimate of this sort must be made. Based on the detailed analysis of its specific manufacturing overhead costs, the company's cost accountant presents these estimates:

Estimated Manufacturing Overhead Costs for Next Year

Total Fixed Overhead Costs for 45,000 to 55,000 direct labor hours of manufacturing activity	$762,500
Variable Overhead Costs: $2.45 per direct labor hour (on average)	

As mentioned previously, the total fixed overhead cost estimate includes costs such as depreciation on the manufacturing fixed assets, fixed salaries of production supervisors, and the like. Unless the company's total production activity were to drop below 45,000 direct labor hours, the company could not step down (decrease) any of these fixed costs. And, if the total manufacturing output during the year were to require more than 55,000 direct labor hours, then some of the fixed overhead costs would have to be stepped up. The lower to upper boundaries of 45,000 to 55,000 hours is called the *relevant range,* over which total fixed overhead costs are (for all practical purposes) fixed and constant. Total *variable* overhead costs includes things such as power usage and lubricants, which tend to vary in close proportion to the total number of direct labor hours worked during the year. Hence, the variable overhead costs *per direct labor hour* remain constant (for all practical purposes).

Allocating *variable* manufacturing overhead costs based on the average $2.45 per direct labor hour is straightforward. If for example, a particular job order requires 100 direct labor hours, then this production lot should be charged with $245 of the variable overhead cost: ($2.45 per hour × 100 hours). On the other hand, how much *fixed* overhead cost should be allocated to this specific job order? The basic accounting procedure is to spread the *total* fixed overhead costs to each hour of direct labor, that is, to charge an equal "share" of the total fixed overhead to each direct labor hour. In this example the fixed overhead per direct labor hour is determined as follows:

Computation of Fixed Manufacturing Overhead per Direct Labor Hour

Budgeted (or Estimated) Total Fixed Costs for Year			
Budgeted (or Estimated) Direct Labor Hours To Be Worked During Year	=	$\dfrac{\$762,500}{50,000 \text{ hours}}$ =	$15.25 Fixed Overhead per direct Labor Hour

The term *burden rate* refers to the total amount of fixed overhead and variable overhead costs charged to each hour of direct labor, which is the basis of overhead costs allocation in this example. The term "burden" is used because each hour of direct labor is *burdened* or *loaded* with its share of the company's total manufacturing overhead costs during the year. Thus, the burden rate in this example is

Computation of Burden Rate
(Based on Direct Labor Hours) for Coming Year

Fixed Overhead Burden Rate:	$762,500/50,000 hours	= $15.25 per hour
Variable Overhead Burden Rate		= 2.45 per hour
Total Overhead Burden Rate		= $17.70 per hour

For example, if a particular job order requires 2140 direct labor hours, then this cost accumulation unit would be charged with $37,878 of the company's total overhead costs: ($17.70 × 2140 direct labor hours = $37,878). For another example, if one of the company's production departments worked a total of 5300 direct hours during the year, then this department would be charged with $93,810 of the total overhead costs: ($17.70 × 5300 direct labor hours = $93,810).

Application of Burden Rate to Products

During the year accounting entries are made to charge overhead costs to the job orders being worked on during the period (or to production departments) based on the number of direct labor hours of each cost accumulation unit. The general form of this entry is as follows:*

Debit (+) Work-in-Process
      Inventory $ (see explanation)

Credit (−) Manufacturing
      Overhead Costs $ (see explanation)

ILLUSTRATIVE ENTRY TO SHOW THE APPLICATION OF MANUFACTURING OVERHEAD COSTS TO PRODUCTS

Application of manufacturing overhead costs to particular job orders or production departments, based on number of direct labor hours worked on each job order or in each production department; the total overhead cost applied is equal to:

(Total number of direct labor hours × $17.70) = $ Total

It should be emphasized that no entry is made to the Work-in-Process Inventory account, unless the same cost is entered in a separate job order cost sheet or in a department cost summary report for the period—see Exhibit 12.2 for a job order cost sheet illustration. Ideally, the total of all overhead cost application entries during the year should exactly clear out the Manufacturing Overhead Costs account, and should reduce it to a zero balance by the end of the year. That is, the actual total manufacturing overhead costs recorded during the year, if everything goes according to plan, would be exactly the amount budgeted. And, the actual total direct labor hours worked during the period would be the number planned at the start of the period. But usually this is not the case.

Disposition of Underapplied Manufacturing Overhead Costs

In most situations the budgeted (or estimated) manufacturing overhead costs for the year are more or less than the actual total overhead costs for the period. *And,* the total number of direct labor hours worked is more or less than the total predicted at the start of the year. To illustrate one possible situation of this kind, Exhibit 13.1 shows the *summary* of entries to the Manufacturing Overhead Costs account for the year for the same example discussed in the preceding

* Instead of a direct credit (decrease) to the Manufacturing Overhead Costs account, the Manufacturing Overhead Cost Applied account may be credited. The balance in this account is then closed to the Manufacturing Overhead Costs account at the end of the year.

EXHIBIT 13.1
Summary of Entries to Manufacturing Overhead Costs
Account During the Year

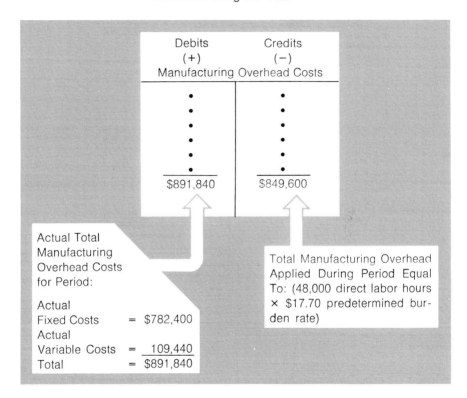

	Debits (+)	Credits (−)
		Manufacturing Overhead Costs

Debits (+)   Credits (−)
Manufacturing Overhead Costs

•   •
•   •
•   •
•   •
•   •
•   •
$891,840 $849,600

Actual Total Manufacturing Overhead Costs for Period:

Actual Fixed Costs = $782,400
Actual Variable Costs = 109,440
Total = $891,840

Total Manufacturing Overhead Applied During Period Equal To: (48,000 direct labor hours × $17.70 predetermined burden rate)

section. The dots extending down in each column indicate that there were many entries during the period to charge (debit) overhead costs into the account, and there were many entries to apply overhead out of the account to the Work-in-Process Inventory account. Only the cost totals for the year are relevant here.

In this example there is a $42,240 debit balance left in the Manufacturing Overhead Costs account at the end of the year (before any end-of-year adjustments): ($891,840 actual overhead − $849,600 applied overhead = $42,240). This is the excess of actual overhead costs that was not applied (allocated to the products worked on during the period). This remaining balance is called *underapplied overhead*. In the reverse case, more total overhead cost is applied (taken out of the account) than the actual total overhead costs during the year; this difference is called *overapplied overhead*.

The main accounting question in this situation is what to do about the underapplied overhead cost of $42,240. To help answer this question, the underapplied overhead is analyzed as is shown in Exhibit 13.2. Based on this analysis, notice that the company spent $8160 less than budgeted for variable overhead

EXHIBIT 13.2
Analysis of Underapplied Overhead Costs

Variable Overhead Costs
    Budgeted Costs: ($2.45 per hour × 48,000 hours worked) = $117,600
    Actual Costs: ($2.28 per hour × 48,000 hours worked) =   109,440

    Variance: ($0.17 per hour × 48,000 hours worked) = $ 8,160 (a)

Fixed Overhead Costs
Spending Variance:
    Budgeted Costs: (Total hours worked is in relevant
                      range for fixed costs.) $762,500
    Actual Costs: 782,400
    Spending Variance: $ 19,900 (b)
Volume Variance:
    Budgeted Costs: (50,000 hours × $15.25 per hour)   = $762,500
    Applied Costs: (48,000 hours × $15.25 per hour)   = 732,000
    Variance: (2,000 hours × $15.25 per hour)   = $ 30,500 (c)

                                                Overhead Cost
                                              Overapplied (+)
                                              Underapplied (−)

Summary
  (a) This favorable spending variance causes
       total overhead costs to be overapplied   +$ 8,160
  (b) This unfavorable spending variance causes
       total overhead costs to be underapplied   − 19,900
       Net spending variance   −$ 11,740
  (c) This unfavorable volume variance causes total
       overhead costs to be underapplied   − 30,500
  Total amount underapplied   −$ 42,240

costs during the year, but that it spent $19,900 more than budgeted for fixed overhead costs, which taken together gives a net *spending variance* of $11,740 more than budget. The unfavorable *volume variance* is because the company's actual production output during the year required 2000 hours less than budgeted. Hence, *fixed* overhead costs were not applied (allocated) to these 2000 unworked hours, which means that $30,500 ($15.25 × 2000 hours) had "no place to go," and thus this amount is still in the account at year-end.

One possible accounting procedure at the end of the year is to recompute the overhead burden rate, and then to adjust the amount of overhead costs originally charged to the various job orders or production departments during the year based on this *revised* burden rate. By using the *actual* total overhead costs and the *actual* direct labor hours, the revised burden rate is:

Computation of Revised Burden Rate at Year-end

$$\frac{\text{Actual Overhead Costs}}{\text{Actual Direct Labor Hours}} = \frac{\$891,840}{48,000 \text{ hours}} = \$18.58 \text{ revised burden rate}$$

Following this procedure, the amount of overhead cost charged to each direct labor hour would be adjusted upward by $.88 ($18.58 revised − $17.70 original), to charge each production lot with the actual overhead cost per direct labor hour worked during the year. *If* this procedure were followed then the underapplied overhead would be disposed of by the following entry made at year-end:

Debit (+) Cost of Goods Sold
Debit (+) Finished Goods Inventory   } 42,240
Debit (+) Work-in-Process Inventory

    Credit (−) Manufacturing Overhead Costs   42,240

To adjust burden rate from $17.70 per direct labor hour originally applied to $18.58 actual per hour.

DISPOSITION OF UNDERAPPLIED MANUFACTURING OVERHEAD COST

To make this entry, the company would have to know how many direct labor hours were charged to products that have already been sold by the end of the year; how many hours were charged to products still in the ending inventory of finished goods at year-end; and how many hours were charged to products still in process of manufacture at year-end. Probably most of the products to which overhead was applied during the year have been sold by the end of the year, and thus the largest part of the $42,240 underapplied overhead would be charged to Cost of Goods Sold expense. For example, assume that of the 48,000 direct labor hours worked during the year, 8000 hours are in the ending inventories, which means that 40,000 of them were charged to products that were sold during the year. Thus $35,200 ($.88 × 40,000) of the total amount of underapplied overhead costs would be charged to the Cost of Goods Sold expense in the entry shown above. However, this disposition procedure usually presents many practical problems. A company may be reluctant to go to the trouble of determining how many direct labor hours are in the ending inventory if it has many different products in the finished goods ending inventory, which came from many different job orders completed during the year. A practical expedient is simply to charge off *all* the underapplied overhead balance to the

Cost of Goods Sold Expense for the year. In this example the entry for this "shortcut" would be:

Debit (+) Cost of Goods Sold Expense	42,240	ALTERNATIVE
		DISPOSITION OF
Credit (−) Manufacturing Overhead Costs	42,240	UNDERAPPLIED
		MANUFACTURING
Charge-off of all underapplied overhead to expense.		OVERHEAD COST

There are many practical pressures for taking this "easy way out," even though theoretically this disposition of underapplied overhead is open to criticism, since the ending inventories do not include the full, actual cost of manufacturing overhead costs during the year.

A more serious accounting question arises in those situations in which the total direct hours worked during the year is 10 to 20% less than predicted for the year. In this example, notice that the total actual direct labor hours worked is 2000 less than planned, which is only 4% less than the total 50,000 hours budgeted for the period. In other words, 4% of the manufacturer's production capacity (in terms of direct labor hours) stood idle during the period. Should the cost of unused capacity be loaded onto the actual hours worked? It can be argued that the cost of the 2000 hours of unused capacity should be charged off as a period cost, that is, to an expense account. We explained previously that the total *fixed* manufacturing overhead costs for the year are the cost of production capacity for that year. However, this does not necessarily mean that if 4% of capacity is idle during the period, then exactly 4% of the total fixed manufacturing overhead cost for the period is the cost of this unused capacity. This general problem is discussed in further detail in the last section of this chapter (starting on page 452).

Recording the Completion of Products

Reaching the End of the Production Process

Assuming that manufacturing overhead cost has been properly applied to the various cost accumulation units, and that the direct costs have been properly identified with the job orders or production departments, then all the manufacturing costs are accumulated for each production lot. Eventually the lot reaches the end of the production line and is finished. Frequently the last step in the manufacturing process is the final inspection of the products, to make certain that all product specifications and quality standards are met. This final inspection step may cause some of the products to be rejected. These "substandard" products are reworked, are sold as "seconds" as is, or possibly are junked.

The additional cost of reworking a *normal* percentage of defective units, or the cost of a normal amount of units that are junked can be included in the total production cost, which is divided by the final number of good units that pass inspection. For instance, it may be normal to have to rework 5% of the units in a job order, or to reject on average 2% of the units that are not reworked. In both of these cases, assume that the job order consists of 100 units that come to the final inspection point. The rework cost of the 5 units would be loaded into the total production cost, which is divided by the 100 units (assuming the 5 reworked units pass inspection). In the other case, the total production cost is divided by the 98 units that pass inspection.

Job Order Manufacturing Systems

Usually the entire batch of products making up one job order come off the production line together—all the units in the production lot are finished at the same time. Until that point, the job order is still in process. Most job order manufacturers prepare weekly or monthly a source document called a *production report* (or some similar title), which summarizes the costs and quantities of *all* job orders *completed* during the period. The information for this production report comes from the separate job order cost sheets that are prepared during the production process of each job order. On receipt of the production report for the job orders completed during the period, the following basic entry is recorded:

Debit (+) Finished Goods Inventory	xxx,xxx.xx	
Credit (−) Work-in-Process Inventory	xxx,xxx.xx	COMPLETION OF JOB ORDERS
Completion of job orders during period; total cost of each job order and total quantity of each job order is taken from job order cost sheet for each.		

The total cost accumulated on each job order cost sheet is divided by the total quantity of finished units from the job to determine the cost per (finished) unit. A copy of the job order cost sheet could serve as the detailed inventory record for the Finished Goods Inventory account. Alternatively, a company may prepare a briefer and more condensed *inventory stock record* from the job order cost sheets, such as is illustrated later in the chapter (see Exhibit 13.3).

Continuous Processing Manufacturing Systems: Equivalent Units Computation

In contrast to a job order manufacturing system, a continuous processing manufacturing system requires additional accounting steps in determining the cost of products completed during the period. A job order has a definite starting point and a definite ending point, and each job order is a separate cost accumulation unit (production batch). Most continuous processing manufacturing companies are organized into two or more production departments, each of which performs a specialized function or series of operations in the total flow and sequence of manufacturing the products. Each production department is a separate cost unit (or center) for purposes of assigning raw material and direct labor costs, and for allocation of overhead costs.

The total manufacturing costs of *each* production department for each period (usually a month) must be determined and recorded. Each production department adds to the total cost of the manufacturing of the products, and each department's cost of working on the products has to be accurately and completely accounted for. When one production department completes its work on the products, the products are transferred to the next production department in the manufacturing process. A *cost transfer entry* is made when products are transferred from each department to the next so that the cumulative production cost of the units stays with the products as they move through the manufacturing process. At the end of the last department the total cost of the products is accumulated on one document, and thus it is readily accessible to determine the full (cumulative) cost of the finished products. These interdepartmental cost transfer entries are somewhat complex and are *not* shown. Interdepartmental cost transfer entries are one difference between a job order and continuous processing manufacturing systems.

In the continuous processing manufacturing situation the products keep "rolling off" the production line without stop (in many cases). Consider, for example, a mass-produced packaged breakfast cereal. The food company continuously manufactures these items. It divides its manufacturing stream into certain time periods, most often a month or a week. All the products worked on during this time interval are treated as one production lot, or one output batch. Indeed, consumer packaging laws require some products to be dated, so that the consumer can tell the freshness of the product. This has been a standard practice for photographic film products for many years. Each roll of film has a code number as well as an expiration date beyond which the manufacturer does not recommend using the film to achieve the best results.

During each period all costs identified with or allocated to each production department are recorded in a separate cost accumulation account for each department. Hence, the total cost of *all* production activity of each department for each period is determined. Assume that a particular department started the period with no products in process. But there is a quantity of work-in-process at the end of the period. That is, in this department are products that are only partially completely at the end of the period; therefore, they have not yet been transferred out. Thus some of this departmnt's total manufacturing cost for the period should be charged to its ending work-in-process—not all of the total cost should be charged to the units completed and transferred out. However, these partially completed units cannot be equated with the (100%) completed units that were transferred out during the period.

The accountant converts the number of in-process units (the partially completed units) into an equivalent number of finished units, which are called *equivalent units*. This conversion into equivalent units has been explained in Chapter Four (see Exhibit 4.2 in particular). However, a brief review may be helpful. Assume that this department has 9000 units still in-process at the end of the period, and that during the period the department transferred out a total of 27,000 (completed) units. The department's total production costs for the period are:

**Department's Total Production
Costs for Period**

Raw materials	$66,600
Direct labor	13,500
Overhead	10,800
Total costs	$90,900

It is not correct to divide the total cost of $90,900 by the total number of units processed, which is 27,000 units completed and transferred out plus the 9000 units not completed and still in-process at the end of the period. The cost accountant estimates the percentage of completion for each manufacturing cost for the units still in-process at the end of the period.

All raw materials are added in the first step of this department's production process; so, as far as the raw materials cost is concerned, the units in-process are 100% complete. Hence, the raw material cost per unit is the same whether it was completed and transferred out or is still in-process at the end of the period. The raw material cost is $1.85 per unit, which is ($66,600 divided by 36,000 units, that is, the 27,000 units transferred out plus the 9000 units in-process). But with respect to the direct labor and overhead costs the in-process units are only one third complete, which means roughly that they are only one third through this department's manufacturing operations. Hence, the 9000 in-process units are multiplied by one third to get 3000 equivalent units. These 3000 equivalent units are added to the 27,000 completed units which were transferred out during the period to get a total of 30,000 units that is then divided into the direct labor cost and overhead costs for the period. This gives $.45 direct labor cost per unit ($13,500/30,000 units) and $.36 overhead cost per unit ($10,800/30,000 units).

In summary, each completed unit would be charged with $1.85 raw material cost, $.45 direct labor cost, and $.36 overhead cost, for a total of $2.66 per unit. Hence, the 27,000 units completed and transferred out would be charged with $71,820 of the department's total cost for the period: ($2.66 × 27,000 = $71,820). The work-in-process ending inventory would be charged with the remainder, or $19,080: ($90,900 total cost − $71,280 charged out). This remaining balance for the work-in-process ending inventory can be double checked as follows:

Computation of Work-in-Process Ending Inventory Cost

Raw material cost	$1.85 per unit × 9,000 units 100% complete	= $16,650
Direct labor cost	.45 per unit × 9,000 units ⅓ complete	= 1,350
Overhead cost	.36 per unit × 9,000 units ⅓ complete	= 1,080
Total cost		$19,080

Eventually the products reach the end of the last department, and essentially the same entry shown above for the job order system (see page 447) is made to transfer the cost of the products from the Work-in-Process Inventory account to the Finished Goods Inventory account.

Recording Cost of Goods Sold

The starting point for determining the cost of goods (finished products) sold are the per unit costs for each production lot that have been entered in the product's inventory stock record. Recall that at the point of completion of the production lot an entry is made to transfer the cost of the lot to the Finished Goods Inventory account (see page 447). At this point the total quantity of units, per unit cost, and total cost, is entered in an inventory sock record for the product. For one of the products manufactured by the company, assume that five job orders for it were completed during the year. The inventory stock record for this product is shown in Exhibit 13.3. The question marks in the sales column raise the question regarding how much cost should be removed from the Finished Goods Inventory account at each point of sale.

EXHIBIT 13.3
Inventory Stock Record Illustration

Completion Date of of Produc- tion Lots	Acquisitions			Sales		
	Quantity Produced	Cost per Unit	Total Cost	Date of Sale	Quantity Sold	Cost Removed
Beginning Balance	2,000	$14.85	$29,700			
March 19	4,000	15.05	60,200			
				April 5	4,500	?
May 8	6,500	15.30	99,450			
July 13	3,400	15.45	52,530			
				July 23	10,000	?
October 4	6,200	15.35	95,170			
				November 28	7,500	?
December 18	2,800	15.80	44,240			

The manufacturer in this example possibly could wait until the end of the year, and then could determine the total cost of all 22,000 units sold during the year (which is called the periodic inventory method). More likely, however, the manufacturer would make an entry for each sale as soon as, or shortly after, the date of sale (which is called the perpetual inventory method). Consider the first sale of 4500 units on April 5. According to the FIFO method the cost of this quantity of goods sold would be determined as follows (see Exhibit 13.3 for data):

Computation of Cost of Goods Sold by FIFO Method

2,000 units @ $14.85	=	$29,700
2,500 units @ $15.05	=	37,625
4,500 units		$67,325

Alternatively, according to the LIFO method the same 4500 units would be costed out as follows (see Exhibit 13.3 for data):

Computation of Cost of Goods Sold by LIFO Method

4,000 units @ $15.05	=	$60,200
500 units @ $14.85	=	7,425
4,500 units		$67,625

According to the third common method, the Average Cost method, the cost of the 4500 units sold is determined as follows (see Exhibit 13.3 for data):

Computation of Cost of Goods Sold by Average Cost Method

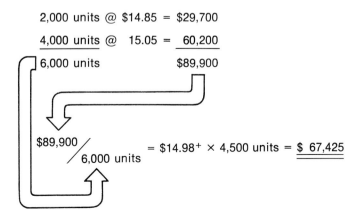

2,000 units @ $14.85 = $29,700

4,000 units @ 15.05 = 60,200

6,000 units $89,900

$89,900 / 6,000 units = 14.98^+$ × 4,500 units = $ 67,425

Since a familiarity with the three inventory cost methods is assumed, no further discussion is offered regarding how each method would apply to the other two sales during the year. It should be pointed out, however, that the Average Cost method shown here is called the *moving* average method. A new average is computed for each sale, based on the balance in the inventory account after the last sale plus any additions to the stock of this product since then. For the second sale (July 23), the cost balance carried forward after the first sale plus the two additions since then is the total cost for the determination of the average cost per unit. Likewise, the LIFO method shown above is the perpetual LIFO method, since an entry to remove the cost of goods sold is made at each point of sale. The periodic LIFO method, applied to the entire year by making one summary Cost of Goods Sold Expense entry at the end of the year, would give different results in most cases.

There is no agreement regarding the best *general* inventory cost method. Different companies use different methods. Indeed, some manufacturers use FIFO for some products and LIFO for other products. Since LIFO is permitted for federal income tax purposes, and since manufacturing costs per unit have steadily increased in most industries, many companies prefer LIFO to minimize their current taxable income. The chief complaint against it is that this method, after several years of use, may leave quite "old" cost values in the ending inventory. These old cost values may be as much as one fourth or one third below the current manufacturing cost of the products. In short, the ending inventory cost value may be seriously understated relative to current manufacturing costs. On the other hand, the advocates of LIFO argue that it gives a better matching of cost of goods sold against the sales revenue for the period to measure net income, because the most recent costs of manufacturing the products is charged to Cost of Goods Sold Expense.

The Problem of Fixed Manufacturing Costs Reconsidered: The Direct Costing Alternative

Full Cost Absorption Costing: The Generally Accepted Inventory Cost Valuation Method

For inventory cost valuation purposes generally accepted accounting principles require the inclusion of *all* manufacturing costs in the total cost assigned or allocated to the products manufactured, which means that *fixed manufacturing costs* must be included as well as all variable manufacturing costs. As we have already explained in this chapter, fixed manufacturing costs are allocated to each production lot worked on during the year through the use of a burden rate application procedure. In this manner each production lot "shares and shares alike" in the absorption of the total fixed manufacturing costs of the year. In fact, allocating fixed manufacturing costs to the products being manufactured is called *absorption costing,* or to be more precise *full cost* absorption costing.

Beginning in Chapter Two and continuing through Chapter Eight, our discussion and analysis centers on one particular company, a manufacturer of one product, which serves as the main example for many different aspects of management accounting. The cost valuation of the company's work-in-process and finished goods inventories has not been greatly emphasized, although occasional reference is made to the ending inventory cost determination. The previous chapters stress the preparation and analysis of accounting reports to managers; the precise details regarding inventory cost valuation are not usually of major importance to managers. However, the basic data for the company's December 31, 1975 and 1976 inventories are shown in Exhibit 4.2 in Chapter Four, and should be reviewed at this point.

First, notice that the company in the example uses LIFO for its work-in-process and finished goods inventories. (Raw materials, being purchased rather than manufactured, are not of any concern here.) Exhibit 13.4 shows how the LIFO cost values of the company's ending inventories for 1975 and 1976 are determined; this exhibit basically is a rearrangement of Exhibit 4.2 that is more useful to the following discussion. (Both the work-in-process and the finished goods inventories are grouped together for convenience of showing the computations.)

Second, notice the amounts of manufacturing fixed costs included in the company's inventories. Inventories increase by 25,000 units in 1975, so $43,125 of 1975's manufacturing fixed costs are allocated to this increment to the inven-

EXHIBIT 13.4
Computations of Cost Values for Work-in-Process and
Finished Goods Inventories

	Total Units (Work-in-Process and Finished Goods Combined)	Variable Cost per Unit	Total Variable Cost	Fixed Cost per Unit	Total Fixed Cost	Total Cost
Beginning inventory start of 1975	100,000 units	$10.600	$1,060,000	$1.725	$172,500	$1,232,500
Increase in inventory during 1975	25,000 units	10.600	265,000	1.725	43,125	308,125
Ending inventory, at close of 1975	125,000 units		$1,325,000		$215,625	$1,540,625
Increase in inventory during 1976	12,500 units	11.350	141,875	1.816	22,700	164,575
Ending inventory, close of 1976	137,500 units		$1,466,875		$238,325	$1,705,200

Notes:
(1) The company uses the LIFO method; hence, the increase in inventories during the year is treated as an additional layer to be added to the beginning inventory. The entire year is treated as one manufacturing period in this example, so the costs per unit for the whole year are multiplied times the number of units of increase during the year.
(2) See Exhibits 4.1 and 4.2 for source of information regarding manufacturing costs each year.

tories. In 1976 the inventories increase by 12,500 units, so $22,700 of the fixed costs for the year are "absorbed" by this increase in the inventories. In other words, instead of charging off *all* the fixed manufacturing costs of each year against that year's sales revenue, part of each year's fixed costs are allocated to the increase in inventories during the year.

There are two main arguments for this accounting procedure. First, part of the company's production capacity during each year is necessary to build up its inventories, and thus part of the fixed manufacturing costs for the years should be allocated to the increase of inventories. The increase of inventory are products not yet sold; hence, it would be premature to charge any manufacturing costs of producing these units against sales revenue until they are sold. Second, there is *full cost* logic of inventory costing. All manufacturing costs should be included; leaving out manufacturing fixed costs is no more logical than leaving out direct labor costs, it is argued. Therefore, all units produced during each year, whether sold during the year or still on hand at year-end in inventory, should "share and share alike" in the absorption of the year's total fixed manufacturing overhead costs.

A General Warning About the Full Cost Absorption Costing Method

There is little doubt that (full cost) absorption costing is the generally accepted method of accounting for manufacturing fixed costs—for purposes of reporting inventory cost values and for measuring net income in the external financial statements published by companies—and to determine taxable income. However, the logic of the absorption costing method does not require that the products actually manufactured during the year absorb *all* of the fixed overhead cost, *regardless of what percentage of production capacity was utilized during the period.* For example, assume a company has a fixed manufacturing cost commitment of $1 million for the coming year and that this provides 1 million direct labor hours of capacity. Thus at full capacity each direct labor hour is charged with a fixed manufacturing cost burden rate of $1. Assume, however, that the company has a very poor year, operates at only 50% capacity, and is not able to step down any of its manufacturing fixed costs. Does this mean that each direct labor hour should be charged with a fixed manufacturing cost burden rate of $2 per hour ($1,000,000/500,000 actual hours worked)? This would *double* the fixed manufacturing cost to each production lot worked on during the year. To the contrary, there is good argument for charging off a large part of the fixed manufacturing cost as an expense or *period cost,* since 50% of the company's production capacity for the year was not used.

As discussed above, a company determines its fixed overhead burden rate based on an *estimate* of its *production capacity* for the year. This manufacturing capacity estimate takes into account the available floor space, machine hours, labor hours, and the like that are provided by the company's existing manufacturing facilities and its present work force. The theoretical maximum production output that could be achieved from its production facilities and work force is called *ideal capacity.* Ideal capacity assumes that the company could squeeze the last ounce of efficiency out of each and every machine, square foot of space, and hour of labor, and also assumes that there would be no breakdowns, lost time, wasted space, and so on. In most situations the company backs off from such an unrealistic capacity measure. Instead, it adopts a more realistic *practical capacity* estimate for the year to determine its fixed manufacturing overhead cost burden rate. Practical capacity allows for some normal amount of "inefficiency" as a result of occasional machine and equipment breakdowns and malfunctions, some small amount of wasted floor space, some tolerable amount of employee deadtime, and so on.

A company's *actual* total production output for the year may fall short of its practical capacity estimate. Thus at year-end there would be some amount of underapplied fixed overhead. As discussed above (see pages 442 to 446), one method of disposing of underapplied overhead cost is to charge the entire amount to Cost of Goods Sold Expense, or to some other manufacturing expense for the year. This disposition is especially justified in those situations where there is a *substantial* amount of underapplied fixed manufacturing overhead.

Referring to the previous example on page 441, the company determines its fixed overhead burden rate of $15.25 per direct labor hour based on a practical capacity estimate of 50,000 direct labor hours for the year. Assume, for example, that the company works only 35,000 direct labor hours and that its total fixed overhead costs remain at the amount originally budgeted for the year ($762,500). In this instance, there would be an unfavorable volume variance of $228,750: ($15.25 fixed burden rate per hour $\times$ 15,000 unworked hours = $228,750). Thus there would be underapplied fixed overhead of this amount. This amount should be charged off to an expense (not necessarily the Cost of Goods Sold Expense). Putting it another way, the company should not charge more than $15.25 fixed cost overhead per direct labor hour to the products in ending inventory. If this fixed cost per direct labor hour lid is put on product cost, then underapplied fixed overhead cost has to be expensed.

The Direct Costing Method: An Alternative Inventory Cost Valuation and Profit Measurement Procedure

As we emphasize many times, fixed costs should be separated from variable costs in accounting reports to managers. Therefore, it is taken for granted that there is no serious argument against the segregation of fixed and variable costs in management reporting and analysis. Indeed, the first management profit performance statement introduced in Chapter Four (see Exhibit 4.1) distinguishes between fixed and variable costs. More to the point, the contribution margin format for the management profit performance statement is based mainly on the segregation of fixed and variable costs (see Exhibit 4.5). In particular, notice in Exhibit 4.5 for 1975 that $43,125 of the year's total manufacturing fixed costs is absorbed by the increase of inventories, so that this amount is subtracted from the total fixed costs for the year. And in 1976, $22,700 is deducted from the year's total fixed manufacturing costs, which is the amount of fixed cost absorbed by the increase of inventories. These fixed cost amounts charged to the increase of inventories each year can also be seen in Exhibit 13.4, which shows the cost components of the inventories.

In both 1975 and 1976, we can see that the largest part of the year's fixed manufacturing cost is charged off against sales revenue. However, a small part is carried forward in the inventories' cost value. In a sense each year is "relieved" of the amount of fixed cost inventoried instead of expensed. In sharp contrast, one school of thought argues that fixed manufacturing costs should be accounted for entirely as a period cost (expense), and that none of the manufacturing fixed costs should be included as product costs. *All* fixed costs would bypass the inventories accounts, and would be charged off immediately to expense. This suggested method is called *direct costing* or *variable costing,* since only variable manufacturing costs would be charged to the products manufactured. Direct costing has been rejected for inventory cost valuation and periodic profit measurement purposes in external financial reports and in federal income taxation returns.

There are two main differences caused by the direct costing method. In this example the company's operating profit each year would be reduced because all of each year's total manufacturing fixed costs would be expensed to that year, and none would be absorbed by the increase in inventories, which is shown as follows:

Determination of Operating Profit According to Direct Costing Method

	1975	1976
Operating profit determined by the absorption costing method (see Exhibit 4.5)	$731,000	$977,900
Fixed manufacturing costs absorbed by increase in inventories during the year (see Exhibit 13.4)	43,125	22,700
Operating profit determined by the direct (variable) costing method	$687,875	$955,200

Second, the ending inventories of work-in-process and finished goods would be valued at the variable cost amounts shown in Exhibit 13.4 which, as we can observe are considerably less than the full cost amounts determined by the absorption costing method. For instance, at the end of 1976 the ending inventories would be reported at $1,466,875 by the direct costing method compared with $1,705,200 by the absorption method.

As a general rule, if fixed manufacturing costs per unit are stable or increasing, then the absorption method will show larger operating profit in years when inventories increase and smaller operating profit in years when inventories decrease. However, there are two reasons why in most cases the differences in operating profit may not be too material. First, fixed manufacturing costs in many situations are the smallest part of total manufacturing costs; variable manufacturing costs are the largest part. Second, the increase or decrease of inventories during the year as a percentage of total inventories sold during the year usually is not very large. Frequently examples are used to demonstrate the differences between direct costing and variable costing that exaggerate these two factors. In these "extreme" examples, fixed costs are made a large part of total manufacturing costs. Even more objectionable, the increase or decrease of inventories during the year is made to be 25% or even 50% of the total inventories sold during the year. In these relatively rare cases the two methods would give widely different results.

Summary (Chapters Twelve and Thirteen)

Although the "ideal" situation might be to hold no inventories, as a practical matter almost all manufacturers carry stocks of raw materials, usually have some products still in process of production at the end of the period, and maintain quantities of finished goods. Therefore, determining inventory cost values are very important for asset valuation and profit measurement reasons. Ending inventory accounting errors affect two periods—the periods just ending and the next period. The importance of managers knowing product costs has already been discussed in previous chapters.

The essential idea of manufacturing cost accounting is to match the manufacturing costs of the period to the production lots worked on during the period. A production lot may be a job order, which is a separate batch or group of products that moves through the manufacturing process as a distinct work order. On the other hand, continuous processing manufacturing systems are organized into separate production departments, and manufacturing costs are first identified or allocated to each of the production departments. Then, the costs of that department's operations for the period are matched with the products moving through that department. In either type of manufacturing system there are three basic types of manufacturing costs—raw materials, direct labor, and indirect manufacturing costs that are called overhead costs.

Once the choice between the FIFO, LIFO, or Average Cost methods has been made, it is usually not too difficult to match raw materials costs to the production lots being worked on, although there may be abnormal wastage or spoilage of raw materials which should be excluded from the raw materials cost assigned to a production lot. Likewise, direct labor by its very nature can be identified with particular job orders or specific production departments. However, the fringe benefits costs of direct labor are more difficult to account for in the same manner as the gross wage cost of direct labor for each week or month. Some or most of the fringe benefits costs may be treated as overhead costs.

Because of their indirectness, manufacturing overhead costs must be allocated (distributed) to the production lots worked on during the period. The basic procedure is to develop a burden rate which is then applied to production lots based on a common denominator of manufacturing activity among all the production lots, such as direct labor hours. However, the application of overhead costs during the year may not allocate all the actual manufacturing costs for the year. There may be underapplied (unallocated) manufacturing overhead costs at the end of the year. Theoretically the underapplied overhead costs amount should be allocated among the cost of goods sold expense and the ending inventories of work-in-process and finished goods. As a practical short cut, all of the underapplied overhead costs amount simply may be charged to the cost of goods sold expense for the year. (Underapplied fixed overhead costs due to idle capacity should be charged to expense in any case.)

Generally accepted accounting principles require that all manufacturing costs, including fixed costs, be included in the cost values accumulated in the work-in-process and finished goods inventories. This is called the full cost absorption costing method—the product costs absorb all manufacturing costs reasonably related to production of the products. However, the full cost absorption method does not mean that the cost of excess idle capacity should be loaded in the cost of the products manufactured during the year. In other words, the conventional absorption costing method is not blind to the situation in which there are unused fixed manufacturing costs during the year as a result of a large percentage of idle manufacturing capacity. The fixed manufacturing cost allocated to each unit of product manufactured during the year should be based on the company's total practical capacity for the year. The unallocated remainder of fixed manufacturing costs for the year caused by unused capacity should not be inventoried but, instead, should be charged off to expenses in the year the costs are incurred.

The direct (or variable) costing method would treat *all* fixed manufacturing costs as period costs, not as product costs. Inventories would be valued at their variable costs of manufacture only; no fixed costs would be allocated to the product costs. This suggestion has not met with general acceptance. Indeed, the direct costing method is not allowed for federal income tax purposes, which undoubtedly discourages the use of this inventory cost valuation method. The direct costing method can be seriously objected to on grounds of understating the full manufacturing cost of products. Also, the direct costing method seems to ignore the fact that manufacturing capacity is needed to build up inventories, as well as to produce inventories sold during the year. Last, the direct costing method should not be confused with the contribution margin format of presenting management profit performance reports, such as is shown in Chapter Four. The separation of fixed from variable costs and the determination of contribution margins is very useful for management decision making; there is no doubt about this point. But the direct costing method goes beyond this separation in management reports and involves a major conceptual difference in inventory cost valuation and periodic profit measurement.

Questions

13. 1 (a) "Almost all manufacturing overhead costs are *fixed* costs. Do you agree? If not, cite examples of variable overhead costs.
    (b) "Almost all manufacturing overhead costs are *indirect* costs." Do you agree? If not, cite examples of direct overhead costs.

13. 2 (a) What is the main characteristic and nature of the Manufacturing Overhead Cost account?
    (b) Could the debit or credit balance in this account properly be carried forward from one year to the next?

13. 3 (a) Why is direct labor hours usually a reasonably satisfactory common denominator or general index of manufacturing activity for the purpose of overhead cost allocation?
    (b) Does a company have to use one and only one common denominator base for all overhead costs allocation? Explain.

13. 4 What is a burden rate? What does "burden" mean? What does "rate" refer to?

13. 5 (a) What are three different reasons for underapplied overhead?
    (b) Would these same three reasons possibly result in overapplied overhead?

13. 6 (a) "All of the underapplied overhead balance at year-end should be charged to Cost of Goods Sold Expense for the year." Do you agree? Explain.
    (b) "All of the overapplied overhead balance at year-end should be charged (that is, credited) to Cost of Goods Sold Expense for the year." Do you agree? Explain.

13. 7 Assume that a job order's total production cost is $15,288 which is normal for the 1000 units included in this job order. However, the final inspection rejected 320 of these units which were not reworked and were sold as "seconds" and "thirds" for total revenue of $2000. Normally ony 2.0% of the units in these types of job orders are rejected. How would you account for this situation? Explain fully.

13. 8 What are two basic differences in accounting procedures between a job order and a continuous processing manufacturing system?

13. 9 Assume a production department in a continuous processing manufacturing system had no beginning or ending work-in-process inventory In this case would it be necessary to compute equivalent units? Explain.

13.10 (a) If several job orders were completed during the year, and If the cost per unit from each job order was higher than the preceding job order, then which inventory method is the best one to determine the cost of goods sold?
    (b) If the per unit costs dropped with each successive job order, then which inventory method is best?

13.11 (a) What are the basic arguments in favor of full cost absorption costing for inventory valuation and profit measurement purposes?

(b) What are the basic arguments against full cost absorption?

(c) In which situations would direct costing and full cost absorption make no difference?

13.12 Assume that a company uses direct costing. Would the company still have to choose between FIFO, LIFO, or Average Cost direct costing?

13.13 Why are differences in annual operating profit between the full cost absorption and direct costing methods usually not very material? Is this also true for differences in inventory cost values?

13.14 "I don't see why FIFO direct costing isn't acceptable, since LIFO full cost absorption costing could give lower inventory cost values in many cases." How would you answer this?

Problems

P13. 1 As is explained in Chapter Twelve (see Exhibit 12.2 in particular), a separate job order cost sheet is prepared to record all the details of raw materials, direct labor, and manufacturing overhead costs that are assigned or allocated to each individual job order worked on during the period. Presented below is summary information from all these job order cost sheets for each of the three products manufactured by the company during the year just ending. To keep the amount of computations and "pencil pushing" in this problem to a reasonable level, it is assumed that these products are the only ones processed during the year, although you realize, of course, that an actual company may produce hundreds or even thousands of different products. However, the basic procedures of accounting for manufacturing overhead costs can be learned with three products, as well as from 30, 300, or 3000.

The raw material and direct labor costs for the year have already been recorded during the year, and accordingly these costs have been entered in the job order cost sheets. This problem is not concerned with the accounting entries and procedures for these prime costs, which is the subject of the preceding chapter. This problem is concerned primarily with manufacturing overhead costs. Therefore, assume that all the raw material and direct labor cost entries already have been recorded properly. These prime costs also have been recorded into the job order cost sheets, and from these accounting records for the job orders the following summary is given:

Manufacturing Activity During the Year	Total Quantity of Finished Units of All Jobs	Raw Materials		Direct Labor	
		Total Quantity (in lb)	Total Cost	Total Number of Hours	Total Cost
All Job Orders for Product A	10,000	51,250	$ 71,750	9,500	$ 59,375
All Job Orders for Product B	20,000	99,750	219,450	61,750	469,300
All Job Orders for Product C	15,000	76,350	114,525	23,750	197,125

At the beginning of the year the company budgeted its manufacturing overhead for the coming year as follows

Total *fixed* overhead costs over the production output
range from 90,000 to 110,000 direct labor hours = $570,000

Total production output for year in terms of
direct labor hours to be worked = 100,000 hours

Variable manufacturing overhead costs = $2.30 per direct labor hour

Information about the company's actual manufacturing overhead costs for the year is summarized as follows.

(a) Depreciation is recorded by the straight-line method; the total depreciation on its manufacturing fixed assets for the year is $102,000.

(b) Total property taxes on its manufacturing real estate for the year is $29,000.

(c) For the year the total salaries of the nonproduction line employees who are paid a fixed salary per month is $419,000. (To simplify assume all this total amount is paid in cash during the year.)

(d) The total of other out-of-pocket *fixed* overhead costs during the year is $43,750 (which is paid entirely in cash).

(e) The total cost of power usage (primarily electricity and gas) for this year is: 95,000 machine hours × $1.40 = $133,000. Assume that this amount is paid entirely in cash during the year. Also, assume that one direct labor hour requires one machine hour of power usage.

(f) The total of other out-of-pocket *variable* overhead costs paid in cash during the year is $71,250.

Required:

(1) Record the actual manufacturing costs for the year, which are listed in (a) to

(f) above, in general journal form. Explanations under each of these entries are *not* necessary.

(2) In general journal form record a *summary* entry for the year to apply manufacturing overhead to the job orders worked on during the year. Include in the explanation for this entry the computations of the burden rate at the beginning of the year which is used to apply overhead for the year to the various job orders processed during the year.

(3) In general entry form make a *summary* entry to record the completion of the job orders of each product during the year. There are no jobs in process at the end of the year. In other words, all the job orders were completed during the year.

(4) Assume, to simplify, that the company had no beginning inventories of finished goods of the three products at the start of the year. Sales of each product during the year are

$$
\begin{aligned}
\text{Product A} &= \ \ 9{,}000 \text{ units} \\
\text{Product B} &= 15{,}000 \text{ units} \\
\text{Product C} &= 12{,}000 \text{ units}
\end{aligned}
$$

Record the cost of goods sold in a *summary* entry for the year, based on the application of overhead costs at the predetermined burden rate established at the start of the year. In your explanation for this entry, briefly show how you determined the cost of each product sold.

(5) Prepare a brief summary analysis to explain the difference between the actual total manufacturing overhead cost for the year, and the total overhead costs applied during the year that is based on the predetermined burden rate established at the start of the year.

(6) This part of the problem concerns the disposition of the over- or under-applied overhead for the year, as the case may be.

(a) Assume the company does *not* want to revise the overhead cost applied to the job orders manufactured during the year. Record in general journal entry form the year-end entry to dispose of the over- or under-applied overhead.

(b) Assume the company *does* want to revise the overhead cost applied to the job orders manufactured during the year-end entry to dispose of the over- or under-applied overhead. Record in general journal entry form the year-end entry to dispose of the over- or under-applied overhead.

P13. 2 Certain amounts in the accounts shown below have been extracted from all the many entries to each account during the year. These amounts are the summary of the entries to the accounts for a particular job order that was started and completed during the year. The job order called for 1000 units to be manufactured. Since the final inspection usually rejects about 5 bad units for every 100 good units accepted, the company prepared the job order for 1050 units and, sure enough, at the final inspection point 50 units from this job order were rejected and thrown away.

Raw Materials Inventory		Direct Labor Cost Clearing	
	24,930		37,800

Manufacturing Ovehead Costs		Work-in-Process Inventory	
	32,400	24,930	
		37,800	
		32,400	
			95,130

Finished Goods Inventory	
?	
(See below)	

Required:

(1) Determine the cost per unit of the product manufactured by this job order. If you make any arbitrary assumptions or follow any arbitrary procedures to determine this cost, mention them.

(2) The burden rate applied to this job order was $4.05 per direct labor hour, which includes variable overhead of $1.35 per hour. If the company had budgeted total output (of all products for all job orders) for the year of 150,000 direct labor hours, compute the budgeted total *fixed* overhead cost for the year. Show your work clearly.

P13. 3 The purpose of this problem is to demonstrate certain differences between the generally accepted full cost absorption inventory cost valuation method and the direct (variabe) cost method. Assume the following costs for a company during the first two years of manufacturing and selling a *new* product. During each year the company continues to sell their other products, of course.

New Product Costs	Year One	Year Two
Manufacturing Costs		
Raw materials	$1.00 per unit	$1.10 per unit
Direct labor	$2.50 per unit	$2.75 per unit
Variable overhead	$0.50 per unit	$0.55 per unit
Fixed overhead[a]	$280,000	$176,000
Marketing, Administration, and General Costs		
Variable	$2.00 per unit	$2.20 per unit
Fixed[b]	$150,000	$165,000

[a] This is that part of the company's total fixed overhead costs for the year that are allocated to the production of this particular product based on the number of direct labor hours required in the manufacturing of this product each year. The company as a whole had no over- or underapplied fixed overhead costs either year. In other words, in each year the company's production capacity is fully utilized (for all the several products manufactured by the company), and the company's fixed overhead actual costs were exactly as predicted in establishing the fixed overhead burden rate at the beginning of the year.

[b] This is the part of the company's total fixed nonmanufacturing costs for the year that is allocated to the sales of this particular product, based on the number of units sold during the year.

During year one the company sold 100,000 units at $10 per unit sales price, and during year two the company sold 100,000 units at $11 sales price per unit. During year one, the first year of manufacturing this product, the company produced 140,000 units; during year two the company produced only 80,000 units in order to reduce the inventory quantity to a more reasonable ratio of sales volume. The company uses the FIFO inventory method for all its products.

Required:

(1) Determine each year's profit from this new product according to the conventional full cost absorption inventory cost valuation method. To answer this part of the problem prepare a condensed profit performance statement for this product down to the operating profit line.
(2) Determine the operating profit for each year from this product according to the direct (variable) costing method. To answer this part of the problem, prepare a condensed profit performance statement for the product down to the operating profit line.

(*Note:* This part of the problem raises the question whether or not fixed costs should be allocated to product lines for measuring the profit from each product line when the direct costing inventory valuation method is used.)

(3) Prove the difference in each year's operating profit from this product between the absorption cost method and the direct costing method.
(4) Do your results in parts (1) and (2) agree with the general rule stated on page 456 in the chapter that ". . . if fixed manufacturing costs per unit are stable or increasing, then the absorption method will show larger operating profit in years when inventories increase and smaller operating profit in years when inventories decrease"?

P13. 4 This company manufactures products that require handling very heavy raw materials. Thus the company needs a great deal of materials handling equipment such as forklift trucks, overhead hoists, and conveyor systems. Also many direct labor operations are required in the production process. While many overhead costs depend primarily on the weight of the raw materials handled, many others depend primarily on the direct labor hours required to process the raw materials. Rather than separate its overhead costs into two groups, the company prefers to allocate all overhead costs on one common basis. For the coming year the company's accounting department has prepared the following budgeted estimates, based on the sales forecast and production output forecast for the year:

Total pounds of raw material	5,300,000
Total direct labor hours	500,000
Total fixed manufacturing overhead costs	$9,010,000
Total variable manufacturing overhead costs:	
Per pound of raw material handled	$ 2.120
Per direct labor hour worked	$22.472

Notice that variable overhead costs are expressed on *alternative* bases. Variable overhead can be measured as either $2.120 per pound of raw material handled, or as $22.472 per labor hour worked (but *not* as the total of the two).

Required:

(1) Compute the (total) burden rate that would be applied to job orders based on:
   (a) Raw material weight.
   (b) Direct labor hours worked.
(2) Information about two different job orders for the same product completed during the year is as follows:

	First Job Order	Second Job Order
Number of units produced	10,000 units	15,000 units
Raw material cost	$38,250	$59,670
Raw material weight	85,000 pounds	132,600 pounds
Direct labor cost	$57,375	$84,240
Direct labor hours	10,625 hours	15,600 hours

Determine the total manufacturing overhead cost allocated to each job order as well as the total manufacturing overhead cost per unit of finished product if overhead costs are applied on the basis of:
   (a) Raw material weight.
   (b) Direct labor hours worked.

P13. 5 At the start of 1976 this company adopted an overhead burden rate of $3.60 per direct labor hour based on a total production output estimate of 25,000 units of finished product for the year and a total fixed overhead cost estimate of $275,625. This fixed overhead cost estimate is for an output range from 100,000 direct labor hours to 120,000 hours. On average, 4.5 hours of direct labor are required per unit of finished product. The company maintains two manufacturing costs accounts—one in which actual fixed overhead costs are accumulated during the year, and a second in which actual variable overhead costs are accumulated during the year. As overhead is allocated to job orders during the year, the company credits the Manufacturing Overhead Costs Applied account. At the end of 1976 the company's general ledger accounts include the following:

	Year-end Balance	
Account	Debit	Credit
Fixed manufacturing overhead costs	$282,132	
Variable manufacturing overhead costs	$132,768	
Manufacturing overhead costs applied		$398,304

The company actually produced 24,000 units of product during the year which required 110,640 direct labor hours.

Required:

(1) Analyze the difference between the actual total manufacturing overhead costs for the year and the total manufacturing overhead costs applied during the year. (See Exhibit 13.2 for example.)
(2) Assume that one eighth of the year's total production output is on hand at year-end in the ending finished goods inventory, and that the company uses the FIFO method. (There is no work-in-process.) Record the proper entry at year-end 1976 to dispose of the underapplied overhead cost:
   (a) If the revised burden rate is used to adjust inventory cost.
   (b) If the underapplied overhead cost is charged off entirely to expense in 1976.

P13. 6 Refer to Problem 13.5; the same information regarding the company's predetermined burden rate is assumed. In this present problem, however, it is assumed that the company produced 18,000 units of finished products through the end of September 1976, but that starting October 1 the company's entire production work force went on strike and the strike lasted through the end of December. The company shut down its entire production activity during this three-month strike period. However, it was not able to reduce its fixed overhead costs tor 1976, since the strike was not predicted and since the company was unwilling to lay off any production supervisors and managers. The strike was settled December 31, 1976, and the union employees should reutrn to work immediately. At year-end 1976 the company's general ledger accounts include the following:

Account	Year-end Balance	
	Debit	Credit
Fixed manufacturing overhead costs	$282,132	
Variable manufacturing overhead costs	99,576	
Manufacturing overhead costs applied		$298,728

The company, as noted above, produced 18,000 units of product during the first nine months of the year which required 82,980 direct labor hours.

Required:

(1) Analyze the difference between the actual total manufacturing overhead costs for the year and the total manufacturing overhead costs applied during the year. (See Exhibit 13.2 for example.)
(2) In this case would you think it proper to recompute a revised burden rate based on the actual output of 18,000 units and to adjust the company's ending finished goods inventory by using the revised burden rate? (Assume that one eighth of the year's output is on hand in ending inventory and that the company uses the FIFO method.) Explain fully.

P13. 7 Please refer to Problem 13.5; the same information regarding the company's predetermined burden rate is assumed. In this present problem, however, it is assumed that the company experienced unusually large and unexpected sales demand. The company pushed output over its normal product capacity by working many hours of overtime, and produced 28,000 units of finished product during the year. As a result, fixed overhead costs had to be increased because additional supervisory employees were hired. Also, some variable overhead costs depend directly on the gross wages paid to production line workers, and since some direct labor hours were paid on an overtime basis (150% of the normal hourly rate) some, although not all, of the variable costs increased. At year-end 1976 the company's general ledger accounts include the following:

Account	Year-end Balance	
	Debit	Credit
Fixed manufacturing overhead costs	$303,338	
Variable manufacturing overhead costs	157,620	
Manufacturing overhead costs applied		$464,688

The company, as noted above, produced 28,000 units of product during the year which required 129,080 direct labor hours

Required:

(1) Analyze the difference between the actual total manufacturing overhead costs for the year and the total manufacturing overhead costs applied during the year. (See Exhibit 13.2 for example.)

(2) In this case would you think it proper to recompute a revised burden rate based on the actual output for the year and to adjust the company's ending inventory of finished goods by using the revised burden rate? (Assume that one eighth of the year's output is on hand in ending inventory and that the company uses the FIFO method.) Explain fully.

P13. 8 A company manufactures two basic products, called X and Y in this problem. During the year the company completed several job orders of each product: 45,000 units of product X and 72,000 units of product Y were produced. Manufacturing overhead costs are applied to both products based on direct labor hours worked. The direct labor cost per hour is the same for manufacturing both products. The total prime costs for the total output of each product for the year are:

	Product X	Product Y
Raw Materials	$106,200	$226,800
Direct labor	68,640	137,280

The total manufacturing overhead costs for the year are $315,240, which means that underapplied overhead costs at year-end are $6360.

Required:

(1) Determine how much overhead costs have been applied to the total output of each product during the year. Show your computations clearly.

(2) Assume that the variable overhead cost burden rate equals 50% of the of the direct labor cost per hour, and that there is no over- or underapplied variable overhead cost for the year. Determine the actual fixed overhead costs for the year.

P13. 9 This company continuously produces a relatively low priced product in large quantities. Its manufacturing process is organized into four production departments through which the products flow in sequence. For convenience these four departments are called Production Department Nos. 1, 2, 3, and 4 in this problem. Most of the raw materials are started in process in Department No. 1, although some additional raw materials are issued to Department No. 2. No raw materials are added during processing in Departments Nos. 3 and 4. The summary of the manufacturing cost entries for the entire year in each production department's Work-in-Process inventory account are shown below.

Work-in-Process Department No. 1

Debit		Credit	
Beginning Balance	—0—		
Raw Materials	$ 425,000	Transferred Out	$ 543,900
Direct Labor	82,000		
Overhead	36,900		

Work-in-Process Department No. 2

Debit		Credit	
Beginning Balance	—0—		
Raw Materials	$ 82,000	Transferred Out	$ 973,900
Direct Labor	240,000		
Overhead	108,000		
Transferred In	543,900		

Work-in-Process Department No. 3

Debit		Credit	
Beginning Balance	—0—		
Direct Labor	$ 344,000	Transferred Out	$1,472,700
Overhead	154,800		
Transferred In	973,900		

Work-in-Process Department No. 4

Debit		Credit	
Beginning Balance	—0—		
Direct Labor	$ 418,000	Transferred Out	$2,078,800
Overhead	188,100		
Transferred In	1,472,700		

Normally the company shuts down its production line during the last week of the year for the annual maintenance work and safety check of all machinery and equipment. Thus at year-end there usually is no work-in-process inventory. During the year the company's total output was 25,000 units of finished products.

Required:

(1) Determine the average cost per unit of each finished product manufactured during the year, including a breakdown in terms of raw materials, direct labor, and overhead costs per unit.

(2) The company applies overhead costs equal to 45.0% of direct labor costs in each department; variable overhead costs were predicted to be $.30 for each dollar of direct labor cost during the year. The company's actual output for the year is exactly equal to that forecast at the start of the year, when the predetermined burden rate was computed, and the company's actual direct labor cost per unit finished during the year is exactly as predicted. Based on this information, determine the estimated total fixed manufacturing overhead costs for the year used in establishing the burden rate at the start of the year.

P13.10 This company operates a machine shop. In March 1976 the company was low bidder on a contract to deliver 600 units of kartz by May 15 at a contract price of $200 each. The company's estimate of the costs to manufacture each unit of kartz was:

40 pounds of materials at $1.50 per pound	$ 60
20 hours of direct labor at $4.00 per hour	80
Manufacturing overhead (40% variable)	30
Total cost	$170

Inventories on hand at April 1 included 30 completed kartz which already had been transferred to finished goods inventory, 70 kartz 60% processed, and 2000 pounds of materials at a cost of $3000. Production during March was at estimated costs. During April 500 kartz were started in production, and 450 kartz were completed and transferred to finished goods. The work-in-process inventory at April 30 was 10% processed. All material is added when a kartz is started in production. The materials inventory is priced under the FIFO method.

The following information is available for the month of April:

(a) Materials purchased:

Pounds	Amount
8,000	$12,000
8,000	12,800
4,000	5,600

(b) Materials requisitioned and put into production totaled 21,000 pounds.

(c) The direct labor payroll amounted to $37,296 for 8880 hours.

(d) Since the Kartz contract represents the only products processed during April, all overhead costs for the month are charged to the kartz units being worked on. Actual manufacturing overhead incurred, including indirect labor, totaled $13,125 and was charged to the Overhead-in-Process account.

(e) Accounts employed by the company include Material-in-Process, Labor-in-Process, Overhead-in-Process, Work-in-Process Inventory, Finished Goods Inventory, and Materials inventory. The first three accounts are closed monthly to the Work-in-Process Inventory account.

(f) As stated above, 450 units were completed during April and transferred to finished goods. The company uses the FIFO inventory method.

Required:

Set up a T account for each of the following accounts; enter the beginning balance and the summary of the entries to each account during the month, including the month-end closing entries to the Work-in-Process Inventory account. (Show your computations clearly for each entry in the accounts as well as for the beginning balances.)

Materials Inventory
Materials-in-Process
Labor-in-Process
Overhead-in-Process
Work-in-Process Inventory
Finished Goods Inventory

Determine the cost of each finished unit of kartz manufactured during the month. Show each cost component that makes up the total cost per unit of finished product.

P13.11 An analysis of the company's three ending inventory accounts' balances reveals the following.

Inventory Account	Cost			
	Raw Materials	Direct Labor	Applied Overhead	Total
Raw Materials	$212,415	$ —0—	$ —0—	$212,415
Work-in-process	71,400	22,050	8,820	102,270
Finished goods	382,347	262,395	104,958	749,700

During the year the company recorded total cost of goods sold expense of $4,998,000; the cost makeup of this total expense is in the same proportions as that shown above for the Finished Goods inventory account ending balance. Because of a strike during the last three months of last year, the company started this year with no work-in-process or finished goods inventories. The ratio of raw material to direct labor cost has been constant through the year for all goods completed. Manufacturing overhead is applied as a percentage of direct labor cost, which is credited directly to the Manufacturing Overhead Costs account.

Shortly before the close of the year the company's accountant noticed that the debit balance in the company's Manufacturing Overhead Costs account was unusually large, so he investigated. He found that in establishing the predetermined burden rate at the start of the year certain fixed overhead costs were *not* included in the computation. If these omitted costs had been included, then the balance in the Manufacturing Overhead Costs account would have been zero by year-end. Since the costs were not included in the burden rate computation, the debit balance is $135,583.

Required:

(1) Make the appropriate adjusting entry required at year-end to dispose of the underapplied overhead cost for the year. Show your computations clearly.

(2) *All* raw materials are issued to production as the first step of starting the manufacturing process. Knowing this, determine the percentage of completion regarding the direct labor and overhead costs of the work-in-process at the end of the year.

(3) If the average direct labor cost per hour for the year is $5 and if the variable overhead burden rate applied was $1.25 per direct labor hour, determine the total fixed overhead costs that were used in establishing the company's burden rate applied during the year (excluding the $135,583 additional fixed overhead costs discussed above).

P13.12 A certain job order was started in process on Thursday, March 11, 1976. It will require all of the company's production facilities and work force while it is being processed; no other job orders will be worked on while this job order moves through the production process. *All* raw materials are issued to production on the first day. This job order should take 45 working days to complete. The company operates its production plant 5 days each week, Monday to Friday. For all practical purposes an equal amount of work is done each working day, since the company has an experienced, stable size work force. At March 31, 1976 the company prepares the first quarter production reports, which includes this particular job order that is still in process at this date, of course. Pertinent information for this in-process job order is as follows:

	Costs to Date
Raw materials	$ 68,000
Direct labor	23,400
Variable overhead applied	11,700
Fixed overhead applied	12,750
Total	$115,850

At this time, March 31, 1976, the company's sales manager needs an estimate of the cost per unit of finished product to be produced by this job order. Starting April 1, 1976 you know that the company's entire direct labor force will receive a cost of living wage increase of 2.5%, which should cause the variable overhead per direct labor hour to increase 2.0%. Fixed overhead costs, at least over the next three months, should not increase.

Required:

(1) Assuming that 12,500 units of finished product are to be produced by this job order, determine the estimated cost per unit produced by this job order. Show your computations clearly.

(2) Determine the company's total fixed overhead costs for the year, which was used to establish the fixed overhead burden rate.

P13.13 This company started to manufacture a new product early in the year. Four job orders for this new product were started and completed during the year. The costs of each successive job order are as follows:

	Job Order No. 1	Job Order No. 2	Job Order No. 3	Job Order No.4
Raw materials	$10,000	$10,000	$10,000	$10,000
Direct labor*	36,000	28,800	23,040	18,432
Overhead	18,000	14,400	11,520	9,216
Total cost	$64,000	$53,200	$44,560	$37,648
Number of units	1,000	1,000	1,000	1,000
* Direct labor hours	8,000	6,400	5,120	4,096

The company applies overhead based on direct labor hours. Notice the "learning curve" effect in each successive job order processed. This means that as a result of prior experience, there is a learning process—prior mistakes are avoided and other improvements occur. Consequently the second job order required only 80% of the direct labor hours as the first job order, and the third job order required only 80% of the direct labor hours as the second job, and so on. The production manager predicts that there will be little if any additional learning curve benefits byeond the fourth job order.

Required: Assume the company sold 2500 units of the new product during the year and has 1500 units on hand in its ending finished goods inventory. Which inventory method, FIFO, Average Cost, or LIFO, is the most appropriate? In your answer, explain why you decided aganist the other two mothods. Also, show the computation of the cost of goods sold expense and ending inventory cost value. Explain fully.

P13.14 The main purpose of this problem is to contrast the direct (variable) costing inventory valuation method with the full cost absorption method. For this purpose all manufacturing costs and other operating expenses are held constant over a four-year period, although you realize of course, that most (if not all) costs and expenses change over time. However, cost and expense changes year to year would confuse the analysis in this problem. Thus, make the following assumptions:

(a) The company manufactures and sells just one product.
(b) The company started business in early January 1974.
(c) The sales price per unit sold is a constant $100 in all four years.
(d) The company built a production plant and installed machinery and equipment that provides a maximum annual output capacity of 120,000 units under normal and usual conditions. There have been no additions or retirements of any fixed assets during the company's first four years of business.
(e) The production quantities and sales quantities each year are:

	1974	1975	1976	1977
Total quantity produced	120,000	120,000	120,000	120,000
Total quantity sold	100,000	115,000	120,000	130,000

(There is no work-in-process at the end of any year.)

(f) The variable manufacturing costs per unit produced are $30 in all four years.
(g) The total fixed manufacturing overhead cost is $2,400,000 in each of the four years.
(h) The variable selling, administration, and other nonmanufacturing costs per unit sold are $20 in all four years.
(i) The total fixed selling, administration, and other nonmanufacturing costs is $1,794,000 in each of the four years.

Required:

(1) Prepare brief but adequately detailed profit performance statements for the four years (1974 to 1977) down to the operating profit before interest and income tax according to:
(a) The full cost absorption inventory cost valuation method.
(b) The direct (variable) costing method.
(2) Analyze and explain the difference in operating profit between the two methods for each year.
(3) Analyze and explain the difference in operating profit from 1975 to 1976 if
(a) The full cost absorption method is used.
(b) The direct (variable) costing method is used.

P13.15 Please refer to Problem 13.14; the same company and assumptions are used for this problem, with one important difference. Instead of the production and sales quantities given in information item (e) in Problem 13.14, assume the following:

	1974	1975	1976	1977
Total quantity produced	120,000	60,000	120,000	120,000
Total quantity sold	60,000	100,000	120,000	140,000

(There is no work-in-process at the end of any year.)

Required: Prepare brief but adequately detailed profit performance statements for the four years (1974 to 1977) down to the operating profit before interest and income tax line according to:

(1) The full cost absorption inventory cost valuation method, with a normal production capacity assumption of 120,000 units per year; and,
(2) The direct (variable) costing method.
(3) Comment on the problem you see in 1974 with the use of the full cost absorption method.

P13.16 This company started to manufacture a certain product six years ago. In each year only one large job order was processed to manufacture all the quantity of the product needed that year. Although not a "hot" item, this product has shown a steady sales growth. During each of the six years the company increased the finished goods inventory quantity of this product. The company uses the LIFO inventory cost method. In brief, the entries to the finished goods inventory account for this particular product through the end of the most recent year, December 31, 1977, are as follows:

Finished Goods Inventory—This Product

1972	10,000 units	$ 50,000	1972	8,000 units	$ 40,000
1973	10,500 units	58,800	1973	10,000 units	56,000
1974	12,500 units	75,000	1974	12,000 units	72,000
1975	15,750 units	99,225	1975	15,000 units	94,500
1976	21,250 units	144,500	1976	20,000 units	136,000
1977	25,000 units	175,000	1977	24,000 units	168,000

Required:

(1) Determine the cost of goods sold expense for this product for each of the six years that would have been reported to management according to the FIFO inventory method, and determine the FIFO cost value of the December 31, 1977 finished goods inventory of this product.
(2) For insuring this part of the company's total inventory of finished goods during 1978, which per unit cost value is most relevant?
(3) For making sales price decisions during 1978, which cost value per unit is most relevant?
(4) Assume that during the early part of 1978 the company manufactures a Job order of 30,000 units of this product for a total cost of $222,000. As a result of an unexpected surge in the sales demand for the product late in 1978, the company sold all of its stock of this product, so that at the end of 1978 it has a zero quantity of this item on hand. Based on the cost of the

1978 job order, the company established the sales price of this product to equal 150% of the manufacturing cost per unit. This is the normal practice of this company which has been followed in each of the six years the product has been manufactured.

(a) How much gross profit from the sale of this product in 1978 would be reported to the managers in this situation? Do you have any objection to this amount? Would you attach a special explanation or interpretation for the managers? Explain fully.

(b) Early in 1979 the company plans to manufacture a job order large enough to bring the finished goods inventory quantity of this product back up to normal level. In other words, the 1979 job order will be large enough to replace the stock of inventory that was sold late in 1978, as well as to cover 1979 expected sales demand. Because of this some of the company's managers argue that, somehow, the replacement cost of the normal inventory quantity that was sold out late in 1978 should be recognized. Do you know of any accounting procedures that would do this? Explain fully.

Chapter Fourteen

Standard Cost Systems

STANDARD COST SYSTEMS

General Concept and Role of Standards

The general concept of a standard of performance is very important in management planning and control. Generally speaking, a standard can be thought of as a measure or test of achievement that can be and should be attained. A standard is the bench mark against which actual performance can be compared. Thus the standard can be used as the reference point to measure a shortfall or deficiency of performance, and to raise questions such as: "What went wrong, and why?" and, "How can things be improved next period?" On the other hand, if actual performance is better than standard, then the standard is the reference point for measuring the added margin of success or the "surplus of achievement."

Certainly the use of standards of one sort or another is found in most areas of a business organization. For instance, a standard of safety for employees may be expressed as zero accidents, or zero workdays lost because of accidents. A company may adopt a standard of, at least, a 15% annual rate of net income on its stockholders' equity. A rate of 2% or less of defective units may be established as the production standard for manufacturing its products. A turnover rate of 5% or less among its employees for the year may be a standard expected by a company. Indeed, it is difficult to think of any area of a typical business where the managers responsible for the performance of this segment of the organization do not use several standards. In short, the term "standard" can have a rather broad and diverse meaning.

In contrast, the term *standard cost system* has a more limited meaning. This term refers to the methods and procedures for the development and management use of standard costs for certain operations of a business. Basically, standard costs are *carefully predetermined cost measures* that are based on the conditions and circumstances expected to prevail over the coming period. A standard cost, in other words, is a "scientific" or "engineered" measure of the cost of an operation or series of operations that form a distinct unit of activity, which can be and should be achieved during a coming period. The main application of standard cost systems by most companies has been in the manufacturing area of operations .

In the manufacturing area there is a convenient and obvious focal point for standard costs—each product or batch of products being manufactured. Also, production costs are usually larger than the costs of marketing products or the administration costs of an organization. (It is true that manufacturing costs of some products are less than their marketing costs, but this is not very typical.) Thus the main concern of this chapter is with the development, implementation, and uses of manufacturing standard costs (and variances of actual costs from standard costs).

The logic and uses of standard cost systems are applicable in the other areas of operation as well, that is, in the broad areas of marketing and administration. But standard costs are usually more developed and more widely used in the manufacturing area. For one reason, work measurement and the development of efficiency indexes are more difficult in the nonmanufacturing areas. For instance, what is the standard number of letters that the typing pool should turn out per hour? What is the standard number of pounds that an employee working on the delivery dock should handle per hour? What is the standard number of miles that a salesman should drive per sale, or in total per year? No doubt, most companies expect certain performance standards or quotas to be met by employees in nonmanufacturing areas. The general concepts and procedures of standard costs, which are discussed for manufacturing operations below, also apply to nonmanufacturing operations, although each different operating area presents special problems.

Advantages and Disadvantages of Standard Cost Systems

There are several important management reasons or advantages for the development and use of standard costs. First, the development and construction of standard costs requires the close study, analysis, and evaluation of the manufacturing operations of the company relative to the facilities, resources, practices, and purchase market conditions that are expected during the coming period. In other words, to build up a standard cost "forces" managers to take a careful and fairly detailed look at how things are being done, and which input factors (raw material, labor skills, etc.) are being bought in what kind of supply markets. Based on this scrutiny of the company's manufacturing methods and procedures, the managers must establish, *in advance,* specific measures of performance—both in terms of physical measures of efficiency (or productivity) *and* in terms of purchase prices of the particular input factors being used. In short, managers are directed toward the key question: "What *should* costs be, given all the relevant factors that determine the final outcome of the costs?"

Once developed, standard costs become the bench marks or yardsticks against which actual cost performance can be compared. In particular, deviations (called variances) of actual costs from standard costs signal "out of control" situations, which may deserve the immediate attention and action of managers. Deviations from standards provide valuable feedback information for review and control of performance. Control decisions and actions require, first of all, information to act on, which in turn means that the manager needs a system or method to evaluate actual performance relative to the goals, objectives, policies, and performance standards of the specific operations and activities under the manager's sphere of responsibility and authority.

If properly developed, a standard cost is the best available measure against which actual cost performance can be compared. There seem to be only two basic practical alternatives to a standard cost (for comparison of actual cost performance): (1) past (historical) cost performance; and, (2) some current subjective individual measure of cost performance that is adopted by the manager (usually somewhat arbitrarily). In short, standard costs provide a more useful reference point for judging actual cost performance for the basic purpose of controlling cost performance. There are other important uses of standard costs as well.

Standard cost information is quite useful in several areas of management decision making, such as setting sales price targets for the next period, the comparative analysis of alternative manufacturing methods and facilities that should be considered, and so on. Standard costs are usually better than actual costs for decision making purposes. Standard costs are the planned *future* costs for the coming period of time such as three months or longer. Actual costs, if you stop to think about it, are *historical* costs of *past* periods. Decisions can only affect future action and results, not the past results. Managers need to focus on predicted future costs; they should not assume that historical costs will be the same in the future. Standard costs are usually the best sort of predicted future costs that are available to managers.*

Also, actual costs usually are different from period to period; hence, the historical cost pattern is one of fluctuation. In contrast, a standard cost is a *stabilized* cost during the future period to which it applies. Managers find a stabilized cost more convenient to deal with in their decision analysis. Last, it should be mentioned that standard costs are the backbone of a formal budgeting system, which is discussed in Chapters Six and Seven. You may want to review briefly the section in Chapter Six dealing with estimating costs (pages 193 to 198), to appreciate this remark.

Despite the important advantages of standard cost systems, some disadvantages exist that managers should be aware of and should weigh in their decision regarding whether to adopt a standard cost system. One way or another, a standard cost system runs parallel to the company's actual cost system. The company, in other words, must collect two sets of cost data—the standard costs of the operations and the actual costs. This additional "second layer" of data requires more recordkeeping and data processing costs. Also, quite a bit of management time and effort goes into the development of standard costs, as well as the interpretation of variances of actual costs from standard costs. Managers should always ask whether this time could be better spent elsewhere doing something else.

A standard cost system may become an end in itself, rather than the *means* of better management decision making and control. Once developed and estab-

---

* Not all future costs to be recorded are necessarily relevant to special decision situations. See Chapter Eleven for discussion of relevant cost analysis.

lished as part of a company's way of doing things, a standard cost system tends to become *institutionalized,* that is, becomes a precedent for what is the "right" way for getting things done in the organization. Unless a standard cost system is clearly worthless (not very likely), it is difficult to abandon. Various persons in the organization who are most directly involved in the preparation of the standards develop *vested interests* in the standard cost system. Usually they are not willing to give-up; they probably would resist any attempts to do so. Actually, there may be resistance even to proposed changes or modifications, since it is more comfortable and easier to keep the system running in the same way as before. Organizational "fossilization" tends to freeze a standard cost system, as well as many established procedures and policies of a company.

Although the general idea of a standard cost is very persuasive in the abstract, in the more concrete, detailed, and practical circumstances of the "real world," standard costs are not all that easy to determine. Setting standards is usually based on arbitrary methods, to some degree. Usually some degree of "guessing" is built into the standards. In other words, two different managers or accountants setting the same standard may arrive at different cost measures to some extent. Although not a perfect comparison, the development of standard costs is like two different accountants deciding which inventory cost accounting method is best for a company. One may choose FIFO and the other may prefer LIFO, *given the same set of facts.* In using standard costs, managers should be aware that the standards may be "conservative" or "liberal." That is, the standards may be set tight or loose. They may be rather difficult to achieve. Or, they may be relatively easy to achieve and to surpass. This is especially important in the interpretation of variances of actual costs from standard costs, which is discussed later in this chapter.

Also, the setting of standards may not have the best motivation effects on those whose performance is judged by the standards. How would you like to be held accountable for achieving a standard that you think is not fair? What would be your behavior response? You might think of ways to fool the reporting of actual cost performance, such as shifting hours you save on one job order to other job orders which are going over standard, so that all your job orders come in very close to standard. This may look better, at least in your opinion, than a report that shows some jobs considerably under standard and some considerably over standard. You may prefer to be thought of as a consistent performer than as an erratic performer. Yet, on the other hand, a standard that you think is fair might be a very important incentive that you are willing to work hard to achieve. Without this incentive your performance might not be as good. There is a great sense of satisfaction in achieving a demanding yet achievable goal. Furthermore, having the standard in the open is a good way to communicate and to make clear that you have achieved the goal, which might otherwise go unnoticed by your superiors.

In summary, a standard cost system is a useful management tool, but the cost of using the tool and the problems inherent in using the tool should be carefully considered by managers. Ideally, top level managers should apply some sort of *cost-benefits analysis* to decide whether a standard cost system should be adopted or continued by the company. Do the benefits (discussed above) outweigh the cost and disadvantages? Obviously many companies have decided that the cost and troubles of a standard cost system are more than offset by its advantages for their decision making and control purposes. Standard costs are especially useful in formal budgeting systems. The basic alternative to a standard cost system, keep in mind, is an historical cost system. Generally speaking, historical costs must be updated for *current* management decisions that activate the *future* performance of the company. A standard cost system may not be perfect, but it may be the best practical method and approach available for management control and for management decision making; both of which by their very nature are future directed.

Development of Standard Costs

As explained in Chapters Twelve and Thirteen, the costs of manufacturing a product consist of:

1. *Direct* (or *prime*) *costs:* These are the costs of the raw materials that go into the product, and the costs of the direct labor operations of working the raw materials and handling the products; these costs can be directly identified with the products being manufactured.
2. *Overhead* (or *indirect*) *costs:* These are all other manufacturing costs that cannot be directly associated with particular production lots, and which must be allocated among the production lots on some reasonable basis.

The production lot may be a job order, which moves through the manufacturing process as a separate batch, or it may be the output of a production department over a certain period of time (frequently a month) in the case of a continuous manufacturing processing system. Since it is easier to follow the trail of a job order through the accounting cycle, this type of production lot is used as the example to illustrate standard cost entries in the discussion that follows.

To determine the standard cost of a product means to identify each and every input factor that goes into the production of the product, and for each input factor to develop a *quantity* standard and a *price* standard (or dollar cost per unit of the input). The quantity standard is a measure of how many units of this input factor should be used to manufacture the product; in essence, it is a productivity standard, or an efficiency standard. For raw materials, for instance, each separate raw material item that goes into the manufacture of the product must be identified specifically, and the precise quantity of each raw material item has to be measured. The price standard is a dollar measure of how much each unit of each input factor should cost. Consider direct labor cost, for instance. For each specific step or direct labor operation in the manufacturing process, the wage rates of the specific employees who will work on the products must be determined.

Standard Cost Example Introduced

It would be very cumbersome to introduce a completely realistic example of how a standard cost system works. Usually there are many separate input factors required to manufacture a product. For instance, there may be 10 or more separate raw material items, 20 or more separate direct labor steps in the manufacture of the product, and there may be 30 or more distinct manufacturing overhead cost items, some of which are variable costs and some of which are fixed costs. A large number of factors would make an example very tedious to follow. To keep the example within manageable limits, therefore, a hypothetical example is introduced with a relatively few separate input factors. The *standard cost sheet* for this example is shown as Exhibit 14.1. It is for a job order for 1000 units of a particular product to be manufactured during the coming period.

EXHIBIT 14.1
Illustration of a Standard Cost Sheet: Job Order No. 3A

```
                       JOB ORDER NO. 3A
               Quantity: 1,000 units of this product

Raw Materials
   Item A:    (2,500 lb × $10.00/lb)          =   $25,000
   Item B:    (5,000 sq ft × $2.00/sq ft)     =    10,000
   Total Raw Materials                                          $35,000

Direct Labor
   Step One:  (1,400 hr × $3.75/hr)           =   $ 5,250
   Step Two:  (  400 hr × $6.25/hr)           =     2,500
   Total Direct Labor                                           $ 7,750

Variable Manufacturing Overhead
   Electrical Power Usage:
            (5,000 kW-hr × $0.05/kW-hr)        =   $   250
   Machinery Parts and Supplies:
            (1,400 mach. hr × $2.50/mach. hr)  =     3,500
   Total Variable Overhead                                      $ 3,750

Fixed Manufacturing Overhead
   (1,800 direct labor hours × $5.00 standard
      fixed burden rate)                       =                $ 9,000
Total Standard Cost of Job Order                                $55,500
          Standard Cost per Unit: $55,500/1,000 = $55.50
```

Raw Material and Direct Labor Standards

The determination of quantity standards and price standards for the prime manufacturing costs requires the careful and detailed analysis of each raw material component and each separate labor operation. For this reason these standards are sometimes called *engineered* standards, since the production engineering staff of the company or other production management experts usually are involved in determining the quantity standards, and they also determine the specifications of the materials purchased, and so on. Clearly cost accountants need to understand the company's manufacturing process. But in developing quantity and price standards, the cost accountant must rely on those managers who decide how to manufacture the products, who purchase the raw materials inputs, and who supervise the labor operations. Thus the managers who design the plant layout, who schedule the production activity, who direct the purchase of the raw materials, who assign workers to particular work stations, and the like, are key sources of information in the development of the quantity and price standards for prime costs.

The quantity standard and the price standard for each raw material item and for each separate labor operation present their own specific problems. It is difficult to generalize thoroughly about how these standards are reached. There are some common problems, however. Raw material quantity standards depend on assumptions about what is considered a normal percentage of wastage due to shrinkage, scrap, spoilage, and damage in the handling, storage, and working on the raw materials. Usually there is a normal percentage of wastage of each raw material item because of unavoidable causes inherent in the manufacturing process. In the example the quantity standard is 2500 pounds of raw material item A (see Exhibit 14.1), even though not all of the 2500 pounds ends up in the 1000 units of finished product. That is, this quantity standard allows for normal wastage due to cutting and trimming to size. Likewise, there is a wastage allowance for the other raw material item in the example.

Each direct labor quantity standard also depends on assumptions about the time it takes the job order to move through each work station, and just how fast and efficiently employees are expected to work. In most cases there is some allowance for "downtime" or other nonproductive time during which no work is being done on the products. Beyond a reasonable and normal allowance for downtime, managers and the cost accountant should draw a line and treat additional time as truly wasteful. The qualifications and skills of the employees at each work station along the entire production process, and the rates of pay of each job grade or job classification must be identified. If the company's employees are unionized, then the labor contract in force for the coming period is the main information source to determine the labor wage rates.

Manufacturing Overhead Standards

Variable overhead costs can be separated into their quantity and price standards, although not as easily as prime costs. In the example the company is able to meter the amount of electrical power for each machine or work station in its plant. On this basis each job order passing through each work station can be allocated its share of electrical power cost. The second variable overhead cost in this example (see Exhibit 14.1) is a charge for short-lived machinery parts and supplies, which includes items such as drill bits, blades, and the like that wear our roughly in proportion to the number of hours of use of the machines. These items have to be replaced as soon as they break or when they become too worn for further use. For comparison, tires on a truck wear out more or less in direct proportion to the number of miles driven. Likewise, many machines and other types of production equipment wear out certain parts in a fairly close proportion to the hours of use of these assets.

The two variable overhead costs in this example have a reasonably clear basis of allocation to each job order. Many variable overhead costs, on the other hand, are more difficult to trace or to identify with specific job orders. These indirect overhead costs vary in proportion to the company's *total* production activity for the period, but it is not practical to determine a different method of allocation for each and every indirect variable overhead cost. A more practical solution is to charge most (perhaps all) variable overhead costs to individual job orders on the basis of a common denominator among all the job orders, such as the number of direct labor hours or the total weight of the raw materials of each job order, which is the burden rate approach discussed in Chapter Thirteen (pages 440 to 442).

The nature of *fixed* manufacturing costs has been discussed in previous chapters. Only certain relevant points are mentioned here. One fundamental idea is that fixed manufacturing costs are incurred by a company to provide production *capacity* for a given time period (usually one year). The measurement of production capacity seldom is easy or obvious. As we mention in Chapter Thirteen (page 454), a company's theoretical maximum production output is called ideal capacity. This is a total output level that would be possible *if* all manufacturing resources were operated at peak efficiency continuously throughout the entire year (although the company may not need all of this production capacity during the year). Usually a more realistic, practical, and "normal" measure of capacity will be adopted, one that allows for some degree of nonutilization of the company's plant, equipment, and work force. Raw material standards allow for some percentage of normal wastage of the materials as unavoidable in most production processes. Likewise, some wastage of a company's theoretical maximum production capacity is normal and unavoidable in most practical manufacturing situations.

Given that the managers have adopted a realistic practical measure of production capacity, the next question concerns the predicted or budgeted production output for the coming period. Assume for purposes of this example that the practical production capacity of the company's plant and facilities is 50,000 direct labor hours for the coming year. The theoretical maximum capacity is more than this. But the production vice-president's best estimate is that 50,000 direct labor hours is the maximum volume of activity that could be achieved under normal operating conditions. However, in this example the production output schedule for the coming year (based on budgeted sales volume) requires only 45,000 direct labor hours. In other words, the company knows in advance that there will be 5000 direct labor hours of unneeded production capacity available during the coming year. The company's managers are unwilling to step down any of the fixed overhead costs, since the sales and production volumes are predicted to increase the following year, and they want to remain at the present capacity level to be prepared for this future increase in sales.

In this example, assume that the company's total fixed manufacturing costs are budgeted at $225,000 for the coming year. Which of the following two fixed manufacturing cost burden rates should be adopted as the standard cost?

Alternative Computations of Fixed Manufacturing Costs Standard Burden Rate

Alternative No. 1: Based on Total Available Capacity

   $225,000/50,000 direct labor hours = $4.50 per hour

Alternative No. 2: Based on Budgeted Need for Capacity

   $225,000/45,000 direct labor hours = $5.00 per hour

We observe in the standard cost sheet for the job order in this example (Exhibit 14.1) that the $5 standard fixed overhead burden rate is decided on. In essence, therefore, the cost of the unused production capacity for the coming year, 5000 direct labor hours in this case, is being loaded on the planned production of 45,000 direct labor hours.

The fixed overhead cost standard burden rate can be objected to on the grounds that the cost of the 5000 direct labor hours of excess capacity (for the coming year) should be charged to expense, and should not be charged to the various production lots during the coming year. This argument favors the $4.50 standard fixed cost burden rate. Also, the $5 fixed cost burden rate is troublesome in another respect. If the company were to increase its production output to 50,000 direct labor hours during the coming year, then its total fixed manufacturing costs should *not* increase. If the company's actual production output required 50,000 direct labor hours during the coming year, then at $5 per hour $250,000 of fixed overhead costs would be applied to the production lots worked on during the year, which would result in overapplied fixed overhead cost for the year. In any case, the company decides to use 45,000 direct labor hours to determine the standard fixed overhead burden rate, which gives $5 per direct labor hour.

Recording Standard Costs and Variances

A standard cost system can be implemented in two basic ways:

1. The *actual* manufacturing costs, and only these actual costs of each production lot are accumulated in the accounts, as explained in Chapters

Twelve and Thirteen. Then, the actual costs are compared with the standard cost sheets for each production lot so that the appropriate variances can be determined. The standard cost sheets and the variance reports are "off to the side" of the actual cost entries and accounts. Standard costs and variances are *not* entered in the double-entry general ledger accounts of the formal recordkeeping system of the company.

2. *Standard* costs are entered in the inventory accounts, and the variances of actual costs from standard costs are also entered in accounts. In this way the variances and standard costs become part of the formal double-entry recordkeeping accounts of the company. This method involves certain differences and additional procedures in contrast with the basic cost accounting cycle explained in Chapters Twelve and Thirteen. These differences and procedures are described in the remainder of this chapter.

In the following discussion one summary entry is made for each cost factor. In actual practice, many entries are made during the manufacturing process, which may stretch over several weeks. To illustrate the essential steps of recording standard costs in the accounts, it is appropriate to make summary entries spanning the entire production cycle of the job order.

Purchase and Issue of Raw Materials

The following entry records the purchase of the raw materials needed for this job order. Notice that the company buys larger quantities of these materials than the quantities needed for this *one* job order. Some of the same materials are used for other job orders.

Debit (+) Raw Materials Inventory—Item A	41,600	
Debit (+) Raw Materials Inventory—Item B	15,200	
Credit (+) Accounts Payable		56,800

PURCHASE OF RAW MATERIALS

Purchase of raw materials for inventory, some of which will be issued to the job lot in the example:

Item A: (4,000 lb × $10.40/lb) = $41,600
Item B: (8,000 sq ft × $1.90/sq ft) = $15,200

The total issues of the two raw material items to this job order over the entire production process on the job is summarized as follows:

Summary of Raw Materials Quantities Issued to Job Order

	Standard	Actual Issuance
Raw Material Item A:	2500 lb	2600 lb
Raw Material Item B:	5000 sq ft	5100 sq ft

The actual purchase prices of these two raw materials are shown in the entry made above to record the purchase. For Item A the actual purchase price is more than the standard price. Based on this actual price and quantity information, as well as the standard cost sheet information (Exhibit 14.1), the summary entry shown below is made to record the issue of raw materials to this job order, *and* to record the raw material variances. Notice in particular the computations of the raw material price and quantity variances, which are recorded in the variance accounts.

The Work-in-Process Inventory account is charged with the raw material *standard cost* for the job order. Differences between the actual cost of raw materials issued to the job order and the standard raw material cost are recorded in either the price variance account, or in the quantity variance account. In brief, the difference between the actual purchase and the standard price of each item is multiplied times the actual quantity of the item used to determine the price variance of each item. The two price variances are summed to get the total raw material price variance for the job order. The excess of the actual quantity used over the standard quantity allowed for each raw material item is multiplied by the standard price of each item to determine the quantity variance for each item. The two quantity variances are summed to get the total quantity variance for the job order.

Debit (+) Work-in-Process Inventory (at Standard)	35,000.00
Debit (+) Raw Materials Price Variance	530.00
Debit (+) Raw Materials Quantity Variance	1,200.00
Credit (−) Raw Materials Inventory Item A	27,040.00
Credit (−) Raw Materials Inventory Item B	9,690.00

RECORDING ISSUANCE OF RAW MATERIALS TO JOB ORDER AND RAW MATERIALS VARIANCES

Issues of raw materials to Job Order No. 3A. Work-in-Process Inventory is charged with standard cost of raw materials, according to the standard cost sheet for this job order (see Exhibit 14.1). Differences between standard cost and actual cost of materials used are computed as follows: (+ =actual more than standard; − =actual less than standard)

Raw Materials Price Variance
Item A: (+$0.40/lb × 2600 lb used)	=	+$1,040.00
Item B: (−$0.10/sq ft × 5,100 sq ft used)	=	− 510.00
Total (Net) Variance		+$ 530.00

Raw Materials Quantity Variance
Item A: (+100 lb × $10.00/lb)	=	+$1,000.00
Item B: (+100 sq ft × $2.00/sq ft)	=	+ 200.00
Total Variance		+$1,200.00

Recording the raw materials entry shown above has two main effects. First, the Work-in-Process Inventory is charged with the *standard* raw materials cost of the job order. When the job order is completed, the Finished Goods Inventory account also will be recorded at standard cost. In other words, product costs are "standardized" in the inventory accounts. If another job order of the same product is processed during the period, this second job order would be entered in the inventory accounts at the *same* standard cost per unit. In short, managers can look at the inventory balances and know that these cost values are stated at the standard costs established for the products. The second main effect is that the variance accounts are ready sources of information for reporting exceptions or deviations from performance standards in management accounting reports. The variances do not have to be computed at a later time; the amounts are already entered in the accounts.

Raw materials *price variances* are primarily the responsibility of the managers in the company's purchasing department. The price variances for the job order would raise questions such as: Why was the purchase price for Item A 40 cents more than the standard price for this item? Why was there a cost savings of 10 cents per square foot on Item B? Price variance information accumulated in the price variance accounts is reported to the purchasing managers, as well as being reported to the managers who review their performance. The raw materials price variance on this particular job order would be included in the regular monthly or quarterly report on the total raw materials price variance for all the production activity during the entire period.

Raw materials *quantity* variances are primarily the responsibility of production managers and supervisors, and these variances (if significant) are investigated by them to determine the reasons. The reason may be the improper handling of the raw materials, or the poor performance by the workers on this particular job order. Raw materials quantity variances are more of an *internal* variance, compared with price variances. Quantity variances depend on the manager's ability to control the efficiency of using raw materials, such as preventing abnormal wastage and shrinkage, and avoiding damage to the raw materials during the production process.

Last, notice that *unfavorable* variances are *debits* to the variance accounts. Unfavorable means an excess of actual cost over standard cost. The excess of actual cost over standard cost, which otherwise would be debited (+) to the Work-in-Process Inventory account, is instead debited to the variance accounts. Favorable variances are just the reverse. In that case, the standard cost is debited to the Work-in-Process Inventory account, even though the actual cost is less than the standard cost. Hence, the credits to the variance accounts make up the difference as it were. (The entry below to record overhead costs includes favorable variances.)

Direct Labor Cost

The entry shown below summarizes the direct labor cost for the job order in this example. Certain aspects regarding the computation of the direct labor cost variances shown in the entry deserve brief mention. Differences between the actual wage rates per hour and the standard wage rates are multiplied times the *actual* number of labor hours worked, to determine the labor *wage rate* variances. The separate wage rate variances for each labor step are summed to determine the total wage rate variance for the job order. The difference between the actual number of hours worked and the standard hours allowed for each labor step is multiplied times the *standard* cost per hour to determine the labor *efficiency* variances for each labor operation. These separate variances are summed to determine the total efficiency variance for the job order.

Debit (+) Work-in-Process Inventory
        (at Standard)   7,750.00
Debit (+) Direct Labor Price (or
        Wage Rate) Variance   368.75
Debit (+) Direct Labor Efficiency
        (or Quantity) Variance   406.25

    Credits (Cash, short-term liabilities,etc.)   8,525.00

Based on direct labor source documents, such as time cards, the total hours and wage rates chargable to Job Order No. 3A are:

    Step One: (1,550 hr × $4.00/hr)   = $6,200.00
    Step Two: (375 hr × $6.20 hr)   =   2,325.00
    Total Actual Direct Labor Cost $8,525.00

In contrast, the standard quantities and standard wage rates for this job order are as follows (see standard cost sheet, Exhibit 14.1):

    Step One: (1,400 hr × $3.75/hr)   = $5,250.00
    Step Two: (400 hr × $6.25/hr)   =   2,500.00
    Total Standard Direct Labor Cost $7,750.00

The direct labor variance accounts are computed as follows: (+ =actual more than standard; − =actual less than standard)

Direct Labor Price (or Wage Rate) Variance
    Step One: (+$0.25 × 1,550 hr)   =   +$387.50
    Step Two: (−$0.05 ×   375 hr)   =   −   18.75
                             $ 368.75

Direct Labor Efficiency (or Quantity) Variance
    Step One:(+150 hr × $3.75/hr)   =   +$562.50
    Step Two: (− 25 hr × $6.25/hr)   =   − 156.25
    Total (Net) Variance   +$406.25

RECORDING DIRECT LABOR COST TO JOB ORDER AND DIRECT LABOR VARIANCES

As in the case of the raw material variances, one purpose of recording the direct labor cost variances in the accounts is to have this information readily available for reporting to those managers responsible for control of direct labor wage rates and efficiency. The direct labor variances for this job order would be combined with the variances on the other job orders processed during the period in reporting to the managers responsible for direct labor performance. The pattern of direct labor variances for the period may show, for example, that some jobs have relatively small unfavorable efficiency variances and that other jobs have relatively small favorable efficiency variances, such that the net effect of all the efficiency variances for the period is negligible. Some random deviation or fluctuation of actual hours worked from the standard hours allowed is not unusual for most jobs. However, if the monthly direct labor variance report shows that a majority of the job orders have unfavorable efficiency variances, or if certain jobs have relatively large efficiency variances, then the responsible managers should investigate and determine the reasons.

Variable Manufacturing Overhead Costs

In this example two variable overhead costs are included in the standard cost job sheet (see Exhibit 14.1). Each of these variable overhead costs is expressed in terms of a quantity standard and a price (or purchase cost) standard. These variable overhead costs variances can be computed in much the same manner that is used for raw materials and direct labor. The entry below summarizes the variable overhead costs allocated to this job order and the recording of the variable overhead variances.

We emphasize again that in this example each variable manufacturing overhead cost is allocated *separately* to the job order. For instance, electrical power is measured according to the number of machine hours that each job order requires. In actual practice a manufacturer usually has many different variable overhead costs, and it may not be practical to allocate each specific overhead cost on a different and separate basis. Furthermore several kinds of variable overhead costs are very indirect; there is no obvious basis for allocation of these costs to particular job orders (or production departments). In short, in actual practice many different variable overhead costs may be grouped together and allocated on one common basis, such as the direct labor hours of each particular job order.* Electrical power costs, for instance, may be included with

* In this case the entry to record the application of variable overhead costs to each job order would be based on the *standard* variable overhead cost burden rate per direct labor hour. Any efficiency variance would be recorded at the time of making the entry, since the application of the burden rate is based on the actual number of hours worked. But the price (spending) variance could *not* be recorded at the time of making the entry. Rather, the total spending variance for the entire period would be determined at the end of the period. The total actual variable overhead costs debited (+) to the Variable Overhead Costs account during the period is compared with the total costs credited (−) from the account during the entire period. This is the total spending variance for the period, which is *not* allocated to specific job orders. Instead, it is the total spending variance for the entire period for all the job orders worked on during the period.

Debit (+) Work-in-Process Inventory
        (at Standard)   3,750.00
    Credit (−) Variable Manufacturing
            Overhead Costs   3,175.00
    Credit (−) Variable Overhead Price
            (or Spending) Variance   560.00
    Credit (−) Variable Overhead
            Efficiency Variance   15.00

Based on allocation schedules for period, the following actual variable overhead costs are allocated to this job order:

Electrical Power Usage:
    (4,700 kW-hr @ $0.05/kW-hr)   = $ 235.00

Replacement Parts and Supplies:
    (1,400 mach. hr @ $2.10/mach. hr) =   2,940.00

Total Actual Variable Overhead Cost $3,175.00

In contrast, the standard quantities and per unit costs are as follows (see the standard cost sheet, Exhibit 14.1):

Electrical Power Usage:
    (5,000 kW-hr @ $0.05/kW-hr)   = $ 250.00

Replacement Parts and Supplies:
    (1,400 mach. hr @ $2.50/mach. hr) =   3,500.00

Total Standard Variable Overhead Cost $3,750.00

The variable manufacturing overhead variances are computed as follows:
(+ = actual more than standard; − = actual less than standard)

Variable Overhead Price (or Spending) Variance
    Replacement Parts and Supplies:
        (−$0.40 × 1,400 mach. hr)   =   −$560.00

Variable Overhead Efficiency Variance
    Electrical Power Usage:
        (−300 kW-hr × $0.05/kW-hr)   =   −$ 15.00

RECORDING
VARIABLE
OVERHEAD
COST TO
JOB ORDER
AND
VARIABLE
OVERHEAD
VARIANCES

follows (see the standard cost sheet, Exhibit 14.1):

many other variable overhead costs, all of which are allocated on the direct labor-hour basis. (In some situations, the number or weight of raw materials required for each job order, or processed by each production department, may be the more logical basis for the composite-group allocation of variable overhead costs.) In passing, it should be mentioned also that there is nothing wrong with the allocation of some variable overhead costs on an item-by-item basis, and with the composite-group allocation of the remainder of the variable overhead costs.

In the above entry, which records the variable overhead costs allocated to the job order in the example, notice the credit (−) of $3175.00 to the *Variable* Manufacturing Overhead Costs account. It is assumed that the company accumulates actual variable manufacturing overhead costs in this account. As the specific job orders to which the variable overhead costs should be charged are identified, an entry is made to remove the costs from this account. In short, a *separate* account is assumed for the *variable* manufacturing overhead costs, which means that *fixed* overhead costs are accumulated in another overhead costs account.

The reporting of overhead cost variances depends on the organizational structure of the company. The managers responsible for controlling these costs, of course, are the proper persons to receive the monthly variances reports. Generally speaking, monthly variance reports are prepared that cover all the job orders processed during the manufacturing period, with emphasis on the significant variances.

Fixed Manufacturing Overhead Costs

In this example the company's total fixed manufacturing overhead costs for the year are allocated to the job orders based on each job order's direct labor hours. Fixed overhead of $9000 is allocated to this job order based on the 1800 standard direct labor hours allowed for this job at the standard fixed overhead burden rate of $5 per hour. As we have already observed in recording the direct labor cost, the *actual* total direct labor hours worked on this job order is 1925 hours: (1550 hours for Step One plus 375 hours for Step Two = 1925 hours—see entry on page 491). For most job orders the actual hours probably will be somewhat more or somewhat less than the standard hours allowed. Hence, the question arises: Should the standard fixed overhead burden rate be multiplied by the *actual* number of direct labor hours *or* by the *standard* number of direct labor hours for each job order? There are good arguments on both sides of this question.

On the one hand, it can be argued that the company's fixed costs are the same amount as long as its total output for the year stays within the relevant range of production activity for which the fixed costs were budgeted. The fact that more direct hours are required than the standard hours allowed for the job order should not increase the company's total fixed overhead costs for the year, unless the excess hours force total fixed costs up to a higher plateau. This line of reasoning takes the point of view that a direct labor hour is simply a convenient common denominator among all the production lots so that total fixed manufacturing costs for the year can be allocated or "divided up" among the different production lots processed during the period. If this allocation is carried out on the basis of the *standard* number of direct labor hours allowed for each production lot, the correct total amount of fixed overhead cost should be distributed among all the production lots worked on during the year, as long as *on average* the company can keep to the standard hours allowed for all the production lots processed during the year.

The other side of the argument is that the unfavorable labor efficiency variance of 125 hours (1925 actual hours − 1800 standard hours) of this job "uses up" some of the company's production capacity available during the year. Therefore, this job order should absorb more of the total fixed manufacturing cost than originally allowed for it (based on the standard number of direct labor hours), since these "extra" 125 hours are not available for working on other job orders during the period. This is true. But, other jobs may require less actual hours than the standard. In most normal situations, unfavorable labor efficiency variances of some jobs are offset by favorable efficiency variances of other jobs (unless standards on all jobs are set very tight and are difficult to achieve).

The procedure adopted here is to allocate fixed manufacturing cost on the basis of the *standard* number of direct labor hours allowed for each job order. As is explained in more detail below, this seems to be the better approach because the total utilization of production capacity over the entire year is analyzed at one time rather than on a job-by-job basis. Also, all costs are recorded at standard to the inventory accounts. Thus the following entry is made to charge (apply) fixed manufacturing costs to this one particular job order:

Debit (+) Work-in-Process Inventory		
(at Standard)	9000.00	
Credit (−) Fixed Manufacturing		
Overhead Costs		9000.00

APPLICATION OF FIXED OVERHEAD TO JOB ORDER

Application of fixed manufacturing overhead costs to this job order, based on standard fixed overhead burden rate multiplied times the standard number of direct labor hours as follows:

($5.00 × 1800 hours) = $9000.00

Notice in this entry that no variances are recorded at the time of making the entry. Instead, at the end of the year, variances are recorded for the *total* fixed manufacturing costs for the entire year. To explain: assume that for the year as a whole the *Fixed* Manufacturing Overhead Cost account shows the following (variable overhead costs are accumulated in a separate account, as explained above):

Summary of Fixed Manufacturing Overhead Costs for Year

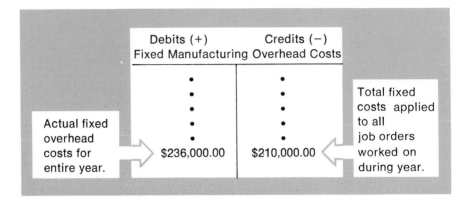

The debits (+) to the account during the year are the actual costs recorded, such as depreciation on production machinery and equipment, real estate taxes and production supervisors' salaries. The total of the credits (−) to the account is the total of all fixed overhead costs applied to the many different job orders worked on during the year, such as the entry for the particular job order example shown above. This total amount applied is equal to the *standard* fixed burden rate times the *standard* number of direct labor hours of each and every job order worked on during the year. Therefore, the details of the total are as follows:

$$\left[\begin{array}{c} 42{,}000 \text{ standard number of direct} \\ \text{labor hours of all job} \\ \text{orders during the year} \end{array} \times \begin{array}{c} \$5.00 \text{ standard fixed} \\ \text{burden rate} \end{array} \right] = \underline{\underline{\$210{,}000.00}}$$

At the end of the year there is an underapplied (debit) balance in the account of $26,000: ($236,000 actual costs − $210,000 applied costs). This remaining balance is "cleared out" by the following entry, which also records the fixed manufacturing cost variances for the entire year:

Debit (+) Fixed Overhead Capacity
      Variance   15,000.00
Debit (+) Fixed Overhead Spending
      Variance   11,000.00
    Credit (−) Fixed Manufacturing
        Overhead Costs   26,000.00

Removal of remaining balance (underapplied overhead) in the account, and recording of variances which are computed as follows:

RECORDING TOTAL FIXED OVERHEAD VARIANCES FOR THE YEAR

Fixed Overhead Capacity (or Volume) Variance

Total Direct Labor Hours Budgeted	=	45,000 hours
Actual Total Direct Labor Hours, at Standard Hours for Each Job	=	42,000 hours
Unused (or Idle) Capacity	=	3,000 hours

(3,000 hr unused capacity × $5.00/hr burden rate) = $15,000.00

Fixed Overhead Spending Variance

Total Fixed Overhead Cost Budgeted for Year	=	$225,000.00
Actual Fixed Overhead Costs Recorded for Year	=	236,000.00
Excess of Actual Costs over Standard Costs	=	$ 11,000.00

The unfavorable spending variance of $11,000 is straightforward. It is simply the excess of the actual fixed overhead costs recorded during the year over the total cost budgeted for the year. Of course, the managers responsible for controlling these costs would investigate which specific fixed costs are most seriously over budget, and why.

The interpretation of the capacity variance, on the other hand, is not so cut-and-dried. First, the $15,000 unfavorable capacity (or volume) variance does *not* mean that this exact amount is a good measure of the fixed cost that could have been saved or avoided if management had known in advance that only 42,000 direct labor hours (at standard) would be needed during the year. In other words, the $5 per hour fixed overhead burden rate is an *average*, arrived at by dividing the budgeted fixed costs of $225,000 for the year by the 45,000 direct labor hours that were available during the year. (Keep in mind that any measure of capacity is somewhat arbitrary to begin with). It should not be thought that each and every unit of capacity, starting with the first, up to and including the 45,000th unit of capacity, involves an incremental cost of exactly $5.

Fixed costs are very "lumpy"—in most instances a company must add rather large increases of capacity at a time, such as purchasing a (whole) machine. The company cannot buy a fraction of one machine, for example. Likewise, one additional (full-time) fixed salary production supervisor usually must be hired. Usually a company cannot add a fraction of one additional supervisor. This works the same way on the downside as well: the company cannot "shave off" exactly one unit, or even 100 units, or maybe not even 1000 units of capacity. Furthermore, the cost of each additional "chunk" of capacity is not necessarily the same as the previous "chunk." In short, the $15,000 unfavorable fixed overhead capacity variance probably is *not* equal to the amount of fixed overhead cost that could have been saved or avoided if the company had scaled down its capacity at the start of the year.

A second major point of interpretation of the fixed manufacturing overhead cost capacity variance concerns the use of the *standard* number of direct labor hours allowed for each job as the basis for allocating (applying) fixed overhead costs to the job orders worked on during the year. As is discussed above, the alternative is to use the *actual* number of direct labor hours for each job order, which may be more or less than the standard number of direct labor hours allowed. For instance, assume that the actual total number of direct labor hours worked over the year is 43,000 hours, which is 1000 hours more than the total number of direct labor hours allowed at standard. Given these facts the capacity variance for the year could be recorded at $10,000, instead of the $15,000 amount shown in the above entry. That is, 1000 of the 3000 hours shown in the capacity variance computation in the above entry is an inefficient utilization of capacity, but a utilization nonetheless. Hence, the capacity variance could be recorded as $10,000 (2000 unused hours × $5 standard fixed cost burden rate), and a fixed overhead efficiency variance account could be debited (+) for $5000 in the entry (1000 hours over standard × $5 standard fixed cost burden rate).

Managers should keep in mind that the fixed overhead capacity variance is a convenient but *arbitrary* cost measure of unused capacity (assuming an unfavorable variance). The capacity variance, in short, is equal to the standard fixed overhead costs burden rate multiplied times the number of unused direct labor hours during the year. The unused number of hours, as explained above, may be capacity less the number of standard hours allowed for the jobs worked on during the year, or may be capacity less the actual number of hours worked during the year. Probably it is more useful for managers to focus on the *percentages* of unused hours of capacity, rather than on a dollar measure of the capacity variance. Unused hours of production capacity are very important in decisions regarding the future expansion (or contraction) of a company's production plant and facilities. Finally, the analysis of unused production capacity must be considered in light of the actual sales volume performance for the year, especially if the budgeted sales volume was not reached. The unfavorable production capacity variance may be due simply to the failure to reach the budgeted sales volume, and thus production volume must be reduced to avoid accumulating excess inventories.

Disposition of Standard Cost Variances

One disadvantage of recording standard costs in the inventory accounts and recording deviations of actual costs from standard costs in the several variance accounts, is that the variances accounts must be disposed of at the end of the accounting period (usually at year-end). The variance accounts are like revenue and expense accounts in one respect. The variances accounts relate to the manufacturing activity of one period, and at the end of the period the variances have served their information purpose and do *not* carry forward to the next year. The accountant has to close out these accounts. Generally, there are two basic alternatives for disposition of the variances:

1. Close the net total of all the variances to the Cost of Goods Sold Expense, thereby leaving the inventory accounts at their standard costs; or,

2. Allocate the variances' balances between the ending inventory accounts and Cost of Goods Sold Expense, so that the ending balances in the inventory accounts are stated at their actual costs.

To illustrate these two alternatives, consider the job order example discussed over the last several sections and the eight variance accounts that have been debited or credited for the differences between actual costs and standard costs. Six of the variance accounts (all but the two fixed overhead variance accounts) are directly related to this job order, which are the variable costs of the job order. These six variance accounts are the first concern. If all the 1000 units produced by this job order have been sold by the end of the year, then clearly the six variable cost variances recorded in the previous entries should be charged to the Cost of Goods Sold Expense for the period. This entry would be as follows (see previous entries for the recording of the variances):

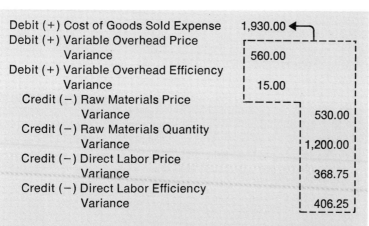

Debit (+) Cost of Goods Sold Expense   1,930.00
Debit (+) Variable Overhead Price
    Variance   560.00
Debit (+) Variable Overhead Efficiency
    Variance   15.00
Credit (−) Raw Materials Price
    Variance   530.00
Credit (−) Raw Materials Quantity
    Variance   1,200.00
Credit (−) Direct Labor Price
    Variance   368.75
Credit (−) Direct Labor Efficiency
    Variance   406.25

CLOSING OUT THE VARIANCE ACCOUNTS BY CHARGE TO COST OF GOODS SOLD EXPENSE

The net total of the six variances is an unfavorable $1,930.00, which is charged to the Cost of Goods Sold Expense account, since all the units of this job order have been sold.

We can see that, after recording this entry, each of the six variable variance accounts recorded for this one job order would be reduced to a zero balance (and thus closed out), and that the net total of all six of the variances ($1930) "ends up" in the Cost of Goods Sold Expense account. After this entry is recorded, in other words, the Cost of Goods Sold Expense account is the same as if the actual costs had been recorded to the inventory accounts in the first place.

In contrast, assume that of the 1000 units produced by this job order, only 900 units are sold by the end of the period; there are still 100 of these units in the ending finished goods inventory. It can be argued, with strong logic, that one tenth of the $1930 net total unfavorable variance should be charged to the ending inventory of these units. In many practical situations, however, the company may not go to the trouble of restating all of the many different products in its ending inventory to an actual cost basis. Thus the same entry shown above may be recorded, which theoretically understates the ending inventory of these 100 units by $193. That is, the standard variable cost of the 100 units is $193 less than the actual variable cost. On the other hand, there is the argument that the standard cost of a product is the preferred basis for inventory valuation, since this is what the cost *should* have been.

Last, there is the need to dispose of the two *fixed* overhead cost variances. (See the entry on page 497 that records these two variance accounts for the year.) As is explained above, fixed cost variances are aggregate variances for the entire period. This is in contrast to the variable variances which are directly related to particular job orders. It can be argued that part of each fixed cost variance for the year should be allocated to the ending inventories of the various products manufactured during the year, to put the ending inventory products on an actual cost basis. However, the more expedient procedure of simply charging all the fixed overhead variances to the Cost of Goods Sold Expense for the period is not an uncommon practice. This means that the products in the ending inventory include fixed overhead cost based on the *standard* fixed overhead cost burden rate, even though the actual burden rate may be somewhat higher or lower.

To summarize briefly, by the end of the year the variance accounts have served their purpose for collecting information about deviations of actual costs from standard costs during the period. Thus the variance accounts are closed out and are not carried forward to next year. In most situations the preferred method is to adjust the ending inventory accounts from their standard costs to their actual cost basis by the allocation of the appropriate fraction of the variance accounts' balances to the ending inventory accounts. But the practical expedient of closing all variance accounts' balances to the Cost of Goods Sold Expense account, if done consistently every year, usually involves no serious disadvantages and simplifies the recordkeeping process.

Summary

Standard costs are predetermined measures of how much costs during a future period should be, based on the detailed analysis and forecasts about purchase prices, efficiency performance levels, output levels, and all other relevant factors that are expected to prevail during the coming period. Standard costs are the logical outgrowth of the general use of performance standards which is found in most areas of business management. The development of standard costs forces a detailed critical evaluation of the company's methods of operations. A close scrutiny of this kind may otherwise be avoided by managers. The main development of standard costs has been in the manufacturing area of operations, although the logic and reasons for standard costs apply with equal force in the other operating areas of the business. In the production area, there is an obvious focus for standard costs—the product being manufactured.

The standard cost for a (finished) product is the composite total of the specific standards for each raw material item, each labor step or operation, and the various overhead costs. With respect to variable manufacturing costs, the basic procedure is to develop a quantity standard and a purchase price standard for each factor. The actual quantity of each factor used is compared with the standard quantity allowed, and the difference is then multiplied by the standard purchase price of the factor to determine the quantity (or efficiency) variance. The actual purchase price per unit of the factor is compared with the standard purchase price per unit and the difference is multiplied times the actual quantity of the factor used, to determine the spending (or price) variance. The fixed cost capacity variance, on the other hand, depends on the total actual utilization of production capacity during the year compared with the company's practical capacity planned at the start of the year. The fixed cost spending variance is the difference between the actual total fixed costs for the year the total fixed cost budgeted for the year.

Standard costs can be kept on a "memo" basis only, and actual manufacturing costs are recorded in the manner explained in Chapters Twelve and Thirteen. The standard costs sheets for each production lot are used as a reference to determine variances of actual costs from the standard costs. Alternatively, standard costs can be recorded in the company's inventory accounts, which means that differences between actual and standard costs are recorded in variance accounts. These variance accounts are readily accessible sources of information for reporting this information to those managers responsible for controlling the costs. If this second alternative is followed, at the end of the year the variance accounts' balances have to be disposed of by closing entries. The net total variance for the year may be charged entirely to the Cost of Goods Sold Expense account, although it can be argued with strong logic that ending inventories should be restated and put on an actual cost basis, which means that part of the net total variance for the year should be allocated to the ending inventories.

Questions

14. 1 (a) What are "standards" in the general, broad sense of the term?
    (b) What are standard costs?

14. 2 "Standard costs apply only to manufacturing products." Do you agree? Explain.

14. 3 (a) What are the principal advantages and management reasons for developnig and using standard cost systems?
    (b) What are the main disadvantages of standard cost systems?

14. 4 The importance of a "fair" standard for employee motivation is discussed briefly in the chapter. What is a "fair" standard? How would you, as a manager, know when the standard is not fair?

14. 5 Which, generally, would be more difficult to develop a standard cost for: a product the company has manufactured for several years, or a new product the company has never before manufactured?

14. 6 A company has not updated its standard costs for its products for three years. What problems would this probably present?

14. 7 A company has just negotiated a new three-year labor contract with its production employees. How would this new contract be important in developing standard costs?

14. 8 "Standard costs, being future costs, are relevant costs." Do you agree? Explain.

14. 9 What are the essential steps in setting prime cost standards?

14.10 Why is a general burden rate approach adopted for variable manufacturing overhead standard costs, instead of using a separate basis of allocation for each variable overhead cost?

14.11 "In setting its standard fixed overhead cost burden rate a company should use its ideal capacity." Do you agree? Explain.

14.12 (a) What are the two ways in which a standard cost system can be implemented in the actual recordkeeping process of a company?
    (b) Do the two alternative methods result in different variances between actual and standard costs?

14.13 Could raw materials' price variances be recorded at the time of purchase? What are the reasons for this timing of the entry, instead of waiting until the materials are issued to job orders as shown in the chapter?

14.14 What are the two basic ways or approaches to allocate variable overhead costs to production lots? Does the recording of variable overhead spending variances depend on which method is used?

14.15 Should fixed overhead (at the standard burden rate) be allocated to specific job orders based on their actual or their standard number of direct labor hours (assuming this is the basis of allocation)? Discuss briefly.

14.16 "An unfavorable fixed overhead capacity variance indicates poor management planning." Do you agree? Explain.

14.17 What is done with standard cost variances at the end of the year?

Problems

P14. 1 The standard cost sheet of a particular job order for 1000 units of a certain product manufactured during the year is as follows in summary:

Raw Materials:	(200 lb × $18.00/lb)	=	$1600	
Direct labor:	(500 hr × $4.75/hr)	=	2375	
Prime costs				$3975
Overhead costs:				
Variable:	(200 lb × $2.25/lb)	=	$ 450	
Fixed:	($4.00 per direct labor hour × 500 hr)	=	2000	
Total overhead costs				$2450
Total all costs				$6425

You should notice that variable overhead costs are allocated based on the weight of raw material whereas fixed overhead costs are allocated on the basis of direct labor hours.

The actual prime costs assigned to this job order, which was completed during the year, can be determined from the following information;

Raw materials   210 pounds at $17.50 average cost per pound
Direct labor   480 hours at $4.90 average cost per hour

Required:

(1) Compute the raw materials and the direct labor variances of actual costs assigned to the job from the standard costs allowed for the job. Show your computations clearly.

(2) Assume that 750 of the units produced by this job order were sold before year-end; the other 250 units are still in the company's ending inventory of finished goods of course.

Required: Make a journal entry to dispose of the prime cost (raw materials and direct labor) variances for this job order.

(3) Without any other information than that given above, can you compute any of the overhead variances? Explain.

P14. 2 To begin this problem, refer to the overhead standard costs for the job order example in Problem 14.1. This job was one of hundreds processed by the company during the year. In total, for all the jobs processed during the year the company used 47,300 pounds of raw materials compared with 45,000 pounds "allowed" for all the jobs. In other words, the standard quantity of raw materials that should have been used (at standard) was 45,000 pounds. The actual total of all variable overhead costs for the year was $104,533. The company established its fixed cost overhead burden rate based on a practical normal production capacity of 125,000 direct labor hours for the year. The actual total direct labor hours worked during the year was 120,000 hours. The total hours "allowed," based on the standard direct labor hours for each job processed during the year, was 118,000 hours. The actual total of all fixed overhead costs for the year was $531,000.

(1) *Required:* Compute the variable overhead cost variances of actual from standard for the entire year. Show your computation clearly.

(2) *Required:* Compute the fixed overhead cost variances of actual from standard for the entire year. Show your computations clearly.

P14. 3 Duke Manufacturing Co., Inc. (an actual company by the way) reported the following inventories in its Balance Sheets for December 31, 1973 and 1972:

	December 31	
Inventories:	1973	1972
Finished Goods	$ 98,174	$ 85,034
Work-in-process	386,515	348,935
Raw materials	356,474	319,533
	$841,163	$753,502

Footnote (1) in its financial report is quoted as follows

"Inventories are stated at . . . cost (first-in, first-out) . . . such cost generally representing as to finished goods and work in process, standard manufacturing cost, exclusive of manufacturing overhead. The estimated manufacturing overhead excluded from inventories as at December 31, 1973 and 1972 amounted to approximately $122,000 and $112,000, respectively."

Required:

(1) Is the company's cost accounting procedure regarding manufacturing overhead a generally accepted accounting method? Discuss briefly.
(2) What are some possible reasons why the company follows the accounting practice of excluding manufacturing overhead costs from its finished goods and work-in-process inventories?
(3) Determine how much different the company's operating profit (before interest and income tax) would have been in 1973 if the company had used the full cost absorption inventory cost valuation method.
(4) Compare the company's finished goods inventory with its work-in-process inventory. Even allowing for the exclusion of manufacturing overhead costs, would you estimate that the company has a short manufacturing cycle or a rather long manufacturing process?

P14. 4 This company follows the practice of recording manufacturing costs at standard in its work-in-process and finished goods inventory accounts and of recording differences between actual costs and standard costs in appropriate variance accounts. The following standard cost sheet has been prepared for a particular job order that the production plant is about ready to begin:

Standard Cost Sheet—Job Order No. A153

Number of finished units to be produced: 10,000 units					
Raw material:	14,500 pounds	×	$2.60 per pound	=	$37,700
Direct labor:	2,750 hours	×	$5.20 per hour	=	14,300
Overhead:	2,750 hours	×	$2.08 per hour	=	5,720
Total					$57,720

Overhead is not applied to the job order until the point when the job order is completed and transferred to the finished goods inventory warehouse. At that time, the total number of direct labor hours assigned to the job order is known and one summary entry for overhead is made.

The actual prime costs charged to Job Order A153 through the point of completion of the job were:

Raw materials	15,080 pounds at total cost of $39,962
Direct labor	2,700 hours at total cost of $13,905

Required:

Make a summary entry for each prime cost factor to record the cost of processing the job order through the point of completion. Also make a summary entry to apply the appropriate amount of overhead cost to the job order. Show your computations of the prime cost variances clearly. Overhead cost variances cannot be recorded based on the information that is available above. Last, make the entry to record the completion of the job order.

P14. 5 For the year just ended this company applied a standard burden rate of $8.50 based on standard direct labor hours, which was based on a standard total fixed overhead cost for the year of $360,000 and a standard normal production capacity of 80,000 direct labor hours. No overhead cost variances have been recorded yet. Based on an analysis of the production reports for the year and the overhead account, the following information is available.

	At Standard	At Actual
Variable overhead costs	$300,000	$315,400
Fixed overhead costs	$360,000	$368,000
Direct labor hours	75,000	76,000

During the year all overhead applied is credited directly to the Manufacturing Overhead Costs account.

Required:

(1) Determine the debit (or credit) balance in the Manufacturing Overhead Costs account at year-end before any entries are made to record the overhead variances for the year.

(2) Make an entry to record the various overhead variances for the year, thereby reducing the balance in the Manufacturing Overhead Costs account to zero.

P14. 6 At the end of the year, before any final entry to dispose of the variance accounts is made, the company's general ledger accounts included the folowing (ending balances only are shown):

Raw Materials Price Variance		Raw Materials Quantity Variance		Direct Labor Price Variance	
58,000			1,400	9,500	

Direct Labor Efficiency Variance		Variable Overhead Price Variance		Variable Overhead Efficiency Variance	
14,720			9,800	7,500	

Fixed Overhead Capacity Variance		Fixed Overhead Spending Variance	
27,500			1,500

Required:

(1) Identify which of the above are favorable variances and which are unfavorable.

(2) Record the entry at year-end to dispose of the variances if the inventory accounts are *not* adjusted to the actual cost basis.

(3) Record the entry at year-end to dispose of the variances if the inventory accounts are adjusted to the FIFO actual cost basis. To simplify, assume that the company manufactures and sells only one product on a continuous processing basis. Information about the company's production and inventory position is as follows:

Beginning work-in-process inventory (50% complete with respect to all manufacturing costs)	1,000 units
Beginning finished goods inventory	12,500 units
Total number of products completed (finished) during the year	50,000 units
Ending work-in-process inventory (75% complete with respect to all manufacturing costs)	1,000 units
Ending finished goods inventory	15,000 units

P14. 7 At the beginning of this year the company established the following standard cost for Product X.

	Prime Cost	Manufacturing Burden—50%	Total
Material A	$10.00		$10.00
Material B	5.00		5.00
Material C	2.00		2.00
Direct Labor—Cutting	8.00	$4.00	12.00
Direct Labor—Shaping	4.00	2.00	6.00
Direct Labor—Assembling	2.00	1.00	3.00
Direct Labor—Boxing	1.00	0.50	1.50
Total	$32.00	$7.50	$39.50

The year's budget called for the manufacture of 10,000 of Product X at a total cost of $395,000 at standard. The following variance accounts relating to Product X appear on the books at the end of the year, with the reasons for each variance briefly explained:

	Debit	Credit
Material price variance:		
Due to a favorable purchase of total requirements of Material A; this probably was a one time, unusual situation in purchasing the raw material item		$19,500
Material usage variance:		
Excessive waste during period; this problem is receiving the attention of the production manager	$ 3,000	
Labor rate variance:		
5% wage increase to direct workers	7,500	
Labor productivity variance:		
Due to shutdown caused by strike	15,000	
Burden variance—fixed overhead		
Due to shutdown caused by strike	6,000	
Burden variance—variable overhead		
Due to permanent savings in costs of certain services		12,000
Totals	$31,500	$31,500

Required: Based on the above information, prepare a revised standard cost sheet for Product X for the coming year.

P14. 8 Ross Shirts, Inc., manufactures men's shirts for large retail stores. Ross produces a single quality shirt in lots to each customer's order and attaches the store's label to each. The standard costs for a dozen shirts are:

Direct materials	24 yards @ $ .88	$21.12
Direct labor	3 hours @ 3.92	11.76
Manufacturing overhead	3 hours @ 2.00	6.00
Standard cost per dozen		$38.88

During October 1976 Ross worked on three orders for shirts. Job cost records for the month disclose the following.

Job Lot No.	Total Units in Lot	Material Used	Hours Worked
30	1,000 dozen	24,100 yards	2,980
31	1,700 dozen	40,440 yards	5,130
32	1,200 dozen	28,825 yards	2,890

The following information is also avaliable:
(a) Ross purchased 95,000 yards of material during the month at a cost of $85,120. The materials price variance is recorded when goods are purchased, so all inventories are carried at standard cost.
(b) Direct labor incurred amounted to $44,000 during October. According to payroll records, production employees were paid $4 per hour.
(c) Overhead is applied on the basis of direct labor hours. Manufacturing overhead totaling $22,800 was incurred during October.
(d) A total of $288,000 was budgeted for overhead for the year 1976 based on estimated production at the plant's normal capacity of 48,000 dozen shirts per year. Overhead is 40% fixed and 60% variable at this level of production.
(e) There was no work-in-process at October 1. During October, lots 30 and 31 were completed and all material was issued for lot 32, which was 80% completed as to labor.

Required:

(1) Prepare a schedule computing the standard cost for October 1976 of lots 30, 31, and 32.
(2) Compute the materials price variance for October and indicate whether the variance is favorable or unfavorable.
(3) Prepare schedules that compute the following (and indicate whether the variances are favorable or unfavorable) for each lot produced during October:
   (a) Materials quantity variance in yards.

(b) Labor efficiency variance in hours.

(c) Labor rate variance in dollars.

(4) Prepare a schedule computing the total manufacturing overhead spending and capacity variances for October, and indicate whether the variances are favorable or unfavorable.

P14. 9 The company has a theoretical maximum production capacity of 210,000 units per year. Normal capacity is regarded as 180,000 units per year. Standard variable manufacturing costs are $11 per unit. Fixed factory (manufacturing) overhead is $360,000 per year. Only manufacturing costs are standardized. Variable selling expenses are $3 per unit, and fixed selling expenses are $252,000 per year. The unit sales price is $20.

The operating results for 1976 are: sales, 150,000 units; production, 160,000 units; beginning inventory, 10,000 units; and the net unfavorable variance from standard of all variable manufacturing costs is $40,000 (including both spending and efficiency variances). All variances are written off as additions to (or deductions from) standard cost of sales.

Required: [For (1), (2), and (3) assume no variances from standards for manufacturing costs.]

(1) What is the break-even point expressed in dollar sales?

(2) How many units must be sold to earn a net income of $60,000 per year?

(3) How many units must be sold to earn a net income of 10% on sales?

(4) Prepare net income statements for 1976, based on actual costs of course, according to the following (ignore interest and income tax expenses):

(a) Conventional (full cost absorption) costing method.

(b) "Direct" costing method.

(5) Briefly account for the difference in operating profit between the two income statements.

P14.10 The Longhorn Manufacturing Corporation produces only one product, Bevo, and accounts for the production of Bevo by using a standard cost system for prime costs but not for overhead costs. At the end of each year, Longhorn prorates all variances among the various inventories and cost of sales. Because Longhorn prices its inventories on the first-in, first-out basis and all the beginning inventories are used during the year, the variances that had been allocated to the ending inventories are immediately charged to cost of sales at the beginning of the following year. This allows only the current year's variances to be recorded in the variance accounts in any given year.

Following are the standards for the production of one unit of Bevo: 3 units of item A @ $1 per unit; 1 unit of item B @ $.50 per unit; 4 units of item C @ $.30 per unit, and 20 minutes of direct labor @ $4.50 per hour. Separate variance accounts are maintained for each type of raw material and for direct labor. Raw material purchases are recorded initially at standard. Manufacturing overhead is applied at $9 per actual direct labor hour but is not related to the standard cost system. There was no overapplied or underapplied manufacturing overhead at December 31, 1975.

After proration of the variances, the various inventories at December 31, 1975 were priced as follows:

Raw Material

Item	Number of Units	Unit Cost	Amount
A	15,000	$1.10	$16,500
B	4,000	0.52	2,080
C	20,000	0.32	6,400
			$24,980

Work-in-Process

9000 units of Bevo which were 100% complete as to items A and B, 50% complete as to item C, and 30% complete as to labor. The composition and valuation of the inventory follows:

Item	Amount
A	$28,600
B	4,940
C	6,240
Direct Labor	6,175
	$45,955
Overhead	11,700
	$57,655

Finished Goods

4800 units of Bevo composed and valued as follows:

Item	Amount
A	$15,180
B	2,704
C	6,368
Direct Labor	8,540
	$32,792
Overhead	16,200
	$48,992

Following is a schedule of raw materials purchased and direct labor incurred for the year ended December 31, 1976. Unit cost of each item of raw material and direct labor cost per hour remained constant throughout the year.

Purchases

Item	Number of Units or Hours	Unit Cost	Amount
A	290,000	$1.15	$333,500
B	101,000	0.55	55,550
C	367,000	0.35	128,450
Direct Labor	34,100	4.60	156,860

During the year ended December 31, 1976, Longhorn sold 90,000 units of Bevo and had ending physical inventories as follows.

Raw Materials

Item	Number of Units
A	28,300
B	2,100
C	28,900

Work in Process

7500 units of Bevo which were 100% complete as to items A and B, 50% complete as to item C, and 20% complete as to labor, as follows:

Item	Number of Units or Hours
A	22,900
B	8,300
C	15,800
Direct Labor	800

Finished Goods

5100 units of Bevo, as follows:

Item	Number of Units or Hours
A	15,600
B	6,300
C	21,700
Direct Labor	2,050

There was no overapplied or underapplied manufacturing overhead at December 31, 1976.

Required:

Answer each of the following questions. Supporting computations should be prepared in good form.

(1) What was the charge or credit to cost of sales at the beginning of 1976 for the variances in the December 31, 1975 inventories?

(2) What was the total charge or credit to the three material price-variance accounts for items A, B, and C for the year ended December 31, 1976?

(3) What was the total charge or credit to the three material quantity variance accounts for items A, B, and C for the year ended December 31, 1976?

(4) What was the total charge or credit to the direct labor rate variance account for the year ended December 31, 1976?

(5) What was the total charge or credit to the direct labor efficiency variance account for the year ended December 31, 1976?

P14.11 The questions of this problem are based on the following information.

Tolbert Manufacturing Company uses a standard cost system in accounting for the cost of production of its only product, product A. The standards for the production of one unit of product A are as follows.

Direct materials:	10 feet of item 1 at $.75 per foot and 3 feet of item 2 at $1 per foot
Direct labor:	4 hours at $3.50 per hour
Manufacturing overhead:	Applied at 150% of standard direct labor costs

There was no inventory on hand at July 1, 1975. Following is a summary of costs and related data for the production of product A during the year ended June 30, 1976.

100,000 feet of item 1 were purchased at $.78 per foot.

30,000 feet of item 2 were purchased at $.90 per foot.

8,000 units of product A were produced, which required 78,000 feet of item 1, 26,000 feet of item 2, and 31,000 hours of direct labort at $3.60 per hour.

6,000 units of product A were sold.

At June 30, 1976 there are 22,000 feet of item 1, 4000 feet of item 2, and 2000 completed units of product A on hand. All purchases and transfers are "charged in" at standard.

Required: Select the correct answer from the four choices; show your computations.

(1) For the year ended June 30, 1976 the total debits to the raw materials account for the purchase of item 1 would be:
   a. $75,000.
   b. $78,000.
   c. $58,500.
   d. $60.000.

(2) For the year ended June 30, 1976 the total debits to the work-in-process account for direct labor would be:
   a. $111,600.
   b. $108,500.
   c. $112,000.
   d. $115,100.

(3) Before allocation of standard variances, the balance in the material usage variance account for item 2 was
   a. $1000 credit.
   b. $2600 debit.
   c. $ 600 debit.
   d. $2000 debit.

(4) If all standard variances are prorated to inventories and cost of goods sold, the amount of material usage variance of item 2 to be prorated to raw materials inventory would be
   a. $0.
   b. $333 credit.
   c. $333 debit.
   d. $500 debit.

(5) If all standard variances are prorated to inventories and cost of goods sold, the amount of material price variance for item 1 to be prorated to raw materials would be
   a. $0.
   b. $647 debit.
   c. $600 debit.
   d. $660 debit.

P14.12 The Groomer Company manufactures two products, Florimene and Glyoxide, used in the plastics industry. The company uses a flexible budget in its standard cost system to develop variances. Relevant data follow.

		Florinene	Glyoxide
Data on standard costs:	Raw material per unit	3 pounds at $1.00 per pound	4 pounds at $1.10 per pound
	Direct labor per unit	5 hours at $2.00 per hour	6 hours at $2.50 per hour
	Variable factory overhead per unit	$3.20 per direct labor hour	$3.50 per direct labor hour
	Fixed factory overhead per month Normal activity per month	$20,700 5,750 direct labor hours	$26,520 7,800 direct labor hours
	Output produced in September	1,000 units	1,200 units
Costs incurred for September:	Raw material	3,100 pounds at $0.90 per pound	4,700 pounds at $1.15 per pound
	Direct labor	4,900 hours at $1.95 per hour	7,400 hours at $2.55 per hour
	Variable factory overhead	$16,170	$25,234
	Fixed factory overhead	$20,930	$26,400

Required: Select the correct answer from the four choices given; show your computations.

(1) The total variances to be explained for both products for September are
   a. Florimene, $255 favorable; Glyoxide, $909 unfavorable.
   b. Florimene, $7050 favorable; Glyoxide, $6080 favorable.
   c. Florimene, $4605 favorable; Glyoxide, $3131 favorable.
   d. Florimene, $2445 unfavorable; Glyoxide, $2949 unfavorable.
(2) The labor efficiency variances for both products for September are
   a. Florimene, $195 favorable; Glyoxide, $510 unfavorable.
   b. Florimene, $1700 favorable; Glyoxide, $1000 favorable.
   c. Florimene, $200 favorable; Glyoxide, $500 unfavorable.
   d. Flormiene, $195 favorable; Glyoxide, $510 favorable.
   e. None of the above.
(3) The labor rate variances for both products for September are
   a. Florimene, $245 favorable; Glyoxide, $370 unfavorable.
   b. Florimene, $200 favorable; Glyoxide, $500 unfavorable.
   c. Florimene, $1945 favorable; Glyoxide, $630 favorable.
   d. Florimene, $245 unfavorable; Glyoxide, $370 favorable.
(4) The spending variances for variable overhead for both products for September are
   a. Florimene, $490 unfavorable; Glyoxide, $666 favorable.

    b. Florimene, $167 unfavorable; Glyoxide, $35 unfavorable.
    c. Florimene, $170 unfavorable; Glyoxide, $34 unfavorable.
    d. Florimene, $1900 favorable; Glyoxide, $1960 favorable.
    e. None of the above.

P14.13 Conti Pharmaceutical Company processes a single compound product know as NULAX and uses a standard cost accounting system. The process requires preparation and blending of three materials in large batches with a variation from the standard mixture sometimes necessary to maintain quality. Conti's cost accountant became ill at the end of October, and you were engaged to determine standard costs of October production and to explain any differences between actual and standard costs for the month. The following information is available for the Blending Department.

(a) The standard cost card for a 500-pound batch shows these standard costs:

	Quantity	Price	Total Cost
Materials:			
Mucilloid	250 pounds	$ .14	$35
Dextrose	200 pounds	.09	18
Ingredients	50 pounds	.08	4
Total per batch	500 pounds		$ 57
Labor:			
Preparation and blending	10 hours	$3.00	30
Overhead:			
Variable	10 hours	$1.00	10
Fixed	10 hours	.30	3	13
Total standard cost per			
500 pound batch			$100

(b) During October 410 batches of 500 pounds each of the finished compound were completed and transferred to the Packaging Department.
(c) Blending Department inventories totaled 6000 pounds at the beginning of the month and 9000 pounds at the end of the month (assume both inventories were completely processed but not transferred, and that they consisted of materials in their standard proportions).
(d) Inventories are carried in the accounts at standard prices. During the month of October these materials were purchased and put into production:

	Pounds	Price	Total Cost
Mucilloid	114,400	$.17	$19,448
Dextrose	85,800	.11	9,438
Ingredients	19,800	.07	1,386
Totals	220,000		$30,272

(e) Wages paid for 4212 hours of direct labor at $3.25 per hour amounted to $13,689.

(f) Actual overhead costs for the month totaled $5519.

(g) The standards were established for a normal production volume of 200,000 pounds (400 batches) of NULAX per month. At this level of production, variable factory overhead was budgeted at $4000 and fixed factory overhead was budgeted at $1200.

Required:

(1) Prepare a schedule that presents the computation for the standard cost of October production itemized by components of materials, labor, and overhead.

(2) Prepare schedules computing the differences between actual and standard costs and analyzing the differences as:
   (a) Materials variances (for each material) caused by
      Price differences.
      Usage differences.
   (b) Labor variances caused by
      Rate difference.
      Efficiency difference.
   (c) Overhead variances caused by
      Price factors.
      Volume or efficiency factors.

P14.14 The Jones Furniture Company uses a standard cost system in accounting for its production costs. The standard cost of a unit of furniture is as follows:

Lumber, 100 feet @ $150 per 1000 feet		$15.00
Direct labor, 4 hours @ $5.00 per hour		20.00
Manufacturing overhead:		
Fixed (15% of direct labor)	$3.00	
Variable (30% of direct labor)	6.00	9.00
Total unit cost		$44.00

The following flexible monthly overhead budget is in effect:

Direct Labor Hours	Estimated Overhead
5,200	$10,800
4,800	10,200
4,400	9,600
4,000 (normal capacity)	9,000
3,600	8,400

The actual unit costs for the month of December were as follows:

Lumber used (110 feet @ $120 per 1000 feet)	$13.20
Direct labor (4¼ hours @ $5.20 per hour)	22.10
Manufacturing overhead ($10,560 ÷ 1200 units)	8.80
Total actual unit cost	$44.10

Required: Prepare an analysis of each actual cost variance from standard cost for the month of December.

P14.15 The Bronson Company manufactures a fuel additive that has a stable selling price of $40 per drum. Since losing a government contract, the company has been producing and selling 80,000 drums per month, which is only 50% of normal capacity. Management expects to increase production to 140,000 drums in the coming year. You have been asked to review some computations made by Bronson's cost accountant. Your analysis discloses the following about the company's operations:

(a) Standard costs per drum of product manufactured:

Materials:		
8 gallons of miracle mix	$16	
1 empty drum	1	
Total	$17	
Direct labor—1 hour	$ 5	
Factory overhead	$ 6	

(b) Costs and expenses during September:

Miracle mix:
500,000 gallons purchased at cost of $950,000; 650,000 gallons used
Empty drums:
94,000 purchased at cost of $94,000; 80,000 used
Direct labor:
82,000 hours worked at cost of $414,100
Factory overhead:

Depreciation of building and machinery (fixed)	$210,000
Supervision and indirect labor	
(part fixed and part variable)	460,000
Other factory overhead (variable)	98,000
	$768,000

(c) Other factory overhead was the only actual overhead cost that varied from the overhead budget for the September level of production; actual other factory overhead was $98,000 and the budgeted amount was $90,000.
(d) At normal capacity of 160,000 drums per month, supervision and indirect labor costs are expected to be $570,000.
(e) None of the September cost variances are expected to occur proportionally in future months. For the next fiscal year, the cost standards department expects the same standard usage of materials and direct labor hours. The average prices expected are: $2.10 per gallon of miracle mix, $1 per empty

drum, and $5.70 per direct labor hour. The current flexible budget of factory overhead costs is considered applicable to future periods without revision.

Required:

(1) Prepare a schedule computing the following variances for September:
    (a) Materials price variance.
    (b) Materials usage variance.
    (c) Labor rate variance.
    (d) Labor usage (efficiency) variance.
    (e) Budget (or spending) overhead variance.
    (f) Volume (capacity) overhead variance.
    Indicate whether variances were favorable or unfavorable.
(2) Prepare a schedule of actual manufacturing cost per drum of product expected next year at production level of 140,000 drums per month by using the following cost categories: materials, direct labor, fixed factory overhead, and variable factory overhead.

Chapter Fifteen

Contemporary Developments and Certain Other Aspects of Management Accounting

CONTEMPORARY DEVELOPMENTS AND CERTAIN OTHER ASPECTS OF MANAGEMENT ACCOUNTING

In this chapter we survey briefly the important contemporary developments in management accounting, as well as certain other aspects of the discipline. The first section summarizes the main functions of a company's cost accounting system which, properly speaking, can be viewed as the keystone of its management accounting system. Actually, until fairly recently, a company's cost accounting system was viewed as the sum and substance of its management accounting system; the two terms were used almost interchangeably. But this narrow view of management accounting is held by very few managers and accountants today. Even a cursory review of recent and current management accounting journals, articles, and books makes clear just how broad the field of management accounting is considered at the present time.

Brief Summary of a Company's Cost Accounting System: Diverse but Compatible Functions

A company's cost accounting system is not the whole of its management accounting system. But its cost accounting methods and procedures are an absolutely essential part of its management accounting system, which should be adequate for servicing management's many different needs for cost information. A useful point of departure for this chapter is to review the basic functions of a company's cost accounting system, which are discussed in previous chapters. The term *system* is used to emphasize one important point. A company must carefully plan, organize, and supervise its cost accounting methods and procedures to service fully the demands of managers for cost measurements and information; there must be a *system* in the fullest sense of this term.

In general, a company's cost accounting system has three basic functions:

1. Determination and accumulation of product costs for *inventory valuation* and for internal and external *profit and net income measurement and reporting* for the company as a whole. A manufacturer cannot prepare its internal or external financial statements and accounting reports for the entity without knowing the cost values of its beginning and ending inventories. The financial position of the company, its gross profit, its operating profit, and its final net income for each period cannot be determined with-

out knowing the costs of manufacturing products, part of which are in the work-in-process and finished goods inventories at the beginning and end of the period. As is explained in Chapters Twelve and Thirteen, a manufacturer matches raw material and direct labor costs to the production lots being worked on, and the company allocates manufacturing overhead costs in some reasonable manner to the production lots, so that the total (full) cost of manufacturing each production lot can be determined. In short, to prepare internal (management) and external (investor) periodic accounting reports, a company must necessarily establish a cost accounting system whereby its manufacturing costs are properly measured each period and are properly identified or allocated to the products being manufactured.

2. Determination and measurement of *production and other operating costs* for the preparation of the *regular periodic management accounting reports* within the organization. In contrast to financial statements for the entity as a whole, these internal accounting reports and analyses are much more detailed, focus on each source of operating profit or each organizational unit, and stress the behavior of costs. Usually these internal accounting reports are designed to facilitate *comparative analyses* by managers. Managers need regular periodic accounting reports that compare actual profit and return on investment performance against past performance and budgeted (or planned) performance for the current period. These basic routine accounting reports are essential for management control. For instance, managers must know how actual cost performance compares with what costs should be, or at least with what costs were last period. Only in this way can significant deviations or variances be identified, so that managers are alerted to those specific operations and performance areas that need attention and improvement. Without this cost information, management quite literally does not know what is going on. These regular periodic accounting reports direct managers' attention to *specific* problems that should be investigated.

3. Determination and measurement of *relevant costs for special decision situations* that fall outside the information provided by the routine periodic accounting reports to managers. Management accountants should meet the information demands of the special, nonrecurring type of decision situations that call for certain cost information not regularly reported to managers, and which may not be available in the historical based accounting records of the company. Frequently these special decisions are of an *explorative* nature. That is, the manager is looking beyond what the company is now doing and is considering possible changes. For example, assume that the production manager has noticed from the routine periodic accounting reports that the cost of a certain raw material item is increasing at a much higher rate than any other manufacturing costs. This may trigger the manager into exploring the possibility of manufacturing this particular raw material item instead of purchasing it.

Since the company in the past has not manufactured this raw material item, this decision situation calls for cost estimates and forecasts that are not found in the historical cost records of the company. Only the historical purchase costs of this raw material item are stored in the company's accounting system. Furthermore, the manager must make a new sort of comparative analysis—the predicted cost of continuing to buy the item is compared with the future cost of manufacturing the item. There are many such "special" or nonroutine decision-making demands on the company's accountants, which go beyond the basic accounting procedures and reports. (See Chapter Eleven for review of these special decision situations.) Not all this special cost information can or should be captured in the company's basic cost accounting methods and procedures. In this sense the relevant cost information for special decision situations cannot be "systematized." Rather, the company's basic cost accounting system, which is developed to service functions (1) and (2), should be open-ended and accessible enough to facilitate function (3) as well.

In summary, a company's cost accounting system should be multipurpose—different costs are needed for different purposes, that is, different methods of cost analyses and different cost measurements are necessary for different purposes. Functions (1) and (2) should never prevent the management accountant from supplying new costs and different analysis of old costs for special management decisions. But, this is easier said than done. A company's cost accounting system may tend to become oriented *exclusively* to the routine and repetitive demands on the system. In recording the actual costs of the transactions and operations of the company, costs are usually classified in the journal entries and accounts so that they can be properly assigned or allocated to particular products or to specific operating departments in the organization. This is entirely proper for inventory valuation, profit measurement, and the preparation of the regular accounting reports to managers. But a special decision situation may arise that needs relevant cost information classified on a different basis. For example, the decision maker may need to know those costs that could be avoided in the future if the company were to make certain changes in its method of operations. It is unlikely that the actual costs already recorded in the accounting system would be classified on the basis of which costs would be avoidable under certain circumstances and which would not. The management accountant would have to analyze and reclassify the costs into those that would be avoidable and those that would not be.

Management Information Systems: The Same as Management Accounting Systems or Something More?

In recent years the term "management information system" has caught the imagination of many writers, and is enthusiastically adopted in current management and accounting publications. There are almost as many meanings for the term as there are authors. The general concepts and assumptions behind this "buzz word" promise much, perhaps too much. In the extreme, some writers take it for granted that a complete, perfect, and relatively inexpensive management information system is feasible and practical, and is just around the corner for those bold enough to adopt such a course. This seems far too optimistic, to say the least. Yet, it is hard to fault the basic theory and the essential logic of the discussion of management information systems (MIS).

The main problem is how to translate MIS theory into actual practice. Clearly good decisions depend on having and using good information, and rejecting bad information. Indeed, one of the most basic functions of a manager is to know what information is needed for each decision, to know the sources of the information, and to know how to assess the validity, credibility, and accuracy of the information from each source. But to pretend that *all* the many diverse types of information needed for *all* the decisions made by *all* the managers throughout the entire organization can be systematized, and that this information can be put into a formal communication network within a business organization, seems naive and unrealistic if not a dangerous illusion.

On the other hand, there is no doubt that *some* of the information needed by management decision makers in the organization can be and should be systematized, mainly to assure that certain basic information does, in fact, flow into the hands of these decision makers which otherwise might be overlooked. In other words, there is consistent and regular need for certain types of basic information by management decision makers. It would be foolhardy not to make sure that this information is captured, processed, and reported to the decision makers. A system should be established for the collection and communication of this management information. Once established, the MIS should free managers to concentrate their time and efforts on getting the other types of information that are relevant to their decisions and that cannot be systematized. An excellent short discussion summarizing many important points about management information systems is found in a recent article by Colbert, excerpts of which are reproduced in Exhibit 15.1.* As Colbert himself probably would admit, his article is just the tip of the iceberg and does not do justice to the many practical problems of implementing an MIS in an actual company.

Curiously, many articles and books about management information systems say very little about the *management accounting system* of a company. If it is mentioned at all, the management accounting system usually is maligned and frequently dismissed as being largely useless and irrelevant. This attitude is not only unfair, but also seems to be based on ignorance of what a management accounting system is and does for managers. Actually, it seems to be to a matter of definitions. Evidently many writers assume that the term "accounting" is rather limited, whereas the term "information" is all-inclusive. The more types of information that are assumed to be within the scope of a MIS, then the less likely would anyone (even accountants) be to identify it as a manage-

---

* Bertram A. Colbert, "Pathway To Profit: The Management Information System" *The Price Waterhouse Review*, Spring 1967, pages 6-8.

ment *accounting* system. There is no doubt that the management accounting system is an essential part of a more broadly conceived management information system. Most managers, it seems fair to assume, are not too concerned about which term is used. Rather they are concerned with results, that is, getting all the relevant information they need from the management "accounting/information" system, whichever term is used.

Thrust of Management Science, Operations Research, and Quantitative Methods of Analysis on Management Accounting

Over the past two to three decades there has emerged what truly can be called a new field of study or a new discipline that deals with the broad area of decision processes and decision analysis primarily from the mathematical and statistical points of view. The most common terms used to describe this rather diverse body of methodology are *management science* (MS) and *operations research* (OR), although the terminology is not yet completely agreed on. Management science is the term used here. (Systems analysis, quantitative methods, and other terms are used also; no attempt is made here to differentiate among the various terms.) The basic thrust of management science is to bring more sophisticated and more powerful analytical methods to bear on many decision problems. The stress is on *formal models,* which are put in a mathematical and/or probabilitistic framework. Mathematical and/or statistical techniques of analysis are used to find the best or optimal solution to the problem. The *scientific method* is the guiding philosophy behind these methods of structuring and analyzing problems.

Management science can be viewed as a "bag of analytical tools" that are designed especially to deal with two pervasive and fundamental characteristics of many management decision problems—*risk* and *complexity.* Loosely speaking, risk means that the manager does not know for certain what will happen in the future. Obviously, cause and effect relationships change over time (to some degree), and these changes cannot always be predicted in advance. Also, most of the variables and factors that are relevant to a decision tend to fluctuate and do not remain constant over time. The decision maker must predict the values or other measures of these variables and factors over the future time-frame of the decision. Many of them do not follow a constant pattern or a consistent formula of behavior over time. All is not chaos, however. Usually the decision maker can do two things to deal with fluctuation of the variables and factors that are relevant to the decision.

First, a *range* of future values (or other measures) can be determined (or guessed at). The lowest possible value and the highest possible value can be estimated, below which and above which there is very little chance of occurrence. Within this range of possible values, some values (usually those in the middle of the range) are more likely to occur than others (usually the extreme values). Based on either an intuitive approach or a more explicit method, the

EXHIBIT 15.1

What is a management information system?

A management information system, simply, is an organized method of providing each manager with all the data and only that data which he needs for decision, when he needs it and in a form which aids his understanding and stimulates his action.

Such a system:

1. Considers the full effect of a decision in *advance* by supplying complete, accurate and timely data for use in the planning and decision-making processes.
2. Eliminates from the planning and decision-making processes the problems associated with the use of inconsistent and incomplete data by providing a means for preparing and presenting information in a uniform manner.
3. Uses common data and methods in the preparation of long-range and short-term plans.
4. Identifies, structures and quantifies significant past relationships and forecasts future relationships through the use of advanced mathematical techniques in analyzing data.
5. Merges financial and production data to produce significant measures of performance to facilitate planning decisions with minimum processing of data.
6. Recognizes the needs of all corporate units so that the requirement of each are met with a minimum of duplication while serving the corporation as a whole.
7. Reduces the time and volume of information required to make decisions by reporting to each level of management only necessary degrees of detail and usually only the exception from the standard or norm.
8. Utilizes personnel and data processing equipment effectively so that the optimum in speed and accuracy is achieved at the lowest cost.
9. Requires that the data be presented to those responsible for the decision-making and planning processes in a form which minimizes the need for analysis and interpretation.
10. Provides flexibility and adaptability to change.

The concept of management information is one that would be equally valid if the company were small or large, or if the data were obtained and processed through the most simple manual means or through the most sophisticated computer. Management must, to design a system, select at each level of control only the data that is required. The data must be presented in a manner which facilitates understanding and action, and provides a measure of effectiveness of the action which has been and is being taken.

Symptoms of information hunger

Most growing companies and many mature companies show certain symptoms or clear indications of what we can call "information hunger." Some of these symptoms may, of course, arise from sheer poor management, even when the information system is adequate, but we have listed them here simply because they are so frequent and often so baffling even to competent managers. Many managers simply do not realize that the information on which they are basing even their most routine decisions may be dangerously inadequate or misleading and that their information system is simply not geared to the needs of their company. Let us turn to Chart 4 and consider the 25 symptoms any or any combination of which may indicate an inadequate information system.

In the operational aspect of the business, they range from large inventory adjustments to a sterile R and D program; in the human aspect from inability to note the significance of certain financial indicators to overloaded briefcases and poring over reports at midnight.

Any executive will do well to study these symptoms and note whether his organization exhibits one or more of them. A study of the present scope of management information in the typical enterprise as shown in Chart 5 and a comparison of the typical management informational efforts with the values to be received through each shown in Chart 6 show that in the typical organization management is either using its information facilities too narrowly or has not developed facilities of the necessary scope and significance to insure the enterprise's future. As indicated, most managements devote 90% of their efforts to the securing of information which will enable them to operate and control and only about 5% of their efforts to securing the necessary information to meet competition and another 5% to meet future needs. These proportions do not make the organization adaptable to change and may lead to such stagnation or such poor preparation that a competitors' new product or a change in consumer's tastes and needs may knock the enterprises right out of the ball game.

EXHIBIT 15.1

What kinds of information should managers have?

What, then, are the kinds of information which managers need? They can be grouped into three major categories: information which various company executives require for operation and control; information required to assess future action, and information required to assess or compare performance by the company in competition or within the industry.

CHART NO. 4
SYMPTOMS OF AN INADEQUATE MANAGEMENT INFORMATION SYSTEM

OPERATIONAL	PSYCHOLOGICAL	REPORT CONTENT
Large physical inventory adjustments	Surprise at financial results	Excessive use of tabulations of figures
Capital expenditure overruns	Poor attitude of executives about usefulness of information	Multiple preparation and distribution of identical data
Inability of executives to explain changes from year to year in operating results	Lack of understanding of financial information on part of nonfinancial executives	Disagreeing information from different sources
Uncertain direction of company growth	Lack of concern for environmental changes	Lack of periodic comparative information and trends
Cost variances unxeplainable	Executive homework reviewing reports considered excessive	Lateness of information
No order backlog awareness		Too little or excess detail
No internal discussion of reported data		Inaccurate information
Insufficient knowledge about competition		Lack of standards for comparison
Purchasing parts from outside vendors when internal capability and capacity to make is available		Failure to identify variances by cause and responsibility
Record of some "sour" investments in facilities, or in programs, such as R & D and advertising		Inadequate externally generated information

CHART NO. 5
PRESENT SCOPE OF
MANAGEMENT INFORMATION

FINANCIAL	40
LOGISTICS	40
PERSONNEL	5
MARKETING	5
RESEARCH AND DEVELOPMENT	5
ALL OTHERS	5
	100%

CHART NO. 6
TYPICAL MANAGEMENT INFORMATIONAL EFFORTS
VERSUS MANAGEMENT INFORMATION NEEDS

EFFORT TO OBTAIN	INFORMATION ABOUT	VALUE FOR MANAGEMENT
5	FUTURE	25
5	COMPETITION (External)	15
90	SELF (Internal)	60
100%		100%

decision maker can develop a *probability distribution* of future values (measures) for each relevant factor. Many decision makers operate with an intuitive feel or a subjective sense of these probability distributions, instead of attempting to quantify the probabilities in some manner. One approach is simply to choose the *one* value that is thought to be the most likely of being true in the future. This is called a *point* estimate, since one particular point in the range of possible values of the factor is selected to the exclusion of all others.

On the other hand, it may be possible to develop a probability *distribution* for the range of possible future values for each relevant variable. For example, one value may be given a .25 (25%) probability of occurrence, another a .20 (20%) probability of occurrence, and so on, across the range of values for the variable. In most instances certain values are given higher probability weights than others—assigning each value an equal chance of occurrence is not too usual. Several management science techniques work with these probability distributions, such as queueing (waiting line) theory, and other probabilistic models and methods. The usefulness of these probabilistic methods depends heavily on the reliability and accuracy of the probability weights assigned to each variable's future values. For instance, assume we want to determine the best betting strategy for playing craps in Las Vegas. The probability of each possible number on a roll of the dice is rather definite and can be determined accurately, assuming a fair pair of dice, of course. But in most practical business decision situations, probabilities are not as easily determined. In short, there is always the question: What is the probability that the probability distribution is correct?

When a decision problem is said to be complex, this usually means that there are many different relevant variables and a large number of interactions among them. Also complexity may mean that there are a relatively large number of alternative solutions or mix of solutions. Complexity may also mean that serious difficulties exist with respect to expressing the goals, purposes, and objectives of the decision in meaningful, concrete, and operational terms, especially if there are two or more goals that are not entirely consistent with one another. *Linear programming* is perhaps the best-known management science method for dealing with complex problem situations that concern the allocation of limited resources to many different alternative possible uses, to achieve an overall optimal result subject to many restraints. For example, a company may have 5 manufacturing plants in different locations and 20 widely distributed inventory warehouses across the country. The basic problem is to decide how much each plant should ship to each warehouse, given the transportation costs between each plant and each warehouse, and given the production capacities of each plant and the storage limits of each warehouse. All of this should be done at the lowest total cost and still meet the sales demands for the number of units needed at each warehouse. The number of feasible solution combinations in such a problem situation is staggering. Linear programming models and techniques can deal with problems of this kind, assuming that adequate and accurate cost and other accounting information is available.

Some authors of management science articles and books have gone out of their way to "bad-mouth" management accounting for ignoring the development of these mathematical and quantitative methods. They criticize management accountants for failing to understand enough about management science so that useful cost and other accounting information can be supplied to decision makers who are using management science methods. Some of this criticism is justified. But some of their comments are based on a rather glaring ignorance of management accounting. Management accountants have, to some extent, recognized the importance and management use of management science methods. For instance, the professional organization of management accountants (the National Association of Accountants, or NAA) offers education and training courses that include many management science topics.

Regarding developments in the field of management science (MS), there seem to be two major questions the managment accountant should answer. (1): Which MS methods are actually being used by managers? (2): How and where are these quantitative methods being used? Some management science models and techniques involve more theory than practice; many of the methods advocated in MS publications are not being used in actual practice. It is unfair to blame management accountants for not responding to untried MS theory. On the other hand, some management science methods have found widespread use, such as linear programming, statistical analysis of cost behavior, statistical control charts, and PERT. These methods call for relevant cost and other accounting information. Clearly management accountants should respond to these demands. However, in some companies the top management may not view this as a function of management accounting. In other cases management accountants themselves are to blame because they have balked at accepting these new responsibilities.

The prevailing view, at least in authoritative professional accounting publications, is that management accountants should welcome these challenges and should expand the traditional boundaries of their field to include active participation in the use and development of management science methods by decision makers. Indeed, Part 5 of the national examination prepared by the Institute Of Management Accounting (established by the NAA) for the Certified Management Accountant (CMA) certificate covers decision analysis, including modeling and information systems. Part 2 of this examination covers organization and behavior.

Relevance of Behavioral Sciences to Management Accounting

For many years management accountants have been aware of the impacts of budgets on people in the organization, the problems regarding the effects of setting and adopting standards on motivation, and that the management accounting reporting system should be based on the organizational structure and the distribution and departmentalization of authority and responsibility in the organization. More recently, however, professional management accounting publications are paying increasing attention to the behavioral sciences. It would be unusual today to find a management accountant who has not at least heard and read something about the relevance of behavioral sciences to management accounting. Psychology, sociology, and communication (to name only three) abound with theories and research findings that have direct bearing on management accounting. Indeed, a good part of the research over the last two to three decades in these disciplines has been dircted to organizations, large groups, and small groups, as well as to motivational and behavioral theory of the individual, all of which are highly relevant to business management and administration.

In his book, *Management Accounting And Behavioral Science,* Caplan contrasts what he considers to be the traditional management accounting model, involving the assumptions about the role of accounting, with his view of the modern organization theory model (see Exhibit 15.2).* Many would disagree with both sides of Caplan's contrast of the traditional accounting model and the modern organization theory model. However, the important point is that this sort of concern and argument is now taken very seriously, whereas not so many years ago there was very little interest and debate. An enormous difficulty facing management accountants is the huge volume of research and publications in the diverse fields of behavioral sciences that should be searched for relevance to management accounting. Psychology is an obvious field to examine, but this discipline is subdivided into many specialized areas, and in each area there are several journals and many books published each year. Then, there are many conflicting or diverse theories and models of human behavior, as individuals and in organizations.

Nevertheless, the management accountant of today would do well to keep abreast of developments in the behavioral sciences that have bearing on management accounting. Fortunately, professional accounting publications, as well as several other "nonexpert" popular magazines which are now available, provide an abundant source of information. As with management science, the main problem facing management accountants is not really learning about the behavioral sciences. The main problem is the application and implementation of their theories and research findings in the day-to-day practice of management accounting.

For example, consider the importance of *goal congruence* in the organization, which roughly speaking means keeping all managers and organization units working together in harmony towards the organization's goals. The company's accountants should avoid any accounting practice that encourages discongruence, and they should adopt accounting methods that foster goal congruence. One accounting practice that comes under heavy criticism from the standpoint of goal congruence is the allocation of noncontrollable costs to a manager's department (or other type of responsibility unit). For instance, assume that a company has established 20 sales territories, each under the authority and control of a sales manager. All the company's advertising, on the

---

* Edwin H. Caplan, *Management Accounting And Behavioral Science* (Addison-Wesley, 1971), pages 42-44.

EXHIBIT 15.2

ASSUMPTIONS ABOUT THE ROLE OF ACCOUNTING

The Traditional Management Accounting Model

A. The primary function of management accounting is to aid management in the process of profit maximization.

B. The accounting system is a goal-allocation device which permits management to select its operating objectives and to divide and distribute them throughout the firm, i.e., assign responsibilities for performance. This is commonly referred to as "planning."

C. The accounting system is a control device which permits management to identify and correct undesirable performance.

D. There is sufficient certainty, rationality, and knowledge within the system to permit an accurate comparison of responsibility for performance and the ultimate benefits and costs of that performance.

E. The accounting system is neutral in its evaluations—personal bias is eliminated by the objectivity of the system.

The Modern Organization Theory Model

A. The management accounting process is an information system whose major purposes are: (1) to provide the various levels of management with data which will facilitate the decision-making functions of planning and control; and (2) to serve as a communications medium within the organization.

B. The effective use of budgets and other accounting planning and control techniques requires an understanding of the interaction between these techniques and the motivations and aspiration levels of the individuals to be controlled.

C. The objectivity of the management accounting process is largely a myth. Accountants have wide areas of discretion in the selection, processing, and reporting of data.

D. In performing their function within an organization, accountants can be expected to be influenced by their own personal and departmental goals in the same way that other participants are influenced.

Modern business organizations are highly complex, and their managements must continually operate under conditions of uncertainty and limited rationality. There is absolutely no way in which any information system, including accounting, can possibly record and report all of the variables affecting an organization. Therefore, a tremendous amount of selection and abstraction is bound to occur. Moreover, management accountants are subject to the same kinds of drives and needs as are other members of the organization. All of this suggests that management accounting systems could not, even under the best of circumstances, achieve the degree of certainty, neutrality, and objectivity that is often attributed to them. To the extent that management accounting fails to live up to its image in this regard, it can be anticipated that certain problems will arise for the organization. For one thing, organization members are often subject to evaluations based on information produced by the accounting system. These individuals are likely to be confused and frustrated by a flow of seemingly precise and exact accounting data which they can neither understand nor explain but which, nevertheless, are used to determine whether they are performing their tasks properly. Another problem is that managers who depend on accounting data for decision making may be misled because they fail to recognize the limitations of the data. An essential step in minimizing these difficulties would be a broader educational program by accountants to inform management at all levels of the inherent limitations of accounting data and the fact that such data may not be as precise or as complete as they appear at first glance.

One additional comment regarding the role of accounting is worth noting. As members of the organizations which they serve, management accountants can be expected to seek such psychological and social objectives as security, esteem, and influence. In some instances, they might also be expected—as suggested by the discussion of subunit goals—to view the success of the accounting department and the technical perfection of the accounting process as ends in themselves. These observations offer at least a partial explanation for what has been described as the "watchdog" attitude of accountants. While this attitude is inconsistent with modern views of management accounting, it is undoubtedly true that some accountants still see their function as primarily one of criticizing the actions of others and placing responsibility for failures to achieve certain desired levels of performance. This is unfortunate, because management accounting systems which reflect such an attitude are bound to be a significant source of frustration and conflict within an organization.

other hand, is in national magazines and on national television, so the company has centralized its advertising functions in one home office department. The territory sales managers provide only advisory input into the advertising decisions made by the company's advertising managers. In this situation the company's advertising costs are noncontrollable to each territory's sales manager. Yet, the advertising benefits sales in all territories, and probably benefits some territories more than others. Hence, top management is considering the allocation of the company's total annual advertising expense among the 20 sales territories.

The following methods for allocating the total national advertising expense for the year have been suggested.

1. Charging an equal amount of the total annual expense to each sales territory, that is, 5.0% of the total to each territory.

2. Charging each dollar of sales revenue in all territories with an equal amount of the total advertising expense, so that if one territory generates, say, 6.35% of the company's total sales revenue for the year, then this territory would be allocated 6.35% of the total advertising expense.

3. Determining the advertising cost for each individual product advertised and charging each territory's sales revenue from each product its proportionate share of the total advertising expense for each product. If one territory sells, say, 5.83% of the company's total sales of a patricular product, this territory would be allowed 5.83% of this product's total advertising cost for the year. Each territory's total sales would have to be broken down by each product sold for this allocation method.

4. Charging an equal amount of the total annual advertising expense to each salesman employed in the sales territories, so that if one territory has 20 salesmen and another has 10, the first would be allocated twice the amount of advertising expense.

5. Charging an equal amount of advertising expense to each dollar of *budgeted* sales revenue in each territory. Each territory's sales budget (quota) is determined at the start of the year, based on market research and the past sales experience in that territory.

There are several other possible allocation methods, but the five listed above are sufficient to illustrate the problems of cost allocation. Each allocation method has some logic to it. There are many arguments in favor of one method over the others. The important point is not which method is "right" from a theoretical accounting point of view but, instead, which method encourages the best goal congruence of the 20 sales managers to make the best use of the company's advertising efforts during the year. One argument is that centrally controlled expenses should *not* be allocated at all, since the sales managers cannot be held responsible for the advertising expense, and they would resent any noncontrollable expense being charged against "their" sales revenue.

The Different Types of Responsibility Centers in the Business Organization: Implications for Management Accounting

Basic Types of Responsibility Centers

If one looks down and across the organizational structure of a business enterprise, one sees different types of management *responsibility centers* in the organization. The term "responsibility center" refers to any distinguishable separate organization unit, department, division, branch, territory, office, or the like. Business organizations (almost any type of organization for that matter) are subdivided into management responsibility centers, usually based on the specialization of functions and duties of the managers and other employees in each of these organizational subunits.

One way to identify the management responsibility centers in a business organization is to look at the company's organization chart. (For the top part of such an organization chart see Exhibit 1.4 in Chapter One.) A major task of a company's management accountants is to design accounting reports that are relevant, useful, and *most appropriate* for the nature and span of authority of each responsibility center. This guiding principle is called *responsibility accounting*, which is discussed briefly in Chapter One (see pages 17 to 18). Here we examine more closely the nature of responsibility centers and the accounting reports appropriate for each type.

Presumably the scope of authority and responsibility of each management position in the organization is clearly defined and is understood throughout the organization. Presumably the relationships and flow of communication (both formal and informal) among managers and among the separate responsibility centers is well defined and is closely adhered to throughout the organization. These are questionable presumptions, to be sure. The dynamics of an organization cannot be ignored. It has been observed that the members of an organization constantly "reorganize" its structure and processes. Thus to some degree, organizational relationships and communication patterns constantly change over time, and are dependent both on the personalities and styles of behavior of those particular managers who occupy positions of authority, and on how they relate to one another. Yet there usually is a reasonably stable ongoing subdivision of the management activity in the business organization.

The following discussion assumes fairly well defined responsibility centers in the organization, that is, centers of activity, duties, and functions for which particular managers have specific authority and responsibility. The responsibility centers in a business organization generally can be classified into four types from the point of view of designing accounting reports to the managers of these organizational units: (1) revenue centers, (2) cost centers, (3) profit centers, and (4) Investment centers.

Revenue Centers

A revenue center is a responsibility center for which sales revenue is the primary responsibility and which has little or no responsibility for costs, except for direct selling expenses such as salesmen's travel expenses, entertainment of customers, and certain advertising and promotion costs. The typical sales department or sales territory fits this description, and consists of several salesmen and a general sales manager of the unit. These front-line sales managers need very detailed sales reports that break out the quantity and prices of each specific model and each size of each product sold during the period. These sales reports frequently include summaries of the sales by each salesman, and may also include the total sales during the period to each customer or to each types of customer. Actual sales performance may be compared with budgeted sales for the period or with other types of sales quotas in these periodic sales reports. The sales reports usually include detailed information on sales returns, price adjustments and allowances, and the like. Also those particular expenses under the sales manager's control would be included in the regular periodic accounting reports to the managers.

Cost Centers: The Problems of Joint Cost Allocation

A *cost center,* as the name implies, is an organizational unit whose activities, functions, and operations require the expenditure of costs that are far removed and too distant from sales revenue sources to allow any matching of their costs with the company's sales revenue. The *staff departments* of the typical business organization are prime examples of cost centers, such as a company's legal office, its public relations department, its data processing department, its accounting department, and others. These cost centers provide essential services to carry on the operations of the company. One of the primary responsibilities of the general manager of the cost center is to maintain the quality of these services at a reasonable cost. The periodic accounting reports to managers of cost centers usually include a very detailed breakout of the costs for the period. In these reports each cost line may be compared with the budgeted cost for the period, and they usually include a comparison with last period's cost. Most often these periodic cost reports show both the costs of the latest period (for example, a month), and the year-to-date cost totals (with appropriate comparison with budget and/or last period).

Some costs are direct and clearly assignable to the particular cost center. For instance, consider a company's data processing department cost center. The salaries of the card punchers, machine operators, programmers, and other employees working in the department are direct costs of the center. Likewise, the rental payments or depreciation of the computer hardware equipment are direct costs. But what about the depreciation of the company's building in which the data processing department is located? Should some of the electricity cost of the month be allocated to the data processing department? The data processing department manager probably has no authority or responsibility for building occupancy costs. If indirect costs are allocated to a cost center, costs which the manager of the cost center has little or no authority or responsibility for, then these allocated costs should be clearly separated from the direct costs for which the manager does have control responsibility.

Whether or not to allocate *common* or *joint costs* of a company which by their very nature are quite indirect to any particular cost center or revenue center is a difficult question. The allocation of a company's national advertising expense to its sales territories is discussed above (see pages 531 to 532). For another example, consider a company all of whose operations are contained in one large building that occupies an entire city block. The company is organized into many different revenue and cost centers. Each year this company receives one real estate tax bill for its entire land and building property. Should this company-wide joint cost be allocated among the various revenue centers and cost centers that occupy the building?

It seems that some reasonable basis of allocation of the annual real estate bill could be worked out, for example, one based on the square footage of space occupied by each revenue center or each cost center. If the data processing department uses 10,000 square feet and the total building has 500,000 square feet of space, then the data processing department cost center could be charged with (10,000/500,000) or 2% of the real estate tax expense for the year. If all such joint or common costs were allocated in some manner, then each cost center and each revenue center absorb their "fair share" of these costs. The company would have a "full cost" measure for each cost center and for each revenue center. On the other hand, allocation methods are usually arbitrary to one degree or another. And, the managers of the revenue and cost centers have little or not control over these indirect costs. In short, whether to allocate non-controllable joint costs and how to allocate these costs is a difficult management decision.

Profit Centers and Investment Centers

A *profit center* is an organizational department or division whose general manager has direct profit performance responsibility. This means that a profit center not only has organizational responsibility for generating sales revenue but also has control over its manufacturing costs of the products being sold and over most, if not all, of the selling costs of making the sales. For example, one of the major divisions of a company may manufacture and sell a particular line of products; this is the prime example of a profit center. Internally a profit center may be divided into sales centers and cost centers.

An *investment center* is a profit center—or perhaps two or more profit centers grouped together—which also has management responsibility and control over the assets that are used to carry on its sales, manufacturing, and other operations. In essence, an investment center is a relatively self-contained, autonomous "mini company" within the business organization. The periodic accounting reports to managers of profit centers follow the basic format illustrated in preceding chapters (see Exhibits 4.1 and 4.5 in particular). Investment center managers also receive asset investment reports that show the asset balances being used by the center, including inventories, fixed assets, and accounts receivable. Profit center accounting reports are limited to total profit and profit ratio measures. Investment center accounting reports also include return on investment performance measures.

Whether within the organization there are profit centers and investment centers depends mainly on the management philosophy of the company. Some companies follow a policy of decentralization, that is, of dividing the company into fairly autonomous divisions. Each division has direct profit responsibility and has the authority to make most decisions without clearing them with headquarters. This organizational structure consists of profit and investment centers. On the other hand, some companies follow a tight policy of centralization. All important decisions are centralized in headquarters at the top management level. It is difficult in these cases to find any of its organizational units that are truly profit centers or investment centers in the complete sense of these terms. The organizational units would be either cost centers or revenue centers. In highly centralized business organization structures, managers do not have coordinated responsibility for *both* sales revenue and costs except at the top management level.

In summary, the design of the management accounting reports for each responsibility center in the business organization are (or should be) based on the organizational character and nature of that organizational unit. If the department or division is an autonomous segment of the business which is accountable for its sales, costs, profit, and return on assets performance, then it is an investment center. If, on the other hand, the responsibility center has limited authority and is subject to decision control from above by a top level centralized group of managers, then the department is a cost center or revenue center.

Last, certain basic problems of preparing management accounting reports for profit and investment centers should be mentioned briefly. One problem, already discussed above regarding cost centers, is the allocation of *joint costs* among two or more profit centers or investment centers. Since allocated costs are not under the direct control of the managers of profit and investment centers, and since they reduce the reported profit performance of these centers, the managers are quite sensitive to the fairness of joint cost allocation methods. For investment centers there is also the problem regarding whether and how to allocate certain general company-wide *assets* among two or more investment centers. Should the corporate headquarters' fixed assets be allocated to the various investment centers in the organization that are located elsewhere? If so, how?

Profit centers and investment centers may engage in transactions among themselves. There are problems in accounting for these interdivisional transactions, in particular regarding how to establish *transfer prices* for the products or services being "bought" and "sold" between the responsibility centers. One investment center, for example, may sell its products to outside customers as well as to other organization units in the company. A paper company may sell its paperboard to outside customers and also may sell the same products to another division of the company which manufactures paper container products. Assume both the papermill division and the container division are investment centers. What price should the selling unit be given credit for when selling to another unit within the organization? Should the selling unit charge its normal price to show a normal profit margin on the sale? Or, should the products be sold at cost? Then, there is the question whether the cost of capital rate for one investment center should be higher or lower than another investment center. For instance, many companies have established separate finance companies to loan money to their customers to enable the customers to purchase its products on long-term credit terms. These finance companies are separate investment centers in the organization. The cost of capital to the finance company may be lower than the company's cost of capital rate.

Legal and Regulatory Aspects of Cost Accounting

In designing its cost accounting methods and procedures, and in deciding on joint cost allocation methods in particular, a company is not free to do just as it pleases. Federal and state laws have a bearing on these accounting decisions. The federal income tax law requires that the full cost absorption cost method be used for the determination of the cost of work-in-process and finished goods inventories for measuring taxable income. (See Chapter Thirteen for discussion.) A company must follow reasonable methods of allocation of manufacturing overhead costs among its production output.

If a company contracts with the federal government, there are many rules and regulations that are part of the contract that govern permissible cost accounting methods and procedures. The Cost Accounting Standards Board was established by Congress in 1970 to develop cost standards and principles for government contract work. Evidently these standards and principles will have a broad influence and authority that goes beyond government contract work. Some believe that pronouncements by the CASB may eventually become generally accepted cost accounting principles, comparable in authority to generally accepted accounting principles.

Also, in 1936 Congress passed the Robinson-Patman Act, which prohibits price discrimination by companies if the effects are to lessen competition. The act does not prohibit price differences between customers buying the same product that can be justified on the basis of differences in the costs of manufacture or the cost of distribution of the products to the customers. But the company is forced on the defensive, if challenged, to justify the sales price differences relative to its cost differences. The Federal Trade Commission has brought many cases of alleged unlawful price discrimination that companies have had to defend in legal proceedings, not always successfully it should be added. Finally, many states have laws that prohibit selling products below cost, although cost is not necessarily well defined in the state laws.

In Conclusion: The General Applicability of Management Accounting Concepts and Analytical Methods to Nonprofit Motivated Entities

The main orientation of this book concerns the profit motivated business entity that manufactures and sells products. However, the concepts and methods discussed throughout apply to other types of profit motivated business entities, including service companies, financial institutions, and the like. Of course, these concepts and methods must be applied somewhat differently in each case. Designing management accounting methods and reports for an airline is quite different from designing them for a commercial bank, a supermarket chain, or a greyhound racetrack.

Also, management accounting theory and methods are just as useful to *nonprofit* motivated organizations, agencies, and institutions, such as universities, hospitals, state government departments and agencies. It is fair to say that management accounting for nonprofit entities is on the whole *more* difficult than for business entities. There, the connection between revenue sources and the costs of providing the services by the nonprofit organization is usually more indirect. Measuring benefits and setting performance standards for the many diverse services provided by a typical nonprofit entity is preplexing. For example, measuring the quality and quantity of services and other benefits provided by a municipal government, and comparing these measures with the costs of providing these services is very difficult. As the general public becomes more aware of and more demanding regarding the public environment, ecology, and energy conservation, cost-benefit studies and analyses will obviously become increasingly important. Management accounting theory and analysis has much to offer in these areas of public concern and governmental decision making.

Questions

15. 1 (a) What are the three basic functions of a company's cost accounting system?
   (b) Can all three functions be served equally well? Doesn't one function have to suffer so that the other two can be done well?

15. 2 "Costs once recorded are historical and therefore irrelevant to current management decisions; therefore, the historical based cost records are only useful for external financial statement reporting and for income tax." Do you agree? Explain.

15. 3 "A management accounting system is a subset of the company's more general management information system." Do you agree? Explain.

15. 4 What are some key symptoms of an inadequate management information system?

15. 5 Give several examples of management information that can be and probably should be systematized, and some examples of management information that either cannot be or probably should not be.

15. 6 (a) Briefly, what are two basic characteristics of many management decisions that cause serious analysis problems?
   (b) How do managers attempt to deal with these characteristics in their decision analyses?

15. 7 What is a probability distribution? How are these useful in management decision analysis?

15. 8 Should management accountants "get into" management science and quantitative analysis models and methods? Explain.

15. 9 "The behavioral sciences are generally irrelevant to the actual practice of management accounting; study of the behavioral sciences is primarily for managers not accountants." Do you agree? Explain.

15.10 Refer to the quotation from Dale in Chapter One (pages 0 to 0) regarding the basic functions of management. What is the relevance of behavioral science to these functions? Briefly explain.

15.11 What is goal congruence? What is the relevance of this organizational behavior concept to management accounting?

15.12 Consider the five different method for allocation of the company's national advertising expense to its 20 sales territories (see page 000). For each allocation method:
(a) What is the strongest argument in favor of the method?
(b) What is the strongest argument against the method?
(c) If you were president of the company would you even allocate the advertising expense? Explain.

15.13 (a) What are the four basic types of responsibility centers in a business organization?
(b) What are the main differences in the accounting reports to each type of responsibility center?

15.14 Does whether the company adopt a centralized or decentralized organization structure affect its management accounting system? Explain.

15.15 Assume that one investment center in an organization sells its products to outside regular customers and occasionally sells some of the same products to another investment center in the company. Should the selling unit charge its normal sales price to the buying unit, or should the units be sold at cost? Briefly explain your points of argument.

15.16 Which management account concept do you think is more relevant to a *nonprofit* organization: the fixed-variable cost distinction or return on investment? Explain.

Problems

P15. 1 Shown below are three-year comparative net income statements for a particular company that manufactures and sells just one product. During these three years this company has been in a most unusual situation—a noninflation economic environment. Sales volume and production output has increased each year. But almost everything else that affects profit performance (except volume) has remained constant. In particular, the sales price, variable costs per unit, total fixed operating costs, interest rate, and income tax rate have been constant during this three-year period. In fact, even the *quantity* of inventories at the at the end of each of the last four years has remained constant. The cost per unit of inventory has decreased, however, since the same total fixed manufacturing cost each year is spread over a larger volume of output each year. The beginning and ending inventories shown in the Net Income Statements below are *entirely* finished goods inventory; there is no work-in-process at the end of any year.

NET INCOME STATEMENTS

	Two Years Ago	Last Year	This Year
Sales revenue	$2,500,000	$2,750,000	$3,300,000
Cost of goods sold:			
Beginning inventories	$ 375,300	$ 373,750	$ 362,500
Manufacturing costs	1,495,000	1,595,000	1,815,000
Total	$1,870,300	$1,968,750	$2,177,500
Ending inventories	373,750	362,500	343,750
Cost of goods sold expense	$1,496,550	$1,606,250	$1,833,750
Gross profit	$1,003,450	$1,143,750	$1,466,250
Marketing expenses	$ 475,000	$ 505,000	$ 571,000
Administration and general expenses	447,450	457,450	479,450
Total	$ 922,450	$ 962,450	$1,050,450
Operating profit	$ 81,000	$ 181,300	$ 415,800
Interest expense	40,000	44,000	52,800
Net income before income tax	$ 41,000	$ 137,300	$ 363,000
Income tax (at flat 48% rate)	19,680	65,904	174,240
Net income	$ 21,320	$ 71,396	$ 188,760

Required: All of the following parts to this problem are based on the three-year comparative net income statements and the introduction to these statements given above. Except for whatever additional information is given with each part below, you must "dig out" the necessary information from the statements and introduction to the problem. Answer the parts in the order given. The information supplied with each part is cumulative; that is, a later part may build on the information given in an earlier part.

(1) Determine the annual total fixed costs in each operating area (manufacturing, marketing, and administrative and general). Also, explain how the variable costs in each operating area behave.

(2) Compute the company's break-even sales revenue for each year, or to be more precise the break-even sales revenue that would cause exactly a zero operating profit (before interest and income tax expenses are considered).

(3) The company uses the FIFO full-cost absorption cost method for determining its ending inventory cost each year. All of the manufacturing costs of that year are treated as one production lot for determining the per unit cost of the products manufactured that year. The company's production output quantity This Year (but *not* Last Year or Two Years Ago) is exactly equal to 100.0% of its practical manufacturing capacity.

   (a) At what percentage of manufacturing capacity did the company operate Last Year and Two Years Ago? Only show the correct fraction for each year; you do not need to bother to divide the fraction to find the final answer.

   (b) If the company had expensed as a period cost each year the proportionate share of its manufacturing capacity cost of the unused capacity in that year (instead of the method reflected in the Net Income Statements above), determine the amount of the cost of goods sold expense that should have been recorded each year (including the charge off for idle capacity).

   (Hint: the ending inventory cost value at the end of This Year is based on 100.0% utilization of production capacity.)

(4) Restructure This Year's net income statement following the contribution margin format and the direct costing method for inventory valuation, down to the operating profit line in the statement. You do *not* have to explain any difference in the operating profit in this statement compared with the operating profit in the Net Income Statement given at the start of the problem.

P15. 2 The following report is reproduced from the August 1973 issue (Volume 50, No. 4) of the "Clients' Service Bulletin," which is published by The American Appraisal Company, Inc. (the company's headquarters are in Milwaukee, Wisconsin).

Market Value of a Going Concern

The study most often made by The American Appraisal Company, Inc. is the valuation of the business enterprise, either closely held or publicly traded, as a whole. A business enterprise may be defined as the combination of all tangible and intangible assets into a producing economic unit. Determining the market value of a going concern is a vigorous intellectual pursuit, requiring appraisers to balance the values of all underlying assets so they properly reflect each one's proportionate contribution to total entity value.

The following is a brief resume of how such a study is made:

Market value of a going concern is often expressed as the present worth of potential earnings. Thus an investigation and analysis is made of many facets of the operation and its industry, some of them being the adequacy and capacity of the underlying assets, the financial condition of the company, its working and long term capital needs, its past operating results and future prospects, and any pertinent internal or external economic factors. In addition, a comparative evaluation is made with the operating results of comparable companies in the same or a similar line of business.

To obtain information about an enterprise, the property is inspected and discussions held with top level management and with personnel in finance, marketing, engineering, production, and research.

Each part of this study offers the following data:

OPERATING FACILITIES—An engineering analysis permits determination of the:

- Desirability of the plant site with respect to location, transportation, parking, and future expansion

- Condition and utility of buildings, efficiency of plant layout, adequacy of office space and warehousing; ability to manufacture competitive products to meet sales forecasts
- Age, condition, and utility of machinery and equipment, and efficiency of production process
- Availability of skilled labor force, state of labor relations, and outlook
- Competence of plant management
- Capital investment necessary to provide facilities adequate for generating projected revenues

BUSINESS ANALYSIS—Studies are made of:

Manufacturing process
- capacity to meet market demands
- research and development programs
- technical know-how of personnel

Product Lines
- relative compatibility
- raw materials used
- length of conversion period
- quality control standards
- obsolescence

Marketing organization
- location of markets served
- sales and distribution methods
- market penetration and consumer acceptance
- effectiveness of advertising and sales promotion
- competition and trends within industry
- general direction of economy

INTANGIBLE ASSETS—Investigation identifies and, when possible, establishes an economic life for:

- Assembled organization
- Leasehold interests

- Product design and development
- License agreements for franchises
- Long term purchase or supply contracts
- Patents and patent applications
- Secret formulas and processes
- Trademarks and copyright
- Mailing lists
- Investment opitons
- Goodwill and other intangible assets

An evaluation may then be made of the relative significance and contribution of each intangible asset to the total business enterprise.

FINANCIAL ANALYSIS—Operating and financial records are examined to:

Measure
- operating performance
- working capital and debt service requirements
- capital investment returns
- revenue growth rates
- status and trends of profitability

Adjust reported earnings for
- method of valuing inventory
- depreciation policy
- capital and business expense practice
- executive compensation
- any extraordinary items

Project earnings to reflect
- revenue growth trends

- operating cost increases
- pricing policies

COMPARATIVE ENTERPRISES—Industry trends and specific similar enterprises are analyzed to determine the closest comparatives, and the following market ratios are developed for each:

Aggregate market value of stock to
- net profit
- cash flow
- dividends
- net worth

Aggregate market value of invested capital to

- debt free net profit
- cash flow

The quality and trend of operating results of the enterprise being appraised become evident during the course of the comparative analysis, as do trends in net worth and dividends paid.

Further analysis of these results permits appropriate adjustments to the market multiples or ratios selected for application to the historical and projected performances of the enterprise being valued, which, adjusted for risk and tempered to reflect the judgment of the appraiser, result in the final opinion of value.

Required: Read the report by The American Appraisal Company, and then answer these questions:
(1) Which of the many different factors listed in the report are most directly related to a company's management accounting system, and would be included in the regular periodic accounting reports to managers of the company?
(2) Notice under the heading *Financial Analysis* that the report states "... Adjust reported earnings for ..." Why would these five items have to be adjusted? What is the purpose of these"adjustments"?

(3) Would you consider this report a fairly good checkoff list of the key management factors that determine the success of a company?

(4) Would two different appraisers of the same company, both following the approach suggested in the report, come up with the same or very close total market value appraisals of a going concern?

P15. 3 The following excerpts are taken from an article in the March 23, 1974 issue of *Business Week* (pages 62 and 64) entitled "A 'Holes' Committee To Plug Profit Leaks."

Required: If the "holes committee" works so well for this company, shouldn't all companies at least give it a try? Discuss. What impact might such a committee have on a company's management accounting system?

> Mallinckrodt Chemical Works is not the first company to try to create an image designed to appeal to Wall Street, but few have become so adept at the game as the St. Louis pharmaceutical and chemical producer. Since investors pay a premium for steady earnings growth, Mallinckrodt's management goes to unusual lengths to avoid unpleasant surprises, to investors as well as to itself. It even has a committee of top executives that deals with profit leaks if all its other controls should fall . . .

> Under standard accounting systems, most companies monitor sales and profit trends monthly. At Mallinckrodt, each division produces a readout every five days on sales and also on income against budget. In effect, each division is a profit center with an earnings projection that is never more than about a week old. The system has been in operation for some six years. "It has paid off," says Thayer (Chairman and Chief Executive, Harold E. Thayer), "especially during this period of shortages, rising prices, and changing market conditions. With prices changing so quickly, you no longer can afford to wait 30 days to be informed."

> Thayer set up the internal accounting system so reporting responsibility rests squarely upon his 12 division managers and the two group vice-presidents who oversee them . . . Twice a year the divisions calculate their return on investment for each of their businesses, and every 90 days each division manager re-projects his budget for the next four quarters.

> At Mallinckrodt, that is just the beginning of controls. Thayer's fetish for avoiding surprises prompted him three years ago to set up what company people call the "holes" committee. Thayer explains, "This committee watches for holes through which profits can leak." . . .

> Thayer claims it has unlimited authority to poke into any area of the company to correct dubious practices . . .

> So far the holes committee has looked into about 30 activities, including inventory control, microfilming records, and product liability. It is now making a detailed review of the company's insurance policies to determine every potential liability . . .

The company still has a way to go in improving its profit margins and its return on equity, but the trend in both has been mostly up for a decade. In 1964 the company earned only 3.3% on sales, but last year the figure was up to 6.6%. Return on investment rose from 4.9% to 11.9% in the same period. Thayer hopes to keep those figures moving up.

P15. 4 Select the best answer choice for each of the following questions, which relate to a variety of managerial accounting problems. In determining your answer to each question, consider the information given in the preceding lettered statement of facts.

(a) The Zel Company, a wholesaler, budgeted the following sales for the indicated months:

	June 1977	July 1977	August 1977
Sales on account	$1,500,000	$1,600,000	$1,700,000
Cash sales	200,000	210,000	220,000
Total sales	$1,700,000	$1,181,000	$1,920,000

All merchandise is marked up to sell at its invoice cost plus 25%. Merchandise inventories at the beginning of each month are at 30% of that month's projected cost of goods sold.

(1) The cost of goods sold for the month of June 1977 is anticipated to be
   a. $1,530,000.
   b. $1,402,500.
   c. $1,275,000.
   d. $1,190,000.
   e. None of the above.

(2) Merchandise purchases for July 1977 are anticipated to be
   a. $1,605,500.
   b. $1,474,400.
   c. $1,448,000.
   d. $1,382,250.
   e. None of the above.

(b) The following annual flexible budget has been prepared for use in making decisions relating to product X.

	100,000 Units	150,000 Units	200,000 Units
Sales volume	$800,000	$1,200,000	$1,600,000
Manufacturing costs:			
Variable	300,000	450,000	600,000
Fixed	200,000	200,000	200,000
	500,000	650,000	800,000
Selling and other expenses:			
Variable	200,000	300,000	400,000
Fixed	160,000	160,000	160,000
	360,000	460,000	560,000
Income (or loss)	$ (60,000)	$ 90,000	$ 240,000

The 200,000-unit budget has been adopted and will be used for allocating fixed manufacturing costs to units of product X; at the end of the first six months the following information is available:

	Units
Production completed	120,000
Sales	60,000

All fixed costs are budgeted and incurred uniformly throughout the year and all costs incurred coincide with the budget.

Over- and underapplied fixed manufacturing costs are deferred until year-end.

(3) The amount of fixed factory costs applied to product during the first six months under absorption costing would be
    a. Overapplied by $20,000.
    b. Equal to the fixed costs incurred.
    c. Underapplied by $40,000.
    d. Underapplied by $80,000.
    e. None of the above.

(4) Reported net income (or loss) for the first six months under absorption costing would be
    a. $160,000.
    b. $80,000.
    c. $40,000.
    d. ($40,000).
    e. None of the above.

(5) Reported net income (or loss) for the first six months under direct cost would be

a. $144,000.
b. $72,000.
c. $0.
d. ($36,000).
e. None of the above.

(c) The following inventory data relate to the Shirley Company:

Inventories

	Ending	Beginning
Finished goods	$95,000	$110,000
Work in process	80,000	70,000
Direct materials	95,000	90,000

Costs Incurred During the Period

Cost of goods available for sale	$684,000
Total manufacturing costs	654,000
Factory overhead	167,000
Direct materials used	193,000

(7) Direct materials purchased during the year were
   a. $213,000.
   b. $198,000.
   c. $193,000.
   d. $188,000.
   e. Nonc of the above or not determinable from the above facts.

(8) Direct labor costs incurred during the period were
   a. $250,000.
   b. $234,000.
   c. $230,000.
   d. $224,000.
   e. None of the above or not determinable from above facts.

(9) The cost of goods sold during the period was
   a. $614,000.
   b. $604,000.
   c. $594,000.
   d. $589,000.
   e. None of the above or not determinable from above facts.

(d) Carey Company sold 100,000 units of its product at $20 per unit. Variable costs are $14 per unit (manufacturing costs of $11 and selling costs of $3). Fixed costs are incurred uniformly throughout the year and amount to $792,000 (manufacturing costs of $500,000 and selling costs of $292,000). There are no beginning or ending inventories.

(10) The break-even point for this product is

        a. $3,640,000 or 182,000 units.
        b. $2,600,000 or 130,000 units.
        c. $1,800,000 or 90,000 units.
        d. $1,760,000 or 88,000 units.
        e. None of the above.

(11) The number of units that must be sold to earn a net income of $60,000 for the year before income taxes would be

        a. 142,000.
        b. 132,000.
        c. 100,000.
        d. 88,000.
        e. None of the above.

(12) If the income tax rate is 40%, the number of units that must be sold to earn an aftertax income of $90,000 would be

        a. 169,500.
        b. 157,000.
        c. 144,500.
        d. 104,777.
        e. None of the above.

(13) If labor costs are 50% of variable costs and 20% of fixed costs, a 10% increase in wages and salaries would increase the number of units required to break even (in fraction form) to

        a. 807,840/5.3.
        b. 831,600/5.78.
        c. 807,840/14.7.
        d. 831,600/14.28.
        e. None of the above.

P15. 5 Select the best answer for each of the following questions relating to a variety of managerial accounting problems.

(1) A planned factory expansion project has an estimated initial cost of $800,000. Using a discount rate of 20%, the present value of future cost savings from the expansion is $843,000. To yield exactly a 20% time-adjusted rate of return, the actual investment cost *cannot* exceed the $800,000 estimate by more than

        a. $160,000.
        b. $20,000.
        c. $43,000.
        d. $1,075.

Items 2 and 3 are based on the following information:

Standard costs and other data for two component parts used by Griffon Electronics are presented below:

	Part A4	Part B5
Direct material	$ .40	$ 8.00
Direct labor	1.00	4.70
Factory overhead	4.00	2.00
Unit standard cost	$5.40	$14.70
Units needed per year	6,000	8,000
Machine hours per unit	4	2
Unit cost if purchased	$5.00	$15.00

In past years, Griffon has manufactured all of its required components; however, in 1977 only 30,000 hours of otherwise idle machine time can be devoted to the production of components. Accordingly, some of the parts must be purchased from outside suppliers. In producing parts, factory overhead is applied at $1.00 per standard machine hour. Fixed capacity costs, which will not be affected by any make-buy decision, represent 60% of the applied overhead.

(2) The 30,000 hours of available machine time are to be scheduled such that Griffon realizes maximum potential cost savings. The relevant unit production costs which should be considered in the decision to schedule machine time are
   a. $5.40 for A4 and $14.70 for B5.
   b. $5.00 for A4 and $15.00 for B5.
   c. $1.40 for A4 and $12.70 for B5.
   d. $3.00 for A4 and $13.50 for B5.

(3) If the allocation of machine time is based upon potential cost savings per machine hour, then Griffon should produce
   a. 3500 units of A4 and 8000 units of B5.
   b. 6000 units of A4 and 8000 units of B5.
   c. 6000 units of A4 and 3000 units of B5.
   d. No units of A4 and 8000 units of B5.

Items 4 and 5 are based on the following information:

Expected annual usage of a particular raw material is 2,000,000 units, and the standard order size is 10,000 units. The invoice cost of each unit is $500, and the cost to place one purchase order is $80.

(4) The average inventory is
   a. 1,000,000 units.
   b. 5,000 units.
   c. 10,000 units.
   d. 7,500 units.

(5) The estimated annual order cost is
   a. $16,000.
   b. $100,000.
   c. $32,000.
   d. $50,000.

(6) Adams Corporation has developed the following flexible-budget formula for annual indirect-labor cost:

$$\text{Total cost} = \$4,800 + \$0.50 \text{ per machine hour}$$

Operating budgets for the current month are based upon 20,000 hours of planned machine time. Indirect-labor costs included in this planning budget are
a. $14,800.
b. $10,000.
c. $14,400.
d. $10,400.

Items 7 and 8 are based on the following information:

Gyro Gear Company produces a special gear used in automatic transmissions. Each gear sells for $28, and the Company sells approximately 500,000 gears each year. Unit cost data for 1976 are presented below:

Direct material	$6.00	
Direct labor	5.00	

	Variable	Fixed
Other costs:		
Manufacturing	$2.00	$7.00
Distribution	4.00	3.00

(7) The unit cost of gears for direct-cost-inventory purposes is
a. $13.
b. $20.
c. $17.
d. $27.

(8) Gyro has received an offer from a foreign manufacturing to purchase 25,000 gears. Domestic sales would be unaffected by this transaction. If the offer is accepted, variable distribution costs will increase $1.50 per gear for insurance, shipping, and import duties. The relevant unit cost to a pricing decision on this offer is
a. $17.00.
b. $14.50.
c. $28.50.
d. $18.50.

Items 9 and 10 are based on the following information:

From a particular joint process, Waktins Company produces three products, X, Y, and Z. Each product may be sold at the point of split-off or processed further. Additional processing requires no special facilities, and production costs of further processing are entirely variable and traceable to the products involved. In 1976, all three products were processed beyond split-off. Joint production costs for the year were $60,000. Sales values and costs needed to evaluate Watkins' 1976 production policy follow:

Product	Units Produced	Sales Values at Split-Off	Additional Costs and Sales Values if Processed Further	
			Sales Values	Added Costs
X	6,000	$25,000	$42,000	$9,000
Y	4,000	41,000	45,000	7,000
Z	2,000	24,000	32,000	8,000

Joint costs are allocated to the products in proportion to the relative physical volume of output.

(9) For units of Z, the unit production cost most relevant to a sell-or-process-further decision is
   a. $5.
   b. $12.
   c. $4.
   d. $9.

(10) To maximize profits, Watkins should subject the folowing products to additional processing
   a. X only.
   b. X, Y, and Z.
   c. Y and Z only.
   d. Z only.

P15. 6 Select the best answer for each of the questions below, which relate to a variety of management accounting problems. In determining your answer to each question, consider the information given in the preceding lettered statement of facts or data.
   (a) The following information is available for Keller Corporation's new product line:

Selling price per unit	$ 15
Variable manufacturing costs per unit of production	8
Total annual fixed manufacturing costs	25,000
Variable administrative costs per unit of production	3
Total annual fixed selling and administrative expenses	15,000

There was no inventory at the beginning of the year. During the year 12,500 units were produced and 10,000 units were sold.

(1) The ending inventory, assuming Keller uses direct costing, would be
    a. $25,000.
    b. $32,500.
    c. $27,500.
    d. $20,000.
(2) The ending inventory, assuming Keller uses absorption costing, would be
    a. $32,500.
    b. $27,500.
    c. $20,000.
    d. $25,000.
(3) The total variable costs charged to expense for the year, assuming Keller uses direct costing, would be
    a. $110,000.
    b. $100,000.
    c. $117,500.
    d. $80,000.
(4) The total fixed costs charged against the current year's operations, assuming Keller uses absorption costing, is
    a. $35,000.
    b. $40,000.
    c. $25,000.
    d. $15,000.

(b) The Butrico Manufacturing Corporation uses a standard-cost system which records raw materials at actual cost, records materials-price variance at the time that raw materials are issued to work in process, and prorates all variances at year end. Variances associated with direct materials are prorated based on the direct-material balances in the appropriate accounts, and variances associated with direct labor and manufacturing overhead are prorated based on the direct-labor balances in the appropriate accounts.

The following information is available for Butrico for the year ended December 31, 1976

Raw-materials inventory at December 31, 1976	$ 65,000
Finished-goods inventory at December 31, 1976	
Direct material	87,000
Direct labor	130,500
Applied manufacturing overhead	104,400
Cost of goods sold for the year ended December 31, 1976	
Direct material	348,000
Direct labor	739,500
Applied manufacturing overhead	591,600
Direct-material price variance (unfavorable)	10,000
Direct-material usage variance (favorable)	15,000
Direct-labor rate variance (unfavorable)	20,000
Direct-labor efficiency variance (favorable)	5,000
Manufacturing overhead incurred	690,000

There were no beginning inventories and no ending work-in-process inventory. Manufacturing overhead is applied at 80% of standard direct labor.

(5) The amount of direct-material price variance to be prorated to finished-goods inventory at December 31, 1976, is a
   a. $1740 debit.
   b. $2000 debit.
   c. $2610 credit.
   d. $3000 credit.

(6) The total amount of direct material in the finished-goods inventory at December 31, 1976, after all variances have been prorated is
   a. $86,130.
   b. $87,870.
   c. $88,000.
   d. $86,000.

(7) The total amount of direct labor in the finished-goods inventory at December 31, 1976, after all variances have been prorated is
   a. $134,250.
   b. $131,850.
   c. $132,750.
   d. $126,750.

(8) The total cost of goods sold for the year ended December 31, 1976, after all variances have been prorated is
   a. $1,682,750.
   b. $1,691,250.
   c. $1,683,270.
   d. $1,693,850.

(c) Tomlinson Retail seeks your assistance to develop cash and other budget information for May, June, and July 1976. At April 30, 1976, the company had cash of $5,500, accounts receivable of $437,000, inventories of $309,400, and accounts payable of $133,055.

The budget is to be based on the following assumptions:

I. *Sales*
   a. Each month's sales are billed on the last day of the month.
   b. Customers are allowed a 3% discount if payment is made within ten days after the billing date. Receivables are booked gross.
   c. Sixty percent of the billings are collected within the discount period, 25% are collected by the end of the month, 9% are collected by the end of the second month, and 6% prove uncollectible.

II. *Purchases*
   a. Fifty-four percent of all purchases of material and selling, general, and administrative expenses are paid in the month purchased and the remainder in the following month.
   b. Each month's units of ending inventory is equal to 130% of the next month's units of sales.
   c. The cost of each unit of inventory is $20.
   d. Selling, general, and administrative expenses of which $2000 is depreciation, are equal to 15% of the current month's sales.

Actual and projected sales are as follows:

1976	Dollars	Units
March	$354,000	11,800
April	363,000	12,100
May	357,000	11,900
June	342,000	11,400
July	360,000	12,000
August	366,000	12,200

(9) Budgeted cash disbursements during the month of June 1976 are
    a. $292,900.
    b. $287,379.
    c. $294,900.
    d. $285,379.

(10) Budgeted cash collections during the month of May 1976 are
    a. $333,876.
    b. $355,116.
    c. $340,410.
    d. $355,656.

(11) The budgeted number of units of inventory to be purchased during July 1976 is
    a. 15,860.
    b. 12,260.
    c. 12,000.
    d. 15,600.

P15. 7 Instructions: Select the BEST answer for each of the questions below.

(1) Which of the following statements is true for a firm that uses "direct" (variable) costing?
    a. The cost of a unit of product changes because of changes in number of units manufactured.
    b. Profits fluctuate with sales.
    c. An idle facility variation is calculated by a direct cost system.
    d. Product costs include "direct" (variable) administrative costs.
    e. None of the above.

(2) When a firm prepares financial reports by using absorption costing, it may find that
    a. Profits will always increase with increases in sales.
    b. Profits will always decrease with decreases in sales.
    c. Profits may decrease with increased sales even if there is no change in selling prices and costs.
    d. Decreased output and constant sales result in increased profits.
    e. None of the above.

(3) An accountant would typically have the following in mind when referring to the "margin of safety":
   a. The excess of budgeted or actual sales over the variable costs and the fixed costs at break-even.
   b. The excess of budgeted or actual sales revenue over the fixed costs.
   c. The excess of actual sales over budgeted sales.
   d. The excess of sales revenue over the variable costs.
   e. None of the above.
(4) Which of these alternatives would decrease contribution per unit margin the most?
   a. A 15% decrease in selling price.
   b. A 15% increase in variable expense.
   c. A 15% increase in selling price.
   d. A 15% decrease in variable expense.
   e. A 15% decrease in fixed expenses.
(5) If fixed costs decrease while variable cost per unit remains constant, the new variable contribution margin in relation to the old will be
   a. Unchanged.
   b. Higher.
   c. Lower.
   d. Indeterminate.
   e. None of the above.

(6) On the Profit/Volume chart above.
   a. The areas XX and YY and the point K represent profit, loss, and volume of sales at break-even point, respectively.
   b. The line O-Z represents the volumes of sales.
   c. The two lines O-M and N-Z represent fixed costs.
   d. The line M-N represents total costs.
   e. None of the above is true.
(7) The vertical scale represents
   a. Volume of sales.

      b. Units produced.

      c. Profit above O and loss below O.

      d. Contribution margin.

      e. None of the above.

(8) In break-even analysis, a number of assumptions typically are made. Which of the following assumptions typically is *not* made.

      a. Volume is the only relevant factor affecting cost.

      b. No change between beginning and ending inventory.

      c. The sales mix will be maintained as volume changes.

      d. Prices of cost factors fluctuate proportionally with volume.

      e. None of the above.

(9) To which of these independent variables would "setup" expense probably have the closest relationship?

      a. Machine hours.

      b. Direct labor hours.

      c. Number of shop orders.

      d. Direct labor cost.

      e. Number of employees.

(10) Which of the following expenses should not be on a monthly cost control report of a department manager?

      a. Department labor costs.

      b. Department supplies costs.

      c. Depreciation cost on departmental equipment.

      d. Cost of material used in the department.

      e. None of the above.

(11) A management purpose for allocating joint costs of a processing center to the various products produced is

      a. To develop accurate processing cost variances by product.

      b. To report more correct standard product costs for comparative analysis.

      c. To establish inventory values for unsold units.

      d. To record accurate cost of sales by product line.

      e. None of the above.

(12) Unabsorbed overhead costs in an absorption costing system are

      a. Fixed factory costs not allocated to units produced.

      b. Factory overhead costs not allocated to units produced.

      c. Excess variable overhead costs.

      d. Costs that cannot be controlled.

      e. None of the above.

(13) Which of these variances is least significant for cost control?

      a. Labor price variance.

      b. Material quantity variance.

      c. Overhead budget variance.

      d. Overhead volume variance.

      e. Labor quantity variance.

The following statement applies to questions 14 to 16.

In analyzing the relationship of total factory overhead with changes in direct labor hours, the following relationship was found to exist: $Y = \$1000 + \$2X$

(14) Y in the above equation is an estimate of
   a. Total variable costs.
   b. Total factory overhead.
   c. Total fixed costs.
   d. Total direct labor hours.
   e. None of the above.

(15) The $2 in the equation is an estimate of
   a. Total fixed costs.
   b. Variable costs per direct labor hour.
   c. Total variable costs.
   d. Fixed costs per direct labor hour.
   e. None of the above.

(16) The use of such a relationship of total factory overhead to changes in direct labor hours is said to be valid only within the relevant range. The phrase "relevant range" means
   a. Within a reasonable dollar amount for labor costs.
   b. Within the range of observations of the analysis.
   c. Within the range of reasonableness as judged by the department supervisor.
   d. Within the budget allowance for overhead.
   e. None of the above.

P15. 8 This company compensates its field sales force on a commission and year-end bonus basis. The commission is 20% of standard gross margin (planned selling price less standard cost of goods sold on a full cost absorption basis), contingent on collection of the account. Customer's credit is approved by the company's credit department. Price concessions are granted on occasion by the top sales management, but sales commission are not reduced by the granting of such discounts. A year-end bonus of 15% of commissions earned is paid to salesmen who equal or exceed their annual sales target (quota). The annual sales target is usually established by applying approximately a 5% increase to the prior year's sales.

Required:

(1) What features of this compensation plan would seem to be effective in motivating the salesmen to accomplish company goals of higher profits and return on investment? Explain.

(2) What features of this compensation plan would seem to be countereffective in motivating the salesmen to accomplish the company goals of higher profits and return on investment? Explain.

INDEX